THE BEST PLAYS OF 1973–1974

THE
BURNS MANTLE
YEARBOOK

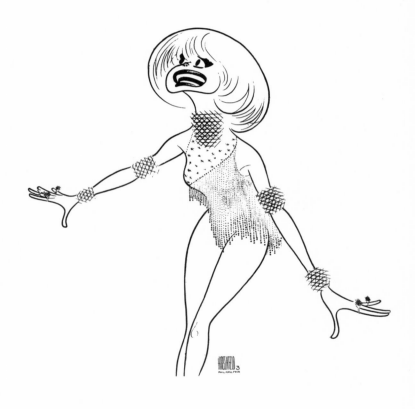

THE
BEST PLAYS
OF 1973-1974

EDITED BY OTIS L. GUERNSEY JR.

*Illustrated with photographs and
with drawings by* **HIRSCHFELD**

DODD, MEAD & COMPANY
NEW YORK • TORONTO

EDITOR'S NOTE

THE subject of each succeeding *Best Plays* volume is the same: theater in its most professional aspects. The early Burns Mantle volumes covered only Broadway; over the years the focus has widened to include the tributary New York theater and the national and international scene. Our focus always changes slightly with each passing year, following closely wherever the theater's development may lead.

This year it's that indefinable area known as "off off Broadway" or "OOB" for short that is demanding extra attention. OOB lacks the formalities (usually) of firm commitments such as managerial contracts, opening nights and regular schedules, so that it cannot possibly be reported in the formal way we outline the clearer silhouettes of Broadway and off Broadway in this volume. OOB has become something of a Presence in the New York midst, however, and is more and more to be taken into account in any seasonal summary. The year's best new American play *(The Sea Horse)* originated off off, as did two others of the ten Best Plays. And the size of OOB is getting to be as impressive as its creative potential. The Theater Development Fund lists over 80 producing organizations on its OOB roster, and the OOB Alliance lists over 50—and they aren't all the same, and there are many more (estimates run as high as 220). And if OOB is large, and creative, it also tends to be elusive. Many, even most of its hundreds and hundreds of programs come and go without leaving a wrack of information behind. It's not uncommon for the cast, the director, the performance schedule, the title, the script—especially the script—to change materially from day to day. Trying to get a definitive picture of off off Broadway is recording a river in still photos—the snapshot is obsolete before it can be developed.

The one relatively stable element of OOB is the producing organization like La Mama or Circle Theater or Theater at St. Clement's. Most OOB production takes place under one of these wings. In an effort to meet their wonderful challenge of vital theater, we have expanded our OOB coverage in *The Best Plays of 1973–74* to include more than 70 of these (last year there were 45) in the listing of "other" New York programs which follows our "Plays Produced off Broadway" section. Each entry gives the producing organization's name, its esthetic specialty or goal and the name of its principal director, followed by a sampling of its 1973–74 programs with the emphasis on new scripts as they occur. The organizations were selected for listing on the basis of 1) the existence of some production activity in 1973–74, 2) a demonstrated degree of professionalism and/or creativity and 3) the availability of accurate information about their work (undoubtedly there are others which deserve inclusion on our list; here's hoping they'll establish communication so that we can include them next year). The icing on this rapidly rising OOB cake in our volume is an article reporting the most talked-of successes (apart from the obvious ones like those transferred to commercial production) of the year by Gloria Gonzalez, a much-produced, often-discouraged but still-persevering off-off-Broadway playwright.

From abroad, *The Best Plays of 1973–74* has the uniquely comprehensive coverage of the theater in London, Paris and other Continental centers by Ossia Trilling, our European editor, in listings (prepared with the much-appreciated assistance of Anne Doggett) and articles, including a special comment on the London scene by the distinguished British playwright Arnold Wesker. Exceptional success on the London stage is spotlighted by what we call "Trilling's Top Thirty," our editor's selection of London's 30 best 1973–74 shows, with complete casts and credits of these bests appearing in the London production roster.

Ella A. Malin's incomparably thorough listing of professional theater from coast to coast in the U.S.A. and Canada is preceded this year by an article by the distinguished playwright Israel Horovitz, giving his impression of what it is like to have major works premiered far from Broadway at major regional theater centers. Additional copious thanks are due to Rue Canvin for her compilations of the necrology and books and records listings, plus other editorial chores; and to Stanley Green for his informative section on major cast replacements in the long-run hit shows and touring attractions.

Jonathan Dodd of Dodd, Mead & Company, the publishers of this volume annually for 55 years, and the editor's own meticulously hard-working wife are the beginning of a long, long list of people who deserve the gratitude of both reader and editor for their invaluable contributions to this volume: Henry Hewes, Bernard Simon of *Simon's Directory,* Mimi Horowitz of *Playbill,* Hobe Morrison of *Variety,* Clara Rotter of the New York *Times,* Ralph Newman of The Drama Book Shop, and as always the many people in the theatrical production offices whose help was essential in collecting accurate information about all the shows. Al Hirschfeld's drawings are welcome aboard as a true adornment of the voyage. So are the examples of the year's outstanding designs by Tony Walton and Pearl Somner and the photos of the theater in New York and across the country by Martha Swope, Friedman-Abeles (Joseph Abeles and Sy Friedman), Richard Brasten, Martha Holmes, Bert Andrews, Ken Howard, Nat Newman, Claire Henze, William L. Smith, Andy Hanson, James Fry, Clifford L. Moore, David Robbins, Greenberg-May, Glen E. Erikson and Robert C. Ragsdale.

Most of all we have the dramatists to thank, not only the authors of the Best Plays synopsized in this volume and the ones that came close, but all dramatists successful or otherwise who insist on making their sacrifice of time and talent at the very root of the theatrical process, keeping our theater very much alive under any and all circumstances. We hope each and every one of them has a script ready for next season when we will all be looking forward to America's Bicentennial just over the horizon, when Watergate will be a subject for dramatizations instead of news stories, and when the only thing certain about the theater is that it will continue to fulfill exciting new destinies which the future surely holds in store.

OTIS L. GUERNSEY Jr.

June 1, 1974

CONTENTS

Drawings by HIRSCHFELD

CONTENTS   xi

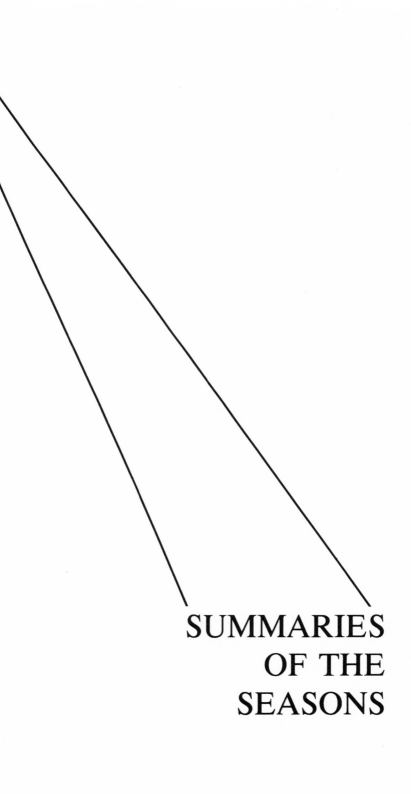

SUMMARIES
OF THE
SEASONS

○
○
○
THE SEASON IN NEW YORK

○
By Otis L. Guernsey Jr.
○
○

THE most indelicate theatrical season since Sodom and Gomorrah has left us
wondering what the New York stage plans to do for an encore. In 1973–74 we
saw a naked man mount a naked woman in a Broadway show, hardly a believable
illusion, more like watching a third-rate magician attempt the Indian Rope Trick
—success was clearly impossible. Off Broadway we saw a naked man pretend he
was going to mount another naked man for an entire act (actors playing the
French poets Verlaine and Rimbaud) in what was certainly the superlatively
cathartic sequence of the year, though perhaps not for the first reason that comes
to mind. It aroused real pity for the actors, not as characters but as human beings,
for their defenseless and prolonged exposure in this impossible context.

In another Broadway session we saw a virile young man murder a handsome
young woman and bear away her naked corpse to have his necrophiliac way with
it offstage, in a rare instance of modesty if not of the highest behavioral standards.
The human form was in conspicuous display all over town, even if it necessitated
the intrusion of a spurious gesture like the violent baring of a lady's breasts in
When You Comin' Back, Red Ryder? This sculptured asset was attractively
showcased in *Ulysses in Nighttown,* but the image that the Joycean nightmare
insisted on leaving with us wasn't the gentle curve of naked, reflective Fionnuala
Flanagan as Molly Bloom. Oh no, it was, rather, this same lady's intimate contact
with a chamber pot on the stage—and, finally, the androgynous side show of Swen
Swenson costumed in black lace panties and black leather jock strap, heavily
eye-shadowed and cracking a whip.

The 1973–74 season was blatant verbally as well as epidermically. The descriptions of male homosexual practises in *Find Your Way Home* and of child molestation in *Short Eyes* spared few sensibilities. The vital forces of these two Best Plays
absorbed and transcended any shock in their subject matter, however. *Find Your
Way Home* is a drama of love and loneliness, not sex, and *Short Eyes* is a drama
of man's inhumanity to man, not perversion. The revival of *Ulysses* or David
Rabe's new *Boom Boom Room* were earthbound to the sensationalism of their
subject matter, but the Hopkins and Piñero plays easily lifted the weight of their
physical imagery. So did *Creeps,* a sensitive script about prejudice against people
who are "different" (in this case spastics), though it was anything but attractive
in a filthy men's room setting, with all the concomitant action the place implies.

Add to all this the year's other immoderate conceits, such as the ballad about
venereal disease in *Over Here!* and exploration of other dark corners of the human
experience in the neuroses in *Bad Habits,* the cruel disillusionment in *Red Ryder*

3

The 1973–74 Season on Broadway

PLAYS (10)

Children of the Wind
Veronica's Room
Vivian Beaumont:
  Boom Boom Room
What the
  Wine-Sellers Buy
SHORT EYES
  (transfer)
THE GOOD DOCTOR
Thieves
An American
  Millionaire
My Sister, My Sister
BAD HABITS
  (transfer)

MUSICALS (9)

Raisin
Molly
Gigi
Lorelei
Rainbow Jones
Sextet
Over Here!
Ride the Winds
The Magic Show

REVUES (1)

Good Evening

FOREIGN PLAYS IN ENGLISH (8)

Crown Matrimonial
Full Circle
The Au Pair Man
FIND YOUR WAY HOME
The Freedom of the City
NOEL COWARD IN TWO KEYS
My Fat Friend
JUMPERS

SPECIALTIES (7)

An Evening With
  Josephine Baker
Liza
Clarence Darrow
Music! Music!
Words and Music
Sammy
Will **Rogers** U.S.A.

REVIVALS (19)

Circle in the Square:
  Uncle Vanya
  The Waltz of the
    Toreadors
  The Iceman Cometh
  Scapino
The Desert Song
A Streetcar Named Desire
New Phoenix:
  The Visit
  Chemin de Fer
  Holiday
The Pajama Game
City Center Company:
  Three Sisters
  The Beggar's Opera
  Measure for Measure
  Scapin
  Next Time I'll Sing
    to You
*A Moon for the
  Misbegotten*
Candide
  (transfer
Ulysses in Nighttown
The Dance of Death

HOLDOVER SHOWS WHICH BECAME HITS DURING 1973–74

A Little Night Music
Sugar
The **River Niger**

Categorized above are all the plays listed in the "Plays Produced on Broadway" section of this volume.
Plays listed in CAPITAL LETTERS have been designated Best Plays of 1973–74.
Plays listed in *italics* were still running June 3, 1974.
Plays listed in **bold face type** were classified as hits in *Variety's* annual list of hits and flops published
  June 5, 1974 or judged likely to become hits

and the shame lurking under the urbanities of Noel Coward's *Song at Twilight,* and you have maybe the century's best prototype for the famous sarcastic Jerry Herman lyric "Oh, what a lovely theatrical season we've had!"

Whatever the character of the 1973–74 season in New York, it can't be blamed on or credited to the eminent American dramatists. They took all too little part in shaping the stage material this year. Only one American Broadway play made the list of the Best Plays, and that was the special case of Neil Simon's Chekhov adaptation, *The Good Doctor.* Four American off-Broadway scripts made the Best Plays list—Terrence McNally's *Bad Habits,* Mark Medoff's *When You Comin' Back, Red Ryder?* Miguel Piñero's *Short Eyes* and Edward J. Moore's *The Sea Horse*—but the latter three were the professional playwriting debuts of first-time-outers. It was as though virtually the whole American playwriting establishment had suddenly vanished, leaving the theaters gaping empty, to be filled only by the tentative first efforts of newcomers or the imported creativity of the British *Noel Coward in Two Keys, Find Your Way Home* by John Hopkins (a newcomer) and *Jumpers* by Tom Stoppard on Broadway and David Storey's *The Contractor* off, plus the short-lived Canadian play *Creeps* by David E. Freeman, his first in New York. Such was the makeup of the Best Plays list this year: five foreign plays and five American; five U.S. playwriting debuts and five established authors, three of them British; six off Broadway and only four on; all straight plays, no musicals, in a year which saw stage musical invention at a low level. Even among the shows that came close to making the best list, foreign scripts like *The Au Pair Man, My Fat Friend* and *The Freedom of the City* held a conspicuous place along with *Veronica's Room, What the Wine-Dealers Buy, A Breeze From the Gulf, The Enclave* and *Thieves.* If this was a Rabelaisian, nay, a Bacchanalian, season, it wasn't because the American dramatist took a forceful position on sex, violence or any other subject.

The reach and the grasp of Broadway seemed to diminish somewhat in 1973–74, but the volume of production repeated that of last season: 54 shows, including as "Broadway" offerings those offered under special contracts at the smaller Times Square theaters like the Bijou and the Little. Thus the dropoff from 84 productions in 1967–68, 76 in 1968–69, 68 in 1969–70, 56 in 1970–71, 56 in 1971–72 and 54 in 1972–73 seems to have bottomed out. It took a lot of revivals (19) to bring that 1973–74 total up to 54, however, as there was a marked drop in new American play production: from 16 last year to 10 this, from 13 musicals to nine. New foreign plays in English doubled from four last year to eight this, materially helping Broadway to make a season of it.

The worst attenuation continued to take place in the all-important matter of playing weeks (if ten shows play ten weeks, that's 100 playing weeks). According to *Variety's* figures, Broadway hit another new low in playing weeks in 1973–74 of 852, as compared with 878 or 889 (as variously reported) in 1972–73 and 1,092 in 1971–72, way off the 1960s plateau of 1,200 playing weeks. The total 52-week gross was up slightly according to *Variety's* figures, however, to $46,250,772 from less that $44 million last season, but way off the $52.3 million the previous year and the record $59 million in 1967–68. This increased Broadway gross may have occurred because of a slight increase in the proportion of more expensive shows to less expensive ones, or even maybe a small rise in attendance, but it wasn't because of a rise in the top ticket price, which hung in there for still another year at $15.

It was on the road, not on Broadway, that the most noticeable drop took place of more than $10 million, to a total 52-week 1973–74 gross of $45.3 million as compared with almost $56 million last year. *Variety* attributes this 18 per cent drop to "the dearth of multiple-company touring musicals such as *Hair* and *Godspell,* which bolstered the totals substantially in recent seasons." For that matter, almost the same could be said of Broadway itself, where the presence of three or four blockbusting musical holdovers brought crowds into the theater district and padded the totals for season after season in the 1960s.

Ups and Downs

This was just another year in the life of *The Fantasticks* off Broadway, the all-time longest-running show of record in the professional New York theater, which began its run May 3, 1960 and now 14 years later is closing in on its 6,000th performance. It was a vintage year in the professional life of Debbie Reynolds, who set what must be an all-time record week's legitimate stage gross in *Irene:* $355,000 for 6 performances at the 12,000-seat open-air Municipal Opera in Forest Park, Ill., far outstripping the putative runner-up, Carol Channing's $252,000 road week in *Lorelei.* Miss Reynolds's *Irene* also set a mark to shoot at in future Minskoff Theater bookings, $144,731 for one week's gross.

This was also a vintage year for Liza Minnelli, who shook up Broadway with her $413,000 take in a personal appearance at the Winter Garden, setting a number of impresarios scrambling for other stars who might be able to fill a big legit house with a solo show. Josephine Baker wasn't quite able to hack it at the Palace, but Sammy Davis Jr. packed the Uris for two weeks with a version of his night club act, and Sammy Cahn turned out to be an engaging personality as well as a gifted lyricist in *Words and Music,* a one-man show devoted to his works. Frank Sinatra was another hit solo attraction, but he didn't venture into a Broadway house; he stopped uptown at Carnegie Hall for a sellout one-night stand at $100–$150 a ticket.

The returns won't be in on this season's successes for a while yet (it takes longer than ever for a show to recoup its production cost), though *Lorelei* came to town trailing a golden $5 million gross from its long road stint, and the hit British revue *Good Evening,* with Peter Cook and Dudley Moore repeating some of the song and satire gems from *Beyond the Fringe* together with new sparklers, recouped before the snows melted and had reached the $40,000 profit mark on its $120,000 investment. Off Broadway, the success story of *El Grande de Coca-Cola* was writ large, but in relatively small numbers: 112 per cent profit on an initial investment of $30,000. Meanwhile, *Sleuth* finally closed after 1,222 cat-and-mousey performances and a profit of $1,700,000 on its $150,000 investment; *Pippin* was passing the $1,188,000 profit level; and Broadway's all-time longest-run show, *Fiddler on the Roof,* touring, reached $4,515,000 profit on its $375,000 investment, and still

JAMES COOK, SEAMUS O'BRIEN, PHIL KILLIAM, SHARON WERNER, ROBERT BRIGHAM AND HAL ROBINSON IN "THE FANTASTICKS." THE MUSICAL CELEBRATED ITS 15TH YEAR IN MAY OF 1974. THE SHOW'S PRODUCERS, ROBERT TANNENHOUSE AND LORE NOTO, ARE SHOWN LOWER LEFT.

counting. In this connection, *Variety* published a summary of Harold Prince's record as the producer of 20 shows including *Fiddler* and *A Little Night Music* in 21 seasons. Prince has scored 11 hits in his 20 tries (and two of the others still have a chance to get into the black), for an 84.87 per cent return, or a net profit of $5,868,000 on a total investment of $6,915,000.

Bad news happens faster and is more quickly reported in *Variety's* estimates. Sixteen unsuccessful 1972–73 musicals had lost their backers a total of $6,150,000 when all was said and done and the last one, *Seesaw,* had finally gone on the road. This *succes d'estime* was figured as the most expensive of the 16, a $1,250,000 loss (a show can loose much more than its original investment by staying open and fighting a losing cause in the Broadway theater, where a near-hit can be something like a second-best hand in poker. *Variety* estimated that *Seesaw* lost $750,000 in addition to its production cost of $500,000). Losses on the unsuccessful 1973–74 musicals as reported by *Variety* amounted to $2,040,000 as of our press time, as follows: *The Desert Song* $200,000; *Rachael Lily Rosenbloom and Don't You Ever Forget It* (which closed in previews at the Broadhurst) $500,000; *Molly* $600,000 (on a $400,000 investment); *The Pajama Game* $300,000; *Gigi* $440,000. Still another failed musical, *Rainbow Jones,* closed after only one Broadway performance, with no estimate of its loss available.

Among the straight Broadway plays, what there was of them, *Children of the Wind* was the shortest-lived with only 6 performances. The most expensive failures according to *Variety* estimate, however, were *Boom Boom Room,* the David Rabe play that cost Joseph Papp's group an estimated $250,000 at Lincoln Center, *Full Circle* and *Crown Matrimonial* at deficits of $150,000, *Veronica's Room,* the Ira Levin thriller which ran a respectable 75 performances but dropped $125,000 of its $225,000 cost, and *Freedom of the City* at the $100,000 level. Off Broadway there were two plays and two musicals which came and went for only one performance each: *The Boy Who Came to Leave, The Indian Experience* and the musicals *Kaboum!* and *Pop* which went the way of their titles.

In this season which saw more revivals produced at the Broadway level than the combined Broadway total of American plays and musicals, there was heavy reliance on the strength of our acting establishment to carry the season along. It was fully justified in the performance. The vivid personal images were topped by Michael Moriarty as the hustler in *Find Your Way Home,* Jason Robards and Colleen Dewhurst as O'Neill's star-crossed lovers in *A Moon for the Misbegotten,* Lewis J. Stadlen's Dr. Pangloss in *Candide* and Julie Harris's threadbare queen in *The Au Pair Man.* They also included, in no special order, the Nicol Williamson and George C. Scott portraits in the ensemble of Mike Nichols's outstanding *Uncle Vanya* . . . George Grizzard as Edward VIII and Patrick Horgan as his brother the Duke of York in the *Crown Matrimonial* ensemble . . . Eileen Heckart as a lethal witch under Ellis Rabb's direction in *Veronica's Room* . . . Dick A. Williams as a drug pusher, preening like a peacock in *What the Wine-Sellers Buy* under Michael Schultz's direction . . . Popular visitors Peter Cook and Dudley Moore in the many guises of their revue *Good Evening* . . . Carol Channing, again Lorelei Lee in *Lorelei,* and Zero Mostel, again Leopold Bloom in *Ulysses in Nighttown* . . . Christopher Plummer, Rene Auberjonois and company as directed by A.J. Antoon in *The Good Doctor* . . . Hume Cronyn with Jessica Tandy and Anne Baxter in a pair of Noel Coward reflections staged by Vivian Matalon . . . Brian Bedford extracting every thunderbolt of apocalyptic gallows humor from his role of a professor in *Jumpers* . . . *The Contractor* ensemble meticulously directed by Barry Davis, as well as The Family ensemble of *Short Eyes* as staged by Marvin Felix Camillo, the off-Broadway *Moonchildren* ensemble under John Pasquin's direction, the *Chemin de Fer* ensemble directed by Stephen Porter and the fluttering *Fashion* ensemble directed by Anthony Stimac . . . Samuel E. Wright as a Pullman porter and Janie Sell as a Nazi spy, backing up Maxene and Patty Andrews in *Over Here!* under Tom Moore's direction . . . Henry Fonda's fine-grained, persistent portrayal of Clarence Darrow in a "one-character play" and Jane Marla Robbins's of Fanny Burney and others in the one-woman *Dear Nobody* . . . Mark Baker as the ultimate bumpkin, Candide, and Alfred Drake as the ultimate sophisticate in *Gigi* . . . The delightful *My Fat Friend* trio of Lynn Redgrave, George Rose and John Lithgow . . . The elder Redgrave, Michael, visiting Brooklyn with the Royal Shakespeare productions, and another British visitor to both Brooklyn and Manhattan, Jim Dale, in the title role of the Young Vic's *Scapino*. . . Virginia Capers as a matriarchal rock of ages and Ralph Carter as her solemn grandson in *Raisin,* staged by Donald McKayle . . . Frank Coppola and Marilyn Child leading the way surely through the dark forest of *The Faggot* . . . Scott McKay and Ruth Ford as troubled parents troubling their son (Robert Drivas) in *A Breeze From the Gulf*. . . Kevin Conway as the troublemaker of *When You Comin' Back, Red Ryder?*. . . David Downing as hero and Al Freeman Jr. as villain of the symbolical *The Great Macdaddy,* directed by Douglas Turner Ward . . . *The Dance of Death* ensemble (Robert Shaw, Zoe Caldwell, Hector Elizondo) . . . Doug Henning's truly amazing illusions in *The Magic Show* . . . Conchata Ferrell and Edward J. Moore in *The Sea Horse* . . . And last but by no means least, the pendulous feat of James Earl Jones, who swung from one extreme of style as *King Lear* in the Central Park production to another as Hickey in the Circle in the Square revival of *The Iceman Cometh.*

A director who scored twice this season was Harold Prince, who provided the year's top musical staging in *Candide* and also put on a notable revival of *The Visit* in New Phoenix repertory. Robert Moore was also doubly effective in musical and straight categories with *Lorelei* and *My Fat Friend.* Edwin Sherin added *Find Your Way Home* to his summer *King Lear,* and A.J. Antoon directed Simon and Strindberg. Other outstanding 1973–74 directors in addition to those named in the preceding paragraph were Jose Quintero, who turned his revival of O'Neill's *A Moon for the Misbegotten* into the the the hit of the season; Marshall W. Mason, orchestrating two characters supremely skillfully in *The Sea Horse;* and Robert Drivas, who also scored a kind of double this year, playing a leading role in *A Breeze From the Gulf* and then directing *Bad Habits.* The only Broadway director to win an Academy Award for movie acting this year was John Houseman, who by the way also staged two 1973–74 shows: City Center Acting Company's *Measure for Measure* and the Fonda *Clarence Darrow.*

Joseph Papp limited himself to two directing stints *(Boom Boom Room* and *As You Like It),* but he was the busiest of producers as he took over the legit theaters at Lincoln Center in addition to his nest of theaters in the Public downtown and the action at the Delacorte in Central Park. Not counting workshop or experimental productions, Papp produced 15 shows during the 1973–74 season: three in Central Park, six at the Public Theater, four (not counting a transfer) at the Beaumont and two in the Newhouse (formerly the Forum). They weren't all good, but they all had a vitality, a thrust; and certainly Papp enjoyed his share of success this season with one Best Play, the Critics Award-winning *Short Eyes,* and several that came close, including *The Au Pair Man, What the Wine-Dealers Buy* and *The Killdeer.* No one who likes theater could fail to applaud Papp's energetic determination to lift the American theater out of its doldrums into the heavens, single-handed if necessary.

A little off-off-Broadway troupe under the artistic direction of Marshall W. Mason, The Circle Repertory Theater Company, was even more successful, or luckier, or whatever, in finding new scripts. They stole a big piece of the show last year with *The Hot l Baltimore* and an even bigger piece this year with *Red Ryder* and *Sea Horse,* first produced at the Circle Theater and subsequently elevated to commercial status. In the opinion of the *Best Plays* editor, they were certainly 1973–74's two best American scripts. Orin Lehman had a hand in the off-Broadway presentation of *The Sea Horse* (together with Kermit Bloomgarden and Max Allentuck), and he also produced *Creeps* off Broadway, so that together with Circle Repertory he has the distinction of producing two Best Plays this season.

The Robert Kalfin-Michael David-Burl Hash Chelsea Theater Center also had a shining year with the importation of *The Contractor* and the hit revival of *Candide* with a new book (both Critics Award winners, but the latter ineligible for Best Play status, not only because it is clearly not a new work but also because it was a Best Play of its premiere year, 1956–57). Other impresarios whose taste and judgment helped light up the all too dimly-lit 1973–74 skies were Elliot Martin *(Red Ryder* and *A Moon for the Misbegotten),* Adela Holzer *(Bad Habits),* Richard Barr and Charles Woodward *(Noel Coward in Two Keys),* Rick Hobard *(Find Your Way Home),* Alexander H. Cohen *(Good Evening, Words and Music, Ulysses* and the Tony Awards TV show), Emanuel Azenberg and Eugene V. Wolsk *(The Good Doctor),* Bruce Mailman and Richard Lipton *(The Faggot),* Steve Steinlauf *(Moonchildren)* and R. Scott Lucas *(Fashion).* Theodore Mann's and Paul Libin's Circle in the Square, the New Phoenix under the guidance of T. Edward Hambleton, Michael Montel, Harold Prince and Stephen Porter, John Houseman's City Center Acting Company and Gene Feist's Roundabout also contributed whole schedules of distinction to the New York theater.

Among designers, Tony Walton stood out for the second straight year for two Chekhovian environments, *Uncle Vanya* and *The Good Doctor.* His strong straight-play competition included Douglas W. Schmidt's *Veronica's Room,* John Conklin's *The Au Pair Man,* Santo Loquasto's *What the Wine-Sellers Buy,* William Ritman's *Find Your Way Home,* Peter Larkin's *Thieves,* Doug Higgins's *Total Eclipse,* Robert Randolph's *The Enclave* and Bill Stabile's *Red Ryder.* The outstanding musical designs were Franne and Eugene Lee's *Candide* and Schmidt's *Over Here!,* with Robert U. Taylor's *Raisin* and Oliver Smith and Oliver Messel's *Gigi* in close contention, with Pearl Somner's *Ulysses in Nighttown* designs clearly tops in straight-play costumes.

While this gilded group of actors, directors, producers and designers was finding a portion of success on the troubled stages of 1973–74, often in revivals, what were the playwrights doing? Researching the back alleys of the Casbah for ever more bizarre experiences to color their future work? Just sitting around waiting for better times? Well, a handful of them—Ira Levin, David Rabe, Neil Simon, Herb Gardner, Murray Schisgal—were hanging in there on Broadway, in each case with a script that was of more than passing interest, and the same was true of Terrence McNally, Mart Crowley, Arthur Laurents, Ed Bullins and a few others off Broadway. They helped keep the franchise for the American playwriting establishment at this dismal time when every empty theater presents a temptation for someone to tear it down for real estate development.

Where where the others? Well, Arthur Miller was teaching at Michigan, experimenting there with a new work in progress and adapting his *The Creation of the World and Other Business* into a musical called *Up From Creation*, apparently just for the hell of it. Tennessee Williams was experimenting off off Broadway and working on a new play for possible production by David Merrick (who was off somewhere making a movie). Edward Albee was teaching, experimenting with off-off-Broadway production and getting a new play ready. Sidney Kingsley and Jules Feiffer were trying to cast new scripts. Jerome Lawrence and Robert E. Lee were teaching, directing and writing books. Lanford Wilson was acting in an off-off-Broadway revival. Frank D. Gilroy and Robert Anderson were writing movies. Israel Horovitz was having the first of a nine-play series produced on regional stages (an article by him evaluating this experience appears in this volume as the introduction to our section on "The Season Around the United States"). John Guare was trying out a new play in Chicago. Etc., etc., etc.

On the Broadway musical stages it was much the same story. The shows that counted were more nostalgic than inventive. All leaned heavily on a well-remembered score, playscript or performance, and the major one that could be classified "original"—*Over Here!*—was the most nostalgic of all. The likes of *Raisin* and *Lorelei* helped keep audiences coming to Broadway, but the most inventive element of our proud Broadway musical theater in 1973–74 was the new staging of *Candide*. Off Broadway was the showcase for the most imaginative new musical material this year, with Al Carmines's *The Faggot*.

Where were our Broadway musical authors? Well, Stephen Sondheim and Burt Shevelove were staging their own idea of Aristophanes's *The Frogs* in the Yale swimming pool (and Sondheim wrote some new lyrics for *Candide*). Jerry Herman was working on *Mack and Mabel* for future production. Mary Rodgers and Sheldon Harnick did the score for a new Bil Baird marionette show, *Pinocchio*. Richard Rodgers, Jerry Bock, Tom Jones, Harvey Schmidt, Lee Adams, John Kander and all the others who could be mentioned were between shows, we must suppose. The stalwarts who put in an appearance with Broadway material included Jule Styne, Betty Comden, Adolph Green, Hugh Wheeler, Alan Jay Lerner, Frederick Loewe, Stephen Schwartz (and Sammy Cahn in person), and they deserve our applause both for the substance and value of their work and for helping to keep some of the streets lighted.

One of the reasons why so few ventured forth this season was that the dramatist's so-called "chance to fail" is shrinking fast in the modern commercial theater. It can be said that off off Broadway offers the American playwright his chance to succeed, as witness the progress of a *Red Ryder,* a *Sea Horse* or a *Short Eyes* as they evolve from the seething OOB embryo. The chance to fail is quite another matter, however. It is or should be a function of the commercial, not the experimental, theater, as important to its vitality and development as to the business of drilling oil wells: the established producer and dramatist's chance to fail in the center ring, in a full-scale commercial production with no effort spared, without causing irreparable damage to the financial or ego structures. Under modern pressures, this chance to fail has all but disappeared from Broadway and is fading fast off Broadway. What is left of it can be preserved only by means of at least partial subsidy (as in the case of David Rabe and *Boom Boom Room*)—subsidy either by an enlightened, arts-conscious public, or by setting aside a portion of the profits from commercial-theater hits, or both.

And speaking of hits, as we have noted in past *Best Plays* volumes, a "hit" in the true Broadway meaning of the word isn't merely a show that is hard to get into on Friday night, but a show which pays off its production cost (it may be easy to get into but become a "hit" by virtue of a movie sale or a profitable road tour). In recent seasons, however, the word "hit" has been losing a lot of its magic. With higher costs hopefully compensated by longer runs, few productions, however popular, reach the break-even point in the season in which they opened. And very often New York doesn't have the first or last word on a playscript as it once did. A good script ignored on Broadway for some strange or special reason (as *Moonchildren* was the first time around) may take on an illustrious life elsewhere on world stages or in other media. So we make no special point in this resume about which 1973-74 offerings were "hits" and which were "flops" except that this information is recorded in the one-page summary of the Broadway season accompanying this report.

The ultimate insignia of New York professional theater achievement (we insist) is not the instant popularity of the hit list, but selection as a Best Play in these volumes. Such selection is made with the script itself as the primary consideration, for the reason (as we have stated in previous volumes) that the script is the very spirit of the theater, the soul in its physical body. The script is not only the quintessence of the present, it is most of what endures into the future.

So the Best Plays are the best scripts. As little weight as humanly possible is given to comparative production values. The choice is made without any regard whatever as to a play's type—musical, comedy or drama—or origin on or off Broadway, or popularity at the box office or lack of same.

The Best Plays of 1973-74 were the following, listed in the order in which they opened in New York (an asterisk * with the performance number signifies that the play was still running on June 3, 1974):

The Contractor
(off Broadway; 72 perfs.)

The Good Doctor
(Broadway; 208 perfs.)

Creeps
(off Broadway; 15 perfs.)

When You Comin' Back, Red Ryder?
(off Broadway; 201* perfs.)

Find Your Way Home
(Broadway; 135 perfs.)

Bad Habits
(off B'way & B'way; 126* perfs.)

Noel Coward in Two Keys
(Broadway; 106* perfs.)

Short Eyes
(off B'way & B'way; 80* perfs.)

The Sea Horse
(off Broadway; 52* perfs.)

Jumpers
(Broadway; 48 perfs.)

Broadway

The best of bests in this problematical year, all things considered, was a Broadway offering (albeit a foreign script), *Noel Coward in Two Keys,* an eight-year-old British program. Being the work of a master dramatist, it shrugged off its age as a matter of no consequence in a sparkling Richard Barr-Charles Woodward production which enjoyed the services of the original London director, Vivian Matalon. In the 1966 London production there were three plays divided into two evening's programs: *Shadows of the Evening* (about a terminally ill man determined to reconcile his wife and his mistress to the fact of his impending death, so that they could all get some fun out whatever time he had left); *Come Into the Garden Maud* (about the liberation of a henpecked American millionaire); and *A Song at Twilight* (about the previously hidden but now surfacing homosexuality of an internationally famous writer). On Broadway, the first was dropped and the third abridged slightly to make a single, also memorable, evening of Noel Coward in top form in the twilight of his own years, dwindling down to a precious few that ended with his death in Jamaica in March 1973. Coward played the male parts in London as Hume Cronyn did in New York. The characters have differing conflicts and personalities, but they are all men of distinction coping grandly with a climax in their lives, in an elegant Swiss hotel suite which was the same set for all three plays. In the two plays done in New York, Coward makes the direct statement that vanity and greed are eventually self-defeating (in *Maud*); and that in all forms of love, honesty is the best policy (in *Twilight*). The larger implication of the total program was even more striking. Coward's characters insist on maintaining standards of excellence even though all about them may be crumbling, and so did Coward as a playwright—standards of characterization, manner, wit, *mise-en-scene* and everything else that goes into an evening of theater. This is finished work with a high polish, of a kind all too seldom encountered on the stages of today. Hume Cronyn playing wide open as two husbands, Jessica Tandy as two wives—one selfish, the other managerial—and Anne Baxter as two intruders—one loving, one designing—served the play very well on the three points of Coward's triangles. *Noel Coward in Two Keys* (London title: *Suite in Three Keys*) was the last but certainly not the least of the now-treasured works in the canon of this great 20th-century playwright.

Easily the next-best of the year's Broadway productions was another script by an English author, John Hopkins, this one bearing down very firmly on the matter of homosexuality. This subject pained the characters in Coward's play; not so in Hopkins's *Find Your Way Home.* Here homosexuality is a matter of devouring involvement, with Michael Moriarty in a brilliant portrayal (the best male performance in a season of exceptionally good performances) of a young man who, when suddenly suddenly deserted by his lover without explanation, was so agonizingly bereaved that he could ease the pain only by immolating himself in the extreme degradations of a hustler. When his lover—a husband who finally decides to leave his wife—returns as unexpectedly as he once left, the homosexual hustler begins a long climb back from the pit into which he has sunk, toward some kind of daylight. The dialogue of Hopkins's play is vividly (and to some, shockingly) explicit about physical homosexual practises. His play is not so much about homosexuality, however, as it is about love and the consequences of its deprivation. It's obviously difficult for a playwright to deal objectively with such matters —discussing, recriminating, threatening, surrendering—without resorting at times to the literary tactics of soap opera (and commentators have been quick to point out that Hopkins is an experienced TV writer). For the most part, however, the English author of *Find Your Way Home* kept his play from being spoiled by this taint, in a forthright script which had its world premiere in this New York production.

Still another British play imported to Broadway made its way onto the Best Plays list: Tom Stoppard's *Jumpers* which may turn out some day to be the play of the decade if someone finds a way to communicate to an audience the full depth and breadth of its witticisms and conundrums on the subject of God, the universe and the true meaning and value of human life on earth. When in the last scene the heroine, a neurotic but appealing musical comedy star, sings the deceptively simplistic lyric line "Two and two make roughly four," this is a staggeringly comprehensive philosophical observation which can be appreciated only if the listener has noted and understood clearly the meaning of all the verbal stunts which have gone before in Stoppard's scintillating but difficult play.

The problem is that in this production *Jumpers* never seemed clear about anything, in particular 1) whether it really wanted to be a play at all and 2) if so, what kind of a play it wanted to be. On the surface it showed itself an extremely loose-jointed absurdist farce collected in setpieces unrelated in style, or, apparently, any sort of useful "plot". There was a nugget hidden in each and every segment, however, in a play that dares greatly and is great or nothing. The "jumpers" of the title are acrobats, college professors who are also gymnasts, to make a kind of running pun of mental and physical agility. A murder takes place in the first scene and the corpse keeps bobbing up. Sportive sex also breaks out here and there, but the heart of the matter lies in the philosophical dissertations of a logician (Brian Bedford) preparing to debate the existence of God, and in the distressed cries of his wife, the singing star, protesting that astronauts have robbed the moon of its Juneyness. The sheer joyous acrobatics of Stoppard's language invite comparison with a Coward or a Wilde. Bedford's interpretation was perfect, combining as it did a meticulous articulation with an absent-minded-professor appearance and manner. The Stoppard-Bedford combination worked well enough in this New York (via Washington) production to whet the appetite for a fuller realization of the entire play some day, if indeed that is possible.

If there was any large mass of solid worth in this Broadway season, it was the group of attractive foreign plays lined up behind the three foregoing. First there was Royce Ryton's *Crown Matrimonial,* the abdication of Edward VIII (played by George Grizzard) as witnessed from the point of view of Queen Mary and others in her drawing room. This British script was somewhat bloodless, not being able to introduce the key character of Wallis Warfield into the exclusively royal circle, but it came to life in a scene depicting the distress of the Duke and Duchess of York (Patrick Horgan and Ruth Hunt) upon learning that duty would call them away from their private family life to sit on the uncomfortable throne. Another British script, Charles Laurence's *My Fat Friend,* was a platform on which to display the entertaining performances of Lynn Redgrave as a compulsive eater nevertheless determined to lose weight for love's sake, George Rose as her middle-aged and devoutly homosexual boarder who urges her toward her heterosexual goal with fast friendship and an even faster wit, and John Lithgow as a young Scottish square, also a boarder, who does all the cooking and all the straight lines. Under Robert Moore's light directorial touch, these three provided a textbook example of soap-bubble entertainment.

Another foreign script adept at managing the flash and flow of language was Hugh Leonard's *The Au Pair Man,* with Julie Harris and Charles Durning as character symbols of British royalty declining in everything but pride, still served by loyal, subservient, but perhaps a bit restless Irish vigor. This two-character play took place in a set designed by John Conklin to symbolize British imperialism crumbling around the regal lady and her au pair man as they move through their intricate charade (for example, she is always seeking to borrow his pen, his literary tradition, to use as her own). It was a clever piece, acted as carefully as it was directed by Gerald Freedman, much the best of the 1973–74 plays originated at the Vivian Beaumont.

Two other imports were of a darker hue. Brian Friel's *The Freedom of the City,* set amidst the present Irish troubles, might have enjoyed a longer run in easier times. It searched deep inside the lives of three innocent victims of overzealous police action—two men and a woman who take refuge in the town hall during a Londonderry demonstration and are shot dead as they emerge, bewildered and unarmed. Friel uses a flashback technique he has used before (in *Lovers*) to shine the special lighting of hindsight on the ambitions and emotions of the living from the ironical vantage point of death. A special technique, equally ironic, was also useful to Peter Stone's adaptation of Erich Maria Remarque's play *Full Circle,* about the fall of Berlin in 1945. The play points to the similarity between totalitarian systems, Nazi and Communist, by emphasizing the identical nature of the last-gasp Gestapo actions in the early scenes and the first-blush-of-victory actions of the conquering Russians in the final scenes, with the identical actors playing the two sets of violent characters, wearing two sets of uniforms but a single set of values.

The best American play of the Broadway season was undoubtedly but not surprisingly Neil Simon's *The Good Doctor,* a collection of 11 sketches suggested by the life, career and stories of Anton Chekhov. Chekhov's point of view as a story-teller is what gives this program whatever unity it possesses, at it deals with one after another of the social and emotional characteristics of his highly class-conscious Russian society. It is Chekhov's sense of humor which Simon obviously admires most, and obviously there is no one better qualified to make the translation from printed page to an entertaining evening of theater, enhanced by Christopher Plummer's vigorous portrayal of the Russian writer, plus strong acting support in various roles by the entire ensemble: Rene Auberjonois, Barnard Hughes, Marsha Mason and Frances Sternhagen. Other embellishments were a concert of atmosphere-establishing music and songs written for the play by Peter

RENE AUBERJONOIS, CHRISTOPHER PLUMMER, FRANCES STERNHAGEN, BAR-
NARD HUGHES AND MARSHA MASON IN NEIL SIMON'S "THE GOOD DOCTOR"

Link (with lyrics by Neil Simon) and a colorful and versatile Tony Walton set.
In *The Good Doctor,* Simon wasn't exactly writing a play in the fullest sense of
the word, but he kept a curtain up on 1973–74 Broadway to excellent advantage
and lengthened his incredible chain of successes.

Herb Gardner's *Thieves* was also a series of episodes, comments on life today
in harried New York City, strung together on a thread of a plot about a young
wife (Marlo Thomas) who is considering getting both an abortion and a divorce.
Even in 1970s New York it is fairly obvious how that little difficulty is likely to
be resolved; meanwhile Gardner does his thing in arresting monologues like that

of the brother in his *A Thousand Clowns* and of the hot dog stand operator in his *The Goodbye People*. Here in *Thieves* it is the young wife's father, a cab driver played to the hilt by Irwin Corey, who pours out a parent's ultimate position statement on married daughters who contemplate abortions; and there's also a fumbling tramp (William Hickey) who talks to himself a lot about the difficulty of working up some kind of specialty which will bring him success in his chosen occupation: panhandling. *Thieves* was constructed like a string of beads; it was the baubles that counted for something, not the connections.

Ira Levin's *Veronica's Room* was the year's best-made American play to reach Broadway. This was a melodrama about a heroine's visit to a strange, gloomy mansion whose occupants (Arthur Kennedy and Eileen Heckart) aren't the friendly fatherly and motherly couple they at first seem to be. It was a melodrama with a difference, however, in that our foolhardy heroine (Regina Baff) does *not* escape the clutches of the villains, and it turns out that their deeds are motivated by a variety of dark perversions—which may have confused some but surprised nobody in this season of 1973–74. The old couple, it turns out, are an incestuous brother and sister who have produced a necrophiliac offspring upon whom they dote, in an atmosphere so noxious that murder seems almost a cleansing act. With Ellis Rabb directing a fine cast (whose fourth member was Kipp Osborne as the son), *Veronica's Room* was a raw, red helping of evil served up for the pure flavor of it.

Still another well-made American play, Ron Milner's *What the Wine-Sellers Buy* produced on Joseph Papp's Lincoln Center schedule, dramatized the dilemma of a black youth at the crossroads: shall he choose the strait, narrow and seemingly hopelessly, permanently deprived path of righteousness his good mother has taught him to take, or shall he listen to the blandishments of the flashy, high-heeled and well-heeled pusher next door and go for the bread, even if he must pimp his own fiancee to get it? Dick A. Williams made the most of the dope peddler—in a key of never-failing amusement at the ease with which evil seems always to get the upper hand—under Michael Schultz's careful direction. With this effective slice-of-life drama; with *The Au Pair Man;* with A.J. Antoon's firmly-staged revival of *The Dance of Death;* with the transfer uptown of the Best Play *Short Eyes* following its acclaimed debut downtown at the Public Theater; and, yes, even with David Rabe's controversial new play *Boom Boom Room,* Joseph Papp's first season at the Vivian Beaumont was one of adventure for the Lincoln Center subscription audiences (and audiences who aren't adventurous don't belong at Papp productions). They said it couldn't be done, but Papp has done it; he brought the Beaumont into the mid-1970s, without any major sacrificing of standards downtown. The only feat Papp was unable to accomplish in 1973–74 was dominate his rivals with a single, towering piece of theater as he has done in the past (though at least he won a Critics Award with *Short Eyes*). Rabe's *Boom Boom Room* was supposed to be that piece of theater, and there is disappointment only, not dishonor, in its failure to live up to great expectations. A random account of how a go-go dancer became entrapped in life and in her unrewarding profession, with sharp flavorings of promiscuity, incest, homosexuality, etc., etc., this play set out to explore some rugged terrain of human experience, apparently without the proper equipment, the emotional experience and/or insight, to accomplish its mission. Any idea of Rabe's is obviously worth trying onstage, however, and the only unworthy element of the whole experiment was the public outcry raised by Papp over Clive Barnes's put-down review in the New York *Times*. What should be borne in mind through such trying episodes is that Rabe will write another play; Papp and Barnes, each an adept in his own field, will continue to live eyeball-to-eyeball; and maybe the next time out everyone will cover himself with exceptional distinction.

Other American playwrights who ventured Broadway this season with less than happy results were Jerry Devine with *Children of the Wind,* a dark show-biz drama about an actor attempting a comeback, and Murray Schisgal with *An American Millionaire,* a black farce about violence, affluence and assorted hapless maladies of our time. On the fringe of Broadway at the Little Theater appeared Ray Aranha's *My Sister, My Sister,* a play about a black woman growing up in the white-dominated South of the 1950s, in a series of sensitized episodes flashing backward and forward over her life. This play was first produced in regional theater by the Hartford, Conn., Stage Company and made its way to 44th Street via an off-off-Broadway tryout at U.R.G.E.N.T., in the feeder mechanism which is becoming so important to today's theater.

The dropoff in new Broadway musical production from 13 in 1973 to nine this year was matched by a drop in voltage. Revivals have loomed over the musical stage in recent seasons, but in each year there was at least one new work with greater stature than the old: *No, No, Nanette* had its *Follies* and *Irene* its *A Little Night Music*. This season, however, there was nothing new on Broadway that could stand up to the revival of *Candide. Over Here!* came the closest, though its concept was so nostalgic that it certainly *seemed* like a revival. It provided a vehicle for a Broadway appearance of the two surviving Andrews Sisters, Maxene and Patty, with a Will Holt book about World War II G.I.s to be trained and entertained, and a Richard M.-Robert B. Sherman score to entertain them. Patricia Birch's dances were an amusing evocation of the jitterbug era, with Samuel E. Wright, John Mineo and Ann Reinking most notably putting the choreography into action. The show also had a "big band" in full view of the stage, and it had Janie Sell acting out its musical comedy version of a Nazi spy and finally providing a third note of harmony in the Andrews Sisters' song numbers. These two great performers sang up a storm on Broadway, including what they called a "third act," with the Andrews Sisters stepping out of character and doing a medley of their old hits after the last line of the book was finally out of the way, nostalgically evocative of that rhythmic and harmonic perfection once attained by adding the now-stilled voice of LaVerne. *Over Here!* was warm, it was fun in an undemanding sort of way, but hardly a flagship show for an entire Broadway season.

Raisin, the Tony Award winner, also had its moments in a Robert Nemiroff-Charlotte Zalzberg-Judd Woldin-Robert Brittan musical rendition of Lorraine Hansberry's prizewinning play *A Raisin in the Sun,* about a black family upwardly mobile in the Chicago of the 1950s. Virginia Capers as a loving and understanding mother and grandmother and Ralph Carter as the child of the family came on with particularly engaging performances. Performance was the thing in *Lorelei,* too, as Carol Channing returned to town in the justly famous person of Lorelei Lee. Subtitled "Gentlemen Still Prefer Blondes," this show goes back to Lorelei as a widow "remembering" some of her 1920s *Gentlemen Prefer Blondes* adventures, almost a revival but not quite with its four new numbers by Jule Styne, new lyrics by Betty Comden and Adolph Green and new book material by Kenny Solms and Gail Parent. Another old-fashioned concept cloaked with some novelty on the musical stage this season was *The Magic Show,* an effort to set the amazing feats of an accomplished illusionist (Doug Henning) within the context of a Broadway musical. It was a good try, with lively, contemporaneous Stephen Schwartz musical numbers and fantastically adept acts of "magic" by its star, but it suffered from that old infirmity, book trouble.

Two other old friends, *Gigi* and *Molly* found Broadway less hospitable. *Gigi* was an adequate stage adaptation by Alan Jay Lerner and Frederick Loewe of their hit movie musical, with Alfred Drake impeccable in the Maurice Chevalier role, but stage audiences responded less than enthusiastically to its live presence in their midst. Likewise the effort to transpose Molly Goldberg to the musical stage, with Kay Ballard in the role created and made famous in every entertainment medium by Gertrude Berg, met with little success. The same was true, alas, in the case of *Ride the Winds,* with John Driver music, lyrics and book about an 11th century Samurai, on view for only 3 performances. And finally on the 1974 musical scene, intricate sexual pairings did not help *Sextet* nor animal fantasies rescue *Rainbow Jones* down on the bottom of this all too meager heap.

The 1973–74 Broadway specialty list included *Music! Music!,* a tuneful cavalcade of American music from late 19th century New Orleans jazz to rock 'n' roll, number upon number of old favorites staged by Martin Charnin with footnotes by Alan Jay Lerner. Also prominent in this category were the previously-mentioned semi-concert appearances of Josephine Baker, Liza Minnelli, Sammy Davis Jr. and Sammy Cahn (and it's getting harder and harder to draw the fine line of definition between a Broadway solo "show" and a concert which happens to take place in a Broadway theater. The Tony Awards committee reached across that line to hand a special award to Bette Midler for playing the Palace in what was styled, reviewed and has to be categorized as a concert rather than a Broadway show.)

There were no such reservations about still another solo, Henry Fonda's appearance as Clarence Darrow in a one-man show billed as "a play by David W. Rintels." Fonda evoked the personality of this dynamic lawyer who dared mightily and could laugh at his own shortcomings. The performance seemed so smoothly accomplished, so effortlessly and at the same time perfectly done, that the star's physical collapse which ended the show's Broadway run came as a surprise as well as a sorrow. Star and playwright were capable of calling up in the audience's imagination many of the characters to whom or about whom Darrow was speaking when he wasn't addressing the audience directly: defendants, plaintiffs, judges, juries, even wives. *Clarence Darrow* was well conceived, well acted and crisply directed by John Houseman, one of the year's most satisfying entertainments. In another specialized performance, James Whitmore portrayed Will Rogers in a one-man show adapted and staged by Paul Shyre, dropping in on Broadway following a long cross-country tour.

There was a tremendous amount of important additional action on Broadway this season in the form of revival production, including *A Moon for the Misbegotten* and *Candide,* to be taken up in the next section of this report. Meanwhile, here is where we list the *Best Plays* choices for the top individual achievements of 1973–74. In the acting categories, clear distinctions among "starring," "featured" or "supporting" players cannot possibly be made on the basis of official billing, in which the actor may appear as a "star" following the title (which is not true star billing), or as an "also starring" star, or any of the other typographical ego gimmicks. Here in these volumes we divide acting into "primary" and "secondary" roles, a primary role being one which carries a major responsibility for the play; a role which might some day cause a star to inspire a revival in order to appear in that character. All others, be they as vivid as Mercutio, are classed as secondary. Our problem is not definition but an embarrassment of riches as we proceed to narrow the choice to a single best in each category.

Here, then, are the Best Plays bests of 1973–74:

PLAYS

BEST PLAY: *Noel Coward in Two Keys* by Noel Coward

BEST AMERICAN PLAY: *The Sea Horse* by Edward J. Moore

ACTOR IN A PRIMARY ROLE: Michael Moriarty as Julian Weston in *Find Your Way Home*

ACTRESS IN A PRIMARY ROLE: Colleen Dewhurst as Josie Hogan in *A Moon for the Misbegotten*

ACTOR IN A SECONDARY ROLE: George Rose as Henry in *My Fat Friend*

ACTRESS IN A SECONDARY ROLE: Jessica Tandy as Anna-Mary Conklin and Hilde Latymer in *Noel Coward in Two Keys*

DIRECTOR: Jose Quintero for *A Moon for the Misbegotten*

SCENERY: Tony Walton for *Uncle Vanya* and *The Good Doctor*

COSTUMES: Pearl Somner for *Ulysses in Nighttown*

MUSICALS

BEST MUSICAL: *The Faggot* by Al Carmines

BOOK: *Candide* by Hugh Wheeler

MUSIC: Al Carmines for *The Faggot*

LYRICS: Al Carmines for *The Faggot*

ACTOR IN A PRIMARY ROLE: Lewis J. Stadlen as Dr. Voltaire, Dr. Pangloss, etc. in *Candide*

ACTRESS IN A PRIMARY ROLE: Carol Channing as Lorelei Lee in *Lorelei*
ACTOR IN A SECONDARY ROLE: Ralph Carter as Travis Younger in *Raisin*
ACTRESS IN A SECONDARY ROLE: Virginia Capers as Lena Younger in *Raisin*
DIRECTOR: Harold Prince for *Candide*
CHOREOGRAPHER: Patricia Birch for *Over Here!* and *Candide*
SCENERY: Eugene and Franne Lee for *Candide*
COSTUMES: Franne Lee for *Candide*

Revivals on and off Broadway

An enormous proportion of the 1973–74 New York theater's effectiveness was achieved under the heading of revivals. Broadway's biggest straight-play hit was a revival: the superb Jose Quintero staging of Eugene O'Neill's *A Moon for the Misbegotten* showering credit on all participants including Colleen Dewhurst in an earth-mother portrayal of Josie Hogan—easily the best starring female performance of the year—and Jason Robards as James Tyrone Jr. in an equally telling performance which was as near to the year's best as makes very little difference, with Ed Flanders in powerful support as Phil Hogan. Not since *That Championship Season* (which closed this year after 844 performances) has a drama established itself as a sellout hit on Broadway, and very seldom has a revival achieved such status without the presence of an overwhelmingly popular star; still less a revival of a play whose emotional tensions can be summed up under the pejorative contemporary meaning of the word "heavy" and which wound up its original 68-performance run with only an indifferent reputation as a second-rate item in O'Neill's first-rate canon. Then along came Quintero to change this duckling into a swan of swans.

But this was that kind of a season for revivals. The most popular Broadway musical, too, was a revival: *Candide,* the 1956 Leonard Bernstein-Lillian Hellman-Richard Wilbur musical which has built up more renown over the intervening years with its original cast recording than it ever did in its 73-performance first run on Broadway. This year it reappeared with a new book by Hugh Wheeler adapted from the Voltaire work and added lyrics by Stephen Sondheim and John Latouche, all restaged with the golden touch of Harold Prince. This revamped *Candide* was first tried out off Broadway at Chelsea Theater Center in Brooklyn, then moved to Broadway as the musical of the year. It still is as it was in 1956 (when it was named a Best Play of its season) a musically and verbally sophisticated satire on concepts of good and evil in human affairs—the "newness" of the 1974 *Candide* is more conceptual than spiritual. The book covers about the same ground, taking Candide through his episodes of adventure, from gullible pupil of Dr. Pangloss ("All for the best in the best of all possible worlds") to disillusioned but still hopeful man of the world ready to shed pretension and concentrate on making his own little garden grow.

Lewis J. Stadlen, the Groucho Marx of *Minnie's* and the nephew of *The Sunshine Boys,* was perfect as Dr. Pangloss and other dryasdust pontificaters, in the year's top musical performance. Mark Baker as Candide was somewhat more effective and Maureen Brennan as Cunegonde less so than the players in the original production, winning one and losing one in the comparison. Physically, this *Candide* concept was volatile, with the action taking place all over the auditorium (including sometimes its ceiling) and with the spectators seated in clumps all over the place, some of them in direct contact with the action. The show adapted itself to last year's radical physical alterations of the Broadway Theater for and by *Dude,* so that some good can be said to have finally come out of that debacle. If they don't tear down the Broadway, it is now a handy tool for shaping a new kind of theater, a sort of architectural blendor capable of stirring the performers and the audience together in one great intermingled unit of experience, as in this resounding *Candide.*

Another conspicuous Broadway revival was *Ulysses in Nighttown,* a segment of James Joyce's masterpiece dramatized by the late Marjorie Barkentin for off-Broadway presentation in the 1958–59 season and now remounted on Broadway with Zero Mostel playing Leopold Bloom as he did in the first production. As I indicated in the opening paragraphs of this report, I found it more vulgar than effective (except in the quality of performance and design, most notably the costumes by Pearl Somner). This play needed to soar to high reaches of imagination if its excursion into one man's overblown vision of a red light district was going to work on the stage. It was cruelly pulled back down to earth time after time, however, by grossly insensitive stress on the body's orifices and protuberances. If *Ulysses* is ever revived successfully, Zero Mostel may be the one to play it, but there has to be a better way to stage it.

The Circle in the Square began the 1973–74 season (which by tradition is dated from June 1) with a masterful revival of *Uncle Vanya* staged and co-adapted by Mike Nichols, with standout performances by Nicol Williamson as Voinitsky and George C. Scott as Astrov, designed by Tony Walton at the top of his form—the first and surely one of the best shows of the year. Circle in the Square followed with two more top-drawer revivals on its 1974 schedule: *The Waltz of the Toreadors* as interpreted by Anne Jackson and Eli Wallach under Brian Murray's direction, and *The Iceman Cometh* staged by the Circle's own Theodore Mann, with James Earl Jones a resonant Hickey. With programs such as these, it's almost incredible that Circle in the Square was brought to the edge of oblivion this season because of financial difficulties, which seem to be the common lot in this decade of our discontent and disorientation. As we went to press, the group was still the subject of much concern among theater folk but was equipped for the beginning, at least, of another season in 1975. They were enjoying an extra boost in both box office and prestige from their guest production from overseas, the Young Vic's popular *Scapino* with Jim Dale captivating Broadway audiences in the title role of this version of Molière's hardy farce, which had already made a hit off Broadway earlier in the season as a guest production at the Chelsea Theater Center.

Solidly mounted revivals of *A Streetcar Named Desire* (last year's Lincoln Center production restaged for downtown by Jules Irving) and *The Pajama Game* (staged and enhanced with some new material by George Abbott) ventured into the commercial fray of Broadway and emerged with honor but not much glory.

An earlier effort to breathe life into *The Desert Song* seemed too little and too late, and its sister revival production of *The Student Prince* closed on the road.

The luck of the Broadway draw was much better in the organizational revival productions like those of New Phoenix with three treasures of the stage offered in repertory: Friedrich Duerrenmatt's *The Visit* directed by Harold Prince (a New Phoenix artistic director), Philip Barry's still-charming *Holiday* and Feydeau's *Chemin de Fer,* a fugue of flirtation expertly played by Rachel Roberts and the other members of the repertory ensemble under Stephen Porter's direction. Likewise, John Houseman's City Center Acting Company enjoyed a good season at the Billy Rose Theater with a versatile program of *Three Sisters, The Beggar's Opera, Measure for Measure, Scapin* (in a special performance for children) and *Next Time I'll Sing to You,* the difficult Shakespeare play directed most successfully by Houseman himself.

In case you weren't counting, that makes 19 Broadway revival productions in 1973–74, three more than last season even in this year of attenuated action in the large theaters. In the smaller ones, the story was the same. Off Broadway came up with 22 revivals, three more than last year. Shakespeare predominated in this area, with the productions last summer of *As You Like It,* the James Earl Jones *King Lear* and a return engagement of *Two Gentlemen of Verona* in Central Park at the Delacorte, and with innovative New York Shakespeare productions of *Troilus and Cressida* (staged as camp) and *The Tempest* in Lincoln Center's small theater, formerly the Forum, now renamed the Mitzi E. Newhouse Theater in recognition of its new namesake's thoughtful and bounteous patronage. (This group also put on *Macbeth,* but only as a workshop production.)

Shakespeare was also prominently on display in the offerings of four visiting English troupes imported by the Brooklyn Academy of Music in association with Brooklyn College, creating a series of cultural events that would have parted the waters of the East River to make way for theatergoers migrating to Brooklyn, were there not already a sufficiency of bridges and tunnels for this purpose. The first group of English visitors to the Academy's Opera House was the Royal Shakespeare Company with its production of *Richard II* under John Barton's direction, with Ian Richardson and Richard Pasco alternating as Richard and Bolingbroke who deposes him, as though to place double emphasis on the mutability of human affairs. In the Academy's smaller Leperq Space, three members of the British company performed a "new" work, *Sylvia Plath,* a stage arrangement and presentation of selections from that poet's writings.

The next group to fly the Union Jack over Brooklyn's cultural center was the two-year-old cooperative ensemble called the Actors Company playing the second *King Lear* of the season in repertory with a little-known Chekhov play *The Wood Demon, The Way of the World* and a novel and challenging program of verbal acrobatics called *Knots,* created by the Scottish philosopher R.D. Laing.

The third group to arrive in Brooklyn was the Young Vic with *The Taming of the Shrew* in repertory with their *Scapino* (which was later brought to Broadway by Circle in the Square) and Terence Rattigan's amusing bit of 1930s fluff

French Without Tears. Finally there came to Brooklyn another Royal Shake-speare troupe headed by Michael Redgrave and Sara Kestelman in two remark-able anthology programs: *The Hollow Crown,* a compendium of writings and statements by kings and queens of England and about them by Shakespeare and other observers, which played once before in New York in 1963; and a brand new anthology, *Pleasure and Repentance,* a collection of writings about the ways of love from Sir Walter Raleigh up to and including the Beatles.

Our own leading off-Broadway troupe, the Roundabout Theater Company under the persistent and consistently able direction of Gene Feist and Michael Fried, presented New York with yet another busy, distinguished season. This was the group's longest year, beginning in early summer with Pinter's *The Caretaker* starring William Prince and continuing into April with W. Somerset Maugham's *The Circle* with Natalie Schafer, Christopher Hewett and David Atkinson. The three Roundabout programs in between were *Miss Julie* on a bill with the Ameri-can premiere of a short French madame-and-butler farce called *The Death of Lord Chatterly,* by the French author Christopher Frank; another Strindberg, *The Father,* with Robert Lansing as the Captain; and a Chekhov, *The Seagull,* both the latter adapted by Feist, who directed all the programs except the double bill, which was directed by Henry Pillsbury. This worthy troupe, which has taken the word "Repertory" out of its name probably because it now schedules its programs seriatim, is to off Broadway what the New Phoenix and City Center are to Broadway itself, a going and active concern which does not always touch the heights with each production but does sometimes, and which maintains those standards of taste and performance which give New York theater its good name.

The straight-play revival hit of this off-Broadway season was *Moonchildren* by Michael Weller, a darkish comedy about 1960s undergraduates clinging to the last few weeks of the fantasy life they've created for themselves in their dormitory, with its special language and code of behavior, before being thrust out into what is clearly going to be a painfully cold world. This play was first produced on Broadway in 1972, the New York playwriting debut of its gifted author, but it survived only 16 performances—mostly because at that time audiences were fed up with hearing about the exploits of rebellious youth on every hand and were loath to expose themselves to it further, voluntarily, as entertainment. *Moonchil-dren* was named a Best Play of its season, though, and now it has become a solid commercial hit off Broadway, as directed by John Pasquin. Parenthetically, its author fared less well this season with a new effort to castigate Vietnam policies and events in the form of the musical *More Than You Deserve,* produced for a short run at the Public Theater.

Finally among this year's off-Broadway revivals, there were two productions at opposite ends of the stylistic scale: the Greek Art Theater's *Medea* and a return engagement of the revue *Jacques Brel Is Alive and Well and Living in Paris,* which already made off-Broadway history in its first run of 1,847 performances. The ever-increasing energy devoted to breathing new life into the theater's past is a flower in the thistle of the modern theater's environment. As the volume of new work shrinks, the volume of revivals apparently expands (to 41 this year from a combined Broadway and off-Broadway total of 35 last year). The prominence of the revival schedule was on the rise this season, too, with productions like *A Moon for the Misbegotten, Candide, Moonchildren* and the distinguished British visitors, plus the solid, steady contributions of Circle in the Square, New York Shakespeare, New Phoenix, City Center and Roundabout, maintaining a strong presence of legitimate theater all over town. As Walter Kerr has noted, maybe New York doesn't want or need a permanent repertory company because it already *is* a permanent, active repertory theater. For example, here's a summary of what was going on in 1973–74, a list of this Broadway and off-Broadway season's revived authors in alphabetical order, with the titles of their revived works:

Anthology (various authors)
The Hollow Crown
Jean Anouilh
The Waltz of the Toreadors
Marjorie Barkentin
Ulysses in Nighttown
Philip Barry
Holiday
Anton Chekhov
The Seagull
Three Sisters
The Wood Demon
Uncle Vanya
William Congreve
The Way of the World
Friedrich Duerrenmatt
The Visit
Euripides
Medea
Georges Feydeau
Chemin de Fer
John Gay
The Beggar's Opera
W. Somerset Maugham
The Circle
Molière
Scapin
Scapino (twice)
Musicals (various authors)

Candide (twice)
The Desert Song
Jacques Brel, etc.
The Pajama Game
Two Gentlemen of Verona
Eugene O'Neill
The Iceman Cometh
A Moon for the Misbegotten
Harold Pinter
The Caretaker
Terence Rattigan
French Without Tears
James Saunders
Next Time I'll Sing to You
William Shakespeare
As You Like It
King Lear (twice)
Measure for Measure
Richard II
The Taming of the Shrew
The Tempest
Troilus and Cressida
August Strindberg
The Dance of Death
The Father
Miss Julie
Michael Weller
Moonchildren
Tennessee Williams
A Streetcar Named Desire

Off Broadway

The nitty gritty of the contemporary New York theater's economic and artistic problems is exposed off Broadway, where costs have risen in multiples, not just percentages (it cost seven times as much to produce Mart Crowley's three-character *A Breeze From the Gulf* off Broadway in 1973–74 as it did to produce his nine-character *The Boys in the Band* in 1968, $70,000 vs. $10,000). The volume of off-Broadway production was bound to fall off this season, and it did: straight-play programs in English from 37 last season (and 52 the season before) to 35 this year; new American plays from 28 last year (and 43 the season before) to 27 this year; new musicals from 19 down to six. Revivals were up slightly, as previously noted, from 19 last season to 22 this year. The overall total of off-Broadway programming has been recorded in recent *Best Plays* volumes as follows: 119 in 1969–70, 95 in 1970–71, 87 in 1971–72, 87 in 1972–73 and 76 in 1973–74 (a steady decline, though the inference to be drawn isn't quite as simple and straight-lined at it looks at first glance, perhaps, when you take into consideration the average quality level of the productions over the years, the length of runs, percentage of subsidy, etc. Even the term "off Broadway" has fluctuated in definition somewhat as time passed. By "off Broadway" in this volume we mean those English-language productions offered in houses of 299 seats or less, usually under the organizational umbrella of the League of off-Broadway theaters and usually located in midtown Manhattan, which have Equity casts, plan to play regular full-week schedules of performances open to the public and to public scrutiny by inviting reviews. A few others which don't qualify technically are included at the editor's discretion, sometimes because they are visitors from abroad or because they have found their way onto other major but less precise lists of "off Broadway" shows and therefore would be expected to appear on this one.)

Certainly there doesn't seem to be any parallel waning of artistic standards off Broadway. On the contrary, six of the 1973–74 Best Plays had their initial commercial-theater productions off Broadway, the largest number in the history of this 55-year old series: *The Contractor, When You Comin' Back, Red Ryder?, Creeps, Bad Habits, Short Eyes* and *The Sea Horse.* It is significant of the new era that two of these were pre-tested foreign scripts, two were transfers pre-tested off off Broadway in Circle Theater productions and a fifth was produced organizationally—that is, as part of the schedule of a semi-subsidized organization, rather than as an individual production standing on its own commercial feet. Of this year's half dozen Best Plays off Broadway, only one, *Bad Habits,* made it solo. There could hardly be a more persuasive illustration of the great value of experimental facilities to develop new works, either in the form of the off-off-Broadway work-in-progress production or under the umbrella of a subsidy.

Off Broadway's 1973 best-of-bests was *The Sea Horse,* the best American play of the whole New York year, a remarkably sensitive portrayal of a persistent wooing. She (Conchata Ferrell) is the owner-manager of a waterfront bar; built like a beer barrel and sleeps in the barroom loft, often alone. He (Edward J.

Moore), a seaman with a flair for engines, and a stubborn wooer with an almost limitless supply of compassion, enjoys the lady's favors—such as they are—but is finally determined to persuade her to marry him and hack at least a thin portion of happiness out of their lives, if it takes him all night from closing time to opening time the next day (as it does). She has seen her beloved father killed by a drunken customer and has learned everything about how to survive and sometimes even enjoy herself, except how to love. He knows that their best hope lies in making a commitment to each other for better or worse, and he means to get "yes" for an answer even though it is like trying to milk a water buffalo; her skin is thick enough to resist all but the most pointed emotional penetration. His isn't, and this situation, plus the skill of the two actors and the Marshall W. Mason direction, provided a very full two acts of theater, even with only two people onstage. Mason is the artistic director of off off Broadway's Circle Repertory Theater Company, which launched last year's *The Hot l Baltimore* and this year's *Red Ryder* and *Sea Horse,* all transferred to commercial productions after their worth was proven at the Circle. *The Sea Horse* opened off Broadway as the work of one "James Irwin," which turned out to be a *nom de plume* for its co-star, Edward J. Moore, who had written the play as a vehicle for his own performance but didn't see fit to run double jeopardy as both actor and author. He succeeded admirably in both persons, reminding us that perhaps the good old practise of writing for specific actors, a la Shakespeare, Molière, etc., should be put to use more often in the modern theater.

The first of the Circle's two plays to graduate into the commercial theater this season and reach Best Play status was *When You Comin' Back, Red Ryder?,* another debut of a new American playwright, Mark Medoff (that new growth *will* continue to appear, no matter what), and another strong piece of conventionally styled playmaking. Red Ryder—the hero of a once-popular Western comic strip—ain't never comin' back to the pages of your local newspaper or anywhere else, the author is saying, nor is any other symbol of America's lost innocence in this era of disillusionment. Medoff's characters are collected in a third-rate diner in the Southwest, across the street from a motel just off the highway. Among them are a couple of dreamers (Bradford Dourif as the night man, still clinging to pieces of the Red Ryder ideal, and Elizabeth Sturges as a day waitress making the best of her sorry lot), a couple of doers (Robyn Goodman as a concert violinist and James Kiernan as her attendant husband) and a catalyst (Kevin Conway as a drug-smuggling bully who terrorizes all the others in the manner of *The Petrified Forest* and takes pleasure in smashing each and every one of their Red Ryder hopes and pretensions because he has long since lost the last vestige of his own). Bill Stabile's flyblown cafe set, Kenneth Frankel's direction and the performance of a closely-knit cast all contributed to the very great effectiveness of Medoff's play. Set in the late 1960s, *Red Ryder* might be summed up as the embitterment and self-destruction of one of the mid-1960s *Moonchildren,* a resolution which offers itself all the more readily because Conway was an unforgettable image in the Broadway production of the Michael Weller play.

A third off-Broadway Best Play by a new author was *Short Eyes,* which climbed the ladder all the way up in a single season. It began with an off-off-

The 1973–74 Season off Broadway

PLAYS (27)

The Boy Who Came to Leave
Nellie Toole & Co.
Nourish the Beast (return engagement)
A Breeze From the Gulf
American Place:
House Party
Bread
A Festival of Short Plays
The Year of the Dragon
Public Theater:
Lotta
Barbary Shore
Les Femmes Noires
SHORT EYES
The Killdeer
The Enclave
WHEN YOU COMIN' BACK, RED RYDER?
Felix
BAD HABITS
Ridiculous Theater:
Hot Ice
Camille
Negro Ensemble:
The Great Macdaddy
A Season-Within-a-Season:
Black Sunlight
Nowhere to Run, Nowhere to Hide
Terraces
Heaven and Hell's Agreement
Once I Saw a Boy Laughing
THE SEA HORSE
A Look Back at Each Other

MUSICALS (6)

The Faggot
Antiques
More Than You Deserve
Fashion
Kaboom!
Pop

REVUES (3)

Sisters of Mercy
The Indian Experience
Let My People Come

FOREIGN PLAYS IN ENGLISH (8)

The Death of Lord Chatterly
Chelsea:
THE CONTRACTOR
Total Eclipse
The Foursome
CREEPS
Royal Shakespeare:
Sylvia Plath
Pleasure and Repentance
Knots

FOREIGN-LANGUAGE PRODUCTIONS (2)

The Man From the East
Le Roi Se Meurt

REVIVALS (22)

Delacorte:
As You Like It
King Lear
Two Gentlemen of Verona
Roundabout:
The Caretaker
Miss Julie
The Father
The Seagull
The Circle
Candide
Medea
Moonchildren
Newhouse:
Troilus and Cressida
The Tempest
Royal Shakespeare:
Richard II
The Hollow Crown
Actors Company:
The Wood Demon
King Lear
The Way of the World

SPECIALTIES (8)

Young Vic:
The Taming of the Shrew
Scapino
French Without Tears
Jacques Brel Is Alive and Well, etc.

Nicol Williamson's Late Show
I Love Thee Freely
Baird Marionettes:
The Whistling Wizard, etc.
Pinocchio
Dear Nobody
I Am a Woman
The Wild Stunt Show
Ionescopade

Categorized above are all the plays listed in the "Plays Produced off Broadway" section of this volume.
Plays listed in CAPITAL LETTERS have been designated Best Plays of 1973–74.
Plays listed in *italics* were still running June 1, 1974.

Broadway production by the Theater of the Riverside Church, then moved to off Broadway in its New York Shakespeare Festival production downtown at the Public Theater where it won considerable acclaim including the Drama Critics Award for the best American play of the year, and finally moved up to Broadway status when the Papp organization transferred it uptown to the Vivian Beaumont for an extended run. *Short Eyes* is a drama of life in prison, with inmates divided into three ethnic cliques—white, black and hispanic—living in close quarters in an uneasy truce. Their single point of agreement, of temporary solidarity, is their hatred of any child-molester, or "short eyes," who is an untouchable pariah in their tripartite society. This play was written by a former convict, Miguel Piñero, who was still on parole at the time of his play's opening (c.f. his personal history in the biographical sketch which accompanies the synopsis of *Short Eyes* in this volume). His cast off off, off and on Broadway was an ensemble brought together not only in the unified effort of performance but also united by their past as members of a prison theater workshop called The Family, many of whose members continued to work together on the outside under the guidance of Marvin Felix Camillo, who brought them to Riverside as a resident company and directed *Short Eyes* on all its stages.

The bulk of the off-Broadway schedule downtown at the Public was exploratory, reaching, purposeful, never scaling as high a peak as *Short Eyes,* which could and should not be expected of a large production schedule of not-necessarily-finished work. There were new plays by Robert Montgomery *(Lotta)* and Jay Broad (*The Killdeer,* drawing a bead on a suburban Willie Loman); the Michael Weller-Jim Steinman musical *More Than You Deserve;* a Jack Gelber adaptation of Norman Mailer's *Barbary Shore,* a study of Marxism veneered with mystery drama; and *Les Femmes Noires,* details of the contemporary black experience in a script by Edgar White. The Joseph Papp organization did more than its share for the New York theater in 1973–74 and had its share of success, while establishing a powerful momentum of production all around the town.

A fourth American off-Broadway Best Play was the work of the distinguished professional Terrence McNally, who in his new comedy *Bad Habits* turned his laser beam onto the opposing forces of self-indulgence and self-denial. The medium for his message is the nursing home, in this case an unmatched pair of them, and the types of patients—alcoholics, eternal misfits, deviates, etc.—who might avail themselves of their services. Like two other of the year's Best Plays *(Noel Coward in Two Keys* and *The Good Doctor),* McNally's is a program of short plays, two one-acters set in sanatoria with opposite theories of treatment: in *Ravenswood* anything goes, patients are put on soothing high-cholesterol diets and encouraged to do and/or have their thing, whatever it may be; in *Dunelawn* nothing goes except a shot of tranquillizing drug which turns the most eccentric and difficult patients into identical vegetables. The two plays are a unit, however, in making their author's observation that in the long run it may perhaps be more bearable to suffer the consequences of, say, smoking than to suffer the dehumanizing frustration of not smoking (figuratively, not literally—as in other McNally comedies there is little to be learned about the taste of *Bad Habits* by studying the list of its ingredients). An ensemble juggled the eight extravagant characterizations in each play under the direction of Robert Drivas, who has starred in McNally plays in his time and is comfortable with the basically black-comic McNally style. At season's end *Bad Habits* moved to Broadway, but I am happy to have made its acquaintance in a smaller theater, with actors brushing by me up and down the aisle, in close contact with its pleasantly weird sense of values.

Chelsea Theater Center weighted its schedule with imports this season, most notably *The Contractor,* a 1970 play by David Storey, written the year before his Critics Award-winning *Home* but only now reaching New York in the Chelsea production which won the Critics Award for the best of bests in 1973–74. In this play as in his others, Storey distills the most acidulous implications from what appears to be the most watery of situations, as assoi .ed workmen put up a marquee for the wedding party of their boss's daughter and then take it down again the day after the ceremony (the wedding party itself doesn't take place on stage, only the preparation and aftermath). Into this tiny frame Storey gets a huge chunk of the contemporary scene with its haves and have-nots, workers and drones, rough diamonds and smooth-polished obsidians. The contractor himself is the tent-pole character—it is his workmen, his tent, his daughter, an allegory of his life that is passing before his eyes as the marquee goes up and down. A major challenge of this play is to personify every member of a variegated company, and the acting ensemble under Barry Davis's direction, led by John Wardwell as the contractor, met the challenge admirably.

Candide, also a Critics Award-winner, was Chelsea's only American work on its 1973–74 schedule. One of its other imports was Christopher Hampton's *Total Eclipse,* a play about the strong attachment between the French poets Verlaine and Rimbaud in which the Messrs. Christopher Lloyd and Michael Finn played just about the whole second act naked in a succession of bedrooms (like *Candide, Total Eclipse* experimented with a multiplicity of acting areas interspersed with the audience seating, so that the action moved from place to place freely, in the style of a novel). Chelsea wound up its season going from the ridiculous to the ridiculous with *The Wild Stunt Show,* a zany topical revue which originated as a popular touring entertainment for London pubs and streets.

Another foreign script which made the Best Plays list in an off-Broadway production was *Creeps,* a study of nerve-damaged spastics written by a Canadian, David E. Freeman. *Creeps* was a hit and an award-winner in Toronto, after which it was produced in Washington, D.C. at the Folger Theater before its arrival in New York for an unfortunately short run of 15 performances. Its author is himself a cerebral palsy victim (see the biographical sketch accompanying the synopsis of *Creeps* in the Best Plays section of this volume), but his play makes no special plea—quite the contrary. *Creeps* isn't about handicaps—its characters have pretty much learned to live with theirs—but about prejudice, as a group of men with various muscle and speech infirmities gathers in the filthy washroom of a "sheltered workshop" for the handicapped to discuss their principal grievance: the so-called "normal" members of society, even the members of their own families, look on them as pariahs to be hidden away in the attic or in institutions. Once in a while they are permitted to become the objects of organized charity, but they are never to be treated as human beings or allowed to develop their own capacities in their own way. *Creeps* is a strong play by a gifted author who at this writing already has another hit in Canada. Once again we can report that it was very capably interpreted by another of those solid ensemble casts we've enjoyed this season, this one under the direction of Louis W. Scheeder. The fact that this play was so short-lived in the New York commercial theater was regrettable but understandable—how do you convince audiences they *must* go see a play demonstrating the consequences of crippling illness and taking place in an extraordinarily filthy men's room? Nevertheless this was a wonderfully moving work, a small but insistent concept which no doubt will have a life of its own in the world theater repertory.

Neither American Place nor the Negro Ensemble Company produced one of the Best Plays this season (though a 1973 NEC graduate, *The River Niger,* won the 1974 Tony), but they brought on some of the better off-Broadway offerings. The NEC's *The Great Macdaddy* was an imaginative musical parable of the black experience, with Macdaddy (David Downing) wandering across the U.S.A. looking for an old friend named Wine (Graham Brown) but generally finding nothing but trouble caused by villainous Scag (Al Freeman Jr.). It was a rare instance of a black Morality play in which Whitey is not the only evil. NEC simultaneously put on what it called *A Season-Within-a-Season,* a series of four new plays presented in limited rather than full-scale engagements. It was preparing to round off its production year with the full-scale production of a new Charles Fuller script as the season ended.

American Place put on the new Ed Bullins, *House Party,* like so much of his recent work a series of vignettes or statements about the black experience as he witnesses it. In this case it was framed in the theater as a kind of night club show. The American Place schedule also included David Scott Milton's *Bread* and a one-act play program of scripts by William Hauptman, Lonnie Carter and Maria Irene Fornes. The last and most effective of the organization's new-play programs was *The Year of the Dragon* by Frank Chin (author of *The Chickencoop Chinaman*), a study of two generations of a San Francisco Chinatown family, with a predictably bitter indictment of the restricted quality of life imposed on such a family by a combination of its own traditions and those of American society.

In addition, American Place's production of last year's Steve Tesich family comedy *Baba Goya* returned for an off-Broadway run as an individual presentation at the Cherry Lane under the new title *Nourish the Beast.* Toward the end of the season American Place's director, Wynn Handman, announced that his group, which helped pioneer the concept of the playwright's workshop and showcase, had now been joined by so many other organizations devoted to the identical cause that it would now adopt a new policy called "Resurgence": the production of past works which for some reason or another may not have received as much attention as they deserved the first time around and merit a new hearing. Next season's first "Resurgence" production will be S.J. Perelman's *The Beauty Part,* a 1962 Broadway *succes d'estime.*

Charles Ludlam's well-established off-off-Broadway troupe, the Ridiculous Theater Company, surfaced in the commercial theater with the wild and woolly

Hot Ice, a spoof of corpse-freezing, detective fiction and just about everything else in a putative theft-and-murder mystery written and direct by Ludlam and catering expertly to the special taste for theatrical camp. Ludlam ended his season by playing Camille in his own vision of the Alexandre Dumas play done by his company in their usual outlandish style.

After the phenomenal success a few seasons ago of his *The Boys in the Band,* Mart Crowley's second New York-produced play, *A Breeze From the Gulf,* aroused great expectations. They weren't entirely fulfilled by this too-introspective study of a boy's growing up with the burden of a boozy father and neurotic mother, even though the acting of the three characters by Robert Drivas, Ruth Ford and Scott McKay was first-rate. The greatest expectation of all was satisfied, however: *A Breeze From the Gulf* was a more than routinely interesting play by an author who turns out to be a new playwright in the full meaning of the word, not just a fluke of one-time success. Another more than routinely interesting off-Broadway script was *The Enclave* by the distinguished dramatist Arthur Laurents. The enclave of his title is a mews which a close-knit group of friends plans to renovate and settle as their own private little island in the sea of the city —until the group is suddenly fragmented under the blow of learning that one of them plans to come out of the closet as a homosexual and live openly in their midst with his lover. The New York production of *The Enclave* (following one last season at the Washington, D.C. Theater Club) included a Robert Randolph set ingeniously adaptable to all the various homes. An effort at ensemble performing didn't quite come off, however; the supposedly very strong rapport among these characters at the beginning of the play was never convincing.

Also on the list of off-Broadway's one-at-a-time productions in 1973-74 was E.A. Whitehead's play *The Foursome* about the battle of the sexes, imported for a short run. A Peter Keveson psychological thriller which had premiered in West Germany, *Nellie Toole & Co.,* was remarkable more for the offstage incident it provoked than for anything it developed onstage. The actress Sylvia Miles so resented John Simon's review that upon meeting him at a party a few days after the opening she anointed him with a plate of food.

Musical production was more satisfying off Broadway than on, even with the season's attenuated volume. The year's best musical, *The Faggot,* sprang to life out of the mind of Al Carmines, the regisseur of the Judson Poets' Theater, who wrote, directed and performed in the show both in its original off-off-Broadway phase and later as it graduated to a commercial production for a run of 182 performances. It was a series of comments on homosexuality aimed as humor, as pathos, as historical reference to such as Oscar Wilde and Catherine the Great, and, in its best sequence, as the emotional undercurrent in various modern situations. *The Faggot* was a show of strength for the musical theater, as Carmines brought poetry, melody and sympathy to his complex subject.

Off Broadway's other standout new musical was *Fashion,* based on the 19th Century comedy by Anna Cora Mowatt in an adaptation by Anthony Stimac (who also directed), with Don Pippin music and Steve Brown lyrics. This show was subtitled "A New Style Musical Comedy," and it was indeed a triumph of tongue-in-cheek style perfectly comprehended and performed by every member of the company in every corner of the production. The antique comedy is about a would-be lady of fashion whose financier husband has cooked his books in order to keep her in clothes and parties; she in her turn is easy prey for a bogus count and other designing persons. The heart of the joke in this version, though, is that the whole show is presented as a run-through by a modern Long Island ladies' dramatic society doing an early American script, with all the roles played by women except for the one male hired by the society to "direct" the show. *Fashion* had only one dimension of music played on a piano at the side of the stage, but it had an extra dimension of satire realized in such performances as Rhoda Butler's Snobson, the financier's scheming clerk, or Henrietta Valor's Trueman, a wealthy friend from the West who is a square shooter and figures heavily in the denouement (and it *was* a rich, ripe, 19th century-type denouement, not just an ending).

Off Broadway was dotted with outstanding specialty shows, too, throughout the season. No sooner had the *Uncle Vanya* revival established itself as a Broadway hit than one of its stars, Nicol Williamson, hired a small hall across town and performed nightly an after-theater mix of narrative poetry, songs and sketches under the title *Nicol Williamson's Late Show*. It was a popular success, as was Jane Marla Robbins's "one-woman play" about the noted 18th century wit, Fanny Burney, and those who moved through her world. Love letters of the Brownings were dramatized in *I Love Thee Freely*, and Viveca Lindfors brought in her one-woman program of sketches by and about women, *I Am a Woman*, for a limited engagement. The Bil Baird Marionette Theater opened a new hit for its repertory, a puppet musical version of *Pinocchio* created by an illustrious team of musical theater dramatists: Jerome Coopersmith (book), Mary Rodgers (music) and Sheldon Harnick (lyrics).

The foreign-language visitors this year were *The Man From the East*, a Japanese musical production of the Red Buddha Theater with a rock score by Stomu Yamash'ta, and the Tréteau production in French of Ionesco's *Exit the King*. There wasn't much to shout about in the category of off-Broadway revues, the one notable occurrence being the production of Earl Wilson Jr.'s *Let My People Come*, self-described as "A sexual musical," which opened in January at the Village Gate but steadfastly refused to formalize its existence and invite the critics to an opening night; instead, it merely allowed its "previews" to fade imperceptibly into a run.

If any single rung in a ladder can be said to be the most important, then surely off Broadway was the major rung in the ladder of legitimate stage production in 1973–74. It came up with six of the Best Plays and the best new musical. As an arena of experimental activity it was shrinking, but it was still able to provide a few of the theater's most illustrious artists with the opportunity to try out a *Candide* or a *Bad Habits* before committing them to the siege perilous of the Broadway showplace. It proved hospitable to imported, pre-tested scripts as well as to the work of new, scarcely-fledged American playwrights emerging from off off Broadway as from a hatching egg. Off Broadway's most conspicuous flaw, the rising cost of production, is shared by every other segment of the live performing arts, including, probably, the blind street minstrel who has to pay more these days for his dog's food. But off Broadway's 1973-74 honors were handsomely won, and deserve our enthusiastic applause.

Offstage

Along Broadway the principal subjects of conversation and concern were about the same as everywhere else: Watergate and finances. There wasn't anything much the theater could do about the former except discuss it, but a lot was done about financing in efforts to energize both the box office and the subsidy sources.

The season's major achievement in this area was TKTS, the ticket booth in Duffy Square which distributes unsold seats for same-day Broadway and off-Broadway offerings at half price plus a small service charge which goes to maintain the booth. This Times Square Theater Center was opened June 25, 1973 under the sponsorship of state and city agencies and the Theater Development Fund, which manages it. The booth was an instant success and soon was credited with handling a significant proportion of the New York commercial theater's weekly gross. By the end of 1974, *Variety* estimated, TKTS had distributed 409,886 tickets for gross receipts of $1,860,568—or about 4 per cent of the total gross during the time period covered by the estimate. A TDF survey conducted by William J. Baumol came to the conclusion that this TKTS business represented a net increase in the size of the theater's audience, drawing patrons who probably would not otherwise have bought theater tickets.

One prominent Broadway production, *The River Niger,* the eventual 1974 Tony winner, refused to participate in TKTS, twofers or any other plan to fill empty seats at cut-rate prices. The show closed in November and went on tour rather than trying to stay open in New York by means of the sales plans. Its management, the Negro Ensemble Company, is making a special effort to attract to the theater new audiences from the black community; and, as an NEC spokesman stated in *Variety,* the organization's artistic director, Douglas Turner Ward, made the decision not to offer cut-rate tickets because he felt that "selling individual tickets on a cut-rate basis to some, while haphazardly excluding others, constitutes a breach of faith with those who buy at regular prices." Mr. Ward had insisted that regular box office prices at *The River Niger* be as low as possible from the very beginning of its Broadway run. The NEC to the contrary notwithstanding, TKTS is proving to be a real boon to the theater at a very difficult time.

The 1973-74 shows aided by TDF in the form of direct subsidy of ticket purchases to the tune of about $150,000 were *Nourish the Beast, Chemin de Fer, The Visit, A Moon for the Misbegotten, When You Comin' Back, Red Ryder?, Ulysses in Nighttown, Jumpers, The Sea Horse* and *My Sister, My Sister.* TDF also continued its subsidy of off off Broadway by means of cut-rate vouchers for tickets (with TDF making up the difference at the box office). TDF put $100,000 into this plan this year, double last year's allotment for OOB audience-building.

The National Endowment and the New York State Arts Council came through with proportionate shares of subsidy for the New York theater, the sums increasing in 1973-74 as they have in past years, but nowhere near as fast as the needs of those putting on live entertainment. A survey conducted in 1973 by a Louis Harris affiliate, the National Research Center of the Arts, estimates that about 64 per cent of American taxpayers would be willing to pay $5 extra annually to support the arts (the per capita Federal support is now averages out to less than 25 cents a year). If that 64 per cent handed out $5 apiece next year, it would amount—the survey estimated—to about $495.5 million, as compared with $60.7 million actually allotted to the National Endowment for fiscal 1974. New York State's allotment to arts subsidy is to be $34.1 million in 1974–75, more than double the $15 million distributed the previous year.

The season's most conspicuous need was that of Circle in the Square, which fell behind to the extent of $191,110 in its operating budget of $1,560,000 on Broadway. The distinguished producing organization was forced to cancel a scheduled production of a musical version of *Look Homeward, Angel* and make known its distress. It was saved from threatened extinction by aid from various sources including $17,500 from a $50-a-seat "Save the Circle" benefit put on by Broadway show folk. The popularity of the Young Vic production of *Scapino* which the Circle imported to substitute for *Look Homeward, Angel* as the fourth show of their subscribers' season also helped give the organization a timely boost.

Among gimmicks dreamed up to stimulate theatergoing was the free taxi service offered by the long-run Micki Grant musical *Don't Bother Me, I Can't Cope.* Ticket purchasers from all New York City boroughs except Staten Island were offered a free taxi ride one way, either to the theater or home after the show. Staggering curtain times was another means of catering to the customers (some like them early, some like them late). A new agreement with the stagehands permits the curtain to be raised at any hour, so long as it comes down before 11:30. As a general rule in 1973–74 the Broadway straight plays moved their curtains back to 8 p.m., while the musicals held to 7:30.

A more comprehensive idea was outlined by Lee Adams in the Autumn issue of the *Dramatists Guild Quarterly* in an article suggesting it might be advantageous for large corporations to sponsor the production of, not industrial or direct-advertising shows, but major Broadway productions. The show would be a form of institutional advertising while running in New York; when the show goes on tour it becomes a strong force of local promotion and company prestige —and image-building. The Adams program, Sponsored Theater, was in the discussion stage as of the season's end.

The legitimate playhouses themselves were a focus of rising concern in 1973–74. One of them—the versatile and useful Mercer Arts Center—suffered physical collapse in August when its Siamese twin, the Broadway Central Hotel, fell down. The theater complex had to be abandoned by the four off-Broadway shows then playing therein (*One Flew Over the Cuckoo's Nest, El Grande de Coca-Cola, The Proposition* and *Tubstrip,* which previewed for a while but never formally opened). The knowledge that theaters were crumbling downtown was not much eased by the thought that new ones were a-building uptown. The new Uris, Circle in the Square and Minskoff Theaters have proved usable but never quite comfortable for their inhabitants. The Uris is cavernously hard to fill even with a musical and may commit itself mostly to dance and concert productions next season. The

Circle in the Square, too, is overlarge for the theater-in-the-round concept of its design. The approach to the Minskoff's auditorium is dominated through hugh glass windows by Broadway advertising displays, which have never been noted for their good taste; and its stage floor proved too rigid for dancers (alterations were made to correct this during a week's layoff of its incumbent *Irene*).

The deepest concern, though, was reserved for the encroachment of real estate interests into the Times Square area, threatening its glamor, prestige and very survival as an oasis of entertainment, of human architectural scale, of contemplative design in the midst of a broadening desert of uninteresting, intrusive, steel and glass monster office buildings. The announcement in the summer of 1973 that a planned 54-story, block-long hotel-office-store complex will further intrude on the theater district turned threat into dismal reality. This monster tower is to displace the Morosco on 45th Street and the Helen Hayes on 46th Street (and not incidentally the Bijou and Victoria Theaters and the Piccadilly Hotel). The Morosco (in bad repair) and the Hayes (with an obsolete balcony structure) are hard to defend except on the urgent general principle that the American theater needs an inviolate district in New York. The defense was only perfunctory when it came time to hold hearings on the new project. Since then, Drama Desk, the organization of theater journalists, has formed a Committee for the Preservation and Development of Theater Facilities which, along with other alerted groups, will conceivably prevent the easy planning-away in future of more of our valuable theaters to serve the artistically destructive purposes of real estate profits. Meanwhile, the city planners are giving serious consideration to major physical improvements in the Times Square area, including the construction of a large pedestrian mall on the Broadway side of the double avenue from 45th to 48th Streets.

Among theater organizations busy doing their thing in 1973–74 was Actors Equity, which added new impetus to the commercialization of the off-Broadway theater—with all the attendant cost/price problems which that entails—by pressing the League of off-Broadway Theaters and Producers for a jump in actors' wages during early winter negotiations for a new three-year contract. Equity, cognizant of the profits which can accrue to a big off-Broadway hit, was asking for a $12.50 weekly raise in each of the three years of the contract (the previous off-Broadway actor's minimum was $125 to $200 weekly, depending on box office receipts). The managers, cognizant of the tremendous odds against achieving hit status today off Broadway and the rising cost of production sapping off Broadway's strength of experimentation, stood firm enough so that a strike almost took place. It was avoided when both sides agreed to submit the matter to binding arbitration, which decided on a minimum sliding from $127.50 to $175 over the three years, graduated upward to $210 to $245 when the box office receipts of an off-Broadway show reach $13,000 weekly—at which point the off Broadway and Broadway actors' minimum become equal. In another part of its thickening forest, Equity established dinner-theater weekly acting minimums of $136 to $176. As for off off Broadway and Equity, Edward Albee delivered the word to a Drama Desk discussion meeting also attended by Donald Grody, Equity's executive secretary: "Leave us alone . . . ignore us . . . make out we don't exist.

Just leave us alone." And, just after the end of the season, Equity came to a new agreement with the League for Broadway minimums rising to $285 in three years (and scaled from $347.50 to $395 on tour).

On behalf of the League of New York Theaters, Alexander H. Cohen once again surrounded the Tony Awards ceremony with a most attractive TV presentation. His theme this year was "homecoming"—that is, former stage people who have drifted into other media coming back to Broadway to participate in Tony night—and no doubt many TV viewers were astonished at the parade of top TV talent who once carried spears on Broadway. As usual, the Tonys themselves were the subject of a qualification hassle. This time it was a question of what is or is not a revival, involving *Candide, Ulysses in Nighttown, Lorelei* and *A Moon for the Misbegotten*. Such matters have always been decided *in camera* by the panel of critics making the nominations in any one year. This year, when a planned rules change would have permitted the self-interested members of the League of New York Theaters to make these decisions, there was an outcry of protest which caused the League's Tony administrative committee to revert to the old rule.

In the opinion of the *Best Plays* editor all the above shows are revivals, with the exception of *Lorelei*. The Tony nominators passed in *Ulysses* because it had appeared only off, never on, Broadway. The New York Drama Critics Circle in its turn ruled out *Ulysses* but passed in *Candide* as a "new" musical and gave it their best-musical award, a fact which reflects great credit on the quality of that show but little on the Critics' extra-esthetical judgment. The Tony committee's judgment can also be brought into question because the best Broadway play of the year, *Noel Coward in Two Keys*, wasn't even nominated in its category (it probably wouldn't have won against *The River Niger*, a beautiful play of *last* season, not this one, in every sense of the word except the confused technicalities of Tony Award qualifications). Since the Pulitzer committee copped out with no award, 1973–74 cannot be classified as a good year for prizes.

Richard Watts Jr., distinguished drama critic of the New York *Post*, announced his retirement following the end of the 1973–74 season. Watts pioneered movie criticism beginning in 1924 on the *Tribune*. He succeeded Percy Hammond as drama critic of the *Herald Tribune* in 1936. After serving in missions to Dublin and China in World War II, he joined the *Post* as drama critic in 1946, continuously sustaining his well-deserved reputation as one of the leading critics of his generation. He will continue to write a column for the *Post* but will pass along the daily reviewing chore. Elsewhere among what is customarily but somewhat erroneously styled the critical fraternity, Clive Barnes of the *Times* moved up to succeed Henry Hewes as president of the New York Drama Critics Circle, and Douglas Watt of the *Daily News* was elected to succeed Barnes as vice president. And, organization-wise, representatives of various theater interests convened in Princeton, N.J. just after the end of the season, the first week in June, to discuss the theater's problems and goals including urban decay, inflation, younger audiences and the methods of financing and subsidizing shows. Since it was called the First American Theater Congress (FACT), its name implies that there will be a second one next year. As was to be expected, the assemblage brought forth many ideas but no solutions.

If this Congress tended to magnetize the disparate, disassociated theater groups and bring them together, so did the persistent presence of porno in the Broadway area. They rallied as if confronted by a common enemy when an effort was made to give over one of the theaters in their midst to pornographic homosexual films (it ran only one day). It seemed as though all Broadway and city agencies under both Mayors Lindsay and Beame were in continuous session trying to work out new ways to "clean up" the Times Square area, which was always very well policed in 1973–74 and seemed to be a completely peacable environment if you ignored occasional culture shock brought on by visual contact with the area's more colorful inhabitants. On this same subject, Drama Desk polled its membership as to whether new restrictions should be placed on porno. It found that the theater press considers the possibility of censorship far more dangerous than the effects of permissiveness in nudity, language and even hard-core pornography.

In this matter of censorship, a development of great potential significance to the theater as to the other arts was the apparent danger that the June 1973 Supreme Court *Miller v. California* decision, holding that obscenity should be defined by contemporary community standards in individual localities rather than by any national standard, might lead to oppressive and unconstitutional local censor attacks on books, movies and even plays. The Jules Feiffer film *Carnal Knowledge* was actually suppressed in a Georgia court decision*. The distinguished general counsel of the Authors League and the Dramatists Guild, Irwin Karp, filed a brief on behalf of these writers' organizations in the Supreme Court in the summer of 1973 urging a rehearing of the Court's *Miller v. California* decision. Here is an outline of Mr. Karp's clarification of this very important censorship development, in excerpts from his brief:

> There is a serious threat—as evidenced by the *Carnal Knowledge* decision —that legislators, prosecutors and judges have not understood (1) that the literary, artistic, political or scientific value of a book is not to be determined by "community standards"; and (2) that a book or film which has "serious" literary or artistic value is (under the guidelines) still protected by the First Amendment against suppression, even though it be patently offensive or pruriently appealing.
>
> These misinterpretations of the guidelines will produce statutes, prosecutions and convictions that violate the First Amendment as construed by *Miller*. Booksellers, librarians and theater owners who are threatened, prosecuted or convicted because of these erroneous interpretations will suffer substantial and unredressable injury—if the Court waits long months or years until the consequences of the misinterpretations are presented to it by appeals from unconstitutional convictions.

The brief also stated that courts and legislators have erroneously assumed that "local" rather than state-wide community standards may now be applied:

*Later overturned by unanimous decision of the U.S. Supreme Court

We believe that in *Miller* this Court sanctioned the use of statewide community standards, but did not hold that "local community standards" could be applied. It is essential that this be made clear, as soon as possible. The Authors League has expressed its view that even 50 state-wide standards will restrict dissemination of books and films that can only be produced if they may be distributed to national audiences. But the application of innumerable "local community" standards would produce a massive crazy-quilt of censorship that would suppress—on a vast scale—the distribution of books and films of substantial literary and artistic value, which deal with sexual themes.

The brief also urged the Court to make it clear on rehearing that localities may not legislate their own standards of "obscenity" under the new ruling but must use the three points of the *Miller* decision in the same way that the *Roth* guidelines had previously been used:

A state cannot classify a work as "obscene" unless: taken as a whole, it appeals to prurient interest; *and* its description or depiction of specifically defined sexual conduct is patently offensive; *and* the work, taken as a whole, *also* lacks serious literary, artistic, political or scientific value.

The impossibility of defining "serious value" by the personal standards of individuals or majorities of groups or fluctuating community mores was stressed:

A *lack* of literary, artistic, scientific or political value is not to be determined by applying a "community standard"; and is not to be determined by the subjective "literary" or "artistic" judgments of the jurors, trial judges or appellate justices.

Jurors and judges who might not personally consider that *Ulysses* had serious literary or artistic value, if they read it, would nonetheless concede that it had recognized "literary" value—in the eyes of critics, scholars and other literary experts. . . . The recent decision of the Supreme Court of Georgia, in the *Carnal Knowledge* case, indicates the need for clarification of the "serious value" standard.

. . . . . Lack of scientific and literary value cannot be established by majority vote, which is essentially what the "consensus" of community standards reflects. Moreover, majorities (per se) are not qualified to pass judgment on the literary or artistic value of books. Example: in a 1969 Gallup poll, 58 per cent of the adults polled said "they had never read a book from cover to cover . . ."

Notable celebrations this season included the dedication of a room in the New York Public Library's theater collection at Lincoln Center to the distinguished actress Katharine Cornell and her husband Guthrie McClintic. Miss Cornell, whose last stage appearance was in *Dear Liar* in 1961, was too ill to attend the April 24 event (she died soon afterward at her home at Martha's Vineyard). Many other notables were present, however, at the dedication of this large reading room featuring displays of Cornell-McClintic memorabilia. George Gershwin, too, was celebrated in all kinds of observances of the 75th anniversary of his birth—Sept. 26, 1973—including concerts, sing-alongs, exhibitions, a Gershwin stamp, special record albums and five books.

That's how it went in the New York theater of 1973–74. We are almost half a century removed from the peak years of the mid-1920s when there were more than 200 Broadway shows annually; a quarter of a century removed from the booking jams, ticket-icing, etc. of the 100-plus show years at the turn of the mid-century. Here in the 1970s Broadway production has attenuated to barely 50, including only eight new American plays, like the tip of a south-drifting iceberg melting in the hotter and hotter sun.

What we should bear in mind is that half a century ago there was no bottom to the iceberg worth mentioning; no great mass of theater activity hidden under the glitter of Broadway. If the stage's tip has shrunk by one-half or three quarters, its hidden mass has grown hugely, until now there is in New York City within any 12 months a volume of legitimate stage activity that includes hundreds and hundreds and hundreds of "productions" off off Broadway in numbers that would have been unimagineable by any theatergoer of the 1920s. Granted, our commercial managers are bearing greater and greater financial burdens, and for some reason our better-known dramatists seem to have taken the year off in 1973–74. But if ever an iceberg was ready with hidden substance to rise and replace its melting tip, our theater is. If ever it held promise, it is now.

THE 1973–74 SEASON OFF OFF BROADWAY

By Gloria Gonzalez

Journalist and author of many off-off-Broadway productions

REPORTING on off off Broadway is about as much fun as organizing a rent strike. Your chance of pulling it off to the satisfaction of all is equal to winning a conviction against your landlord. Considering that approximately 1,500 new plays are produced each year in an environment that stretches from prison to a church basement, it would take ten full-time critics (with only a half-hour lunch break) to cover the territory.

What is off off Broadway? There are various yardsticks: productions which are not covered by the major critics; "showcases" limited to 12 performances; anything done up or above street level from the Bowery to Riverdale; theater where no one gets paid—or any enclosure where you can gather four people to watch a 15-character play.

Actually, off off Broadway is about the only place left where you can produce a 15-character play—providing you can find a stage large enough to support their combined weight. Actors and directors aren't paid, the playwright doesn't have to worry about his audience catching its train (since they're all related and car pooled together); there are no ushers to pay overtime, and you don't have to vacate the premises for a janitor because the stage manager (if you have one) sweeps up once a week.

It is the best—and worst—of all worlds.

Off-off-Broadway playwrights are full-time doctors, surgeons, typists, newspaper reporters, hairdressers, IBM clerks, lawyers, sales ladies, nurses, decorators, waiters, telephone repairmen—and the lucky ones collect unemployment insurance so they can stay home and write.

Some, like Miguel Piñero, are former convicts. His prison play *Short Eyes* won this year's Drama Critics prize for the best American play in a commercial Joseph Papp production, but it was first produced off off Broadway at the Riverside Church Theater. Directed by Marvin Felix Camillo, the play evolved from the Family, a theater workshop at the Bedford Hills Correctional Facility in New York. The theater workshop came about following a visit by Camillo, who brought his visiting street theater into various prisons, including Sing Sing. The response to Camillo's street theater was so favorable that the Bedford Hills warden asked him to set up a workshop. With the help of actress Colleen Dewhurst, who attended a workshop production, The Family was formed. As the inmates were released from jail, Camillo would meet with them and continue his theatrical teachings. By the spring of 1973, The Family was performing in high schools and churches.

Playwright Piñero, on parole from Sing Sing for armed robbery, joined the group at its new headquarters at Riverside Church. He had a prison play called *Short Eyes* and the new repertory company had on-the-job training. Piñero reports—with obvious delight—that during the casting call for his play his parole officer showed up to audition for a part. How would you like to be the playwright in that situation?

The Off-Off-Broadway Alliance, an organization of nearly 60 theater groups, drew newspaper headlines May 4 when it sponsored an all-day parade, festival, carnival and open-air theater at the plaza in Lincoln Center. Mayor Abraham D. Beame officially changed the street name of Broadway to Off Off Broadway, and speeches were made in support of the movement. Hundreds of playwrights, producers, directors, actors and stage personnel participated in the festivities aimed at attracting new audiences to the basements and lofts.

And what a show it was! Each theatrical group set up its own booth and outdid each other in attracting the attention of the casual and curious visitors. There were male transvestites garbed in gold capes covering a pink-feathered G-string; a 250-pound man wearing a white ballet costume, platinum wig and puffing on a cigar; an extremely large black man in a pink silk outfit with a shocking pink wig and matching lipstick; a white flour-faced girl with a headpiece of grapes . . . a beautiful Oriental girl stunning in a white lace gown and matching parasol . . . some clowns and jugglers . . . folk singers . . . and a white-robed male impaled on a cross.

A pedestrian was heard to comment: "If this is off off Broadway, I'll stick to television."

Various productions were presented throughout the day beneath open-air domes decorated with balloons. Most productions were well attended, and spectator and performer alike appeared to enjoy themselves. The festival drew coverage from all the major newspapers, and the consensus seemed to amount to a hit production. Much of the success of the endeavor should be credited to Ms. Virginia Kahn, executive director of the Alliance.

Regarding the 1973–74 off-off-Broadway season per se: while it is impossible to single out all productions of merit, there were some that aroused special affection. Certainly one of the most impressive was *The Women's Representative* by Sun Yu, directed by Pamela DeSio, performed at the Nighthouse. It opened in May, 1973 and ran eight months. This is a prize-winning Communist Chinese play with a Women's Lib theme, laced with wit and tenderness.

Also noteworthy was *Poe: From His Life and Mind* by Stanley Nelson, directed by Marjorie Melnick at Theater 77. The play is a biographical drama in which characters from Poe's life are intermingled in a kind of fantasia with the characters that Poe created.

The Color of a Mind by Roma Greth, directed by Martin Oltarsh, was produced at the Cubiculo. The play is a very sensitive portrayal of the world of a retarded girl.

In a much lighter vein was *Marjorie Daw*, with music, book and lyrics by Sally Dixon Wiener, presented at Theater at Noon under the direction of Miriam Fond. The lilting turn-of-the-century musical came complete with an English butler and quill pens. It is the story of a love affair conducted through the mails—with a bright touch of mistaken identity.

No off-off-Broadway season can be complete without a new play by the prolific Donald Kvares (if they ever have a Kvares play festival, bring food for a month). Don is now happily ensconced at Theatre 77 where this year his musical *Mushrooms* was presented under the able direction of Ted Mornel. Through the years, Kvares has impressed many critics and audiences, and his plays are insured of a faithful following.

Other productions that generated interest during the year were: *I Am a Woman*, a compilation drawn from the works of a dozen playwrights, directed by Paul Austin at Theater in Space; *The Cowgirl and the Tiger*, a children's musical by Wallace Gray, music and lyrics by Hank Beebe, directed by Howard Lipson at the 13th Street Theater Repertory Company; *Under the Bridge There is a Lonely Spot With Gregory Peck*, a comedy-drama by Helen Duberstein, directed by Neil Flanagan for the Theater for the New City; *Sheba*, a musical by Hazel J. Bryant, directed by Helaine Head at the Afro-American Total Theater; *The Guest*, by Pedro Juan Soto, directed by Reynaldo Arana for the Puerto Rican Traveling Theater, and *The Same Old Story (the same old history) Right*, written and directed by Elizabeth Pasquale at the Byrd Hoffman School of Byrds.

An enthusiastic reception was given *La Celestina*, a production of the Spanish Theater Repertory Company which presented Fernando de Roja's 475-year-old "play." It is actually a novel in dramatic form of love and passion which is performed with "an odd blend of laughter and guts", according to the New York *Post.*

In an experimental move, Folk City, a Sixth Avenue night club which claims to have started the careers of Simon and Garfunkle—and also Dylan—started a policy of presenting plays prior to its evening folk and rock concerts. The first play produced was *Lonely Friends* by Edna Schappert, directed by Sammy Eneff, four short plays billed as "a few fables for humans." The main characters include ice cubes, pandas, an onion seed and a strawberry seed. The theme is loneliness and the difficulties encountered in saying, "I love you."

It is evident that off off Broadway is becoming a strong movement in terms of audience attendance and participation. In 1972, the Theater Development Fund poured $50,000 into off off Broadway with its vouchers which persons could buy at 50 cents each and the theater owners could redeem for $2. From June 1973 through June 1974, the TDF vouchers were purchased at 80 cents apiece and redeemed at $2.50, subsidizing off off Broadway to the tune of $100,000. Ms. Peregrine Whittlesey, who designed and operates the project, expects that its budget will be doubled again to $200,000 during fiscal 1974–75. As of July 1, the cost to the theatergoer of the OOB voucher goes up to $1 each.

"Our program was so successful from the very beginning that we had to put hundreds of people on a waiting list," said Ms. Whittlesey. She is confident that all persons seeking vouchers in the future will be accommodated. TDF subsidized 105 OOB groups by means of vouchers last season.

Why are audiences suddenly clamoring for off-off-Broadway tickets? "For the simple reason that a lot of it is worth going to see, and also people like to support their community theaters," said Ms. Whittlesey. She also said that teachers bring busloads of students to productions, which in turn builds a future audience for the theater. TDF draws its financial support from many private sources including the Edna McConnell Foundation, which made an initial investment of $130,000 to get the voucher system started.

So . . . with all the attention and financial support now being given the lofts, basements and churches of off off Broadway . . . it appears the movement will continue to thrive and grow. One can only hope that its growing pains do not one day cause it to limp alongside Broadway and off Broadway. The pitfalls are there. So we watch and wait and cheer the stepchild on.

THE SEASON AROUND THE UNITED STATES

with

A DIRECTORY OF PROFESSIONAL REGIONAL THEATER

INTRODUCTION: NOTES ON WORKING IN REGIONAL THEATERS

By Israel Horovitz

Playwright, author of *The Indian Wants the Bronx, Line, Alfred the Great,* etc.

I'LL change the names to protect the innocent. Let's say it happened in Bellows Falls.

The director of the Bellows Falls Rep, a Mr. Molloy, I suppose, was invited to a meeting of the theater's Steering Committee. The committee chairman, a Mr. Cappella, I suppose, made Mr. Molloy an invitation he couldn't refuse.

Cappella's words follow in, roughly, this order: Mr. Molloy, you'll notice, please, that we shut the door and it's locked, too. Which means you couldn't get out of the room until we say okay. Which also means you'll have to listen. Mr. Molloy, you're a good speaker, in fact you're a terrific speaker, so you'll have to keep your good speaking mouth closed and just listen because if you don't . . .

Molloy shuddered.

. . . we'll never get said what we got to get said. Okay?

Molloy acquiesced. He nodded to let them know.

Good. Now, Mr. Molloy, you'll see that we're all familiar faces. Local people, therefore good people. We're businessmen, Mr. Molloy. We don't come to your theater because we want to: we come to your theater because our wives make us. Like I said before and you've always known, we're businessmen: tired and looking for rest and relaxation. At the end of a tough business day, a play is not the thing, believe me . . .

(The background to this scene needs to be inserted here: two years ago, Molloy introduced Euripides to Bellows Falls, with a modern-dress production of *Iphigenia in Aulis*. One year ago, as though now a Molloysian tradition, Euripides appeared again with Gilbert Murray's seldom-performed translation of *Rhesus*. Just one week ago, Molloy announced next year's season to include Jean Anouilh's *Antigone*.)

. . . Molloy? Are you paying attention, Molloy? When you're a tired business-man and you got to go to a theater because of your wife, what you want to see (as long as you *got* to see *something*) is something a little dirty, also very funny and a little sexy and maybe smutty. You know what I mean?

A pause was wasted on Molloy.

Now then. Two years ago, you put on a Greek play by what's-his-name about a young woman. You remember? We hated it, Molloy. It was boring and stupid. Okay, we said, give him another chance. So we did and you put on still another play by your friend, this one worse.

Now we got crazy and we formed this Steering Committee just for this purpose.

We waited for your brochure to go to the printer, who sent the copy right over to me and I called this meeting. Mr. Molloy, we see you got another Greek play on the list for next year and we got to talk about it.

Cappella affected a fiendishly friendly smile.

We know you got to please all kinds of ethnic groups of people when you run a theater in a community like ours. I mean, everybody ain't the same, right? But, Molloy, I got just one question that I'd like you to answer, okay?

How many Greeks do you think we got here in Bellows Falls, anyway?

*   *   *

Rien, as the French say, *n'est simple*.

I have used regional theaters in America for my new plays during the past three or four years, five or six plays. It is not that I've wanted to avoid New York, so much as I've needed the use of acting companies, which seem to be non-existent in New York. It is also not that I have avoided the commercial theater nearly as much as the commercial theater has avoided me.

Let me be specific.

In 1971 or so, I began work on a nine-act trilogy, *The Wakefield Plays* of which part one is *Alfred the Great;* part two *Our Father's Failing*, and part three *Alfred Dies*. The entire work is set in my home town, Wakefield, Mass., and concerns itself mostly with a man named Alfred who has been evidently quite successful in a big city and has now, at age 40, returned home to his small town.

Before showing any of the work to anybody, I completed first drafts of all three plays. At Christmas time, 1971, I showed the first draft of the first play, *Alfred the Great*, at an invitational reading, in English, at the American Center for Artists and Students, Boulevard Raspail, Paris, which was then run by my friend Henry Pillsbury.

After extensive rewriting, I sent a second draft of that play to the Eugene O'Neill Memorial Theater Foundation, Waterford, Conn., to be staged during the 1972 National Playwrights Conference there. Lloyd Richards accepted the work as a special project and assigned the script, not surprisingly, to James Hammerstein, who had, to date, directed nine of my plays. The O'Neill Foundation is, I think, the mother of all regional theaters in America as far as a single source of new plays for regional theater production is concerned.

No less than ten regional theater directors were present for the reading of *Alfred the Great* at O'Neill. Jules Irving was also present, then representing Lincoln Center. Mr. Irving asked for an option on the work within five minutes of the third act curtain. He offered production in the Forum Theater of each of the three plays, one a year for three consecutive years. In the fourth year there would be a full production in the Vivian Beaumont Theater. A company of four actors would be assigned to me for continuing work on the trilogy.

I accepted. Irving vanished mysteriously from Lincoln Center. The plays were never done there.

Ken Costigan, one of the directors of the Pittsburgh Playhouse, had seen the O'Neill reading. He'd also asked my agent for an option on the play. When he was told that the Lincoln Center project had, as they say, fallen through, he set up a production period for *Alfred* almost immediately.

I completed a new draft of the play prior to Pittsburgh, and another after that production.

The Pittsburgh production was a success with both critics and audience. The text was sent by my agent, Mary Dolan, to several New York commercial producers. It was rejected by all.

The second play of the trilogy, *Our Father's Failing*, was rewritten and submitted to the O'Neill Theater for the 1973 National Playwrights Conference. Once again, Lloyd Richards accepted the play as a special project. Alexander H. Cohen, the Broadway producer, was there at the *Our Father's Failing* presentation. He, like Irving before him, asked within minutes of the final curtain for production rights to the plays. He was to produce *Alfred the Great* on Broadway, opening in September 1973. But an agreement between Mr. Cohen and me was not, finally, possible, and once again it was a regional theater that stepped forward with both simple and agreeable terms. This time it was the Trinity Square Repertory Company, Providence, R.I., under the direction of Adrian Hall. Hall was led to the play by Sally and Joseph Dowling, Providence people who work at no salary for the Trinity theater, who happened to be present for *Alfred* rehearsals in 1972 and returned for *Our Father's Failing* in 1973, bringing Hall *et al* along with them. With Hammerstein directing, we went into rehearsal almost immediately.

The Providence production was also successful, which is to say that Providence, like Pittsburgh, has asked to continue showing *Alfred* in its repertory and, in addition, has asked for production rights to the remaining two plays.

In the meantime, Charles Bowden has taken a Broadway option on *Alfred* and shows every indication of actually getting the play open. But three years have passed in the waiting and, really, without the interim productions in Pittsburgh and Providence, I wonder how much interest there would have been on anyone's part, mine included.

Gordon Davidson, the marvelous man who runs the Mark Taper forum in Los Angeles, had a good experience with my play *Line* in his experimental theater program back in 1970. He got in touch with me at the O'Neill in 1973, and we talked of the possibility of presenting *Line* in the regular Mark Taper Forum season, which would necessitate my creating a companion play for *Line,* which has a running time of one hour. I suggested to Davidson that he might *commission* a new play from me for for that purpose; nothing terribly newsworthy, but I think that there was a token payment of $250. But the *idea* of the commission was solid enough. Like most writers, I respond to deadlines. Once Davidson created the deadline, I got to work on the new text. At this writing in late spring of 1974 I am scheduling my second trip to Los Angeles to work at the Taper on that text. Actors are secured for each reading there. Both Gordon Davidson and Edward Parone have given substantial amounts of time to me in the refinement of the script.

The point is this: I cannot imagine a commercial manager in New York being able to create the work construct as did Davidson and Parone in Los Angeles, Costigan in Pittsburgh, Hall in Providence, or Lloyd Richards and George White in Waterford. Lamentable, but true. Not to say there aren't places to work in New York. To the contrary, I do some first drafts in New York, in readings. The Manhattan Theater Club, since the entrance of Lynne Meadow as director, has become a receptive, pleasant place to work. Edward Berkeley's Shade Company is a treasure, as is Marshall W. Mason's Circle Theater. But, frankly, working in New York with unfinished texts is, well, dangerous. Critics and producers poke around. The risk that the text will open publicly, without ever really being finished, is all too high. Furthermore, the few theaters in New York with acting companies are the last to be able to pay actors. There is no one more easily distracted than the actor in New York who is working without salary. The same actor, paid, in Providence, Pittsburgh, Waterford, Los Angeles, wherever, is a veritable workhorse. Understandable, Lamentable. All things considered, actors are really quite wonderful about work on new texts, but often feel they are "being taken advantage of" . . . because they are.

I must note here the enormous distinction between a regional theater production during which I actually attend rehearsals, and another during which I am not present at all. The latter, for me, is like one of Bishop Berkeley's falling forest trees; it is unheard and does not really exist. The part of me that is interested in that sort of disconnected production is not my most attractive part. And this is to note that I am very pleased to go out of New York with a new play and actually get to work with a resident company in a regional theater. This may not seem surprising, in light of this report thus far, but most regional theater directors have been rather surprised by my sincerity in this matter. And while this work/travel scheme has been expecially good for me, I'm not certain that it will please other writers. Nor am I certain that it is a fundamentally good scheme for regional theaters.

Consider this: regional theaters, when they work, exist for their own communities. The Trinity company must please Providence people, finally, if that theater is to survive. Using Providence as an example, at Brown University in that city there are several good writers employed as teachers of literature. Two of them have written plays. Each of the two is capable of writing excellent plays, but each needs support from the Trinity company, in the form of continuing productions. Pittsburgh has its own writers, as does Los Angeles. Perhaps the real purpose of regional theater should be to develop writers and directors and actors from that community, *for* that community. I don't suggest that theaters limit themselves to local writers—hardly. But I have found it a bit curious over the years that Los Angeles writers often have the premieres of their plays in other cities. (One Los Angeles playwright's work was recently given its first production in Paris. A Providence writer spent a year as playwright-in-residence with a theater in San Francisco.)

Unfortunately, regional theater directors have gotten much too much praise from their boards of directors for looking way beyond their community. This is to say that the only *real* assurance a regional theater man has of his contract being renewed (other than a money-making season, which is clearly impossible) is a record of having started plays that went on to New York productions, preferably Broadway and commercial success. This reality has altered the taste of many a regional theater director in choosing new plays for a new season. If Broadway represents mediocre thinking, as indeed it does, then how awful is it to think of the regional theaters as the possible source? Yet the problem is real. Regional theater directors, by and large, are like prudes of the 1950s: they want only virgins, only premieres. (If a student were to check the history of *Alfred the Great* carefully, he would see that it was given four separate world premieres before its world premiere in New York.) Here I submit that if regional theaters are to contribute substantially to the development of new plays, their boards of directors and artistic directors must be anxious to advertise and produce new *drafts* of plays. They must be educated to understand that a fifth draft is far more valuable, far more finished, than a first draft. This can be carried to a far more exciting idea: a play that opened too soon on Broadway and was not really finished is usually doomed to be buried, sometimes not even published. A regional theater could encourage a playwright with such a play to work on the play for production *and publication,* using its success in that regional theater to encourage other productions in other regional theaters. New York should be only one stopover in the travels of a play. No such journey should either begin or end in New York, any more than a playwright should live his or her entire life in New York, without venturing out and beyond. But this is also to suggest that actors and directors and writers who center their lives in any one place should, from time to time, stray from that center. Change, I believe, begets change. And Bellows Falls, like New York, is certainly a nice place to visit . . .

A DIRECTORY OF PROFESSIONAL REGIONAL THEATER

Including selected Canadian programs and selected programs for children

Compiled by Ella A. Malin

Professional 1973–74 programs and repertory productions by leading resident companies around the United States, plus major Shakespeare festivals including that of Stratford, Ontario (Canada), are grouped in alphabetical order of their locations and listed in date order from May, 1973 to June, 1974. This list does not include Broadway, off-Broadway or touring New York shows, summer theaters, single productions by commercial producers or college or other non-professional productions. The directory was compiled by Ella A. Malin for *The Best Plays of 1973–74* from information provided by the resident producing organizations at Miss Malin's request. First productions of new plays—American or world premieres—in regional theaters are listed with full casting and credits, as available. Figures in parentheses following title give number of performances and date given is opening date, included whenever a record of these facts was obtainable from the producing managements.

Augmented reports on other than regional theater production in Los Angeles by Rick Talcove and Washington, D.C. by Jay Alan Quantrill are included under those cities' headings in this listing.

Summary

This Directory lists 370 productions of 336 plays (including one-acters and workshop productions) presented by 39 groups in 61 theaters in 40 cities (36 in the United States and four in Canada) during the 1973–74 season. Of these, 160 were American plays in 133 full productions and 27 workshop productions. Seventy-four were world premieres, 15 were American or North American premieres. Frequency of production of individual scripts was as follows:

    2 plays received 4 productions *(The Hot l Baltimore, The Tooth of Crime)*
   12 plays received 3 productions *(Waiting For Godot, As You Like It, The Taming of the Shrew, Othello, A Midsummer Night's Dream, The Seagull, Private Lives, The Miser, Oedipus Rex, That Championship Season, Inherit The Wind, Jacques Brel Is Alive And Well And Living In Paris)*
   39 plays received 2 productions
  283 plays received 1 production

Listed below are the playwrights who received the greatest number of productions. The first figure is the number of productions; the second figure (in parentheses) is the number of plays produced, including one-acters.

Shakespeare	34	(19)	Pinter	3	(3)
Chekhov	10	(7)	Strindberg	3	(3)
Molière	9	(5)	Horovitz	3	(2)
Williams	8	(6)	Miller, Jason	3	(1)
Coward	8	(5)	Sophocles	3	(1)
O'Neill	7	(6)	Ayckbourn	2	(2)
Shaw	7	(6)	Chase	2	(2)
Shepard	7	(4)	French	2	(2)
Beckett	6	(4)	Gogol	2	(2)
Ibsen	6	(4)	Lawrence, D.H.	2	(2)
Brecht	5	(4)	Nichols	2	(2)
Wilson	5	(2)	O'Casey	2	(2)
Abbott	4	(2)	Osborne	2	(2)
Lawrence & Lee	4	(2)	Perr	2	(2)
Albee	3	(3)	Pirandello	2	(2)
Miller, Arthur	3	(3)	Warren	2	(2)
McNally	3	(3)	Wilder	2	(2)

ABINGDON, VA.

Barter Theater: Main Stage

(Artistic director-manager, Rex Partington.)

LIFE WITH FATHER (32). By Howard Lindsay and Russel Crouse. June 5, 1973. Director, Laurence Hugo; scenery, Bennet Averyt; lighting, David Mazikowski; costumes, Marianne Powell-Parker. With Laurence Hugo, Ludi Claire, Barbara Tarbuck, Gwyllum Evans.

THE HOSTAGE (16). By Brendan Behan. June 19, 1973. Director, Ken Costigan; scenery, Bennet Averyt; lighting, David Mazikowski; costumes, Marianne Powell-Parker. With Brendan Fay, Barbara Tarbuck, Dorothy Marie, Michael Tolaydo, Sarah Burke.

COCKTAILS WITH MIMI (14). By Mary Chase. July 3, 1973 (world premiere). Director, Owen Phillips; scenery, Bennet Averyt; lighting, David Mazikowski; costumes, Marianne Powell-Parker.

Paul Hanson	David Darlow
Mimi Ralston	Ann Buckles
Edith Ralston	Eda Zahl
Lucy White	Dorothy Chace
Burt Evans	Ed Bordo
Mrs. Carlton De Vries	Dorothy Blackburn
Mrs. Clyde Elliot	Georgia Heaslip
Clyde Elliot	Raf Michaels
Judge Leland Calthorpe	Gwyllum Evans
Eudorra Calthorpe	Dale Carter Cooper
Lester Calthorpe	Josef Warik
Waiter	Mark Leonard

Time: The present. Place: Suburb of a city in the Far West of the United States. Act I: The library of Mimi Ralston's home, late afternoon of a day in late spring. Act II: The same, a few minutes later.

THE IMAGINARY INVALID (18). By Molière; adapted by Allen Lorenson. July 17, 1973. Director, John Olon; scenery, Raymond C. Recht; lighting, David Mazikowski; costumes, Marianne Powell-Parker. With Max Gulack, Harriet Nichols, Carolyn Porter, Joseph Warik, Charles Thomas Harper.

NIGHT MUST FALL (16). By Emlyn Williams. August 21, 1973. Director, Kenneth Frankel; scenery, Thomas Stolz; lighting, Myron White; costumes, Marianne Powell-Parker. With Dale Carter Cooper, Barbara Tarbuck, George C. Hosmer, Josef Warik, Gwyllum Evans.

CANDLE-LIGHT (16). By Siegfried Geyer; adapted by P. G. Wodehouse. September 4, 1973. Director, Rex Partington; scenery and lighting, Raymond C. Recht; costumes, Marianne Powell-Parker. With George C. Hosmer, David Darlow, Barbara Tarbuck.

THE SUBJECT WAS ROSES (16). By Frank D.

Gilroy. September 18, 1973. Director, Ken Costigan; scenery, Bennet Averyt; costumes, Marianne Powell-Parker. With James Glenn, Dorothy Marie, Gaetano BonGiovanni.

THE MARRIAGE-GO-ROUND (16). By Leslie Stevens. October 2, 1973. Director, Kenneth Frankel; lighting, Myron White; costumes, Marianne Powell-Parker. With Dalton Dearborn, Frederica Minte, Gayle Kelly Landers, Rex Partington.

THE VOICE OF THE TURTLE (24). By John van Druten. October 16, 1973. Director, Owen Phillips; scenery, James Franklin; lighting, My-

ron White; costumes, Marianne Powell-Parker. With Elaine Kilden, Gayle Kelly Landers, James Secrest.

CANDIDA (6). By George Bernard Shaw. May 3, 1974. Director, George Touliatos; lighting, Myron White; costumes, Sigrid Insull. With Cleo Holladay, Michael Tolaydo, Rex Partington.

SCAPIN (16). By Molière. May 17, 1974. Director, Rex Partington; scenery, Bennet Averyt; lighting, Myron White; costumes, Sigrid Insull. With John Medici, Nancy Snyder, Max Gulack, Gwyllum Evans, David Darlow.

Barter Theater: Barter Playhouse—Children's Theater

THE FROG PRINCE (16), June 20, 1973; WHO AM I (21), July 14, 1973, directed by Barbara Tarbuck.

Barter Theater: Barter Playhouse—Intern Ensemble

BY WAY OF INTRODUCTION (39). June 21, 1973. THE OLD LADY SHOWS HER MEDALS by J. M. Barrie; THE BEAR and THE MARRIAGE PROPOSAL by Anton Chekhov, directed by Dorothy Marie. THE MAN WITH THE FLOWER IN HIS MOUTH by Luigi Pirandello, FUMED OAK by Noel Coward, THE STRONGER, by August Strindberg, directed by Owen Phillips.

COLLISION COURSE (25). August 2, 1973.

STARS AND STRIPES by Leonard Melfi and TOUR by Terrence McNally, directed by Owen Phillips. WANDERING by Lanford Wilson and COWBOYS #2 by Sam Shepard, directed by David Darlow. CHUCK by Jack Larson and JEW! by Harvey Perr, directed by Dorothy Marie.

THE NATURE OF COMEDY, created by the Intern Ensemble, directed by Dorothy Marie (11 tour performances). October 16, 1973.

Note: Members of the Barter Intern Ensemble were selected by auditions from all over the country to participate in a two-year training/performance program leading to the formation of a resident repertory company. Productions are designed by the Ensemble; scenery by Thom Hanson.

ASHLAND, ORE.

Oregon Shakespearean Festival: Elizabethan Theater

(Founder, Angus L. Bowmer; producing director, Jerry Turner; general manager, William W. Patton.)

AS YOU LIKE IT (29). By William Shakespeare. June 23, 1973. Director, Pat Patton.

THE MERRY WIVES OF WINDSOR (28).

June 24, 1973. Director, Thomas B. Markus.

HENRY V (29). By William Shakespeare. June 25, 1973. Director, Laird Williamson.

Oregon Shakespearean Festival: Angus Bowmer Theater

THE DANCE OF DEATH (20). By August Strindberg. June 24, 1973. Director, Jerry Turner.

THE ALCHEMIST (20). By Ben Jonson. June 25, 1973. Director, Laird Williamson.

OTHELLO (20). By William Shakespeare. June

26, 1973. Director, Laird Williamson

Designers: scenery, Richard L. Hay; lighting, Steven A Maze; costumes, Jean Schultz Davidson. Summer acting company: Harry Anderson, Denis Arndt, Powers Boothe, Jeffrey Brooks, Franklin Brown, Elizabeth Cole, Steven Crenshaw, Timothy D'Arcy, Evan Davidson, Philip

Davidson, Joseph V. De Salvio, Dan Desmond, Michael Eagan, James Edmondson, William Evans, Carolyn Gillespie, Alex Gillis, Lynette Godsey, Jo Goff, Douglas Hadley, James Harbour, Glenn Holland, Will Huddleston, Arnold Hummasti, Dan Johnson, Sherril Kannasto, Jason Lee, Aldena Leonard, Richard Leonard, Sandy Lynch, Margit Moe, Laurie Monahan, Garry Moore, Paul Myrvold, Sylvia Myrvold, Mark Murphey, Pat Patton, Kristin Patton, Shirley Patton, Richard Riehle, Neil Savage,

Karen Seal, Peter Silbert, Ernie Stewart, Mary Turner, Denene von Glan, Laird Williamson, Cal Winn, Michael Winters.

WAITING FOR GODOT (12). By Samuel Beckett. November 2, 1973. Director, Andrew J. Traister; scenery, Richard L. Hay; lighting, Stephen A. Maze; costumes, Robert Hines. With Jeffrey Brooks, James Edmondson, Richard Riehle, Cal Winn.

Oregon Shakespearean Festival: Stage II—Angus Bowmer Theater

A FUNNY THING HAPPENED ON THE WAY TO THE FORUM (12). Book by Burt Shevelove and Larry Gelbart; music and lyrics by Stephen Sondheim. March 8, 1974. Director, Jerry Turner; choreography, James Edmondson; musical director, Todd Barton.

TWO GENTLEMEN OF VERONA (15). By William Shakespeare. March 9, 1974. Director, Laird Williamson.

HEDDA GABLER (12). By Henrik Ibsen; translated by Michael Meyer. March 9, 1974. Director, Margaret Booker.

THE TIME OF YOUR LIFE (13). By William

Saroyan. March 10, 1974. Director, Pat Patton.

Designers: scenery, Richard L. Hay; lighting, Steven A. Maze; costumes, Richard Hieronymus, John David Ridge, Robert Hines. Spring acting company: Neville Archambault, Denis Arndt, Jeffrey Brooks, Franklin Brown, David Q. Combs, Joseph V. De Salvio, le Clanche du Rand, James Edmondson, Douglas Hadley, Christine Healy, Will Huddleston, Mary Alice Kurr, Judith Metskas, Margit Moe, Michael Kevin Moore, Mark Murphey, Susan Opdenaker, Shirley Patton, Richard Riehle, Diane Salinger, Warner Shook, Peter Silbert, Ernie Stewart, Mary Turner, Laird Williamson, Cal Winn.

BALTIMORE

Center Stage

(Producing director, Jacques Cartier; managing director, Peter W. Culman; productions consultant, John Stix.)

THE HOT L BALTIMORE (33). By Lanford Wilson. October 26, 1973. Director, John Stix; scenery and lighting, Raymond C. Recht; costumes, Laura Crow. With Heather Macrae, Glenn Walken, Eunice Anderson, Paul Benedict.

UNCLE VANYA (26). By Anton Chekhov. November 30, 1973. Director, Jacques Cartier; scenery and lighting, Raymond C. Recht; costumes, Linda Fisher. With Page Johnson, Paul Benedict, Pamela Burrell, John Eames, Marcia Jean Kurtz.

WHO'S AFRAID OF VIRGINIA WOOLF? (26) By Edward Albee. January 8, 1974. With James Pritchett, Gabrielle Strasun, Susan Sharkey, W. T. Martin.

HAY FEVER (17). By Noel Coward. February 9, 1974. Director, Jacques Cartier; scenery and

lighting, Raymond C. Recht; costumes, Linda Fisher. With Peter Bailey-Britton, Myra Carter, K. T. Baumann, Julia Curry, Dale Hodges, Michael Lewis, Richard Lieberman, Vivienne Shub, Michael Tolaydo.

A VIEW FROM THE BRIDGE (16). By Arthur Miller. March 9, 1974. Director, Michael Murray; scenery and lighting, Raymond C. Recht; costumes, Jean Levine. With Frank Savino, Maureen Silliman, Janet Sarno, Richard Dmitri.

HAPPY BIRTHDAY, WANDA JUNE (16). By Kurt Vonnegut Jr. April 6, 1974. Director, Carl Schurr; scenery and lighting, Raymond C. Recht; costumes, Jean Levine. With Don Plumly, Tanny McDonald, James L. Pryor, Henry Strozier, Lori Ehudin, Wil Love.

OUTSTANDING PERFORMANCES, 1973-74

Jason Robards (foreground) as James Tyrone Jr., Ed Flanders as Phil Hogan and Colleen Dewhurst as Josie Hogan in *A Moon for the Misbegotten*

Michael Moriarty as Julian Weston in *Find Your Way Home*

Julie Harris as Mrs. Rogers in *The Au Pair Man* (FAR RIGHT)

Carol Channing as Lorelei Lee in *Lorelei* (FAR LEFT)

Dick A. Williams as Rico in *What the Wine-Sellers Buy*

Brian Bedford as George in *Jumpers*

Kevin Conway as Teddy in *When You Comin' Back, Red Ryder?* (FAR RIGHT)

Conchata Ferrell as Gertrude Blum in *The Sea Horse* (FAR LEFT)

Henry Fonda as Clarence Darrow in *Clarence Darrow*

Hume Cronyn as Hugo Latymer and Jessica Tandy (FAR RIGHT) as Hilde Latymer in *Noel Coward in Two Keys*

Lewis J. Stadlen as the Sage in *Candide* (FAR LEFT)

Christopher Plummer as the Narrator in *The Good Doctor*

Virginia Capers as Lena Younger in *Raisin*

George Rose as Henry in *My Fat Friend* (FAR RIGHT)

Jim Dale as Scapino in *Scapino*

Eileen Heckart as The Woman in *Veronica's Room* (FAR LEFT)

NOEL COWARD IN TWO KEYS—*Above and left,* Hume Cronyn as two husbands, Anne Baxter as two visitors and Jessica Tandy (*above right*) as one of the two wives in the program of Noel Coward plays, *Come Into the Garden Maud* (*above*) and *A Song at Twilight* (*left*)

FIND YOUR WAY
HOME—Jane Alexander
and Lee Richardson
(*right*) as husband and
wife and Lee Richardson
and Michael Moriarty
(*below*) as lovers in the
play by John Hopkins

CHEKHOV DESIGNS BY TONY WALTON—
At top of this and facing page, examples of the indoor and outdoor phases of Tony Walton's set for *The Good Doctor. At left,* a Walton costume sketch for Astrov in *Uncle Vanya* and *at right,* two of his sketches for Helena's costumes in the same production. *Below,* a photo of Walton's model for the *Uncle Vanya* set

JUMPERS—Brian Bradford as a professor and Jill Clayburgh as his wife, a singer. A group of gymnasts, the "jumpers" of this Tom Stoppard play, appear in the background, *left*

Other new British plays on Broadway were *My Fat Friend* (*right,* with George Rose, Lynn Redgrave and John Lithgow) and *Crown Matrimonial* (*below,* with Eileen Herlie as Queen Mary, George Grizzard as Edward VIII, and Ruth Hunt and Patrick Horgan as Duke and Duchess of York)

BOOM BOOM ROOM—*Above,* Charlotte Rae, Charles Durning and Madeline Kahn in the new David Rabe play produced by Joseph Papp at Lincoln Center

THIEVES—*Below,* Richard Mulligan and Marlo Thomas in the new comedy by Herb Gardner

Above, James Whitmore as Will Rogers in one-man show

VERONICA'S ROOM—Kipp Osborne, Regina Baff, Eileen Heckart and Arthur Kennedy in the play by Ira Levin

GOOD EVENING—Dudley Moore and Peter Cook in the *On Location* skit from their revue

Right, Liza Minnelli on Broadway in her one-woman show

MUSICALS

OVER HERE—*Left,* Ann Reinking and John Mineo in a jitterbug number (with choreography by Patricia Birch) from the musical harking back to the World War II home front

Below, the Andrews Sisters, Patty and Maxene, in the foreground of the *Over Here* company

LORELEI—Carol Channing (*center*) surrounded and uplifted by admirers in the new musical adventures of Lorelei Lee of *Gentlemen Prefer Blondes*

RAISIN—*Below,* Ralph Carter leads the congregation in a song number from the musicalization of Lorraine Hansberry's *A Raisin in the Sun*

FASHION—Ty McConnell and Sandra Thornton in the foreground of this musical-zation of a 19th century American comedy, in which all the male roles but one were played by actresses

THE MAGIC SHOW—*Below,* zig-zagging a lady (Dale Soules) was one of magician Doug Henning's (*left*) tricks, scrutinized by a skeptical rival (David Ogden Stiers, *right*) in the musical-with-magic

CANDIDE—*Above,* the classroom scene (with Mark Baker, Deborah St. Darr and Lewis J. Stadlen) from the new production of the 1956 musical with a new book by Hugh Wheeler

THE PAJAMA GAME—*Below,* Cab Calloway and chorus in the Broadway revival of the 1954 musical, staged by George Abbott

WHEN YOU COMIN' BACK, RED RYDER?—Kevin Conway (*foreground*) and, *left to right,* Robyn Goodman, James Kiernan, Bradford Dourif (*standing*), Elizabeth Sturges, Addison Powell, Joe Jamrog and Kristin Van Buren in the Mark Medoff play

THE SEA HORSE —
Above, Edward J. Moore
and Conchata Ferrell in the
two-character play written
by Mr. Moore under the
nom de plume "James Irwin"

CREEPS—*Left,* Steven Gilborn (*top*) and Bruce Weitz
as cerebral palsy victims in
the Canadian play by David
E. Freeman

PUBLIC THEATER

Two of Joseph Papp's New York Shakespeare Festival downtown productions are pictured on this page. *Above,* the winner of the Critics citation as best American play, *Short Eyes,* with Kenny Steward, Joseph Carberry, Tito Goya, Ben Jefferson, Felipe Torres and Bimbo. *At right,* Barbara Barrie and Ralph Waite in *The Killdeer*

THE CONTRACTOR—*Above,* George Taylor, Kevin O'Connor, Michael Finn and Joseph Maher in the British play by David Storey, winner of the Critics Award for best of bests

BAD HABITS—*Below,* entire cast in the *Dunelawn* segment of Terrence McNally's program: Paul Benedict, Cynthia Harris, Doris Roberts, J. Frank Lucas, Michael Lombard, Henry Sutton, F. Murray Abraham, Emory Bass

A BREEZE FROM THE GULF—*Above,*
Scott McKay, Robert Drivas and Ruth Ford in
Mart Crowley's family drama

HOUSE PARTY—*Below,* Starletta De Paur,
Verona Barnes and Mary Alice in the Ed
Bullins play at American Place

DEAR NOBODY — *Above,*
Jane Marla Robbins in her
one-woman show

THE GREAT MACDADDY—*Left,* Al Freeman Jr. surrounded in a scene from the Negro Ensemble Company production

THE FOURSOME—*Below,* Lindsay Crouse and Matthew Cowles in the British import by E. A. Whitehead

THE ENCLAVE — *Below,* a scene from the Arthur Laurents play, with Tom Happer, Barton Heyman and Peg Murray

REVIVALS

THE TEMPEST — *Right,* Sam Waterston and Christopher Allport in the N.Y. Shakespeare Festival production at Lincoln Center

MOONCHILDREN—*Left,* Kenneth McMillan is surrounded by students, the Moonchildren of the title of Michael Weller's play, revived off Broadway

O'Neill was conspicuously in revival on Broadway with Colleen Dewhurst and Jason Robards (*left*) in *A Moon for the Misbegotten* and James Earl Jones as Hickey in *The Iceman Cometh*

THREE SISTERS—*Below,* Mary-Joan Negro, Mary Lou Rosato and Patti Lu Pone (seated) in City Center Acting Company repertory

THE CIRCLE—*Below,* David Atkinson, Natalie Schafer and Christopher Hewett in the Roundabout Theater production of the Maugham comedy

MARY DRISCOLL
COURTROOM SCENE

On this page is a sampling of sketches by Pearl Somner for her *Ulysses in Night-town* costume designs

ULYSSES IN NIGHTTOWN—Zero Mostel as Leopold Bloom (*center,* with moustache) is surrounded by the citizens of Nighttown as he fantasizes the pangs of childbirth. Costume design sketches appear on opposite page

THE WALTZ OF THE TOREADORS—Eli Wallach and Anne Jackson in Circle in the Square's revival of the Anouilh play

BRITISH VISITORS

THE WOOD DEMON — *Above,* Sheila Reid and Ian McKellen in The Actors Company production of a seldom-produced Chekhov play

Left, Brenda Bruce (facing camera) in the Royal Shakespeare Company's *Sylvia Plath,* adapted from the works of the late poetess; *below,* a scene from Royal Shakespeare's *Richard II,* with Ian Richardson as Bolingbroke, Sebastian Shaw as York and Richard Pasco as Richard

A SAMPLING
OF NEW PLAYS IN
REGIONAL THEATERS

LOS ANGELES — *Left,* Joe Flynn in Jules Tasca's *The Mind With the Dirty Man* at Mark Taper Forum. *Below,* Norbert Weizer (Dr. Faustus), William Hunt (Mephostophilis) and Michael Dawdy (Christopher Marlowe) in Michael Monroe's *Dominus Marlowe/ A Play on Dr. Faustus,* a Los Angeles Critics Circle Award winner

PROVIDENCE—New plays produced this season by the Trinity Square Repertory Company included (above) Stuart Vaughan's *Ghost Dance,* with Barbara Orson, George Martin and Richard Kneeland, directed by the author, and (*right*) Israel Horovitz's *Alfred the Great,* with (clockwise from *top*), George Martin, Naomi Thornton, Nancy Chesney and Richard Kneeland

SEATTLE—*Left,* Sylvia Sidney in *A Family and a Fortune,* adapted by Julian Mitchell from Ivy Compton-Burnett's novel, at Seattle Repertory Theater

DALLAS—*Right,* Ken Latimer in the title role of *Jack Ruby, All-American Boy* by Jack Logan in association with Paul Baker, at Dallas Theater Center

CLEVELAND—John Bergstrom, Allen Leatherman and Douglas Jones in the world premiere production of Kevin O'Morrison's *The Morgan Yard* at Cleveland Play House

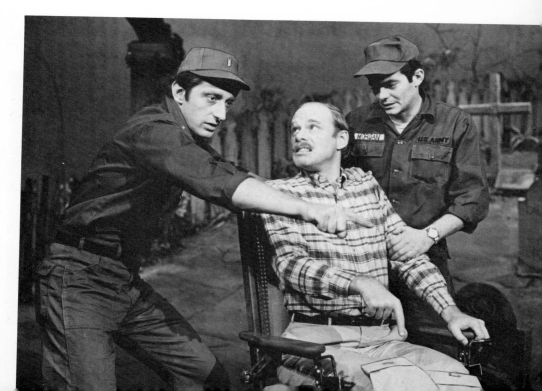

MILWAUKEE — *Left,* Robert Jorge as prosecutor and Robert Lanchester as Roger Casement in *Prisoner of the Crown* by Richard F. Stockton, in the Milwaukee Repertory Theater production

PRINCETON—Anthony McKay, Virginia Downing and Christopher Murney in D. H. Lawrence's *The Daughter-in-Law* at the McCarter Theater

HARTFORD—*Above,* Seret Scott and Jessie Saunders in the Hartford Stage Company's world premiere of Ray Aranha's *My Sister, My Sister*

SARASOTA—*Right,* Walter Rhodes in Asolo State Theater's professional American premiere of Carl Zuckmayer's *The Devil's General*

ABINGDON, VA.—*Right,* David Darlow and Ann Buckles in *Cocktails With Mimi* by Mary Chase, at the Barter Theater

BUFFALO—*Right,* Lynne Thigpen and Avon Long in a stage adaptation of Truman Capote's *Other Voices, Other Rooms* at Studio Arena

CANADA

Left, Bernard Hopkins in *Queer Sights* by Frank McEnaney at Vancouver's Playhouse Theater Center; *below,* John Gardiner, Felix Mirbt, Carole Galloway and Ann Rushbrooke in Henry Beissel's *Inook and the Sun* at Stratford, Ont.

Center Stage: Children's Theater

SAINT GEORGE AND THE DRAGON, musical comedy adaptation by Carl Schurr. Oc- tober 1973-May 1974, 114 performances touring the elementary schools.

Note: Center Stage's theater was completely destroyed by fire on Jan. 10, 1974. *Virginia Woolf,* the production which had just opened, was immediately transferred to the Baltimore Museum of Art and then to the College of Notre Dame, where the rest of the season was performed.

BOSTON

Theater Company of Boston: Loeb Drama Center

(Artistic director, David Wheeler; managing director, Peggy Forbes.)

CAT ON A HOT TIN ROOF (22). By Tennessee Williams. May 22, 1974. Director, David Wheeler; scenery, John Thornton; lighting, Maureen Gibson; costumes, Marianne Powell-Parker. With Lauri Peters, Lance Henriksen, Jean David, Gil Rogers.

Theater Company of Boston: Kresge Auditorium MIT

MISS JULIE by August Strindberg and THE DUMBWAITER by Harold Pinter (22). June 13, 1974. Director, David Wheeler; scenery, Don Beamon; lighting, Jack Peers; costumes, Wendy Russell. With Lauri Peters, Lance Henriksen, Joan Tolentino, Jan Egleson, Lane Smith.

BUFFALO

Studio Arena Theater

(Executive producer, Neal Du Brock.)

OTHER VOICES, OTHER ROOMS (30). By Truman Capote; dramatization, Anna Marie Barlow. October 4, 1973 (world premiere). Director, Melvin Bernhardt; scenery, John Conklin; lighting, David Zierk; costumes, Steven B. Feldman; music and sound, James Reichert.

Joel . . . . David Aaron
Idabel Thompkins . . . . . . Swoosie Kurtz
Roberta V. Lacey . . . . Bryna Weiss
Sam . . . . .James DeMunn
Jesus Fever . . . . Avon Long
Florabel Thompkins . . . . . .Irene Arranga
Amy . . . . .Nancy Franklin
Zoo . . . . .Lynne Thigpen
Randolph . . . . John Harkins
Little Sunshine . . . . Arnold Johnson
Mr. Sansom . . . . .Burgess Maynard
Miss Wisteria . . . . Yvonne Moray
The play takes place in Mississippi during a summer in the late 1930s. One intermission.

A STREETCAR NAMED DESIRE (30). By Tennessee Williams. November 2, 1973. Director, Jerome Guardino; scenery, Douglas F. Lebrecht; lighting, David Zierk; costumes, Steven B. Feldman. With Jon Voight, Dorothy Tristan, Anthony Costello, Hershey Parady.

FUNNY FACE (30). Music, George Gershwin; lyrics, Ira Gershwin; book, Fred Thompson, Paul Gerard Smith. December 6, 1973. Director-adapter, Neal Du Brock; scenery and lighting, David F. Segal; costumes, Steven B. Feldman; musical supervision and arrangements, William Cox; songs and dances, Edward Roll. With Susan Campbell, Jerry Dodge, Pat Sysinger, Anthony S. Teague, Susan Watson, Ronald Young.

THAT CHAMPIONSHIP SEASON (30). By Jason Miller. January 3, 1974. Director, Warren Enters; scenery and lighting, James Tilton; costumes, Steven B. Feldman. With David Ford, Richard Greene, Ben Hayes, James O'Reilly, Jess Osuna.

FLINT (30). By David Mercer. January 31, 1974 (American premiere). Director, Warren Enters; scenery and lighting, James Tilton; costumes, Steven B. Feldman.

Eric Swash . . . . Lance Brilliantine
Ossian Flint . . . . Kenneth Mars
Dixie O'Keefe . . . . Niki Flacks
Esme Flint . . . . Betty Lutes
Victoria . . . . Maureen Hurley
Dr. Colley . . . . Richard Neilson
Mr. Hodge . . . . .Tom Mardirosian
Fireman 1 . . . . Jack R. Marks

Fireman 2 . . . . Steve Demler
Bishop . . . . .Bob Moak
Maurice . . . . .Ray Hill
Inspector Hounslow . . . . . . Geoff Garland
Waiter . . . . Thomas M. Fontana
Act I, Scene 1: A church in North Kensington,
London. Scene 2: The Vicarage, later that day.
Scene 3: The church, two weeks later. Scene 4:
The vestry, immediately thereafter. Scene 5: The
Vicarage, moments later. Act II, Scene 1: The
Bishop's residence, the next day. Scene 2: The
vicarage, later the same day. Scene 3: The vicar-
age, still later. Scene 4: The church hall, several
days later. Scene 5: The journey, over several
months. One intermission.

THERE'S A GIRL IN MY SOUP (30). By Terence Frisby. February 28, 1974. Director, Stuart

Bishop; scenery, Larry Aumen; lighting, Peter
Gill; costumes, Steven B. Feldman. With Van
Johnson, Vicki Kaywood, Bob Moak.

THE MISER (30). By Molière; translated by
Wallace Fowlie. March 28, 1974. Director, War-
ren Enters; scenery and lighting, Michael Sharp;
costumes, Steven B. Feldman. With Donald
Moffat, Tandy Cronyn, Ronald Bishop, Gwen
Arner, George Ebeling.

OH COWARD! (24). Words and music by Noel
Coward. April 25, 1974. Devised and directed by
Roderick Cook; scenery, Helen Pond, Herbert
Senn; lighting, F. Michell Dana; musical director
and arranger, Rene Wiegert. With Roderick
Cook, Charlotte Fairchild, David Holliday.

Studio Arena—Children's Theater

CAROLS AND CAROUSELS: A Christmas
celebration (12). Christmas, 1973. Director, Tom
Mardirosian; lighting, Peter Gill.

HANSEL AND GRETEL (4). Music by Engel-
bert Humperdinck. April 19, 1974. Performed by
Jim Menke's Marionettes.

BURLINGTON, VT.

Champlain Shakespeare Festival: University of Vermont Arena Theater

(Producer-director, Edward J. Feidner; designers, Donald A. Rathgeb, Barry L. Cohen, Nanalee
Raphael.)

A MIDSUMMER NIGHT'S DREAM (18). By
William Shakespeare. August 8, 1973. Director,
Edward J. Feidner. With Michael Diamond,
Glynis Bell, Randy Kim, Marjorie Lyne Feiner,
Jennifer Reed, Philip Oxnam, Morgan Donohue,
Thomas Wagner.

ROMEO AND JULIET (14). By William
Shakespeare. August 11, 1973. Director, Ada

Brown Mather. With Randy Kim, Marjorie
Lyne Feiner, Glynis Bell, Dennis Boutsikaris,
Michael Tolaydo, Morgan Donohue, Michael
Diamond.

RICHARD III (13). By William Shakespeare.
August 17, 1973. Director, Edward J. Feidner.
With Randy Kim, Bruce Thomson, Jennifer
Reed, Marjorie Lyne Feiner, Philip Osnam.

CHICAGO

Goodman Theater Center: Goodman Memorial Theater

(Artistic director, William Woodman; managing director, John Economos.)

THE FREEDOM OF THE CITY (44). By Brian
Friel. October 9, 1973 (American premiere). Di-
rector, William Woodman; scenery, David Jen-
kins; lighting, F. Mitchell Dana; costumes, Al-
icia Finkel.
The Dead:
Doherty, Elizabeth
  Marigold . . . . .Frances Hyland
Fitzgerald, Adrian Casimir . . Lenny Baker
Hegarty, Michael . . . . . .Allan Carlsen
The Law:

Judge . . . . Maurice D. Copeland
Constable . . . . Charles W. Noel
Scientific Experts:
  Prof. Cupley . . . . .Edward Meekin
  Dr. Winbourne . . . . James Miller
The Church:
  Father Brosnan . . . . . . Fred Michaels
The Army:
  Brig. Johnson-Hansbury . .Anthony Mockus
  Corporal . . . . .Timothy W. Oman
  Press Officer . . . . Stephen Parr

Soldiers . . . .Timothy Himes, Ian Williams
The Observers:
Liam O'Kelly . . . . Frank Miller
Balladeer . . . . Bob Swan
Lecturer, Prof. Dodds . . . David Whitaker
Time: 1970. Place: Londonderry, Northern Ireland. One intermission.

A DOLL'S HOUSE (44). By Henrik Ibsen; translation by Christopher Hampton. November 20, 1973. Director, Tormod Skagestad; scenery, John Scheffler; lighting, G. E. Naselius; costumes, Alicia Finkel. With Carole Shelley, Phillip Kerr, Anthony Mockus.

THE TOOTH OF CRIME (44). By Sam Shepard. January 8, 1974. Director, Michael Kahn; scenery, John Kasarda; lighting, Gilbert V. Hemsley Jr.; costumes, John David Ridge. With Charles Siebert, Cynthia Dalbey, Jack Wallace, Michael Houlihan.

TO BE YOUNG, GIFTED AND BLACK (44). By Lorraine Hansberry; dramatized by Robert Nemiroff. February 19, 1974. Director,

Patrick Henry; scenery, Joseph Nieminski; lighting, Daniel Adams; costumes, Andrea Kalish. With Reuben G. Greene, Colostine Boatwright, Myron Natwick, Kristine Cameron, Connie Mango, Amanda Ambrose, Noreen Walker, Larry D. Riley, Jackie Taylor.

HENRY IV (44). By William Shakespeare; adaptation of *Henry IV, Parts 1 and 2* by Richard Matthews. March 29, 1974. Director, William Woodman; scenery and lighting, Peter Wexler; costumes, Virgil Johnson. With David Selby, Tom Atkins, Jack Roberts, George C. Hearn, Lu Ann Post, Karen Shallo.

GUYS AND DOLLS (44). Book by Jo Swerling and Abe Burrows; music and lyrics by Frank Loesser; based on a story and characters by Damon Runyon. May 10, 1974. Director, Gene Lesser; scenery, James E. Maronek; lighting, William Mintzer; costumes, Nancy Potts; choreography, Elizabeth Keen; musical director, David Richards. With Don Perkins, Sheilah Rae, Mary Louise, Terry Deck, Paul Zegler, Eugene J. Anthony.

Chicago Theater Center: Children's Theater

THE WIND IN THE WILLOWS (29). By Kenneth Grahame; adapted by Joseph Baldwin. October 20, 1973. Director, Joseph Slowik; scenery, Nancy Long; lighting, Phillip A. Evola; costumes, Niki Rudisill. With Michael Cullen, Kip Gillespie, Richard Grusin, Barbara Kingsley.

THE EMPEROR'S NEW CLOTHES (29). By Allen Lorensen; adapted from the story by Hans Christian Andersen. December 8, 1973. Director, Ned Schmidtke; scenery, David Emmons; lighting, James F. Highland; costumes, Julie A. Nagel. With Greg Sullivan, Vincent Guasteferro, Timothy R. Smith, Judy Fields.

APPLESEED (32). By Ed Graczyk; music and

lyrics by Errol Pearlman. January 26, 1974. Director, Bella Itkin; scenery, Gregory Buch; lighting, Steve Burgess, G. E. Naselius; costumes, Susan Lopez; choreography, Estelle Spector. With Brian Clare, Drapel Townsend, Ronald Smith, Danny Woodard, Adrian Smith.

THE LION WHO WOULDN'T (29). Book and lyrics by Gifford W. Wingate; music and additional lyrics, David Coleman. March 23, 1974. Director, Kelly Danford; scenery, Brad Loman; lighting, James F. Highland, William C. Fox; costumes, Gay Crusius; choreography, Gisli Bjorgvinsson, Bobbie Kingsly, Frank Ventura. With Ted Wass, Gisli Bjorgvinsson, Vincent Guasteferro, Judy Fields.

Note: The Goodman Theater Center also presented a subscription series at the School of Drama Studio Theater: *She Stoops to Conquer* by Oliver Goldsmith, directed by Eleanor Logan, November 2, 1973; *Right You Are if You Think You Are* by Luigi Pirandello, translated by Eric Bentley, directed by Charles McGaw, November 30, 1973; *The Killer* by Eugene Ionesco, translated by Donald Watson, directed by Joseph Slowik, February 1, 1974; *As You Like It* by William Shakespeare, directed by Jack Jones, March 1, 1974; *Catch-22* by Joseph Heller, directed by James F. Engelhardt, April 5, 1974; *Summer Brave* by William Inge, the rewritten and final version of *Picnic.,* directed by Bella Itkin, May 3, 1974.

CINCINNATI

Playhouse in the Park: Robert S. Marx Theater

(Artistic director, Harold Scott; managing director, Sara O'Connor.)

KISS ME, KATE (22). Book by Bella and Samuel Spewack; music and lyrics by Cole Porter. June 21, 1973. Director, Word Baker; scenery, Tom Oldendick; lighting, John Gleason; costumes, Caley Summers. With David Canary, Joy Franz, David Mack, Gene Wolters, June Gable.

THE TEMPEST (32). By William Shakespeare. October 4, 1973. Director, Garland Wright; scenery, Robert Yodice; lighting, Arden Fingerhut; costumes, Lewis Rampino. With James Ray, Harold Scott, Hannibal Penney Jr., Michele Shay.

OLD TIMES (32). By Harold Pinter. November 8, 1973. Director, Harold Scott; scenery, John Scheffler; lighting, John Gleason; costumes, Lewis Rampino. With Carolyn Coates, James Ray, Ronnie Claire Edwards.

HARVEY (33). By Mary Chase. January 3, 1974. Director, John Going; scenery, Tom Oldendick; lighting, John Gleason; costumes, Lewis Rampino. With James Noble, Dee Victor, Lynn Milgrim, Leta Bonynge.

MONKEY MONKEY BOTTLE OF BEER HOW MANY MONKEYS HAVE WE HERE? (32). By Marsha Sheiness. February 21, 1974 (world premiere). Director, Harold Scott; scenery, John Scheffler; lighting, John Gleason; costumes, Lewis D. Rampino.

Lynn . . . . Helene Friedman
Evans . . . . .Deloris Gaskins
Luther . . . . Diane Danzi
Amber . . . . .Rosemary DeAngelis
Lewis . . . . Peggy Kirkpatrick
Todd . . . . Jean DeBaer

Joe . . . . Marc Jefferson
    Time: The present. Place: A private clinic, late morning. One intermission.

WAITING FOR GODOT (32). By Samuel Beckett. March 28, 1974. Director, Harold Scott; scenery, Eric Head; lighting, Arden Fingerhut; costumes, Lewis D. Rampino. With Leland Moss, Earle Hyman, Henry Kaimu Bal, David Sabin, Ethan Tucker.

TRAVELLERS (32). Book and lyrics by Corinne Jacker, music by Jonathan Tunick, May 2, 1974 (world premiere). Director, Tony Giordano; scenery, John Scheffler; lighting, John Gleason; costumes, Lewis D. Rampino; musical director, Frank Vincent.

Lillian . . . . Marian Mercer
Stephen . . . . David Snell
Leon . . . . Ed Hall
Baby . . . . Leland Moss
Nan . . . . .Pamela Hall
Dora . . . . Eda Reiss Merin
Ken . . . . Steve Schochet
    Musicians: Piano, Frank Vincent; drums, Randall Bass; bass, David Stallsmith.
    Place: A playground in Central Park. Act I: Noon, a day in early May. Act II: Evening the same day.
    Musical Numbers—Act I: "Aldebaran," "Ambivalence," "I Have To Move," "Tree Song," "Will You Bring Me," "I Must Think," "Tomorrow," "Come To My World," "This Afternoon." Act II: "If The Meat Is Rotten," "Lao Tzu," "Discovering Stars," "If The Meat Is Rotten" (Reprise), "Spinning," "Remember The Details," "Death Song," Finale.

Playhouse In the Park: Shelterhouse Theater

A MEMORY OF TWO MONDAYS (12). By Arthur Miller. May 3, 1973. Director, Kent Paul; scenery, Peter Larkin; lighting, Dwight Werle; costumes, Maggie Bodwell. With William Carden, Joseph Lambie, Celia Howard, Kathryn Baumann, Clarence Felder.

THE LONG VOYAGE HOME, BOUND EAST FOR CARDIFF, IN THE ZONE (12). By Eugene O'Neill. May 17, 1973. Director, Kent Paul; scenery, Peter Larkin; lighting, Dwight Werle; costumes, Maggie Bodwell. With

Michael Medieros, Celia Howard, Kitty Soodek, Edwin Owens, Dermot McNamara, Joseph Lambie, Clarence Felder, Bill DaPrato.

THE CASE OF THE CRUSHED PETUNIAS, MOONY'S KID DON'T CRY, PORTRAIT OF A MADONNA (12). By Tennessee Williams. May 31, 1973. Director, Pirie MacDonald; scenery, Peter Larkin; lighting, Dwight Werle; costumes, Maggie Bodwell. With Celia Howard, Robert Burgos, Jeanne Rostaing, Kelly Walters, Edwin Owens.

CLEVELAND

The Cleveland Play House: Euclid-77th Street Theater

(Producing Director, Richard Oberlin.)

THE FRONT PAGE (29). By Ben Hecht and Charles MacArthur. October 19, 1973. Director, Thomas Gruenewald; scenery, Richard Gould; lighting, Larry Jameson; costumes, Joe Dale Lunday. With James Broderick, Victor Caroli, Jo Farwell, Julia Curry.

IN FASHION (31). Book, Jon Jory; music, Jerry Blatt; lyrics, Lonnie Burstein. November 30, 1973. Director-choreographer, Dennis Rosa; scenery, Richard Gould; lighting, Larry Jameson; costumes, Joe Dale Lunday; musical director, Donna Renton. With Phillip Piro, Michelle Reilley, Hal Robinson, Norm Berman.

COUNT DRACULA (34). By Ted Tiller; based on the novel by Bram Stoker. January 11, 1974. Director, Larry Tarrant; scenery, Richard Gould; lighting, William J. Plachy; costumes, Estelle H. Painter. With Daniel Mooney, Katherine Bruce, Jonathan Farwell, Richard Halverson.

PRIVATE LIVES (29). By Noel Coward. February 22, 1974. Director, Paul Lee; scenery, Richard Gould; lighting, Larry Jameson, costumes, Joe Dale Lunday. With Barrie Youngfellow, Richard Halverson, Jonathan Farwell, Margaret Hilton.

BORN YESTERDAY (30). By Garson Kanin. April 5, 1974. Director, Edmund Lyndeck; scenery, Richard Gould; lighting, John Rolland; costumes, Joe Dale Lunday. With Kerry Slattery, Jonathan Farwell, Daniel Mooney.

The Cleveland Play House: Drury Theater

THE SCHOOL FOR WIVES (18). By Molière; translated into English verse by Richard Wilbur. October 20, 1973. Director, Dennis Rosa; scenery and lighting, Richard Gould; costumes, Estelle H. Painter. With Richard Halverson, Jonathan Farwell, John Bergstrom, Brenda Curtis, Michelle Reilley, Phillip Piro.

A TOUCH OF THE POET (29). By Eugene O'Neill. November 9, 1973. Director, Paul Lee; scenery, Richard Gould; lighting, William J. Plachy; costumes, Bernadette O'Brien. With Edmund Lyndeck, Brenda Curtis, Margaret Hilton, Marjorie Dawe.

LOOK BACK IN ANGER (27). By John Osborne. December 21, 1973. Director, Douglas Seale; scenery, Richard Gould; lighting, David Eisenstat; costumes, Harriet Cone. With Victor Caroli, Barrie Youngfellow, Robert Allman.

HAMLET (36). By William Shakespeare. February 1, 1974. Director, J. Ranelli; scenery and costumes, Fred Voelpel; lighting, William J. Plachy. With James Sutorius, Peggy Roeder, Edmund Lyndeck, Jo Farwell, Robert Allman, John Bergstrom, Dale Place.

ROSENCRANTZ AND GUILDENSTERN ARE DEAD (20). By Tom Stoppard. March 15, 1974. Director, J. Ranelli; scenery and costumes, Fred Voelpel; lighting, William J. Plachy. With Douglas Jones, Phillip Piro, Victor Caroli, James Sutorius, Peggy Roeder, Edmund Lyndeck, Jo Farwell.

The Cleveland Play House: Brooks Theater

THE REMOVALISTS (24). By David Williamson. October 26, 1973 (American premiere). Director, Larry Tarrant; scenery, Joe Dale Lunday; lighting, John Rolland; costumes, Bernadette O'Brien.

Sergeant Dan Simmonds . Richard McKenzie
Constable Neville Ross . . . . James Sutorius
Kate LePage . . . . Myrna Kaye
Fiona Carter . . . . Peggy Roeder
Kenny Carter . . . . Douglas Jones
Rob, the Removalist . . . . James Bartz
  Place: Melbourne, Australia. Act I: A suburban police station, Thursday morning. Act II:

The Carters' flat, Friday evening.

THE MORGAN YARD (14). By Kevin O'Morrison. December 14, 1973 (world premiere). Director, Jonathan Farwell; scenery and lighting, Richard Gould; costumes, Estelle H. Painter.

Jess . . . . Douglas Jones
Lt. Bonheur . . . . John Bergstrom
Mayor Hesseltine . . . . Robert Snook
Carrie Morgan . . . . Evie McElroy
Orpha . . . . Jo Farwell
Barry B . . . . Allen Leatherman

Place: The Morgan Yard, a private burial ground in the Missouri Ozark Mountains.

Time: A day in late summer, 1970. Two intermissions.

Cleveland Play House: Children's Theater

(Director, Jo Farwell; designer, Eugene Hare.)

THE EMPEROR'S NEW CLOTHES (2), dramatized by Allen Lorensen; December 27, 1973.

THE GOLDEN GROTTO OR BRACKO, THE PRINCE FROG (3). April 13, 1974.

DALLAS

Dallas Theater Center: Kalita Humphreys Theater

(Managing director, Paul Baker.)

MARY STUART (33). By Friedrich von Schiller; translated by Stephen Spender. June 5, 1973. Director, Ken Latimer; scenery, Peter Wolf; lighting, Allen Hibbard; costumes, Kathleen Latimer. With Mary Sue Jones, Norma Moore, Steven Mackenroth, Michael Dendy.

NIGHT WATCH (33). By Lucille Fletcher. July 17, 1973. Director, John Figlmiller; scenery, Yoichi Aoki; lighting, Robert Dickson; costumes, Mary Sue Jones. With Mona Pursley, Chelcie Ross, Synthia Rogers.

JOHN BROWN'S BODY (15). By Stephen Vincent Benét. September 11, 1973. Director, Judith Davis; scenery, Sam Nance; lighting, Robyn Flatt; costumes, Cheryl Denson; projections, John Figlmiller; music, Fenno Heath; choral director, Sharon West. With Tom Cantu, Herman Wheatley, Cecilia Flores and members of the company and of the Janus Players.

HADRIAN VII (33). By Peter Luke; based on *Hadrian the Seventh* and other works by Fr. Rolfe (Baron Corvo). October 9, 1973. Director, Ken Latimer; scenery and costumes, Kathleen Latimer; lighting, Robyn Flatt. With Randy Moore, Gary Moore, John Hallowell Jr., Barry Hope, Jacque Thomas, Brian O'Reilly.

A MIDSUMMER NIGHT'S DREAM (39). By William Shakespeare; music and lyrics by Randolph Tallman and Steven Mackenroth. November 20, 1973 (world premiere). Conceived and directed by Randloph Tallman and Steven Mackenroth; scenery, Linda Blase; lighting, Sam Nance; costumes, John Henson; choreography, Margaret Tallman, John Stevens

Theseus	Barry Hope
Hippolyta	Diana Devereaux
Egeus	John Henson
Hermia	Zoe Conner
Lysander	Richard F. Ward
Helena	Margaret Tallman
Demetrius	Tony Kish
Oberon	Chelcie Ross
Puck	Steven Mackenroth
Titania	Linda Daugherty
Oregano	Norma Moore
Mustardseed	Cindy McHugh
Moth	Sara Hess
Peaseblossom	Elta Blake Snyder
Cobweb	Mary Rohde
Peter Quince	John Stevens
Nick Bottom	Herman Wheatley
Francis Flute	Jesse Y. Ramos
Robin Starveling	Lyle Maurer
Tom Snout	Greg Poe
Snug	Randolf Pearson

The Nightmares: Keyboards, Beth Kathleen Logue, John Stevens; guitar and vocal, Randolph Tallman; bass guitar, James Smith; drums, Greg Devereaux.

Musical Numbers—Act I: "The Magic Play," "The Call," "Love Surround You," "Love Surround You" (Reprise), "The Course of True Love," "Happy Some Others," "I Am Puck," "Consequence," "Oberon Flower-Squeezing," "What Is Love," "The Chase," "Woosel Cock," "Titania to Bottom." Act II: "Puck Shuffle," "Quadrangle," "Puck Lullaby," "Consequence" (Reprise), "Spirit of Peace and Love," "Shadows."

THE CRUCIBLE (39). By Arthur Miller. January 15, 1974. Director, Michael Dendy; scenery, Sallie Laurie; lighting, Randy Moore; costumes, Judith Rhodes. With Tim Green, Louise Mosley, Roselee Blooston, John Hallowell Jr., Norma Moore, Bryant J. Reynolds, B. J. Theus.

JACQUES BREL IS ALIVE AND WELL AND LIVING IN PARIS (39). By Eric Blau and Mort Shuman, based on Brel's lyrics and commentary; music by Jacques Brel. March 5, 1974. Director, Joe Bousard; designer, Nancy Levinson; lighting, Randy Moore; choreography, Cindy McHugh. With John Henson, Synthia

Rogers, Mary Rhode, Chelcie Ross, Randolph Tallman, Sharon West.

JACK RUBY, ALL-AMERICAN BOY (33). By John Logan, in association with Paul Baker. April 23, 1974 (world premiere). Director, Paul Baker; scenery, Peter Wolf; lighting, Robyn Flatt; costumes, Kathleen Latimer; projections, Nancy Levinson; sound, Tuna Howell; choreography, Chastity Fox; assistants to the director, Bryant J. Reynolds and Linda Daugherty.
Jack Ruby . . . . Ken Latimer
P.T. . . . . Randy Moore
Willard . . . . Herman Wheatley
Honey Suckle . . . . Chastity Fox (Margaret Tallman)
Wendy Winchester . . . . . . Cindy McHugh
Sandy . . . . Cecilia Flores
Dumplin' . . . . Catherine Mackenroth
Jan . . . . Cindy Holden

Barbie Dahl . . . . Linda Daugherty
Brenda Gayle Burns . . . . . Claudia Latimer
Statue of Liberty Mime, . . . Rebecca Ramsey
Jack Ruby Mime . . . . Greg Deveraux
Dan . . . . Chris McCarty
Anna . . . . Renee Welte
Police Chief . . . . Barry Hope
Lee Harvey Oswald . . . . .B.J. Theus
Prosecutor . . . . Preston Jones
Sheba . . . . Joy Sue Marie
Others: Ronni Lopez, Polly Holliday, Karyl Kesmodel, Diane Crane, Chantal Westerman, Sara Hess, Margie Reese, Tim Green, James Crump, Lyle Maurer, Melvin Kramer, Steve Lovett, Tom Cantu, Gerald Gines, Debbie Waddell, Michael Mullern, William Smotherman, John Hallowell Jr., James Smith, Paul Dollar, Steven Hetzke.
Act I: October, 1963. Act II: November 22–24, 1963. Act III: January, 1967.

Dallas Theater Center: Down Center Stage

GETTING TO KNOW THE NATIVES (15). By Daniel Turner. October 30, 1973 (world premiere). Director, Bryant J. Reynolds; scenery, Yoichi Aoki; lighting, John A. Black; costumes, Daryl Conner.
Jarlath Breen . . . . John Figlmiller
Carita Breen . . . . Deborah Mogford
Clement Rose . . . . Allen Hibbard
Misty Rose . . . . Sue Ann Gunn
Visitor . . . . John A. Black
One intermission.

THE LAST MEETING OF THE KNIGHTS OF THE WHITE MAGNOLIA (19). By Preston Jones. December 4, 1973 (world premiere). Director, Paul Baker; scenery, Mary Sue Jones; lighting, Allen Hibbard; costumes, Cindy Holden.
Ramsey Eyes . . . . Ted Mitchell
Rufe Phelps . . . . Lewis Cleckler
Olin Potts . . . . Sam Nance
Red Grover . . . . Ken Latimer
L. D. Alexander . . . . Preston Jones
Skip Hampton . . . . James Crump
Col. J. C. Kinkaid . . . . Randy Moore
Lonnie Roy McNeil . . . . . . Keith Dixon
Milo Crawford . . . . Robert Dickson
Time: 1962. Place: Bradleyville, Texas, pop. 6,000, somewhere between Big Spring and Abilene on the old highway. One intermission.

DEAR LUGER (15). By Kerry Newcomb. January 8, 1974 (world premiere). Director, John Stevens; designer, Yoichi Aoki; lighting, Sam Nance; sound, Sue Ann Gunn.
Ado . . . . Mark Stevenson
Eva . . . . Daryl Conner
Herm . . . . John A. Black

Voice . . . . Joseph Nilson
Place: A stone bunker. Time: April 30. No intermission.

LU ANN HAMPTON LAVERTY OBERLANDER (15). By Preston Jones. February 5, 1974 (world premiere). Directors, Paul Baker and Preston Jones; scenery, Mary Sue Jones; lighting, Allen Hibbard; costumes, Kathleen Latimer.
Lu Ann . . . . Sallie Laurie
Billy Bob . . . . Charles Beachley
Mom . . . . Synthia Rogers
Skip . . . . James Crump
Dale . . . . Barry Hope
Red . . . . Ken Latimer
Rufe . . . . Tommy Kendrick
Olin . . . . Sam Nance
Corky . . . . Chelcie Ross
Milo . . . . Robert Dickson
Charmaine . . . . Rebecca Ramsey
Place: Bradleyville, Texas, pop. 6,000, somewhere between Big Spring and Abilene on the old highway. Act I: The Hampton home, 1953. Act II: Red Grover's bar, 1963. Act III: The Hampton home, 1973.

CURIOUS IN L.A. (15). By Glenn Allen Smith. March 12, 1974 (world premiere). Director, Ken Latimer; scenery, Yoichi Aoki; lighting, Robert Duffy; costumes, Daryl Conner.
Freddy Foster . . . . Preston Jones
Chip . . . . Clay Broussard
Grandmother . . . . Lynn Trammell
Merrianne . . . . Judith Davis
Harry . . . . Drexel H. Riley
Betty Lou . . . . Robyn Flatt
Place: The living room of a bungalow, somewhere in the vast sprawl of Los Angeles. Act I:

A late afternoon in winter. Act II: A few minutes later. Act III: A few minutes later.

FUSE (15). By Sally Netzel. April 9, 1974 (world premiere) Director, Sally Netzel; scenery, Yoichi Aoki; lighting, Allen Hibbard; costumes, Cheryl Denson; projections, Linda Blase.
Harold . . . . Richard F. Ward
Molly . . . . Diana Devereaux
Prince . . . . Paul Callihan

Ali . . . . Greg Poe
Debra . . . . .Mona Pursley
Iris . . . . Denise Waters
Daddy . . . . Brian O'Reilly
Carla . . . . .Mary Sue Jones
Bill . . . . John A. Black
Dr. Rosewald . . . . John Figlmiller
    Place: A warehouse for scientific equipment, a weekend, late evening. One intermission.

Dallas Theater Center: Children's Theater

PINOCCHIO October 20, 1973; THE CHRISTMAS NIGHTINGALE December 15th, 1973; AESOP'S FALABLES January 26, 1974;

ALADDIN AND HIS WONDERFUL LAMP March 30, 1974. (9 each)

HARTFORD

Hartford Stage Company

(Producing director, Paul Weidner; managing director, Terence C. Murphy.)

MY SISTER, MY SISTER (44). By Ray Aranha. September 28, 1973 (world premiere). Director, Paul Weidner; scenery, Lawrence King; lighting, Larry Crimmins; costumes, Kathleen Ankers.
Sue Belle . . . . Seret Scott
Mama . . . . Barbara Montgomery
Evalina . . . . Jessie Saunders
Jesus . . . . .Daniel Snyder
Eddie . . . . .David Downing
    Specters: Gertrude Blanks, Bob Bright, Arnold Canty, Lorraine Henry, Larry Pertilla, Robbie Stevenson.
    Time: The late 1950s. Place: The South. One intermission.

GETTING MARRIED (44). By George Bernard Shaw. November 9, 1973. Director, Douglas Seale; scenery, Marjorie Kellogg; lighting, Larry Crimmins; costumes, Jane Greenwood. With Myra Carter, Bernard Frawley, Ted Graeber, Tana Hicken, Russell Nype, Richard Pilcher.

UBU ROI (44). By Alfred Jarry; translated by Paul Weidner. January 27, 1974. Director, Paul

Weidner; scenery and costumes, John Conklin; lighting, Larry Crimmins. With Richard Pilcher, Henry Thomas, Ted Graeber, David O. Peterson, Bernard Frawley.

ARSENIC AND OLD LACE (44). By Joseph Kesselring. February 8, 1974. Director, Eve Collyer; scenery, Lawrence King; lighting, Larry Crimmins; costumes, Kathleen Ankers. With Virginia Payne, Ruth Maynard, Jack Murdock, Tony Aylward, Tana Hicken.

A TOUCH OF THE POET (44). By Eugene O'Neill. March 29, 1974. Director, Paul Weidner; scenery, Marjorie Kellogg; lighting, Peter Hunt; costumes, Caley Summers. With Paul Sparer, Tana Hicken, Maureen Quinn, Barbara Caruso, Jack Murdock.

THE SCHOOL FOR SCANDAL (44). By Richard Brinsley Sheridan. May 17, 1974. Director, Paul Weidner; scenery, Kathleen Ankers; lighting, Larry Crimmins; costumes, Caley Summers. With Barbara Caruso, Jack Murdock, Robert Moberly, Tana Hicken, Chris Sarandon, Virginia Downing.

Note: Hartford Stage Company presented four productions by its Touring Theater from October 15 through the spring season. Plays were *One Wore Blue and One Wore Gray, Tales in a Teahouse, On the Season* and *Folklorico.*

HOUSTON

Alley Theater: Large Stage

(Producing director, Nina Vance.)

INHERIT THE WIND (38). By Jerome Lawrence and Robert E. Lee. October 18, 1973. Director, Robert E. Leonard; scenery, William Trotman; lighting, Jonathan Duff; costumes, Barbara Cox. With Paul C. Thomas, Bruce Hall, John Mansfield, Clint Anderson.

AH, WILDERNESS! (38). By Eugene O'Neill. November 29, 1973. Director, Beth Sanford; scenery and costumes, John Kenny; lighting, Paul Gregory. With Harry Townes, Timothy Wayne-Browne, Gertrude Glynn, Bettye Fitzpatrick, Deborah Gwillim.

A MIDSUMMER NIGHT'S DREAM (38). By William Shakespeare. January 17, 1974. Director, Robert E. Leonard; scenery and lighting, William Trotman; lighting, Jonathan Duff; costumes, Barbara C. Cox. With Lilliam Evans, Anthony Manionis, John Mansfield, Susan Andre, Lane Davies, Glynis Bell.

COMEDY OF MARRIAGE, originally titled

Play Strindberg (38). By Friedrich Durrenmatt. February 28, 1974. Director, Robert Symonds; scenery, John Kenny; lighting, Paul Gregory; costumes, Barbara C. Cox. With Priscilla Pointer, Robert Symonds, William Trotman.

COUNT DRACULA (38). By Ted Tiller, adapted from the novel by Bram Stoker. April 12, 1974. Director, William Trotman; scenery, John Kenny; lighting, Jonathan Duff; costumes, Barbara C. Cox; magic advisor, Jerry Jones. With David Wurst, Donna O'Connor, Jonathan Harker, Robert Symonds.

THE DECLINE AND FALL OF THE ENTIRE WORLD AS SEEN THROUGH THE EYES OF COLE PORTER (38). A revue conceived and assembled by Ben Bagley. May 23, 1974. Director, Beth Sanford; scenery, John Kenny; lighting, Jonathan Duff; costumes, Barbara C. Cox. With Georgia Creighton, Vivian Lee Davis, Chesley Santoro, Spence Jackson, Robert R. Kaye.

Alley Theater: Arena Stage

THE PURIFICATION (29). November 23, 1973. Director, Nina Vance; scenery, William Trotman; lighting, Jonathan Duff; costumes, Barbara C. Cox. With Robert Cornthwaite, Glynis Bell, William Trotman, Margo McElroy, Bruce Hall.

Note: Alley Theater again presented its children's theater production *The Yellow Brick Road,* adapted from the *Wizard of Oz* by Iris Siff for 4 performances. Following an unprecedented run on its Large Stage, Alley Theater remounted its production of *Jacques Brel* for an additional run in the Arena Stage on July 6, 1973.

KANSAS CITY, MO.

Missouri Repertory Theater: University of Missouri

(Artistic director, Patricia McIlrath; designer, Richard Ferguson-Wagstaffe.)

STRAIGHT UP (16). By Syd Cheatle. June 28, 1973 (American premiere). Director, Vincent Dowling; lighting, Joseph Appelt; costumes, Judith Dolan; sound, Bruce Richardson.

Beryl Sedley	Harriet Levitt
Father Hooligan	Robert Smith
Ned	Michael Mertz
Sandra Sedley	Priscilla Lindsay
Mick	Steven Ryan
George Sedley	John Q. Bruce, Jr.

The action takes place in the living room of the Sedley home in S. E. London, England. Time: The present. Act I: Early evening. Act II: Night, three weeks later. Act III: The next morning.

Two intermissions.

PYGMALION (15). By George Bernard Shaw. July 5, 1973. Director, Patricia McIlrath; lighting, Joseph Appelt; costumes, Douglas A. Russell. With Robert Scogin, Art Ellison, Michael Mertz, Robert Elliott, Sally Mertz.

ONE FLEW OVER THE CUCKOO'S NEST (18). By Dale Wasserman; based on the novel by Ken Kesey. July 12, 1973. Director, Thomas Gruenewald; lighting, Joseph Appelt; costumes, Judith Dolan. With Claude Woolman, Ronetta Wallman, Robert L. Smith, Michael Mertz,

Steven Ryan, Hannibal Penny Jr., Robert Elliott, Robert Scogin, Priscilla Lindsay.

OTHELLO (15). By William Shakespeare. July 19, 1973. Director, John O'Shaughnessy; lighting, S. O. Butler; costumes, Douglas A. Russell. With Hannibal Penney Jr., Sally Mertz, Claude Woolman, Harriet Levin, Steven Ryan.

HEDDA GABLER (14). By Henrik Ibsen; new version by Christopher Hampton. August 2, 1973. Director, Thomas Gruenewald; lighting,

Joseph Appelt; costumes, Judith Dolan, Douglas A. Russell. With Valerie von Volz, Steven Ryan, Sally Mertz, Robert Smith, Claude Woolman.

JABBERWOCK (14). By Jerome Lawrence and Robert E. Lee; based on the life and writings of James Thurber. August 9, 1973. Director, Alan Schneider; lighting, Joseph Appelt; costumes, Douglas A. Russell. With Robin Humphrey, Michael Mertz, James Daniels, Robert Smith, Art Ellison, Priscilla Lindsay.

LAKEWOOD, OHIO

Great Lakes Shakespeare Festival: Lakewood Civic Auditorium

(Producer-director, Lawrence Carra; designers, Frederic Youens, William French, Warner Blake.)

TWELFTH NIGHT (19). By William Shakespeare. July 6, 1973. Director, Lawrence Carra; music, Klaus George Roy. With Page Johnson, Anne Dockery, John Newton, Daniel Mooney, Carol Mayo Jenkins, Janet Hayes, Charles Berendt.

TARTUFFE (20). By Molière. July 12, 1973. Director, John Beary. With John Newton, Kermit Brown, Janet Hayes, Robert Allman.

A MIDSUMMER NIGHT'S DREAM (16). By William Shakespeare. July 26, 1973. Director, Lawrence Carra. With Page Johnson, Anne Dockery, Charles Berendt, Norma Joseph, Carol

Mayo Jenkins, Brendan Griffin, Daniel Mooney.

MUCH ADO ABOUT NOTHING (13). By William Shakespeare. August 9, 1973. Director, Paul Lee. With Carol Mayo Jenkins, Kelly Fitzpatrick, Anne Dockery, Gregory Lehane, Robert Allman.

THE ITALIAN STRAW HAT (12). By Eugene Labiche; translated and adapted by Mary Fournier. August 23, 1973. Director, Lawrence Carra; music, Frederic Koch. With Gregory Lehane, Kermit Brown, Robert Allman, Keith Mackey, Carold Mayo Jenkins.

LOS ANGELES

Center Theater Group: Ahmanson Theater

(Managing director, Robert Fryer.)

CYRANO DE BERGERAC (48). By Edmond Rostand; translated by Brian Hooker. October 16, 1973. Director, Joseph Hardy; scenery, H. R. Poindexter; lighting, H. R. Poindexter, Donald Harris; costumes, Lewis Brown. With Richard Chamberlain, Werner Klemperer, Kurt Kasznar, Jane Connell, Robert Burr, Victor Garber, Joan Van Ark.

FINISHING TOUCHES (48). By Jean Kerr. December 4, 1973. Director, Joseph Anthony; scenery and lighting, Ben Edwards; costumes, Jane Greenwood. With Barbara Bel Geddes, Robert Lansing, Gene Rupert.

SAINT JOAN (48). By George Bernard Shaw. January 29, 1974. Director, Arvin Brown; scenery, John Conklin; lighting, Tharon Musser; costumes, Frank Thompson. With Sarah Miles, Richard Thomas, Ken Ruta, James Naughton, John Schuck, Joseph Maher, Scott Thomas, Keene Curtis.

THE TIME OF THE CUCKOO (48). By Arthur Laurents. April 2, 1974. Director, Joseph Hardy; scenery, Harry Horner; lighting, H. R. Poindexter; costumes, Joel Schumacher. With Jean Stapleton, Cesare Danova, Patty McCormack, Ernest Thompson, Charlotte Rae, Jack Manning, Tamara Toumanova.

Center Theater Group: Mark Taper Forum

(Artistic director, Gordon Davidson; director, New Theater For Now, Edward Parone.)

THE HOT L BALTIMORE (48). By Lanford Wilson. August 2, 1973. Director, Marshall W. Mason; scenery, Archie Sharp; lighting, H. R. Poindexter; costumes, Noel Taylor. With Christopher Lloyd, Jennifer Salt, Margaret Linn, Ted LePlat, Alan Oppenheimer.

THE MAHAGONNY SONGPLAY by Bertolt Brecht, translated by Michael Feingold, music by Kurt Weill; and THE MEASURE TAKEN by Bertolt Brecht, translated by Eric Bentley, music by Hanns Eisler (54). November 1, 1973. Director, Edward Payson Call; scenery and costumes, Sally Jacobs; lighting, Gilbert V. Hemsley Jr; choreography, Wally Strauss; musical director, Conrad Susa. With Karen Morrow, Harold Brown, Darrell Sandeen, David Cryer, LaVerne Williams, Peter Colly.

HAMLET (54). By William Shakespeare. March 14, 1974. Director, Gordon Davidson; scenery and lighting, Peter Wexler; costumes, Noel Taylor. With Stacy Keach, Kitty Winn, Salome Jens, Harris Yulin, Jeff Corey, Peter Nyberg.

THE CHARLATAN (54). By Derek Walcott; music by Galt MacDermot. May 23, 1974 (world premiere). Director, Mel Shapiro; scenery, Dan Snyder; lighting, Tharon Musser; costumes, Sandra Stewart.

Corpie	Cleavon Little
Heckler	Thomas M. Pollard
Andrea Holley	Paula Kelly
Dr. Theodore Holley	Murray Matheson
Henderson Josephs	Lou Gossett
Robert Martin	James Woods
Policeman	Larry Simpasa
Clarissa Holley-Upshot	Ruth Ford
Heloise Upshot	Dori Brenner
Dr. Mamamba	Sherman Hemsley
Francisco Elias	Len Lesser
Brig. John Calthorpe Upshot	Ivor Barry
Orange Vendor	Sylvia Soares

Street People: Jon Cedar, Ronald Yates Warden.

Musical conductor, pianist, organist, Gildo Mahones; bass, Clint Houston; acoustical guitar, Pete Fox; drums, congas, Bennie Parks; steel drums, percussion, Robert Greenridge.

Time: Carnival Eve, the present. Place: A street and a painter's attic in Belmont, Port-of-Spain, Trinidad.

Center Theater Group: Mark Taper Forum, New Theater For Now—Stage B 20th Century Fox

TADPOLE (6). By Jules Tasca. September 18, 1973 (world premiere). Director, Edward Parone; scenery, David Barber; lighting, John De Santis; costumes, Robert P. Ryan.

Policeman	Jon Barron
Andy	Curt Conway
Skip	George Furth
Jimmy	Laurence Luckinbill
Colleen	Marian Mercer
Amy	Ruth Nelson
Messenger	Lou Wagner

Two intermissions.

AFTERNOON TEA by Harvey Perr and THE GLEANERS by David Danielson (6). September 25, 1973 (world premiere). Director, Gordon Hunt; scenery, Michael Devine; lighting, Martin Aronstein; costumes, William Barbe.
Afternoon Tea:

Rachel	Barbara Colby
Aaron	Ron Rifkin

The Gleaners:

Black Girl	Shirley Jo Finney
Mrs. Haney	Karen Morrow
Shurlee	Sharon Ullrick

THE COLLECTED WORKS OF BILLY THE KID (6). By Michael Ondaatje October 2, 1973

(U. S. premiere). Production conceived and directed by John Dennis; scenery and visual effects, Kristine Haugan; lighting, Lawrence Metzler; costumes, Juliellen Weiss.

Pat Garrett	John Beck
John Chisum	Herb Foster
Sally Chisum	Keetje Hunt
Billy Wilson	John A. Koch
Tom O'Folliard	Hal Landon, Jr.
Angie Dickenson	Lee McCain
Charley Bowdre	Michael McNeilly
Dave Rudabaugh	Jack Nance
Billy the Kid	Mark Wheeler.

One intermission.

THE KRAMER (6). By Mark Medoff. October 9, 1973 (world premiere). Director, Robert Greenwald; scenery, Russell Pyle; lighting, Daniel Adams; costumes, Terence Tam Soon.

Toshio Uichi	Robert Ito
Judy Uichi	Joanna Miles
Bart Kramer	Ron Rifkin
Carol May Malin	Julie Rogers
Edward Bowers	Joseph R. Sicari
Art Malin	Todd Susman
Ellie Perry	Barbette Tweed

One intermission.

Center Theater Group: Mark Taper Forum, New Theater For Now—Coffee House Theater

L.A.W.O.M.A.N. (6). Conceived by Lawrence Sacharow; written by Hesper Anderson. September 20, 1973 (world premiere). Director, Lawrence Sacharow; lighting, Ron Rudolph; entrance environment, Janice Lester, Nancy Youdelman; environmental artist, Suzanne Lacey. With Argus, Kashka Bartusick, Elizabeth Bakewell, Emylin Bronstein, Kris Kirsten, Janet Laken, Donna Latrell, Carol Richard.

The play is loosely based on improvisations on the lives of the ensemble. No intermission.

Center Theater Group: Mark Taper Forum, New Theater For Now—Mark Taper Forum Theater

THE TOOTH OF CRIME (6). By Sam Shepard. September 19, 1973. Director, Robert Greenwald; scenery, Russell Pyle; lighting, Martin Aronstein; costumes, Terence Tam Soon. With William Callaway, Michael Christopher, Nedra Deen, Brad Jose, James Keach, Kendrew Lascelles, Michael Lerner.

TWENTY-THREE YEARS LATER (6). By Michael Weller. September 26, 1973 (world premiere). Director Lee D. Sankowich; scenery, Archie Sharp; lighting, John De Santis; costumes, Juliellen Weiss.

Jack	Hal England
Tom	Robert Fields
Sarah	Erin Fleming
Thakkir	Martyn Green
Mandy	Ruth McDevitt
Gloria	Joyce Van Patten
Jamie	Chip Zien
Rufus	Putty

WHAT THE WINE-SELLERS BUY (6). By Ron Milner. October 3, 1973 (world premiere). Director, Michael A. Schultz; scenery, Archie Sharp, B. B. Neel; lighting, Martin Aronstein; costumes, Andrea Lilly.

Mrs. Copeland; Candy	Gloria Edwards
Party Girl #2	Lorraine Fields
Party Girl #1	Angela Gibbs
George	Kirk Kirksey
Old Bob	Charles Lyles
Party Boy; Wino	Johnny Ray McGhee
Mrs. Harris; Neighbor Lady	Mae Mercer

Mrs. Carlton	Juanita Moore
Hustler; Detective #1	Garrett Morris
Cab Driver; Wino	Will Richardson
Melvin	Lonny Stevens
Jim Aaron	Lance Taylor Sr.
Mae	Della Thomas
Steve	Glynn Turnman
Joe	Ray Vitte
Marilyn	Shirley Washington
Rico	Dick A. Williams
Coach; Detective #2	Bill Wintersole

Two intermissions.

CONFESSIONS OF A FEMALE DISORDER (6). By Susan Miller. October 10, 1973 (world premiere). Director, Edward Parone; scenery and visual effects, Kristine Haughan; lighting, Lawrence Metzler; costumes, Pete Menefee.

Ronnie	Barra Grant
Cheerleader #1	Nedra Deen
Cheerleader #2	Laura Campbell
Cheerleader #3	Katharine Dunfee
Mother	Lesley Woods
Coop	Penelope Windust
Liz	Julie Mannix
Doctor	Gene Elman
David	Michael Cristofer
Mitch	Mark Wheeler
Letterman #1	David Gilliam
Letterman #2	Jon Barron
Letterman #3	Richard Gilliland
Evelyn	Melissa Murphy

One intermission.

Note: Mark Taper Forum also presented an improvisational theater project in the fall of 1973 and the spring of 1974; and a Forum Laboratory which presented *The Romance and Tragedy of Pioneer Life* by John Dennis (June 22, 1973); *Or Req* by Ronn Smith (July 13, 1973); *Canadian Gothic* by Johanna Glass (November 20, 1973); *Ajax* by Maya Angelou (February 5, 1974).

The Season Elsewhere in Los Angeles
By Rick Talcove

Theater critic of the Van Nuys, Calif. *Valley News.*

The key word in describing native Los Angeles theater during 1973–74 is "breakthrough." Never before had local companies asserted themselves with such artistic confidence, staging both new and traditional works with a flair that often left the larger, well-subsidized playhouses trailing behind. Naturally, not every small theater effort was earthshaking in either conception or execution; nevertheless, talent and craftsmanship were nearly always interesting, and in many cases truly impressive.

Two productions managed to dominate the smaller theater scene: the ProVisional Ensemble's *Dominus Marlowe* and the Pasadena Repertory Company's staging of David Storey's *In Celebration.* Artistically, the shows couldn't have been farther apart. Michael Monroe's *Dominus Marlowe* was a startling, pageant-like exploration of what might have gone on the mind of Christopher Marlowe just moments after his death. Monroe pitted the playwright as an intellectual pawn of his own creations: Mephostophilis (sic) and Faustus. Flamboyant in its larger moments while profound in its smaller scenes, *Dominus Marlowe* developed over its three-month run into the first really successful merging of poetic drama with counter-culture theater . . . and the effect was exhilarating, to say the least.

In Celebration, perhaps the least-admired full-length play by David Storey, was just tempting enough to producer Duane Waddell and director Gil Dennis for them to pursue—and win—the play's American premiere rights. Concerned with the stiff reunion among three sons at their parents' 40th anniversary, the play carried Storey's heightened realism to new boundaries. When the unmarried industrial relations sibling remarked, "It's less embarrassing to *be* married than not to be," there was no doubt that this "unpopular" play had found its proper berth. The professionals in this production illuminated the script under Dennis's quietly understanding direction, and when the playwright himself conferred his own letter of approval, the triumph of Pasadena Rep's *In Celebration* was just about complete.

The late William Inge figured prominently during the season with the Contempo Theater's production of *The Last Pad* and the MET Theater, under James and Nancy Gammon, discovering theatrical gold by offering three definitive revivals of Inge plays: *The Dark at the Top of the Stairs, Picnic,* and *Bus Stop;* the latter production taking no less than five Los Angeles Drama Critics Circle awards—a belated tribute to a fine playwright, but a tribute nonetheless.

Free Shakespeare came to Los Angeles's Pilgrimage Theater with the first Free Shakespeare Festival offering a sparkling revival of *As You Like It* featuring a prominent cast taking well-deserved bows under Alfred Ryder's adroit staging. The most neglected play of the year was Gardner McKay's *Sea Marks,* a fine, sensitive script that succumbed through inexperienced management. No such fate befell Milt Larsen's Mayfair Music Hall, a Santa Monica-based recreation of the traditional English vaudeville entertainment that spotlighted such figures as Beatrice Kay, Martyn Green and Nick Lucas during its first successful year of operation.

The following is a selection of the most noteworthy Los Angeles productions staged during the year. The list does not include the numerous touring shows nor the Center Theater Group productions at the Ahmanson and the Mark Taper (see the Regional Theater listing above). A plus sign (+) with the performance number indicates the show was still running on June 1, 1974.

DOMINUS MARLOWE/A PLAY ON DOCTOR FAUSTUS (74). By Michael Monroe. July 27, 1973 (world premiere). Director, Steve Kent; scenery and lighting, John Sefick; costumes, Ted Schell. Produced by the ProVisional Theater Foundation at the Odyssey Theater.

Hider	Candace Laughlin
Chorus; Mephostophilis	William Hunt
Thomas Kyd; Faustus	Norbert Weizser
Ingram Friser; Green Devil	Joseph Hudgins
Nicholas Skeres; Blue Devil	Darrell Larson
Robert Poley; Red Devil	Richard Serpe
Christopher Marlowe	Michael Dawdy

Sundry Devils Elinor Graham, Larry Hoffman
One intermission.

AS YOU LIKE IT (24). By William Shakespeare. September 3, 1973. Director, Alfred Ryder; scenery, Russell Pyle; lighting, Donald Harris; costumes, Joe I. Tompkins. With Penny Fuller, Kristoffer Tabori, Joan Van Ark, Roscoe Lee Browne, William Schallert, John Ritter, Dran Hamilton, Robert Burr. Produced by the Los Angeles Free Shakespeare Festival at the Pilgrimage Theater.

I DO! I DO! (32). Musical with book and Lyrics by Tom Jones; music by Harvey Schmidt; based on *The Fourposter* by Jan de Hartog. June 20, 1973. Director, Gower Champion; scenery, Oliver Smith; costumes, Bill Hargate; lighting, Jean Rosenthal. With Carol Burnett, Rock Hudson. At the Huntington Hartford Theater.

GONE WITH THE WIND (64). Musical with book by Horton Foote; music and lyrics by Harold Rome; based on the novel by Margaret Mitchell. August 28, 1973 (American premiere). Director, Joe Layton; scenery David Hays; costumes, Patton Campbell; lighting, H.R. Poindexter. At the Dorothy Chandler Pavilion.

Scarlett O'Hara	Leslie Ann Warren
Rhett Butler	Pernell Roberts
Melanie Hamilton	Udana Power
Ashley Wilkes	Terence Monk
Mammy	Theresa Merritt
Prissy	Cheryl Robinson
Belle	Ann Hodges

One intermission.

THE LAST PAD (54). By William Inge. June 14, 1973. Director, Keith Anderson; scenery, John Retsek; lighting, Conrad Penrod; costumes, Candice Taylor. With Nick Nolte, Henry Polic

II, James Matz. Produced by Thomas Quillen at Contempo Theater.

A FLEA IN HER EAR (38). By Georges Feydeau; adapted by Carol Johnston. November 11, 1973. Director, Joseph Ruskin; scenery, L5ooie Mawcinitt; costumes, Victoria Carroll and Victoria DeKay. With John Ashton, Harvey Gold, Victor Holchak, Victoria Carroll, Lillian Garrett, Michael Prichard. At Company of Angles.

A VIEW FROM THE BRIDGE (121). By Arthur Miller. November 3, 1973. Director, Tony Carbone; scenery, Will Eyerman and John Banicki, costumes, Mary Taylor; lighting, Will Eyerman. With Ed Knight, Isa Crino, Deemarie Michaels, Terence Evans, Kevin May, Edmund D. Towers. At the Onion Company-Zephyr Theater.

BUS STOP (41). By William Inge. August 10, 1973. Director, James Gammon; scenery, Richard McGuire; lighting, Stephen Whittaker. With Belinda Balaski, Kiva Lawrence, John Mitchum, C.J. Hincks, Frederic Downs, Max Baer, Timothy Scott, Alan Vint. At the Met Theater.

DARK AT THE TOP OF THE STAIRS (45). By William Inge. January 5, 1974. Director, Timothy Scott; scenery, Richard McGuire. With Carol Vogel, James Gammon, Belinda Balaski, Dermott Downs, John Schwartz, Joanne Moore Jordan, John Gregory, Jill Voight, Danny Driggins. At the Met Theater.

PICNIC (29+). By William Inge. April 6, 1974. Director, James Gammon, scenery, Richard McGuire. With Nick Nolte, C.J. Hincks, Belinda Balaski, Peggy Stewart, Viola Kates-Stimpson. At the Met Theater.

IN CELEBRATION (34). By David Storey. November 16, 1973 (American premiere). Director, Gill Dennis; scenery, Howard Whalen; lighting, Julia Huntsman. At Pasadena Repertory Theater.

Steven Shaw	Jack Provost
Mr. Shaw	Howard Whalen
Mrs. Burnett	Lenore Woodward
Mrs. Shaw	Marie Peckinpah
Andrew Shaw	Robert Baron
Colin Shaw	Duane Waddell
Mr. Reardon	Dennis Jopling

One intermission.

SEA MARKS (21). By Gardner McKay. February 20, 1974 (American premiere). Director, Gardner McKay; scenery and lighting, John Nance. Produced by Patti Gilbert at Hollywood Center Theater.

Colm . . . . Joshua Bryant
Timothea . . . . Jane Merrow
    One intermission.

THE ROCKY HORROR SHOW (88+). Musical with book, music and lyrics by Richard O'Brien. March 22, 1974 (American premiere). Director, Jim Sharman; scenery, Brian Thomson; costumes, Sue Blane; lighting, Chipmonck. Produced by Lou Adler at the Roxy Theater.

Frank . . . . Tim Curry
Narrator . . . . Graham Jarvis
Brad . . . . B. Miller
Janet . . . . Abigale Haness
Magenta . . . . Jamie Donnelly
Rocky . . . . Kim Milford
Riff-Raff . . . . Bruce Scott
Columbia . . . . Boni Enten
Eddie; Doctor Scott . . . . Meat Loaf
    One intermission.

LOUISVILLE, KY.

Actors Theater of Louisville: Pamela Brown Auditorium

(Producing director, Jon Jory.)

LONG DAY'S JOURNEY INTO NIGHT (34). By Eugene O'Neill. September 27, 1973. Director, Jon Jory; scenery, Paul Owen; lighting, Geoffrey T. Cunningham; costumes, Kurt Wilhelm. With Victor Jory, Jean Inness, Tom Atkins, Michael Gross, Leta Anderson.

RENDEZVOUS (35). By Jon Jory, adapted from Monsieur Chasse! by Georges Feydeau; translated by Frederic Mullett. November 1, 1973 (American premiere). Director, Sue Lawless; lighting, Geoffrey T. Cunningham; costumes, Kurt Wilhelm.
Moricet . . . . Eric Tavaris
Leontine . . . . Peggy Cowles
Duchotel . . . . Jeffrey Tambor
Jean-Paul . . . . Michael Gross
Babette . . . . Leta Anderson
Cassagne . . . . Sandy McCallum
Mme. Latour Du Nord . . . Zouanne Henriot
Commissioner Bridois . . . . . . Irwin Atkins
1st Officer . . . . Greg Bell
    Time: 1895. Place: Paris. Act I, Scene 1: The home of Monsieur and Madame Duchotel. Scene 2: Moricet's bachelor apartment that same night. Act II: The Duchotel residence the morning after.

TARTUFFE (34). By Molière; English verse translation by Richard Wilbur. December 6, 1973. Director, Jon Jory; scenery and costumes, Paul Owen; lighting, Geoffrey T. Cunningham. With Jeffrey Tambor William Cain, Hope Alexander-Willis, Michael Gross, Leta Anderson.

ONE FLEW OVER THE CUCKOO'S NEST (34). By Dale Wasserman, based on the novel by Ken Kesey. January 10, 1974. Director, Jeffrey Tambor; scenery, Paul Owen; lighting, Geoffrey T. Cunningham; costumes, Kurt Wilhelm. With Adale O'Brien, William Cain, Greg Bell, Sandy McCallum, Ken Jenkins.

THE JOURNEY OF THE FIFTH HORSE (34). By Ronald Ribman, based on Turgenev's Diary of a Superfluous Man. February 14, 1974. Director, Jon Jory; scenery, Paul Owen; lighting, Geoffrey T. Cunningham; costumes, Kurt Wilhelm. With Jeffrey Tambor, Lee Anne Fahey, William Cain, Vaughn McBride.

THE MIRACLE WORKER (36). By William Gibson. March 21, 1974. Director, William Cain; scenery and lighting, Paul Owen; costumes, Kurt Wilhelm. With Peggy Cowles, Dawn Massie, Susan Cardwell Kingsley, Sandy McCallum.

CHIPS 'N' ALE (35). By Jon Jory and Anne Croswell, based on Oliver Goldsmith's She Stoops To Conquer; music by Jerry Blatt; lyrics by Anne Croswell. April 25, 1974 (world premiere). Director, Jon Jory; scenery, Paul Owen; lighting, Geoffrey T. Cunningham; costumes, Kurt Wilhelm; musical arrangements, Peter Howard; choreography, Paul Godkin.
Mr. Hardcastle . . . . Jack Bittner
Mrs. Hardcastle . . . . Adale O'Brien
Constance Neville . . . . Leta Anderson
Kate Hardcastle . . . . Teri Ralston
Bet Bouncer; Sample . . . . Tinker Gillespie
Tony Lumpkin . . . . Allan Gruet
Percy; Muggins . . . . Daniel Davis
Stingo; Roger . . . . David Eric
Jack Slang; Diggory . . . . . . Tom Sinclair
Young Marlow . . . . Patrick Tovatt
Hastings . . . . Michael Gross
Sir Charles Marlow . . . . . . William Cain
    Time: 1773. Place: England, in and around the Hardcastle country estate. One intermission.
    Musical Numbers—Act I: "Chips 'n' Ale," "Give Me The Innkeeper's Daughter," "Up Bluebird Hill," "A Love-e-ly Affair," "Who Needs Gems?," "Madam, I—," "Jewels," "A

Simple Girl," "Jewels (Reprise)," "To Catch A Man." Act II: "Tell Me About Your Childhood," "The Final Straw," "A Lovely Affair (Reprise)," "The Letter," "Oh Lud! Oh Law!," "The Most Beautiful Thing," Finale.

Actors Theater of Louisville: Victor Jory Theater.

THE BOOR by Anton Chekhov; translation by Gary Barker and MAN OF DESTINY by George Bernard Shaw (12). October 9, 1973. Director, Jon Jory; scenery, Paul Owen; lighting, Geoffrey T. Cunningham; costumes, Kurt Wilhelm. With Jeffrey Tambor, Lee Anne Fahey, William Cain, Irwin Atkins, Peggy Cowles.

PLAY STRINDBERG (12). By Friedrich Durrenmatt. October 23, 1973. Director, Charles Kerr; scenery, Paul Owen; lighting, Geoffrey T. Cunningham; costumes, Kurt Wilhelm. With William Cain, Adale O'Brien, James J. Lawless.

LAST OF THE RED HOT LOVERS (27). By Neil Simon. November 6, 1973. Directors, Vaughn McBride, Adale O'Brien; scenery, Paul Owen; lighting, James Stephens; costumes, Jan Kastendieck. With G. W. Bailey, Kay Erin Thompson, Lee Anne Fahey, Mary Shelley.

THE BOYS IN THE BAND (37). By Mart Crowley. March 19, 1974. Director, Charles Kerr; scenery, Paul Owen; lighting, James Stephens; costumes, Kurt Wilhelm. With Michael Thompson, Gordon L. Fox, Scott Porter, Elliott Moffitt, Gary Garth.

Actors Theater of Louisville: Children's Theater

RUMPELSTILTSKIN (9). Book and lyrics by Vaughn McBride; music by Charles Kerr. October 13, 1973.

THUMBELINA (11). By Jerry Blatt, with Lonnie Burstein. November 10, 1973.

A CHRISTMAS CAROL (20). By David Ball and David Feldshuh; a story-book version with music. December 8, 1973.

SAINT GEORGE AND THE DRAGON (9). By Carl Schurr. February 16, 1974.

GABRIEL GHOST (9). By Peggy Simon Trakt-

man, Sue Lawless, Phil Gilbert. March 23, 1974.

CINDERELLA (8). By Vaughn McBride and Charles Kerr. April 27, 1974.

Director, Vaughn McBride; musical director, Kathleen Brown, choreographer, Janet Kerr; scenery, Paul Owen; lighting, Geoffrey T. Cunningham, James Stephens; costumes, Kurt Wilhelm, Ann Shanto.

Company: Mary Jo Begley, Deirdre Bryant, Richard Flanders, Janet Johnson, Dana Kyle, Jeremy Lawrence, Steven Males, E. Allen Stevens, Eric Uhler, Deborah Watassek.

Note: Actors Theater of Louisville also toured productions of *Dames At Sea* (October 18, 1973) and *The Apple Tree* (April 9, 1974).

MILWAUKEE

Milwaukee Repertory Theater Company: Todd Wehr Theater

(Artistic director, Nagle Jackson; managing director, Charles Ray McCallum.)

PRISONER OF THE CROWN (50). By Richard F. Stockton, based on a story by Richard T. Herd. October 5, 1973 (American premiere). Director, Nagle Jackson; scenery and lighting, Christopher M. Idoine; costumes, James Edmund Brady.

Cast: Juror, Casement—Robert Lanchester; Juror, M.P., Prisoner Neill, Dr. Prentiss, Warder—Jim Baker; Juror, Hall, Doctor—Montgomery Davis; Juror, Ryan, Shorter, Court Clerk—Robert Dawson; Juror, Keeper of Rolls, Scotland Yard Clerk, 1st Tower Guard, 1st Parchment Guard, American Reporter—Robert Ground; Juror, Smith—Robert Jorge; Juror, Sullivan, Constable Riley, Prison Governor—Durward McDonald; Juror, Blackwell—William McKereghan; Juror, Reading, Thomson, Herbert Samuel—David O. Petersen; Juror, Sentry, Sgt. Hearn, Tower Sentry, Prisoner Egan, Morgan, Records Clerk—Michael Pierce; Juror, Quinn, Allen, Edward Grey, 2d Parchment Guard—Richard Risso; Juror, Robinson, Artemis Jones, 2d Tower Guard—Jack Swanson; Bailiff—Nagle Jackson; Custodian—Ray Johnston.

Time: June 29, 1916. Place: The Jury Room of the Old Bailey in London and in the minds of the Jurors. One intermission.

KNOCK (50) By Jules Romains. November 23, 1973. Director, Thomas Gruenewald; scenery, Stuart Wurtzel; lighting, Christopher M. Idoine; costumes, James Edmund Brady. With Richard Risso, Durward McDonald, Montgomery Davis, Penelope Reed.

OUR TOWN (53). By Thornton Wilder. January 11, 1974. Director, Nagle Jackson; scenery and lighting, Christopher M. Idoine; costumes, James Edmund Brady. With Durward McDonald, Judith Light, Robert Ground, Jim Baker, Ruth Schudson.

THE TRAGICALL HISTORIE OF DOCTOR FAUSTUS (50). By Christopher Marlowe. March 1, 1974. Director, Nagle Jackson, scenery, Christopher M. Idoine; lighting, Ken Billington; costumes, James Edmund Brady. With Richard Risso, G. Wood, John Hancock, Durward McDonald, Richard Loder.

LA TURISTA (50). By Sam Shepard. April 19, 1974. Director, John Lion; scenery, John Jenson; lighting, Christopher M. Idoine; costumes, Ellen M. Kozak. With Woody Eney, Jeffrey Tamber, Cheryl Anderson.

THE LITTLE FOXES (50). By Lillian Hellman. June 7, 1974. Director, Richard Risso; scenery and lighting, Christopher M. Idoine; costumes, James Edmund Brady. With DeAnn Mears, Donald McDonald, G. Wood, William McKereghan, Anne Shropshire.

Milwaukee Repertory Theater Company: Court Street Theater

BILL #1 (17). April 25, 1974. AN OCCASIONAL PIECE SUITABLE TO OPENINGS OF THEATERS by Nagle Jackson; director Nagle Jackson; scenery and lighting, Richard H. Graham; costumes, Ellen M. Kozak and Gerald Pannozzo. With the 1974 Court Street Company. THE SERVICE FOR JOSEPH AXMINSTER by George Dennison. Director, Penelope Reed; scenery and lighting, Richard H. Graham; costumes, Ellen M. Kozak. With Susan Schoenfeld, Montgomery Davis, G. Wood, Judith Light, John Hancock. THE COLLECTION by Harold Pinter. Director, William McKereghan; scenery and lighting, Richard H. Graham; costumes, Gerald Pannozzo. With Richard Risso, Jack Swanson, Elaine Dale, Joe Laur.

BILL #2 (18). May 15, 1974. PLAY by Samuel Beckett. Director, Montgomery Davis; scenery and lighting, Richard H. Graham; costumes, Ellen M. Kozak. With Richard Loder, Durward McDonald, Penelope Reed, Judith Light. SEVERAL OBJECTS PASSING CHARLIE GREELEY by Carl Larsen. Director, Nagle Jackson; scenery and lighting, Richard H. Graham; costumes, Ellen M. Kozak. With Penelope Reed, Richard Loder, Elaine Dale. WHISPER INTO MY GOOD EAR by William Hanley. Director, Fredric H. Orner; scenery and lighting, Richard H. Graham; costumes, Gerald Pannozzo. With Jim Baker, John Hancock.

Milwaukee Repertory Theater Company: Young People's Theater

THE DIARIES OF ADAM AND EVE, two stories by Mark Twain, adapted by Josephine Nichols. October 27, 1973, on tour to schools and organizations throughout Wisconsin. Director, Nagle Jackson; costumes, James Edmund Brady. With Martha J. Tippin, Jerry Brown.

Note: Milwaukee Repertory Theater Company also toured *Adaptation* by Elaine May and *The Golden Fleece* by A.R. Gurney Jr. from April 17 until June 1, 1974.

MINNEAPOLIS

The Guthrie Theater Company: Guthrie Theater

(Artistic director, Michael Langham; managing director, Donald Schoenbaum.)

BECKET (32). By Jean Anouilh. June 27, 1973. Director, David Feldshuh; scenery and costumes, Lewis Brown; lighting, Gilbert V. Hemsley, Jr. With Peter Michael Goetz, Kenneth Welsh, Bernard Behrens, Pauline Flanagan, Nicholas Kepros, Cynthia Wells.

OEDIPUS THE KING (20). By Sophocles; adapted by Anthony Burgess. June 28, 1973. Director, Michael Langham; scenery and costumes, Desmond Heeley; lighting, Richard Borgen. With Kenneth Welsh, Pauline Flanagan, Nicholas Kepros, Paul Ballantyne, James Cahill.

THE GOVERNMENT INSPECTOR (33). By Nikolai Gogol; adapted by Peter Raby. July 17, 1973. Director, Michael Langham; scenery, John Jensen; lighting, Gilbert V. Hemsley Jr.; costumes, Tanya Moiseiwitsch. With Bernard Behrens, Paul Ballantyne, Barbara Byrne, Sheriden Thomas.

JUNO AND THE PAYCOCK (31). By Sean O'Casey. September 6, 1973. Director, Tomas MacAnna; scenery, Tomas MacAnna; lighting, Duane Schuler; costumes, Jack Edwards. With Pauline Flanagan, Larry Gates, Ivar Brogger, Barbara Bryne, James Cahill, Dennis Jay Higgins, Sheriden Thomas.

I, SAID THE FLY (26). By June Havoc. September 20, 1973 (world premiere). Director, Eric Christmas; scenery, John Döepp; lighting, John Döepp, Gilbert V. Hemsley Jr.; music, Dick Whitbeck.

Big Gurn	Kenneth Welsh
Fanny Brads	June Havoc
Bunty Brads	Lee Allen
Harry Marvel	Art Kassul

Alma Marvel	Barbara Bryne
And Company	Dori Brenner
Gentle Julia	Marie Lillo
Pancho Mexicali	Oliver Cliff
Bercovici	Paul Nickabonski
The Juggler	Libby Dean

Others: Harold Dixon, Wilberto Rosario, Joy Javits, Donna Haley, Douglas Hamilton, Gerald J. Quimby, Cynthia Wells, Sheriden Thomas, Tom Balstad, Fred Koivumaki, Kim Lockhart.

WAITING FOR GODOT (29). By Samuel Beckett. October 2, 1973. Director, Eugene Lion; scenery, Gregory Hill; lighting, Richard William Tidwell; costumes, Patricia Zipprodt. With Bernard Behrens, Larry Gates, Peter Michael Goetz, Jeff Chandler.

THE MERCHANT OF VENICE (42). By William Shakespeare. November 20, 1973. Director, Michael Langham; scenery, Eoin Sprott; lighting, Gilbert V. Hemsley Jr.; costumes, Sam Kirkpatrick. With Blair Brown, Louis Turenne, James Cahill, Ellin Gorkey, Mark Lamos.

Note: In addition to the main season, the Guthrie Theater toured an original musical presentation, *The Portable Pioneer and Prairie Show* by David Chambers and Mel Marvin, directed by David Hawkanson. Drawn from the history and music of the Midwest states and territories, it is based on two travelling troupes of real Minnesota families, the Hutchinsons of Hutchinson and the Andrews of Mankato. Opening March 29th, 1974 in Hutchinson, Minn., the production played one-night stands in over 50 cities in Minnesota, Iowa, Wisconsin and North and South Dakota.

NEW HAVEN

Long Wharf Theater

(Artistic director, Arvin Brown.)

THE MASTER BUILDER (33). By Henrik Ibsen; adapted by Austin Pendleton. October 12, 1973. Director, Austin Pendleton; scenery, John Conklin; lighting, Ronald Wallace; costumes, Whitney Blausen. With Geraldine Fitzgerald, E. G. Marshall, Gretchen Corbett.

THE WIDOWING OF MRS. HOLROYD (33). By D.H. Lawrence. November 16, 1973 (American premiere). Director, Arvin Brown; scenery, David Jenkins; lighting, Ronald Wallace; costumes, Bill Walker; dialect coach, Elizabeth Smith.

Mrs. Holroyd	Joyce Ebert
Blackmore	Frank Converse
Jack Holroyd	Todd Jones
Minnie Holroyd	Vicky Geyer
Clara	Roberta Maxwell
Laura	Veronica Castang
Holroyd	Rex Robbins
Grandmother	Geraldine Fitzgerald
Rigley	Emery Battis

Mine Manager	William Swetland
Miners	James Herker, James Silverstein

Place: Holroyd's cottage in a North Country mining village. Act I, Scene 1: Evening. Scene 2: Two hours later. Act II: Later that night. Act III: The following evening.

MORNING'S AT SEVEN (33). By Paul Osborn. December 21, 1973. Director, Bill Francisco; scenery, Steven Rubin; lighting, Jamie Gallagher; costumes, Bill Walker. With Nancy Coleman, Carmen Mathews, Tresa Hughes, Shirley Bryan.

A PAGAN PLACE (33). By Edna O'Brien. January 25, 1974 (American premiere). Director, John Lithgow; scenery, Elmon Webb, Virginia Dancy; lighting, Ronald Wallace; costumes, Bill Walker.

Wiley	Stephen Mendillo
Creena	Linda Kelsey
Con	John Braden

Josie . . . . Christina Pickles
Ambie . . . . Sean G. Griffin
Miss Davitt; 2d Nun . . . . . . .Maria Tucci
Father Declan . . . . .David H. Leary
Della . . . . Swoosie Kurtz
Mr. Holland . . . . Louis Beachner
Caimin . . . . Paul Rudd
Aunt Bride . . . . .Mary Fogarty
Petronella; 1st nun . . . . . .Veronica Castang
Dr. Daly . . . . .Edward Grover
Lizzie . . . . Mary Louise Wilson
Emma . . . . Suzanne Lederer
    Men in the Pub: James Harker, James Hummer, John Long, Steve Karp, James Silverstein.
    Place: The environs of Coose, a town and townland in the west of Ireland. One intermission.

THE SEAGULL (33). By Anton Chekhov, translated by Stark Young. March 1, 1974. Director, Arvin Brown; scenery Elmon Webb, Virginia Dancy; lighting, Ronald Wallace; costumes, Bill Walker. With Joyce Ebert, William Swetland, Charles Cioffi, Roberta Maxwell, David Clennon.

THE NATIONAL HEALTH (33). By Peter Nichols. April 5, 1974. Director, Arvin Brown; scenery, Elmon Webb, Virginia Dancy; lighting, Ronald Wallace; costumes, Whitney Blausen. With William Swetland, Richard Venture, George Taylor, Louis Beachner, Stephen Mendillo, Emery Battis, Paul Rudd, Rita Moreno, Olivia Cole, Pamela Payton-Wright, Joseph Maher, George Ede.

THE RESISTIBLE RISE OF ARTURO UI (33). By Bertolt Brecht; translated by Ralph Mannheim. May 10, 1974. Director, Brooks Jones; scenery, John Conklin; lighting, Ronald Wallace; costumes, Ruth Morley; music, Robert Dennis; musical director, Thomas Fay. With David A. Butler, Frank Converse, George Ede Robin Gammell, Michael Granger, Sean G. Griffin, Howard Honig, Dick Latessa, David H. Leary, Suzanne Lederer, Michael Lerner, Joseph Maher, Stephen Mendillo, Lynn Milgram; George Morfogen, Graham Pollock, Paul Rudd, George Taylor, Angela Wood, Edward Zang.

Long Wharf Theater: Young People's Theater

CIRCUS, ADVENTURES IN THE MAGIC CIRCLE, GYPSIES, THE DOORS OF MYSTERY, THE MANY FACES OF JOHNNY APPLESEED. (12 each—four weekends in the theater, then made available for touring). Using a variety of theater techniques including story theater, improvisation, mixed media and audience participation.

Yale Repertory Theater

(Artistic director, Robert Brustein.)

THE TEMPEST (21). By William Shakespeare. October 5, 1973. Directors, Moni Yakim, Alvin Epstein. Scenery and costumes, Michael H. Yeargan; lighting, Barb Harris. With Alvin Epstein, Niki Flacks, Carmen de Lavallade, Stephen Joyce.

DARKROOM (21). By David Epstein. October 19, 1973 (world premiere). Director, Michael Posnick; scenery, Michael H. Yeargan; lighting, D. Edmund Thomas; costumes, Tony Negron; sound, William Otterson; original music, Lenny Hat.
Spoons . . . . Lenny Hat
Tim . . . . John Kuhner
Jake . . . . .Charles Levin
Boo . . . . Niki Flacks
Garvey . . . . Darryl Hill
Maxine . . . . Kate Stewart
Richard . . . . .Tony Roberts
    One intermission.

WATERGATE CLASSICS (21). By Robert Barnett, Robert Brustein, Lonnie Carter, Jules Feiffer, Jeremy Geidt, Jonathan Marks, Philip Roth, Isaiah Sheffer, Maury Yeston. November 16, 1973 (world premiere). Director, Isaiah Sheffer; scenery, Zack Brown; lighting, Dirk Epperson; costumes, Tove Ahlback, Jeanne Button, Michael H. Yeargan; choreographer, Carmen de Lavallade; musical director, Jay Gitlin.
    With Robert Brustein, Alvin Epstein, Carmen de Lavallade, Frederic Warriner, John J. Brown, Norma Brustein, Darryl Hill, Paul Schierhorn, Sigourney Weaver, Diana Belshaw, Joseph Costa, Charles Levin, Kate Stewart, Jeremy Geidt, Stephen Joyce, Jerome Dempsey, Stephanie Cotsirilos, Jonathan Marks.
    Scenes, with acknowledgement to their sources: Prologue—chorus from Shakespeare's *Henry V;* Oedipus Nix—Sophocles's *Oedipus Tyrannos;* Agamilhous Rebound—Aeschylus's *Agamemnon* and Euripides's *Iphigenia in Aulis;* The Tragical History of Samlet—Shakespeare's *Hamlet;* Pledge—the Pledge of Allegiance; Pirate Martha—"Pirate Jenny" from the Brecht and Weill's *The Threepenny Opera;* High Shame —*High Noon;* Waiting for G—Lucky's speech from Beckett's *Waiting for Godot;* Anything Goes—Cole Porter's "Anything Goes"; He Was

a Boy—Blanche's speech from Williams's *A Streetcar Named Desire;* Dick's Last Tape—Beckett's *Krapp's Last Tape;* Somewhere Over the Rainbow—Arlen and Harburg's *The Wizard of Oz;* The President Addresses the Nation (Robert Brustein).

THE TUBS (21). By Terrence McNally. December 21, 1973 (world premiere). Director, Anthony Holland; scenery and costumes, Michael H. Yeargan; lighting, Barb Harris; sound, Fred Goldsmith.

Claude Perkins . . . . Frederic Warriner
Abe; Patron . . . . Joseph Costa
Buff . . . . John J. Brown
Sheldon Farenthold, M.D. . . . Kurt Kasznar
Gaetano Proclo . . . . Michael Vale
Michael Brick . . . . Ted Tally
Arthur Steelwood-Poe . . . . . . Jeremy Geidt
Tiger . . . . Charles Levin
Chris . . . . Eric McFarland
Ritz "Googie" Gomez . Stephanie Cotsirilos
Carmine Vespucci . . . . . Jerome Dempsey
Vivian Proclo . . . . Marion Paone
  Patrons: Peter Benda, David Coffey, Mordecai Newman, John Phillips, Bill Picanza, Ronald Recasner, James R. Shaffer.
  Two intermissions.

THE RISE AND FALL OF THE CITY OF MAHAGONNY (28). Text by Bertolt Brecht; music by Kurt Weill; translated by Michael Feingold. February 1, 1974. Director, Alvin Epstein; musical director and conducter, Otto-Werner Mueller; scenery, Antony Straiges; lighting and projections, D. Edmund Thomas; costumes, Tony Negron. With Kurt Kasznar, Gilbert Price, Jeremy Geidt, Grace Keagy, Stephanie Cotsirilos and Company.

GEOGRAPHY OF A HORSE DREAMER (21). By Sam Shepard. March 8, 1974. Director, David Schweizer; scenery and costumes, William Ivey Long; lighting, Bronislaw Sammler; sound, Steve Pollock; films, David Aschenson. With Berkeley Harris, Michael Vale, Charles Levin, Frederic Warriner, Kurt Kasznar. And AN EVENING WITH DEAD ESSEX By Adrienne Kennedy. Director, Andre Mtumi; scenery and costumes, William Ivey Long; lighting, Bronislaw Sammler; visuals, Karma Stanley; sound, Steve Pollock. With Hannibal Penney Jr., John J. Brown, Pierre Maurice Baston, Darryl Hill, Earnest L. Hudson, Carmen de Lavallade.

SHLEMIEL, THE FIRST (21). By Isaac Bashevis Singer. April 12, 1974 (world premiere). Director, Isaiah Sheffer; scenery, Michael H. Yeargan; lighting, William B. Warfel; costumes, Anthony Straiges; music, Bobby Paul; musical director, Robert Goldstone.

Gronam Ox . . . . Kurt Kasznar
Dopey Lekish . . . . Paul Schierhorn

Zeinvel Nitwit . . . . John J. Brown
Treitel Fool . . . . Jerome Dempsey
Sender Donkey . . . . Mordecai Newman
Shmendrick Numbskull . . . . . Charles Levin
Yenta Pesha . . . . Norma Brustein
Shlemiel . . . . Anthony Holland
Tryna Rytza . . . . Marion Paone
Children of Shlemiel:
  Yokish . . . . Stuart Katz (Brian Drutman)
  Feivish . Danny Brustein (Raphael Sbarge)
  Keile Beile . . . . Deborah Schwartz (Jamie
                                              Luciani)
Chaim Rascal . . . . Berkeley Harris
Yontel . . . . Michael Vale
Yochne Dvosha . . . . Diana Belshaw
Greena Gela . . . . Kate Stewart
  One intermission.

THE FROGS (15). By Aristophanes; adapted by Burt Shevelove; music and lyrics by Stephen Sondheim. May 20, 1974 (world premiere). Direcrer, Burt Shevelove; scenery, Michael H. Yeargan; lighting, Carol M. Waaser; costumes, Jeanne Button; musical director, Don Jennings; choreography, Carmen de Lavallade; orchestrations, Jonathan Tunick. The words of William Shakespeare and Bernard Shaw have been selected and arranged from their works by Michael Feingold.

Dionysos . . . . Larry Blyden
Zanthias . . . . Michael Vale
Herakles . . . . Dan Desmond
Charon . . . . Charles Levin
Hierophantes . . . . Ron Recasner
Aeakos . . . . Alvin Epstein
Handmaiden; Innkeeper's
  Wife . . . . Carmen De Lavallade
Innkeeper . . . . Stephen R. Lawson
Pluto . . . . Jerome Dempsey
William Shakespeare . . . . . . Jeremy Geidt
Bernard Shaw . . . . Anthony Holland
  Guards: Joseph Costa, Jonathan Marks, Gil Rochon III, Paul Schierhorn. Flagbearers: Christopher Brown, Darryl Hill.
  A Band of Initiates—The Singers: Joan Berliner, Peter Bogyo, Alma Cuervo, Franchelle Stewart Dorn, Christopher Durang, Beth Hatton, Brock Holmes, Richard Larsen, Stephen R. Lawson, Susan LeFevre, Robert Picardo, Ron Recasner, Bil Rochon III, Stephen Rowe, Jeremy Smith, Kate McGregor-Stewart, Meryl Streep, David Thomas, Scott Ulmer, Bob Van Nest, Sigourney Weaver, Donald Woodall. The Dancers: Diana Belshaw, Linda K. Harold, Ron Porter, Diana Raffman, Susan Strasburger, Alfonso Wilson, Kathryn Woglom.
  A Splash of Frogs—Steve Edelson (leader), Wade Agurcia, Michael Armstrong, Robert Barnett, Michael Cadden, Jack Callahn, Gary Cavaliere, Peter Crawford, David B. Fisher, Ed Hornsby, Alexander Lawler, Quentin Lawler, Frank Lawlor, Kevin Lawlor, Dave Lichten, Pat Monahan, Ralph Redpath, Curt Sanburn, Ted

Stein, Jose A. Taboada, Richard Taus.

The Orchestra—Members of the Yale University Band: Lori Laitman flute and piccolo; Rami Levin oboe and English horn; Frank Holden, Bill Cobb, Wendy Haskins bassoon; Karen Toupin, Mark Leder French horn; Chris Standlee, James Sinclair trumpet; Tom Olcott, Randy Brion trombone; Peter Wasserman percussion; Roberta Brockman mallets; Bruce Rosenblum string bass; Sarah Cutler harp.

Note: The Yale Repertory Theater and Drama School also presents Yale Cabaret, Experimental Theater, Studio projects and Main Stage productions with students, members of the Repertory Theater and faculty members.

PRINCETON, N.J.

McCarter Theater Company: McCarter Theater

(Artistic director, Louis Criss.)

THE SEA GULL (10). By Anton Chekhov; English version by Jean-Claude van Itallie. October 4, 1973. Director, Louis Criss; scenery, Robert U. Taylor; lighting, John McLain; costumes, Linda Fisher. With Frank Converse, Irene Dailey, Cara Duff-MacCormick, Alice Drummond, I. M. Hobson, Gene Gross.

THE ENTERTAINER (10). By John Osborne. November 15, 1973. Director, Carl Weber; scenery, Robert U. Taylor; lighting, John McLain; costumes, Linda Fisher. With Robert Pastene, Barbara Tarbuck, Alice Drummond.

TWELFTH NIGHT (10). By William Shakespeare. February 14, 1974. Director, Louis Criss; scenery and costumes, Lowell Detweiler; lighting, John McLain. With James Broderick, Ann McDonough, Clarence Felder, I. M. Hobson, Lauri Peters.

THE DAUGHTER-IN-LAW (10). By D. H. Lawrence. March 7, 1974 (world premiere). Director, John Pasquin; scenery, Robert U. Taylor;

lighting, Lowell B. Achziger; costumes, Linda Fisher.

Mrs. Gascoigne . . . . . Virginia Downing
Joe . . . . Christopher Murney
Mrs. Purdy . . . . Anne Sheldon
Minnie . . . . Jobeth Williams
Luther . . . . Anthony McKay
Cab Man . . . . Gordon Gray

Place: A small colliery in the midlands of England between Nottingham and Derbyshire. Act I, Scene 1: Mrs. Gascoigne's kitchen, early afternoon. Scene 2: Minnie Gascoigne's kitchen, early evening. Act II: Minnie Gascoigne's kitchen, late that evening. Act III, Scene 1: Minnie Gascoigne's kitchen, a fortnight later in the afternoon. Scene 2: The same, early morning.

YOU NEVER CAN TELL (10). By George Bernard Shaw. March 28, 1974. Director, Stephen Porter; scenery, Robert U. Taylor; lighting, Marc B. Weiss; costumes, Linda Fisher. With Ann McDonough, Curt Dawson, Paddy Croft, Linda Carlson, James Gallery.

PROVIDENCE, R.I.

Trinity Square Repertory Company: Lederer Playhouse

(Producing director, Adrian Hall.)

BROTHER TO DRAGONS (38). By Robert Penn Warren. October 24, 1973. Director, Adrian Hall; scenery, Eugene Lee; lighting, Richard Devin; costumes, James Berton Harris. With James Eichelberger, Marguerite Lenert, Richard Kavanaugh, Barbara Meek, Ben Powers, John McCrea.

ALFRED THE GREAT (33). By Israel Horovitz. November 28, 1973 (world premiere). Director, James Hammerstein; scenery, Robert D. Soule; lighting, Richard Devin; costumes, James Berton Harris.
Margaret . . . . Nancy Chesney

Alfred . . . . Richard Kneeland
Will . . . . George Martin
Emily . . . . Naomi Thornton

Time: Spring. Place: Home of Will and Margaret, Wakefield, Mass. Act I, Scene 1: Sunday afternoon, the start of it. Scene 2: the following evening. Act II, Scene 1: Late afternoon of the following day. Scene 2: Late night, two days later. Act III: Early the next morning.

FOR THE USE OF THE HALL (37). By Oliver Hailey. January 2, 1974 (world premiere). Director, Word Baker; scenery, Robert D. Soule; lighting, Richard Devin; costumes,

James Berton Harris.
Bess . . . . Nancy Cushman
Allen . . . . Richard Kavanaugh
Charlotte . . . . .Marian Seldes
Terry . . . . Mina Manente
Alice . . . . Nancy Chesney
Martin . . . . David Kennett.
One intermission.

THE TOOTH OF CRIME (34). By Sam Shepard. February 18, 1974. Director, Larry Arrick;

scenery, Robert D. Soule; lighting, Roger Morgan; costumes, James Berton Harris. With Ed Hall, Margo Skinner, Rose Weaver, Daniel Von Bargen, James Eichelberger.

SHERLOCK HOLMES (42). By William Gillette; new adaptation by Dennis Rosa. April 16, 1974. Director, Dennis Rosa; scenery, Robert D. Soule; lighting, Roger Morgan; costumes, Betsey Potter. With Timothy Crowe, George Martin, Richard Kavanaugh, Barbara Orson.

Trinity Square Repertory Company: Lederer Theater

GHOST DANCE (30). By Stuart Vaughan. November 1, 1973 (world premiere). Director, Stuart Vaughan; scenery, Eugene Lee; lighting, Richard Devin; costumes, James Berton Harris; supervision of Dakota songs, Richard Cumming; ethnic dances, Julie Strandberg.
Dr. Charles Eastman   . . William Damkoehler
Kicking Bear . . . . Ed Hail
Porcupine . . . . Bruce McGill
Sgt. Bullhead . . . . Robert J. Colonna
Sitting Bull . . . . Richard Kneeland
Major James McLaughlin . . . George Martin
Gen. Nelson A. Miles . . . . . David C. Jones
"Buffalo Bill" Cody . . . . .Moultrie Patten
Ralph Becker; Col. Edwin
Drum . . . . Timothy Crowe
Marie McLaughlin . . . . . . Barbara Orson
Catherine Weldon . . . . . . .Ann Thompson
Christie Weldon . . . . John Boudreau
(Zachary Miller)
Time: 1890. Place: An Indian burial place on an open South Dakota hilltop. One intermission.

AIMEE (46). Book and lyrics by William Goyen; music by Worth Gardner. December 6, 1973 (world premiere). Director, Adrian Hall; scenery and environment, Eugene Lee; lighting, Richard Devin; costumes, James Berton Harris; musical director, Richard Cumming; dances, Sharon Jenkins.
Aimee—Pamela Payton-Wright; Mama—Marguerite Lenert; Rev. Semple, Elegant, Fireman—Robert Black; Bigboy, Gambler, Four Square—Robert J. Colonna; Man in Whorehouse, Praying Janitor, 1st Newsman, John the Baptist—Timothy Crowe; 1st Policeman, Paul, Sheriff, Praying Janitor, Four Square, (trumpet)

—William Damkoehler; Drunk, 2d Newsman, Elegant, (accordian)—James Eichelberger; Rowdy Heckler, St. Stephen, Praying Janitor, Four Square, (bass drum)—Ed Hall; McPherson, 3d Newsman, Elegant, Fireman—Richard Jenkins; Whataman, Four Square, Ex-drunk, (cymbals)—David C. Jones; Charlie, Simon Legree, Devil, Fireman—T. Richard Mason; Crippled Woman, Woman Sawed in Half, Showgirl—Cynthia McKay; 1st Prostitute, Texas Guinan, Showgirl—Barbara Meek; 3d Prostitute, Lucille Smith—Barbara Orson; 2d Prostitute, Rosie, Margie, (triangle)—Margo Skinner; Nurse, Model, Unwed Mother, (trombone)—Deborah Templin; 2d Policeman, St. Sebastian—Daniel Von Bargen; Girl in Providence, Model, Unwed Mother—Rose Weaver; Temple Members—Jane McDonald, Julie Miterko.
Time: The play moves back and forth in time from 1918 to 1944. Act I: Memorial service for drowned Aimee. Act II: Ransom money service for kidnapped Aimee. Act III: Welcome home, Aimee.
Musical Numbers: "Lullaby of Sister Asleep in the Sea," "Car of Love," "One of Yours," "Heart of Jesus," "Sister Is My Daughter," "Concrete and Steel," "Precious Lady," "Joy Joy Joy," "Woman in a Prison," "Welcome Home," Sister Aimee," "Aimee Is No Angel."

A MAN FOR ALL SEASONS (44). By Robert Bolt. February 21, 1974. Director, Adrian Hall; scenery and environment, Eugene Lee; lighting, Roger Morgan; costumes, James Berton Harris. With Richard Kneeland, Robert J. Colonna, Barbara Orson, Richard Kavanaugh, George Martin, David C. Jones, Richard Blackburn.

ROCHESTER, MICH.

Oakland University Professional Theater Program: Meadow Brook Theater

(Artistic director, Terence Kilburn; managing director, David Robert Kanter.)

THE MEMBER OF THE WEDDING (29). By Carson McCullers. October 11, 1973. Director, Terence Kilburn; scenery and lighting, William

B. Fosser; costumes, Rachelle Dwaihy. With Burniece Avery; Mary Wright, Johnny Doran.

A STREETCAR NAMED DESIRE (29). By Tennessee Williams. November 8, 1973. Director, Charles Nolte; scenery and lighting, William B. Fosser; costumes, Rachelle Dwaihy. With Debra Mooney, Martin Kove, Lee Bryant, John Hallow.

HOW THE OTHER HALF LOVES (28). By Alan Ayckbourn. December 6, 1973. Director, Terence Kilburn; scenery and lighting, Thomas Aston; costumes, Rachelle Dwaihy. With Donald Ewer, Edgar Meyer, Marilyn Meyers, Marianne Muellerleile, Elisabeth Orion, Briain Petchey.

OEDIPUS REX (29). By Sophocles; adapted by Charles Nolte. January 3, 1974 (world premiere). Director, Charles Nolte; scenery and lighting, Thomas Aston; costumes, Rachelle Dwaihy.

Priest	Dennis Romer
Oedipus	Briain Petchey
Creon	Bernard Kates
The Oracle Tiresias	Joel Brooks
Jocasta	Shirley Diercks
Messenger From Corinth	John Crawford
Old Shepherd From Thebes	Fred Thompson
Slave of Oedipus	William Adler

Chorus: Marianne Muellerleile, Nancy Jeris, Fred Thompson, Joel Brooks. Citizens: Carey Yeager, Marlan Moyer.

Time: Remote antiquity. Place: Before the palace of Oedipus, King of Thebes. No intermission.

SPOON RIVER (29). By Charles Aidman; adapted from the poems by Edgar Lee Masters. January 31, 1974. Director, John Ulmer; scenery, Peter Wrenn-Meleck; lighting, James Bryne; costumes, Rachelle Dwaihy. With Elaine Browne, John Crawford, Bernard Kates, David Kroll, Debra Mooney, Marianne Muellerleile.

AS YOU LIKE IT (29). By William Shakespeare. February 28, 1974. Director, Terence Kilburn; scenery and lighting, Thomas A. Aston; costumes, Rachelle Dwaihy. With Maureen Anderman, Leah Chandler, Dennis Romer, Donald Ewer, William Adler.

TEN LITTLE INDIANS (33). By Agatha Christie. March 28, 1974. Director, Terence Kilburn; scenery, Susan Zsidisin; lighting, Thomas A. Aston; costumes, Rachelle Dwaihy. With Dennis Romer, Leah Chandler, John Crawford, Joel Brooks.

I DO! I DO! (29). By Tom Jones and Harvey Schmidt; based on *The Fourposter* by Jan de Hartog. April 25, 1974. Director, Judith Haskell; scenery and lighting, Thomas A. Aston; costumes, Rachelle Dwaihy; musical director, Marsha Whitaker. With Stephen Arlen, Adrienne Angel.

ST. LOUIS

Loretto-Hilton Repertory Theater

(Managing director, David Frank; consulting director, Davey Marlin-Jones.)

DETECTIVE STORY (24). By Sidney Kingsley. October 19, 1973. Director, Davey Marlin-Jones; scenery, Grady Larkins; lighting, Peter E. Sargent; costumes, Lawrence Miller. With Lenka Peterson, Wil Love, Brendan Burke, Joneal Joplin, Arthur A. Rosenberg.

THE IMAGINARY INVALID (24). By Molière; adapted by Miles Malleson. November 23, 1973. Director, John Going; scenery, Grady Larkins; lighting, Peter E. Sargent; costumes, Lawrence Miller. With Arthur A. Rosenberg, Donna McKechnie, Brendan Burke, Lewis Arlt, John Lisbon Wood.

THE HOT L BALTIMORE (24) by Lanford Wilson. December 28, 1973. Director, Davey Marlin-Jones; scenery, Grady Larkins; lighting, Peter E. Sargent; costumes, Lawrence Miller. With Robert Ari, Kathleen Doyle, Gina Petrushka, Barbara Frank, Margaret Winn, Wil Love.

HENRY V (24). By William Shakespeare. January 25, 1974. Dirctor, David Frank; scenery, Grady Larkins; lighting, Peter E. Sargent; costumes, Lawrence Miller. With Lewis Arlt, Brendan Burke, Denise Sachs, Arthur A. Rosenberg, Kathleen Doyle.

IRMA LA DOUCE (24). Book and lyrics by Alexandre Breffort; music by Marguerite Monnot; English book and lyrics by Julian More, David Heneker, Monty Norman. March 1, 1974. Director, Davey Marlin-Jones; scenery, Grady Larkins; lighting, Peter E. Sargent; costumes, Lawrence Miller; musical director and conductor, Salli Parker; mime consultant, Bob DeFrank. With Mickey Hartnett, Arthur A. Rosenberg, Lewis Arlt, Nelson Sheeley.

Loretto-Hilton Repertory Theater: Children's Theater

ANDROCLES AND THE LION (20). Adapted by Bob DeFrank. April 25, 1974. Director, Bob DeFrank. With Arthur A. Rosenberg, Joneal Joplin, Bob DeFrank, Thekla McDevitt.

SAN FRANCISCO

American Conservatory Theater: Geary Theater

(General director, William Ball.)

THE TAMING OF THE SHREW (48). By William Shakespeare. October 20, 1973. Director, William Ball; scenery, Ralph Funicello; lighting, F. Mitchell Dana; costumes, Robert Fletcher. With Marc Singer, Fredi Olster, William Paterson, Claire Malis.

THE HOT L BALTIMORE (25). By Lanford Wilson October 23, 1973. Director, Allen Fletcher; scenery, Robert Blackman; lighting, F. Mitchell Dana; costumes, Robert Morgan. With Ruth Kobart, Nancy Wickwire, Joseph Bird, Ray Reinhardt, Elizabeth Huddle.

YOU CAN'T TAKE IT WITH YOU (19). By George S. Kaufman and Moss Hart. November 6, 1973. Director, Jack O'Brien; scenery and costumes, Robert Blackman; lighting, Fred Kopp. With Anne Lawder, E. Kerrigan Prescott, William Paterson, Deborah May, Marc Singer.

THE MISER (32). By Molière; translated by Donald M. Frame. December 4, 1973. Director, Allen Fletcher; scenery, Ralph Funicello; lighting, T. Mitchell Dana; costumes, Robert Blackman. With Ray Reinhardt, Charles Lanyer, Claire Malis, Elizabeth Huddle.

THE HOUSE OF BERNARDA ALBA (26). By Federico Garcia Lorca; English version by Tom Stoppard. December 18, 1973. Director, Joy Carlin; scenery, Ralph Funicello; lighting, Mitchell Dana; costumes, Robert Morgan. With Ruth Kobart, Nancy Wickwire, Fredi Olster, Barbara Dirickson.

TONIGHT AT 8:30: RED PEPPERS, directed by Paul Blake; FAMILY ALBUM, directed by Edward Hastings; SHADOW PLAY, directed by Paul Blake (25). By Noel Coward. February 12, 1974. Scenery, Robert Blackman; lighting, Fred Kopp, costumes, Robert Morgan. With Charles Hallahan, Judith Knaiz, Ruth Kobart, Ray Reinhardt, Deborah May, Kathryn Crosby, Fredi Olster, Elizabeth Huddle, Paul Shenar.

THE CHERRY ORCHARD (27). By Anton Chekhov; English version by William Ball and Dennis Powers. March 19, 1974. Director, William Ball; scenery, Robert Blackman; lighting, F. Mitchell Dana; costumes, Ann Roth. With Sada Thompson, Peter Donat, Dana Elcar, Claire Malis, Elizabeth Cole, Marc Singer, William Paterson, Nancy Wickwire.

BROADWAY (27). By Philip Dunning and George Abbott. April 2, 1974. Director, Edward Hastings; scenery, Ralph Funicello; lighting, Fred Kopp; costumes, Robert Morgan. With Ray Reinhardt, James R. Winker, Ruth Kobart, Kathryn Crosby, Charles Lanyer.

American Conservatory Theater: Marines' Memorial Theater

OH COWARD! (110). Words and music by Noel Coward. December 1973. Devised and directed by Roderick Cook; scenery, Helen Pond, Herbert Senn; lighting, F. Mitchell Dana; musical director, Joe Speck. With Roderick Cook, Charlotte Fairchild, David Holliday.

WILL ROGERS' U.S.A. (32). Adapted by Paul Shyre. February 26, 1974. Director, Paul Shyre; designer, Eldon Elder. With James Whitmore.

American Conservatory Theater: Guest Production

DON'T BOTHER ME I CAN'T COPE (56). By Micki Grant; conceived and directed by Vinnette Carroll; scenery, H. R. Poindexter; lighting, Ken Billigton; costumes, Noel Taylor. July 21, 1973.

Note: American Conservatory Theater "plays in progress" program presented the following during the 1973-1974 season: *Private Parts* by Stephen Yafa, directed by Paul Blake; *A Bunch of the Gods*

Were Sitting Around One Day by James Spencer, directed by Robert Bonaventura; *The Miss Hamford Beauty Pageant and Battle of the Bands* by T. C. Miller, directed by Allen Fletcher; *Shay* by Anne Commire, directed by Edward Hastings; five one-act plays—*Academy of Desire* by Yale Udoff, directed by Robert Chapline, *And* by Robert Gordon, directed by Raye Birk, *Benito* by Allen Sternfield, directed by Peter Hadreas, *Stamp Before the Rates Went Up* by Joe Landon, directed by Joy Carlin, *Car* by McCrea Imbrie and Neil Selden, directed by Joy Carlin. Also presented was *An Evening With Arthur Miller*, adapted by Lynne Kaufman from his plays and directed by Robert Goldsby, with Peter Donat, Angela Paton, William Paterson; and the A.C.T. Young Conservatory production of *Everyone For Himself, or The Shameless Stage* written and directed by Ross Graham.

SARASOTA, FLA.

Asolo Theater Festival: The State Theater Company

(Artistic directors, Robert Strane, Eberle Thomas; managing director, Howard J. Millman; executive director, Richard G. Fallon.)

THE ROSE TATTOO (21). By Tennessee Williams. June 22, 1973. Director, Robert Strane; scenery, Rick Pike; lighting, Martin Petlock; costumes, Catherine King. With Isa Thomas, Eberle Thomas, Barbara Reid McIntyre.

THE MERCHANT OF VENICE (13). By William Shakespeare. July 27, 1973. Director, Eberle Thomas; scenery, Rick Pike; lighting, Martin Petlock; costumes, Catherine King. With Bradford Wallace, Penelope Willis, Robert Strane, Corie Sims.

TRELAWNY OF THE "WELLS" (20). By Arthur Wing Pinero. February 14, 1974. Director, Robert Strane; scenery, Rick Pike; lighting, Martin Petlock; costumes, Catherine King. With Ellen Novack, Bradford Wallace, William Leach, Walter Rhodes.

PRIVATE LIVES (25). Noel Coward. February 16, 1974. Director, Howard J. Millman; scenery, Rick Pike; lighting, Martin Petlock; costumes, Catherine King. With Jillian Lindig, Robert Strane, Nona Pipes, Henson Keys.

THE DEVIL'S GENERAL (26). By Carl Zuckmayer; adapted by Tunc Yalman from a translation by Ingrid C. and William F. Gilbert. February 22, 1974 (American premiere), Director, Tunc Yalman; scenery, Rick Pike; lighting, Martin Petlock; costumes, Catherine King; sound, Michael Cushman.

Harras	Walter Rhodes
Hansen	William Leach
Korrianke	Henson Keys
Friedrich Eilers	Robert Murch
Pfundtmayer	James Crisp
Hartmann	Stephen Johnson
Writzky; 2d Worker	Denny Albee
Hastenteuffel;	
Air Force Guard	Thomas Busard
Von Mohrungen	Bradford Wallace
Baron Pflungk	John Behan

Dr. Schmidt-Lausitz	Robert Strane
Oderbruch	Philip LeStrange
Anne Eilers	Barbara Reid McIntyre
"Pootsie" von Mohrungen	Nona Pipes
Olivia Geiss	Isa Thomas
Diddo Geiss	Ellen Novack
Lyra Schoeppke	Donna Aronson
Otto; 1st Worker	Ernest Hartman
Francois	Bruce Katzman
Detlev; Police Detective	William Turner
Buddy Lawrence	Burton Clarke

Time: Late 1941, shortly before America's entry into the Second World War. Place: Berlin. Act I: A private banquet room in Otto's restaurant, late at night. Act II: General Harras's studio apartment in a suburb of Berlin, late afternoon, two weeks later. Act III: An office at a military airfield outside Berlin, early morning, ten days later.

BROADWAY (42). By Philip Dunning and George Abbott. March 1, 1974. Director, Howard J. Millman; scenery, Rick Pike; lighting, Martin Petlock; costumes, Flozanne John; choreographer and associate director, Jim Hoskins. With William Leach, Philip LeStrange, Isa Thomas, Jillian Lindig, Robert Murch, Walter Rhodes.

A DELICATE BALANCE (20). By Edward Albee. April 5, 1974. Director, Bradford Wallace; scenery, Rick Pike; lighting, Martin Petlock; costumes, Catherine King. With Isa Thomas, William Leach, Jillian Lindig.

ARSENIC AND OLD LACE (31). By Joseph Kesselring. May 3, 1974. Director, Amnon Kabatchnik; scenery, Rick Pike; lighting, Martin Petlock; costumes, Catherine King. With Isa Thomas, John Behan, William Leach, Barbara Reid McIntyre, Philip Le Strange, Walter Rhodes.

INHERIT THE WIND (22). By Jerome Lawrence and Robert E. Lee. May 31, 1974. Director, Howard J. Millman; scenery, Rick Pike; lighting, Martin Petlock; costumes, Paige Sout-

hard. With William Leach, Bradford Wallace, Stephen Johnson, Nona Pipes.

Asolo Theater Festival: Children's Theater

THE CANTERVILLE GHOST (14). By Oscar Wilde; adapted by Robert Strane and Barbara Reid McIntyre. July 1, 1973. Director, Richard Hopkins; scenery, Rick Pike; lighting, Lee Moffatt; costumes, Mary Gibson; sound, John Edwards. With John Henderson, Christine Smith, William Turner, Ellen Bate.

THE WIND IN THE WILLOWS (20). By Kenneth Grahame; adapted by Moses Goldberg. August 5, 1973. Director, Jon Spelman; scenery, Rick Pike; lighting, Lee Moffatt; costumes, Paige Southard. With Doug Kaye, John Behan, William Turner, Denny Albee.

SEATTLE

Seattle Repertory Theater

(Artistic director, Duncan Ross; producing director, Peter Donnelly.)

JACQUES BREL IS ALIVE AND WELL AND LIVING IN PARIS (24). By Eric Blau and Mort Shuman; based on Brel's lyrics and commentary; music by Jacques Brel. October 17, 1973. Director, Jay Broad; scenery and costumes, John Wright Stevens; lighting, Richard Nelson; musical conductor, Stan Keen. With Leon Bibb, Marni Nixon, Eve Roberts, Clayton Corzatte, Patricia Ann Kern, Orrin Reiley.

THAT CHAMPIONSHIP SEASON (26). By Jason Miller. November 14, 1973. Director, Duncan Ross; scenery and costumes, John Wright Stevens; lighting, Richard Nelson. With Donald Woods, Biff McGuire, Ronny Graham, Clayton Corzatte, David Sabin.

THREE MEN ON A HORSE (26). By George Abbott and John Cecil Holm. December 19, 1973. Director, Robert Loper; scenery, Scott Robinson; lighting, Richard Nelson. With Ronny Graham, Marian Mercer, Robert Moberly.

A FAMILY AND A FORTUNE (26). By Julian Mitchell, adapted from the novel by Ivy Compton-Burnett. January 16, 1974 (American premiere). Director, Duncan Ross; scenery, Eldon Elder; lighting, Richard Nelson; costumes, Janet Christine Warren.

Edgar Gaveston	Larkin Ford
Blanche	Gale Sondergaard
Dudley	Biff McGuire
Justine	Jeannie Carson
Mark	Tobias Andersen
Clement	Robert Moberly
Oliver Seaton	Douglas Seale
Matty Seaton	Sylvia Sidney
Miss Griffin	Inga Douglas
Jellamy	Michael Keenan
Maria Sloane	Gwen Arner

Act I, Scene 1: The Gavestons' dining room, autumn 1901. Scene 2: The lodge of the Gavestons' house, two weeks later. Scene 3: The Gavestons' drawing room, six months later. Scene 4: The same, two months later. Scene 5: Blanche's bedroom that night. Act II, Scene 1: The drawing room one month later. Scene 2: The same, one month later. Scene 3: The same, three months later. Act III, Scene 1: The dining room, next morning. Scene 2, the drawing-room, one month later.

THE SEAGULL (26). By Anton Chekhov; translated by Stark Young. February 20, 1974. Director, Duncan Ross; scenery, Eldon Elder; lighting, Richard Nelson; costumes, Janet Christine Warren. With Nina Foch, Jess Richards, Laurie Prange, Lee Shallat, Paul Roebling.

THE SKIN OF OUR TEETH (26). By Thornton Wilder. March 27, 1974. Director, Edward Payson Call; scenery, Robert Dahlstrom; lighting, Richard Nelson; costumes, Janet Christine Warren. With Biff McGuire, Jeannie Carson, Elaine Kerr, Gun-Marie Nilsson, John Abajian, Angela Wood, Don West.

STRATFORD, CONN.

American Shakespeare Festival

(Artistic director, Michael Kahn; managing producer, Berenice Weiler.)

THE COUNTRY WIFE (33). By William Wycherley. June 1, 1973. Director, David Giles; scenery, Ed Wittstein; lighting, Marc B. Weiss; costumes, Jane Greenwood; With Carole Shelley, Jack Gwillim, Philip Kerr, Christina Pickles.

MEASURE FOR MEASURE (34). By William Shakespeare. June 2, 1973. Director, Michael Kahn; scenery, William Ritman; lighting, Marc B. Weiss; costumes, Jane Greenwood. With Philip Kerr, Christina Pickles, Lee Richardson, David Rounds, Rex Everhart.

MACBETH (30). By William Shakespeare. July 6, 1973. Director, Michael Kahn; scenery, Douglas W. Schmidt; lighting, Marc B. Weiss; costumes, Jane Greenwood. With Fritz Weaver, Rosemary Murphy, Michael Levin, Lee Richardson, Carole Shelley.

JULIUS CAESAR (3). By William Shakespeare. August 1, 1973. Director, Garland Wright; scenery, Robin Wagner; lighting, Marc B. Weiss; costumes, Jane Greenwood. With Wynn Pendleton, Rex Everhart, Philip Kerr, Michael Levin, Lee Richardson.

New Playwright Series: Studio Workshop

THE EVE OF SAINT VENUS by Gregg Almquist, based on a novel by Anthony Burgess. June 14, 1973. Director, Philip Taylor.

KITTY HAWK by Leonard Jenkin. July 12, 1973. Director, Garland Wright.

ST. JAMES PARK by Bruce Serlen, directed by Carole Shelley and EPIC OF BUSTER

FRIEND by Rick Lenz, directed by Michael Kahn. August 2, 1973.

BETTER DEAD THAN SORRY by Charles Durang. August 23, 1973. Directors, Larry Carpenter and Michael Kahn.

Staged reading of SLIPPING BACK by Joseph Maher.

SYRACUSE

Syracuse Stage

(Artistic director, Arthur Storch.)

WAITING FOR LEFTY (27) by Clifford Odets, and NOON (27) By Terrence McNally. March 1, 1974. Director, Arthur Storch; scenery, William Pitkin; lighting, Roger Morgan; costumes, Larry Schultz. With John Carpenter, Ben Kapen, Connie Van Ess, Margaret Impert, Tom Keena, Mitchell McGuire, Phoebe Dorin, Jack Hollander.

AN ENEMY OF THE PEOPLE (27). By Henrik Ibsen; adapted by Arthur Miller. March 29,

1974. Director, George Sherman; scenery, Kenneth E. Lewis; lighting, Roger Morgan; costumes, Lowell Detweiler. With Robert Lanchester, Tom Brannum, Victoria Boothby, Kathy Connell.

OF MICE AND MEN (20). By John Steinbeck. April 26, 1974. Director, Arthur Storch; scenery, William Pitkin; lighting, Roger Morgan; costumes, Whitney Blausen. With Barry Snider, Ron Frazier, Virginia Kiser, James Staley.

WALTHAM, MASS.

Brandeis University: Spingold Theater

ALL THE KING'S MEN. By Robert Penn Warren. October 17, 1973. Director, Charles Werner Moore; scenery, Beth Morgan; lighting, Larry Jaquith; costumes, Marilyn Ree.

THE PERSECUTION AND ASSASSINATION OF JEAN-PAUL MARAT AS PERFORMED BY THE INMATES OF THE ASYLUM OF CHARENTON UNDER THE DIRECTION OF THE MARQUIS DE SADE

(9). By Peter Weiss; English version by Geoffrey Skelton; verse adaptation by Adrian Mitchell. December 5, 1973. Directors, Walter Brazil and Dick Heller; scenery and lighting, Gerry Hariton; costumes, James F. Franklin.

THE MISER (8). By Molière, English adaptation by Miles Malleson. February 26, 1974. Director, Ted Kazanoff; scenery, Laurence W. Jac-

quith; lighting, Elizabeth Morgan; costumes, Gerry Hariton.

OEDIPUS THE KING (11). By Anthony Burgess, translated and adapted from Sophocles. April 23, 1974. Director, Charles Werner Moore; scenery, James F. Franklin; lighting, Marilyn Need; costumes, Charles Otis Sweezey.

Brandeis University: Spingold Theater, Guest Productions

THE THREE SISTERS by Anton Chekhov, THE BEGGAR'S OPERA by John Gay, MEASURE FOR MEASURE by William Shakes-

peare (7). March 11, 1974. The New York City Center Acting Company.

Brandeis University: Laurie Theater

THE DISINTEGRATION OF JAMES CHERRY (4). By Jeff Wanshel. October 10, 1973. Director, James H. Clay; scenery and lighting, Charles Otis Sweezey; costumes, Ted Cohen.

THE PIGEON (4). By Henry Zacchini. November 28, 1973 (world premiere). Director, Jon Yates; scenery, Michael S. Wien; lighting, Elizabeth Morgan; costumes, Laurence Jaquith.

A DAY IN THE DEATH OF JOE EGG (4). By Peter Nichols. February 13, 1974. Director, Dick Heller; scenery, Ted Cohen; lighting, James F Franklin; costumes, Diana Greenwood.

LENNY (4). By Julian Barry; music by David Golub and Steve Wininger. March 20, 1974. Di-

rector, Jon Yates; scenery, Marilyn Reed; lighting, Laurence W. Jaquith; costumes, Wendy Pierson; choreography, Sheldon R. Lubliner.

STATUES by Janet L. Neipris, directed by Sheldon R. Lubliner and OCEANS APART by George Masselam, directed by James Foster Kenney Jr. (4). May 5, 1974 (world premiere). Scenery, Robert Murphy; lighting, Bob Jaffe; costumes, Carol Lynn Talkov.

Brandeis professional acting company: Jack Axelrod, Barbara Bolton, Becky Chancey, Jay Drury, Jay Alan Ginsberg, David S. Howard, Theodore Kazanoff, Ian McElhinney, Randall Merrifield, Barbara Teitelbaum.

WASHINGTON, D. C.

Arena Stage: Kreeger Theater

(Producing director, Zelda Fichandler; executive director, Thomas C. Fichandler.)

KRAPP'S LAST TAPE and NOT I (21). By Samuel Beckett. September 18, 1973. Director, Alan Schneider; technical consultant assistance, Douglas Schmidt, John Gleason. With Hume Cronyn, Jessica Tandy, Joseph Brockett.

OUR TOWN (5). By Thornton Wilder. October 24, 1973. Director, Alan Schneider; scenery, Ming Cho Lee; lighting, Hugh Lester; costumes, Marjorie Slaiman. With Gary Bayer, Dianne Wiest, Robert Prosky, Howard Witt, Leslie Cass, Terrence Currier, Jane Groves.

TOM (38). By Alexander Buzo. December 14, 1973 (American premiere). Director, Alan Schneider; scenery, David Jenkins; lighting, William Mintzer; costumes, Marjorie Slaiman.
Tom . . . . .Stanley Anderson

Susan . . . . Susanne Peters
Ken . . . . Michael Mertz
Carol . . . . .Judith Long
Stephen . . . . .Max Wright
Angela . . . . .Fontaine Syer
    Time: Now or soon. Place: A modern harborside flat in Sydney, Australia. Act I, Scene 1: Monday morning. Scene 2: Following Saturday, late afternoon. Scene 3: Following Wednesday, 6 P.M. Scene 4: A day later, morning. Act II, Scene 1: Following Saturday morning. Scene 2: Tuesday evening, 6 P.M. Scene 3: Saturday morning. Scene 4: A few days later, 2 A.M. Scene 5: A few days later, late afternoon. Scene 6: Friday evening.

LEONCE AND LENA (36). By Georg Buechner; English version by Eric Bentley.

March 15, 1974 (American premiere). Director and designer, Liviu Ciulei; music, Theodor Grigoriu.

King Peter . . . . .Max Wright
Prince Leonce . . . . .Dennis Howard
Princess Lena . . . . Halo Wines
Valerio . . . . John Christopher Jones
Rosetta . . . . Dianne Wiest
Governess . . . . Leslie Cass
Master of Ceremonies . . . .Stanley Anderson
President of the Council;
Schoolmaster . . . . Robert Prosky
1st Valet . . . . Terrence Currier
2d Valet . . . . .David Reinhardsen
1st Policeman . . . . Howard Witt
2d Policeman . . . . Gary Bayer
Ministers of the Council: Michael Haney, Michael Mertz, Gene S. Minlow. Court: Laurent Bishlawy, Charles R. Edwards, John B. Jellison, Jared Matesky. Kurt Orwick, Arnold Victor.
Prologue: Excerpts from *Leonce and Lena,*

Danton's Death, Woyzeck.

IN CELEBRATION by David Storey and RELATIVELY SPEAKING by Alan Ayckbourn (47 in rotation). May 23, 1974. Director, John Dillon; scenery, David Jenkins; lighting, Arden Fingerhut; costumes, Gwynne Clark.
In Celebration
Steven Shaw . . . .Philip Charles MacKenzie
Mr. Shaw . . . . Donald Ewer
Mrs. Burnett . . . . June Hansen
Mrs. Shaw . . . . Katherine Squire
Andrew Shaw . . . . .Stanley Anderson
Colin Shaw . . . . .Paul Collins
Reardon . . . . Terrence Currier
Relatively Speaking
Greg . . . . .Philip Charles MacKenzie
Ginny . . . . .Sara Croft
Philip . . . . Donald Ewer
Sheila . . . . Barbara Lester

Arena Stage: Arena Theater

INHERIT THE WIND (40). By Jerome Lawrence and Robert E. Lee. November 1, 1973. Director, Zelda Fichandler; scenery, Ming Cho Lee; lighting, Hugh Lester; costumes, Marjorie Slaiman. With Robert Prosky, Dorothea Hammond, Dana Elcar, Terrence Currier, Max Wright.

THREE MEN ON A HORSE (39). By John Cecil Holm and George Abbott. December 21, 1973. Director, Norman Gevanthor; scenery, Marjorie Kellogg; lighting, Nora Pepper; costumes, Gwynne Clark. With Richard Bauer, Gary Bayer, Robert Prosky, Mordecai Lawner, Howard Witt.

THE RESISTIBLE RISE OF ARTURO UI (39). By Bertolt Brecht; translated by Ralph Manheim. February 1, 1974. Director, Carl Weber; scenery, Karl Eigsti; lighting, William Mintzer; costumes, Marjorie Slaiman. With Wendell Wright Jr., Max Wright, Robert Prosky, Richard Bauer, Don Plumley, Howard Witt, Stanley Anderson, Dianne Wiest, Leslie Cass.

ZALMEN, OR THE MADNESS OF GOD (39). By Elie Wiesel; adapted by Marion Wiesel from the French translation by Nathan Edelman. May 3, 1974 (English language premiere). Director, Alan Schneider; scenery, William Ritman; lighting, William Mintzer; costumes, Marjorie

Slaiman.
Zalmen . . . . Richard Bauer
The Rabbi . . . . Joseph Wiseman
Chairman, Synagogue Council   Robert Prosky
Srul . . . . Sanford Seeger
Shmuel . . . . Sy Travers
Motke . . . . Michael Mertz
Chaim . . . . .David Reinhardsen
Zender . . . . Glenn Taylor
The Doctor . . . . Mark Hammer
Inspector . . . . Howard Witt
Nina . . . . Dianne Wiest
Alexei . . . . Gary Bayer
Misha . . . . Benjamin G. Chew (John Koch)
The Commissar . . . . Scott Schofield
The Secretary . . . . Nancy Dutton
Avrom . . . . .Michael Gorrin
Feige . . . . Leslie Cass
Cantor . . . . .John B. Jellison
Guards: Michael Haney, Wendell W. Wright Jr. Members of the Congregation: Jonathan Alper, Arnold Victor, Douglas Wager. Visitors to the Service: Jonathan Alper, Bradford Gottlin, Mark Hammer, Wendell Wright Jr.

HORATIO (39). Book and lyrics by Ron Whyte; music by Mel Marvin. June 14, 1974. Director, Charles Haid; scenery, Karl Eigsti; lighting, William Eggleston; costumes, Bruce Harrow; musical director, Mel Marvin. With Tom Barbour, David Murphy, Richard Bauer, Penelope Windust, Max Wright, Gary Bayer.

Kreeger Theater Guest Production: National Theater of the Deaf

OPTIMISM, OR THE MISADVENTURES OF CANDIDE (7). Created by Harold Stone and the National Theater of the Deaf Acting

Company. Also, poems and children's stories (3). By Little Theater of the Deaf.

The New Theater of Washington: Washington Theater Club

(Executive producer, Paul R. Allen; executive director, Hazel Wentworth. This theater is in the process of reorganization and of establishing its theatrical policy. This first season, guest productions were presented, as well as local groups.

INNER CITY (109). By Eve Merriam, music by Helen Miller. July 18, 1973. A production of the Black American and Ebony Impromptu Theater Companies.

WARP (53). By Bury St. Edmund and Stuart Gordon. September 7, 1973. A production of the Georgetown Theater Company.

THOUGHTS (23). By Lamar Alford; additional lyrics by Megan Terry and Joe Tapia. January 23, 1974. An original production of LaMama Jarbor Players.

BEHIND THE BROKEN WORDS (19). Poetry selected and presented by Anthony Zerbe and Roscoe Lee Browne. March 8, 1974.

LET THERE BE LIGHT (24). A light show with quadraphonic sound by the Lumia Company. April 16, 1974.

JACQUES BREL IS ALIVE AND WELL AND LIVING IN PARIS (34). By Eric Blau and Mort Shuman, based on Brel's lyrics and commentary; music by Jacques Brel. A production of Paul K. Cohen Associates.

The Season Elsewhere in Washington

By Jay Alan Quantrill

Drama critic of radio station WAVA and drama critic and editor of *The First Folio*

Audiences in Washington, D.C. go to the theater not so much for the new play, the original statement, or the latest invention, as for an experience. Whether the play be old or new, revised or revived, patrons seem to approach each one as a happening, looking for what is good—to their tastes, of course, not necessarily the critics'. Certainly established stars draw and are needed to fill large theaters. And then, too, we have the subscription audience concept; but which plays they will see is not guaranteed, for as our theater scene has expanded, the uncertainties have increased proportionately. Even Arena Stage now feels free to revise its plan in mid-season if new works become available, or if important performers are suddenly unavailable.

Seventy-two major professional productions played Washington during 1973–74, including ten world premieres, six American premieres, six pre- and 13 post-Broadway touring companies, five non-Broadway touring productions and numerous revivals and assorted bookings from other theaters throughout the country. This includes two Broadway-bound productions on extended tours but does not include professional and semi-professional dinner theaters or summer package shows.

An overview of the season shows promise and dismay. Of the four theaters that came upon the scene as of last season, only the D.C. Black Repertory Company continues as originally planned, though even it is stumbling along, having produced only one show during the entire season. The other—the Mayflower Cabaret

—died in the summer's heat. The Virginia in Alexandria faded but reappeared in the fall with a non-Equity group that soon folded after a rumored loss of $80,000.

The American Theater saw five productions before the operating organization, Chelsea Projects, Ltd., was summarily booted out the door for reported mismanagement. To complete the dismay, the fate of the Washington Theater Club, last reported as waxing, has waned to the point of near-extinction. Steve Aaron made a surprise exit at the end of last season, returning to Juilliard, and the theater has not as yet recovered. A merger with a local group, The New Theater School of Washington headed by Paul Allen, has produced an organization burdened by leftover debts and a desperately small staff. Only three shows of the eight promised ever materialized, and none of the three was very exciting. Both the New Theater at the Theater Club and the D.C. Black Repertory are confident that there is a future for them, however.

The Kennedy Center consolidated its position as one of the two real pacesetters in Washington theater (Arena Stage being the other). They began the fall season with a Shakespeare and the Performing Arts Festival. It was a month-long offering of theater, opera, dance and music inspired or written by the bard, but it was mostly dull, except for the one brilliant theater-piece devised by Christopher Plummer called *Love and Master Will,* in which Plummer was dazzlingly matched with Zoe Caldwell. It was truly one of the finest evenings of the season.

After that, the Center brought on a balanced mixture of goods and bads, highlighted by the Quintero *A Moon for the Misbegotten,* and Tom Stoppard's *Jumpers.* Neither of these shows would have played anywhere, including New York, had they not originated at the Kennedy Center in Washington. This illustrates the beginning of the fulfillment of the purpose of the Center. Besides productions like *The Prodigal Daughter* with Wilfrid Hyde-White and *The Headhunters* with the season's best performance by Anthony Quayle, many other works have gotten much-needed support from our audiences and Kennedy Center Productions, Inc. that has literally given them a chance to live.

The Headhunters inaugurated a scheme which portends great things if continued as predicted. The show was given a two-week tryout engagement at the University of Tennessee at Knoxville. It drew packed houses, provided professional actors and a living playwright for seminars, and when the play opened in Washington we were not forced to suffer the break-in pains that resulted from unprepared openings like that of *Jumpers,* which experience initiated this collegiate tryout plan. Next season will see more of the same, with some shows playing as many as five colleges, says Roger L. Stevens, chairman of the Center.

The extended tour plan continued this season as Alice Faye and John Payne in *Good News,* another of Harry Rigby's period revivals, and *A Community of Two,* a Jerome Chodorov vehicle for Claudette Colbert's return to the stage, passed through Washington on the long road which may end at Times Square.

After a summer-long run of *Raisin* (which was then re-mounted for proscenium stage and Broadway), the Arena Stage organization travelled to Moscow and Leningrad with their productions of *Our Town* and *Inherit the Wind.* The company has had an exciting season under the direction of Alan Schneider (Zelda

CLAUDETTE COLBERT IN "A COMMUNITY OF TWO" BY JEROME CHODOROV

Fichandler being on her first well-earned sabbatical in 24 years), though the results for the audiences were somewhat bizarre. A production like *Leonce and Lena* under director Liviu Ciulei was artistically a profound experience, but it was disquieting for many patrons. *The Madness of God* by Elie Wiesel was a passionate undertaking, yet it was less than satisfying theater. The combined selection of works was daring; the overall effect was uneven but enlightening. As the season drew to a close, a long-planned mini-repertory series of two plays opened in the Kreeger under the direction of very young and very talented John Dillon (who also directed a major American premiere at the Folger Theater Group this season). David Storey's compelling *In Celebration* and Alan Ayckborn's occasionally funny *Relatively Speaking* were both perfectly mounted with only a few directorial problems.

The Folger Theater Group led off with a moving production of the Canadian play *Creeps* (which was selected for transfer to off Broadway) and followed it with *Edward G., Like the Film Star* and a romping fine production of *The Inspector General.* The season closed with an interesting attempt to redefine the form of musicals in an adaptation of *Love's Labor's Lost,* which failed in most departments. The Folger demonstrated an adventurous spirit, though, that has won them larger and larger audiences; they are looked toward for the fresh and new and the honesty of effort that becomes a solid operation. They are one of the promising ventures on the Washington scene.

The Olney Theater presented its usual five-play summer season in 1973. Without question the most exciting production was Hugh Leonard's new play *Da,* which starred John McGiver. It is concerned with returning after the departure of loved ones, coming to terms with your memories. Stephen Joyce played the younger man with authority and compassion, and McGiver played his "da." McGiver and director James D. Waring repeated their success with this show at the Dublin Festival in the fall. The rest of the Olney season was far above average, as usual.

The National Theater, about which the Nederlanders have become totally disenchanted, actually had a better than average season with such as *The River Niger* and *Noel Coward in Two Keys.* Ford's Theater began its season with the end of one fluke and ended with what looks like the beginning of another. *Godspell* closed on Sept. 16 after 625 performances, setting a record that will probably last a long time in this city of two-to-eight-week engagements. Hopefully, the profits from *Godspell* will support other worthy endeavors. The other fluke is *Don't Bother Me, I Can't Cope* which opened in April to heavy advances, universal praise and long lines at the box office.

In between *Godspell* and *Cope* came an array of entertainments, particularly *American Revolution, Part I,* a concoction of history and "story theater" which Paul Sills and company could still rescue if they'd spend the time. It was to be the first of three for the bicentennial; its prospects now seem flat as a pancake. A revival of Gershwin's *Funny Face* was the best of all revivals from *Nanette* to *Good News.*

Activity elsewhere was on the increase in Washington. The Waay (sic) off Broadway Theater opened in the Southeast section of town adjoining a gay bar and offering theater for the gay community on an Equity guest-artist contract basis. *Tubstrip* and a female impersonator led the season. An all-male version of *The Women* is scheduled for the end of the season.

Catholic University's Hartke Theater didn't have a single professional show this year, much to the chagrin of its subscribers, and area college theater had little to tell about, except for a superb production of *Ah, Wilderness!* which Father Hartke directed and which is now touring Hungary.

American Theater

CERVANTES (24). By Norman Corwin. September 6, 1973 (world premiere). Directed by Frank Corsaro; scenery and lighting, Gardner Compton; costumes, Hugh Sherrer; slides, Gardner Compton, Emile Ardolino. With Richard Kiley, John Clarkson, Suzanne Toren, Brad Rüssell, Ronda Saunders. Produced in association with Jerry Hammer; Aaron Fodiman, associate producer.

R. J. (32). Musical fable with book, music, and lyrics by Jill Williams. October 9, 1973 (world premiere). Directed by Gene Persson; scenery,

Richard Ferrer; lighting, Spencer Mosse; costumes, Virginia Carre Magee; musical staging, Sammy Bayes; musical direction and orchestrations, Danny Holgate. With Ruby Persson, Peggy Hagen Lamprey, Richard Kuller, Jay Bonnell, Stephanie Silver, Peter Kastner, Kay St. Germain, Peter Johl.

SOMETHING'S AFOOT (64) Musical with book, lyrics and music by James MacDonald, David Vos, and Robert Gerlach. November 13, 1973. Directed by Tony Tanner; scenery, Raymond T. Kurdt; scenery adaptation and supervision, Richard Talcott; lighting, Alice O'Leary.

Clive	Henry Victor
Lettie	Patti Perkins
Flint	Pierre Epstein
Hope Langdon	Barbara Heuman
Dr. Grayburn	Boris Aplon
Nigel Rancour	Gary Beach
Lady Grace Manley-Prowe	Liz Sheridan
Col. Gillweather	Gary Gage
Miss Tweed	Lu Leonard
Geoffrey	Steve Scott

Time: Late spring. Place: Rancour's Retreat, a country estate in the English lake district, the entrance hall.

Musical Numbers—Act I: "A Marvelous Weekend," "Something's Afoot," "Carry On," "I Don't Know Why I Trust You (But I Do)," "The Man With The Ginger Moustache," "Suspicious." Act II: "The Legal Heir," "You Fell Out Of The Sky," "Dinby," "I Owe It All," "New Day."

A Chelsea Projects, Limited production, in association with Arch Lustberg and Jerry Schlossberg; associate producer for the American Theater, Dennis Weiss. Originally produced at the Goodspeed Opera House.

THE RAINBOW RAINBEAM RADIO ROADSHOW (32). Musical with music and lyrics by James Rado; book by James Rado and Ted Rado. January 22, 1974. Directed by Steven Margoshes; scenery, Richard Ferrer; lighting, Alice O'Leary; sound, Otts Munderloh; music supervised and arranged, Steven Margoshes. With James Rado, Jozella Reed, Helen Gelzer, Robert Adler, Bert Ossorio, Karen Buhari, Herbert G. Goldman. Produced by Chelsea Projects, Ltd. and Ted Rado; Dennis Weiss, associate producer for the American Theater.

THURBER (24) A evening of works by James Thurber, selected by William Windom. February 19, 1974. Director, Mark Nevas; lighting, Greg Lindsley. With William Windom. Produced by arrangement with Kolmae-Luth Entertainment, Inc.

D.C. Black Repertory

CHANGES (47) Musical with book by Motojicho; music and lyrics by Valerian E. Smith. December 6, 1973 (world premiere). Directed by Motojicho; scenery, James Hooks; lighting, Ves Weaver; costumes, Quay Darnes Truitt; choreography, Louis Johnson, Mike Malone; musical director, Valerian E. Smith; sound, Bob Doughtry.

Gertrude	Janifer Baker
Madame Pethro; Model	Vikki Baltimore
Rupert B. Taylor	Clyde Jacques-Barrett
Bobby Hutchins; Ojenke	Sugar Bear Willis
Dahabu	Lyn Dyson
Richleux	Mike Hodge
Jake Jackson	Kene Holliday
Mae	Rosie Lee Horn
Tessie	Kiki Shepard
Nate Norton	Chester Sims
Ray	Jaye W. Stewart
Susie Brown	Lynn C. Whitfield

Henry	Robert Whitson

Prologue: Dark city street. Act I, Scene 1: Construction site. Scene 2: Adrienne's bedroom. Scene 3: Ray's Place. Scene 4: Ma Bess's front room/phone booth. Scene 5: Baker home. Scene 6: Construction Site. Scene 7: Funeral procession. Scene 8: Construction Site. Act II, Scene 1: Henry Smith and Susie Brown's apartment. Scene 2: Baker home. Scene 3: Ray's Place. Scene 4: Madame Pethro's parlor. Scene 5: Public park. Scene 6: Finale.

Musical Numbers—Act I: "Black Lullaby," "Rhyme Time," "Can't Be Nobody Else," "God, Watch My Child," "Amy's Song," "At This Point In Time," "Mississippi Mud." Act II: "That's Henry," "Intangible Things," "She Noticed Me," "Change Your Name," "Yoruba Chant," "Yoyo," "Understand Me," "My Mother's Face," "Black Child."

Ford's Theater

THE AMERICAN REVOLUTION, PART I (27). Created by Paul Sills; written by Paul Sills and Arnold Weinstein; music by Tony Greco; lyrics by Arnold Weinstein; based on the poems of Philip Freneau (1752-1832).

Sam Adams; Robinson	Severn Darden
Son of Liberty; Mitchell	Charles Bartlett
John Adams; Doorkeeper	John Brent
James Otis; Capt. Parker; Son of Liberty	Thomas Erhart
Tax Agent; Sewell; Singer; Musician	Richard Fire
John Hancock	Gerrit Graham

Thomas Oliver	Mike Gray
Singer; Musician	Tony Greco
Soldier; Son of Liberty	John Heard
Gov. Hutchinson; Porter	Anthony Holland
Dr. Joseph Warren	Stephen Keep
Paul Revere; Gov, Bernard	Richard Libertini
Macintosh; Officer; Son of Liberty	Jess Nadelman
Billy Dawes; Soldier; Son of Liberty	Bill Noble
Bowdouin; Gen. Gage; Son of Liberty	Rex Robbins
Son of Liberty; Soldier	Edward Steif

Hallowell; Phlucker; Monroe . . Tom Towles Col. Dalrymple; Singer . . .Arnold Weinstein Directed by Paul Sills; scenery and lighting, James M. Riley; costumes, Noel Taylor; produced for Ford's Theater by Zev Bufman.

Act I, Part 1: The Stamp Act Crisis, 1765. Part 2: The celebration at Repeal, March 1768. Part 3: Action and reaction. Part 4: The abduction of the Liberty, May 1768. Part 5: The threat of armed occupation, September 1768. Part 6: The arrival of the troops, September 20, 1768. Part 7: The occupied town, September 20, 1768. Part 8: The Boston Massacre, March 5, 1770. Part 9: The quiet years. Act II, Part 1: The Boston Tea Party, December 1773. Part 2: Military government, June 1774. Part 3: The center of danger and honor, February 1775. Part 4: The Massacre Oration, March 1775. Part 5: The deposition of Paul Revere, April 18, 1775.

Part I of three projected parts of an account of the American Revolution using the Story Theater techniques developed by Paul Sills.

FUNNY FACE (23). Revival of the musical with music by George Gershwin; lyrics by Ira Gershwin; book by Fred Thompson and Paul Gerard Smith, adapted by Neil Du Brock. January 2, 1974. Directed by Neil Du Brock; scenery and lighting, David F. Segal; costumes, Steven B. Feldman; musical supervision and arrangements, William Cox; songs and dances staged by Edward Roll. With Susan Watson, Anthony S. Teagle, Tony Tanner, Ronald Young, Susan Campbell, Pat Lysinger.

DON'T BOTHER ME I CAN'T COPE (44+). Musical revue by Micki Grant; conceived by Vinnette Carroll. April, 23, 1974. Directed by Vinnette Carroll; scenery, Richard Ferrer; lighting, Ken Billington; costumes, Noel Taylor; orchestrations and musical direction, Danny Holgate; choral arrangement and direction, Charpman Roberts; choreography, Edmond Kresley. With Salome Bey, Deborah Lynn Bridges, Sheila Ellis, Pat Estwick, Donny Harper, Every Hayes, Clinton Keen, Alton Lathrop, Teri Lindsey, Garrett Morris, Nat Morris, Wyetta Turner, Edmond Wesley. A Ford's Theater presentation by arrangement with Edward Padula and Arch Lustberg of Urban Arts.

Note: The season at Ford's Theater also included guest productions of *El Capitan,* the City Center Acting Company's *Three Sisters, Scapin* and and *The Beggar's Opera* and touring productions of *Will Rogers' U.S.A.* and *Oh, Coward.*

John F. Kennedy Center: Eisenhower Theater

THE WALTZ OF THE TOREADORS. (31). By Jean Anouilh; translated by Lucienne Hill. June 19, 1973. Directed by Brian Murray; scenery and lighting, Clark Dunham; costumes, Joseph F. Bella. With Anne Jackson Eli Wallach, Jay Garner, and Diana Van Der Vlis. A Kennedy Center Productions, Inc. production.

THE PRODIGAL DAUGHTER (39). By David Turner. November 1, 1973 (American premiere). Directed by Stephen Porter; scenery and lighting, Ben Edwards; costumes, Jane Greenwood.

Father Anthony Perfect . Wilfrid Hyde-White
Father Geoffrey Vernon . . . . Stephen Elliott
Father Michael Daley . . . . . .John Lithgow
Christine Smith . . . . . Katharine Houghton
Patrick O'Donnell . . . . Brian Brownlee
Mary Fallon . . . . Janet Grey

Place: The living room of the presbytery of Saint Peter's Church, somewhere in England. A two-act comedy-drama concerning three ministers who are invaded by a young mod housekeeper. Produced for Kennedy Center Productions, Inc. by Robert Whitehead and Roger L. Stevens.

A MOON FOR THE MISBEGOTTEN (24). By Eugene O'Neill. December 4, 1973. Directed by Jose Quintero; scenery and lighting, Ben Edwards; costumes, Jane Greendwood. With Jason Robards, Colleen Dewhurst, Ed Flanders. Produced for Kennedy Center Productions, Inc. by Elliot Martin and Lester Osterman Productions.

JUMPERS (67). By Tom Stoppard (American premiere). Directed by Peter Wood; scenery, Josef Svoboda; lighting, Gilbert V. Hemsley Jr; costumes, Willa Kim.

Dotty . . . . .Jill Clayburgh
Secretary . . . . Joan Byron
Crouch . . . . Walter Flanagan
George . . . . .Brian Bedford
Duncan McFee . . . . Robert Rhys
Archie . . . . .Remak Ramsay
Bones . . . . .Ronald Drake
Clegthorpe . . . . .William Rhys

Jumpers, Chaplains, Ushers, etc: Larry Bailey, Larry Breeding, Mark Hanks, Bobby Lee, James Litten, Eddie Mekka, Ross Miles, Dale Muchmore, Stand Picus, George Ramos, Robert Rhys, Jason Roberts, Russell Robertson, Gordon Weiss.

Produced for Kennedy Center Productions, Inc. by Roger L. Stevens, Frederick Brisson and James Nederlander.

THE AMERICAN COLLEGE THEATER FESTIVAL. Sixth annual two-week festival of ten college productions selected from all over the U.S. brought to the Kennedy Center. THE SOFT TOUCH (3) by Neil Cuthbert. April 15,

1974 (world premiere). Directed by John Betten-
bender; scenery, Joseph F. Miklojcik Jr.; lighting, Michael Tomko; costumes, Vicki McLaughlin.

Wilfred . . . . Bob Harper
Mom . . . . .Maureen Heffernan
Mrs. Crisp . . . . .Sheryl Lee Ralph
Harvey and Frank Likk . . . . . Michael Folie
Blinky . . . . .Bernie Velinsky
Landlord . . . . Fred Sirasky
Mr. Crisp . . . . Eduardo McCormack
Emile . . . . Sidoti
Offstage Voices . . Terry Robak, Maria Matos
TV Announcer . . . . .John Hart
TV Voices . . . . Jule Kane, George Spelvin

Produced by Douglass College, Rutgers University. Winner of ACTF Playwrighting Award.

Two-act farce about a young man who's sleep
is interrupted by various wierd visitations in his
Philadelphia apartment.

Festival program also included *Song of the
Great Land* (1), dramatic chorale covering the
history of Alaska by Frank Brink, April 16, 1974
(world premiere), Alaska Methodist University;
The Mandrake (2), musical adaptation of Machiavelli's play set in the 1890s, book, music and
lyrics by Jerry Rockwood, with additional music
by Thomas Wilt, April 17, 1974 (world premiere), Montclair State College; *Lying in State*

(2), by Lane Batemen, April 18, 1974 (world
premiere), runner-up in the ACTF playwrighting
awards, Southern Illinois University, *Liberty
Ranch* (2) Old West musical version of Oliver
Goldsmith's *She Stoops to Conquer* with book by
Dick Vosburgh, lyrics by Caryl Brahms and N.
Sherrin, music by John Camerons, April 23,
1974 (American premiere), Southern Methodist
University.

THE HEADHUNTERS (40). By Henry Denker
(world premiere). Directed by Anthony Quayle;
scenery, Ben Edwards; lighting, Gilbert V.
Hemsley Jr; costumes, Jane Greenwood.

Pavel Nicolaiavitch
Andreyev . . . . Anthony Quayle
Vera Andreyeva . . . . .Ann Williams
Anna Riabovska . . . . Ruth Nelson
Artur Freeling . . . . .George Voskovec
Krimsky . . . . Fred Major
Yakanov . . . . Sydney Walker
Lev Leonidovich Ziskin . . . . . Curt Dawson
Gorodnov . . . . David Hooks
Brovka . . . . Michael Lewis

Place: The small modest flat of Pavel Andreyev and his wife in an old building in Moscow.
Produced for Kennedy Center Productions, Inc.
by Roger L. Stevens and Richmond Crinkley.

Note: The season at the Eisenhower Theater also included pre-Broadway engagements of *Full Circle*
and *Freedom of the City;* a Jeffrey Hayden production of *Summer and Smoke;* American Shakespeare
Theater productions of *Measure for Measure* and *Macbeth;* and the touring productions of *The Day
After the Fair* and *The Real Inspector Hound.*

John F. Kennedy Center: Opera House

LOVE AND MASTER WILL (5). Chronicle of
love from the works of William Shakespeare; arranged by Christopher Plummer. September 11,
1973 (world premiere). Directed by Christopher
Plummer; lighting, Gilbert V. Hemsley Jr. With
Christopher Plummer, Zoe Caldwell.

Part I: The Engagement. Part II: The Union,
The Consequences and Reunion. Two-character
enactment of love sequences from Shakespeare's
plays and poetry.

SHAKESPEARE DANCE AND DRAMA (7)
Scenes from *A Midsummer Night's Dream,*

Othello and *Romeo and Juliet* by William
Shakespeare and their balletic realizations. Sep-
tember 25, 1973 (world premiere). Staging super-
vised by Michael Kahn; lighting, Gilbert V.
Hemsley Jr.; musical direction, Akiro Endo.
With Maurice Evans, Kathleen Widdoes, Tony
Tanner; and dancers Natalia Makarova, Royes
Fernandez, Keith Lee, Bonnie Mathis, Sallie
Wilson (American Ballet Theater) and Michael
Coleman, Desmond Kelly (Royal Ballet). Pro-
duced for the Kennedy Center by Martin Fein-
stein.

Note: The season in the Opera House also included tryout or touring companies of *A Little Night
Music, The Pajama Game, A Streetcar Named Desire, The Desert Song, The Student Prince, The
Hollow Crown* and *Good News* and the Herb Rogers production of *Show Boat.*

Folger Library Theater Group

CREEPS (35) By David E. Freeman. October
12, 1973 (American premiere). Directed by
Louis Scheeder; scenery, lighting, costumes, David Chapman; movement consultant, Virginia
Freeman.

Pete . . . . Steven Gilborn

Michael; M.C.; Puffo the Clown;
Barker . . . . . .Philip Charles MacKenzie
Tom . . . . .Mark Metcalf
Sam . . . . .Bruce Weitz
Football Player . . . . Bruce Morrow
Astronaut . . . . Roger Ault

Girl; Thelma . . . . Sloane Bosniak
Jim . . . . Richard DeFabees
Saunders . . . . Pat Gerhard
Shriners . . . . . Roger Ault, Bruce Morrow
Carson . . . . Peter Vogt
Place: The men's washroom of a sheltered
workshop for cerebral palsy victims. No inter-
mission. Produced in association with Orin Leh-
man.

EDWARD G., LIKE THE FILM STAR (27)
By John Harvey Flint. December 4, 1973
(American premiere). Directed by John Dillon;
scenery and costumes, Michael Stauffer; lighting,
Betsy Toth.
Edward Morris . . . . Charles Randall
Eileen Morris . . . . Pat Gebhard
Pearson . . . . F. William Parker
Alan Hopkins . . . . Mark Robinson
Elizabeth Hulme . . . . Sara Jane Croft.
Place: In the Morris home in a small town in
England. A man is troubled by his inability to
help when someone is in need. Two intermis-
sions.

THE INSPECTOR GENERAL (28). Farce by
Nicolai Gogol; adapted by Andrew McAndrew.
February 12, 1974. Directed by Paul Schneider;
scenery and lighting, David Chapman; costumes,
Joan Theil. With Stuart Pankin, Richard
DeRusso, Gerald Holmes, Paul Hastings, Nancy
A. Desmond, Mark Robinson, Richard Wright.

LOVE'S LABOUR'S LOST (35). Musical adaptation of the play by William Shakespeare; book
and lyrics by David Vando; music by Bryan Wil-
liams. April 23, 1974 (world premiere). Directed
by Patrick Bakman; scenery, David Chapman;
lighting, William Eggleston; costumes, Dona
Granata; movement, Virginia Freeman; orches-
trations and musical direction, John Edward
Niles.
King of Navarre . . . . Martin Vidnovic
Berowne . . . . Richard Kline
Longaville . . . . John Butz
Dumaine . . . . Roger L. Nelson
The Princess of France . . . . . Meg Bussert
Rosaline . . . . Charlene Harris
Maria . . . . Dorothy Chansky
Katherine . . . . Terri Allen
Don Adriano Armado . . . . . Ronn Robinson
Costard . . . . Mark Robinson
Jacquenetta . . . . Cathy Simpson
Minstrel . . . . Frank Coppola
Place: The park grounds surrounding the
court of Navarre. No intermission.
Musical numbers—"The Edict," "Study,"
"Oath," "Love, You are a Devil!," "Did Not I
Dance with You?," "The Eye of Love," "Cupid's
Curse," "Then Come the Bow," "If Loving You
Makes Me Forsworn," "So Sweet a Kiss,"
"Heavenly Rhetoric," "Alack!, "For Love, First
Learned in a Lady's Eyes," "These Loving
Lords," "Muskovite Masquerade," "Thus Pour
the Stars Down Plagues for Perjury," Finale.

National Theater

NORMAN, IS THAT YOU? (21) Comedy by
Ron Clark and Sam Bobrick. July 3, 1973. Directed by Danny Simon; scenery, lighting, and
costumes, James Riley. With Billy Daniels, Kyle
Johnson, Royce Wallace, Kim Allen, Charlene

Jones. Produced by Gard Productions, Inc. Original black version first presented by Nick Stewart's Ebony Showcase Theater and Cultural Arts
Center in Los Angeles.

Note: The season at the National Theater also included touring productions of *Two Gentlemen of
Verona, Butley, The River Niger, National Lampoon's Lemmings, Noel Coward in Two Keys, Clarence
Darrow, My Fat Friend, That Championship Season* and *A Community of Two.*

Olney Theater

PRIVATE LIVES (21). By Noel Coward. June
5, 1973. Directed by Leo Brady; scenery and
lighting, James D. Waring; costumes, Nancy Desmond. With Robert Millia, Kristina Callahan,
Peter Vogt, Ruby Holbrook, and Joyce Audley.

A VIEW FROM THE BRIDGE (21). By Ar-
thur Miller. June 26, 1973. Directed by James D.
Waring; scenery and lighting, James D. Waring;
costumes, Nancy A. Desmond. With Herb Vo-
land, Meg Myles, Claire Malis, Peter Vogt,
Ralph A. Byers, Nicholas Cosco, Paul R. Hume.

THE MOUSETRAP (21). By Agatha Christie.

July 17, 1973. Directed by John Going; scenery
and lighting, James D. Waring; costumes, Sandra Cannon. With George Taylor, Virginia
Payne, Barbara Caruso, Bruce Gray, Robert Moberly, John Wardwell, Joan Welles, John Wylie.

DA (21). By Hugh Leonard. August 7, 1973
(world premiere). Directed by James D. Waring;
scenery and lighting, James D. Waring; cos-
tumes, Sandra Cannon.
Charlie Now . . . . Stephen Joyce
Oliver . . . . Peter Vogt
Da . . . . John McGiver
Mother . . . . Virginia Payne

Charlie Then . . . . Davis Hall
Drumm . . . . John Wylie
The Yellow Peril . . . . Cecelia Riddett
Mrs. Prynne . . . . .Barbara Caruso
Time: May 1968, and later, times remembered.
Place: The kitchen, and later, places remembered. Concerns a man coming to terms with his reminiscences just after his father's funeral. One intermission.

Summer Shakespeare Festival

OTHELLO (41). By William Shakespeare. July 11, 1973. Directed by Ellie Chamberlain; scenery, Robert Yodice; lighting, Phil Mosbo; costumes, Brooks-Van Horn; music, Bruce McLendon, Jim Smith. With Robert Guillaume, Cara

Wolf Trap Farm Park

THE MOST HAPPY FELLA (8). Musical with book, music, and lyrics by Frank Loesser, based on Sydney Howard's *They Knew What They Wanted.* July 19, 1973. Directed by Jerome Eskow; scenery and lighting, Charles Murawski;

THE TAVERN (21). By George M. Cohan (suggested by a play entitled *The Choice of a Super-Man* by Cora Dick Gantt). August 28, 1973. Directed by Leo Brady; scenery and lighting, James D. Waring; costumes, Jo-Ellen La Rue. With Robert Milli, Barbara Caruso, Peter Vogt, Alan Wade, Cecelia Riddett, Davis Hall, Mary Jane Milli, and Stephen Johnson.

Duff-MacCormick, Tony Tanner, Perry King, Susan Harney.
Produced in association with the National Capital Parks Commission.

costumes, Brooks-Van Horn; choreography, Joyce Trisler; musical direction, Anton Coppola. With William Chapman, Rita Gardner, Jerry Lanning, Pamela Myers, James Tushar, Muriel Greenspon.

WATERFORD, CONN.

Eugene O'Neill Theater Center National Playwrights Conference

(President, George C. White; artistic director, Lloyd Richards; designers, Peter Larkin, Fred Voelpel, John Gleason, Arden Fingerhut.)

Barn Theater (indoors)

CONFESSIONS OF A FEMALE DISORDER (2). By Susan Miller. July 19, 1973 (world premiere). Director, Larry Arrick; dramaturg, Edith Oliver.
Ronnie . . . . Swoosie Kurtz
Cheerleader #1 . . . . . . .Gayle Harrington
Cheerleader #2 . . . . Michele Shay
Cheerleader #3 . . . . Barbara Ramsay
Mother . . . . Jacqueline Brookes
Cop . . . . .Beverly Bentley
Liz . . . . .Deloris Gaskins
Psychiatrist . . . . Peter Turgeon
David . . . . Lenny Baker
Mitch; Ben . . . . .Ben Masters
Letterman #1 . . . . .Richard Ludgin
Letterman #2 . . . . Jon Breuer
Letterman #3 . . . . Bob Oliker
Evelyn . . . . .Rosemary DeAngelis
Cocktail Party Guests: Gayle Harrington, Michele Shay, Barbara Ramsay, Jacqueline Brookes, Richard Ludgin, John Breuer, Bob Oliker.
One Intermission.

MAGRITTE SKIES (2). By Yale M. Udoff. July 24, 1973 (world premiere). Director, Hal Scott; dramaturg, Martin Gottfried.

Diane Moore . . . . Carolyn Coates
John William Moore . . . . . . Jay Garner
Douglas Moore . . . . Lenny Baker
Caroline Moore . . . . .Rosemary DeAngelis
Ralph . . . . .Richard Ludgin
TV Voices: Deloris Gaskins, Beverly Bentley, Michele Shay, James Ray.
Prologue: Morning. Movement I: Late afternoon, same day. Movement II: Early evening, same day. Movement III: Evening, same day. Movement IV: Late evening, same day. Movement V: Early morning, next day. Epilogue: Early evening, a few days later. Two intermissions.

WHAT REASON COULD I GIVE (2). By Daniel Owens. July 26, 1973 (world premiere). Director, Larry Arrick; dramaturg, Dan Sullivan.
Nad Lewis . . . . .Bob Christian
The Couple . . . . . . Juanita Bethea, Charles Holmond
Ormond . . . . Michele Shay
Tease . . . . .Bill Cobbs
Debra . . . . .Deloris Gaskins
Jazz Interpretations . Louis Posner, tenor sax
Two intermissions.

SHAY (2). By Anne Commire. July 28, 1973 (world premiere). Director, Edward Hastings; dramaturgs, Katherine Brisbane, Martin Gottfried.

Shay . . . . Carolyn Coates
Marce . . . . Jacqueline Brookes
Reg . . . . Lenny Baker
Fran . . . . Swoosie Kurtz
Jerry . . . . .Ben Masters
Ed . . . . Peter Turgeon
Mr. Oulette . . . . Jay Garner
Mrs. Oulette . . . . . . Rosemary DeAngelis
1st Voice . . . . Bob Oliker
2nd Voice . . . . Richard Ludgin.
One intermission.

ALICIA (Goin' Thru Changes) (2). By Richard Wesley. August 1, 1973 (world premiere). Director, Hal Scott; dramaturg, Edith Oliver.
Alicia . . . . Michele Shay

Instant Theater (outdoors)

EIGHT BALL (2). By Richard Wesley. August 3, 1973 (world premiere). Director, Hal Scott; dramaturgs, Edith Oliver, Ed Bullins.
Earl David . . . . .Bill Cobbs
Eddie Green . . . . Bob Christian

HOLMES AND MORIARTY, OR AN EXTENSION OF PHILOSOPHY, OR THE RAPE OF MRS. HUDSON (2). By Allen Sternfield. August 6, 1973 (world premiere). Director, Edward Hastings; dramaturg, Dan Sullivan.
Sherlock Holmes . . . . Peter Turgeon
Dr. Watson . . . . Jay Garner
Mrs. Hudson . . . . Jacqueline Brookes
Professor Moriarty . . . . James Ray
Colonel Moran . . . . Michael Sacks
Inspector LeStrade . . . . Bob Christian

Amphitheater (outdoors)

FIX (2). By Mark Eisman; music, Barbara Damashek; lyrics, Mark Eisman. August 2, 1973 (world premiere). Director, Larry Arrick; dramaturgs, Katherine Brisbane, Martin Gottfried.
Ted De Wolf; Congressman   . . . James Ray
Debby . . . . Barbara Ramsay
Karen . . . . Gayle Bruno
Albert . . . . Michael Sacks
Stella Munday . . . . Carolyn Coates
Dr. Joan Wren . . . . .Beverly Bentley
Gepetto Arrovini . . . . Jay Garner
Camille Darwin . . . . Michele Shay
Dr. Amanda Willis . . . . Jacqueline Brookes
Kathy Willis . . . . Swoosie Kurtz
Fr. Paul McKeever . . . . . .Richard Ludgin
Jon . . . . Jon Breuer

Darnell . . . . .Bob Christian
Mae . . . . .Deloris Gaskins
Mrs. Pierce . . . . Juanita Bethea
Policeman #1 . . . . .Jon Breauer
Policeman #2; Marvin   . . .Charles Holmand
Nate . . . . .Bill Cobbs
Nurse . . . . Carol Lawes
T. C. . . . . .Samuel L. Harris III

THE WAKEFIELD PLAYS, PART TWO: OUR FATHER'S FAILING (2). By Israel Horovitz. August 9, 1973 (world premiere). director, Larry Arrick; dramaturgs, Martin Esslin, Dan Sullivan.
Sam . . . . Jay Garner
Pa . . . . James Noble
Alfred . . . . Lenny Baker
Emily . . . . Carolyn Coates
Two intermissions.

THE TRANSFIGURATION OF BENNO BLIMPIE (2). By Albert Innaurato. August 6, 1973. Director, Edward Hastings; dramaturg, Edith Oliver.
Benno . . . . Michael Sacks
Old Man . . . . Lenny Baker
Young Girl . . . . Swoosie Kurtz
Middle-aged Man . . . . .Ben Masters
Middle-aged Woman   . .Rosemary DeAngelis

THE WAKEFIELD PLAYS, PART ONE: ALFRED THE GREAT (1). By Israel Horovitz. August 11, 1973. Director, Larry Arrick.
Margaret . . . . .Beverly Bentley
Alfred . . . . Lenny Baker
Will . . . . James Noble
Emily . . . . Carolyn Coates

Cameraman   . . . . . . .Roger Christiansen
One intermission.

IN THE VOODOO PARLOUR OF MARIE LEVEAU (2). Two plays from a projected trilogy by Frank Gagliano. August 10, 1973 (world premiere). Director, Hal Scott; sound recording, James Reichert; dramaturgs, Martin Gottfried, Martin Esslin.
Gris-Gris
Marie Leveau . . . . .Deloris Gaskins
Beauregard . . . . James Ray
Woman . . . . Michele Shay
Drummer . . . . .Bill Cobbs
Commedia World of Byron B (inspired by a work of Luigi Pirandello)
Byron Beauregard . . . . .Ben Masters

Aurora . . . . Michele Shay
De Pepe . . . . James Ray

One intermission.

Eugene O'Neill Theater Center: Shakespeare and Company

THE TAMING OF THE SHREW (1). By William Shakespeare. July 29, 1973. Barn Theater. THE WINTER'S TALE (1). By William Shakespeare. August 5, 1973. Amphitheater. Director, Tina Packer; text director, Kristin Linklater; commedia tumbling, B. H. Barry; music and songs, Barbara Damashek, Bill Partlan.

With Abraham Alvarez, Dion Anderson, Randal Chicoine, Wilson Dunster, Laura Esterman, Robert Farber, Franklin Getchell, Karen Grassle,, David Harscheid, Terry Hinz, John Christopher Jones, Susan Cardwell Kingsley, Murray Moss, Tina Packer, Ellen Parks, Chuck Richie, R. H. Thomson.

The Eugene O'Neill Theater Center: The National Theater of the Deaf

(Producing director, David Hays.)

OPTIMISM, OR THE MISADVENTURES OF CANDIDE (1). Adapted by the company, under the supervision of Harold Stone; based on the novel by Voltaire; second act introduction by John Guare. September, 1973 (world premiere). Director, Harold Stone; scenery, Alfred Corrado; lighting, Guy Bergquist; costumes, Fred Voelpel.
(The members of the company play a variety of roles, human and otherwise. They are identified here by the first individual character they portray, in order of appearance, as well as any major sustaining role they subsequently play.)
Candide . . . . Tim Scanlon
Pacquette . . . . Linda Bove

Second Maid . . . . Elaine Bromka
Baron Thunder-Ten-Tronkh . Bernard Bragg
Baron's Son . . . . Edmund Waterstreet
Cunegonde . . . . Freda Norman
Baroness . . . . Juliana Field
Dr. Pangloss . . . . Patrick Graybill
Army Recruiter; Cacambo . . . Joseph Sarpy
A Street Cleaner . . . . Rico Peterson
Rich Lady; Old Woman . .Mary Beth Miller
Orator's Wife . . . . Timothy Near
James . . . . Richard Kendall
One intermission.
This production toured the United States during 1973–74.

WEST SPRINGFIELD, MASS.

Stage/West Theater

(Artistic director, John Ulmer; managing director, Stephen E. Hays.)

CAT ON A HOT TIN ROOF (23) By Tennessee Williams. November 9, 1973 (world premiere of new authorized version). Director, John Ulmer; scenery and lighting, Charles G. Stockton; costumes, Susan Glenn Harvuot.
Margaret . . . . Linda Selman
Brick . . . . Armand Assante
Big Mama . . . . Charlotte Jones
Big Daddy . . . . Maury Cooper
Polly . . . . Eloise Weiss
Dixie . . . . Melissa Thea
Trixie . . . . Linda Poleri
Mae . . . . Evelyn Baron
Sonny . . . . Steven Poleri
Gooper . . . . .Peter DeMaio
Buster . . . . .Brett R. Zalkan
Rev. Tooker . . . . .Curt Williams
Dr. Baugh . . . . Edward Holmes
     Time: Mid-1950s. Place: A bed-sitting room and section of the gallery of a plantation home in the Mississippi Delta, an evening in summer.

Two intermissions.

THE DRUNKARD (30). By Bro Herrod and Barry Manilow, based on the melodrama by W. H. S. Smith. December 7, 1973. Director, John Ulmer; scenery and lighting, Charles G. Stockton; costumes, Susan Glenn Harvuot; choreography, Judith Haskell; additional music, Thomas Babbitt. With Armand Assante, Evalyn Baron, Maury Cooper, Peter DeMaio, Tovah Feldshuh, Regina Jean David, Shirley Jean Measures, Linda Selman, Curt Williams.

THE CHERRY ORCHARD (23). By Anton Chekhov. January 11, 1974. Director, John Ulmer; scenery and lighting, Charles G. Stockton; costumes, Betty Williams. With Patricia O'Connell, Linda Selman, Macon McCalman, Louis Edmonds, Betty Williams.

THE WHITE HOUSE MURDER CASE (23).

By Jules Feiffer. February 8, 1974. Director, William Guild; scenery and lighting, Charles G. Stockton; costumes, Susan Glenn Harvuot. With Maury Cooper, Max Gulack, Harry Ellerbe.

THE SHOW-OFF (23). By George Kelly. March 8, 1974. Director, John Ulmer; scenery and lighting, Charles G. Stockton; costumes, Susan Glenn Harvuot. With Dorothy Blackburn, Harry Ellerbe, Eric Tavaris.

PRIVATE LIVES (23). By Noel Coward. April 5, 1974. Director, John Ulmer; scenery and lighting, Charles G. Stockton; costumes, Susan Glenn Harvuot. With Vinnie Holman, Eric Tavaris, Alice Elliott, Curt Williams.

Stage/West Theater: Children's Theater

ANDROCLES AND THE LION (10). December 7, 1973. Director, William Guild; designer, Charles G. Stockton; costumes, Susan Glenn Harvuot; choreography, Jason McAuliffe. With John Shuman, Julia Monroe, Wallace Androchuk.

THE BRAVE LITTLE TAILOR (9). By Aurand Harris, based on The Grimms' fairy tale. April 30, 1974. Director, John Ulmer; scenery, Robert Lunning; lighting, James Riggs; costumes, Susan Glenn Harvuot. With John Shuman, Eric Tavaris, Curt Williams, Vinnie Holman, Betty Williams, Rosanne Falbo.

CANADA

MONTREAL

Centaur Theater

(Artistic director, Maurice Podbrey.)

THAT CHAMPIONSHIP SEASON (32). By Jason Miller. October 18, 1973. Director, Joel Miller; scenery and costumes, Michael Eagan; lighting, Sholem Dolgoy. With Dennis Hayes, Ken James, Richard Kuss, Les Carlson, Maurice Podbrey.

OF THE FIELDS, LATELY (32). By David French. November 22, 1973. Co-produced with Tarragon Theater. Director, Bill Glassco; scenery and costumes, Tiina Lipp; lighting, Carol Manning. With Tim Henry, Florence Paterson, Sean Sullivan, Sandy Webster.

THE TOOTH OF CRIME (32). By Sam Shepard. January 3, 1974. Director, John Palmer; scenery and costumes, Michael Eagan; lighting, Vladimir Svetlovsky; music written, arranged and played by Dionysos. With Janet Barkhouse, Patrick Brymer, George Dawson, Brenda Donahue, Michael Hollingsworth, Gary Reineke, Terrence G. Ross.

THE PROMISE (32). By Aleksei Arbuzov; translated by Ariadne Nicolaeff. February 7, 1974. Director, Maurice Podbrey; scenery and costumes, Marti Wright; lighting, Carol Man-

ning. With Marc Connors, Linda Goranson, Lubomir Mykytiuk.

MR. JOYCE IS LEAVING PARIS (32). By Tom Gallagher. March 14, 1974 (North American premiere). Director, Alan Scarfe; scenery, Felix Mirbt; lighting, Carol Manning; costumes, Louise Lavallee.

James . . . . Neil Vipond
Stanislaus and S . . . . Stephen Markle
B . . . . Kenneth Dight
W . . . . Nuala Fitzgerald
C . . . . John Boylan

Act I: Mid-February 1908, Trieste, the apartment occupied by Stanislaus Joyce (aged 24) and his brother James (aged 26). Act II: December 23, 1939, Paris, a room in the Joyces' recently vacated flat at 34, Rue des Vignes.

YOU'RE GONNA BE ALRIGHT, JAMIE-BOY (32). By David E. Freeman. April 18, 1974. Co-produced with Tarragon Theater. Director, Bill Glassco; scenery and costumes, John Ferguson; lighting, Carol Manning; sound, Richard Carson. With Jayne Eastwood, David Ferry, Lillian Lewis, Chuck Shamata, Hugh Webster.

STRATFORD, ONT.

Stratford Festival: Festival Theater

(Artistic director, Jean Gascon.)

THE TAMING OF THE SHREW (44). By William Shakespeare. June 4, 1973. Director, Jean Gascon; designer, Desmond Heeley; lighting, Gil Wechsler; music, Gabriel Charpentier. With Alan Scarfe, Pat Galloway, William Needles, Powys Thomas, Edward Atienza.

SHE STOOPS TO CONQUER (21). By Oliver Goldsmith. June 5, 1973. Director, Michael Bawtree; designer, Desmond Heeley; lighting, Gil Wechsler; music, Raymond Pennell. With Amelia Hall, Tony Van Bridge, Alan Scarfe, Pat Galloway, Nicholas Pennell, Barry MacGregor, Patricia Collins.

OTHELLO (42). By William Shakespeare. June 6, 1973. Director, David William; designer, Annena Stubbs; lighting, Gil Wechsler; music, Louis Applebaum. With Nachum Buchman, Douglas Rain, Martha Henry, Amelia Hall.

PERICLES (17). By William Shakespeare. July 24, 1973. Director, Jean Gascon; designer, Leslie Hurry; lighting, Gil Wechsler; music, Gabriel Charpentier. With Edward Atienza, Nicholas Pennell, Angela Wood, Pamela Brook, Tony Van Bridge, Martha Henry.

Stratford Festival: Avon Theater

A MONTH IN THE COUNTRY (35). By Ivan Turgenev; translated by Andrew MacAndrew. June 29, 1973. Director, William Hutt; designer, Brian Jackson; lighting, Gil Wechsler. With Kenneth Pogue, Dawn Greenhalgh, Diana D'Aquila, Eric Donkin, Roland Hewgill, Jack Creley.

THE MARRIAGE BROKERS (35). By Nikolai V. Gogol; translated by Alexander Berkman. August 3, 1973. Director, William Hutt; designer, Murray Laufer; lighting, Gil Wechsler. With Leonard Frey, Joseph Shaw, Roberta Maxwell, Sheila Haney.

Stratford Festival: Third Stage Theater

THE COLLECTED WORKS OF BILLY THE KID (23). By Michael Ondaatje; adapted from his book. July 10, 1973. Director, John Wood; designer, John Ferguson; lighting, Gil Wechsler and Mark Hylbak. With Neil Munro, Ted Follows, Michael Donaghue, Nancy Beatty, Cherry Davis.

INOOK AND THE SUN (13). By Henry Beissel. August 1, 1973 (world premiere). Directors, Jean Herbiet, Felix Mirbt; designer, Michel Catudal; lighting, Mark Hylbak; puppets created by Felix Mirbt, assisted by Ian Osgood; special movements, Jill Courtney.

Company of Actors: Carole Galloway, John Gardiner, Andrew Henderson, Sylvia Maynard, Ann Rushbrooke.

Company of Puppeteers: Jill Courtney, Maxim Mazumdar, Felix Mirbt, Ian Osgood, Ann Rushbrooke.

One intermission.

EXILES (11). By Raymond and Beverly Pannell. August 15, 1973 (world premiere). Director, Michael Bawtree; scenery, Eoin Sprott; lighting, Robert Scales; costumes, John Ferguson; photography, Beverly Pannell.

La Cantarina	Janette Moody
Little Boy	Jason Czajkowski
Charlie Quinn	Bob Dermer
Man	Gary Relyea
Woman	Phyllis Mailing
Granpiano	David Schurmann
Bud Gala	Gene Watts
Pierrot	Edward Pierson
La Superella	Candy Kane
Don Balloon	Gary Reineke

Bassoon, John Courtney; violin, Fujiko Imajishi; flute and piccolo, Virginia Markson; veena, M. Ranganathan; koto, Kenneth Richard; cello, Sarah Shenkman; oboe, Sandra Watts.

Self-described as "an opera for the theater." One intermission.

VANCOUVER

The Playhouse Theater Center of British Columbia: Mainstage

(Artistic director, Christopher Newton.)

JULIUS CAESAR (18). By William Shakespeare. October 15, 1973. Director, Christopher Newton; scenery and costumes, Cameron Porteous; lighting, Lynne Hyde. With Derek Ralston, W. Robert Haley, Michael Ball, Yvonne Adalian, Gary Reincke.

LEAVING HOME (18). By David French. November 12, 1973. Director, John Wood; scenery and costumes, Jack Simon; lighting, Frank Masi. With Kate Reid, Leslie Yeo, Rita Howell.

MANDRAGOLA (18). By Niccolo Machiavelli. January 14, 1974. Director, Stephen Katz; designer, Mary Kerr. With W. Powys Thomas, Susan Petrie, Derek Ralston.

A DOLL'S HOUSE (18). By Henrik Ibsen. February 11, 1974. Director, Bill Glassco; scenery and costumes, Cameron Porteous; lighting, Graham Cook. With Blair Brown, W. Powys Thomas, James Hurdle, B. J. Gordon, Derek Ralston.

DUTCH UNCLE (18). By Simon Gray. March 11, 1974 (North American premiere). Director, John Wood; scenery and costumes, Cameron Porteous; lighting, Graham Cook.

Mr. Godboy	Bernard Hopkins
May Godboy	Maggie Askey
Eric Hoyden	Brian McKay
Doris Hoyden	B. J. Gordon
Inspector Hawkins	Frank Kelly
Hedderley	Frank Maraden

Time: The autumn of 1952. Place: The living room of Mr. and Mrs. Godboy in Shepherds Bush, London. Act I, Scene 1: Late afternoon. Scene 2: Half an hour later. Act II: The following afternoon. Act III: A couple of hours later.

QUEER SIGHTS, A MOULDY TALE (18). By Frank McEnaney. April 8, 1974 (world premiere). Director, Christopher Newton; scenery and costumes, Cameron Porteous; lighting, Graham Cook; music, Alan Laing.

Ned	Hank Stinson
Toby Thompson	Neil Munro
Walter	Doug Bowell
Mrs. Tanner	Hilary Nicholls
Belinda	Janis Nickelson
Esmerelda	Alexandra Sellers
Eustace McCracken	Bernard Hopkins
Fob	Bob Dermer
Wallop	Jackson Davies
Soughdough; Dan Victorian Lady;	Brian McKay
Dance Hall Girl	Lesley Rachuk
Bustlin' Bill McCurdy	Frank Maraden
Hank the Tooth	Jim McQueen
Sgt. Steel	Andrew Czaplejewski
Steve	Winston Rekert
Nellie	Janet Wright
Prospector	Robb Smyth

The play takes place in Victoria, B.C., 1897; later it moves into the Klondike. Two intermissions.

The Playhouse Theater Center of British Columbia: Children's Theater

MR. SCROOGE (18). Book and lyrics by Richard Morris and Ted Wood; music and lyrics, Dolores Claman; based on A Christmas Carol by Charles Dickens. December 17, 1973. Director, Christopher Newton. With Graeme Campbell, Susan Anderson, Pat Armstrong, Michael Collins, Wayne Robson.

Note: The Playhouse Theater Center of British Columbia toured three productions to the schools: Reflections by Gloria Shapiro, Reynard by Arthur Fauques and The Amorous Hypocrites by Stephen Katz, based on a traditional commedia dell'arte scenario. The Glass Menagerie by Tennessee Williams, directed by John Wood, toured the province from September 24 to November 2, 1973. At Vancouver City College, two one act plays, Out At Sea and The Party by Slawomir Mrozek, directed by Stephen Katz, were performed from October 30 to November 2, 1973. And, finally, The Playhouse Theater Center's production of A Doll's House by Henrik Ibsen was invited to perform at the National Arts Center in Ottawa from February 11 to March 2, 1974.

WINNIPEG

Manitoba Theater Center: Main Stage

(Artistic director, Edward Gilbert.)

YOU NEVER CAN TELL (27). By George Bernard Shaw. October 19, 1973. Director, Edward Gilbert; scenery, Maurice Strike; lighting, Donald Acaster; costumes, Hilary Corbett. With Paxton Whitehead, Wenna Shaw, Richard Farrell, Patrick Boxhill, Richard Murdoch.

A DAY IN THE DEATH OF JOE EGG (27). By Peter Nichols. November 23, 1973. Director, Edward Gilbert; scenery and costumes, Peter Wingate; lighting, Christopher Lester. With Pat Galloway, John McEnery, Brenda Raynbird.

THE DYBBUK (27). By S. Ansky; new adaptation by John Hirsch. January 11, 1974. Director John Hirsch; scenery and costumes, Mark Negin, Maxine Graham; lighting, Christopher Lester; music director and composer, Alan Laing; lyrics, Tom Hendry. With Roland Hewgill, Michael Granger, Peter Jobin, Marilyn Lightstone, Don Sutherland, Donald Davis.

GODSPELL (27) By John-Michael Tebelak, based upon the Gospel According to St. Matthew; music and lyrics by Stephen Schwartz. February 15, 1974. Director, Dean Regan; designers, Christopher Lester, Tacey Jackson; musical director, William Skolnik. With Barbara Barsky, Karl Blindheim, Derek McGrath.

THE PLOUGH AND THE STARS (27). By Sean O'Casey. March 22, 1974. Director, Edward Gilbert; scenery and costumes, Peter Wingate; lighting, Ken McKay. With Kenneth Welsh, Deborah Kipp, Sheila Haney, Derek Smith, Brian Richardson, Ita D'Arcy.

INDIAN by George Ryga and BLACK COMEDY by Peter Shaffer (27). May 3, 1974. Director, Malcolm Black; scenery and costumes, Peter Wingate; lighting, Christopher Lester. With Johnny Yesno, Dan MacDonald, Edward Greenhalgh, R. H. Thomson, Deborah Kipp, Paddy Croft, Hutchison Shandro.

Manitoba Theater Center: Warehouse Theater

MIME OVER FIVE (12). November 23, 1973. Skits and sketches devised by Adrian Pecknold and the Canadian Mime Theater. With Adrian Pecknold, Paulette Hallich, Ian McKay, Harrow Maskow, Robin Patterson.

ESKER MIKE AND HIS WIFE AGILUK (12). By Herschel Hardin. February 6, 1974. Director, Howard Dallin; scenery and costumes, Grant Guy; lighting, Ken McCay. With Kenneth Welsh, Victoria Mitchell.

YOU'RE GONNA BE ALRIGHT, JAMIE

BOY (12). By David E. Freeman. March 13, 1974. Director, Bill Glassco; scenery and costumes, John Ferguson, Kent McKay. With Jayne Eastwood, David Ferry, Lillian Lewis, Chuck Shamata, Hugh Webster.

JUBALAY (12). By Patrick Rose and Merv Campone. May 8, 1974 (world premiere). Director, Edward Gilbert; scenery and costumes, Peter Wingate; lighting, Ken McKay; choreography, Dean Regan. With Diane Stapley, Patrick Rose, Ruth Nichol, Brent Carver, Merv Campone, Ed Henderson.

Manitoba Theater Center: Children's Theater

WINNIE-THE-POOH (14). By A.A. Milne; adapted by Julian Slade. Director, Arif Hasnain; scenery and costumes, Grant Guy; lighting, Kent McKay. With Heath Lambers, Linda John, Max Tapper, Howard Dallin, Eric Hutt, Marilyn Boyle, Margaret Bard.

THE SEASON IN LONDON

THE PLAYWRIGHT'S OBSTACLE COURSE

By Arnold Wesker

Playwright, author of the 1963–64 Best Play *Chips With Everything* and many other scripts including *Roots, The Kitchen* and *The Four Seasons.*

IN AN article on the theater in these grim years there is room only to be sardonic rather than serious. But we shall begin with an honest enough confession to place us right outside the pale and respect of normal, healthy show-biz folk: We believe the writing of plays to be one of the forms men have come to call art. We believe it profoundly and unequivocally.

For us, then, the theater becomes like an obstacle course. The first obstacle may be one's agent whose love and care, vulnerable and human as these qualities are in all, are heated or cooled by the winds of the moment. As the charts would have us view our worth, so, to these charts, are our agents inexorably drawn—they know not how. They will do what they can but of course there are too many characters, or too many sets, or there's so little interest in politics today or in psychological drama or in plays with words or in words written by playwrights. If only we were actors writing the play, we could pretend we weren't playwrights at all but actors doing it themselves. Everyone should be doing it for himself—excepting the playwright!—as though the creative process were not difficult and intangible but something which took place after adequate market research. But undefenders though the agents may be, they at least love us.

Not so management. To them the playwright is an intruder—the man who doesn't appreciate the favor being done him and who, to boot, is costly. Pompous, presumptuous, illiterate management with its responsibilities to shareholders—as we were solemnly informed by one of them on TV recently. Even artistic directors of subsidized establishments who are responsible to no one excepting remote councils of management, even in them flows an arrogance of such proportions that they can be best described as theatrical terrorists. They think Act I should be dropped or that the last act should have a more dynamic sequel or that the language ought to be less this and more that, or that the play ought really to be about other things. If you are strong and know what you are doing and what the theater is capable of—then you can survive. If not . . .

The third hurdle is more difficult because more natural, more belonging to the real problems inherent in the medium: the director of the play. Some, with modesty, fulfill their role as interpreter. Occasionally we've been helped by the director's attempts to understand *what* it is *we're* trying to communicate and the *way* in which we're trying to communicate it, and he has contributed to clarification of the work. But most directors, uneasily suspecting that the creative act is more worthy than the interpretive one, impose their own smothering voice over that of the playwright and don't interpret but tranform or distort.

Not many weeks ago two young men came from a European country where the theater is of a high standard and proudly informed us that in producing our play *Chips With Everything* they'd taken out the humor in order to make it a more serious work. It didn't occur to them that it might be hurtful to suggest we'd written a frivolous play, or that they were destroying the play's real seriousness by burdening it with pomposity. In which case, one wondered, why did they want to do it in the first place? We've seen productions of our work around the world to make our last hairs stand on end and our hearts heavy. Humorless productions, and thus lifeless; productions where the poetry has been blunted, the rhythm lost, the structure cracked and the meaning ignored; our tried and tempered plays crippled by opportunistic, third-rate imaginations.

Nor does it end there. There is the actor. Heavily thoughtful, lumbering into rehearsal with his independent personality under constant threat, each one his own ponderous Brando. The actor! We have, of course, been frequently blessed with actors who, like some directors, have also modestly accepted their roles as interpreters, risen to great heights and served our plays sometimes better than those plays have deserved. Mostly not, though. One actress we know ruined a director's career. Another actor came to rehearsals drunk, selfishly drove his colleagues into profound insecurity, threatened with a gun, never learned his lines, only ever gave the occasional inspired performance of an amateur, and soon left the run having thrown a fit shortly after the first night. We've just seen a production of *The Kitchen* in another European capital where a small part (in a play of 30 vignettes) was blown up into a pointless aria because the actor said he wanted something more to get his teeth into!

But imagine that agents are our fighting defenders, managements are enlightened and directors and actors are our able colleagues. All should be well. The play is strongly and satisfactorily mounted and—the audience is there. Ah! the audience! Where do they come from and what do they come with? We've all been thrilled—at least once and some more than once—by the sympathetic intelligence of an audience holding its breath when it should, laughing, sighing, murmuring assent or anger where we'd hoped and reacting to the play's end as we'd dreamed. But oh those mindless gigglers, those holier-than-thou condemnators, those sheep who pass their bleating, malformed judgments and their swift opinions one to another. We can touch them with nothing that is not sanctified by the past or blessed by the public's guardians. Which brings us to our next hurdle.

Add to our list a wise and receptive audience. Agent, producer, director, actor, audience—and on our side. What is the sixth Herculean labor? The instant judges! Critics so named, but more reviewers in fact. We have written much about them and by them been hung for it. So rather than use our old, tired, sour words whose tired sourness so tiringly sours us that we have little energy or appetite left to write our plays, here is part of Chapter One of Mr. Fielding's *History of Tom Jones:*

"And here I must desire all those critics to mind their own business, and not to intermeddle with affairs or works who no ways concern them, for till they produce the authority by which they are constituted judges, I shall not plead their jurisdiction."

But of course they never mind their own business and we must survive their censoring little views which, squeezed into the few hundred odd words allowed them by their busy, busy newspapers, become our sentences of life or death.

Hercules had seven labors. So have we. You would think the reviewer was the last. Not so. When only a few years into learning our art there arrive "the aftermath commentators." The league shakers, the sorters, arrangers, classifiers —the top-twenty makers. "Now that the dust has settled," they say, and we are graded up or down before we know our name or why we've been called.

Fortunately, we've managed to last 15 years. Our craft has sharpened, our sensitivity become more subtle, we are satisfied less easily with more and more, we have greater ambition for what we take on, for what we dare to say, and invent for saying it, and our dozen or so plays survive in 15 different languages around the world.

And—one incredible ray of light has broken through into the English theater scene: a complete theater man of real genius from South Africa, Athol Fugard, playwright, director, actor. The Royal Court Theater has this year presented an ambitious season of three of his plays: *The Island, Sizwe Bansi Is Dead, Statements After an Arrest Under the Immorality Act.* All were directed by Fugard. They have poetry, characterization, conflict and social criticism, and they are timeless.

It has confirmed our view that the new direction to be taken (not "one that will revolutionize our theater"—we have learned how slowly so little changes, even when blood is spilt) which will *contribute* to the theater's blood stream is the creation of a writer's theater*, one where the writer will direct, learn to direct, his own play. The theater has only ever been exciting when the work of writers has flourished. The high points in the theater's history have coincided with the discovery of new plays. No group of actors or directors has created a theatrical renaissance—they have contributed to it, but at the center have been the original, creative talents of the writer. Surely, then, there is a place for, and it is time for, the writers to be in control of their own raw materials and the means for their production.

*Editor's note: Anyone wishing to pursue Mr. Wesker's idea for a writer's theater is referred to an article he wrote in the February 1974 *Plays and Players* entitled *The Playwright as Director.*

We wish we were other than a playwright—a novelist, perhaps, in control of our own medium; a singer with only a voice and a guitar to keep in tune; a great teacher; perhaps just a lovely traveler. We're none of these things. Merely a playwright, and that—probably—because we can do nothing else. Let us, then, do nothing else, but let us at least be *complete* theater men and do it fully.

REVIEW OF THE LONDON SEASON

By Ossia Trilling

Author, critic, lecturer, broadcaster; member of the Council of the Critics' Circle; vice president of the International Theater Critics' Association; European Editor of *Best Plays*

HAVING this year, on the insistence of my American editor, made a selection of the best 30 plays of the London year ("Trilling's Top Thirty"), I ought, I suppose, to justify my choice. This is an impossible task, for I have always taken the view that plays or productions, unlike oranges, cannot be graded and priced according to size, color or succulence. Performances may make an impression on the heart or on the mind that sticks, but this is not to say that the harder they stick, the better they are. Nor am I at all sure that length of run, a statistical piece of information for archivists that has always been a feature of *Best Plays*, necessarily indicates superior quality. Take the case of *The Mousetrap*, by Agatha Christie, which has not only broken all records by entering its 23d year, but has also dismayed potential patrons ever since Peter Saunders transferred it from the relatively small Ambassadors Theater to the somewhat larger St. Martin's next door, because they couldn't find it on the playbills: so much so that Mr. Saunders now has to advertise his money-spinning, record-breaking thriller twice over in the daily press, once under each theater, stating that it is no longer at its original home. The Ambassadors now houses quite another kind of show and the lady who takes the cloaks there (and she's been working at this theater even longer than the run of *The Mousetrap*) has been telling patrons how much she misses the original play and how disappointed they are likely to be with its successor which, she says in her bland London accents, "is quite another cup of tea." Clearly, to her, the latter is of a different if not explicitly of an inferior brew. But is it?

The play concerned, or rather the two plays being done in repertory there, are the collective responsibility of the South African playwright Athol Fugard and of the two actors of the Serpent Players of Port Elizabeth who collaborated with him on the text and on its staging, and are now to be seen in them. *Sizwe Bansi is Dead* and *The Island* are plays of quality. I selected the first as one of my top 30 both because of what it says and for the way in which it says it. A glance at the detailed note printed below the entry under Foreign Plays should explain why I, together with the majority of my British colleagues, consider it to be of such importance. I need only add here that it is acted with loving affection by the two black South African actors, John Kani and Winston Ntshona, who portray two very ordinary and not unduly clever human beings living in conditions that would destroy men of less resilience. Also, for all the horror of its implications and the explicit condemnation of the indignity to which the white bosses subject their social and racial underlings, the whole play is tinged with an unsuppressible sense of humour that broadens its humanity. It began life in London at the Royal Court Theater's small stage under the eaves, the Theater Upstairs, and then moved to the larger theater below, where it was joined in repertory by *The Island* and by a third Fugard play which exposes the indignity suffered by the oppressed races in South Africa in a sexual context. Later the first two moved to the West End. There they may not provide quite the same type of thrill which visitors to *The Mousetrap* might be looking for, but they are indisputably among the most thrilling plays to have lent dignity to the private sector of the British theater for as long as I can remember.

Fugard's are political plays, unashamedly so; yet the political element is implicit rather than explicit. There is nothing Brechtian about them, though I feel sure that Brecht, had he been alive, would have welcomed them as warmly as I have done, and for similar reasons. That they should have been first done at the Royal Court is logical, for that theater has been the mainstay of political theater and political drama ever since George Devine revived its fortunes in 1956. This season saw three of David Storey's dramas world premiered there, all three political plays in the widest sense of the word, or at any rate plays with the strongest social conscience. *The Farm* took the spectator back into the Yorkshire ambiance of the author's birth, and into the semi-autobiographical working-class family atmosphere of his youth, which he reproduced with such effortless realism in *In Celebration* in 1969. Some critics have likened it to Chekhov's *Three Sisters,* if only because the family has three daughters and a son and his unsuitable fiancee at odds with one another and with their hopes and ambitions. That may be true, as far as it goes. But the portrait of the besotten working-class father is etched with far less sympathy than in the case of any of Chekhov's gallery of failures. It is much closer, perhaps than even Storey realizes, to some of J.B. Priestley's churlishly stubborn oldsters. The current revival of interest in Priestley's plays in the 80th anniversary year of that Yorkshire writer's birth was not, I believe, accidental. Though no proletarian, Priestley rightly gauged the class discontent of his time, and this is what is giving his plays an unforeseen topicality again. I am thinking of the first-rate revivals of *An Inspector Calls* at the Mermaid and of *Eden End* at the Old Vic, which may well presage a new wave of Priestley's dramas in the British theater in the coming years. Like Storey, Priestley wrote ably-constructed political plays or plays of social protest masquerading as family comedies (or tragedies, depending on where your sympathies lie). Both these were good examples of the genre.

The other two by Storey at the Royal Court were of a different order. *Cromwell,* too, was political, overtly so, if you like, but its form came closer to Brechtian models, and this was heavily accentuated in the "alienation effect" of Anthony Page's direction and Jocelyn Herbert's decor, as well as in the extroverted performances of Albert Finney and others in the cast. Capriciously titled, since Cromwell doesn't appear, the play sought to examine and to arouse resentment in the audience against what can only be described by using that hackneyed phrase "man's inhumanity to man", whether this be practised in 17th century England, or present-day Ireland or the Middle East—the echoes and allusions were undeniable. Storey's *Life Class,* which like *The Changing Room* nicely exploited the nakedness of the human body to bolster a mounting and receding series of events, was also part autobiographical since it drew on the author's own experiences for his portrait of the hero, an art teacher in a Yorkshire art school, who cannot make a go of it. Here the social overtones, as in *Home,* were less conspicuous, but the absorbing realism of the uncouth behavior of an unruly bunch of adolescents, in Lindsay Anderson's production, was at once subtle and vivid.

The other main achievement at the Royal Court, apart from its consistent policy of encouraging and advancing new native and non-native drama, was the rediscovery of D.H. Lawrence's early *The Merry-Go-Round,* to which the director, Peter Gill, did full comic justice considering the awkward change of direction in style as the comedy of working-class cupidity nears its climax. It was one of the productions that British actors took to the biennial Europalia Festival in Belgium, Frank Dunlop's of *Much Ado About Nothing* with the Young Vic Company and the Prospect Theater Company's *The Royal Hunt of the Sun* being two others.

An interesting feature of the season was the success of two newish repertory companies without a permanent base. The first was the aforesaid Prospect ensemble, which created some sort of a record by bringing Toby Robertson's morality version of *Pericles* (as a struggle between good and evil solidly rooted in a brothel setting) to Her Majesty's Theater in the West End for a short season at a time when no other Shakespeare plays where to be seen on any other London stage. The second was the Actors Company, which packed the outlying Wimbledon Theater for eight weeks with a mixed bag from Shakespeare to Feydeau, and from Congreve to Chekhov, and got the same kind of rave notices in the London press as they had in New York during their prior-to-London season at the Brooklyn Academy. Prospect had also taken their *Pericles,* and the Peter Shaffer play, as well as a slightly up-dated *Twelfth Night,* on a successful tour of Europe and Soviet Russia, the first English company ever to perform in Vilnius, the capital of Lithuania. Other British companies also made the grade in their foreign tours this season, witness the Young Vic's visit to the U.S., and a host of smaller, experimental troupes to various festivals in Germany and elsewhere. Among these I might single out (if only because I had witnessed their triumph in person) the eccentrically hilarious improvisational group called *Theater Machine* at the First Festival of Café-Théâtre (or Pub Theater as it is known in Great Britain) staged in the capital of French Britanny, Rennes.

Not that every experimental troupe in Britain has had it all its own way. The Roy Hart Theater, specializing as it does in unorthodox vocal techniques, never managed to gain adequate support on its home ground, despite signal successes in various parts of Europe, and finally moved to a permanent base in France, shaking the dust of England forever from its feet—driven away, perhaps, by some of the most inimical and uncomprehending press notices that any avant-garde group has had to endure anywhere in the world. They will be in good company in France. I refer to the fact that England's Peter Brook is also still rooted in Paris, where just before the season was out he announced that he would begin rehearsals on his own, new version of *Timon of Athens.*

Brook's absence is a loss to both the theaters with which he has mostly worked in England, the National and the Royal Shakespeare Company, though his name still figures on the RSC's programs as co-director of the company together with Peggy Ashcroft and Trevor Nunn, who acts as overall director, and with Peter Daubeny and Peter Hall, who figure as consultant directors. Hall, of course, took over the management of the National on Nov. 1, but he remains allied with the RSC until their new home in the Barbican, masterminded by Hall when he was the RSC's boss, is ready for occupation. Daubeny's contribution during the season was minimal: the absence of the World Theater Season in 1974 was sorely felt, but report had it that work to resume activities in 1975 was well under way. What can one say of the RSC in a year when it presented Trevor Nunn's monumentally monolithic production of the Shakespearean four Roman plays, as they're called? Stylistic homogeneity (first savored in Stratford two years earlier) and visual opulence were their common qualities, and the performances of the casts were frequently invested with rare and welcome histrionic grandeur. Add to this such popular box office hits as Frank Dunlop's side-splitting send-up of the world-famous 70-year-old Sherlock Holmes drama from the pen of an American author-actor (albeit fitted out with a happy ending to which the bachelor detective would most certainly have taken exception), and what could go wrong? Strangely enough, things did not quite go in the RSC's favor as far as box office takings went, though here too, in all fairness, it must be stressed that thanks to the political and industrial turmoil in mid-season and the change of government that ensued, the RSC was not the sole sufferer.

I, for one, welcomed the RSC's second experimental season at the small Place Theater and warmed to Terry Hands's direction of David Rudkin's daunting text and to their joint transposition of the latter's radio play about Roger Casement to the stage. I was deeply moved by the stage version of Sylvia Plath's writings, which was in the repertory that the RSC took with them on their U.S. visit. And I found Philip Magdalany's iconoclastically anti-American *Section Nine* every bit as funny as anything invented by the Marx Brothers or the perpetrators of *Hellzapoppin* to deflate the self-importance of the U.S. establishment, not least when the RSC transferred it to the regular stage at the Aldwych Theater. But the public, seemingly, did not fully share my enthusiasm, any more than they did in the case of David Mercer's satirically apocalyptic *Duck Song* or Peter Barnes's grotesquely ambitious political farce of *The Bewitched,* one of whose few faults was, admittedly, that, at three hours, it went on for one hour too long.

The same criticism might be levelled at *Next of Kin,* the fourth and latest drama of suburban family life by the successful TV dramatist John Hopkins, whose production at the National also marked Harold Pinter's directorial debut there. He, at least, should have been able to trim 60 minutes from the 180 that Hopkins seemed to think were needed to make his points. Maybe the fault lay with the director's inexperience and his fellow-feeling for a fellow-dramatist. *Next of Kin* was a weaker play than it need have been on that account, despite the attraction of the performances and the drama's thematic complexity which, in my case, furnished matter for an animated debate that lasted almost as long afterwards as the play itself. Peter Hall's directorial debut at the National was an equally long-drawn-out production, in his case of *The Tempest.* In this the musicality of the poetry was enhanced by the incidental music of the pop-group Gryphon and Hall's well-known penchant for "operatic" excitements. I found it totally engrossing throughout, and the magical stage effects, invented by John Bury, never less than enthralling, as indeed Shakespeare's text clearly intended them to be. The other novelty under the new regime (though, strictly speaking, it had been promoted by Kenneth Tynan many years ago) was Edward Bond's translation of the Wedekind classic of mistaken middle-class morality and its tyranny over 19th century German adolescence, *Spring Awakening.* Before that, the National had staged *Equus,* Peter Shaffer's pseudo-psychiatric thriller about an adolescent criminal, with its impressive performances by Alec McCowen as the doctor and Peter Firth as the young offender, and two plays which perfectly matched the chameleon-like personality of Laurence Olivier: Trevor Griffiths' *The Party,* in which Olivier, speaking with a broad Glasgow accent, realistically impersonated a Scottish Trotskyite politician, and Eduardo De Filippo's Neapolitan family tragi-comedy *Saturday Sunday Monday,* in which Olivier appeared as the 80-year-old retired hatmaker, itching to get hold of any and every hat he could get his clutches on to subject it clandestinely to the unmentionable hot-iron treatment that only hatmakers know the hidden truth about.

Outside the West End, the most lasting impression was gained at the Greenwich Theater from Jonathan Miller's guest season of three Family Romances, so called presumably because each has the Freudian relationship of a mother and her son at its core: *Ghosts, The Seagull* and *Hamlet,* with the same actors all playing parallel roles in the three families. On the same stage, under different management, I might recall the joyous performance of the 75-year-old Elisabeth Bergner as a crazy Hungarian lady in *Catsplay* and the horrors of the awkward English translation of Genet's *The Maids* and the director's and actresses' extravagantly inept interpretation of it. At the Open Space, Charles Marowitz finally produced the first play by the *Times* (of London) drama critic, Irving Wardle, entitled *The Houseboy,* which oddly coincided with the stage debut as playwright of the drama critic of *Punch* magazine, Jeremy Kingston, with the light-hearted *Signs of the Times,* though no two plays could possibly have been more unlike. Here, too, we saw another Rudkin drama, *Ashes,* with its frank discussion of the problems of sex that evidently shocked some people more than the talk of the obscene terror sown in the streets of Belfast by latter-day so-called Irish patriots, and Arrabal's amalgam of deviant sex and political terror *And They Put Handcuffs on the Flowers,* which was no less intentionally shocking and made Marowitz's version of Ionesco's *Macbett* (the English premiere, at the Globe Playhouse festival on the South Bank) into a tame drawing-room comedy by contrast. The Globe Playhouse still relies on tented premises, but Sam Wanamaker, the American producer behind the scheme, announced plans for a more permanent site for what has become a regular annual event. Other new theaters have come into being on premises formally used as cinemas: the King's Road, where the *Rocky Horror Show* has been keeping the box office staff busy and the producers (and actors) happy for months on end, and the Regent, where Lindsay Kemp's almost all-male camp mime *Flowers* has been doing the same in the former Polytechnic Film Theater. But the threat of closure still hangs over some other theaters, despite concerted efforts by the profession and other interested parties, notably The Criterion in Piccadilly Circus, the Shaftesbury where *Hair* made theatrical history for many years until part of the interior ceiling collapsed this season, and last but not least Joan Littlewood's Theater Royal in London's eastern borough of Stratford-atte-Bowe. This, despite a succession of shows in the familiar Littlewood vein, is now surrounded and totally submerged by high-rise concrete structures, as though in a nightmare movie.

As always, I leave the commercial theater to the last, on the principle, I suppose, that the moneyed classes can take care of themselves. I'm not impugning anyone's artistic integrity or standards in saying this. On the contrary, several private producers, notably Eddie Kulukundis, Michael White and Michael Codron, have contributed as much to the well-being of the theater as the long-established managements, like H. M. Tennent, now wholly American-owned, or others, like John Gale, who tread the well-worn paths. As examples of all three types, I only have to quote such titles as *The Constant Wife, The Waltz of the Toreadors, Henry IV, A Streetcar Named Desire, Absurd Person Singular, In Praise of Love, Dandy Dick, Pygmalion,* or *Design for Living,* all of which rely on star-appeal (Ingrid Bergman, Trevor Howard, Rex Harrison, Claire Bloom, Sheila Hancock, Donald Sinden, Alistair Sim, Diana Rigg and Vanessa Redgrave, respectively); *Why Not Stay for Breakfast?, Snap* (originally entitled *Clap,* but prudence thought better of it), *Two and Two Make Sex,* or *Bordello,* whose titles speak for themselves; or the more or less serious comedies and thrillers representing a more traditional genre, like Peter Nichols's *Chez Nous,* Molnar's *The Wolf,* David Hare's *Knuckle,* or William Douglas Home's *At the End of the Day.* And then there are the musicals, a genre all its own, which defeats analysis, at least as far as I am concerned, for I cannot see why the theater should be packed for *Grease,* or *Pippin,* or *Zorba,* or the revival of *The King and I,* to give four current U.S. examples, or for *Bordello, Cockie, The Card,* or *Billy Liar,* to instance the locally manufactured variety. Public taste cannot be accounted for. A splendid revival of *West Side Story,* no doubt one of the finest present-day musicals by any reckoning, failed to find a West End home after being temporarily lodged in a university theater for several weeks. Or could it be managerial, rather than public, taste that was to blame for this? If I knew the answer to this and kindred questions, I should of course be, not a critic, but a producer. So allow me to stick to my safer and more reliable profession.

Highlights of the London Season

Selected and compiled by Ossia Trilling, who has designated his choice of the 30 best productions of the 1973–74 London season. These 30 appear within the listing in expanded entries, with full casts and credits.

TRILLING'S TOP THIRTY
(listed from left to right in the order of their opening dates)

Absurd Person Singular	*Equus*	*Antony and Cleopatra*
Cromwell	*An Inspector Calls*	*Drums in the Night*
And They Put Handcuffs	*The Constant Wife*	*Sizwe Bansi is Dead*
on the Flowers		
The Farm	*In Praise of Love*	*Cries from Casement*
Section Nine	*Coriolanus*	*Dandy Dick*
The Wolf	*Saturday Sunday Monday*	*The Party*
Sherlock Holmes	*Ghosts*	*The Seagull*
Duck Song	*Chez Nous*	*The Tempest*
A Streetcar Named Desire	*Life Class*	*Next of Kin*
The Bewitched	*Pygmalion*	*Spring Awakening*

OUTSTANDING PERFORMANCES

JANET SUZMAN as Cleopatra in *Antony and Cleopatra*	NICOL WILLIAMSON as Coriolanus in *Coriolanus*	ELISABETH BERGNER as Mrs. Orban in *Catsplay*
LAURENCE OLIVIER as John Tagg in *The Party*	IRENE WORTH as Mrs. Alving in *Ghosts*	NICOLA PAGETT as Ophelia in *Hamlet*
TREVOR HOWARD as General St. Pé in *The Waltz of the Toreadors*	REX HARRISON as Henry IV in *Henry IV*	JOHN GIELGUD as Prospero in *The Tempest*
CLAIRE BLOOM as Blanche Du Bois in *A Streetcar Named Desire*	TAMARA USTINOV as Beattie Bryant in *Roots*	ALAN HOWARD as Carlos II in *The Bewitched*
ALAN BATES as Allott in *Life Class*	DIANA RIGG as Eliza Doolittle in *Pygmalion*	PETER FIRTH as Melchior Gabor in *Spring Awakening*

OUTSTANDING DIRECTORS

TREVOR NUNN *The Romans*	JOHN DEXTER *Equus*	TERRY HANDS *The Bewitched*

OUTSTANDING DESIGNERS

CHRISTOPHER MORLEY *The Romans*	JOHN BURY *The Tempest*	FARRAH *The Bewitched*

OUTSTANDING NEW BRITISH PLAYS

(D)—Playwright's London debut. Figure in parentheses is number of performances; plus sign (+) indicates play was still running on June 1, 1974.

EQUUS by Peter Shaffer. Produced by the National Theater at the Old Vic Theater. Opened July 26, 1973. (Closed March 30, 1974) (60 in repertory)

Martin Dysart . . . . Alec McCowen
Nurse . . . . Louie Ramsay
Hesther Saloman . . . . Gillian Barge
Alan Strang . . . . Peter Firth
Frank Strang . . . . Alan MacNaughtan
Dora Strang . . . . Jeanne Watts
Horseman . . . . Nicholas Clay
Harry Dalton . . . . David Healy
Jill Mason . . . . Doran Godwin
   Directed by John Dexter; design, John Napier;
lighting, Andy Phillips
   Time: The present. Place: Rokeby Psychiatric
Hospital in southern England. One intermission.
   A psychiatric investigation in flashback form
into the motives of an unexplained and particularly brutal criminal assault committed by a teen-ager stable boy on the horses to whom he has been passionately devoted, and into the sexual, moral, religious, social and family influences of his background.

CROMWELL by David Storey. Produced by the
English Stage Company at the Royal Court Theater. Opened August 15, 1973. (Closed September 15, 1973) (28)
Logan . . . . Jarlath Conroy
O'Halloran . . . . Albert Finney
Morgan . . . . Alun Armstrong
Proctor . . . . Brian Cox
Chamberlain; Boatman . . . . Colin Douglas
Moore . . . . John Barrett
Matthew . . . . Marc McManus
Margaret . . . . Anne Dyson
Joan . . . . Frances Tomelty
Kennedy . . . . Martin Read
Broome . . . . .Peter Postlethwaite
Cleet . . . . .Kenneth Colley
Wallace . . . . Alun Armstrong
Drake . . . . Colin Bennett
   Directed by Anthony Page; design, Jocelyn
Herbert; lighting, Andy Phillips.
   An epic, if not an outright pseudo-Brechtian,
drama about divided loyalties, popular ambitions and the human capacity for inflicting hurt and bearing suffering in what might be taken to be a Cromwellian Britain torn apart by civil strife, or other parts of the globe in more recent times. One intermission.

THE FARM by David Storey. Produced by the
English Stage Company at the Royal Court Theater. Opened September 26, 1973. (Closed October 27, 1973) Transferred to Mayfair Theater November 1, 1973. (Closed December 8, 1973) (72)
Wendy . . . . Patricia Healey
Jennifer . . . . Meg Davies
Brenda . . . . Prunella Gee
Mr. Slattery . . . . .Bernard Lee
Mrs. Slattery . . . . Doreen Mantle
Albert . . . . Lewis Collins
Arthur . . . . .Frank Grimes

Directed by Lindsay Anderson; design, Hayden Griffin; lighting, Nick Chelton.
   A drunken Yorkshire farmer tyrannizes over
his family that includes the self-deprecating brother who brings home an unsuitable fiancee who will jilt him before the end, three sisters each with their unfulfilled aspirations, and the ill-used mother who loves her bullying husband in spite of all.
   Act I: Evening. Act II: Next morning. Act III,
Scene 1: Evening. Scene 2: Night. Scene 3: Next morning.

CRIES FROM CASEMENT AS HIS BONES
ARE BROUGHT TO DUBLIN by David Rudkin. Produced by the Royal Shakespeare Company at the Place Theater. Opened October 4, 1973. (Closed December 7, 1973) (9 in repertory)
   With Colin Blakely as Roger Casement,
Darien Angadi, Loftus Burton, Geoffrey Hutchings, Malcolm Kaye, Rosemary McHale, Gerard Murphy, Nicholas Selby, Morgan Sheppard, Margaret Whiting.
   Directed by Terry Hands; design, Terry
Hands, Gordon Sumpter; lighting, Michael Murray.
   Originally commissioned as a radio play by the
B.B.C. and broadcast on Radio 3 on 2/4/73, this stage version, adapted by the author and director, reveals the motives of the Ulsterman whose experiences as a British colonial servant, including the frankly homosexual ones vividly described in his historic diary, converted him into an Irish patriot and earned him a traitor's fate in World War I. One intermission.

THE PARTY by Trevor Griffiths. Produced by
the National Theater at the Old Vic Theater. Opened December 20, 1973. (Closed March 21, 1974) (34)
Angie Shawcross . . . . Doran Godwin
Joe Shawcross . . . . Ronald Pickup
Eddie Shawcross . . . . John Shrapnel
Milanka . . . . .Sarah Atkinson
Sloman . . . . Frank Finlay
Andrew Ford . . . . Denis Quilley
Kate Stead . . . . Rachel Davies
Susie Plaistow . . . . Anna Carteret
Louis Preece . . . . Ram John Holder
Richard Maine . . . . Harry Waters
"Grease" Ball . . . . Desmond McNamara
Jeremy Hayes . . . . Gawn Grainger
Kara Massingham . . . . Gillian Barge
John Tagg . . . . Laurence Olivier
   Directed by John Dexter; design, John Napier;
lighting, Andy Phillips.
   Time: During May 10 and 11, 1968. Place: At
the Shawcross's house, London, SW7. Act I: Friday evening. Act II: 2 a.m. the following morning.
   Kenneth Tynan's swan-song commission for
the National Theater, before leaving after ten

years as its literary manager, this play was written with Laurence Olivier in mind for the leading role of a Scottish Trotskyite labor leader and party official who is invited by a sympathising TV director to a party in his London flat to discuss revolutionary politics in Great Britain with like-minded souls during the debacle of the student revolt in France in May 1968. One intermission.

ASHES by David Rudkin. The scarifying experiences of an Ulsterman whose wife is infertile and whose countrymen destroy life. With Peter McEnery, Lynn Farleigh. (27)

DUCK SONG by David Mercer. Produced by the Royal Shakespeare Company at the Aldwych Theater. Opened February 5, 1974. (Closed April 18, 1974) (30 in repertory)

Herbert Shanklin	David Waller
Eddie Bone	Brian Croucher
Maurice Shanklin	Mark Dignam
Jane Shanklin	Carole Hayman
Wheeler	Arthur Whybrow
Eleanor Jimenez	Elizabeth Spriggs
Lee Mcguire	Gareth Hunt

Directed by David Jones; design, Hayden Griffin; lighting, Stewart Leviton.

Act I, Scene 1: A summer evening, the large studio room in Maurice Shanklin's London house. Scene 2: The same, the next morning. Act II: The same, a moment later.

The author's preoccupations with such topics as colonial genocide, free love, parasitism, women in society, middle-age, approaching death, and the impossibility of writing a tragedy in the absurd present, peers through the surreal story of an elderly, rich English artist's family projected into a cataclysmic situation.

CHEZ NOUS by Peter Nichols. Produced by Michael Medwin for Memorial Enterprises at the Globe Theater. Opened February 6, 1974. (174+)

Dick	Denholm Elliott
Phil	Albert Finney
Diana	Geraldine McEwan
Liz	Pat Heywood
Gunga Din	Denis Carey
Zoe	Beth Porter
Burt	Glenn Beck

Directed by Robert Chetwyn; design, Michael Annals; lighting, Mick Hughes.

Time: The summer of 1973. Place: In a farmhouse in the Dordogne region of southwest France. Act I, Scene 1: Late morning. Scene 2: That afternoon. Scene 3: Later that evening. Scene 4: The next morning. Act II, Scene 1: That afternoon. Scene 2: Early evening the same day. Scene 3: Noon the following day.

A bitter modern comedy in which the facade, behind which two married couples attempt to hide the truth, gradually opens up to reveal beneath in all its glaring painfulness the egotism and thwarted yearnings that have taken the place of true love and loyalty.

KNUCKLE by David Hare. A dead sister's brother returns to the home of his well-to-do, corrupt family to find out why she died. With Edward Fox, Douglas Wilmer, Kate Nelligan, Malcolm Storry. (102+)

LIFE CLASS by David Storey. Produced by the English Stage Company at the Royal Court Theater. Opened April 9, 1974. (Closed May 25, 1974) (48)

Allott	Alan Bates
Warren	Stephen Bent
Saunders	Frank Grimes
Stella	Rosemary Martin
Mathews	Paul Kelly
Brenda	Sally Watts
Carter	David Lincoln
Catherine	Gabrielle Lloyd
Mooney	Stuart Rayner
Gillian	Brenda Cavendish
Abercrombie	Bob Peck
Foley	Brian Glover
Philips	Gerald James

Directed by Lindsay Anderson; design, Jocelyn Herbert; lighting, Nick Chelton.

Act I: Morning. Act II: After dinner.

Inspired by the author's early experiences as an art student, this new realistic drama relates the events of a single day in the studio of an art school in which an art teacher, disappointed both maritally and professionally, in a vain attempt to impart to his pupils the subtleties of their chosen profession, finds himself looking on helplessly at a scene of apparent sexual violence that he has himself provoked and that leads inevitably, if unfairly, to his dismissal.

NEXT OF KIN by John Hopkins. Produced by the National Theater at the Old Vic Theater. Opened May 2, 1974. (9+ in repertory)

Susan Lloyd	Gemma Jones
Brian Lloyd	James Laurenson
Lucy Lloyd	Lynsey Baxter
David Lloyd	Andrew Ashby
Barbara Hayes	Lynn Dearth
Kathleen Shanklin	Antonia Pemberton
James Shanklin	Benjamin Whitrow
Gordon Shanklin	Nicholas Dillane
Nancy Shanklin	Sylvia O'Donnell
Margaret Lloyd	Viola Keats
Stephen Lloyd	Gawn Grainger
Timothy Hayes	John Gregg

Directed by Harold Pinter; design, Timothy O'Brien, Tazeena Firth; lighting, David Hersey.

Act I: Afternoon. Act II: Evening. Act III: Night.

In a suburban family consisting of a widowed mother, her four married children and their grandchildren, the surface family equilibrium is ruffled by explicit revelations of mutual hate and envy and implied secret relationships of illicit love.

THE BEWITCHED by Peter Barnes. Produced by the Royal Shakespeare Company at the Aldwych Theater. Opened May 7, 1974. (13 + in repertory)
The Royal Family:
Philip IV . . . . Mark Dignam
Queen Mariana . . . . Elizabeth Spriggs
Carlos II . . . . Alan Howard
Queen Ana of Neuburg . . Rosemary McHale
Their Attendants:
Sebastien de Morra . . . . . George Claydon
(Peter O'Farrell)
Rafael de Morra . . . . Peter O'Farrell
(George Claydon)
Condesa Belepsch . . . . Janet Henfrey
1st Attendant . . . . Walter McMonagle
2d Attendant . . . . Anthony Nash
3d Attendant . . . . Michael Mellinger
Their Jesuits:
Cardinal Pontocarrero . . . . . Philip Locke
Father Froylan . . . . Joe Melia
Their Dominicans:
Valladares . . . . Mark Dignam
Father Motilla . . . . David Waller
Their Capuchin:
Friar Mauro Tenda . . . . . . Trevor Peacock
Their Nuns of Cangas:
Sister Inez . . . . Joan Morrow
Sister Renata . . . . Edwina Ford
Sister Juana . . . . Madeline Bellamy
Monks: Philip Doghan, Christopher Jenkinson, Walter McMonagle, Joe Marcell, Michael Mellinger, Anthony Nash, Keith Taylor, Arthur Whybrow.
Their Court:
Almirante de Castilla . . . . . Nicholas Selby

Duque de Alba . . . . Tim Buckland
Duque de Medina de la Torres Patrick Godfrey
Comte de Monterrey . . . . . . Lee Crawford
Antonio de Alminda . . . . Philip Manikum
Hieronymous Gongora . . . . . Peter Geddis
Dr. Bravo . . . . Barry Stanton
Dr. Geleen . . . . Sidney Livingstone
1st Lady-in-Waiting . . . Madeline Bellamy
2d Lady-in-Waiting . . . . . . Edwina Ford
3d Lady-in-Waiting . . . . . . Joan Morrow
4th Lady-in-Waiting . . . . . Valerie Verdon
Their Servants:
Theresa Diego . . . . Dilys Laye
Alonso de Alcala . . . . . Arthur Whybrow
Gomez . . . . Christopher Jenkinson
Executioner . . . . Joe Marcell
1st Messenger . . . . Keith Taylor
2d Messenger . . . . . . Michael Mellinger
3d Messenger . . . . . . Philip Doghan
4th Messenger . . . . . . Anthony Nash
Their Subjects:
Diego Lopez Duro . . . . . . Trevor Peacock
Leonora Sanchez . . . . . . Valerie Verdon
Juan Guzman . . . . . . Michael Mellinger
Lucia Guzman . . . . . . Madeline Bellamy
The peasant . . . . John Udall (Howard Hennigan)
Outsiders:
Pierre Rebenac . . . . Walter McMonagle
Old Man . . . . Joe Marcell
Directed by Terry Hands; design, Farrah, assisted by Judith Bland; music arranged and composed by Guy Woolfenden; dances, John Broome; lighting, Stewart Leviton.
A scabrously parodistic pseudo-historical drama about the ludicrous efforts of Church, State, and royal family to get the wife of King Carlos II of Spain, despite his epilepsy, impotence and mental incapacity, to bear him an heir before the War of the Spanish succession overwhelms the realm. One intermission.

POPULAR ATTRACTIONS

TWELFTH NIGHT by William Shakespeare. New Open Air Theater production. With Philippa Gail, Ronald Radd, John Justin, Rowena Cooper, Colin Jeavons. (48)

THE HEROES OF THE ICEBERG HOTEL by Andy Smith. Musical cartoon-strip view of gangsterism and fascism. With David Stockton, Yvonne Gilan. (26)

PLAY with Denise Coffey, KRAPP'S LAST TAPE with Andrew Robertson, COME AND GO and ACT WITHOUT WORDS ONE and TWO with Alun Lewis: a program of plays by Samuel Beckett. Young Vic Beckett season. (6 in repertory)

THE HOUSEBOY by Irving Wardle (D). The

Times drama critic's first play about a university graduate's erotic dreams in a seedy rooming-house run by two middle-aged homosexuals. With Timothy West, Nicholas Selby, Thelma Holt, Philip Donaghy. (25)

THE MALCONTENT by John Marston. Nottingham Playhouse inaugural guest season at Bankside Globe Playhouse's "John Player" Season. With Derek Godfrey, Hazel Hughes. (10)

THE PROVOKED WIFE by Vanbrugh. Greenwich Theater production of Restoration comedy. With Fenella Fielding, Linda Thorson, Sheila Allen, James Grant, David Wood. (21)

SIGNS OF THE TIMES by Jeremy Kingston.

Farcical view of popular journalism and its unforeseen influences all round. With Kenneth Móre, Liza Goddard. (167)

THE ROCKY HORROR SHOW by Richard O'Brien. Rock 'n' roll horror fantasy musical based on the Frankenstein story. With Richard O'Brien, Patricia Quinn. (248+)

NUTS, nightly party of songs, dances, sketches and local news given by Joan Littlewood with words by Chris Allen. With Ken Hill, Jenny Logan. (20)

SQUIRE JONATHAN by John Arden. Revival of Ambiance Theater's 1968 production of Britain's first nudist play, With Ian Trigger, Jenny Lee. (18)

WHO'S WHO by Keith Waterhouse and Willis Hall. A comedy of errors in which Mr. and Mrs. Black are Mr. and Mrs. White or are they? With Francis Matthews, Joe Melia, Judy Cornwell, Josephine Tewson. (94)

TWELFTH NIGHT by William Shakespeare. Globe Playhouse production with a 1920s setting. With Alfred Marks, Bryan Pringle, Dudley Sutton, Amanda Barrie. (15)

THE POPE'S WEDDING by Edward Bond. Exeter Northcott Theater production of Bond's first play of 1962 about a casual marriage in a savage society. With Brian Capron, Alison Stedman, Janette Legge, Nick Brimble. (12)

JUNO AND THE PAYCOCK by Sean O'Casey. Sean Kenny's production of Irish drama, in repertory with COWARDY CUSTARD by Noel Coward from 1972/73 season, directed by Siobhan McKenna after Kenny's untimely death. With Siobhan McKenna, Eithne Dunne. (40 in repertory)

ABSURD PERSON SINGULAR by Alan Ayckbourn. Produced by Michael Codron at the Criterion Theater. Opened July 4, 1973. (378+)

Jane . . . . Bridget Turner
Sidney . . . . Richard Briers
Ronald . . . . Michael Aldridge
Marion . . . . Sheila Hancock
Eva . . . . Anne Calder-Marshall
Geoffrey . . . . David Burke
    Directed by Eric Thompson; design, Alan Tagg; lighting, Mick Hughes.
    Act I: Last Christmas, Sidney and Jane's Kitchen. Act II: This Christmas, Geoffrey and Eva's kitchen. Act III: Next Christmas, Ronald and Marion's kitchen.
    On three consecutive Christmas Eves the tables are farcically and sardonically turned among three couples.

Peter Blythe replaced Richard Briers, Angela Scoular replaced Bridget Turner, Paul Eddington replaced Michael Aldridge, Fenella Fielding replaced Shiela Hancock, Marty Cruikshank replaced Anna Calder-Marshall, Paul Shelley replaced David Burke 4/22/74.

AS TIME GOES BY by Mustapha Matura. New production of 1972 John Whiting Award play by Jamaica Londoner about a West Indian con man in London. With Mona Hammond, T-Bone Wilson. (32)

ANTONY AND CLEOPATRA by William Shakespeare. Produced by the Royal Shakespeare Company in its "The Romans" group of four Shakespeare plays in repertory. With Janet Suzman, Richard Johnson, Corin Redgrave. (46 in repertory)

GLASSTOWN by Noel Robinson. (D). The world of the Brontë family. With Anne Stallybrass, Robert Powell, Angela Down, Vicky Ireland, John Robinson. (47)

ENDGAME by Samuel Beckett. Manchester's 69 Theater Company production. With Wolfe Morris, Trevor Peacock. (23)

MARRIAGES by William Trevor. Revival of earlier lunchtime production, with Isobel Dean, Margaret Ashcroft, in a double bill with A PERFECT RELATIONSHIP, the last ball of an Irish call-girl, with Pauline Delaney, Nigel Stock. (23)

WHY BOURNEMOUTH by John Antrobus. Crazy railroad satire of 1968 revived with new music by Michael Dress. With Leonard Fenton, Hilda Braid, Cheryl Campbell. (25)

AS YOU LIKE IT by William Shakespeare. Open Air Theater production. With Michael Shallard, Martin Potter, Dilys Hamlett. (40)

JULIUS CAESAR by William Shakespeare. Produced by the Royal Shakespeare Company in its "The Romans" group of four Shakespeare plays in repertory. With Mark Dignam, Richard Johnson, Philip Locke, Corin Redgrave, Patrick Stewart, Margaret Tyzack. (42 in repertory)

THE CARD by Keith Waterhouse and Willis Hall, with music and lyrics by Tony Hatch & Jackie Trent. Musical based on Arnold Bennett's novel. With Jim Dale, Millicent Martin, Eleanor Bron (later Dinah Sheridan). (127)

THE WATER BABIES by John Taylor and Ross Taylor. World premiere of musical adaptation of Charles Kingsley's children's book. With Jessie Matthews, Ted Merwood. (66)

FRENCH WITHOUT TEARS by Terence Rattigan. Young Vic production of 1930s comedy. With Denise Coffey, Mel Martin, Hugh Hastings. (41 in repertory)

TITUS ANDRONICUS by William Shakespeare. Produced by the Royal Shakespeare Company in its "The Romans" group of four Shakespeare plays in repertory. With Colin Blakely, Mark Dignam, Judy Geeson, Geoffrey Hutchings, Robert Oates, Tim Pigott-Smith. (30 in repertory)

DECAMERON '73 by Peter Coe. A contemporary look at the erotic literature of the world. With Yasuko Nagazumi, Luan Peters. (88)

ANTONY AND CLEOPATRA by William Shakespeare. Tony Richardson's production for the "John Player" Bankside Globe Playhouse Season. Opened August 9, 1973. (Closed September 1, 1973) (21)

Antony . . . . Julian Glover
Octavius Caesar . . . . David Schofield
Lepidus . . . . John Byron
Sextus Pompeius; Clown . . . . Bob Hoskins
Domitius Enorbarbus . . . . . . Dave King
Eros . . . . Stuart Mungall
Dercetus . . . . Ioan Meredith
Agrippa . . . . Trevor Adams
Proculeius . . . . Roger Lloyd Pack
Thyreus . . . . .Nigel Humphreys
Menas; Schoolmaster . . . . Raymond Skipp
Canidius . . . . Dan Meaden
Alexas . . . . Jeffrey Holland
Mardian . . . . David Foxxe
Cleopatra . . . . Vanessa Redgrave
Octavia . . . . Lorna Edwards
Charmian . . . . .Julie Covington
Iras . . . . Vanessa Furse
Directed by Tony Richardson; design, Brian Thomson; costumes, Maria Björnson; lighting, Claude Manley.

There is no record of the first performance of Shakespeare's tragedy, estimated to date from 1607, in the 17th century. The present revival, in modern dress, with unmistakeable references to the political concepts of latter-day fascism, was staged as part of the 1973 John Player Season under the executive direction of Sam Wanamaker. One intermission.

THE FORM by N.F. Simpson in a double bill with FUNERAL GAMES by Joe Orton, under the generic title AN EVENING OF ECCENTRIC DRAMA. With Ron Cook, Linda Liles. (23)

THE ROYAL HUNT OF THE SUN by Peter Shaffer. Prospect Theater Company production in repertory with PERICLES and TWELFTH NIGHT. With Trevor Martin, Rupert Frazer. (8 in repertory)

AN INSPECTOR CALLS by J.B. Priestley. Produced by the Mermaid Theater Trust at the Mermaid Theater. Opened August 29, 1973. (Closed December 8, 1973) (117)

Arthur Birling . . . . Campbell Singer
Gerald Croft . . . . David Horovitch
Sheila Birling . . . . Sheila Ruskin
Sybil Birling . . . . Elizabeth Tyrrell
Edna, a maid . . . . .Jeanette Ranger
Eric Birling . . . . Edward Hammond
Inspector Goole . . . . .Philip Stone
Directed by Bernard Miles; design, Susan Ayers; lighting, Roger Weaver.

Time: An evening in spring, 1912. Place: All three acts, which are continuous, take place in the dining room of the Birlings' house in Brumley, an industrial city in the North Midlands. Two intermissions.

First performed in London at the Old Vic Theater in 1945 with Ralph Richardson in the title role.

PERICLES, PRINCE OF TYRE by William Shakespeare. Prospect Theater Company production in repertory with THE ROYAL HUNT OF THE SUN and TWELFTH NIGHT, and later revived on its own after successful European tour. With Derek Jacobi, Harold Innocent, Jan Waters. (10 in repertory and 9 +)

TWO AND TWO MAKE SEX by Richard Harris and Leslie Darbon. The sexual patterns of a middle-aged husband. With Patrick Cargill, Jane Downs, Diana King, Terence Alexander. (338+)

TWELFTH NIGHT by William Shakespeare. Prospect Theater Company production in repertory with THE ROYAL HUNT OF THE SUN and PERICLES. With Willoughby Goddard, Derek Jacobi, Harold Innocent, Jan Waters. (7 in repertory)

RELATIVE VALUES by Noel Coward. Revival of 1951 comedy. With Margaret Lockwood, Gwen Cherrell, John Stone, Bryan Stanion. (84)

MR. IVES MAGIC PUNCH AND JUDY SHOW by John Grillo. A clash of ideas in the puppet world. With Ian Ruskin, Jeannie Fisher. (20)

THE CONSTANT WIFE by W. Somerset Maugham. Produced by H.M. Tennent Ltd at the Albery Theater. Opened September 19, 1973. (Closed April 27, 1974) (260)

Mrs Culver . . . . Dorothy Reynolds
Bentley . . . . John Hart Dyke
Martha Culver . . . . Pauline Jameson
Barbara Fawcett . . . . Helen Christie
Constance Middleton . . . . .Ingrid Bergman
Marie-Louise Durham . . . . . Barbara Ferris
John Middleton FRCS . . . John McCallum

Bernard Kersal . . . . Michael Allinson
Mortimer Durham . . . . . Charles Pemberton
Directed by John Gielgud; design, Alan Tagg; costumes, Beatrice Dawson; lighting, Joe Davis.
Time: The late 1920s. Place: John Middleton's house in Harley Street. Act I: The drawing room, a summer afternoon. Act II: The same, a few weeks later, late afternoon. Act III: The same, afternoon, one year later.

First produced by the Charles Frohman Company at the Maxine Elliott Theater, New York in November 1926, with Ethel Barrymore, and Gilbert Miller as director. The London premiere, on 4/6/27 at the Strand Theater, with Fay Compton, was followed by revivals in 1937 at the Globe Theater, with Ruth Chatterton, and in 1946 at the Arts Theater with Marjorie Stewart.

NOT DROWNING BUT WAVING by Leonard Webb. After 20 years of marriage, a mother still feels uncertain of life's meaning. With Geraldine McEwen, Gillian Bailey, John Rogan. (27)

THE SPANISH TRAGEDY by Thomas Kyd. Modern revival of the best-known Elizabethan revenge tragedy. With Another Theater Company. (18)

IN PRAISE OF LOVE comprising AFTER LYDIA and BEFORE DAWN by Terence Rattigan. Produced by H.M. Tennent Ltd. at the Duchess Theater. Opened September 27, 1973. (Closed January 12, 1974) (123)
Before Dawn
The Baron . . . . Donald Sinden
The Lackey . . . . Don Fellows
The Captain . . . . .Richard Warwick
The Diva . . . . Joan Greenwood
Time: The early hours of June 17, 1800. Place: Rome.
After Lydia
Lydia Crutwell . . . . Joan Greenwood
Sebastian Crutwell . . . . Donald Sinden
Mark Walters . . . . Don Fellows
Joey Crutwell . . . . . . .Richard Warwick
Time: The present. Place: North London.

Both plays directed by John Dexter; design, Desmond Heeley; lighting, Andy Phillips.

Before Dawn is a farcical treatment of the story of the beautiful Roman diva and the feared police chief, immortalised by Sardou and Puccini, with an unexpected denouement that reveals the hero as something less than the man he gives himself out to be. *After Lydia* is about the foreign-born wife (a part originally written for Ingrid Bergman) of an apparently egotistical English author who is prevented by her altruistically motivated husband from discovering that she is dying from a fatal disease—or is she?

THE BEVELLERS by Bill Bryden. Ups and downs in a Scottish glass factory. With Andrew Byatt, Leonard Maguire, the author. (22)

THE ELECTRIC ELEMENT by and with Bruce Lacey, the Alberts, the Incredible Time-Machine. An amazing space-fantasy. (42)

AT THE END OF THE DAY by William Douglas Home. An inside look at the home of England's prime minister at election time. With John Mills, Dulcie Gray, Michael Denison, Jack May. (205)

THE MISSING LINK by John Antrobus. Satire on human foibles. With Frank Middlemass, Brian Hall, Pat Keen, Cheryl Campbell, the author. (16)

CARRY ON LONDON by Talbot Rothwell. Revue version of popular TV "Carry On" series. With Sid James, Barbara Windsor, Kenneth Connor, Trudi Van Doorn. (411+)

COUNTRY LIFE by Nicholas Wood (D). The life and work of the English middle classes. With George Cole, Virginia McKenna, John Byron. (28)

MUCH ADO ABOUT NOTHING by William Shakespeare. Frank Dunlop's Young Vic production premiered at the Europalia Festival in Brussels. With Denise Coffey, Ian Charleson, Tamara Ustinov, Roy Hudd, Andrew Robertson. (28 in repertory)

DANDY DICK by Arthur Wing Pinero. Produced by H.M. Tennent Ltd. and Knightsbridge Theatrical Productions Ltd. at the Garrick Theater. Opened October 17, 1973. (Closed March 30, 1974) (165)
Salome . . . . .Lucinda Gane
Sheba . . . . .Gemma Craven
Blore . . . . Charles Lloyd Pack
Mr. Darbey . . . . Barry McGinn
Major Tarver . . . . Geoffrey Beevers
Augustin Jedd, D.D. . . . . . . Alastair Sim
Georgiana Tidman . . . . . Patricia Routledge
Sir Tristram Mardon . . . . . Ralph Michael
Batcham . . . . .Richard Denning
Hannah Topping . . . . Pip Hinton
Noah Topping . . . . .Richard Owens
Directed by John Clements; scenery, Alan Tagg; costumes, Margaret Furse.

Act I, Scene 1: The garden at the deanery, St. Marvell's, morning. Scene 2: The morning room, evening. Act II, Scene 1: "The Strong Box," St. Marvell's. Scene 2: The deanery.

Revival of 1887 farce by England's leading exponent of the genre. Originally produced at the Chichester Festival 7/25/73 as John Clements's final production after eight years as director of the Festival.

LANDSCAPE and A SLIGHT ACHE by Harold Pinter. Royal Shakespeare Company's new coupling of two disturbing dramas. With Peggy Ashcroft, David Waller, Peter Schofield. (14 in repertory)

GET OFF MY BACK! by Terry Greer, Brian Phelan and Johnnie Quarrel. A story of London's dockland. With the Half Moon Theater Company. (26)

CORIOLANUS by William Shakespeare. Produced by the Royal Shakespeare Company at the Aldwych Theater. Opened October 22, 1973. (Closed December 13, 1973) (24 in repertory)
Romans—Patricians:

Caius Martius	Nicol Williamson
Menenius	Mark Dignam
Cominius	Nicholas Selby
Titus Lartius	Walter Brown
1st Senator	John Bott
2d Senator	Martin Milman
3d Senator	Desmond Stokes
4th Senator	Lennard Pearce
5th Senator	Michael Egan
Captain	Christopher Jenkinson
Volumnia	Margaret Tyzack
Virgilia	Wendy Allnut
Martius	Christopher Howard-Lee (Matthew Angel)
Valeria	Edwina Ford
1st Gentlewoman	Madeline Bellamy
2d Gentlewoman	Jill Lidstone

Romans—Tribunes:

Sicinius Velutus	John Nettleton
Junius Brutus	Philip Locke

Romans—Officers:

1st Officer	Sidney Livingstone
2d Officer	Keith Taylor

Romans—Aediles:

1st Aedile	Robert Oates
2d Aedile	Mark Sheridan

Romans—Plebeians:

1st Citizen	Morgan Sheppard
2d Citizen	Arthur Whybrow
3d Citizen	Malcolm Kaye
4th Citizen	Paul Gaymon
5th Citizen	Robert Oates

Citizens: Madeline Bellamy, Edwina Ford, Jill Lidstone, Darien Angadi, Loftus Burton, Eric Carte, Joseph Charles, Sidney Livingstone, Joe Marcell, Gerard Murphy, Tony Osoba, Anthony Rowlands, Mark Sheridan, Keith Taylor.
Corioli—Elders:

1st Volscian Elder	Desmond Stokes
2d Volscian Elder	Lennard Pearce
3d Volscian Elder	Tony Osoba

Corioli—Warriors:

Tullus Aufidius	Oscar James
Tullus Lieutenant	Darien Angadi

Volscian Soldiers: Tony Osoba, Joe Marcell, Joseph Charles, Loftus Burton.

1st Watch	Joe Marcell
2d Watch	Tony Osoba

Corioli—People:

Adrian	Darien Angadi
Volscian Citizen	Tony Osoba
1st Servingman	Loftus Burton
2d Servingman	Joe Marcell
3d Servingman	Joseph Charles
Servingmen	Tony Osoba, Darien Angadi

Citizens: Madeline Bellamy, Edwina Ford, Jill Lidstone, Eric Carte, Michael Egan, Paul Gaymon, Christopher Jenkinson, Malcolm Kaye, Sidney Livingstone, Martin Milman, Gerard Murphy, Robert Oates, Anthony Rowlands, Mark Sheridan, Keith Taylor, Arthur Whybrow.

Directed by Trevor Nunn, with Buzz Goodbody and Euan Smith; designed by Christopher Morley with Ann Curtis; music, Guy Woolfenden; lighting, Brian Harris.

No early performance of this play, written in 1607–08, is recorded. The present production, forming part of the four-part cycle of Shakespeare's plays staged under the heading of *The Romans* at the Royal Shakespeare Theater in Stratford in 1972 under the direction of Trevor Nunn, was transferred to the RSC's London home on 10/22/73 as part of a season of the same four plays, with the permanent setting for all four adapted to suit the new stage and with some cast changes. The play was presented in three parts.

ABELARD AND HELOISE by Ronald Duncan. New production of dramatization of famous love letters. With Pamela Coveney, Denis Goacher. (52)

MACBETH by William Shakespeare. New production by Dolphin Theater company's new director, Peter James, formerly of the Young Vic. With Tom Baker, Sheila Allen, Barrie Rutter. (49)

THE TAMING OF THE SHREW by Charles Marowitz. A new view of Shakespeare's comedy, revived at year's end after a European tour. With Thelma Holt, Nikolas Simmonds, Kay Barlow, Jeremy Nicholas. (50 +)

THE MERRY-GO-ROUND by D.H. Lawrence. Revival of neglected comedy of 1912, after taking part in 1973 Europalia Festival in Brussels. With Anne Dyson, Alex McCrindle, Susan Tracy, Derrick O'Connor. (33)

THE CARETAKER by Harold Pinter. New Young Vic production. With Paul Brooke, Jeremy Irons, Ian Trigger. (20 in repertory)

DESIGN FOR LIVING by Noel Coward. New production of popular 1930s comedy. With Vanessa Redgrave, Jeremy Brett, John Stride, Peter Bayliss. (217+)

SO YOU WANT TO BE IN PICTURES by Peter Rankin (D). Strange events in a film studio in Rome. With Frank Coda, Myfanwy Jenn. (27)

FEMALE TRANSPORT by Steve Gooch. The trials of six women convicts transported to Australia in the 19th century. With Yvonne Gilan, Alan David. (24)

AGAMEMNON adapted by Steven Berkoff from the Aeschylus tragedy. With Alfred Michelson, Milton McCrae, Shelley Lee, the author. (13)

A CHRISTMAS CAROL. Theater Workshop's version of the Dickens story, with music. With Ron Hackett, Jane Briers, John Grillo. (36)

GIVE A DOG A BONE by Peter Howard and George Fraser. Christmas Moral Rearmament pantomime. With Lousie Rush, Gordon Reid, Donald Scott. (77)

THE RUFFIAN ON THE STAIR by Joe Orton in a double bill with THE DUMBWAITER by Harold Pinter. Frederick Proud's revival of two one-act dramas of menace. With John Hurt, Prunella Scales. (20)

COCKIE. Memories from the musical career of C.B. Cochran, based on an anthology from his outstanding productions, by various writers and composers. With Avril Angers, Max Wall. (85)

LARRY THE LAMB IN TOY TOWN by David Wood and Sheila Ruskin. Adapted from Toytown Stories by S.G. Hulme-Beaman, with music by David Wood. With Melody Kaye, Philip Anthony. (54)

WHY NOT STAY FOR BREAKFAST? by Gene Stone and Ray Cooney. An unmarried mother and a bachelor friend who takes pity on her hit it off. With Derek Nimmo, Katy Manning. (194+)

CINDERELLA by Henry Livings. A new view of an old children's story. With Jacqueline Andrews, Richard James. (14)

ONION JACK (AND BONZO) by Stanley Eveling. Exposing the libido of boy scouts, girl guides and their teachers, originally an Edinburgh Festival Traverse Theater production. With Susan Carpenter, Roy Sampson. (24)

TREASURE ISLAND by Hal Shaper (lyrics) and Cyril Ornadel (music). New musical version of the Stevenson book. With Bernard Miles, Spike Milligan. (84)

DICK by Steve Gooch. The story of Dick Turpin, the highwayman. With Jeffry Chiswick, Ken Morley. (24)

KNOTS from the book by R.D. Laing (home truths about human nature) and FLOW (five self-revealing monologues) staged by the Actors Company. With Edward Petherbridge, Ian McKellan, Caroline Blakiston, Paola Dionisotti, Robert Eddison, Robin Ellis. (29)

JACK AND THE BEANSTALK by Dick Park and Dick Hills. The annual Christmas Palladium pantomime. With Frankie Howerd, Dora Bryan, Alfie Bass. (176)

THE DANNY LA RUE SHOW by Brian Blackburn. Spectacular camp 'gay' show. With Danny La Rue, Mike Goddard. (188+)

PETER PAN by James M. Barrie. Christmas revival of Robert Helpmann's production. With Maggie Smith, Dave Allen. (24)

TROUBLE ON THE NIGHT SHIFT by and with Sal's Meat Market, Ray Hassett, John Ratzenberger. Way-out fun show, as a late-night show. (22)

THE FEAST OF FOOLS by Jim Hiley. A bawdy mediaeval romp, originally tried out at Oval Theater. With Incubus, the Balloon and Banana Band, Ernie Wolk, Paddy Fletcher. (37)

THE RAINBOW ROBBERY by Scoular Anderson. The theft of a rainbow causes an upheaval. With the Unicorn Theater Company. (9)

DICK WHITTINGTON AND HIS CAT, devised and directed by Mike Leigh. A way-out version of the picaresque British saga. With Tim Stern, Paul Copley, Julia Coppleman. (32)

THE PAPERTOWN PAPERCHASE by David Wood and Roy Jones. About a salamander's search for glory. With Derek Griffiths, Su Yong, David Delve. (18)

PINOCCHIO adapted by Angela Caldati. New version of popular children's story. With Fiona Fullerton. (18)

SHERLOCK HOLMES by Arthur Conan Doyle and William Gillette. Produced by the Royal Shakespeare Company at the Aldwych Theater. Opened January 1, 1974. (179+ in repertory)

Madge Larrabee	Barbara Leigh-Hunt
John Forman	Harry Towb
James Larrabee	Nicholas Selby
Térèse	Madeline Bellamy
Sidney Prince	Trevor Peacock
Alice Faulkner	Mary Rutherford

Sherlock Holmes . . . . John Wood
Professor Moriarty . . . . Philip Locke
John . . . . Paul Gaymon
Alfred Bassick . . . . Martin Milman
Billy . . . . Sean Clarke
Doctor Watson . . . . Tim Pigott-Smith
Jim Craigin . . . . Peter Schofield
Thomas Leary . . . . . Christopher Jenkinson
'Lightfoot' McTague . . . . Keith Taylor
Parsons . . . . Sidney Livingstone
Sir Edward Leighton . . . . Patrick Godfrey
Count von Stalburg . . . . John Bott
Newsboy . . . . Francis Maguire
Street Entertainers, Visitors to London,
Tradespeople: John Bott, Joseph Charles, Joe
Marcell, Joan Morrow.
Directed by Frank Dunlop; design, Carl
Toms; lighting, Stewart Leviton.
Time: 1891. Place: London. Act I, Scene 1:
Drawing room at the Larrabees, evening: Scene
2: Professor Moriarty's underground office,
morning. Scene 3: Sherlock Holmes's apartments
in Baker Street, evening. Act II, Scene 1: The
Stepney gas chamber, midnight. Scene 2: Doctor
Watson's consulting room in Kensington, the
following evening.
This version opened in New York in 1899,
with the American adaptor in the title role and
was performed on and off for 30 years until 1932.
Gillette last appeared in a radio broadcast of it in
1935, aged 82. This production, the first in London for almost 70 years, joined the RSC's
1973/74 Season 1/1/74.

JUDIES by David Fitzsimmons (formerly tried
out as *Punch and Judy Stories*). Two nymphos
get their just deserts. With John Alderton, Pauline Collins, Paul Angelis, Christine Hargreaves.
(72)

MEASURE FOR MEASURE by William
Shakespeare. Jonathan Miller's modern-dress
production for the National Theater Touring
Company's Mobile Production. With Gillian
Barge, Julian Curry, Alan MacNaughtan. (6 in
repertory)

THE COLLECTOR by John Fowles, adapted by
David Parker. West End revival of drama of a
sexual maniac. With Marianne Faithfull, Simon
Williams. (40)

MONTE PYTHON'S FIRST FAREWELL
TOUR by the Monty Python team. A crazy
show based on the Monty Python TV series.
With John Cleese, Michael Palin. (40)

BRIEF LIVES by Patrick Garland. Revival of
Patrick Garland's production of his own adaptation of *Aubrey's Lives*. With Roy Dotrice. (137+)

THE BLACK AND WHITE MINSTRELS by
C.P. Taylor. Satire on Bohemianism, first seen at

1972 Edinburgh Festival. With Tom Conti,
Harry Mankin, Alan Howard, Taiwo Ajai. (24)

DEAD EASY by Jack Popplewell. A charlady
solves a murder mystery. With Irene Handl, Roy
Kinnear, Patrick Barr. (28)

GENTLEMEN PREFER ANYTHING by Ken
Hill. Man and woman exchange roles. With
James Booth, Diane Langton, Frank Coda. (33)

DICK DETERRED by David Edgar. A musical
skit on the U.S. President. With Gregory Floy,
Brian McDermott, Deborah Grant. (60)

SOMETHING'S BURNING by Ronald Eyre
(D). Are secret police and anarchists inter-
changeable? With Peter Copley, Bill Fraser,
Carol Gillies, Penelope Wilton. (34)

THE TEMPEST by William Shakespeare. Pro-
duced by the National Theater at the Old Vic.
Opened March 5, 1974. (32+ in repertory)
Alonso . . . . Joseph O'Conor
Sebastian . . . . William Squire
Prospero . . . . John Gielgud
Antonio . . . . Cyril Cusack
Ferdinand . . . . Rupert Frazer
Gonzalo . . . . David Markham
Adrian . . . . Peter Rocca
Francisco . . . . Christopher Guard
Caliban . . . . Denis Quilley
Trinculo . . . . Julian Orchard
Stephano . . . . Arthur Lowe
Master of a Ship . . . . Alex McCrindle
Boatswain . . . . James Mellor
Miranda . . . . Jenny Agutter
Ariel . . . . Michael Feast
Iris . . . . Julie Covington
Juno . . . . Dana Gillespie
Others: Dai Bradley, Bryan Brown, Jane Carr,
David Dixon, Colin Fay, Glyn Grain, Patti
Love, Ian Mackenzie, James Mellor, Peter Need-
ham, Judith Paris, Veronica Quilligan, Gerard
Ryder, Keith Skinner, James Smith, Stephen
Williams.
Musicians: Chuck Mallett, Barry Mason, Lau-
rie Morgan.
Directed by Peter Hall; design, John Bury,
lighting, John Bury, Leonard Tucker; music,
Gryphon; movement, Claude Chagrin.
Place: An uninhabited island. The play was
presented in two parts.
First acted in November 1611. This revival
marks Peter Hall's directing debut since taking
over as head of the National Theater and reflects
his special interest in the theatrical effects pecu-
liar to the genre of the masque.

HENRY IV by William Shakespeare. Guy
Sprung's production of both parts as a single
play. With John Abbott, Jeff Chiswick, Maurine
Colbourne, Anna Shaw. (28)

THE IMPORTANCE OF BEING EARNEST by Oscar Wilde. Peter James's production for Dolphin Theater Company. With Louise Purnell, Richard Kay, Polly Adams, Edward Jewesbury. (48)

SNAP by Charles Laurence. A very modern London foursome are embarrassed by an epidemic of gonorrhea. With Maggie Smith, Barry Ingham. (91+)

RUNAWAY by Peter Ransley. A neglected working-class Yorkshire boy runs away from reality and family unpleasantnesses. With Bill Owen, Kevin Moreton, Cherry Morris. (21)

HAMLET by William Shakespeare. Part of the Jonathan Miller repertory season under the title Family Romances (also including Ghosts and The Seagull) at the Greenwich Theater. With Peter Eyre, Nicky Henson. Nicola Pagett, Robert Stephens, Irene Worth. (22 in repertory)

KING LEAR by William Shakespeare. Part of the Actors Company London repertory season (also including The Wood Demon, 'Tis Pity She's a Whore, The Way of the World and Ruling the Roost). With Robert Eddison, Ian McKellen, Edward Petherbridge, Sharon Duce. (25 in repertory)

ROOTS by Arnold Wesker. Bernard Goss's Young Vic production. With Tamara Ustinov, Barry Evans, John Rogan. (12 in repertory)

OLD FRUIT by Christopher Gilmore. What army marrieds were kept in the dark about. With John Justin, Julia Lang. (23)

ROYALTY FOLIES by Anthony Newley, with music by Anthony Newley & John Taylor. Paul Raymond's West End frontal pornographic revue. With Debbie Raymond, Rob Wilder. (117+)

THE MOUSETRAP by Agatha Christie. Veteran thriller re-opened at the St. Martin's Theater next door to the Ambassadors Theater of the original production of 1952. (78+)

'TIS PITY SHE'S A WHORE by John Ford. Actors' Company London repertory season production. With Paola Dionisotti, Ian McKellen, Ronald Radd, John Bennett. (13 in repertory)

FLOWERS, a mime by Lindsay Kemp. Inspired by Genet's Our Lady of the Flowers. With Lindsay Kemp and The Incredible Orlando. (112+)

THE WAY OF THE WORLD by William Congreve. Actors' Company London repertory season production. With Edward Petherbridge, Caroline Blakiston, Margery Mason. (14 in repertory)

THE WILL and THE TWELVE-POUND LOOK by James Barrie. One-acters about the price of material success. With Linda Thorson, Peter Bayliss, Caroline Hunt. (53+)

EDEN END by J.B. Priestley. National Theater production of 1930s Yorkshire comedy. With Michael Jayson, Joan Plowright, Leslie Sands. (20+ in repertory)

BORDELLO by Julian More and Carl Denker. A musical flashback history of the French painter's sentimental voyage through life. With Henry Woolf, Stella Moray, Cristina Avery. (50+)

A GHOST ON TIPTOE by Robert Morley and Rosemary Ann Sisson. A 62-year-old supposedly with a year to live kicks over the traces. With Robert Morley, Ambrosine Philpotts, William Franklyn, Karin Fernald. (42+)

BILLY LIAR by Dick Clement and Ian La Frenais, with music by John Barry and lyrics by Dan Brack. Musical based on the Keith Waterhouse-Willis Hall stage, TV, and screen play, of the adolescent fantasist. With Michael Crawford, Avis Bunnage, Gay Soper, Bryan Pringle. (33+)

OFF THE PEG devised and directed by Gordon Deighton and Victor Spinetti. Gay boys send up show biz. With Rayner Bourton, Rogers and Starr. (29+)

WHO SAW HIM DIE? By Tudor Gates. Cop versus robber with no holds barred. With Stratford Johns, Lee Montague, Elizabeth Wallace, Christopher Guinee. (27+)

NORMAN CONQUESTS repertory of three plays by Alan Ayckbourn: TABLE MANNERS (13+), LIVING TOGETHER (9+) and ROUND AND ROUND THE GARDEN, about the entanglements of a librarian in three different parts of the same house and an adulterous plot foiled. With Tom Courtenay, Penelope Wilton, Michael Gabon.

PYGMALION by George Bernard Show. Produced by Eddie Kulukundis at the Albery Theater Opened May 16, 1974. (19+)

Clara Eynsford Hill	Sarah Atkinson
Mrs. Eynsford Hill	Margaret Ward
Bystander	Dennis Handby
Freddy Eynsford Hill	Anthony Naylor
Eliza Doolittle	Diana Rigg
Col. Pickering	Jack May
Prof. Higgins	Alec McCowen
Sarcastic Bystander	Simon McCorkindale
Mrs. Pearce	Hilda Fenemore
Alfred Doolittle	Bob Hoskins
Mrs. Higgins	Ellen Pollock

Parlormaid . . . . Melanie Peck
Bystanders, Persons in Crowd: Fred Bryant, John Church, Joyce Donaldson, Jack Eden, Tony Leary, Angela Wallbank, Jeremy Wallis.

Directed by John Dexter; design, Jocelyn Herbert, Andrew Sanders; lighting, Andy Phillips.

Act I: Covent Garden. Act II: Professor Higgins's laboratory in Wimpole Street. Act III: Mrs. Higgins's drawing room in Chelsea. Act IV: Professor Higgins's laboratory in Wimpole Street. Act V: Mrs Higgins's drawing room in Chelsea. The play was presented in three parts.

First presented in German at the Hofburg Theater, Vienna on 10/16/13 with Lilli Marberg,

and in English at His Majesty's Theater, London on 4/11/14 with Mrs. Patrick Campbell and directed by the author. The first major revival since John Clements' production on 11/19/53 at the St. James's Theater, London, with Kay Hammond.

THE GREAT SOCIETY by Beverley Cross. The Peasant Revolt of 1381 led by Wat Tyler. With Bernard Miles, Peter Postlethwaite, Gary Raymond, Geoffrey Whitehead. (14+)

THE KING by David Cregan. In good King Arthur's glorious days. With Geoffrey Hutchings, Eliza Ward. (7+)

LIMITED RUNS OF INTERESTING NEW BRITISH PLAYS

EDWARD G, LIKE THE FILM STAR by John Harvey Flint. A middle-aged man playing Santa Claus begins to live. With Robin Bailey, Maureen Pryor. (10)

OFF THE BUS, a mixed open-air bill including HOW DO WE DO IT! NO. 1, GETTING ON THE BUS (PART ONE), GETTING ON THE BUS, HOW DO WE DO IT! NO. 2, HOW TO BREATHE, three sketches by Jim Hiley satirizing children's TV programs, with Kevin Costello, the author; MENDEL & BELLA by Michael Bullock, an elderly Jewish couple chat on a bus; AN AMOUR, by David Halliwell, the meaning of love, with Prunella Scales, Paul Brooke; WE'RE ALL GOING TO SOUTHAMPTON and HELLO MAMA, HELLO PAPA by Michael Stevens; SURRUP by Henry Livings; STRONG RIGHT ARM STUFF by Chris Bailey, all set on a bus and dealing with the delights and anxieties of public transportation travel, created by Ed Berman for the 1973 Festival of London and the Ambiance Theater's Fun Art Bus Company. (18)

THE GHOST OUTSIDE THE MACHINE by John Taylor. A hemmed-in victim of persecution mania. With Barry Grantham, Edmund Dring. (12)

MOTHER'S DAY by James Dawson. A mother-fixated son converses with a ghost. With Anthony Sherwood. (10)

MARRIAGES by William Trevor. A widow comforts a mistress. With Zena Walker, Ann Morrish (later Isobel Dean, Margaret Ashcroft; see under Popular Attractions) (10)

YOU SEE THAT THING IS THIS by Ken Campbell, a cub-master in trouble, with Holly de Jongh, Mark Cooper; in a double-bill with A DISCUSSION by David Halliwell, a discussion

about pre-prandial sexual envy, with Ian Judge, Kate Terriss. (6)

GOOD TIMES by Roy Minton. The encounter of two moral outcasts. With John Junkin, Moira Redmond. (17)

STIFF AND SILENT by John St. Clair. The agony of underpaid hospital servants. With Geoff M. Pocock, David Kandalker, Jim Reville. (17)

TILL DAY BREAK by T-Bone Wilson. Drama of Caribbean's writer's aspirations. With the Keskidee Theater Company. (5)

NUTTERS by J.P. Coterell. A psychiatric escapade. With Richard Howard, Jacqueline da Costa. (15)

TOM BARKER OF CAMDEN—AND THE WORLD by Arnold Hinchcliffe. The epic story of a British "Wobbly." With Charles Turner, Ossie Lewis. (9)

CO-PESSIMISTS by Barry Grantham. The world's ills as a harlequinade. With Ian Armstrong, Richard Gordon, Joan Grantham, Finola Keogh, the author. (10)

THE ENLIGHTENMENT OF THE STRAWBERRY GARDENER by Don Howarth. A wilful bureaucrat's philosophy of behavior. With John Blythe, Peter John. (19)

TOYS OF GOD by Alexander Ward. A crazy host re-enacts the story of the Fall of Man. With Llewellyn Rees, Jane Griffiths. (12)

SCRATCHING THE SURFACE by Elen Bronca. To discover the surprises below. With Meg English, Patrick Rice, Robert Stredder. (11)

MAGNIFICENCE by Howard Brenton. Political parable about injustice arising from the illegal occupation of empty premises by a bunch of radicals. With Kenneth Cranham, Robert Eddison, Carole Hayman. (18)

BEGGAR-MY-NEIGHBOUR by Stephen Powell and Tony Craven. Crime, corruption and sexual passion. With Rayner Bourton, David Fleeshman, David George, Rudi Kilroy. (6)

BERLIN DAYS by Stephen Poliakoff. Two boys in pre-Hitler Germany trapped in a lonely city. With David Haughton, Tony Maples. (8)

WATCH THE WOMAN by Brian Phelan and Oliver Wymark in collaboration with the Common Stock Theater Company. A revue about the womenfolk of an Islington housing estate. With Jane Gibson, Trisha Arnold, assisted by Tom Remilon. (6)

FALL IN AND FOLLOW ME by Billie Colville and Dave Marson. The Children's strike of 1911. With the Half Moon Theater Company. (16)

GONE by Dannie Absie, the dilemma of a suicidal husband, with Paul Weaver, Christopher Masters; and THE OTHER END by Liane Aukin, a wife and the daily help and a husband, with Gillian Jason, Penelope Holt. (15)

HUDSON'S AMAZING MONEY-MAKING STEAM-DRIVEN RAILWAY PANTOMIME by Richard Drain. Story of a Victorian Railroad king. With the York Shoestring Theater Company. (12)

EXCUSES, EXCUSES by David Edgar. A Yorkshire mill hand makes a lone protest against the arbitrary despotism of capitalism. With Tony Milner, David Quilter, Gillian Rhind, Sally Sanders, James Warrior. (19)

WHO WAS JERUSALEM by John Taylor. A marriage gone wrong. With Jennifer Watts, Michael Stock. (12)

WILL THE KING LEAVE HIS TEAPOT by John Grillo. Sexual skit on the monarchy. With Joanna Wake, Alan Thompson, Philip McGough, John Malcolm. (10)

RECITAL by Tom Gallagher. Yet another sex triangle. Kika Markham, Colin Haigh. (11)

SWEET TALK by Michael Abbensetts (D). George Devine Prizewinning Trinidadian author's play about two blacks in London. With Mona Hammond, Alastair Bain, Lee Davis. (17)

LIMBO by Richard Drain. Baudelaire and his mulatto mistress. With Bob Peck, Merdel Jardine. (18)

SEEING RED by and with Sara Boyes, Sue Glanville, Frances Rifkin. A housewife breaks the shackles of male domination. (15)

THE PETTICOAT REBELLION by D. Emyr Edwards. The Suffragette Movement story. With Nichola McAuliffe, Teresa Jocelyn, Julia Swift, Sara Squires. (15)

RAMSAY MACDONALD: THE LAST TEN DAYS by the Belt 'n' Braces Road Show. A politician's downfall. With Gavin Richards, Vari Sylvestre. (12)

FERN HILL TO ST VINCENT. by Michael Mundell. Dylan Thomas's life through his letters. With David Ryall, the author. (20)

BRIGHT SCENE FADING by Tom Gallagher. Edinburgh journalist goes in search of a friend. With Adrienne Hill, Roderic Leigh, Robert Trotter. (17)

THE CHILDREN'S CRUSADE by Paul Thompson. The National Youth Theater production of epic drama of catastrophic 13th century crusade. With the National Youth Theater Company. (12)

THE TRICK by and with Vass Anderson, Ken Gregory. Critique of Metropolitan life. (11)

OPERATION ISKRA by David Edgar. Prophetic view of urban terrorism in England in 1977. With Pat Rossiter, Mike Harrigan, Ian Banforth. (5)

GEORDIE'S MARCH by Peter Terson. Shipyard workers crusade for human rights. With George Irving, Andy Tomlinson. (11)

MR. IVES' MAGIC PUNCH AND JUDY SHOW by John Grillo, with MEET MR. McIVOR by Peter Roche and A DOG'S LIFE by Peter Roche. Triangular entertainment for the young. With the Unicorn Theater Company. (12)

SEX, COLD CANS & A COFFIN by Chris Johnson. A girl sociology student encounters two old cronies. With Denis Carey, Douglas Storm, Jenny McCracken, Edna Doré (11)

ORPHEUS by Ted Hughes, in a double-bill with his THE WOUND. Poetic drama for Gods, puppets and music. With Kay Barlow, Ian Lowe. (12)

THE PORTER'S PLAY by Anton Gill (D). One-night tryout of documentary black comedy set in a hospital porter's messroom. With the Theater Upstairs Company. (1)

TOUCH AND GO by D.H.Lawrence. World premiere of unperformed drama about miners' rights and women's subjection. With the Questors Theater Company. (7)

INSTRUMENT FOR LOVE by Jennifer Phillips. Mrs. Drury's thoughts turn to love on a Glyndebourne Festival lawn. With Gillian Martell, Dallas Cavell. (18)

VINCENT by W. Gordon Smith. Revival of Leicester Theater production of Van Gogh drama. With Tom Fleming. (3)

STAY WHERE YOU ARE by Oliver Wymark. A cruel game of deceptive appearances. With Mairhi Russell, Lolly Cockerell, Douglas Storm, Christopher Ravenscroft. (11)

WAIT TILL THE SON SHINES NELLIE by Lynda Marchal. A matriarch and her two sons. With Jack Allen, Laurence Carter, Barbara Keogh. (13)

HER ORIGINAL BRITISCHEN BOYS by and with Theater Machine Company. A daily changing improvisation on surrealist themes. (12)

ONE WAY TRIP by Bill Shiers. A musical documentary about transportations to Australia. With Shelbourne Youth Theater company. (2)

MRS. ARGENT by Tom Mallin. Traverse Theater Edinburgh Festival production about the recollections of an actress. With Sylvia Coleridge. (8)

THE REIGN OF TERROR AND THE GREAT MONEY TRICK, musical based on Robert Tressel's novel *The Ragged-Trousered Philanthropists*. With the 7:84 Theater Company. (5)

SYLVIA PLATH Royal Shakespeare Company's dramatized setting of the poetess's writings. With Brenda Bruce, Louise Jameson, Estelle Kohler. (7 in repertory)

THE BLACK HOLE WORSHIPPERS by and with the Curved Space Theater Company. Science fiction thriller with music. (5)

A BUNCH OF FIVES, comprising five one-acters: COAL by Robert Holman, a coal-pit disaster (16); FUN by Geoffrey Case, trouble overtakes the circus (17); COME by David Mowat, a heart-rending search (16); TRUE-LIFE by Chris Allen, what the royal camera revealed (16); GRABBERWITCH by Vicky Ireland, a thriller for 5 to 10 year olds. With Brian Deacon, Michael Harbour, Caroline Hunt, Illona Linthwaite, Stephen Bent; latter play with Chris Allen, Kevin Costello, Katie Heyland.

THE ONLY STREET by Tom Gallagher. Dublin Festival drama of a young man who tries to burn his boats. With John Hunt, Maev Alexander, Peggy Marshall. (20)

HOW NOW? by Michael Sharp. Televiewer's encounter with the foe. With Brian Murphy, Eileen Kennally, Yvonne d'Alpra. (18)

TAKE ME TO YOUR LEADER by John Taylor. A view of planet Earth from outer space. With Glen Beck. (5)

THE AMIABLE COURTSHIP OF MIZ VENUS AND WILD BILL by Pam Gems. The sex trip of a tough Westerner. With Donald Sumpter, Lindsay Ingram, Darlene Johnson, Neil McLaughlan. (18)

OLD KING COLE by Ken Campbell. The royal parents marry off their daughter. With Richard Jacques, Gary Fairhall, Jacqueline Andrews, Ian Ruskin, Jeannie Fisher. (20)

UNDER THE BAMBOO TREE by Tina Brown (D). Three-handed 30-minute one-acter about the vicissitudes of matrimony. With Gavin Reed, Mary Hamilton, Olivia Mundi. (12)

HOW SPARKS LEARNT TO FLY by Derek Smith (D). A fanciful view of the British working man. With Michael Graham Cox, Paul Freeman, Brian Poyser. (17)

A LESSON ON BLOOD AND ROSES by John Wiles (D). Gothic political melodrama set in 1848 with modern overtones. With Ben Kingsley, Rosemary McHale, John Wood. (13 in repertory)

THE LOVE OF LADY MARGARET by Bill Morrison. Aristocratic grass widow's sexual daydreams. With Diane Fairfax, Morris Perry, Katherine Stark. (13)

APROPOS OF THE FALLING SLEET dramatized by Alan Brown and Kyra Dietz from *Notes from the Underground* by Dostoyevsky. With Peter Eyre, Robert Stephens, Cherith Mellor. (15)

LOVEFOOD by Dinah Brook, an opulent dream; CRABS by Sally Ordway, a secretary supports her film-making man; MAL DE MERE by Micheline Wandor, a mother fights her devouring offspring. With Andonia Katsaros, Ian Liston, Michael O'Hagan, Maggie Nicholls. (18)

THE BALLAD OF ROBIN HOOD by Tom Kempinski and Roger Smith. A political revue about Ireland. With Corin Redgrave, Tom Kempinski. (11)

KINGDOM COMING by Bill Lyons. The effect of a false alarm of total war on a country family. With Roger Brierley, Richard O'Callaghan, Malcolm Hayes (12)

THE PLEASURE PRINCIPLE by Snoo Wilson. Thwarted desires of the rich and the lowly. With Julie Covington, Dinsdale Landen. (16)

PARADE OF CATS by Jane Wibberly. Are women cats or bitches? And what about men? With Buzz Goodbody, Sue Todd, the author. (12)

TOUCHSTONE AND JACQUES ARE MISSING by Peter Layton. A new version of *As You Like It*. With Sandra Freeman, David Hepworth. (10)

BLACK FEET IN THE SNOW by Jamal Ali. An Indian's ghastly experience in England. With the Keskidee Theater Company. (5)

REDUNDANCY by C.A. Higgins. Triangular sex drama, tinged with blackmail. With Roger Bruce, Richard Gordon, Beverly Walding. (12)

WOKING, WAPPING and BARKING by Brian Crow and Clay Nixon. The destructive brain-washing capabilities of admass society. With Gary Taylor, Cherry Gilliam, Fraser Cains. (11)

PLASTIC BIRTHDAY by John Kane. About a strange case of infanticide. With Illona Linthwaite, Ian Gelder, Murray Brown. (23)

THE SERIAL by Patrick Carter. How foolish can suburbia get? With Doreen Mantle, Elizabeth Knight, Leonard Kavanagh. (12)

THE RED RED ROBIN by Glenn Chandler. New Christmas comedy. With David Kroll, Elaine Brown. (2)

A WET WINTER NIGHT'S DREAM by Jonathan Marshall. Erring prison governor is saved by his charges. With Royce Ryton, Azad Ali, Philip Player, Maxine Howe, the author. (12)

I WANT by Adrian Henri and Nell Dunn, adapted by Terry and Marsha Gardiner and Geoff Cummant-Word from the novel about love upset by class barriers. With Terry and Marsha Gardiner. (12)

THE PROJECT by Denise Deegan. Science fiction version of the Christmas story. With Martin Chambers, Ray Gatenby, Sally Harrison, Mike Reid. (6)

THEATER MACHINE STRUTS ITS STUFF.

Improvised show by and with Ben Benison, Roddy Maude-Roxby, Rick Morgan, John Muirhead. (10)

THE DINOSAURS and CERTAIN HUMILIATIONS by John Antrobus. Is man antedeluvian? and he lets himself be knocked around. With the Theater Machine Company. (12)

MIND YOUR HEAD by Adrian Mitchell, about revolutionary activities on a London bus, with Nicky Henson, Lynda Marchal; and DOUBLE DOUBLE by James Saunders, funny talk in a garage canteen, with Sam Kelly, Ian Taylor, June Watson. (15)

NEW POSITIONS by Norris Harvey. Double bill comprising HOPSCOTCH, on a Women's Lib. confrontation; and A NEW PROFESSION, the danger of the police state. With Charles Blackmore, Heather Granger, Pat Gordon, Brian Twiddy. (9)

AN EVENING WITH THE GLC by David Pinner. Father and son debate today's issues on TV. With Michael Godfrey, Timothy Munro, Brian Badcoe, Tom Durham. (6)

RIB by Tim Rose-Price. Four sides of a mixed-up guy's personality at war. With the New Company.

JOHESUS, an American tries to sell Jesus; and DR. CROAK SENDS HELP, two muddled inventors at work, by Henry Woolf (D). With Barry Stanton, the author. (10)

MIDNIGHT by Mike Stott. A bizarre home in a Covent Garden Café. With Sheila Kelley, Eddie Reindeer, Dennis Tynsley, David Foxxe. (18)

THE GOOD AND FAITHFUL SERVANT by Joe Orton. Stage version of radio play about human pretentions. With Yvonne Antrobus, Billy Hamon. (24)

COLLECTED WORKS by David Mowat. The self-analysis of Sir Thomas Wyatt's would-be biographer. With Richard Kane, Tony Steedman, Louisa Martin, Adrienne Byrne. (22)

THE PIG OF THE MONTH by Jonathan Lynne (D). Radical writer's dialogue with a perplexed policeman. With David Wood, Michael Robbins, Peter Jolly. (6)

PUCKA RI by Michael Flynn and Dave Callinan. New production and rewrite of Edinburgh Festival Fringe Celtic rock musical. With Edinburgh Fringe Theater Company. (12)

LEIR BLINDI adapted by Steven Rumbelow

from *King Lear.* With Bjorg Amadottir, Stuart Cox, Piers Meadly, Tim Jones, David Walsh, Nigel Watson. (21)

SPASM by Michael O'Leary. Drama of isolation. With Carrie Lee Baker, Penny Lincoln, John Vine, James Snell. (18)

GREASY SPOON by and with Spike Milligan, Christopher Langhoun, Pamela Obermeyer, David Freedman, Sue Jones-Davis. Forty minutes of meaty music and saucy sketches. (12)

SCENE by James Dawson, the ritual killing of a child, with Eileen Pollock, John Turnbull; in a double-bill with the Edinburgh Pool Lunch Hour Theater's production of THE MOSHE DAYAN EXTRAVAGANZA by Michael Almaz, the case for Israel, with Tutte Lemkow. (16)

THE BLIND SALAMANDER by Tim Rose-Price. A blind man recovers his sight. With Martin Read, Dennis Clinton. (24)

THE KING AND THE SHIRT dramatization by Matyelok Gibbs, Margot Smith, and Olwen Wymark of classical fables. With the Unicorn Theater Company (16)

ARE YOU HAWK OR DOVE? by Rosalie Alford (D). Seventy-year-old unsuccessful labor candidate's first play, about marital relations. With April Walker, Joy Allen, Ian Price. (1)

BLUBBER by John Grillo. How Blubber saved the world. With Harry Ditson, Carolyn Wilde, Norman Gates. (20)

THE ILLEGAL IMMIGRANTS in a triple-bill with CERTAIN HUMILIATIONS and THE DINOSAURS by John Antrobus. *The Illegal Immigrants* is a study of Indians trying to settle in England. With Ben Benison, Rick Morgan, John Muirhead, the author. (16)

THE MOTOR SHOW by Steve Gooch and Paul Thompson. Sixty years of the automobile industry. With Anne Engel, Jim McManus, Stuart Barren. (15)

BODY AND SOUL by T-Bone Wilson. A black author's cry from the heart. With Claudia Winston, the author. (14)

FOUR FROM THE END by John Chiltern (D). Bridegroom faces an uncertain future. With David Pearl, Jill Richards, Christine Paul, Anthony Trent. (17)

EDITH EVANS. . . . AND FRIENDS by and with Edith Evans. A nostalgic anthology of her favorite roles and poems (11)

SOLZHENITSYN, an anthology devised by Michael Bakewell. With Freddie Jones. (14)

DAVE AND GOLIATH by and with Rod Beddall, Warren Hooper, and Chris Jordan What filthy lucre does to the music industry. With the Nice Pussy group, the authors. (16)

A NAVAL OCCASION by Henry Woolf. Two aging sisters try to recapture the gaiety of bygone days. With Mike Pratt, Bridget Armstrong, Susan Williamson. (18)

THE KING by Stewart Conn. A couple mistreat their gardener. With Michael Keating, Diane Mercer, Christopher Saul. (15)

MEETING ENDS by Francis Warner. 1973 Festival production of author's satire on the permissive society. With Katharine Schofield, Eire Garrett, (21)

THE GENTLE ART OF PORNOGRAPHY, anthology devised by Michael Bakewell and Diana Tyler. With Prunella Scales, Timothy West. (14)

JOHNNY by Robert Thornton (D). 1971 George Devine prizewinning drama about a working lad who learns about life the hard way. With Paul Rosebury, Robert Keegan, Adrienne Bryne. (1)

A 'NEVOLENT SOCIETY by Mary O'Malley (D). The daydreams of three London Jews. With John Clive, Leslie Glazer, Roland Macleod, Penelope Parry. (6)

SAD BEAT UP by Stephen Poliakoff. The violence that accompanies two lads on the run. With Bruce Robinson, Michael Tarn. (10)

THE SALESMAN by Johnny Speaight. Stage version of TV play about a suburban housewife's surprise visitor. With Michael Craze, Denise Dwyer. (8+)

RETROGRIM'S PROGRESS by and with Chris Langham, John Lloyd, Chris Reid. New view of *Pilgrim's Progress.* (17)

A STORM BABY by Terry Meech (D). Events in the life of a black medical student. With the Calabash Artists' Company. (10)

THE DRESSING ROOM by Barry Stacey. Theater agent looks backstage. With David Masterman (later Glyn Sweet), Diana Lambert. (15)

THE RECRUITING OFFICER shamelessly stolen from Farquhar, Brecht and the Ministry of

Defense, by and with the Belt and Braces Company. (5)

SHIVVERS by Stanley Eveling. Glasgow Traverse Theater production of a black comedy about an unwholesome trio. With Anthony Haygarth, Deirdre Costello, Bill Stewart. (18+)

KILL THE KIDS by Herb Greer. American-born London author's satire on the consumer society. With Cherry Gillioam, Leslie Pitt. (14+)

THE BOLTING SISTERS by Olwen Wymark. Two ladies rob a bank. With the Unicorn Theater Company. (11+)

BODYWORK by Jennifer Phillips (D). Two young women go through life. With Polly Adams, Joanna Dunham. (9+)

THE CHESSMASTER by David Shellan (D). Life catches up with an obsessed old man. With Stephen Bateman, Julia Nelson. (9+)

SOME AMERICAN PLAYS PRODUCED IN LONDON

THE MUTATION SHOW, collectively created by the Open Theater. With the Open Theater Company. (7 in repertory)

NIGHTWALK (work-in-progress) devised by Jean-Claude van Itallie, Sam Shepard, Megan Terry, Wallace Stevens, Ted Hughes, Bob Dylan. With the Open Theater Company. (6 in repertory)

TERMINAL, text by Susan Yankowitz. With the Open Theater Company. (4 in repertory)

GREASE by Jim Jacobs and Warren Casey. With Richard Gere, Stacey Gregg. (258)

WEST SIDE STORY by Arthur Laurents, Stephen Sondheim and Leonard Bernstein. With Jim Smilie, Rosamund Shelley, Clovissa Newcombe, Jackie Bristow. (95)

THE HOLY GHOSTLY by Sam Shepard. With Gordon Sterne, Glen Beck, Philip Fowler. (10)

HALLOWEEN by Leonard Melfi. With John Dunhill, June Whitaker. (18)

THE LOVE COURSE by A.R. Gurney Jr. With Michael McClain, Margaret Robertson, Nicolette Marvin, Lee Walker. (11)

FINISHING TOUCHES by Jean Kerr. With Wendy Craig, David Knight. (47)

PARADISE GARDENS EAST by Frank Gagliano. With Helena Stevens, Miles Taylor, Rudi Stussi, Emily Richard, Nigel Anthony. (11)

THE KING AND I by Richard Rodgers and Oscar Hammerstein II. With Peter Wyngarde, Sally Ann Howes. (2684)

SECTION NINE by Philip Magdalany. Produced by the Royal Shakespeare Company at the Place Theater. Opened October 11, 1973. (Closed December 6, 1973) Revived at the Aldwych Theater January 23, 1974. (Closed April

23, 1974) (47 in repertory)

Adrian Mackenzie	Harry Towb
Vivien 532	Judy Geeson
Jasper 906	Geoffrey Hutchings
Marlon 845	Gareth Hunt
Fenwick 747	Stephen Moore
Winifred 601	Margaret Whiting
Sen. Sinclair Caldwell	David Waller
Gen. Enfield Muster	Colin Blakely
Somerset Swayze, MD	Patrick Godfrey
Ubell Untermeyer	Phil Brown
Young Man	Jonathan Kent
Man	Peter Schofield
Attendant	Joe Melia

Section Nine Workers, Marines: Brian Anthony, Christopher Ellison, Nick Llewellyn, David Sparks, Joseph Charles, Lee Crawford, Paul Gaymon, Joe Marcell.

Directed by Charles Marowitz; design, Carl Toms; lighting, Michael Murray.

Place: Washington, D.C. The play was presented in two parts.

World premiere of an American author's pacifist fantasy-comedy staged as part of RSC's experimental season (15 in repertory) and then transferred to the Aldwych (32 in repertory); a gay satire on the C.I.A. in which both cops and spies are after an indiscreetly hidden atomic formula that threatens to destroy the world, if its rulers refuse to love one another.

Trader Selkirk replaced Jonathan Kent 1/23/74. Norman Rossington replaced Colin Blakely.

PIPPIN by Roger O. Hirson and Stephen Schwartz. With Paul Jones, Elisabeth Welch, Diane Langton. (86)

THE RECORDER by Martin Duberman. With Ramsay Williams, Peter Banks. (12)

ELIZABETH I by Paul Foster. With Michael Feast, Carole Hayman, Paul Moriarty, David Sands. (15)

EPIPHANY by Lewis John Carlino. With Barry and Wendy Donelly. (12)

GOMES by David Swift and Sidney Sheldon. World premiere of U.S. drama about a sinister, power-hungry butler. With Roy Dotrice, Rachel Kempson. (5)

ZORBA by Joseph Stein, John Kander and Fred Ebb. With Alfred Marks, Miriam Karlin. (21)

GEOGRAPHY OF A HORSE DREAMER by Sam Shepard. World premiere of commissioned play about the cannibalism of genius. With Kenneth Cranham, Bob Hoskins, Neil Johnston, Stephen Rea. (21)

BOTTICELLI by Terrence McNally and CLERINGER'S TRIAL by Joseph Heller. With John Duttine, John Bay, Steven Samuels. (10)

OH KAY! by P.G. Wodehouse, Guy Bolton and George Gershwin. With Amanda Barrie, Jeremy Child. (98+)

SOMETHING UNSPOKEN by Tennessee Williams. With Marcella Markham, Mavis Villiers (later Gudrun Ure). (28)

THE SHOW-OFF by George Kelly. With Al Mancini, Sue Carpenter, Jo Tillinger, Doreen Mantle. (23)

A STREETCAR NAMED DESIRE by Tennessee Williams. Hillard Elkins' production presented by Bernard Delfont and Richard M. Mills for the Bernard Delfont Organization Ltd. at the Piccadilly Theater. Opened March 14, 1974. (90+)

Negro Woman . . . . Louise Nelson
Eunice Hubbell . . . . Meg Davies
Stanley Kowalski . . . . Martin Shaw
Stella Kowalski . . . . Morag Hood
Steve Hubbell . . . . Bryan Stanion
Harold Mitchell . . . . Joss Ackland
Mexican Woman . . . . Ann Tirard
Blanche Du Bois . . . . Claire Bloom
Pablo Gonzales . . . . Tony Sibbald
A Young Collector . . . . . . Kim Fortune
Nurse . . . . Elspeth MacNaughton
Doctor . . . . Rod Beacham

Directed by Edwin Sherin; design, Patrick Robertson; costumes, Beatrice Dawson; lighting, Richard Pilbrow, Molly Friedel; sound, Antony Horder.

First staged by Elia Kazan at the Ethel Barrymore Theater in New York on 12/3/47. This new production was the first major revival in England since the Laurence Olivier production, based on the Kazan original, at the Aldwych Theater on 10/12/49.

COWBOY MOUTH by Sam Shepard and Patti Smith. With Donald Sumpter, Lindsey Ingram. (10)

LITTLE OCEAN by Sam Shepard. With Caroline Hutchinson, O-Lan Sheppard, Dinah Stabb. (12)

CHILDREN by A.R. Gurney Jr., suggested by a story by John Cheever. World premiere of U.S. drama about how childish adults can be. With Constance Cummings, Toby Robins, Bob Sherman, Sarah Marshall. (38)

NIGHTLIGHT by Kenneth H. Brown. With Maureen Pryor, Myles Reithermann, Sheila Ballantine, Peter Miles. (20)

THAT CHAMPIONSHIP SEASON by Jason Miller. With Broderick Crawford. (30+)

SOME FOREIGN PLAYS PRODUCED IN LONDON

THE MOTHER by Bertolt Brecht, translated by Steve Gooch. With Mary Sheen, Kevin Costello. (18)

PLAY STRINDBERG by Friedrich Duerrenmatt, translated by James Kirkup. With Patrick Allen, Freddie Jones, Yvonne Mitchell. (20)

MACBETT by Eugene Ionesco, adapted by Charles Marowitz. London guest visit of Belgrade Theater of Coventry production, to Globe Playhouse festival. With Harry H. Corbett, Terry Scott, Frances Cuka. (16)

THE REMOVALISTS by David Williamson (D). Australian triple prize-winning drama. With Brian Croucher, Ed Deveraux, Darlene Johnson, Mark McManus. (18)

GBANA BENDU by Yulisa Amadu Maddy. Social satire on African traditions. With the Dark and Light Theater Company. (9)

DUET FOR ONE VOICE by Jean Cocteau, translated by Peter Meyer. With Jane Williams. (10)

THE BACCHAE by Euripides, adapted by Wole Soyinka. With Constance Cummings, Martin Shaw, Paul Curran, John Shrapnel. (18 in repertory)

THE PETTY BOURGEOIS by Maxim Gorki, translated by Margaret Weltlin. With Mary Lewisohn, Nick Stringer, Geoffrey Freshwater. (12)

THAT FUNNY OLD MAN by Tadeusz Rozewicz. With Lee Fox. (17)

MISS JULIE VERSUS EXPRESSIONISM (and THE ZOO STORY by Edward Albee) adapted by Steven Berkoff from Strindberg's drama. With the London Theater Group Company. (23)

TODOS LOS DIAS, CINCO DIAS by Mario Benedetti and TRES HISTORIAS PARA SER CONTADAS by Osvaldo Dragun. With Lucie Guillon, Jorge Bosso. (4)

AUGUSTINE by the Marquis de Sade. With the Curved Space Company. (18)

THE JEWISH WIFE and THE INFORMER by Bertolt Brecht, translated by Eric Bentley. With Nigel Hawthorne, Celestine Randall. (11)

DRUMS IN THE NIGHT by Bertolt Brecht, a new adaptation by C.P. Taylor. Produced by the Traverse Theater Club and Foco-Novo Productions at the Hampstead Theater Club. Opened September 11, 1973.) (Closed September 29, 1973.) (17)

Music Narrator	Andy Smith
Waiter	Ken Morley
Kragler; Balicke	Stephen Rea
Glubb	Christopher Martin
Mrs. B.	Linda Polan
Anne	Petra Markham
Murk	Tom Marshall
Babusch	William Hoyland
Marie	Irene Bradshaw

Directed by Roland Rees; design, Moshe Mussman; lighting, Graeme Dott.

The first London production of the author's first full-length play ever to be staged (in Berlin, 1924) in a new adaptation specially made by the Glaswegian dramatist at the Edinburgh Festival, 1973.

THE SHOEMAKERS by Stanislaw Ignacy Witkiewicz. With Maurice Colbourne, Stafford Gordon, Robin Murphy, Natasha Morgan. (23)

AND THEY PUT HANDCUFFS ON THE FLOWERS by Fernando Arrabal, translated by Charles Marowitz. Produced by the Open Space Theater at the Open Space Theater. Opened September 12, 1973. (Closed October 13, 1973) (28)

Amiel	Antony Milner
Katar	Malcolm Storry
Pronos	Ian McDiarmid
Tosan	Don McIver
Falidia	Carole Hayman
Lelia	Candida Fawsitt
Child	June Page

Directed by Fernando Arrabal and Petrika Ionescu; design, Robin Don; costumes, Linda Hemming; masks, Don McIver; lighting, Jenny Cane.

After staging the world premiere of Charles Marowitz's translation at the O'Casey Theater (Mercer Arts Center) in New York on April 21, 1972, Arrabal was invited by Marowitz to restage it in London. Though his name figures on the program as director, Petrika Ionescu did the actual staging. The play was presented without intermission.

SIZWE BANSI IS DEAD devised by Athol Fugard, John Kani and Winston Ntshona. Produced by the Serpent Players at the Theater Upstairs. Opened September 20, 1973. (90+ in repertory)

Styles	John Kani
Bantu	John Kani
Sizwe Bansi	Winston Ntshona

Directed by Athol Fugard; design, Douglas Heap; lighting, Michael Alston, David Longmuir; assistant designer, Harriet Geddes.

First performed in the Theater Upstairs 9/20/73 for 30 performances (closed 10/27/73); transferred to Royal Court Theater 8/1/74 (18 in repertory) as part of the South African Season, and to the Ambassadors Theater 10/4/74 (42+ in repertory) as part of a two-play season, with *The Island* by the same authors. The play is about the keystone of white control over South Africa's vast black majority, the "Dompass." The endorsements and stamps in this book decide where Africans may live, what work they may do, where they may work, if and where they may move, if, where and when their wives and children may live with them, etc. Serpent Players is a drama group based in the African township of New Brighton, Port Elizabeth. The play was presented without intermission.

ESKER MIKE AND HIS WIFE AGILUK by Herschel Hardin, STRAWBERRY FIELDS by Mike Hollingsworth, BAGDAD SALOON by George F. Walker, PENETRATION by Lawrence Russell, THE NEW STEP by Leonard Cohen (12 each in repertory); I REMEMBER DALI WHEN HE WAS JUST A LITTLE KID AND COULDN'T KEEP HIS NOSE CLEAN by Lawrence Russell (6), WE THREE, YOU AND I by Bill Greenland (9), DEATH by Larry Fineberg (6), THE PRINCE OF NAPLES by George F. Walker (3). Four-week festival of Canadian plays included the above. With the Factory Lab of Toronto Company.

THE MAGIC OF PANTALEONE, a commedia dell' arte entertainment, coupled with THE BALD PRIMA DONNA by Eugene Ionesco. With Brian Protheroe, Robin Scobey, Barbara Berkery. (17)

IN SEARCH OF JUSTICE by Bertolt Brecht, translated by Eric Bentley. With the Moloch Productions Company. (16)

HELLO AND GOODBYE by Athol Fugard. Royal Shakespeare Company revival. With Janet Suzman, Ben Kingsley. (13 in repertory)

THE WOLF by Ferenc Molnar, translated by Henric Hirsch and Frank Hauser. Produced by the Oxford Playhouse Company and by Bernard Delfont and Richard M. Mills for the Bernard Delfont Organization, Ltd. at the Apollo Theater. Opened October 23, 1973. (Closed May 18, 1974) (239)

Zagon . . . . Philip Voss
Mikhal . . . . John York
Head Waiter . . . . Nicholas Amer
Wine Waiter . . . . Brian Carroll
1st Waiter . . . . Patrick Monckton
2d Waiter . . . . Thom Delaney
Groom . . . . Ray Gatenby
Vilma . . . . Judi Dench
Kelemen . . . . Leo McKern
George Szabo . . . . . . .Edward Woodward
Nanny . . . . Gwen Nelson
Maid . . . . .Marilyn Smithwick
Jani . . . . .William or Jeremy Booker
Conductor . . . . Patrick Monckton
Countess . . . . Valerie Lush
Miczi . . . . Gwen Nelson
Secretary . . . . Nicholas Amer
Mrs. Ritter . . . . Joan Ryan
Lackeys: Brian Carroll, Patrick Monckton, Thom Delaney, Ray Gatenby
Directed by Frank Hauser; design, Alix Stone; lighting, Robert Bryan.
Time: 1911. Place: Budapest. Act I: The dining room of a fashionable hotel, February, 7.30 P.M. Act II, Scene 1: The drawing room of the Kelemen's flat, half an hour later. Scene 2: The Countess's Palace. Act III, The Kelemens' flat.

Henric Hirsch and Frank Hauser's adaptation of this famous Hungarian comedy of uxorious jealousy was originally performed at the Oxford Playhouse 9/4/73 and transferred to the Apollo in London 10/23/73, to the Queen's Theater 12/3/74 and to the New London 4/3/74. Originally staged in Budapest in 1912, it was first produced in New York in a translation by Leo Ditrichsen in 1914 by David Belasco and again in 1926 as The Tale of the Wolf.

Milo O'Shea replaced Leo McKern, Prunella Scales replaced Judi Dench, John York replaced Edward Woodward 4/22/74.

CATSPLAY by Istvan Orkeny. With Elisabeth Bergner, Margaret Rawlings, Maggie Fitzgibbon, Harold Kasket. (25)

BIODRAME, incorporating BIODRAME by Serge Behar, MARRIAGE DE LUX by Serge Behar, ICH BIN by Paul Portner. With the Roy Hart Theater Company. (18)

SATURDAY SUNDAY MONDAY by Eduardo de Filippo, English adaptation by Keith Waterhouse and Willis Hall. Produced by the National Theater Company at the Old Vic Theater. Opened November 9, 1973. (Closed February 16, 1974) (35 in repertory)

Antonio . . . . Laurence Olivier
Rosa . . . . Joan Plowright
Peppino . . . . Frank Finlay
Aunt Meme . . . . Mary Griffiths
Attilio . . . . Martin Shaw
Raffaele . . . . David Healy
Roberto . . . . .Gawn Grainger
Rocco . . . . .Nicholas Clay
Guilianella . . . . Louise Purnell
Federico . . . . Clive Merrison
Maria . . . . Maggie Riley
Luigi Ianniello . . . . Denis Quilley
Elena . . . . Jeanne Watts
Virginia . . . . Anna Carteret
Michel . . . . Desmond McNamara
Catiello . . . . Harry Lomax
Dr. Cefercola . . . . David Graham
Directed by Franco Zeffirelli; settings, Franco Zeffirelli; costumes, Raimonda Gaetani; lighting, Leonard Tucker
Place: The Priore family's apartment in Naples. Act I: Saturday. Act II: Sunday. Act III: Monday.

This adaptation was written specially for the National Theater and staged by Franco Zeffirelli at Laurence Olivier's invitation with the company all simulating something approaching Neopolitan accents. The play won for its 74-year-old author the Evening Standard 1974 award for the best play of the season in London. The original play was staged by De Filippo at the Teatro Quirino in Rome in November 1959. It deals with family incomprehension, the conflict between interests and affections within a small group, living at close quarters.

A CONCERT FOR SAINT OVIDE by Antonio Buero Vallejo, translated by Victor Dixon. With the Unity Theater Company. (36)

THE RIDE ACROSS LAKE CONSTANCE by Peter Handke. With Faith Brook, Nicky Henson, Alan Howard, Nicola Pagett. (60)

LIFE IS A DREAM by Calderon de la Barca. With the Another Theater Company. (17)

DALABANI by Mukhtar Mustafa, first performance of Nigerian play about African myths personified, in a double bill with THE TRIALS OF BROTHER JERO by Wole Soyinka. With Frank Cousins, Amadu Maddy. (11)

PRESIDENT WILSON IN PARIS by Ron Blair. With Eleanor Bron, Richard Kane, Clive Revill. (12)

THE MAIDS by Jean Genet. All-male production inhibited by author's agent after opening performance. With Lindsay Kemp, Tony Meyer, David Moyn. (1)

DEATH AND THE DEVIL by Frank Wede-kind. With Nicholas Day, Louise Mansfield. (6)

THE MAZE by Ladislav Smocek. With David Foxxe, Neil McLaughlan, Janet McAdam (11)

HOME LIFE by Georges Courteline and RE-SPECTABLE WOMEN by Georges Feydeau, translated and adapted by David Cohen. With Christopher Benjamin, Penelope Lee, David Nettheim, Tina Greatrex. (12)

THE ISLAND devised by Athol Fugard, John Kani and Winston Ntshona. In Royal Court Theater's South African season, later in reper-tory with *Sizwe Bansi Is Dead* by the same au-thors. Two gaol birds stage a play on Robben Island. With John Kani, Winston Ntshona. (26 + in repertory)

THE HEROES by Claude Duneton, adapted by Alan Drury. World premiere of French drama about linguistics. With Deborah Davies, Edna Doré, Murray Noble. (23)

FREEDOM FROM CLEMENS by Tankred Dorst. With Brendan Ellis, Zelfon Draz, J.A. Cashman. (12)

GHOSTS by Henrik Ibsen, translated by Mi-chael Meyer. Produced by the Greenwich Theater at the Greenwich Theater. Opened Janu-ary 17, 1974. (Closed May 4, 1974) (31 in reper-tory)
Mrs Alving . . . . .Irene Worth
Oswald Alving . . . . .Peter Eyre
Pastor Manders . . . . Robert Stephens
Engstrand . . . . Antony Brown
Regina Engstrand . . . . Nicola Pagett
   Directed by Jonathan Miller; scenery, Patrick Robertson; costumes, Rosemary Vercoe; light-ing, Nick Chelton.
   Staged by Jonathan Miller in a permanent set as part of a three-play season under the generic heading of *Family Romances*, that also included *Hamlet* and *The Seagull*. The first English per-formance of *Ghosts* in 1891 evoked a barrage of highly critical notices. The present production, though using a new translation, was the 27th on the London stage. The play was presented in two parts.

STATEMENTS AFTER AN ARREST UN-DER THE IMMORALITY ACT by Athol Fu-gard. The horror of apartheid. With Yvonne Bryceland, Ben Kingsley. (10 in repertory)

FROM MOSES TO MAO by and with Jérôme Savary's Le Grand Magic Circus of Paris. (70)

THE PIG BANK by Eugene Labiche. With the Half Moon Company. (23)

THE SEAGULL by Anton Chekhov, translated by Elisaveta Fen. Produced by the Greenwich Theater at the Greenwich Theater. Opened Janu-ary 31, 1974. (Closed May 4, 1974) (24 in reper-tory)
Mme. Arkadina . . . . .Irene Worth
Trepliov . . . . .Peter Eyre
Sorin . . . . George Howe
Zaryechnaia . . . . Maureen O'Brien
Shamrayev . . . . Antony Brown
Polena Andryeevna . . . . June Jago
Masha . . . . Nicola Pagett
Trigorin . . . . Robert Stephens
Dorn . . . . Anthony Nicholls
Medviedenko . . . . .Philip Lowrie
Yakov . . . . .Lionel Guyett
Chef . . . . Graham Seed
Housemaid . . . . Jennifer Tudor
   Directed by Jonathan Miller; setting, Patrick Robertson; costumes, Rosemary Vercoe; light-ing, Nick Chelton
   Staged in a permanent setting as part of three-play season under the generic heading of *Family Romances*. This was a reproduction of Jonathan Miller's original production of the play at the 1973 Chichester Festival. The play was presented in two parts.

D'ARTAGNAN AMOUREUX by Philippe Dauchez. With the Atelier Théâtre Mobile of Paris. (3)

THE MAIDS by Jean Genet, translated by Minos Volanakis. With Glenda Jackson, Susan-nah York, Vivienne Merchant. (25)

THE WALTZ OF THE TOREADORS by Jean Anouilh, translated by Lucienne Hill. With Tre-vor Howard, Coral Browne, Zena Walker. (122+)

THE STRANGER by August Strindberg, A TRAGEDIAN INSPITE OF HIMSELF by An-ton Chekhov, THE UNKNOWN GENERAL by René de Obaldia. With Ian Talbot, Christo-pher Streuli, Anne White. (12)

BREMEN COFFEE (Bremer Freiheit) by Rainer Werner Fassbinder, translated by An-thony Vivis. With Leonard Maguire, Linda Mar-lowe (11)

HENRY IV by Luigi Pirandello, translated by Stephen Rich. With Rex Harrison, Yvonne Mitchell, James Villiers. (101)

JEUX ET MASQUES by and with the Mum-menschanz Company of Zurich. (12)

THE SHOW-FACTORY OF THE ABSO-LUTE by Karel Capek. With Student Theater Group of Gliwice, Poland. (2)

THE WOOD DEMON by Anton Chekhov. With Robert Eddison, Marian Diamond, Sheila Reid, Robin Ellis, John Woodvine, Ian McKellen. (13 in repertory)

LET'S GO UNDER THE RAINBOW by Georgi Markhov, translated by Penny Haymen. World premiere of exiled Bulgarian author's drama about events in a terminal ward. With Kurt Christian, Simon Cuff, Julian Somers. (12)

PAINTING A WALL by David Lan (D). World premiere of South African writer's play about the hardships of life in his native land. With Saul Reichlin, Tony Osler, Alex Mavro. (18)

YOU WERE SO SWEET WHEN YOU WERE LITTLE by Jean Anouilh, translated by Lucienne Hill. With Angela Pleasence, Paul Jones. (20)

THE JUMP by Alfio Bernabei. An Italian author's English-language drama about the unsolved Pinelli and Valpreda case in 1969 in Milan. With Maggie Bowman, George Bryson, Raymond Cross. (15)

RULING THE ROOST (Le Dindon) by Georges Feydeau. With John Woodvine, Tenniel Evans, Sheila Reid, Robin Ellis, Caroline Blakiston. (13)

DOMINOES by Khanokh Levin. With John Bluthal, Richard Hampton, Dorothy Vernon. (18)

BIRD CHILD by David Lan. World premiere of South African author's comedy about privilege in a white Cape Town suburb. With Marjie Lawrence, Nigel Hawthorne, Jemoko Debayo, Janette Legge. (16)

SAINT JOAN OF THE STOCKYARDS by Bertolt Brecht. With Rynagh O'Grady, Philip McGough. (18)

NORM AND AHMED by Alexander Buzo. With Terence Bayler, Tariq Yunus. (17)

LES TROIS CENTS DERNIÈRES by and with Rufus, from Paris. (3)

LES CHAISES by Eugène Ionesco. With the Atelier Théâtre Mobile Company of Paris. (3)

ABEL, WHERE IS YOUR BROTHER? by Julius Edliss, translated by Ariadne Nicolaieff. With Leonard Rossiter, Jerome Willis, Rula Lenska. (5+)

SPRING AWAKENING by Frank Wedekind, translated by Edward Bond. Produced by the National Theater at the Old Vic. Opened May 28, 1974. (4+)

Children:

Melchior Gabor	Peter Firth
Moritz Stiefel	Michael Kitchen
Hänschen Rilow	Dai Bradley
Ernst Röbel	Gerard Ryder
Otto	David Dixon
Georg Zirschnitz	Keith Skinner
Robert	Martin Howells
Lammermeier	Christopher Guard
Wendla Bergmann	Veronica Quilligan
Martha Bessel	Jane Carr
Thea	Jenny Agutter
Ilse	Patti Love

Boys in the Reformatory:

Dieter	Rupert Frazer
Reinhold	Ian McKenzie
Rupert	James Smith
Helmut	Glyn Grain
Gaston	Bryan Brown

Parents:

Herr Gabor	Joseph O'Conor
Herr Stiefel	James Mellor
Frau Gabor	Susan Engel
Frau Bergmann	Beryl Reid
Ina Mueller	Judith Paris

Teachers:

Headmaster Sunstroke	William Squire
Prof. Gutgrinder	Kenneth Benda
Prof. Bonebreaker	Alex McCrindle
Prof. Tonguetwister	Stephen Williams
Prof. Flyswatter	Peter Needham
Prof. Thickstick	Kenneth Mackintosh
Prof. Apelard	Colin Fay

Other Adults:

Masked Man	Cyril Cusack
Dr. Lemonade	Daniel Thorndike
Dr. Procrustes	Alan Hay
Rev. Baldbelly	Pitt Wilkinson
Fastcrawler	Alan Hay
Uncle Probst	Peter Rocca
Friend Zieg	Glyn Grain
Locksmith	Pitt Wilkinson

Directed by Bill Bryden; design, Geoffrey Scott; costumes, Deirdre Clancy; lighting, Andy Phillips.

Time: 1891–1892. Place: A provincial town in Germany. The play was presented in two parts.

First staged by Max Reinhardt at the Kammerspiele, Berlin, 11/20/06, *Frühlings Erwachen* was described by its German author as a "Children's Tragedy". It was first produced in London by the Sunday Theater Club at the Grafton Theater 3/29/31, causing a considerable stir because of its author's frank discussion of the sexual problems of adolescents. It was revived in a new translation by Thomas Osborn at the Royal Court Theater 4/4/63 for a Sunday night performance and then put on for a run to members only of the English Stage Society at the Royal Court Theater 4/19/65 to evade the objections of the censorship to its alleged obscenity. A production in German by the Bochum Schauspielhaus Company directed by Peter Zadek was given at the Aldwych Theater 4/24/67 during the 1967 World Theater Season. An earlier plan to stage it at the National Theater was frustrated by the censor's ban before his demise in 1968. Bond's translation was specially done for the National Theater.

LES VEUVES (The Widows) by François Billetdoux. With Olivier Hussenot, and the Espace Cardin Company of Paris.

SUPERMALE by Alfred Jarry. With Christopher Ward, Jill Aplin. (4+)

THE SEASON ELSEWHERE
IN EUROPE

By Ossia Trilling

IN Western Germany the competition between managers to bid for the rights to an increasing number of new dramas by German-speaking authors became a central talking point in theatrical circles, just as the previous years' talk of co-determination and shared responsibility as between management and employees seemed to be dying out. This was not the case in Eastern Germany or East Berlin, where repertorial policy was based on quite different premises, though box office factors must continue to be decisive in both capitalist and socialist systems. So, perhaps, when all is said and done, quality is what counts. The proof of this lay in the continuing success of East European authors in the West. Paradoxically, in the reverse direction, only plays like those of Peter Weiss and other ideologically acceptable writers normally reached Eastern stages. The East German author Plenzdorf's *The New Sorrows of Young W.* continued to be staged throughout the West, alongside the works of Peter Hacks and of such writers, proscribed in the East, as the Czech dramatists Pavel Kahout and Vaclav Havel. These, though silenced at home, found outlets in West Germany: Havel in Baden-Baden where his latest political satire, masquerading as boulevard comedy, *The Saviors,* about the unwelcome intrusion of faceless deliverers from oppression who only substitute one form of dictatorship for another, was given its world premiere; and Kohout in Ingolstadt, represented by the last two one-acters in his trilogy of political menace, *Disaster in the Attic* and *Fire in the Cellar.*

It was no coincidence that the major new works of Western authors also fell into the category of political theater in the widest sense. Hartmut Lange, the East German self-exiled author who has been living in the West for nine years, was responsible for two new plays, one in West Berlin and one in Stuttgart, the former dealing with Stalinism and the latter with the role of the artist in society. *Staschek, or the Life Of Ovid,* in Stuttgart, was a political allegory about the difference between Eastern and Western attitudes, the problem of patronage and the pressures exerted by authority, in which the titular hero, who first made his appearance in Lange's earlier drama of *Marski,* wanders through the ages, meeting poets and philosophers of many lands in his search for identity. A social parable inspired by the Frankenstein legend was Wolfgang Deichsel's latest drama of terror entitled *Terror Cell,* performed at the Frankfurt People's Theater or

129

"TAT", which stands for the "Theater am Turm," of which the writer Rainer Werner Fassbinder became the new manager at the end of the season, and not to be confused with the City Theater where Peter Palitzsch remained in control. Among several outstanding productions at the last-named were *Barbarian Comedy*, adapted and staged by Argentinian director Augusto Fernandes from three one-acters by the Spaniard Ramon del Valle-Inclan, and a modernized version of the 45-year-old *Revolt in the Reformatory* by Peter Martin Lampel (1894–1965), which caused a furore when first staged in 1928 and led to wide-ranging reforms in Germany's penal system and the handling of adolescent delinquents. This, staged by Palitzsch himself, and Wedekind's *Spring Awakening*, also staged with great ingenuity by Palitzsch, went on to receive rave notices at the annual Review of German Theater in Berlin. The former, which shows how exasperated prisoners take their revenge on brutal authoritarianism in an orgy of destruction, had lost none of its irony or topicality. The same may be said of Wedekind's tragedy of puberty, parental ignorance and social oppression.

English authors of political plays, or of plays with a social conscience, were also represented with increased frequency in West German theaters, among them Trevor Griffiths, whose *Occupations* was done simultaneously in Cologne and in Dusseldorf; Edward Bond, whose *Lear* and *The Sea* received numerous productions; and James Saunders, whose Brechtian adaptation of a Kleist novella as *Hans Kohlhaas* seemed tailor-made for the German stage. By contrast, Peter Hacks, whose style has been getting further and further away from the Brechtian idiom of his earlier plays, found a ready response in the case of such poetic dramas as *Adam and Eve*, staged with some imagination by Stephan Stroux in Gottingen within days of its world premiere in Dresden in East Germany, a Marxist morality play on the fall of man, that was subsequently staged at the Thalia Theater in Hamburg and in many other towns. At the Hamburg Schauspielhaus under Ivan Nagel, a richly endowed repertory included the German premieres of Peter Shaffer's *Equus* and David Rudkin's *Ashes,* and a charming vaudeville version of the 19th century Austrian black comedy of *The Man Torn in Two* by Nestroy. An invitation to the English avant-garde director Pip Simmons resulted in an abortive attempt to stage a documentary about the terrorist gang of Baaden-Meinhof, which was prevented by demonstrating left-wingers from ever taking off and eventually saw the light of day in Bochum. The center of gravity, theatrically speaking, remained firmly based in this industrial city under the inspired leadership of Peter Zadek, who, however, decided to share managerial responsibility with two fellow-directors from the end of the season to enable him to devote more attention to directing plays. Among the numerous hits at his theater were the Paul Green-Kurt Weill musical *Johnny Johnson,* the German premiere of the Ben Hecht-Charles MacArthur *The Front Page, King Lear* acted in a movie house in an attempt to gain a new audience for Shakespeare, in which Zadek had a youngish actor, Ulrich Windgruber as Lear and an actress, Hannelore Hoger, as the Fool, Christopher Hampton's *Savages,* and a revolutionary version of Chekhov's *The Seagull,* which was also Zadek's eighth play to be presented at a Berlin Theater Review.

In neighbouring Essen, the retiring director, Erich Schumacher, staged a pallid version of Rolf Hochhuth's anti-NATO comedy *Lysistrate,* which had the women of a Greek island stage a revolt on Aristophanic lines. Ellen Schwiers gave a touching performance in the title role of a Greek pacifist-schoolteacher on the eve of the Colonels' seizure of power; the play opened on the same night in a very different production in Vienna. Despite many critical reservations about Hochhuth's recent dramas, the fact that his *The Midwife* from the previous season broke all records this year by being done in 22 theaters, more often than a play by any other dramatist, not excluding Brecht and Shakespeare, should not go unmentioned.

In Munich where the state and city theaters vie for public support, the stage designer Rudolf Heinrich made his directing debut at the former theater with *Measure for Measure,* while at the latter theatrical history of a sort was made with three productions by guest directors: first, *The Sea,* featuring Lola Muthel as Mrs. Rafi, skilfully directed by the 25-year-old Swiss-born Luc Bondy (this play attracted much attention at the Berlin Theater Review, not least because audiences could compare Miss Muthel's extrovert performance in this play with that of the egocentric Madame Arkadina in the Zadek *Seagull*); secondly, *Joan of the Stockyards,* featuring the East Berlin actress Ursula Karusseit and staged by her husband, the Swiss-born director of the East Berlin Volksbuhne, Benno Besson; and lastly, the poetic production of Elsa Lasker-Schuler's *The Wupper* staged by Adolf Dresen of the East Berlin Deutsches Theater. In Wuppertal itself (where *The Wupper* is set) the novelty was Arno Wustenhofer's sentimental production of the first play of the 23-year-old office clerk Karl Otto Muhl, called *The Walk Along the Rhine,* about a lonely old age pensioner who strikes up a friendship with a young kitchen maid, much to his grown-up children's resentment: a rare play, set in a lower-middle-class milieu with no social axe to grind but with well-observed characters, that was taken up in several other theaters. In Heidelberg the new regime under Horst Statkus got off on the right foot with a riproaring production of Goldoni's *Quarrels in Chioggia* that was followed by an equally popular version of Bulgakov's *The White Guard.*

West Berlin

Hans Lietzau's production of Lange's anti-Stalinist drama *The Murder of Ajax* at the Schiller Theater (with décor by Achim Freyer) was notable for the author's quarrel with the director's interpretation and a half-hearted attempt on his part to have the play stopped by legal process; an attempt from which he shrank at the eleventh hour "in the interest of the actors." In this play the leaders of the Bolshevik Revolution appear as Greek heroes, and though Trotsky can be clearly identified as Odysseus, the masks, some of them equipped with double or triple faces, did not make identification easier. This alone went a long way to support Lange's contention that the political sting had been drawn through an over-esthetic approach. In general esthetic considerations dominated in this company's work, witness Dieter Dorn's outrageously topical twist to Aristophanes's *The Birds,* with sexual and phallic allusions in the costumes (the decor was by Wilfried Minks). The same could be said of Freyer's directorial debut, in the Schlos-spark Theater's production, which he designed himself, of Franz Xaver Kroetz's updated version of Hebbel's *Maria Magdalena,* in which the social satire of the Communist author's message was diluted by the pictorial approach of the (former East Berlin) director-designer. One was grateful, however, for some memorable acting performances, including Ernst Schroder's in the title-role of Bond's *Lear* (with the team of Lietzau and Freyer), Helmut Griem as Ferdinand de Bois d'Enghien in Dorn's uproarious production of Feydeau's *A Flea in her Ear,* both at the Schiller; Martin Benrath's as Butley in Simon Gray's play at the Schlos-spark; and Hanne Hiob's in *Not I* at the Studio Theater, where a production of D.H. Lawrence's *The Daughter-In-Law* also impressed.

Kurt Hubner's first production at the Free People's Theater of *Macbeth* disap-pointed, despite an ambitious attempt to make an artistic splash; the failure was fortunately overshadowed by Wilfried Minks's infinitely more felicitous *Cyrano de Bergerac.* Towards the end of the season striking workers, dissatisfied with the discrepancy in their wages as compared with those of the subsidized theaters, brought home-based activities to a halt and nearly torpedoed the annual Theater Review. An important contribution to the latter, staged not at the Free People's Theater, but at the smaller Tribune, was Gunter Kramer's original production of Strindberg's *Miss Julie,* from Hanover, in which the slow pace and the pictorial element, recalling the angst of a Munch canvas, clearly owed all to the influence of Robert Wilson's stylistic mannerisms. At another private theater, the Forum, Armand Gatti created a theatrical precedent with the world premiere of *Four Schizophrenics in Search of the Country Whose Existence Is Disputed,* which the French author wrote and staged himself in collective collaboration with the actors of the company who literally played themselves and thereby precluded any trans-fer or other production of the play elsewhere.

This year once again, as in earlier years, the theatrical thunder in West Berlin was stolen by the "Schaubuhne am Halleschen Ufer," with two productions: Peter Stein's of Labiche's *The Piggy Bank,* which, in Karl-Ernst Hermann's exaggeratedly realistic settings, lasted all of four hours and seemed not a minute too long in its nightmarish presentation of the lengths to which the bourgeois will go to make and to preserve his pile; and with the monumental double bill spread over two evenings with the pretentious title of *Antiquity Project* and performed in the adapted Philips Pavilion of the Trade Fair. This consisted of two four-hour-long performances, respectively entitled *Exercises for Actors* and directed by Stein in a set devised by Karl-Ernst Hermann and *The Bacchae* directed by Klaus-Michael Gruber in a set devised by Gilles Ailland and Eduardo Arroyo, each with costumes by Moidele Bikel. (All three were selected by the jury as Berlin's contribution to the Theater Review). In Part I the actors showed how man becomes aware of his body and how this leads to "play" in the theatrical sense. On a dust-laden arena (surrounded by patiently choking spectators when the actors rushed about) the company went through their paces and performed unspeakable indignities on the human body, male and female, that culminated in the sealing-up of an Aeschylean Prometheus in a plaster cage. In Part II they acted on a slatted wooden floor, which at one point was torn up and almost demolished, while Bruno Ganz, as King Pentheus, naked but for a leather phallus enclosing his genitals, battled with his equally naked antagonists in the Euripidean tragedy. It came to a climax with the primal scream that Edith Clever's Agave, bloodstained (literally) from head to foot, utters in her agonized realization that she has destroyed the fruit of her own womb. This utterly disciplined if decidedly exacting example of ritualistic theater was able to win over only the most devoted supporters of the company.

East Berlin

Benno Besson's Volksbuhne company still leads in the East Berlin theatrical stakes as far as originality, artistic achievement, adventurousness in repertory and acting talent go. Examples were his highly stylized production, using a flexible tented ceiling to effect scene changes, of Hacks's *Margaret of Aix,* starring Ursula Karusseit in the title role, and a fascinatingly original version of Ibsen's *The Wild Duck,* which holds the characters up to scorn as never before, designed by Pieter Hein and staged by Manfred Karge (who played Hjalmar Ekdal on the opening night) and Matthias Langhoff. At the Berliner Ensemble, alongside Gisele May and Jutta Hoffmann in the female leads in Wolfgang Pintzka's sober realization of Shaw's *Mrs. Warren's Profession,* there were Ruth Berghaus's characteristically spectacular production of Heinar Muller's stage version of the Soviet writer Fyodor Gladkov's 1920s novel of Russia under the Nepmen, *Cement* (to which special interest was added because of a competing version of the same work on East German TV); and a courageous original attempt to give to Wedekind's *Spring Awakening* a new look by casting the adolescents' roles from local school children, among whom, for all the naturalness of the others, the most theatrically persuasive was given by Brecht's granddaughter, Johanna Schall, as Ilse.

At the Deutsches Theater the best productions of the year were Adolf Dresen's of *The Man from Outside;* a Soviet drama by Ignati Dvoretski, about the clash between conservative and progressive values in a socialist industrial situation, featuring Klaus Piontek in the title role; and Horst Schonemann's of a new version of Goethe's *Gotz von Berlichingen,* with Hilmar Thate as the tragic rebel hero, which attempts not always successfully to gain more sympathy for the protagonist than his 20-year-old creator had intended.

Switzerland and Austria

The announcement that Gerhard Klingenberg, of the Vienna Burgtheater, would be taking over the management of the Zurich Schauspielhaus in 1977, two years after next year's departure of the 71-year-old incumbent, Harry Buckwitz, left as many questions unanswered as it posed. Meantime, undeterred, Buckwitz continued to meet the demands of his patrons with a series of well balanced artistic productions, among which the European premiere of Arthur Miller's *The Creation of the World and Other Business,* directed by Leopold Lindtberg, and the German premiere of Jason Miller's *That Championship Season,* directed by Michael Kehlmann, vied in popularity with Polish guest-director's Jerzy Jarocki's unorthodox production of Chekhov's *Three Sisters,* Buckwitz's own of *Hamlet,* staged in a decor by Wilfried Minks, and East Berlin guest director Manfred Wekwerth's of Gorki's *Yegor Bulichov and Others,* performed in an imposing multiple revolving set by Hans-Ulrich Schmuckle, and with the director's wife, Renate Richter, as guest star in the leading female role. The series of late-night studio performances, that included the world premiere of *The Third Breast,* a symbolical dramatic parable of human affliction, by the Polish playwright Ireneusz Iredynski, led Buckwitz to introduce a regular studio program on outlying subsidiary stages. Two interesting events in Basel were the world premiere of Heinrich Heinkel's two-hander about two selfish oldsters who get on one another's nerves, entitled *Olaf and Albert,* staged by Werner Duggelin, and Niels-Peter Rudolph's lively version of *Spring Awakening.* Together with Hans Hollamann's intensely tragic version of Schnitzler's *Liebelei* from the preceeding season, they made up Basel's two contributions to the Berlin Theater Review.

The *pièce de résistance* in Switzerland, however, proved to be the Austrian playwright Peter Handke's latest play, *The Unreasonable Ones Die Out,* staged by his countryman, the retiring manager of the Theater am Neumarkt in Zurich, Horst Zankl, as a world premiere, because the Berlin Schaubuhne, who had originally planned to be the first to do it, were not ready in time; and, in fact, even later productions of the play, in Dusseldorf and Wiesbaden, got to first base before them. Handke's allegorical tragi-comedy portrays the suicide of a big-time Brechtian capitalist, and Zankl uses masks and other alienation effects in an effort, that only partially comes off, to make the point, that maybe Handke wasn't altogether trying to make, that the entrepreneur is an anchronism.

Though the Austrian-born manager of Hamburg's Thalia Theater, Boy Gobert, had been tipped as Klingenberg's successor as head of the Burg Theater, the die had not been cast as the season ended. Klingenberg continued his policy of having foreign or non-resident guest directors to stage plays at his two theaters, the Burg proper and the smaller Akademie Theater. In this category were the perfectionist Austrian manager of the East Berlin Comic Opera, Walter Felsenstein, who returned to the legitimate theater by staging Kleist's *Kathchen von Heilbronn* at the Burg in Rudolf Heinrich's sets as a piece of old-fashioned realistic theater and with the father-and-daughter team of Attila and Maresa Horbiger in the leads. Italy's Roberto Guicciardini was responsible for the fairy-tale drama *The Magic Bird* by Carlo Gozzi in Lorenzo Ghiglia's magical decor, and Claus Peymann staged the world premiere of the Austrian's Thomas Bernhardt's latest drama of death and decay, *The Hunting Party,* in which the role of the disgusted artist in a dying society is given an ironical twist at a party in which a card-playing artist and his hostess-partner are contrasted with her dying husband, a former Nazi general unaware of his impending doom. Barbara Petritsch was the star of Peter Loschak's version of Hochhuth's *Lysistrate* at the Volkstheater, which also gave the world premiere of another Austrian playwright's latest drama, Harald Somner's paraphrase of *William Tell* about the supineness of the petty bourgeoisie in the face of a neo-fascist revival, entitled

I Tell You, I've Nothing Whatever Against the Government. Two superb productions at the Salzburg Festival merit special mention: Rudolf Noelte's of *Le Misanthrope* and Giorgio Strehler's two-part version of the chronicle plays of Shakespeare, which, as *The Game of Power,* featured Michael Heltau as Henry IV and Andrea Johnson as Queen Margaret.

France

The appointment of Alain Peyrefitte as Cultural Minister to succeed Maurice Druon did little to allay dismay at internal cultural policy until the death of President Pompidou and new elections gave promise of a more enlightened successor. Ariane Mnouchkine's company had to draw in its horns through lack of an adequate subsidy, but hope was not altogether abandoned. Jack Lang's plans for rebuilding the Palais de Chaillot were given the go-ahead signal. At the small stage, untouched by builders, and in the foyer, as well as rented premises, he was able to realize such ambitious plans as a production of *Princess Turandot* by the Romanian guest director Lucian Pintilie, derived from the text by Carlo Gozzi and the operatic version of Puccini, with Andrea Ferreol, star of the film *La Grande Bouffe,* supported by 15 dwarfs. Lang also presented Claude Régy's wordless musical about "birth, copulation and death," called *Blood Red* and designed by Eduardo Arroyo; a *Troilus and Cressida* staged by the American director Stuart Seide; the Javanese choreographer-director Kusina Sardono's production of a Balinese ritualistic dance drama *The Witch of Dirah,* with an Indonesian troupe (which was also on tour in Italy and performed in Florence during the 1974 Theater Festival and International Conference on Asian Theater); and Antoine Vitez's dramatization for children of the Gospel of St. John as *The Miracles.*

At the subsidized theaters it was the mixture as before. The Comédie Française attempted with only limited success to repeat the previous year's formula by inviting the English director Terry Hands back to Paris to put on a French version of his Stratford hit production of *Pericles.* Better received were, at the parent theater, Raymond Rouleau's new production of Giraudoux's *Ondine* starring Isabelle Adjani (who was also seen to advantage in a charming revival of *The School for Wives*) and, at the Odéon, Pirandello's *Henry IV,* René Clair's *The Dutch Courtesan* (his first venture into dramatic authorship) and, as a visiting production, Jean-Claude Grumberg's *Dreyfus,* which packed the house with both Jewish and non-Jewish theatergoers with its compellingly dramatic exposure of the causes of antisemitism. The Théâtre National Populaire returned to Paris yet again with two plays listed in last year's review *(Toller* and *Overboard)* and a new work by Roger Planchon about religious bigotry and exorcism during the days of the Paris Commune entitled *The Black Pig.* The TNP also took part in the Autumn Paris Festival with one of the season's most visually appealing productions, that by Patrice Chéreau of Marivaux's *The Dispute,* which owed a great deal to Robert Wilson's theater and highlighted the class difference and even the race prejudice which Marivaux had indeed been sensitive to but only indirectly condemned. Jorge Lavelli outdid all his previous sensationalism by staging the Argentinian-born cartoonist Copi's latest stage play *The Four Twin Sisters* inside the mirrored basement of the Palace Theater as part of the Autumn Festival, which also offered its patrons such elitist rarities as Andrei Sherban's *Electra* and Jerzy Grotowski's *Apocalipsis Cum Figuris* adapted to the dimensions and ecclesiastical aura of the historic Sainte Chapelle. At the Théâtre de la Ville the great draw was an unusually spectacular adaptation of the Homeric legend of Ulysses by Jean-Michel Ribes, memorable for the endearing frankness with which the encounter between the modest Nausicaa and the naked shipwrecked protagonist was managed. At the Théâtre de l'Est Parisien it was the turn of *The Good Woman of Setzuan* to satisfy its patrons' preference for Brecht.

The financial success of Jean-Louis Barrault in staging the world premiere at his little Récamier Theater of the stage version of *Harold and Maude* gave him the possibility of turning the temporary tented indoor playhouse (which he had pitched inside the disused railroad-station of the Gare d'Orsay a year before) into a permanent home for himself and his company. Here, in Paris's newest and most modern theater, the first in actual fact to be erected in the capital since before the war, the veteran actor-producer carried on, regaining fully the prestige he had thrown away in 1968, with a regular alternating repertory on the big stage and studio productions on the smaller one, without benefit, as of this writing, of government subsidy, except what every other private producer obtains when staging new plays in France. In the season's commercial sector, experiments included new works by Manet, Arrabal, and Ionesco, while the boulevard repertory came up with names like Pierette Bruno, Marcel Mithois, Barillet and Grédy, Félicien Marceau and revivals of ancient, if not quite antediluvian, comedies by Anouilh, Roussin, Bourdet, Guitry, Feydeau and even Sarah Bernhardt, whose authorship of two one-acters, restyled as *La Délirante Sarah* when revived on this occasion, had been lost sight of. Shaw, Simon Gray and William Douglas Home were the main British contribution to the playbills on the boulevard, while the U.S. sent over a steady stream of hits from Neil Simon, via James Goldman, to Tennessee Williams. Among the season's curiosities were an all-male *Salome* (by Oscar Wilde); Peter Handke's *The Ride Across Lake Constance* at the Espace Cardin, made no more comprehensible by its all-star cast; the revival of a play by the Lithuanian-born French *fin-de-siècle* poet Milosz; Dario Fo in a French-language one-man version of his own *Mistero Buffo;* and an unprecedented number of productions of plays by Brecht including several of his early one-acters.

Italy

The Milan Piccolo reopened with the world premiere of *The Wicked Life of the Nobleman Gilles de Rais, Alias Bluebeard, and the Illuminated Life of His King* about the inhumanity of feudal absolutism, by the dramatist and theater critic Massimo Dursi, staged by Giorgio Strehler's former assistant Lamberto Pugelli and with Franco Graziosi giving a sinister performance of the mass-murderer of the title. Strehler's ealier production of *The Threepenny Opera* transferred to an 1,800-seat movie house to meet the demand for seats of the audiences won over by the sensational production, starring Domenico Modugno and Milva. Three regional companies offered exemplary new attractions: the Genovese Stabile, Luigi Squarzina's new productions of *The Caucasian Chalk Circle* with Lea Massari, and *Long Day's Journey Into Night* with Lilla Brignone; the Aquila Stabile, Giancarlo Cobelli's wilful camp version of Tasso's pastoral play *Aminta,* staged as a commentary on a decadent 16th century court; and in Trieste, Edmo Fenoglio's brilliant rendering, with decors by Sergio d'Osmo inspired by Otto Dix, and starring Tino Buazzelli, of Italo Svevo's *Rejuvenation,* in which a latter-day Faust from Trieste shows that there is nothing to choose between the imbecilities of youth and old age.

Luca Ronconi unexpectedly reverted to the picture-frame stage with Middleton's *A Game at Chess;* and the Catholic dramatist Diego Fabbro collaborated with the Marxist Davide Lajolo in writing *The Absurd Vice,* a documentary drama about the Piedmontese Communist resistance fighter and author, Cesare Pavese, with Luigi Vannucchi as the protagonist and the American actress Penny Brown as his American girl friend Constance. Another American actor, playing an American, was Arnold Wilkerson, a black New Yorker who came to Rome and learnt Italian to play a militant black poet in Giuseppe Patroni Griffi's *Plain, Cold-Blooded People,* a squalid drama of homosexual dropouts in present-day Naples, staged by the author. In Rome, the main events included Carmelo Bene's iconoclastic adaptation of Sem Benelli's 65-year-old poetic tragedy *The Banquet of Jests;* Eduardo de Filippo's latest nostalgic comedy *Exams Never End,* in which Eduardo plays his own hero from youth to old age and beyond in his own production; Franco Enriquez's staging of Horvath's *Kasimir und Karoline* in a circus tent, an affair that immediately launched an Italian Horvath wave; Pirandello's *To Find Oneself,* directed by Giorgio De Lullo and starring Rossella Falk at the head of her own company, in the role that the Sicilian author wrote for Marta Abba; and Glauco Mauri's stage version of Beethoven's *Conversational Notebooks,* in which he and his company interpreted the authentic notes written by the composer when he was deaf and needed their aid to communicate.

The Florence Festival opened with a world premiere of a Polish drama, written, designed and staged by Josef Szajna, head of the Warsaw Studio Theater, and entitled *Dante.* Based on *The Inferno,* it had the titular hero and his companions enter the main stage from the circle along a cruciform walkway that supposedly led not into hell, but to its earthly counterpart below. Other items in the festival program were *The Witch of Dira,* from Paris, *Aminta* from Aquila, a play by Kroetz from the Hamburg Thalia Theater, and one by Krleza from Zagreb, as well as Jerzy Grzegorzweski's eye-catching version of Kafka's *Amerika* from Warsaw.

Belgium and Holland

The biennial Europalia Festival in Brussels and other parts of Belgium was devoted to the arts of Great Britain and resulted in visits by the Prospect Theater Company, the Young Vic (which staged Frank Dunlop's *Much Ado About Nothing* there before its London opening) and the Royal Court's production, directed by Peter Gill, of *The Merry-Go-Round* by D.H.Lawrence. It also brought Dunlop to the Belgian National Theater to stage a modern-dress version of *Pericles* there on a stage literally surrounded and played upon by water-jets, and was responsible for a record number of British plays at the Théâtre du Rideau, where Paul Willems's latest whimsical drama *The Mirrors of Ostende* was also later world-premiered.

Two remarkable events in Holland were, one, the production of Gogol's *The Government Inspector* by Czech guest director Jan Grossman and, two, the four-part drama *The Family* by Lodewijk de Boer, which was also acted in French at the Brussels Pocket Theater, on four consecutive nights. The exiled Flemish dramatist Hugo Claus was responsible for two new plays, both premiered in Holland, one called *Blauw Blauw,* about a homosexual entanglement, the other *Pas de Deux,* a backstage two-hander.

Scandinavia

The annual Ingmar Bergman production, the first two parts of the Strindberg trilogy of *To Damascus,* staged as a single three-hour-long play and starring Jan-Olof Strandberg as the autobiographical spiritual pilgrim the author called The Stranger and Helena Brodin as his wife, was the principal event at the Royal Dramatic Theater in Stockholm, whose director, Erland Josephson announced his impending retirement in mid-season. Jan-Olof Strandberg later agreed to take over in 1975. On the same stage Jan Malmsjo appeared as Hamlet in a lengthy but intelligent production by Lars Goran Carlson, and the repertory began to lean heavily on French authors, what with new productions of *Britannicus, The Tidings Brought to Mary* and *Dr. Knock.* Molière's *Don Juan,* directed by Jonas Cornell, was the rival attraction at the City Theater, whose other offerings included Johan Bergenstrahle's adaptation of Selma Lagerlof's *The Atonement of Gosta Berling,* starring Per Myrberg, and the world premieres of two foreign works: Ionesco's children's play *Twixt Heaven and Earth* and Arnold Wesker's *The Wedding-Feast,* based on a Dostoyevsky story but transposed to a class-ridden Anglo-Jewish industrial milieu. The Gothenburg City Theater's inspired production of Strindberg's *Gustav III,* effectively staged by Lennart Hjulstrom, earned an invitation to the 1974 Edinburgh Festival.

In Copenhagen, at the Royal Theater, Ernst Bruun Olsen's latest verse drama *The Lickspittle,* staged by the author, about a schoolmaster with sexual and other hangups, proved disappointing by contrast with his earlier plays and despite first-rate performances. On its studio stage, *The Myths,* by the 35-year-old Ulla Ryum, a series of monologues in a launderette set in the future in a world beset by pollution, heralded the arrival of a promising new talent.

At Oslo's New Norwegian Theater it was Liv Ullman's turn to enliven a new production, in the New Norwegian language (which she had to learn for the occasion), of Ibsen's *A Doll's House.*

In Finland, interest was divided equally between the capital and Turku. In Helsinki, it was two new productions at the National Theater by Jack Witikka of Bulgakov's *Molière,* and by Jussi Tapola of Euripides's *Hippolytus,* that made the largest splash—closely followed by the late Hella Wuolijoki's peasant drama *Hate From Niskavuori,* directed by Edvin Laine. Laine was also responsible for the uproarious production of Maiju Lasila's turn-of-the-century peasant farce *Borrowing Matches,* staged with great panache during the Tampere Theater Festival at the Pyynikki Park Theater, where the audience, seated on a rotating auditorium, witnessed the comic events of the action on the surrounding circumferential acting-area and in the woodland beyond. The Turku City Theater offered its audiences Ralf Langbacka's meticulously Brechtian production of *Galileo Galilei* and Kalle Holmberg's of the world premiere of *The Wind From the Plain,* adapted by Australian-born Alan Seymour from the Turkish novel by Yashar Kemal, about the hardships of life in a peasant community in turn-of-the-century Anatolia.

Eastern Europe

The Moscow Art Theater celebrated its 75th anniversary by taking over as its third stage a brand new building on the Tverskoi Boulevard. Here the most highly praised new production was that of Antonio Buero Vallejo's Spanish drama about Goya, *Sleeping Reason,* staged by Oleg Yefremov. Yefremov's production of *Solo for a Striking Clock* by the Slovak author Osvald Zahradnik featured some of the company's best-known veteran players in this drama about a reunion of old folk. The Sovremmenik (Contemporary) Theater also acquired new premises—on the site of the former "Kolizei" movie house which was also that of Moscow's earliest 18th century playhouse—opening with *The Bolsheviks* by Mikhail Shatrov, whose most recent drama, called *Tomorrow's Weather* and directed by Galina Volchyok, was set in an automobile factory in the town of Togliatti and dealt with factory production problems that were resolved at the final curtain as the 500,000th Shiguli was driven onstage. At the same theater the Leningrad guest director Georgi Tovstonogov staged *Balalaikin and Company,* Sergei Mikhalkov's stage version of the 19th century novel *Contemporary Idyll* by Saltykov-Shchedrin, about the marriage of an eminent lawyer to a woman of easy virtue and a pretext for a critique of bourgeois hypocrisy. Yuri Liubimov celebrated the tenth anniversary of the Taganka Theater by putting on *Comrade, Believe . . . ,* a collage of Pushkin writings compiled by Liudmila Tselikovskaya and the director, who also announced that he is planning new productions of Brecht's *Turandot,* an adaptation of Bulgakov's novel of *The Master and Margarita* and of Dostoyevsky's *The Devils.* At the Drama Theater on the Malaya Bronnaya Anatoli Efros staged Molière's *Don Juan,* with two actors alternating in the title role; and, at the Maly, Boris Ravenskikh directed a revival of Alexei Tolstoy's *Tsar Fyodor Ioannovich* starring Innokenti Smoktunovski. Back in Leningrad at his Gorki Theater Tovstonogov mounted a musical adaptation of the 19th century Georgian classic by Avksenti Tsagareli, *Khanuma,* a love story among Georgian princes who are manipulated by the female Figaro-like servant of the title. A surprising arrival at the Drama and Comedy Theater in the same city was the Russian premiere of Agatha Christie's *The Mousetrap.*

The best news from Czechoslovakia was the partial reinstatement of Otomar Krejca, who directed *Platonov* by Chekhov at the small outlying S.K.Neumann Theater, to which he was due to be attached for the time being. On the other hand, dramatists like Havel and Kohout, and Krejca's former literary director, Karel Klaus, were still without work. The plays of Mrozek, too, were once again staged in Poland and at the Contemporary Theater, where he had originally put on the world premiere of *Tango,* Erwin Axer staged Mrozek's latest drama about the problem of individual freedom in the face of totalitarian imperatives, entitled *A Happy Event* and first done in West Germany the year before. At the National, two of Poland's foremost comic actors, Wojciech Semion and Wojciech Pszoniak provided most of the belly laughs in Adam Hanuszkewicz's hilarious production of *The Government Inspector,* which made a nice contrast to his own part-romantic, part-satirical adaptation of Slowacki's poem of *Beniowski,* in which Daniel Olbrychski personified the ranting hero. The regulars, like Wajda, Jarocki and Swinarski were all represented by new productions, either in Warsaw or in Cracow—notably Jarocki, who staged Rozewicz's dramatic lampoon on the political and cultural establishment *On All Fours* with eclat at the Dramatic Theater in the capital, and *The Wedding,* by Gombrowicz (making a belated re-appearance on the stages of his fatherland) in Cracow, where Wajda was responsible for *November Night* by Wyspianski and Swinarski for the same writer's *The Liberation,* a discussion about theater in the manner of Brecht's *Selling Brass.* Elsewhere in Warsaw, Jerzy Grzegorzewski fulfilled the brilliant promise of last year's *Amerika* by Kafka with a no less exciting *Ulysses in Nighttown* (at the Ateneum); and, at the Studio Theater, Szajna opened and shut the season with *Replika 4,* an almost wordless collage of memories of Nazi death-camps and Occupation agonies, and the new *Dante.*

In Budapest the National Theater's main claim to seasonal fame was Tamas Major's production of Miklos Hubay's latest drama, *Theater on a Whale's Back,* a pseudo-historial inquiry into the nature of treachery. All the characters in Zoltan Varkonyi's amusing production of Istvan Orkeny's latest absurdist comedy at the Pest Theater, the small stage of the Vigszinhaz, called *Blood Relations,* have the same name and all are railroad employees in this satire on the suppression of the private sphere in human affairs. After a gap of 20 years the 50-year-old Ferenc Bessenyi reappeared as a much maturer Othello in Otto Adam's new production of Shakespeare's tragedy, at the Madach Theater, by contrast with the much younger Iago (Peter Huszti) and Iago's shrewd though ill-treated spouse (Eva Almassy). Another great acting performance was turned in by Iren Psota at the Thalia, this time in Kazimir Karolyi's bawdy adaptation of Diderot's *Les Bijoux Indiscrets,* retitled *The Talking Jewels.* The season's highlight in Bucharest was the opening of the new premises of the National with *The Pathetic Symphony,* Aurel Baranga's political satire set in the liberation year of 1944; another satire, on totalitarianism, set this time in the future, was Horia Lovinescu's *Paradise,* and two further popular draws were Paul Everac's joyous contemporary comedy *Life is Like a Carriage* and Lucian Giurchescu's new production of Caragiale's classical comedy *A Stormy Night.* Back in the saddle at the Bulandra City Theater, Liviu Ciulei staged a production in the round of Titus Popovici's *Power and Truth,* in which a Communist Party secretary reviews his past. At the same theater Moni Ghelerter put on *Pygmalion,* with Mariana Mihuts as Eliza. Dinu Cernescu returned to the 150-seat Cellar Theater, attached to the C.I. Nottara Theater, to stage, virtually in and around the audience, a claustrophobic and de-romanticized version of *Hamlet* starring Stefan Iordache as the Prince and Anda Caropol as Ophelia.

Highlights of the Paris Season

Selected and compiled by Ossia Trilling

OUTSTANDING PERFORMANCES

MICHEL GALABRU as Tibulus in *The One-Eyed Man*	SIMONE VALÈRE as Candida in *Candida*	DOMINIQUE PATUREL as Zanetto and Jonino in *The Venetian Twins*
GENEVIÈVE FONTANEL as Lucienne and Agnès in *This Godawful Mess!*	BERNARD FRESSON as Butley in *Butley*	LUDMILA MIKAËL as Thaïsa and Marina in *Pericles, Prince of Tyre*
MADELEINE RENAUD as Maude in *Harold and Maude*	LOUIS DE FUNÈS as General St. Pe in *The Waltz of the Toreadors*	MARIE BELL as Lady Belmont in *Lloyd George Knew My Father*
CLAUDE RICHE as Jean de la Fontaine in *Jean de la Fontaine*	DANIEL IVERNEL as Gaston in *Traveller Without Luggage*	EDWIGE FEUILLÈRE as Eléonore in *The Lion in Winter*
ISABELLE ADJANI as Ondine in *Ondine*	FRANÇOIS CHAUMETTE as Henry IV in *Henry IV*	MICHEL AUCLAIR as Léviné in *Toller*

OUTSTANDING DIRECTORS

PATRICE CHÉREAU *The Dispute*	JORGE LAVELLI *The Four Twin Sisters*	LUCIAN PINTILIE *Princess Turandot*

OUTSTANDING DESIGNERS

RICHARD PEDUZZI *The Dispute*	YANNIS KOKKOS *The Odyssey at Tea-Time*	TIMOTHY OBRIEN and TAZEENA FIRTH *Pericles, Prince of Tyre*

OUTSTANDING NEW FRENCH PLAYS

(D)—Playwright's Paris Debut

LE BORGNE (The One-Eyed Man) by Eduardo Manet. Cuban-born writer's allegorical drama about the second coming in ancient Rome, originally world-premiered by the Belgian National Theater of Brussels. With Michel Galabru, Sacha Pitoëff, Francis Lemaire, Jacques Rosny.

SMOKING, OU LES MAUVAIS SENTIMENTS (Tuxedoes, or Ill-matched Love) by Jean-Pierre Bisson. Wife-swapping and other encounters among the rich on a luxury cruise. With Jean-Paul Zennacker, Pierre Arditi, the author.

LES QUATRES JUMELLES (The Four Twin Sisters) by Copi. Argentinian-born French cartoonist's symbolical drama about the continual death and resurrection of self-destroying women. With Daisy Amias, Myriam Mezières, Anna Prucnal, Lilliane Rovère.

L'HOMME EN QUESTION (The Man It's All About) by Félicien Marceau. Cynical hero looks back on his life and exchanges views with a female alter-ego. With Bernard Blier, Martine Sarcey.

C'EST LA GUERRE, MONSIEUR GRUBER (This Means War, Mr Gruber) by Jacques Sternberg (D). Belgian author's first French play about a latter-day Everyman threatened with annihilation. With Georges Chamarat, Michel Etcheverry, André Reybaz, Gérard Caillaud.

CE FORMIDABLE BORDEL (This Godawful Mess!) by Eugene Ionesco. Rumanian-born French Academician's satirical view of this godawful world of ours. With Eléonore Hirt, André Thorent, Geneviève Fontanel, Yves Bureau, Odile Mallet, Jacques Mauclair.

DREYFUS by Jean-Claude Grumberg. A group of Jewish actors in pre-war Poland re-enact the story of Dreyfus in an atmosphere of inter-war antisemitism. With the Théâtre du Lambrequin company.

L'ODYSSÉE POUR UNE TASSE DE THÉ (The Odyssey at Tea-Time) by Jean-Michel Ribes. Strip cartoon retelling of the Homeric story of Ulysses for kids and adults. With Claude Vega, Geneviève Page, Michel de Ré, Laurence Vincendon, Pierre Santini.

CÉRÉMONIE POUR UN NOIR ASSASSINÉ (Ceremony for a Slaughtered Black) by Fernando Arrabal. The Spanish-born dramatist's latest cry-from-the-heart against racial intolerance. With Jean Turlier, Issa Diop.

LA CATIN AUX LÈVRES DOUCES (The Sweet-Lipped Harlot) by René Clair (D). The famous film director's first stage play loosely based on Marston's The Dutch Courtesan. With the Young National Theater company.

LE COCHON NOIR (The Black Pig) By Roger Planchon. While the bloody events of the Commune ravage Paris in 1871, an exorcist exercises his skill on a casual agricultural worker who has run amok. First staged in Caen in November 1973, Planchon's latest play formed part of the Théâtre National Populaire's 1974 season in Paris. With the Théâtre National Populaire company of Villeurbanne.

PAR-DESSUS BORD (Overboard) by Michel Vinaver. Musical about the struggle of a national industry against the encroaching power of supranational capitalist conglomerates. With Roger Planchon's Théâtre National Populaire company from Villeurbanne.

POPULAR ATTRACTIONS

L'ÉTOURDI (The Roughneck) by Molière. With the Théâtre National de Strasbourg company.

TURCARET by Alain René Lesage. New production of classic satire on greed. With Micheline Presle, Gérard Lartigau.

LE MARI DE LA VEUVE (The Widow's Husband) by Alexandre Dumas père. Revival of a romantic classic. With Gérard Bayle, Fabienne Mai.

LA CONFUSION CRÉE L'ORGASME (Confusion Provokes Orgasm), twelve sketches from William Shakespeare to Alfred Jarry. With Christiane Casanova, Claude Bouchéry, Yves Savel, Christian Pereira.

CONVERSATION DANS LE LOIR-ET-CHER (Conversation in Loir-et-Cher) Stage adaptation of some of Paul Claudel's writings from the 1920s. With Raphael Andia, Silvia Monfort.

LE CHÂTEAU DANS LES CHAMPS (The Castle in the Fields) by Bernard Chartreux. When a peasant lad becomes a prince. With the Théâtre de la Reprise company.

CIEL, MON MARI (Heavens, My Husband) by Francis Garnung. An unwanted intrusion. With Pierre Bourduge, Monique Canal, Henri Gilabert.

LA VALSE DES TORÉADORS (The Waltz of the Toreadors) by Jean Anouilh. Revival of black comedy. With Louis de Funès, Luce Garcia-Ville, Mony Dalmès.

UNE ROSE AU PETIT DÉJEÛNER (A Rose for Breakfast) by Barillet and Grédy. Catherine and Nicolas in search of love. With Francis Perrin, Mariana Falk.

LE VOYAGEUR SANS BAGAGE (Traveller Without Luggage) by Jean Anouilh. Revival of comedy. With Daniel Ivernel, Francine Bergé.

L'ÉCOLE DES FEMMES (The School for Wives) by Molière. New Comédie Française production. With Michel Aumont, Isabelle Adjani.

LE BEAU ROLE (The Dream Part) by Ada Lonati and Georges Bellair. An actress gives an audition. With Ada Lonati.

NID D'EMBROUILLES (Nest of Intrigue) by Claude Magnier, adapted from a comedy by Alvaro de Laiglesia. Would-be investor employs a medium and learns the truth. With Michèle Sand, the author.

FRACASSE, adapted from Théophile Gautier's *Le Capitaine Fracasse,* by Serge Ganzl. With Jean-Claude Drouot and the Centre Dramatique National company of Lyons.

LES PATIENTS (The Patients) and BOUTIQUE FERMÉE (Closed Shop) by Jacques Audiberti. Revival of two satirical one-acters. With Gilles Lalande, Daniel Langlet.

L'HÔTEL DU LIBRE ÉCHANGE (Hotel Paradiso) by Georges Feydeau. New production of celebrated classical farce. With Jean-Claude Brialy, Micheline Boudet, Michel Roux, Jean Parédès.

L'ARNACOEUR (The Kill-Heart) by Pierrette Bruno. A modern Don Juan exploits a lady of easy virtue. With Roger Carel, Jean-Pierre Darras, the author.

DOUCHKA by Charles Aznavour and Georges Garvarentz. Musical about the French fleet docking in St. Petersburg. With Marcel Merkes, Paulette Merval. Gerard Chapuis.

DOM JUAN by Molière. Roger Mollien plays the lead and directs his own company in a new production of the classic.

LA PLACE ROYALE by Corneille. Hubert Gignoux's new production at the Théâtre de l'Est Parisien. With the Théâtre de l'Est Parisien company.

J'AI CONFIANCE EN LA JUSTICE DE MON PAYS (I Believe in My Country's Justice) by Alain Scoff. An investigation into a police scandal. With the Théâtre Bulle company.

MADAME SANS-GÊNE by Victorien Sardou and Émile Moreau. Revival of famous 19th century comedy. With Jacqueline Maillan, William Sabatier, Pierre Trabaud, Alain Mottet.

LA DISPUTE by Marivaux. Patrice Chéreau's radical adaptation of 18th-century allegory for the Théâtre National Populaire of Villeurbanne. With Mabel King, Thomas Anderson, Hugues Quester, Hermine Karagheuz.

LES CAPRICES DE MARIANNE and ON NE SAURAIT PENSER À TOUT (You Can't Think of Everything) by Alfred de Musset. Two new Comédie Française productions. With Francis Huster, Alain Feydeau, Bérengère Dautun.

LA SITUATION EST GRAVE MAIS PAS DESESPÉRÉE (Things Could Be Worse) by Paul Germont. An Englishman's home isn't always his castle. With Claire Maurier, Bernard Lavalette, Christian Alers, Pasquali.

L'ARC DE TRIOMPHE by Marcel Mithois. The rise and rise of a sempstress. With Sophie Desmarets, Louis Velle.

L'ÎLE DES ESCLAVES (Slave Island) by Marivaux, with Jacques Destoop, Dominique Rozan, and LES FOURBERIES DE SCAPIN (The Pranks of Scapin) by Molière, with Alain Pralon, Paul Noëlle. New Comédie Française double bill.

MISS MADONA, the Théâtre du Chêne Noir Company of Avignon's 1973 Festival production.

VENDREDI, OU LA VIE SAUVAGE (Man Friday, or Life in the Raw) by Antoine Vitez. Adaptation of Michel Tournier's novel. With Katharina Renn.

ABRAHAM ET SAMUEL by Victor Haïm. Comédie Française production of a modern Morality about a Jewish thief. With Jean-Paul Roussillon, Michel Aumont.

L'EXCÈS (Excess) by Philippe Adrien. Adapted from Georges Bataille's novel. With Jean-Pierre Joris, Françoise Giret.

GOB, OU LE JOURNAL D'UN HOMME NORMAL (Gob, or the Diary of a Normal Man) by and with the Marchands de Ville Company. A collective journey through Gob's diary.

JEAN DE LA FONTAINE by Sacha Guitry. Revival of popular pre-war comedy. With Claude Rich, Marie Daems.

L'OR ET LA NEIGE (Gold and Snow) by Paul Paléologue. The wages of egotism. With Blanche Rayne, Fanny Robiane.

LA COMPLICE (The Accomplice) by Luc-Claude Thomas. Crime doesn't pay. With Gérard Barray, Corinne Marchand.

LES NUITS D'UN PRÉSIDENT (A President's Nights) by François Sourbier. Farce based on a de Sade story. With Inès Nazaris, Gilbert Beugniot, Sylvie Lacontaine.

LA DÉLIRANTE SARAH (Delirious Sarah) by Sarah Bernhardt. New production of the famous actress's two short dramas L'AVEU (The Confession) and DU THÉÂTRE AU CHAMP D'HONNEUR (From the Theater to the Field of Honour). With Pierre Spivakoff, Gérard Dessalles, Juliette Carré.

LE POIGNARD MASQUÉ (The Hidden Dagger) by Anicet Bourgeois. Cloaks and daggers in 16th century Venice. With Jean-Pierre Dervieux, Jacques Seiler, Jacqueline Staup.

LES FAUSSES CONFIDENCES (The False Confessions) by Marivaux. New production at the Théâtre de l'Est Parisien. With Geneviève Page, Béatrice Bretty, Michel de Ré.

TOHU-BOHU by Christian Kursner. A con man sets up in the seduction business. With Bruno Balp, Marie-Thérèse Orain, the author.

L'ESCARGOT ÉCOSSAIS (Scotch Snail) by Dominique Nohain. A police inspector vanishes. With Roger Crouzet, the author.

KHOMA by Irène Lambelet and Jean Philippe Guerlais. Based on the works of Henri Michaux. Withe the Orbe-Théâtre company.

L'ANNONCE FAITE À MARIE (The Tidings Brought to Mary) by Paul Claudel. Jean Térensier's new production of famous religious drama. With Maud Rayer, Aravni Mérian.

VIRGULE (Comma) by Roger Hanin. How middle age affects two couples. With Madeleine Robinson, Roger Dumas, Sylvie Joly, the author.

LE RETOUR DE MISS UNIVERS (The Return of Miss Universe) by Guénolé Azerthiope. How to bring up the failures of the Miss Universe

Contest. With the Fénoménal Bazaar Illimited company.

BODY by Rezvani. An erotic dream. With Nicole Evans.

LA TOUR DE NESLES by Alexandre Dumas père. Adapted and staged by Alec-Pierre Quince, from the classic novel. With Colette Renard, Jacques Boloin, Jean-Pierre Rambal.

BARNUM, OU SI LES REQUINS ÉTAIENT DES HOMMES (Barnum, or If Sharks were Men) by Ulysse Renaud. A foreign industrialist buys up a French factory. With the Théâtre du 11 company.

LES TROIS MOUSQUETAIRES by Francis Lopez. A Western-musical version of the famous Dumas story. With Mario Brunini, Maria Candido, Maurice Baquet, Jeanne-Marie Proslier, Jacques Chazot.

LE GRAND GUIGNOL REVIENT (The Return of Grand Guignol) by Gerard Croce. Comprising L'HORRIBLE FIN DU DOCTEUR GUILLOTIN (The Horrible End of Dr. Guillotin), LES BOUCHERS DE WHITECHAPEL (The Butchers of Whitechapel), LE BAL DES FOUS (The Madmen's Ball). With Jean-Pierre Vaguer, Georges Zicco, Liza Viet.

LE CAVALIER SEUL (The Lone Rider) by Jacques Audiberti. New production of author's drama of the Crusade of Mirtus of Languedoc. With Marcel Maréchal's Compagnie du Cothurne of Lyons.

DEUTSCHES REQUIEM (If Hitler Were Still Alive) by Pierre Bourgeade. With Daniel Benoin's Théâtre de l'Estrade company.

ARLÈNE SUPIN CHEZ LES MARTIENS (Arlène Supin visits Mars) by Marc Jolivet. A science fiction musical comedy. With Pierre Jolivet, Rosine Cadoret, Michel Torent.

DÎNER AVEC M. ET MRS. Q (Dinner with Mr. and Mrs. Q) by Augustin Gomez-Arcos. Political truth is stranger than fiction. With Henry Courseaux, Jacques Bayon, Rafaël Gozalbo.

VERMEIL COMME LE SANG (Blood Red) by Claude Régy. A wordless musical based on a Grimm fairy tale. With Patrice Hardouin, Jean-François Bayonne.

PROTÉE (Proteus) by Paul Claudel. New production of satirical skit on the Trojan War. With Bernard Lavalette, Maurice Teynac, Martine Sarcey, Jacques Rosny.

PASIPHAË and LE CHANT DE MINOS (The

Song of Minos) by Henry de Montherlant. New production of rarely seen one-act variants on classical themes. With Fanny Robiane, Evelyn Proudhom, Luce Berthommé.

LE VERS SOLITAIRE (The Tapeworm) by Daniel Laloux. A mother's son trapped in a vicious circle. With the author.

LE MARI, LA FEMME ET LA MORT (Husband, Wife and Death) by André Roussin. Revival of famous 20-year-old comedy. With Jacqueline Gauthier, Jacques Morel, Pasquali.

QUI RAPPORTERA CES PAROLES? (Who'll tell the story?) by Charlotte Delbo. Twenty-two women fight for their freedom. With Edith Scob, Annie Bertin, Dominique Blanchar, Monique Fabre.

ONDINE by Jean Giraudoux. Raymond Rouleau's new production for the Comédie Française. With Isabel Adjani, François Chaumette, Jacques Toja, Nicolas Silberg, Geneviève Casile.

LE PRINCE TRAVESTI (The Prince Disguised) by Marivaux. Daniel Mesguich's new production with the Théâtre du Miroir company.

LES HORSAINS (The Outcasts). A collective production by and with Jean-Paul Cisife, Jean-Claude Bois, Jean-Louis Terrangle, Raphaël-Francis Mattei, Christian Zanetti. Are homosexuals the outcasts of today?

MOZART, OU LE REQUIEM INACHEVÉ (Mozart, or The Unfinished Requiem) by Gabrielle Dalret. The life and death of Mozart. With Catherine Brieux, Louise Debrakel, Roger Montsoret.

LE CITRON AUTOMATIQUE (The Clockwork Lemon) by Francis Perrin. A comic revue for five clowns. With Bernard Alane, the author.

CHEZ PIERROT by Jean-Claude Grumberg. A down-and-out barkeeper and his three down-and-out customers while away the time waiting for the return of the long-lost prodigal son. With Maurice Bénichou, Étienne Bierry, Pierre Frag, Michel Robin.

LES CHANTS DE MALDOROR (The Songs of Maldoror) adapted from Lautréamont by Pierre Boutron. With Jacqueline Staup, Jean-Pierre Joris

EN ATTENDANT GODOT (Waiting for Godot) by Samuel Beckett. New production with songs by Alfred Vigny. With Jacques Salmon, Thierry Destrez, Georges Desmeliers, Jean Chevrin.

FILS CARLOS DÉCÉDÉ (Carlos Son Deceased) by Betty Raffaelli, Joseph Guglielmi, Michel Raffaelli. Arrested in France, a Portuguese worker takes his own life. With Betty Raffaelli, Jean-Pierre Laurent, Christian Bouillette.

CET ANIMAL ÉTRANGE (This Strange Animal) by Gabriel Arout. A new production of drama based on Chekhov short stories. With Maïa Simon, Philippe Mercier.

ISABELLA MORRA by André-Pieyre de Mandiargues (D). Jean Louis Barrault's production of Goncourt prizewinning novelist's first play about the cruel revenge of three 16th century Italian brothers on their innocent sister. With Annie Duperey, Dominique Santarelli, Yves Gasc.

DO YOU SPEAK MARTIEN? by Marc Jolivet. Musical inter-spatial science fiction nonsense comedy. With Pierre Jolivet, Patrick Olivier, the author.

LOCOS (Crazy People) by and with the Atelier de l'Épée de Bois Company. The rule of madness and violence leads to death.

APPELEZ-MOI MAÎTRE (Call me Master) by Jean-Marie Cornille. This way madness lies. With the author.

LES MOROT-CHANDONNEUR (The Morot-Chandonneur Family) by Bernard Minoret and Philippe Julian. The scandalous story of a famous French family. With Annie Noelle, André Fetet, Gérard Maro, Jacques Morineau.

LE SEXE FAIBLE (The Weaker Sex) by Edouard Bourdet. New production of popular inter-war-years comedy. With Lise Delamare, Jean-Laurent Cochet, Michel Le Royer, Odile Mallet.

LES MIRACLES devised by Antoine Vitez. The Gospel according to St. John adapted for children. With the Théâtre National de Chaillot Children's Theater Company.

LE LÉGATAIRE UNIVERSEL (The Residuary Legatee) by Jean-François Regnard and LES MARRONS DU FEU (Chestnuts in the Fire) by Alfred de Musset. New Comédie Française double bill. With Jean-Paul Roussillon, Denise Gence, Francis Huster, Virginie Pradal.

DEUX CLOWNS (Two Clowns), comprising L'HOMME À LA VALISE and LES ASSIETTES (The Man with the Suitcase and The Plates) by Pierre Byland and Philippe Gaulier. A farrago of fun in sketch form. With the authors.

MOI, PIERRE RIVIÈRE adapted by Frank

Oger and Catherine Oudina from the 1835 journal of a murderer describing his triple crime. With Jean-Denis Meunier, the authors.

QU'EST-CE-QUI FRAPPE ICI SI TÔT? (Who's That Knocking So Early?) by Phillippe Madral. Horrible case based on an authentic Italian crime. With Patrick Chesnais, Nadia Taleb.

LA RAISON DU PLUS FORT (Might Is Right). Collective anti-war drama staged by Charles Grau-Stef. With Gérard Maro, Brigitte Carva.

LA TRAVERSÉE DU XXe SIÈCLE EN CHANTANT (Through the 20th Century in Song). From Paul Delmet to present times. With Jean Nohain, Mathé Altéry, Lucien Cupi.

LA POLKA by Patrick Modiano (D). An old man reviews his life. With Malka Ribowska, Jean Leuvrais.

MADAME LE SOCIÉTAIRE (The Actress of the Comédie Française) devised by Jean-Marie Sénécal and Yves Jacquemard. The story of makeup. With Marc Monjou, Jean de Schryver.

SOME AMERICAN PLAYS PRODUCED IN PARIS

ONTOLOGICAL-HYSTERIC THEATER devised and directed by Richard Foreman. With an all-French French-speaking cast.

THE LION IN WINTER by James Goldman. With Edwige Feuillère, Paul Guers.

MEDICINE SHOW and FROGS. With the Medicine Show Theater Ensemble of New York.

THE KARL MARX PLAY by Rochelle Owens. With the American Place Theater company.

PARADISO XX by and with the Earth Theater of Cynthia Briggs.

THAT SIMPLE LIGHT MAY RISE OUT OF COMPLICATED DARKNESS. With the Bread and Puppet Theater of New York.

THE SUNSHINE BOYS (Charlie et Bobby) by Neil Simon. With Jacques Fabbri, Alfred Adam.

CHRISTMAS STORY. With the Bread and Puppet Theater Touring Company.

HAROLD AND MAUDE by Colin Higgins,

adapted by Jean-Claude Carrière (staged world premiere of an American film). With Madeleine Renaud, Daniel Rivière, Yves Gasc, Jean-Pierre Granval, Jean-Louis Barrault.

ONE FLEW OVER THE CUCKOO'S NEST by Dale Wasserman. With Françoise Christophe, Michel Auclair.

THE GINGERBREAD LADY by Neil Simon. With Paul Le Person, Christiane Minazzoli.

COLD BUCK by John Fitzgerald. With Mike Marshall, Dolly West.

SOMETHING UNSPOKEN by Tennessee Williams. With Frédérique Ruchaud, Reine Bartève.

EPIPHANY by Lewis John Carlino. With Stephane Meldegg, Christine Théry.

THE PEDESTRIANS and THE VELDT by Ray Bradbury. With Feodor Atkine, Corinne Deforges, Bernadette Lonpret.

HOTEL VIRGINIA by Jack Fitzgerald. With the Paris English Theater company.

SOME OTHER FOREIGN PLAYS PRODUCED IN PARIS

LIOLÀ by Luigi Pirandello. With the Teatro Stabile company of Catania.

MIN FARS HUS (My Father's House) based on Dostoyevsky. With the Odin Teatret of Holstebro, Denmark.

LES 120 JOURNÉES DE SODOME D'APRÈS SADE (120 Days of Sodom According to Sade). With the Beat 72 company of Rome.

LA PARLERIE DE RUZANTE QUI REVIENT DE GUERRE (Ruzante's Address on Coming Home from the War) by Angelo Beolco. With Alain Halle-Halle, André Lacombe, So-

lange Oswald, Alain Ilan.

LA GRANDE IMPRÉCATION DEVANT LES MURS DE LA VILLE (Great Speech before the City Walls) by Tankred Dorst. With Solange Oswald, Alain Ilan, Alain Halle-Halle, André Lacombe.

TÊTES RONDES, TÊTES POINTUES (Roundheads and Peakheads) by Bertolt Brecht. With the Gennevilliers Theater company.

LUX IN TENEBRIS by Bertolt Brecht. With Dominique and Laurence Doré.

RUBEZAHL (SCÈNES DE DON JUAN) (Scenes From the Life of Don Juan) by Milosz (Oscar Vladislav De Lubicz-Milosz). With Pascale de Boysson, Laurent Terzieff. LE PROMÉTHÉE ENCHAÎNÉ (Prometheus Bound) by Aeschylus. With the Antique Theater company.

LES RIVAUX D'EUX-MÊMES (The Venetian Twins) by Carlo Goldoni. With Dominique Paturel, Nelly Benedetti, Michèle Grellier.

DEVANT LA PORTE (Outside the Door) by Wolfgang Borchert. With Daniel Postal, Marie-Thérèse Normant.

ROMEO AND JULIET by William Shakespeare, adapted by Jean Vauthier. With the Robert Hossein company.

NE COUPEZ PAS MES ARBRES (Lloyd George Knew My Father) by William Douglas Home. With Marie Bell, Robert Lamoureux, Pierre Bertin.

YERMA by Federico Garcia Lorca. With the Nuria Espert company from Spain.

MISS JULIE by August Strindberg. With Luce Berthommé, Henry Pillsbury, Cléo Athanasiou.

LA NOCE CHEZ LES PETITS BOURGEOIS (The Petty Bourgeois Wedding) by Bertolt Brecht. With the Vincent-Jourdheuil company.

APOCALIPSIS CUM FIGURIS by and with Jerzy Grotowski's Laboratory Theater from Wroclaw.

CANDIDA by George Bernard Shaw. With Jean Desailly, Simone Valère, Claude Dauphin, Dominique Leverd.

LEONCE AND LENA and WOYZECK by Georg Buechner. With the Ménagerie Théâtrale company.

LE NUAGE AMOUREUX (The Cloud in Love) by Nazim Hikmet. With the Théâtre de Liberté company.

LA BONNE ÂME DE SÉ-TCHOUAN (The Good Woman of Setzuan) by Bertolt Brecht. With Anne Doat, Michel de Ré.

ET MOI AUSSI, JE PARLE DE LA ROSE (I, Too, Speak of the Rose) by Emilio Carballido. With the Comédie de Saint Étienne company.

ELECTRA by Sophocles. With Andrei Serban's company from La Mama, New York.

LES BELLES SOEURS (Sisters-in-Law) by Michel Tremblay. With the Deux-Chaises company of Quebec.

BUTLEY by Simon Gray. With Bernard Fresson, Nelly Vignon.

SALOME by Oscar Wilde. With Gilbert Beugniot, Philippe Miglioli, Pierre Nayaert, Daniel Abjean, Sylvestre Laboue, Louis Tilly.

EN PLEINE MER (On the High Seas) by Slawomir Mrozek. With Jean-Paul Bourdeaux, Gilbert François, Pierre Trapet.

LA FEMME DE SOCRATE (Socrates's Wife) by Denis Kollatos. With Arlette Baumann.

HENRY IV by Luigi Pirandello. With François Chaumette, Jacques Toja, Rosy Varte.

LE CYCLE DE CUCHULAIN (Four Cuchulain Plays) by W.B. Yeats. With the Théâtre Oblique company.

MISTERO BUFFO by Dario Fo. With the author.

THE TEMPEST by William Shakespeare. With the Ensemble Théâtral de Gennevilliers company.

LA CHEVAUCHÉE SUR LE LAC DE CONSTANCE (The Ride Across Lake Constance) by Peter Handke. With Jeanne Moreau, Delphine Seyrig, Michaël Lonsdale, Sami Frey, Gérard Depardieu.

PERICLES, PRINCE OF TYRE by William Shakespeare. Terry Hands's second production at the Comédie Française based on the Stratford original of 1968. With Michel Aumont, François Beaulieu, Ludmila Mikaël.

LE JOURNAL D'UN FOU (The Diary of a Madman) by Nicolai Gogol, adapted by and with Alain Illel.

LA PRINCESSE TURANDOT by Carlo Gozzi and Giacomo Puccini. Devised and directed by Lucian Pintilie. With a company of dwarfs.

CHAMAN HOOLIGAN by and with the Théâtre Laboratoire Vicinal of Brussels.

LE SUICIDE by Nikolai Erdman. With Jean-Louis Barrault, Marie-Hélène Breillat, Serge Franklin.

LE RÉVIZOR (The Government Inspector) by Nikolai Gogol. With the Théâtre de l'Unité company.

LES MÉFAITS DU TABAC (The Evils of Tobacco) by Anton Chekhov. With Guy Piér-
auld.

LA TRAGÉDIE OPTIMISTE (The Optimistic
Tragedy) by Vsevolod Vishnevsky. With the Vincent-Jourdheuil company.

LA SORCIÈRE DE DIRAH (The Witch of
Dirah) by Kusimo Sardono. With the Indonesian
Theater Company from Java, produced by the
Théâtre National de Chaillot of Paris.

THE TAMING OF THE SHREW by William
Shakespeare. With the Hédoné company.

PANTAGLEIZE by Michel de Ghelderode.
With the Cercle d'Art Populaire company.

IL CHASSE LE DIABLE (Driving the Devil
Out) by Bertolt Brecht. By the Arquebuse
Group.

LE CHAMP DE MORTS (The Field of the
Dead) by Edgar Lee Masters, adapted and translated from the *Spoon River Anthology*. With Jo-
sine Comellas, Gabriel Gascon and their company, from Canada.

LE SOLEIL SE COUCHE (Sundown) and ES-
CORIAL, double bill by Michel de Ghelderode.
With Marcel Lupovici, André Cazalas, Jacques
Roux.

TAMBOURS DANS LA NUIT (Drums in the
Night) by Bertolt Brecht. With the Théâtre de la
Reprise company.

KNOTS by R.D. Laing. With Kari Sylwan, Karin Thulin.

LES PROPRIÉTAIRES DES CLEFS (The
Keepers of the Keys) by Milan Kundera. With
Anne Doat, Robert Lombard.

LES MIGNONS ET LES GUENONS (Lovelies
and Dowdies) with the Cricot 2 Theatre from
Warsaw.

VINCENT ET L'AMIE DES PERSONNA-
LITÉS (Vincent and the VIP's Girl Friend) by
Robert Musil. With Dominique Paturel, Lau-
rence Bourdil, Jean-Pierre Moulin, Armand
Meffre.

TOLLER by Tankred Dorst. With Michel Auclair, Patrice Chéreau and the Théâtre National
Populaire company of Villeurbanne.

TROILUS AND CRESSIDA by William
Shakespeare. With Thierry Fortinaux, Laurence
Roi.

GRÂCITÉ (The Heart of Greece) by Yannis
Ritsos. Jacques Lacarrière's stage version of a
Greek patriot's poems. With the Young National
Theater company.

LES AFFAIRES MIRABOLANTES DU ROI
DES ALLUMETTES (Ivar Kreuger's Swindles)
by Jan Bergquist and Hans Bendrik. With Mario
Santini, Philippe Dauchez.

ANTIGONE by Bertolt Brecht. With Michel
Caccia, Françoise Selgeirolles. COMME LE
CORPS EST NU (How Naked the Corpse Is) by
and with the L.A.H. company from Argentina.

LIMITED RUNS OF INTERESTING NEW FRENCH PLAYS

LE DERNIER SORTI NETTOIE LA SALLE
(Last Out, Cleans the Place Out). Songs and
sketches by a troupe of clowns. By Luis Rego and
Jean-Luc Voulfow. With Luis Rego, Alain Le-
cointe.

LYCÉE THIERS, MATERNELLE JULES
FERRY (Thiers School, Jules Ferry Kindergar-
ten) by Xavier Pommeret. An upper-class cadet
learns the truth about the Commune. With
Jeanne-Marie Legendre, Bernard Malaterre.

MODEL BOY, OU AIMEZ-VOUS LE THÉ
AU JASMIN? (Model Boy, or Do You Like Jas-
min Tea?) by Yves Jacquemard and Jean-Michel
Sénécal. A quadrangular homo-erotic thriller.
With Isabelle Ehni (later Hélène Duc), Thierry
Dufour, the authors.

CHÉRI by Colette, adapted from the famous
novel of that name. With Inès Lazaris, Guy
Fournier.

LA BALLADE DE MAMAN JONES (The
Ballad of Mother Jones) by Catherine de Seynes.
The story of the U.S. Labor Movement. With the
Quatre Chemins Theater company.

AH! AH! AH! (SOURIEZ, NOUS FERONS LE
RESTE) (Smile and we do the rest) by and with
the Montreuil Theater School company.

HISTOIRE DU FABULEUX CAGLIOSTRO
(The Story of Cagliostro the Fabulous) by Roger
Defossez. Based on the Alexandre Dumas story.
With the Festival du Marais company.

HENRY III ET SA COUR (Henry III and his
Court) by Mario Franceschi. Based on the Alex-
andre Dumas story. With Yves Gasc, Nathalie
Nerval, Benoit Allemane.

IL PLEUT, SI ON TUAIT PAPA-MAMAN
(It's Raining, What About Doing Pa and
Ma In?) by Yves Navarre. A bitter bill with

lots of sugar. With the Festival du Marais company.

LA LÉGENDE DE EANNAH (Eannah's Legend) by Katiana Kowalski. With Hideyuki Yano, the author. An erotic fairy story.

À LA PETITE CUILLER (At the Little Spoon) by and with Pierre Louki.

L'HONNEUR DES CIPOLINO (The Honor of the Cipolino Family) by Jean-Jacques Bricaire and Maurice Lasaygues. Passion and love in present-day Sicily. With Harry-Max, Ginette Leclerc, Jacques Alric.

À LA NUIT LA NUIT (Tonight All Night) by François Billetdoux. A whore and her client. With Jacques Charby, Vera Gregh.

CLARA, OÙ EST CARLA? (Clara, Where Is Carla?) by Luis Campodonico. Where has my wife gone? With François Campo, Martine Vatel, Maxence Mailfort.

7 FOIS LA FOUDRE (Seven Times Thunder) by Etienne Rebaudengo (D). The dangers of atomic warfare. With Henri Crémieux, Jany Holt, Paul Le Person.

LA TRAGIQUE HISTOIRE ET LA FIN LAMENTABLE DU DR. FAUST (The Tragic History and Lamentable End of Dr. Faust) by Alain Recoing. Anthology of various versions of the Faust legend. With Marie-José Bloncourt, Gérard Weiss, the author.

TERRE (Earth) A collective drama about hunger and drought. With the Atelier de l'Epée de Bois Company.

PLAIDOYER POUR AUGUSTE (In Defense of August) by Camillo Baciu. Four military men take the stand. With Jacques Cancellier, Gérard Louault, Paul Pidancet, Jacques Ebner.

CHRONIQUES MARTIENNES (Martian Chronicles) by Louis Pauwels, adapted from Ray Bradbury's novel. The conquest of Mars. With the Guy Shelley Théâtre Poétique National company.

UN PETIT NID D'AMOUR (A Little Love-Nest) by Georges Michel. An absurd love story. With the Compagnie du Parnasse

PHILIPPE PÉTAIN by Dimitri Kollatos. What made Petain tick. With Arlette Baumann, Hélène Boitel, Jean-Marc Grangier.

LA B.I.D. (The I.D.B.) by Marianne Sergent and Aravni Merian. Crazy events in the cellar of the International 'Defense' Bank. With Marianne Sergent, Evelyne Grandjean, Zézette le Douarin.

C'EST DU BOIS QUI POURRIT (It's Rotting Wood) by Jean-René Toussaint. Human beings are nothing but rotting wood. With Guéry Burtin, the Author.

SUR LA PISTE (On the Runway) by Eduardo Manet. The absurd adventures of an incompatible couple, by the Cuban-born French writer. With Maria Laborit, Roger Mollien.

LE RÉSEAU DE LA VEUVE NOIRE (The Black Widow's Net) by Xavier Pommery. Something is rotten in the State of the U.S. With Paul Vial, and the Comédie de Saint-Étienne Company.

L'ÉCOLE DES BOURREAUX (School for Butchers) by Henri Lavagne (D). Revolutionary killers change places with their victims. With Erika Maaz, Paul Queret, Gérard Ruinet.

LES FÊTES SECRÈTES (Secret Holiday) by Jean-Manuel Florensa. A strange journey in mysterious company. With Jean-Claude Falet, Marie-Hélène Bonnet.

LE JOUR DE LA DOMINANTE (The Day of the Stronger) by René Escudié (D). A patient's dream in a psychiatric ward. With the Théâtre Éclaté Company from Annecy.

PROMÉTHÉE-PROIE (Prometheus-Prey) by Yves de la Croix (D). New view of an ancient Greek legend. With the La Torque company.

SI ON CAUSAIT . . . (If Only We'd Talk . . .) by and with the Théâtre d'Apremont company. Theater arguments that never meet.

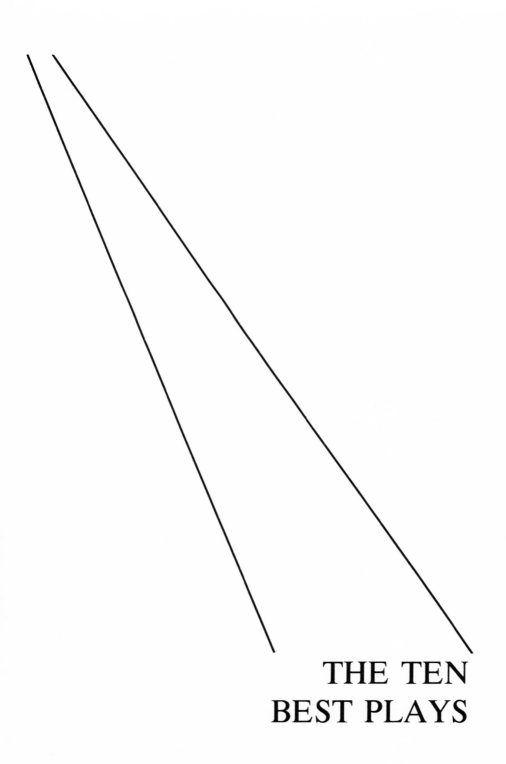

THE TEN
BEST PLAYS

Here are the synopses of 1973–74's ten Best Plays. By permission of the publishing companies which own the exclusive rights to publish these scripts in full in the United States, our continuities include many substantial quotations from crucial/pivotal scenes in order to provide a permanent reference to the style and quality of each play as well as its theme, structure and story line.

Scenes and lines of dialogue, stage directions and description quoted in the synopses appear *exactly* as in the stage version unless (in a very few instances, for technical reasons) an abridgement it indicated by five dots (. . . . .). The appearance of three dots (. . .) is the script's own punctuation to denote the timing of a spoken line.

THE CONTRACTOR

A Play in Three Acts

BY DAVID STOREY

Cast and credits appear on page 382

DAVID STOREY was born in 1934 in Wakefield, Yorkshire, the third son of a British coal miner. He was educated at Wakefield Grammar School, and he showed such promise as an athlete that at 17 he was signed to a contract with the Leeds Rugby League Club. He was admitted to the Honors Geography School at Reading University but decided at the last minute to study art and won a scholarship to the Slade School of Art in London and managed to pay back most of his signing bonus to the professional rugby group. He graduated in painting and exhibited in London with other Yorkshire artists. He still paints in his spare time, but he finally decided that writing was to be his medium of expression.

Storey worked for four years as a secondary school teacher in London's East End while writing seven novels which failed to satisfy even himself ("I was getting a bit wild, before I started getting on," he confided to an interviewer). His eighth, This Sporting Life, *was published in 1960, won the Macmillan Fiction Award and was made into a movie in 1963 by Lindsay Anderson, who has also directed some of Storey's plays. His published work includes four more novels:* Flight Into Camden, Radcliffe, Pasmore *and* A Temporary Life.

Eight years after he first wrote it, in 1966, Storey's first play The Restoration of Arnold Middleton *was produced in London by the Royal Court. His other London productions were* In Celebration *(1969, with an American premiere this season in Los Angeles),* The Contractor *(1970),* Home *(1971, and making the author's American stage debut in in November, 1971, winning him a Best Play citation and the New York Drama Critics Award for the best play of the 1970–71*

Broadway season) and The Changing Room *(1972, with an American premiere at the Long Wharf Theater in New Haven, Conn. in November, 1972 in a production which was transferred to Broadway and won another Best Play citation and Critics Award for the best play of 1972–73).*

Storey makes it three Best Play citations and three Critics best-of-bests Awards in a row with The Contractor, *which had its American premiere at the Long Wharf Theater in November, 1971 and finally reached New York this season in The Chelsea Theater Center production off Broadway. Storey lives in the Hampstead section of London with his wife and four children.*

Time: The present

Place: The lawn of Ewbank's house in Yorkshire

ACT I

Morning, late summer

SYNOPSIS: In the center of a featureless green lawn and against a cloudless sky stand three poles (or, in some productions, a single pole) about twenty feet high to which are attached numerous ropes and other gear to be used in raising a party tent. The construction foreman, Kay, *"a big man, hard, in his 40s, dressed in working trousers and a jacket, not at all scruffy,"* appears and checks the poles and ropes, which he has set up the day before. He is followed by one of his workmen, Marshall, *"a thin, rather lightweight Irishman, pleasant, easygoing, with no great appetite for work."*

The contractor who owns their construction company, Ewbank, comes in. *"He's a solid, well-built man, broad rather than tall, stocky. He's wearing a suit, which is plain, workmanlike and chunky; someone probably who doesn't take easily to wearing clothes, reflecting, perhaps, the feeling of a man who has never really found his proper station in life."* The tent is being prepared for a wedding, and Ewbank is the father of the bride-to-be. This is his lawn (and he warns Kay to be careful not to damage it) in front of his house (offstage left), his tent and his party.

Soon another workman, Fitzpatrick, *"a hard, shrewd Irishman, independent",* comes in eating a sandwich. Marshall is eating too. So is a third workman, Bennett, *"a fairly anonymous person, prefers to be inconspicuous, that is, without being overlooked. He'll do whatever is asked of him, no more and occasionally, if he's sure it'll cause no trouble, a little less,"* who is carrying a pole and thus has his sandwich stuffed in his mouth. He makes a big show in front of Ewbank of the heaviness of the pole.

FITZPATRICK: That's a lovely house you have there, Mr. Ewbank. *(Gestures off.)*

MARSHALL: Beautiful . . . ! Beautiful.

EWBANK: And I'll bloody well keep it that way if I've half a chance.

FITZPATRICK *(to Marshall):* He wouldn't be letting us in there, now, that's for sure. To warm up by the fire.

MARSHALL: Toes and fingers.

FITZPATRICK: Toes and fingers.

> *They laugh.*

MARSHALL: Just look, to God. *(Holds up his fingers.)* They're dropping off.

EWBANK: I came down to give you all a warning. Before you start. That house, now, is full of people.

MARSHALL *(looks up):* People . . .

EWBANK: Relatives of mine. It overlooks the lawn.

FITZPATRICK: It does. It does. *(To Marshall.)* How long's he had it?

EWBANK: And I don't want you, Fitzpatrick, up to your usual habits. Piddling all over the place, for one thing, whenever you feel like it. And language. I'd appreciate it very much, Kay, if you saw to it that they watched their tongues.

KAY: Aye. Right.

FITZPATRICK: You do that, Kay.

EWBANK: And for another thing, Kay: this lawn.

> *Paul comes in.*

FITZPATRICK: Don't tell me, now. *(Stoops. Examines grass.)* He has.

MARSHALL: Numbered every blade.

FITZPATRICK: Lettered every scratch.

EWBANK: Right. I think you know what's what.

The man who has just entered, Paul, is Ewbank's son, *"a bit slighter in build than his father, feckless, a little uncoordinated, perhaps. He's dressed in a shirt and slacks, the former unbuttoned and showing an apparent indifference to the chill of the morning. His initial attitude, deliberately implanted, is that of a loafer."* Ewbank warns Paul to keep out of the workmen's way but introduces him to the foreman Kay. Paul lifts one of the poles, demonstrating—to his father's surprise —that he might be capable of doing a man's work if he wanted to.

Ewbank's daughter Claire comes in. She is younger than Paul, *"easygoing, yet never anxious to be imposed upon. She's wearing jeans and a sweater which show a regard for practicality rather than fashion."* Claire surveys the work in progress for her wedding. Paul offers to help if needed, but Kay is noncommittal. Again Ewbank warns Kay about the men's behavior; he doesn't want them to do anything that might shock his elderly parents, who are here for the ceremony.

The Ewbank family departs, as Fitzpatrick and Marshall carry on some more tent poles and then pause for a breather. They gossip with Bennett about the Ewbanks. Paul, they decide, is educated—unlike his father—an intellectual who's never done a real day's work. Ewbank's big house, they decide, was built at low-paid labor's expense (Fitzpatrick quotes: "The windows bright with our sweat/The concrete moistened by our sorrows.")

Kay is going about his business, never breaking the rhythm of his efforts, occasionally prodding the others to keep them to the business at hand. Another workman, Glendenning, who has been busy closing the gates after all the tent materials have been brought into place, comes in to join the others.

> *Glendenning is perhaps in his early 20s, a good-natured, stammering half-wit. He wears overalls, well-worn but scrupulously clean, and considerably too large for him. A big pair of boots stick out from underneath; something, altogether, of a caricature of a workman. He has entered, carrying a fourteen-pound sledge hammer over one shoulder, and several marquee stakes over the other.*

GLENDENNING: I . . . I . . . I . . . I . . . I . . . I . . .

MARSHALL *(sings to tune of "Down Mexico Way")*: Ay, yi, yi, yi . . . Ay, yi, yi, yi!

GLENDENNING: I . . . I . . . I . . . I'm going to n . . . n . . . n . . . *nnnnn* . . . knock in some . . . *sssss* . . . stakes.

BENNETT: Stakes!

FITZPATRICK: Stakes, bejesus.

KAY *(matter of fact)*: You bloody idiot.

GLENDENNING: W . . . wwww . . . what?

MARSHALL: He said: "You bloody idiot."

GLENDENNING: Wa . . .

BENNETT: The stakes, man. The stakes.

> *Glendenning looks at the stakes. He gazes at them for a while.*

GLENDENNING: W . . . wwww . . . what?

KAY *(going, casual)*: Fitzpatrick. Bennett . . . Come on, now. Come on. *(He goes.)*

FITZPATRICK: You don't knock stakes in here.

MARSHALL: You don't at all.

GLENDENNING: What? *(He looks up at the poles.)*

BENNETT: Not in Mr. Ewbank's lawn.

MARSHALL: No, no.

FITZPATRICK: He's planted this, he has, with special grass. *(Gestures at house.)* You've to step over it . . . like walking on a cloud. Here, now. Here. Look at this . . .

> *Fitzpatrick tiptoes to and fro so that Glendenning might see.*

Kay calls to them from offstage, but they continue making game of Glendenning, threatening him with what Ewbank might do if he saw those stakes. Glendenning listens to them carefully, but he doesn't seem to mind their joking at his expense.

Kay comes back carrying the first piece of canvas to be stretched on the poles. Glendenning wonders how they're going to keep the tent up without stakes, and it turns out that the day before Kay and Bennett implanted stakes in the flower beds around the lawn, "Each one disguised, very nearly, as a flower."

Working together, this crew—which is of course completely familiar with the details of the job—spreads and shackles the pieces of canvas. *"Gradually, in spite of their chatter, the pace of work has begun to assert itself."* The canvas is clean and white, the tent made brand new by Ewbank especially for his daughter's wedding. The details of setting bolts, pole rings, etc. continue as the men chatter about marriage and bachelorhood. As they are working at the foot of the poles, an old man enters.

> *Old Ewbank has come on. In his late 60s, wearing a tweed suit: gnarled. An old artisan. He wanders across absent-mindedly, lighting his pipe.*

OLD EWBANK: Have you seen an old piece of rope lying around? . . . About this length.

MARSHALL: What?

OLD EWBANK: Here. About this thick. *(Makes a circle with thumb and finger which he adjusts with some care.)*

MARSHALL: No, no, I don't think I have . . .

OLD EWBANK: Water? You couldn't rot it if you tried.

MARSHALL: Oh . . .

OLD EWBANK: No damn stamina. Resilience: nothing. *(He walks off.)*

FITZPATRICK: And who the hell was that?

MARSHALL: I've no idea. *(Laughs.)*

FITZPATRICK: Well, now. This is the funniest place I've ever seen.

KAY: Right, then . . . let's have it up.

FITZPATRICK: Up?

MARSHALL: Up?

FITZPATRICK: Glenny, now—that's you he means.

> *They laugh.*

KAY: Right, then. Shoulder height . . . fasten off.

> *Between them, having spread out the canvas—two middle pieces and an end—they haul it up to shoulder height, the sections fastened together by the collars. They fasten the ropes off, through holes in the base of the tent poles, and begin to lace the sheets of canvas together.*

Talking as they work, they remember Ewbank's indignation recently when a beggar asked him for a penny. Glendenning tries to join the conversation but becomes the object of the others' gibes as soon as he opens his mouth. He manages to observe that if he had a daughter he'd want her to get married in a tent like this. Kay has four daughters, but Glendenning wouldn't want to marry one of them. He is attracted by Ewbank's daughter, the bride-to-be.

Glendenning is sent off by his teasing colleages to fetch "a glass hammer and rubber nails," while Kay brings on the canvas walling for the marquee and spreads it out. When Glendenning returns he is not at all upset by the joke played on him; he is as good-natured as he is simple-hearted. As they all continue working under Kay's direction, Fitzpatrick makes an admiring comment about Ewbank's wife, and this sets off the give-and-take of conversation which serves as an audio background to the physical labor, sometimes progressing steadily on a single theme, sometimes disjointed, like the work itself; sometimes benign, but more often barbed.

KAY: Either way, one wife, after a couple of years, is very much like another.
FITZPATRICK: Is that so, now. Is that a fact?
KAY: It is.
FITZPATRICK: You've seen old Ewbank's wife, then, Marshy?
MARSHALL: What? What? Where's that? *(Looking quickly round. They laugh.)*
FITZPATRICK: Bloody nig-nog, man.
MARSHALL: Oh. Aye.
FITZPATRICK: You don't think much to her, Marshy?
MARSHALL: Do I not? *(Laughs.)*
FITZPATRICK: Seen better, have you Marshy?
MARSHALL: Seen better? I should think I have.
BENNETT: And where would that be, Marshy?
MARSHALL: Around, I think. Around.
BENNETT: Around? Around where, then Marshall?
MARSHALL: One or two places I have in mind.
>   *They laugh.*
BENNETT: The places Marshall hangs around I'd be surprised if you'd find a woman there at all.
FITZPATRICK: Is that a fact, now Benny. I'm not so sure of that.
MARSHALL: Won't find Bennett there, now: that's for sure.
FITZPATRICK: Find Bennett some places I wouldn't care to mention.
>   *They laugh.*
Seen him one night . . . now, where was it? . . . taking out his dog.
MARSHALL: A dog?
FITZPATRICK: Fine little mongrel . . . Black and white, now . . .
MARSHALL: Wags its tail.
FITZPATRICK: Wags its tail, you're right.
KAY: Right, then . . . are you ready? . . . . .

In spite of this running stream of conversation, in which each man must play his part and keep to his pecking order, the tent is finally ready to be pulled up. With a man at each rope, Kay gives the signal: "Heave . . . heave . . . heave!" The canvas roof rises to the top of the poles, *"The ropes are fastened off: threaded through holes in the pole for that purpose, then knotted, the men going to put in the side poles as they finish, hoisting up the edges of the tent. . . . . Kay has started 'dressing off' the ropes, wrapping them off, naval fashion, around the foot of the poles."* Fitzpatrick whistles and sings to warn of the approach of Ewbank, on an inspection visit. Ewbank accuses the men of loafing on the job. His comment is merely a boss's reflex, and the men's work rhythm is unaltered by it.

EWBANK: That's a nice bit of canvas, Kay.
KAY: It is. *(Nods, looking up at it.)*
EWBANK: They don't make them like that no more. *(Gestures at tent.)* 'Least not if I can help it. *(Laughs at his own humor.)* It'd be too damn expensive.
KAY: Aye, it would.
EWBANK *(pleased, contemplating):* Would you believe it?

KAY: Aye?

EWBANK: It's the first time I've hired a bit of my own tenting. It'll go down in the books you know. Pay meself with one hand what I tek out with the other.

KAY: Aye! *(Laughs dutifully.)*

EWBANK: I'll never do it again. Never. Never have to.

KAY: No. Well. It's worth making a splash.

EWBANK: Splash? By God, this is a bloody thunderclap! It's not just the tent I'm paying for. God, Christ. I wish it was. No. No. *(To men.)* Hang it! Hang it! Hang it! Hang it! *Hook it up!* That's what they're there for. *(To Kay.)* Three or four hundred people here. Bloody string orchestra. Waiters. Chef. I could buy four marquees with what I've laid out here . . . Ah, well. That's another matter. *(Looks round, examining canvas.)* Let's hope it keeps fine.

Ewbank sympathizes with Kay's having four daughters to provide weddings for. He warns Kay to take special care in setting down the floor (the men are finishing the walling, leaving one side open to bring the floor through). Ewbank's firm has 34 tents rented out this week alone. This piece of canvas is inscribed along one of the seams "Made by F. Ewbank to commemorate the wedding of his daughter Claire."

Claire herself comes in and wanders around the tent, inspecting it, informing them that the others are coming down to see how the job is progressing.

EWBANK: They don't need any supervision. Not with Kay. How long've you been with me? Three years. That's about as long as anybody in this place. They don't stay long. I employ anybody here, you know. Anybody who'll work. Miners who've coughed their lungs up, fitters who've lost their fingers, madmen who've run away from home. *(Laughs.)*

> As the men go in and out they gaze over at Claire, Fitzpatrick still whistling his tune whenever he appears.

They don't mind. They know me. They can soon get shut. I've the biggest turnover of manual labor in this town. I take on all those that nobody else'll employ. See that?

> He indicates the inscription on the tent.

CLAIRE: You'll look well if we put it off.

EWBANK: Put it off? You'll not get this chance again. Not from me. Not from him either. *(He thumbs off, to Kay.)* She's marrying a bloody aristocrat, Kay. He's so refined if it wasn't for his britches he'd be invisible.

CLAIRE: Not like somebody else we know . . .

Ewbank is a rough-and-ready type and is glad to admit it. He warns Fitzpatrick not to "sir" him. His son Paul comes in expecting his father to have joined the workers, but Ewbank is an artisan who has already done his work in making the tent, not one of the workers who puts it up. Paul offers his services to Kay; his father used to let him help out at half a crown an hour, so Paul is familiar with the work. Paul helps Glendenning carry in battens while Ewbank, Kay and Claire depart.

Paul joins the men in admiring the workmanship of the tent. Glendenning confides to Paul that because of his handicap he probably couldn't get a job anywhere else. He would like to have a taste of Paul's occupation, which seems to be not doing anything at all, just loafing.

The groom-to-be, Maurice, enters wearing *"a jacket and flannels, a bit crumpled. He's tall, perhaps with a moustache; fairly ordinary and straightforward."* He is looking for Claire and warns of Old Ewbank's approach, as Paul continues laying flooring. Maurice begs a cigarette from the men, and Fitzpatrick obliges, Maurice promising to return the favor. To Maurice, the process of raising the tent and holding the ceremony seems "a lot of fuss." Glendenning has gone out and come back carrying a 14-pound sledge hammer, and now he proudly marches up and down with it over his shoulder, showing off for Paul's benefit.

Old Ewbank enters with his wife, *"in her 60's, a small, practical, homely person."* The old man cannot keep away from the job. Meanwhile, Kay comes in, takes the hammer from Glendenning and stops his military pacing. Old Ewbank tells them all how he used to be a ropemaker but began making tents in his old age and passed on the skill to his son.

OLD EWBANK: Ropes. That's my trade. Nowt like it.

PAUL *(calling):* I should get out of here, Gran. Something's likely to fall on his head.

   A section of floor, in fact, has narrowly missed Old Ewbank's head.

OLD MRS. EWBANK: I will. I will . . . I never knew you were employed here, Paul.

PAUL: I don't know . . . Got to find your natural level, Gran.

OLD MRS. EWBANK: I've heard that before, I think, somewhere else—

PAUL: Aye. I believe you have. *(Laughs.)*

OLD EWBANK *(to Bennett):* The best education money can buy. That's my grandson. Oxford. Cambridge. University College. All the rest. Ask him about anything and he'll come up with an answer.

BENNETT: Oh. Aye . . .

OLD EWBANK: Not got his father's skill.

FITZPATRICK *(joining in):* No?

OLD EWBANK: Sure? I am. He couldn't thread a needle. . . . .

Old Mrs. Ewbank leads Old Ewbank off as the men comment on the old man's indomitable pride. Fitzpatrick is curious about Paul's education, about the bridegroom's profession (a doctor) and the bride's accomplishments (a nurse), but somewhat facetious in his comments. Fitzpatrick and Marshall identify themselves as honest Irish working men, Bennett as English stock, to which Fitzpatrick comments, "English born, English bred:/Long in the leg and thick in the head."

Having finished laying the floor, the men take a breather. But Kay wants the tent lining brought under cover before they rest, and the men go off to do this. Mrs. Ewbank, Paul's mother, comes in and inspects the half-raised marquee, remembering how a workman once lost a finger because of an unattended splinter from the flooring.

PAUL: Dangerous job.

MRS. EWBANK: Yes.

> *She walks on after a moment, looking round. Sees inscription overhead, on the canvas.*

I didn't know he'd written that.

PAUL: All done by stencils.

MRS. EWBANK: Is that it? *(Gazes up at it.)*

PAUL: Takes it all to heart.

MRS. EWBANK: Yes. He does. *(Pause.)* Why? Don't you like it? *(Casual, pleasant.)*

PAUL: I don't know. *(Shrugs, laughs.)* I suppose I do . . . Frank by name . . . *(Imitates Ewbank's voice.)*

MRS. EWBANK: But not by nature.

PAUL: No?

MRS. EWBANK: No.

The men are heard offstage joking with Glendenning. Mrs. Ewbank guesses that her son plans to go away somewhere when all this is over—he doesn't quite know where yet. Mrs. Ewbank goes off as the men come in carrying bags of canvas. They go out again leaving Paul alone, sitting on a bag of canvas, pensive, abstracted, whistling a melancholy tune as the lights slowly fade. *Curtain.*

ACT II

Afternoon of the same day

Fitzpatrick, Marshall and Bennett are installing the green, yellow and white muslin lining. This fabric too was made especially for this occasion. Fitzpatrick remembers his first sight of a tent—of a field of tents—while in the army; he was thinking what a pity it was that they would have to be taken down some day.

They question Kay about his past, hinting that he was in prison before he came to work for Ewbank. As usual, Kay remains riveted to the job, enigmatic, refusing to take any bait whatsoever. The men raise and fasten the muslin, admiring it as it is pulled into place.

Glendenning comes in eating a large bun Mrs. Ewbank has given him. In exaggerated fashion, the men pretend to be disappointed that Glendenning didn't share his prize with his friends. Kay and Bennett set about bringing in the tent's furniture—white metal chairs and tables. Fitzpatrick and Marshall manage to make Glendenning unhappy by describing a bun with cream and strawberries they are not going to share with him. Glendenning finally is so unhappy that he weeps, as Ewbank enters roaring about the men wearing their boots while walking on the marquee's floor. Ewbank has been drinking, though not very much, but as Bennett takes his shoes off the other men pretend to be singing drunkenly.

Ewbank ignores this, admiring the nearly-completed tent. He placates Glendenning by sending him off on an errand.

Paul comes in, in shirt-sleeves hanging loosely down, his hands deep in his pockets, standing in the door, stooping slightly.

PAUL: I've had me snap. I've had me rest. Now. Where would you like me?

EWBANK *(looking up):* There's nowt in here for you, lad.

PAUL: I don't mind. I'll give a hand.

EWBANK: There's no need.

PAUL: No, no, I understand. Nevertheless . . . I'll do whatever it is I'm able.

He goes to dress the muslin ropes on the main poles.

EWBANK: Marshall. Fetch in the walling. You can start hanging that.

Marshall gets up and goes out.

(To Kay.) Keep that evenly spaced there, Kay.

KAY: Aye. We'll have it straight. Don't worry.

Arranging muslin. Ewbank stands gazing round, a little helpless.

EWBANK: Aye, well . . . *(Looks at his watch.)* I'll look in again in a few minutes. I shan't be long. *(Goes.)*

Marshall comes in with the sack containing the muslin walling.

BENNETT *(working with his back to the door):* Has he gone?

MARSHALL: You can breathe again, feller. *(To Paul.)* No disrespect, mind, to you at all.

PAUL: No, No. None at all.

FITZPATRICK: What're you going to be at the wedding, then?

PAUL: Oh, I don't know.

FITZPATRICK *(cheerful):* Not the best man, then?

PAUL: I might well be that.

They laugh.

FITZPATRICK: What did you study at the school, then?

PAUL: Nothing much.

MARSHALL: Nothing much, to God. You better not tell him that.

Gestures at house. They laugh.

They are hanging muslin walling, and Fitzpatrick confesses his onetime ambition to become a criminal lawyer. Bennett complains of rheumatism. The workmen tell Paul about Kay's past, and they all wonder what sort of crime he committed to land himself in jail. Fitzpatrick prods the imperturble Kay, trying to make him talk.

FITZPATRICK: Kay is a very hard man. You'll get nothing out of him. He didn't suffer all that, you know, in vain. *(Friendly.)* Isn't that right, Kay?

Kay, unmoved until now, has gone on with his work, not even looking up. Now, however, he pauses. He looks up very slowly.

KAY: And what sort of suffering have you done, Fitzpatrick?

FITZPATRICK: Suffering? By God. I'm suffering every day.

MARSHALL *(laughs, snorting):* All day. Seven days a week. Fifty-two weeks in the year.

KAY: Aye. Between one bottle and another. One barroom and the next.

FITZPATRICK: Me? I hope you heard all that. I wouldn't touch a drop of liquor.

Marshall snorts again.

I mean, dropping no names, Kay, and all that there and that, aspersions of that nature would be better cast in a different direction altogether. *(Gestures at the house.)*

KAY: Some people have a grievance. And some of them haven't.

FITZPATRICK: And what is that supposed to mean?

Kay looks at Paul, then looks away. The others look at Paul.

PAUL: Don't mind me. I'm easy.

KAY: Bennett. Mind that walling.

FITZPATRICK: Are you frightened of telling us something, Kay?

KAY: If you want to work, Fitzpatrick, work. If not, the best thing you can do is to clear off altogether.

Kay returns to hang and arrange muslin walling.

FITZPATRICK: Ay. Ay, now. Those are very strong words. *(To Marshall.)* Very strong words indeed.

MARSHALL: If it wasn't for the fact that no trade union would have us . . .

FITZPATRICK: I'd repeat that to the man in charge.

MARSHALL: The top official.

FITZPATRICK: Right away.

MARSHALL: Intimidation . . .

FITZPATRICK: Suppression of the right to labor.

KAY: You wouldn't know a piece of work, Fitzpatrick, if you saw it. The bloody lot of you . . . *(Gestures at the house.)* Poor sod.

Glendenning comes in with some chocolate which he happily breaks into pieces and shares with the others. The bride and groom come onto the scene and comment on Paul's work. Rather bluntly, Fitzpatrick asks Claire and Maurice, "What's it like, then, to be the happy couple? The blushing bride and the handsome groom?" They take it in good part, even when Fitzpatrick goes on to comment on Claire's beauty and beg a cigarette of Maurice.

Stammering, Glendenning asks about Ewbank; he has been sent to get tobacco for him and insists on delivering it in person. Old Ewbank comes in and wanders around, fingering a short piece of rope, showing it off to the others and boasting of how rope was made by hand in the old days, wishing he were still working. Mrs. Ewbank comes in and advises her son Paul not to get in the workmen's way.

Ewbank comes in carrying some of the marquee's finishing touches: boxes to enclose the bottom of the poles and muslin to drape the tops. He curses the others for walking on the floor with their shoes, but there is nothing personal in his remarks. His wife goes off to make tea.

Old Ewbank is reminiscing to nobody in particular about his working days; Fitzpatrick is softly singing his drinking song; Bennett is complaining of a splinter in his foot; Ewbank is consulting with Kay. Glendenning is trying to deliver the tobacco to a preoccupied Ewbank, and Claire and Maurice lead Old Ewbank off toward the house.

GLENDENNING: I . . . I . . . I . . . I . . .

EWBANK: What? What? What?

He's busy getting the muslin drapery ready to take up the ladder.

BENNETT: He's brought you your tobacco, Mr. Ewbank.
EWBANK: What? . . . Oh.
> *Pauses. Then takes it.*
Aye. You're a good lad.
GLENDENNING: I . . . I . . . I . . . I . . .
EWBANK: Did you buy yourself some chocolate?
GLENDENNING: Aye.
> *Marshall whistles "Down Mexico Way" refrain.*
EWBANK *(to Fitzpatrick):* Hold it. Hold it. Hold it. Hold it. God damn and
blast . . .
> *Ewbank has turned to the ladder and begun to mount it, hammer in one hand, drapery in the other. All the men now, but for Glendenning and Fitzpatrick, who is holding the ladder, are working, watching Ewbank at the same time.*
FITZPATRICK *(sings):*
Somebody has had a tipple . . .
Somebody has had a drop . . .
PAUL: I think we've had enough of that.
FITZPATRICK: What . . .?
PAUL: I think we've had enough of it.
FITZPATRICK: I was just . . . *(To Marshall.)* I have a very melodious voice.
> *Bennett snorts.*
MARSHALL: He has. It's right.
> *Fitzpatrick shrugs. Paul goes back to work. Fitzpatrick, so the others can see, sings silently, mouthing the words hugely.*
KAY: All right, Fitzpatrick. You've had your laugh.
EWBANK *(above):* Hold it. God damn and blast.

Ewbank finishes draping the muslin, and Paul moves in and holds the ladder for his father to come down. Ewbank orders Paul to go fetch the flowers, assuring his son that he is aware of everything that is going on here, every nuance, so that the men can put nothing over on him while Paul is absent. Paul goes, while Ewbank gets back onto the ladder, now held by Fitzpatrick. Ewbank finishes the work (as Paul starts bringing in flowers), descends the ladder safely and orders Fitzpatrick to do the draping of the last pole.

Ewbank, looking around at the nearly-finished tent, comments, "I shall never do it again, never." The others are busy doing various chores while Old Mrs. Ewbank comes in carrying a flowering plant which she contributes to the decoration. She admires Paul's skill at arranging the other flowers. Marshall is polishing the floor. Kay and Glendenning bring in the rest of the furniture.

Ewbank hurries them all at their tasks; he wants the job over and done with. They clear away their tools, bags, etc., and finally there is the finished work with its new canvas gleaming and floor shining and Paul arranging the last of the flowers. Ewbank is still fussing over details as the men clear away all extraneous materials. For a moment father and son are alone, and Ewbank asks Paul, "Do you ever fancy this job?" Paul shakes his head, no.

The workmen, Glendenning included, come in to say goodnight, to wish the family good luck, and slowly depart, leaving father and son alone once again.

Ewbank and Paul stand silently in the tent. Vaguely they look around.
EWBANK: You know. You mustn't mind them. *(Gestures off.)*
PAUL: Oh . . . *(Realizing.)* No.
EWBANK: They've a mind for nowt, you know.
PAUL: Yes . . . *(Nods.)*
EWBANK: It'll not happen again, you know.
       Paul Looks up at him.
(Gestures round.) This.
PAUL: There'll not be the chance.
EWBANK: Too bloody old to start again.
PAUL: Aye.
EWBANK: Ah . . . Well, then . . .
       Pause.
PAUL: Aye . . . Well . . . I'll go and fetch some flowers.
       Paul goes. Ewbank stands gazing at the tent.

Old Mrs. Ewbank brings in a plant, and Mrs. Ewbank follows her, joining Ewbank in admiring the tent. Claire and Maurice come in and pronounce it "lovely." Old Ewbank wanders in vaguely, bringing another piece of his hand-made rope. Claire and Maurice and Paul and his mother pantomime dancing, so that Old Ewbank believes they are dancing to music which he cannot hear.

Paul hands his mother over to his father, who takes her around the floor in a waltz. *"Ewbank's dancing is heavy, firm and implacable, entirely characteristic of himself."* Old Ewbank, his mind wandering, blames the machines for destroying the old values of workmanship.

OLD EWBANK *(holding rope):* A bit of pressure, and they come to pieces in your hand.
OLD MRS. EWBANK: I'll take him in and let him lie down.
EWBANK: Aye . . . he needs looking after.
OLD EWBANK: I worked thirty or forty hours a day.
OLD MRS. EWBANK: He means at weekends.
OLD EWBANK *(going):* What? If I'd had any more I'd have given him a bit . . .
OLD MRS. EWBANK: Oh, well. We might find a piece or two you've forgotten.
OLD EWBANK: By God. They are. One glance and they damn well come apart.
       They go. Ewbank sits in silence.
MRS. EWBANK: Well, then . . .
       Pause.
PAUL: I'll go in and wash up. *(Looking at his hands.)*
MAURICE: Yes. Well, I better be getting home . . .
CLAIRE: I'll get your things.
MAURICE *(to Mrs. Ewbank):* I'll see you later. This evening.

MRS. EWBANK: Yes. Later on.
CLAIRE: And tonight, try and stay . . .
MAURICE: What?
CLAIRE: Sober.
    They go. Ewbank and Mrs. Ewbank are left alone. They are silent.
MRS. EWBANK: Well. All ready.
EWBANK: Aye.
    They are silent.
MRS. EWBANK: Are you coming in? *(Ewbank looks up.)* Spend your last
evening with your daughter.
EWBANK: Aye. *(He looks up at the finished tent.)*
MRS. EWBANK: We'll manage.
EWBANK: Aye. We'll make a damn good job of it. *(Half laughs.)* . . . We will.
MRS. EWBANK: Well, then. *(Going.)* Aren't you coming?
    *Goes. Ewbank gazes round, picks up the old piece of rope Old Ewbank
    has left. Gazes round. Rises. Goes. Slowly the light fades. Curtain.*

ACT III

Morning, two days later

The wedding has taken place; bride, groom, orchestra and guests have departed, and *"the tent has suffered a great deal. Part of the muslin drapery hangs
loosely down. Similarly, parts of the lining round the walls hang down in loose
folds."* Even the dance floor has been disturbed, and there are tables lying on their
sides among the empty bottles, napkins, streamers, etc.

The workmen and Kay come in and survey the scene. The revels now have
ended, obviously, and it is time for the men to dismantle the tent they have so
painstakingly erected. Picking up bottles, Fitzpatrick tests them for dregs and
finds a sip here and there; so does Marshall. Kay orders Glendenning to start
taking away chairs, but Fitzpatrick tells him to go fetch a hammer.

    *Glendenning immediately puts down the chair he's carrying, nods, and
    goes quickly outside.*
BENNETT: You want to leave him alone . . .
MARSHALL: What?
BENNETT: Glendenning.
MARSHALL: Ah, now. Go jump on your bloody head.
BENNETT *(backs down):* God. It's freezing. *(Shivers.)*
    They continue working. Kay has begun to take down the muslin walls.
KAY: Marshall, will you bring in the muslin bags.
MARSHALL: Aye. Aye. *(To Bennett.)* It's me today. Fitzpatrick, no doubt it'll
be you tomorrow.
FITZPATRICK *(looking round again):* Good God, you know, but this is a bloody
mess.
BENNETT: Aye, aye . . .

They proceed with taking down the tent and skipping from subject to subject in their comments. As they continue to make jokes at Glendenning's expense, Bennett tells Fitzpatrick to leave the youngster alone, and Fitzpatrick calls him "dictatorial" and "censorious." Fitzpatrick suggests that there is a hidden reason for Bennett's customary ill humor: his wife left him for another man.

BENNETT: Your mouth's going to open too wide one of these days, Fitzpatrick.

FITZPATRICK: It'll be all the easier to let the truth come flying out.

BENNETT: And for me to put my fist inside it.

FITZPATRICK: Since when has a man like me let a man like you put his fist inside my mouth?

Marshall laughs. Bennett tenses but doesn't answer.

KAY: Fitzpatrick, get out, and load the truck outside.

FITZPATRICK: On my own? God damn it. I'm only human.

MARSHALL: Almost.

FITZPATRICK: Almost *(Going.)* It's a hard bloody life is this: walk the straight and narrow and you end up working by yourself. *(He goes.)*

MARSHALL: Well. Well. Now there's a thing. *(Tuts away to himself.)* Revelations.

BENNETT: And it's not only Fitzpatrick.

MARSHALL: Not only what?

BENNETT: Who'll feel the end of this *(Holds up his fist.)*

MARSHALL: What? What? . . . You're not thinking . . . You can't mean it?

Bennett gazes steadily at him, obviously unable to carry out his threat, then turns and goes back to his work.

Good God. He can.

Fitzpatrick can be heard singing outside. Silence for a moment inside the tent.

Do you think now . . .

Bennett looks up threateningly.

(Spreading his arms.) We'd get anything back on the bottles.

They go back to work.

Fitzpatrick comes in and warns them he can hear Ewbank singing up at the house. The men imagine how warm and comfortable Ewbank's circumstances must be, and they skip from subject to subject: how many hours Glendenning sleeps at night, whether Kay has been in prison, whether the wedding celebration reached orgy pitch, whether the bride and bridegroom will be happy, how wives can be unfaithful (this is aimed straight at Bennett, and he feels it).

Kay continually prods them all onward in the task of taking down the tent. Fitzpatrick and Marshall improvise a sort of litany mocking this job and the type of men employed in it.

FITZPATRICK: Some of them . . .

MARSHALL: You're right.

FITZPATRICK: Come here because they're bone idle.

MARSHALL: Like myself you mean.

FITZPATRICK: Like yourself. On the other hand . . .

MARSHALL: Aye . . .

FITZPATRICK: There are those . . .

MARSHALL: Aye . . .

FITZPATRICK: Who have it in them to rise to higher things.

MARSHALL: Higher things. They have.

FITZPATRICK: Who have, within them, Marshy, the capacity to get on.

MARSHALL: They have. They have. You're right.

FITZPATRICK: But who, suddenly—through some calamity on the domestic front . . .

MARSHALL: The domestic front . . .

FITZPATRICK: In a manner of speaking . . .

MARSHALL: In a manner of speaking. That's right.

FITZPATRICK: Lose . . .

MARSHALL: Lose.

FITZPATRICK: All interest in carrying on.

MARSHALL: They do. They do. You're right.

FITZPATRICK: Some terrible calamity overwhelms them . . .

MARSHALL: . . . on the domestic front . . .

FITZPATRICK: And up, into the wide blue yonder . . . all pride and initiative: gone.

MARSHALL: Aye . . . Vanished.

Bennett, now infuriated, threatens them with a rope and shackle. Kay intervenes.

KAY: That's enough, Fitzpatrick.

FITZPATRICK: I was merely ascertainin' the truth of the matter, Kay.

MARSHALL *(to Fitzpatrick):* What's a man's life worth if it's comprised of nothing but untruths and lies?

FITZPATRICK: What is it now, indeed?

KAY: And what's so remarkable about your life, Fitzpatrick?

FITZPATRICK: Remarkable?

KAY: That it gives you the right to go poking so often into other people's.
    Glendenning has come in slowly.
A loud-mouth. A wet rag. That doesn't do a crumb of work unless he's driven to it.

FITZPATRICK: Loud-mouth, now, I might be. And bone-idle.
    Marshall snorts.
But I'm the only one round here who hasn't anything to hide.

KAY: Are you, now. Then you're very lucky. You're a very lucky man, Fitzpatrick. If you don't mind me saying so.

FITZPATRICK: No. I don't mind. I probably am. You're right.
    Marshall laughs.

KAY *(unruffled):* And you think that, then, has some virtue.

FITZPATRICK: Aye. I think it probably has. Meaning no disrespect whatsoever,

(Indicating Bennett.) it was Bennett who pointed out the fact with which, until then, we were unacquainted. Namely that you, Kay, yourself, had been in clink. So what . . . ?

MARSHALL: Some of my best friends are criminals.

FITZPATRICK: What I can't abide is a man who can point his finger at other people but can't bear the same one to be pointed at himself.

KAY: Some people, Fitzpatrick, have injuries that go deeper than you imagine.

Fitzpatrick continues to taunt Kay, not seeing that he has already gone too far. Kay doesn't intend to put up with Fitzpatrick's deliberate trouble-making any longer.

KAY: I think you'd better get home, Fitzpatrick.

FITZPATRICK: What?

KAY: I think you better get off. Come into the office at the end of the week and you'll get whatever you're owed.
  Silence.

FITZPATRICK: Huh. *(Looks round for his jacket.)* Do you mean that?

KAY: I do.
  Fitzpatrick goes to his jacket. He slowly pulls it on.

FITZPATRICK *(to Marshall):* Are you coming?

MARSHALL: Well, now . . . If there's one of us to be out of work . . . better that the other sticks to what he can.

FITZPATRICK *(bitterly):* Aye. I suppose you're right. *(He goes to the door.)* It's amazing, you know . . . the way he surrounds himself with cripples. *(Gestures at the house.)*

KAY: Cripples?

FITZPATRICK: Yourself . . . Bennett . . . Glenny . . . Marshall . . .

MARSHALL: Fitzpatrick . . .

FITZPATRICK: And lastly of course, myself. It qualifies, I suppose, the nature . . . of his warm and understanding heart. Ah, well. You can tell him one thing for nothing. The road up yonder is a harder climb than that. *(Thumbs upwards.)* I'll say goodbye. May God go with you, and treat you more kindly than Himself.
  Taps Glendenning on the shoulder as he goes.
Watch it, Glenny. One day, mind . . . *(Gestures hammer with his hand.)*

GLENDENNING: Aye. *(Laughs.)*
  As Fitzpatrick goes to the door Ewbank comes in.

EWBANK: And where the hell do you think you're going to? God Christ. Just look at the time. Knocking off and they've only been here half an hour.

FITZPATRICK: I've been fired.

EWBANK: Don't be so bloody silly. Get on with this bloody walling . . . God damn and blast. Just look. Covered in bloody muck. *Marshall . . . !* *(Gestures at Marshall to get on with the floor.)* Fitzpatrick . . . let's have it up. *(Indicates floor.)*
  Slowly they go back to their tasks. Kay alone doesn't look up.
Kay, let's have these battens out . . . Good God. We're going to be here all night.

KAY: Bennett . . .

MARSHALL: The couple got off to a happy start then, Mr. Ewbank.
EWBANK: What? . . .
MARSHALL: The happy . . .
EWBANK: Mind your own bloody business. Bennett, I don't call that working. *(To Marshall.)* How the hell would you know that?
MARSHALL: I . . . Me . . . We . . .
FITZPATRICK: Ah, but a great day. Celebratin' . . .
EWBANK: I'll celebrate my boot up your bloody backside, Fitzpatrick. That's what I'll do . . . God Christ. God Christ. They come in here and start telling you what sort of night you've had . . .
KAY: Bennett, over here . . .
They work, silent, taking out the battens and the last of the floor. Ewbank grunts, groans, murmurs to himself.

Marshall tactlessly asserts to Ewbank that Fitzpatrick was truly sacked, and Ewbank's reply is, "There's been nobody sacked from this firm since the day it first began." Ewbank advises Kay to do something about his four daughters, then reminisces about the party and tells the men how he made his speech standing on a table. In response to passing comments by Marshall and Fitzpatrick, Ewbank casually reveals that the crime for which Kay was imprisoned was embezzlement, but "There's nowt for him to embezzle here."

Ewbank tells them that his son Paul is ready to set out on his travels as a member of the wandering younger generation. Old Ewbank comes in and soon is muttering about his rope: "Sheep-nets . . . Fishing boats . . . Dogger Bank, Iceland. Scapa Flow . . . *Greenland.* You'll find bits of rope I made, you know, floating under the North Pole." Old Mrs. Ewbank comes to get him and lead him back to the house.

Fitzpatrick observes that the bridegroom, a doctor, is lucky to have a vocation, and Kay, too, is so dedicated to his task that it seems to be a vocation for him. To Ewbank, it is merely that Kay "knows which side his bread's buttered on." As for the rest of them, they are the debris of society, unemployable by anyone else.

Paul comes in to say goodbye to his father. Their parting is an awkward business, they cannot really communicate to each other except on the subject of money (Paul doesn't need any, he'll manage by himself). Paul says an especially warm goodbye to Glendenning, and then returns to the house, accompanied by his father.

The men have decided that the Ewbanks enjoyed the party. Fitzpatrick enjoys his feeling of being "reinstated." Kay, working with Bennett, advises him not to let Fitzpatrick get under his skin, but Bennett guesses that some day he'll probably kill Fitzpatrick.

The workmen are in the final stages of taking down the canvas and the side poles. Glendenning remarks that if he had a son he'd want him at home, not wandering off, and this draws a series of taunts from the others. Bennett and Fitzpatrick go at each other again, but they're interrupted by the entrance of Ewbank with a bottle, glasses, and pieces of wedding cake. Now that they have finished the job, they can celebrate (the large poles will be left in position to be loaded later on another truck).

Glendenning brings in a table for the tray. During the final business of tidying up the lawn, Ewbank notices that the tent has left a few marks; part of the inevitable price to be paid for everything, he tells Kay.

EWBANK: . . . . . . There's one thing, though . . .
KAY: Aye?
EWBANK: Ah, well . . . *(Uncertain for a moment. Then:)* I came out here, you know, this morning . . . Saw it all . . . Damn near broke my bloody heart . . . You saw it. God. What a bloody mess . . . Seen nowt like it. I haven't.
KAY: S'all made to be used.
EWBANK: Aye. You're right. Doesn't bear much reckoning. Best get on with it while you can.
KAY: Aye. *(Laughs.)*
EWBANK: Did you see much of my son?
KAY: No . . . Not much.
EWBANK: What do you reckon to it, then? Do you know, I've lived all this time —and I know nowt about anything. Least ways, I've settled that. I've come to that conclusion. *(He laughs. Shakes his head.)* A bloody wanderer.
KAY *(watches him):* Your lad?
EWBANK: I've no idea at all. None. Do you know? . . . Where he's off to. I don't think he has himself. His mother sits at home . . . *(Shakes his head.)* The modern world, Kay. It's left you and me behind.
KAY: Aye. Well. It can't be helped.
        They are silent a moment.
EWBANK: Pathetic. *(He looks round.)* A lot of bloody misfits. You could put us all into a string bag, you know, and chuck us all away, and none'd be the wiser.
KAY *(laughs):* Aye, I think you're right.
EWBANK: Aye. *(Laughs.)* Sunk without trace.

The men return, and Ewbank pours drinks all around. They raise a toast to the happy couple and eat their share of the wedding cake. For a moment the others even forget to tease Glendenning, and Fitzpatrick actually puts his arm around him and calls him "A damn fine lad," to which Glendenning responds with his customary "I . . . I . . . I . . I . . . I . . ."

The ritual completed, the workmen file off about their business of trucking the disassembled tent parts back to the yard, where Ewbank will meet them later. Glendenning is the last to go, and Ewbank slips him an extra piece of wedding cake.

Ewbank stands alone, gazing at the bare poles, fastening the remaining ropes hanging from the pulleys. Mrs. Ewbank joins him to tell him that his parents are leaving in a few minutes.

EWBANK: I'll come and see them off.
MRS. EWBANK: He's lost his bit of rope.

EWBANK: I'll cut him off a bit. He'll never know the difference.

MRS. EWBANK: . . . All that smoke . . . like a carpet . . . They had a drink, then.

EWBANK: Aye. Wet the baby's head . . . *(Looks up at her expression.)* Well, I don't know, do I? These days . . . one damn thing . . .
Pause.
Set an example there'll be no stopping. They'll be wanting a sup on every job from now on . . . I don't know. *(Looks down at the view, standing beside her.)* You'd think you'd have something to show for it, wouldn't you. After all this time.

MRS EWBANK: Well, now . . . *(Abstracted.)*

EWBANK: I don't know . . . *(Looks round. Then down at the lawn.)* Made a few marks in that.

MRS. EWBANK: One or two.

EWBANK *(shivers: looks up):* Autumn.

MRS. EWBANK *(abstracted):* Still . . . It's been a good summer.

EWBANK: Aye. Comes and goes.

MRS. EWBANK: What . . . ?
Pause.

EWBANK: Do you know that Kay was had up once for embezzlement?

MRS. EWBANK: They've been had up for a lot of things. The men that work for you.

EWBANK: Aye . . . Nobody else'll have 'em . . . I must be bloody daft. Well. I suppose we better see the old uns off.

MRS. EWBANK: Yes . . .

EWBANK: I don't know . . . What's to become of us, you reckon?
Mrs. Ewbank looks at him, smiles, then shakes her head.
Never do this again, you know.

MRS. EWBANK: No . . . *(She smiles.)*

EWBANK: Me heart wouldn't stand it.

MRS. EWBANK No . . . *(She laughs.)*

OLD MRS EWBANK *(off):* Frank . . . !

EWBANK: Aye, well. *(Half-laughs.)* That's summat.
They turn slowly, arm-in-arm.

OLD MRS. EWBANK *(off):* Frank . . . !

EWBANK: S'all right. We're coming. *(To Mrs. Ewbank.)* Well, then. We better go.
They go. The stage stands empty: bare poles, the ropes fastened off. The light fades slowly. Curtain.

BAD HABITS

A Program of Two One-Act Plays: Ravenswood *and* Dunelawn

BY TERRENCE MCNALLY

Cast and credits appear on pages 366 & 393

TERRENCE MCNALLY was born and grew up in Corpus Christi, Texas. He received his B.A. in English at Columbia, where in his senior year he wrote the varsity show. After graduation he was awarded the Harry Evans Travelling Fellowship in creative writing. He made his professional stage debut with The Lady of the Camellias, *an adaptation of the Dumas story which was produced on Broadway in 1963. His first original full-length play,* And Things That Go Bump in the Night, *was also produced on Broadway, in 1965, following a production at the Tyrone Guthrie Theater in Minneapolis.*

McNally's short play Tour *was produced off Broadway in 1968 as as part of the* Collision Course *program. In the next season, 1968–69, his one-acters were produced all over town:* Cuba Si! *was staged off off Broadway in the ANTA matinee series;* Noon *formed part of the Broadway program* Morning, Noon and Night; *off Broadway an all-McNally program of one-acters—*Sweet Eros *and* Witness*— opened that fall; and in early winter his one-acter* Next *opened with Elaine May's* Adaptation *on a bill which was named a Best Play of its season.*

McNally's second Best Play, Where Has Tommy Flowers Gone?, *had its world premiere at the Yale Repertory Theater before opening off Broadway in 1971. His third,* Bad Habits, *was produced off off Broadway last season by New York Theater Strategy, then and in the present off-Broadway production directed by Robert Drivas. A full-length McNally play,* Whiskey, *was tried out off off Broadway last season at Theater at St. Clement's and another one,* The Tubs, *was done this season at Yale Repertory Theater.*

McNally's works have received many productions in regional theaters as well as in South America and Europe. Two programs of McNally plays, Apple Pie *and* Last Gasps, *have been produced on TV, and he has done screen plays of his own* Sweet Eros *and* Noon. *He is a member of the Actors Studio and the Playwrights Unit and was the recipient of Guggenheim Fellowships in 1966 and 1969 and a CBS Fellowship in 1973.*

RAVENSWOOD

SYNOPSIS: Outdoors, bright sunshine lights a rear wall of lush foliage. A table with chairs and a rolling cart in the foreground hold objects which suggest this mught be the patio of a luxurious resort hotel: champagne, sun tan cream, etc. But this is Ravenswood, a sanitarium, whose attendant, Otto, comes in with flowers for the table. His bearing is Prussian military, and there is German music coming from the cassette recorder Otto carries on a shoulder strap.

April and Roy Pitt arrive at Ravenswood and Otto disappears momentarily to help them with their bags. Roy is carrying tennis equipment and exclaims over Ravenswood's clay court; April is holding her makeup kit. Otto greets them in German and exits with their Vuitton luggage.

APRIL: Jesus, Roy, it's the Gestapo. I just hope this Pepper fellow's all he's cracked up to be.
ROY: I told you. He's just gonna have us talk to each other.
APRIL: We talk to each other all the time. What's he gonna do?
ROY: Listen.
APRIL: Just listen? A hundred and forty-five clams a day and he just listens? I knew I should have checked this guy out first.
ROY: Look what he did for Sandy and Reg.
APRIL: Sandy and Reg are lesbians and they're not in show business. They run a pet shop in Montauk for Christ's sake.
ROY: But they're happy.
APRIL: Sure, they're in dyke heaven, those two. I'm talking about us, Roy.
ROY: So am I, April. You told the answering service where I'd be? I don't want to miss that call from the Coast. *(He exits).*

April follows. Soon after, Jason Pepper, M.D. and Dolly Scupp come in and take possession of the patio. Pepper is *"in an electric wheelchair with a blanket on his lap. Music is coming from a cassette on the chair. Also, the chair has an ashtray, a small shelf on the side for holding a book, a holder for a martini glass and a bell for calling Otto. Dolly Scupp is carrying a shoulder-strap-type handbag and a book. Her right foot is in an orthopedic foot covering."*
Dr. Pepper is consuming a martini and a cigarette as he converses with his visitor. He points out the lake and listens to the rumble of thunder, though he knows it's not going to rain because of the way the platinum plate in his head

feels. The book Dolly is carrying is a Dr. Pepper-authored volume called *Marriage for the Fun of It,* but the doctor intimates to Dolly that the information in it is obsolete, he has learned a lot since he wrote it.

Dolly's husband, Harry, is in Dr. Pepper's care here (though ordinarily he likes to treat couples, not just half of a marriage). Dr. Pepper offers Dolly a cigarette, "a special tobacco, imported from Panama, fertilized with hen feces," but Dolly refuses. She has quit smoking. "During the big scare, huh? So many of you poor bastards did," Dr. Pepper comments, ridiculing the typical family doctors who advise their patients to give up cigarettes.

DOLLY: But surely, Doctor, you're not suggesting that smoking is good for you?

DR. PEPPER: Of course not.

DOLLY: I didn't think so.

DR. PEPPER: What I *am* suggesting is that *not* smoking is conceivably worse.

DOLLY: I don't follow.

DR. PEPPER: Do you want to talk turkey or not, Mrs. Scupp?

DOLLY: Of course I do! And please, call me Dolly.

DR. PEPPER: Hello, Dolly.

DOLLY: Hello.

DR. PEPPER: Well, hello, Dolly.

DOLLY: It's my curse.

DR. PEPPER: You think Dr. Pepper is easy? Now let's start at the beginning and I'll try to keep it in laymen's terms.

DOLLY: Thank you.

DR. PEPPER: Everything in life is bad for you. The air, the sun, the force of gravity, butter, eggs, this cigarette . . .

DOLLY: That drink.

DR. PEPPER: That coffee! Canned tuna fish.

DOLLY: No!

DR. PEPPER: It's true! It's loaded with dolphin meat. There's an article on canned tuna fish in this month's *Food Facts* that will stand your hair on end.

DOLLY: I love tuna fish.

DR. PEPPER: Don't we all?

DOLLY: I don't care what they put in it.

DR. PEPPER: Neither do I. Right now, this very moment, as I speak these words, you're ten seconds closer to death than when I started. Eleven seconds, twelve seconds, thirteen. Have I made my point? Now, how would an ice-cold, extra-dry, straight-up Gordon's gin martini grab you?

He rings the service bell.

DOLLY: I'm afraid it wouldn't.

DR. PEPPER: Ah, vodka is the lovely lady from Scarsdale's poison.

He rings again.

DOLLY: I'm on the wagon.

DR. PEPPER: You don't smoke, you don't drink . . .

DOLLY: And it's Larchmont. And I would like to talk about my husband.

Otto appears and reports the arrival of the Pitts. Otto is ordered to show the Pitts around, but not to offer Mrs. Pitt a rubdown. Dr. Pepper sends Otto off to fetch him another martini (and a glass of water for Mrs. Scupp) and then confides to Dolly that he hates Germans because it was a German—his wife—who pushed him down a short but permanently crippling flight of stairs at the Philadelphia Academy of Music because he had cruelly insulted her singing voice following a concert.

Dolly too has been injured by a spouse: Harry cut off two of her toes with a remote control mower while she was sunbathing. That is why Harry came to Ravenswood. And now, Dr. Pepper believes, Harry is about ready to go home.

Another patient, Hiram Spane of the Newport Spanes, enters *"in a long bath-robe and beach sandals."* Hiram pours himself a champagne and orange juice and is calculatedly rude to Dolly until he learns that she is his friend Harry's wife. Hiram apologizes and indicates to an amazed Dolly that Harry has become a boon drinking companion here at Ravenswood, though he was never a drinker before.

Hiram (who has been a patient here ever since Dr. Pepper opened the place) leaves for the swimming pool just before Francis Tear of the Baltimore Tears enters *"wearing a bathing cap, a bathrobe and rubber bathing shoes."* Francis and Hiram are a couple of sorts, childhood friends who are probably not lovers (Dr. Pepper believes) but have been together for years. Hiram has just told Francis he looks like an embryo, so today they are not speaking. Francis shows off his bathing cap and his shoes, then goes to join Hiram at the pool.

Otto comes in and offers Dolly a rubdown, which she declines. Otto buries his nose in a copy of *Opera News* while Dolly continues her discussion of Harry with Dr. Pepper.

DR. PEPPER: Does Labor Day weekend, 1963, the parking lot outside Benny's Clam Box in Rockport, Maine, do anything for you?

DOLLY: I don't know. Should it?

DR. PEPPER: Think hard.

DOLLY: Benny's Clam Box.

DR. PEPPER: Harry was packing up the trunk of the car and you put the car into reverse.

DOLLY: Oh, that! How did you know?

DR. PEPPER: We have very complete files on our guests here, Mrs. Scupp. Ravenswood is a far cry from the Westchester County Medical Center and your quack G.P. with his Korean war bride and dachshund.

DOLLY: Leave it to Harry to tell you about a silly accident like that.

DR. PEPPER: He was in traction for two months.

DOLLY: I didn't see him back there. What are you driving at, Doctor?

DR. PEPPER: Eight months later you tried to run him over with a golf cart at the Westchester Country Club.

DOLLY: It was an accident. My foot got stuck on the accelerator.

DR. PEPPER: Nobody drives a golf cart on the putting green.

DOLLY: I do! You're making mountains out of mole hills, Doctor. My foot got stuck. I had new golf shoes. What's your point?

DR. PEPPER: A year later he asked you if there was water in the swimming pool before diving in.

DOLLY: I thought he'd asked me should he wash our Puli.

DR. PEPPER: Your Puli didn't end up in White Plains Hospital with a broken leg. Let's talk about the incident at the archery tournament.

DOLLY: Let's not.

DR. PEPPER: It's quite a story.

DOLLY: *His* version.

DR. PEPPER: I'd love to hear yours.

DOLLY: I didn't tell him to change the target when he did.

It wasn't Dolly's fault either, she claims, that Harry fell nearly 600 feet at Acapulco. But Dr. Pepper believes otherwise: "You and your husband have been trying to kill one another since Labor Day weekend, 1963." Dr. Pepper wants to know why. Dolly cites her husband's passion for neatness: He uses coasters everywhere, he straightens the shoes in her closet, he accuses her of putting the toilet paper roll on the dispenser the wrong way. Harry carries neatness to an extreme which Dolly cannot bear. She has noticed how he straightens license plates in public parking lots, but she hasn't noticed whether or not Harry is any good in bed. She especially hates his obsession for collecting and caring for tropical fish.

Dolly is unburdening herself to Dr. Pepper, and she describes some of the other things she hates about Harry: ". . . . . I hate his black Volvo station wagon with the snow tires on in August. He worries about early winters. He worries about everything. We're the only people in Larchmont with draught insurance. I know it's none of my business, but I hate the way he dresses. I hate his big, baggy boxer shorts. The only shoes he'll wear are those big clumpy cordovans. Even on the beach. But my favorite outfit is his 'Genius at Work' barbecue apron he wears over the pink Bermuda shorts and black, knee-high Supphose. Oh, I'm married to a snappy dresser, Doctor. And try taking a trip with him. He reads road signs. Every road sign. Out loud. 'Soft shoulders, Dolly.' 'Slippery when wet, Dolly.' 'Deer crossing, Dolly.' 'Kiwanis Club meeting at noon Wednesday, Dolly.' Who gives a good goddamn? He's not even a member of the Kiwanis Club. Who'd want him? . . . . . Don't get me wrong, Doctor. I love my husband. I just can't stand him. So don't make too much out of that incident with the lawn mower. That was just the straw that broke the camel's back!"

Dr. Pepper warns Dolly that he has done all he can for her husband—the rest is up to her. Harry joins the group, dressed for swimming and carrying a small cardboard box. He is delighted to see his wife Dolly, hugging her before he orders a Bloody Mary from Otto (and the Doctor will have another martini). Harry looks wonderful. Dr. Pepper has put him on the high-cholesterol diet he likes.

Otto goes to make the drinks, and Dr. Pepper follows him, leaving Harry and Dolly alone. Tentatively they approach each other with small talk about the children, the drive down, etc. The box Harry's carrying contains a dead fish, killed by another fish in his aquarium; callously he throws the box over the wall instead of burying his pet ceremoniously, as he was once likely to do.

The lawn mower is waiting in the garage for Harry's return, Dolly tells him. Harry wasn't really trying to hurt her with it, he protests, but Dolly knows better. She asks him why, and Harry tries to tell her.

HARRY: There were a million reasons. It was hot. The refrigerator needed defrosting. The car keys were upstairs when they should have been downstairs. The house was still a mess from your bridge party. You forgot to renew my subscription to *High Fidelity* and they'd sent you three warnings already.

DOLLY: *Hi-Fi Stereo Review.*

HARRY: You knew how much I was looking forward to that comparative analysis of Dolby-ized cassette decks with ferric oxide heads! There was a new water ring on the telephone stand. Things like that.

DOLLY: Did I have the toilet paper on right?

HARRY: As a matter of fact, you did. What happened?

DOLLY: I don't know. I lost my head!

HARRY: Only someone had been playing my stereo. There were fingerprints on my Christmas album.

DOLLY: Who would be playing a Christmas album in June?

HARRY: I didn't say *when* they were put there, I just said I found them.

DOLLY: What were *you* doing playing a Christmas album in June?

HARRY: I wasn't. I just happened to be doing my six-month record cleaning that day. They weren't your fingerprints.

DOLLY: Thank you.

HARRY: They weren't the kids', either.

DOLLY: Well, at least I had the toilet paper on right.

HARRY: I conceded that point.

DOLLY: Well?

HARRY: It was blue!

DOLLY: That's all they had!

HARRY: It was blue! Our bathroom is red! Everything is red! The sink, the tub, the tile, the towels, the shower curtain! You know I don't like a clash. I like everything to match!

DOLLY: That's all they had!

HARRY: You asked me why. I'm telling you why. There were permanent press sheets on the bed.

DOLLY: Cotton's scarce.

HARRY: I can't sleep on permanent press. They're too hot. They're like flame sheets. Things like that. Like I said, it was hot. There were a million reasons. Then, when I saw you staked out on the lawn in your bathing suit, I just kind of lost control with the mower. What was it with me?

DOLLY: The coasters.

HARRY: Even that time in Acapulco?

DOLLY: It was always the coasters.

Harry takes out a cigarette (he has started smoking, too) as Otto comes in with his Bloody Mary. Harry is a bit hung over, he admits, from a wild farewell party for a young couple the evening before at which Harry, who could never dance, rhumbaed all night. Harry feels like a kid again, and he no longer has an urge to murder his wife. He has another surprise for Dolly; he has made an ashtray in the shape of a nude study of Jeanine, his rhumba partner.

Dr. Pepper comes back as Harry runs off to get something else to show Dolly. Dr. Pepper points with pride to the improvement in Harry, but Dolly can remember only that the Doctor has allowed Harry to pay attention to this young woman, Jeanine. Dr. Pepper reminds her: "There are no rules at Ravenswood, Mrs. Scupp. . . . . . That's the secret of my success here, such as it is. I allow everyone to do exactly as he pleases."

Harry comes rushing back with a ukelele and a tap board to show Dolly how his latent song-and-dance talent has emerged under treatment (he is terrible in a rendition of "Aba Daba Honeymoon" but has fun doing it).

Dolly is so angry at the change in Harry that she smashes his ash tray. When Harry advances toward her resentfully, she wards him off with a can of mace. Harry decides to forget the whole thing and join Hiram and Francis down at the pool.

Dr. Pepper observes that maybe it's Dolly who needs treatment now, who needs to find out what it is she likes to do. He sends Dolly off to try to enjoy her day with her husband, and as she goes she confesses that she's beginning to get a bit of a crush on the doctor.

Roy and April Pitt appear briefly, chasing a tennis ball. Dr. Pepper sends Otto for another drink. Hiram and Francis come up from the pool, Francis chortling that both he and Harry beat Hiram in a swimming race. Hiram tries to shrug off the defeat and counters by continuing to insult his friend Francis ("If I'd seen him in that bathing cap, I'd've said he looked like a prophylactic"). Francis, accusing Hiram of being a poor loser, goes into a tantrum, pounding feet and fists on the ground, encouraged by Dr. Pepper to let it all out, hold nothing back.

After the tantrum has passed Francis continues to sulk, complaining that he can't help winning all their contests, it just seems to happen that way. Hiram challenges him to tell Dr. Pepper about the *real* point of contention between them: Celine, a Welsh Corgi they had when they lived on 69th Street. Francis, jealous of the dog's affection for Hiram and angry because it made a mess in his closet, threw the dog out of the window on the 14th floor, Hiram insists. Francis insists it was an accident, the dog jumped out while chasing a fly. The two come to blows. They do little damage to one another and finally collapse with exhaustion as Otto comes in with the drinks and sits down again to his magazine.

FRANCIS: I don't think Ravenswood is working out for us.
HIRAM: Of course Ravenswood isn't working out for us! Why should it?
DR. PEPPER: Did you ever think of getting another dog?
HIRAM: No more dogs. Celine was a terrible shedder.
FRANCIS: Another one would probably just pee in my closet, too.
HIRAM: Or maybe mine next time.
FRANCIS: No more dogs, Hiram? Promise?

HIRAM: The only reason we stay together is because no one else in the world would put up with us.

DR. PEPPER: If you can leave here having realized that much, I'll be satisfied.

HIRAM: *You'll* be satisfied?

DR. PEPPER: And so should you.

HIRAM: We are, I suppose. We are.

FRANCIS: You're the only real friend I've ever had, Hiram.

HIRAM: And I'm sure Dr. Pepper can see why. Help me up, will you? I think I twisted something.

Francis struggles to his feet, then helps Hiram up.

FRANCIS: Are we dressing for lunch?

HIRAM: I don't know about the end of the Baltimore Tear line but the last remaining Newport Spane is . . . . .

As they pick up their drinks a tennis ball bounces in, and the Pitts call loudly and rudely for its return. Hiram responds by shouting an insult and exits with Francis. Roy and April come in; Roy, goaded by April, is looking for the man who just insulted his wife, but Hiram has vanished.

Dr. Pepper greets his new clients. The Pitts, believing they have been recognized as a prominent actor and actress and are about to be lionized, prepare to accept the flattering rewards of celebrity. But such is not the case. They take off their sun glasses, but even with them off Dr. Pepper doesn't recognize the famous Roy Pitt and his wife whose stage name is April James.

DR. PEPPER: And what do *you* do, Mrs. Pitt?

APRIL: What do you mean, "What do I do?" I'm an actress. Thanks a lot, buddy.

ROY: She's an actress.

APRIL: I don't even know you but I really needed that little ego boost.

ROY: Honey, of course he recognized me, my movie was on the Late Show last night, *Cold Fingers.* He probably caught it.

APRIL: God knows you did.

ROY: It's the power of the medium, you know that kind of exposure.

APRIL: *Cold Fingers* should have *opened* on the Late Show.

ROY: Now, don't start with me.

APRIL: Boy, I really needed that little zap.

ROY: He's a dummy.

APRIL: You must have seen me in something. How about *Journey Through Hell* for Christ's sake! You didn't see me in *Journey Through Hell?*

DR. PEPPER: Were you in that?

ROY: That was my beautiful April all right!

APRIL: You bet your sweet ass it was!

DR. PEPPER: That was a wonderful movie, Mrs. Pitt.

APRIL: You see that? Another zap!

ROY: April wasn't in the movie. She created the role off Broadway . . . didn't get the film version!

APRIL: Boy, this is really my day!

April identifies more of her acting work, but Dr. Pepper hasn't seen any of it. Both the Pitts are very much on edge hoping for phone calls from the Coast. In the meantime, they settle for a couple of glasses of Dom Perignon, as April apologizes to Dr. Pepper for shouting at him from the court. They didn't know he was in a wheelchair, and they are quick to assure him that they play lots of benefits—provided their expenses are paid.

Roy stretches out with a sun reflector, as April chats with Dr. Pepper (she still doesn't know who he is): "You're probably wondering what we're doing up here. I know on the surface it must look like we got a model marriage. But believe me, we got our little problems, too. Don't look so surprised. Roy's got an ego on him you could drive a Mack truck with. Show biz marriages ain't nothing to write home about. Half our friends are divorced and the other half are miserable. Naturally, they don't think we're going to make it. Think. They hope. But we're going to show them."

Roy and April quarrel over the use of the reflector—Roy neglected to pack April's. There is obvious rivalry between them in their profession, and it shows in their taunts and gibes. April even takes it amiss when Roy calls her "The best little actress in New York City."

APRIL: As opposed to what? A dwarf?

ROY: If we're going to have a good marriage and, April, I want that more than anything . . .

APRIL: More than you wanted *Lenny?*

ROY: I didn't want *Lenny.*

APRIL: He would've crawled through broken glass for that part!

ROY: I didn't want *Lenny.* Now, goddamnit, shut up!

APRIL: I can't talk to you when you get like that.

ROY: Get like what? You haven't laid off me since we got in the car.

APRIL: You know I'm upset.

ROY: We've all been fired from shows.

APRIL: Before they went into rehearsal?

ROY: Actually, Heather MacNamara isn't a bad choice for that part.

APRIL: She's the pits!

ROY: We're the Pitts! *(Breaking himself up . . .)* We liked her in *The Seagull.*

APRIL: You liked her in *The Seagull.* I'd like her in her coffin.

ROY: Obviously they're going ethnic with it.

APRIL: She isn't even ethnic. She's white bread. I'm ethnic. I want a hit, Roy. I need a hit. I'm going crazy for a hit. I mean, when's it my turn?

ROY: Honey, you're making a shadow.

APRIL: I'm sorry.

ROY: That's okay. Just stick with me, kid. We're headed straight for the top.

APRIL: Roy?

ROY: What, angel?

APRIL: Your toupee is slipping.

Roy clutches at his hairpiece.

Roy wears a piece.

ROY: It's no secret. I've never pretended. It's not like your nose job.

APRIL: Don't speak to me. Just lie there and turn into naugahyde like your mother!

They add a couple more insults before Dr. Pepper interrupts them with a question about how long they've been married (three months, after living together a long time). Dr. Pepper takes out his notebook. Finally the Pitts understand that this man in the wheelchair is Dr. Pepper, and they are ashamed of what they have let him see about themselves.

Hiram and Francis enter in white flannels and striped blazers and sit down to a game of cards. Dr. Pepper introduces the Pitts. Roy remembers that Hiram owes his wife an apology. Hiram's reply to Roy is, "I don't recall speaking to you," but to April he adds, "I've got a foul temper and a vicious tongue. Someone yells 'ball' at me and they start working overtime. And that's about as much of an apology as you're going to get out of me."

Roy hears the phone ringing in the distance and runs off. April tries to show her understanding of Hiram and Francis's relationship to each other—"We have lots of friends like that in the city"—but Hiram puts her down hard.

The Scupps come in with the news that Harry is leaving, pronouncing himself cured, but Dolly is staying. Harry is willing to compromise and Dolly will try, in order to save their marriage, because "We just decided that our marriage was better than no marriage at all." Dolly takes a drag of Harry's cigarette and loves it.

Roy comes back (the phone call was a tentative possibility, but nothing definite). Dolly suddenly recognizes April as someone she has just seen doing a benefit on TV. April gives them all a sample of her act. Dolly feels that she and Harry might have managed better if they'd had more in common, were in the same profession like the Pitts.

Harry lets out a sudden, urgent scream.

DR. PEPPER: How was it?

HARRY: Fantastic.

DOLLY: Is he going to be doing that often?

DR. PEPPER: That depends on you.

DOLLY: If he pulls that in the middle of a board meeting he's going to be looking for a new job.

DR. PEPPER: You might try it yourself some time.

DOLLY: Me? I'm as cool as a cucumber.

DR. PEPPER: What brought that one on, Harry?

HARRY: The truth?

DR. PEPPER: You're still at Ravenswood.

HARRY: I want to shtup Mrs. Pitt.

ROY: Hey!

HARRY: You see how her tennis outfit's all slit up the side? There's no tan line. You know how women who are tan all over drive me crazy, Jason.

ROY: What did you say?

APRIL: It's okay, Roy. He just said he *wanted* to shtup me. He didn't *do* it.

Dolly lets out a sudden, urgent scream.
DR. PEPPER: How do you feel?
DOLLY: Hoarse.
HARRY: You'll get used to it.

Otto comes in with champagne for everybody. They all toast each other, and finally Otto announces lunch. Dolly escorts Harry away to the car. April and Roy go off reassuring each other about their next parts. There is thunder in the air, as Hiram and Francis exit.

Otto offers to wheel Dr. Pepper in to lunch, but the doctor wants no lunch today—he just wants everybody to be happy. "Was ist happy?" Otto inquires and exits. Dr. Pepper, now alone, lifts his glass in a toast to the departing Harry.

In the distance the luncheon guests, now somewhat raucous, can be heard amusing themselves with a chorus of "Aba Daba Honeymoon." Dr. Pepper sings to himself very quietly and slowly the last verse of the song. Curtain.

DUNELAWN

SYNOPSIS: Again, the scene is outdoors at a sanitarium, but this setting is backed not by foliage but by a wall or chain link fence. There is a stone bench at right and a scraggly tree at left.

Nurse Benson strides onstage, followed by Nurse Hedges pushing a medical cart. Nurse Benson gives a sample of her spiel for the patients: "I am your friend. So is Nurse Hedges. But you know something? You are your own best friend. Think that one over."

The loud sound of a whistle is immediately followed by the entrance of the attendant Bruno (*"a horror,"* dirty, disheveled, whistle dangling from his neck) wheeling in a patient, Mr. Ponce (*"a crabby old man"*). Bruno leers meaningfully at Nurse Hedges but is ordered away to fetch other patients by businesslike Nurse Benson.

Nurses Hedges and Benson busy themselves at the cart preparing a syringe, ignoring Mr. Ponce as he pleads with them to bring him something to drink.

PONCE: Liquor! Liquor! I want liquor!
BENSON: Honestly, Becky, I don't know what's gotten into you lately.
HEDGES: I'm sorry.
PONCE: I want a drink, somebody!
BENSON: You're sniveling again, Hedges.
HEDGES: I am?
PONCE: Will somebody please get me a good stiff drink?
BENSON: I'll cure you of that if it's the last thing I do.
HEDGES: I don't mean to snivel. I don't want to snivel. I just do it, I guess.
PONCE: I need a drink! I must have a drink!
BENSON: Well, we'll soon put a stop to that.

HEDGES: You're so good to me, Ruth!
BENSON: I know. Syringe, please.
PONCE: I don't want to stop! I like to drink! It's all a terrible mistake!

When Mr. Ponce sees they mean to administer a syringe, he becomes very agitated and throws off his blanket, revealing that he is wearing a straitjacket and is strapped into the wheelchair. Mr. Ponce's agitation upsets Nurse Hedges, but Nurse Benson remains cool. Just as she threatens to report Mr. Ponce's behavior to Dr. Toynbee, the Doctor himself strolls into view—*"He has sad, benign eyes and a smile to match."* He does not speak, but only looks sadly at his patient, as Nurse Benson reports Mr. Ponce's recalcitrant behavior and suggests that he should be ejected from Dunelawn.

In the presence of Dr. Toynbee, Mr. Ponce changes abruptly from angry to shamefaced. At the suggestion that he leave Dunelawn—when the straps are released and the straitjacket unfastened—he becomes abjectly apologetic and begs forgiveness. He begs them not to send him back to the outside world and its gin mills.

PONCE *(putting the straitjacket back on):* Look, look, see how much I want to stay?
BENSON: Take that off, Mr. Ponce.
PONCE *(to Hedges):* Fasten me up, fasten me up!
HEDGES: Dr. Toynbee?
PONCE: The straps, the straps, just fasten the straps.
HEDGES *(moved):* Poor Mr. Ponce.
BENSON: I wouldn't do that, Hedges.
HEDGES: Dr. Toynbee?
    Dr. Toynbee slowly, sadly, benignly, nods his head. Hedges buckles Mr. Ponce up in the straitjacket.
PONCE: Thank you, Doctor, thank you! . . . . . I'll be good, I'll be better! You'll see, you'll see! This will never happen again. Come on, Benson, you heard the doctor!
BENSON: Surely, Doctor, you're not going to . . . ?
    Again Dr. Toynbee nods his head.
That man is a saint.
PONCE: God bless him.
BENSON: Dr. Toynbee is a saint.
PONCE: I am so grateful and so happy.
BENSON: A saint!
PONCE: I could kiss his hand for this.
    He tries to, and can't.
BENSON: Should I proceed with the injection, Doctor?
    Dr. Toynbee smiles and nods.
Hedges.
    Hedges helps her prepare another syringe as Dr. Toynbee moves to Mr. Ponce and stands directly behind him. He looks down at him and

puts one hand on each shoulder and fixes him with a sad and solemn stare.

PONCE: I can't bear it when you look at me like that. You're so good, Doctor, so good! I know how rotten I am. But some day I'll be able to look you in the eye. I'll make you proud of me. I'll make me proud of me. I don't want to be me any more.

Dr. Toynbee smiles and bends down to Mr. Ponce's ear. When he does finally speak, it is totally unintelligible gibberish.

You're so right, Doctor! Everything you say is so right!

Dr. Toynbee departs with the others' exclamations of his blessedness ringing in his ears. Mr. Ponce begs Nurse Benson to give him the injection quickly before he gets another attack, but Nurse Benson dawdles unfeelingly in conversation with Nurse Hedges about their boss's qualities of perfection. Mr. Ponce cries out for "a Jeroboam of Bombay Gin!" but still Nurse Benson fails to respond. Finally, almost grudgingly, she gives him the drug, and Mr. Ponce is almost instantly content. He wants nothing any longer. He is perfectly relaxed.

The nurses are now free to discuss their own interests, which at the moment center on themselves. Nurse Hedges wishes she were beautiful like Nurse Benson, who will only go as far in returning the compliment as to say that Nurse Hedges is "an adorable person." Nurse Hedges wishes for more than that, however.

BENSON: I said you were adorable.

HEDGES: And I said you were beautiful.

BENSON: It's out of my hands.

HEDGES: It's out of mine too.

BENSON: You're sniveling again.

HEDGES: I know.

BENSON (*pulls Hedges over to the bench and sits her down*): Becky, listen to me. You think I'm beautiful. Thank you. I can accept a compliment. I know I'm beautiful. I can't lie to myself any more. But what good did it do me as far as Hugh Gumbs was concerned?

HEDGES: Such a beautiful name!

BENSON: There you go again, Becky.

HEDGES: I didn't snivel that time.

BENSON: You made a stupid, flattering, self-serving, Minnie Mouse remark, which is much worse. Hugh Gumbs is not a beautiful name and you know it.

HEDGES: I'm sorry. I'll be good. I'll be better. Finish your story.

Hugh Gumbs, it seems, was much beloved by Nurse Benson but turned her down for another woman named Mildred Canby, who has made him unhappy in marriage (apparently she lacked that character, those traditional virtues which —Nurse Benson assures Nurse Hedges—all men would rather find in a woman than beauty). It was because of her experience with Hugh Gumbs that Nurse Benson has made herself over into the 118-pound bundle of perfection she is now.

Hedges also had a man in her life, one Tim Taylor, but lost him. Dr. Toynbee drifts past them reading a book and smiling, and Nurse Hedges gets the notion from a look in Nurse Benson's eye that perhaps she is sweet on the good doctor. Nurse Benson slaps Nurse Hedges for harboring this thought, then slaps her again for good measure, and Nurse Hedges apologizes abjectly for making such a dreadful mistake.

Nurse Benson, it seems, once weighed more than 200 pounds. But she didn't so much change as allow her real self to emerge, just as Mr. Ponce is allowing the non-drinker latent within him to emerge under their care. The "real" Nurse Hedges (Nurse Benson remarks) has big thighs, and there is nothing she can do about that: "You can diet all you want and you're still going to end up with big thighs."

Finding herself sniveling again, Nurse Hedges goes to the cart to prepare a syringe for herself. Nurse Benson takes the drug away from her and, in a nervous reflex, takes out a pack of cigarettes and lights one up—revealing by mistake to a shocked Nurse Hedges that she smokes.

There is another loud whistle, and Bruno enters pushing Mr. Blum in his wheelchair. Again, Bruno leers at Nurse Hedges, then takes out a strictly-forbidden hip flask and has a swig.

BENSON: . . . . . You're a walking, sub-human nightmare, Bruno.
BRUNO *(for Hedges's benefit):* Sure is a hot one coming on. A real scorcher.
BENSON: Must you, Bruno?
BRUNO: Must I what?
BENSON: Stand there like that?
BRUNO *(to Hedges):* Now she don't like the way I stand.
BENSON: It's deliberately provocative.
BRUNO: What is that supposed to mean?
BENSON: Only you're about as provocative to a woman as a can full of worms. Now either get Mr. Yamadoro out here or I'll report you to Dr. Toynbee.
BRUNO: Hold your bowels, Benson.
He is trying to think. He turns to Hedges.
I got desires. That's all I know, I got desires and I like to do 'em.
He goes. Hedges curiously starts to follow. Benson claps her hands, and Hedges joins her.

The second patient, Mr. Blum, ignores Nurse Benson's cheerful greeting and begs her to let him wear her nurse's cap. Nurse Benson threatens to report this backsliding to Dr. Toynbee, but Mr. Blum pleads: "Benson, I haven't been in full drag in six weeks! You know what I was like when Martha brought me here. You've seen how I've changed. You couldn't force me at gunpoint to put your shoes on."

In spite of Mr. Blum's begging, Nurse Benson withholds both her cap and the comforting syringe. The patient is at the height of a nervous crisis, when Dr. Toynbee enters. Again, his presence seems to pour shame on the sinner—Mr. Blum squirms in mortification when Nurse Benson takes off her cap and places it on his head. Doctor Toynbee actually is caused to weep at the sight of such inner torment. He takes the cap off Mr. Blum and hands it back to Benson, *"then turns and talks to Blum. Again we can't understand his gibberish. . . . . Now Blum is the one who is crying. Dr. Toynbee asks for the syringe with a gesture. Benson gives it to him and he injects Blum. Benson wheels Blum next to Ponce, who is beginning to stir restlessly."*

Mr. Ponce mumbles something about a perfect Rob Roy on the rocks, and benignly Dr. Toynbee signals to Nurse Hedges to give him another shot, which she does, with a beginner's difficulty. As Dr. Toynbee leaves, Nurse Hedges is ecstatic at her own accomplishment with the needle (and perhaps a bit drawn to Dr. Toynbee herself) but Nurse Benson brings her down by dashing a glass of water into her face.

A third loud whistle heralds the entrance of Bruno wheeling Mr. Yamadoro. After leering suggestively at Nurse Hedges once more and putting Nurse Benson in her place, Bruno drifts off. The new patient's real name is Vincenzo Luparelli, but he likes to be called Mr. Yamadoro—that's one reason why he's here at Dunelawn.

Nurse Hedges remarks that no one ever seems to get better here, and Nurse Benson punishes her for such *lèse majesté* with a slap and an admonishment that Dr. Toynbee knows what he's doing even if his patients don't. The slap arouses Mr. Yamadoro, who shows some signs of being still interested in pain, even though he protests that he has cured himself of all such urges. To test him, Nurse Benson describes in detail the torture of a beautiful naked woman. Mr. Yamadoro remains outwardly calm through it all, convincing Nurse Benson that he is cured. But when the nurses move away, Mr. Yamadoro confides to the groggy Messrs. Ponce and Blum: "Don't tell Benson, but I just had an orgasm."

When Nurse Hedges comes over to give Mr. Yamadoro his injection he suffers a relapse and tries to bite her, but the needle soon calms him down.

> *Benson and Hedges begin readjusting the wheelchairs. All three patients nod in a drugged stupor.*

BENSON: Look at them. Like babies now. It's a beautiful sight.

HEDGES: Everyone should take Dr. Toynbee's serum. Then the whole world would be perfect. No wars, no greed, no sex. No nothing.

> *Bruno enters with a letter from the office.*

BENSON: Mr. Ponce, Mr. Blum and Mr. Yamadoro are going to be all right, Becky. It's only the Brunos of this world that are hopeless.

BRUNO: Hey, you in the white dress with the bird's legs!

HEDGES: I feel good just looking at them like this.

BRUNO: You want this, tight ass?

> *He shows the letter.*

BENSON: You're looking at the future, Becky.

HEDGES: In our lifetime?

BENSON *(sadly shaking her head):* I'm afraid we're just the pioneers.

BRUNO: Hey, ugly-puss, I'm supposed to give you this.

HEDGES: A perfect world with perfect people.

BENSON: Someone has to do it.

Bruno finally gets through to Nurse Benson that he is carrying an important message about a new patient. After another leer at Nurse Hedges he departs, as Nurse Benson reads the note and discovers that her beloved but lost Hugh Gumbs has just become a patient here at Dunelawn. Nurse Benson rushes off to find him, leaving Nurse Hedges in charge of the patients—and at last alone and unprotected when Bruno comes in to pursue his wooing.

Bruno exposes himself again and again to Nurse Hedges, who, trying desperately to find some sort of defender, lets loose the three patients in the hope that they will help her. They are too tranquillized to do anything, however, and Nurse Hedges's only possible escape is in flight. She runs off with Bruno in hot pursuit.

The three patients are free but don't wish to go anywhere; they merely sit there reminiscing blissfully about experiences of alcohol, transvestism and sado-masochism in their past lives, while Nurse Hedges runs across the stage still pursued by Bruno. Offstage there is a call for help and the sound of tearing cloth, but here all is serene contentment. The saintly Dr. Toynbee's serum has made Dunelawn a heaven on earth for the most troubled spirits.

While the three patients join in a chorus of "Pack Up Your Troubles in Your Old Kit Bag," Nurse Benson wheels in Hugh Gumbs, *still wearing his lice-ridden street clothes* and crying out several times an agonized "Aaaaaaaaaaaa!" Hugh Gumbs wants his injection, but Nurse Benson delays, going over his papers. Hugh admits "You name it and I've got it, done it or used it." He smokes multiple packs of cigarettes daily and never ceases drinking, for the same reason that everybody does everything that's bad for them: "Because they like it! They like it!" Now, however, Gumbs longs for the same treatment the other patients have received.

HUGH *(indicating the others)*: Look at them! How cured they seem!

BENSON: You will be too, Hugh. Excuse me, I meant Mr. Gumbs.

HUGH: That's the first thing I'd like to change about me. My name. How could any woman love a Hugh Gumbs?

BENSON: You mustn't torment yourself like that!

HUGH: I can't help it. I meet a woman and it's fine about the drinking, fine about the smoking, it's even fine about the . . . never mind . . . but when I tell them my name, it's all over. Ask yourself, Nurse, would you want to go through life as Mrs. Hugh Gumbs?

BENSON: Surely there was one woman, somewhere in your life, who didn't mind your name?

HUGH: One. Just one.

BENSON: You see?

HUGH: My mother, for Christ's sake! Please, can't I have my first injection?

BENSON: We're nearly done. A moment ago you said when you met a woman it was "even fine about the . . ." What's your "about the," Mr. Gumbs?

HUGH: I can't tell you.

BENSON: I must have it.

HUGH: Believe me, you don't want it.

BENSON: Mr. Gumbs, I've got to have it.

Dr. Toynbee enters, smiling as usual.

This is Hugh Gumbs, Dr. Toynbee, a new patient. He won't tell me what his worst habit is.

> *Dr. Toynbee goes to Hugh and stands, then bends and mumbles his unintelligible gibberish. Hugh bows his head, deeply ashamed, then motions Dr. Toynbee to lean forward while he whispers his worst habit into his ear, with much pantomiming. Dr. Toynbee straightens up, appalled at what he had just heard, and leaves without even looking at Benson.*

Nurse Benson probes further, prompting Gumbs to think back over the women in his life. Gumbs senses something familiar in the nurse's voice but can't quite place her; meanwhile he admits that there was one notable woman in his life, "intelligent, decisive, yet strangely yielding," and her name is Mildred Canby. Nurse Benson can stand it no longer and brings up her own name, pretending that Gumbs mentioned it when he was brought in, raving. Gumbs remembers a Ruth Benson who was "circus fat," maybe 280 pounds. He also remembers her as "the only person, man, woman or child, I ever asked to take a bath. She used to smoke. Six packs a day minimum, cigarillos. Nicotine stains right up to her elbows! I don't guess she ever drew a sober breath. My main image of her is passed out on the floor like a big rancid mountain. And talk about being a slob! She had dust balls under her bed the size of watermelons. She didn't just have roaches in her kitchen. She raised them. . . . ."

They both had bad habits, they were a lot alike in those days, Gumbs remembers. Nurse Benson draws attention to her good-looking legs. Then she turns her back on Hugh. Her moment has come.

BENSON: Don't you know who I am yet, Hugh? No, don't say anything until I've finished. I'm not going to turn around until you tell me that you want me to turn around. I'm glad you don't recognize me. There's no reason that you should. I did it all for you, Hugh. Hugh Gumbs. Like your name, it wasn't easy. But I didn't mind the suffering, the self-humiliation, the incredible self-discipline. I wanted to torture myself into becoming someone a man like you could love, and I have. Let me finish! I'm brutally honest with myself. That's not enough, I know, but it's a beginning. When I look in a mirror now I can say yes, yes, I like that person. I'm not smug, Hugh, I just know my own worth. For five years I've made myself thoroughly miserable so that today I could make you happy and I did it all for love. *(Pause.)* Now yes or no, Hugh, do you want me to turn around?

> *Pause.*

HUGH: Who are you?

BENSON *(turning to him, ecstatic):* It's me. Ruth.

HUGH: Ruth?

BENSON: Ruth Benson.

HUGH: Fat Ruth Benson?

BENSON: Yes, yes!

HUGH: You don't look like Ruth.

BENSON *(she is so happy):* I know, I know!

HUGH: You don't sound like her, either.

BENSON: Voice lessons, darling.

HUGH: You don't even smell like Ruth.

BENSON: Zest, Dial, Dove, Lava!

HUGH: You have such beautiful legs.

BENSON: I worked for them.

HUGH: Your teeth.

BENSON: All caps.

HUGH: And your . . . *(He indicates her breasts.)*

BENSON: Exercises.

HUGH: Your big, hairy mole.

BENSON: Cosmetic surgery.

HUGH: It's really you?

BENSON: It's really me. The real me and it's all for you, Hugh, I did it all for you.

HUGH: You did?

BENSON: And now that I've found you again I'm not going to let you go this time.

HUGH: You didn't let me go the last time. I let you go.

Hugh is by no means ready to accept Nurse Benson's gift of herself. He insists they could never make a go of it—besides, he is now totally committed to Dunelawn. He doesn't even recognize her, and in their present condition she's obviously too far above him to be an object of his affection: "I didn't love you when you were fat and rotten. I can't love you now that you're beautiful and perfect and have such terrific legs."

Nurse Benson tries to pretend that she has faults, too, but Gumbs knows better. She is an angel now, and he is unworthy. She offers to bring him cigarettes and liquor, she tries kissing him, she will be anything he wants—but all he wants is his injection.

Nurse Hedges comes back with Bruno, her uniform askew, a changed woman, planning to marry Bruno and run off with him to Fort Lauderdale. Nurse Benson tries to slap some sense into her friend, but this time Nurse Hedges slaps back. She doesn't care about self-improvement any longer, and as for Dr. Toynbee, "He gives me the creeps." She tells the patients that if they had any sense they'd come along with her and Bruno in the microbus. Nurse Hedges and Bruno depart, and Hugh Gumbs decides that maybe he'd better not stay at Dunelawn after all.

HUGH: I can't stay here with you, Ruth. I'm not even worthy of Dunelawn. Maybe I'll come back to you one day, a better and worthier man. If not, I know you'll find someone good enough for you.

BENSON: It's a rotten world out there. It'll destroy you.

HUGH: It already has.

> *He starts to go.*

BENSON *(concealing the syringe):* One last kiss.

> *They kiss. Benson has the syringe in her hand, poised to inject him. Dr. Toynbee enters. Benson is mortified.*

Dr. Toynbee! I'm so ashamed. I . . . Mr. Gumbs was just leaving.

HUGH: That woman is perfect!

He goes.

BENSON: I don't know what happened, Dr. Toynbee. I left them with Nurse Hedges and she's gone off to Florida to open a pizza stand with Bruno and the love of my life is gone again and I'm having a nervous breakdown because I don't understand people any more. It's so good here. You're so good. Why would anyone want to leave Dunelawn when all we're trying to do is help them to be perfect?

Benson is shattered. She is holding on to Dr. Toynbee for support. He puts his arm around her and takes her to the wheelchair left empty by Hugh Gumbs.

You're so good, Dr. Toynbee. It's the end of summer.

Dr. Toynbee goes to the cart to get a syringe.

I won't cry. I refuse to cry. It's you and Dunelawn I'm thinking of. Not myself. The world is filled with men like Hugh Gumbs. But someone somewhere is the man for me. Zero defects. No faults, no failings, no fantasies. Where is he, Dr. Toynbee?

Dr. Toynbee injects her. A wonderful smile lights up her face.

Oh yes.

Dr. Toynbee starts fitting Nurse Benson into the straitjacket, as the other patients join in singing "Pack Up Your Troubles in Your Old Kit Bag," joined by even more voices offstage. *"Dr. Toynbee takes a step forward and starts to address us in his unintelligible gibberish, as a few leaves fall from the scraggly tree. Curtain."*

FIND YOUR WAY HOME

A Play in Three Acts

BY JOHN HOPKINS

Cast and credits appear on page 357

JOHN HOPKINS was born in London Jan. 27, 1931 and was educated at a local grammar school and St. Catherine's College in Cambridge. He did his National Service with the Royal Artillery and began writing in 1958. He joined BBC-TV as a writer and contributed many television dramas to both the BBC and independent programming. His TV career highlights have included Z-Cars for which he won a Screenwriters' Guild Award two years running; four TV plays with the portmanteau title Talking to a Stranger; Horror of Darkness *with Glenda Jackson and Nicol Williamson; and two works for TV which Hopkins wrote for his wife, the actress Shirley Knight:* Some Distant Shadow, *in which Miss Knight played an age range from 16 to 35, and the short* The Quiet Earth *which Hopkins directed as well as wrote.*

Hopkins's first play for the stage was This Story of Yours, *produced by the Royal Court Theater in 1969 and subsequently adapted by its author for the screen as* The Offence. *The Hopkinses' first husband-and-wife theater stint was* Economic Necessity, *produced at the Haymarket Theater in Leicester with Miss Knight in the lead. His* Find Your Way Home *had its world premiere in this season's Broadway production, now cited as a Best Play, and his* Next of Kin *was on the National Theater's spring 1974 production schedule under Harold Pinter's direction. He has recently finished a series of seven plays about family life called* Fathers and Families, *and among his movie credits is the screen play for* Thunderball.

Mr. and Mrs. Hopkins have three children and live in London.

Time: The present

Place: A small flat in a large town in the south of England

ACT I

SYNOPSIS: In the main living area of Julian Weston's high-ceilinged furnished flat, the most conspicuous object is a large bed upstage left against a wall on which there is *"a photomontage of faces . . . . . some of the faces are famous actors and film stars, singers. Some of the faces have been cut roughly out of newspapers and a very few stare out of glossy photographs, smiling and posed. The faces are jumbled together without recognizable pattern."* The rest of the furnishings are also a patternless collection including dining table, kitchen equipment, stereo equipment, books and records, a comfortable chair, armoire, etc., but the wall decorations are highly individualistic. A window at right looks out over a series of gardens, the entrance door is upstage center and the bathroom door is at left. The fireplace with its gas heater is placed in the middle of the wall at left with a mirror hanging over it.

At 8 P.M., Julian Weston is stretched out in front of the fireplace listening to rock music. David Powell sits in the center chair watching him. Weston is *"23 years old, just below average height, slender, with very blonde hair,"* while Powell is 30, broad-shouldered, brown-haired, wearing open-necked shirt and corduroy pants.

Weston is telling Powell that he doesn't know the meaning of the word "love." All Powell understands is quick sex. The phone rings, but apparently there's no one on the other end when Weston answers it.

Weston tells Powell he didn't expect him to hang around this flat as though he intended to move in. He "had a sort of more temporary arrangement in mind." Powell replies reproachfully, "You ask people in—you want they should take care of you, when it's dark and you're afraid—you can't just—you know?—when it's got light again and you're not frightened any more—tell them 'out.' "

Powell lives in this same building and doesn't go out anywhere to work (though Weston does). Powell watches while Weston changes the record on the player and moves around the room emptying ash trays, etc. Powell gets up and turns the music off.

> *Powell reaches out suddenly and catches hold of Weston's arm. He holds it tightly, the fingers pressing into the flesh and marking it white. Weston watches Powell calmly, without showing visible reaction to the pain.*

WESTON: Well? If you don't want the goods—you know?—don't muck 'em about.

POWELL: You bother me, Julie. All the time—fussing—you bother me.
WESTON: You bore the shit out of me.
     Silence.
POWELL: You want to fuck?
WESTON: Not particularly.
     Silence.
And now—if you don't mind—
  POWELL: It's colder. Isn't it getting colder?
  WESTON *(harshly):* Will you let go!
     Powell lets go of Weston's wrist. Weston crosses to dining table.
POWELL *(quietly):* Times—and you like to be hurt.
WESTON: Ha!
POWELL: I was reading about that—people—hurting you.
WESTON: Reading? Reading what? What d'you mean?
POWELL: Int'resting. All that stuff. Better than books.
     Silence. Weston opens the door of the armoire and crouches in front of
     it. He reaches into the armoire and pulls out a folder. He looks at the
     mass of notebooks stacked inside it.
WESTON: You bitch. You rotten, filthy bitch. You cunt!
  POWELL: You don't have secrets—I mean—there isn't anything you have to
hide. It's like—I've been inside your head. Inside your body—now—inside your
head.
  WESTON *(shuts armoire door):* You must've known—surely!—reading—
couldn't you see? I didn't mean anyone should read . . .
  POWELL: I wanted you last night. Tonight!—The way I feel tonight—what I
know about you—what happens—thinking . . . If you didn't mean anyone should
read it—how come you wrote it all down? Couldn't you just as well remember
—keep it in your head?
  WESTON *(crosses, sits on foot locker, holding folder close):* I didn't mean anyone
should read it.
  POWELL: Someone—you wanted someone to read it. Maybe not me . . .
  WESTON: Not you.
  POWELL: No—maybe not, but someone—yes?
     Silence
Julie?
     He crosses and kneels beside Weston and puts an arm across his shoul-
     ders, pulling him close towards him, holding him tight.
I'm sorry, Julie.
     He rubs a hand down Weston's arm, comfortingly.
You have to understand—reading those books—it seemed like a chance to know
you—get to know you—and I couldn't stop myself . . . I've watched you—days
and weeks. You must've seen me—you must've known. Didn't you know? Days
—and I've wanted just to come and knock on your door—nights—the nights
weren't any easier. And then—last night . . .
  WESTON *(cold, pulls away):* Last night, darling—I needed something warm in
bed with me—something beside me—something I could touch—reach out and

touch—if I woke in the night and I was scared—something—there—in the darkness—anything, darling—man, woman or dog.
     Crosses to bed, puts folder under mattress, then rises, facing Powell.
You think I'm going to let you fuck me? I mean—now! What are you? Some sort of raving maniac! I wouldn't let you fuck me—as long as you live—one thing you have to know—you'll never—ever, ever, ever—get into me again.

Weston ridicules Powell's powers of love-making: "I've had fellas make you look like a girl." Powell lunges at Weston, who dodges him adroitly. The doorbell rings, and Weston orders Powell out of the flat. Powell is straightening his clothing, as Weston opens the door to Alan Harrison, *"47 years old. He smiles easily, a smile which protects the eyes from showing too much pain, the face from seeming too vulnerable."*

Weston introduces Powell to Harrison as his brother, to save explanations, and identifies Harrison as an old, good friend whom he hasn't seen in almost a year. Harrison remembers that the flat was once furnished differently, with not so much expensive equipment showing. Weston invites him to sit down and take off his coat, while again suggesting that Powell take his leave.

The phone rings—it is obviously someone trying to make contact with Weston, but Weston pretends it's a wrong number. Weston persuades Powell to leave by making him a promise—in words which are supposed to be "family" gossip in order to conceal their true meaning from Harrison—that he will spend the weekend with him.

Once Powell is gone, Weston turns on Harrison and reproaches him bitterly for walking out on him almost a year ago: "Don't come crawling in here with all this humble shit! You went away. You said—end—dead end."

Harrison finally takes off his coat, hangs it up and sits down.

HARRISON: Why did you leave the firm?

WESTON: What did you expect me to do?

HARRISON: I don't want to feel you had to leave—because—you and I—because . . .

WESTON: Oh, my love—your battered, beautiful bleeding heart! I would have left long before, if it hadn't been for you. Most of the time I hated the place and everybody working there. What was I? Sort of a glorified office boy—right? Do this—do that—fetch the tea, lad—shit!—and get anything wrong—like I'd raped the Mother Superior. Didn't I ever tell you? Anyway, I've got a much better job now.

HARRISON: What's that?
     Silence.

WESTON: I don't want to talk about it.

HARRISON: Why not? Where are you working? What're you doing?

WESTON: Most of the time, love—I mean—my main preoccupation—waiting for Mr. Right to come along—riding his great, white charger, wearing his silver, shining armor and waving his ten-foot lance eagerly in my direction. What I do is my affair entirely and nothing to do with you.

HARRISON: No.
WESTON: What are you doing here?
HARRISON: I came to see you.
WESTON: You want to go to bed?
    Silence.
You always did. Hardly inside the door and it was—"Take off your clothes—get into bed"—and getting out again—"Sorry, love—can't stay long tonight—they're expecting me home early."
    Silence. Harrison takes out cigarette lighter.
How are they all at home? I should have asked. How very forgetful of me! What's-her-name—your loving, forgiving wife—how is she?
HARRISON *(lights cigarette):* Jackie . . .
WESTON *(harshly):* I know what her name is.
    Silence.
HARRISON: She's well.
WESTON: And the children—how are they?
HARRISON: They're all right.

Weston speculates that probably the children never realized that Harrison had ever "left" them in mind and heart, because he never physically departed from the family circle. Harrison admits he wasn't strong enough to break with his family. It seemed easier at the time to leave Weston instead. The memory angers Weston: "You always make me feel stupid—in bed and I can make you feel good—then—you can be generous. You can show me—love. You can give—and not explain—make me understand all the giving means—to you—to me—the meaning! I don't give a shit!"

Things have changed, Weston continues, love has been smothered, and perhaps it would be best if Harrison would just leave. Harrison pleads that he never intended to make a complete break, he just needed a trial separation to think things out, but he didn't feel he had the right to ask Weston to wait until he could make up his mind what to do with his life. Now Harrison has finally made his decision: "I want to live with you, Live here—with you—live anywhere."

This announcement brings tears of irony to Weston's eyes. Weston would gladly have waited, had he only known—but now it is too late, too much time has passed, too many things have changed.

Harrison won't take no for an answer, he even shows signs of jealousy of Weston's so-called "brother." Harrison pleads with Weston to talk, so Weston unburdens himself as he moves around, wiping the crumbs off the table with a dishcloth: "I can't trust you, love. You went away. You said you wouldn't—all the same—you did. . . . . I hurt a lot—and I cried—after you left. I used to cry all the time. *(Laughing.)* It got ridiculous. Buses and trains—restaurants—once—I was home—talking to my mother—I started to cry. I said I'd lost my job. I was worried about the rent. She gave me a couple of quid—patted me on the head and told me—'Don't worry.' Poor old thing. I wanted to tell her—'Alan's left me. Gone back to his wife.' Oh, God! Everything there was—I gave it to you—and you went away—and I didn't have it any more. . . . ."

Weston will go to bed with Harrison right now if he wishes, and afterward Harrison must go. But this is not what Harrison wants. The doorbell rings, and Weston goes to dismiss whoever is trying to see him. Weston comes back with a cover story about some woman wanting to look at the flat. Then he immediately confesses that Powell is not his brother, but an unimportant lover. Harrison understands now about the promised weekend, and Weston agrees to break his promise to Powell.

Weston wonders what Harrison has been doing all this time he has been away, whether and where he found love. Finally he blurts out to Harrison that in spite of everything he loves him still. Harrison tries to explain why he went away, reminiscing about making love to women and girls, about the many near-futile games he played, and finally: "I found—there was no one in my life I trusted. No one I could let come close—no one could even understand—no one who knew the simple basic fact—my life—everything—was part of this same lie—this slight —but central!—divergence from the truth. I had contrived an absolute aloneness for myself. Why did I go away? You have to understand, love,—at that time— truthfully, I thought—that was the life I wanted—and most of the time—enjoyed it—It was a sort of death—but locked inside—keeping my head down and my eyes closed—I was happy—and why not! What's so much better here?—out here! —and I'm not happy—more alone—and all the time—aware! *(Silence.)* I did come here tonight—thinking we could make love—and right away—before we talked—before—anything!—make love. That was the fantasy—blanking out thought—and all consideration—just—the memory of every night we spent here."

Weston sees no reason why they can't make love. The phone rings again; it's another "wrong number." Harrison wants Weston to tell what he felt and did the night Harrison left him, but Weston puts him off. They need a drink, Weston insists, and since there's nothing in the flat Weston sends Harrison out to the local pub to get some scotch.

After Harrison goes, Weston starts to remember out loud about the night Harrison walked out. Weston stood in the street in front of Harrison's house until all the lights went out, then sat in a cafe. A man picked him up there, and they went into the park for some rough and unsatisfactory sex. Weston couldn't bear the thought of coming home to the flat he had shared with Harrison, so he spent the night at the house of a friend who insisted on more sex activity, unwanted by Weston.

His reminiscence has become a monologue addressed to the absent Harrison, during which Weston has been making the bed.

WESTON: . . . . . I didn't want to do those things. I didn't want to let them fuck me. They were strangers. I didn't know their names. Why weren't you here to stop me, Alan? If you'd been here . . .
    Pushes himself to his feet and turns away from the bed. He stumbles across the room toward the record-player and starts a record.
They were all friends—good friends—I knew them—really quite well—and they said—"Julie—we're having a party. You're the guest of honor."—and they

laughed. I went to the party with them, and of course there wasn't any party. It was a game they were playing with me—and I knew. Love—I knew it was a game. I always knew! I knew what they had planned and that was my game—played against them—knowing—and letting it happen anyway. They had this plan to rape me. Two of them holding—two of them watching—one of them—and I laughed. What did they think—what was there left to rape? They thought they were so wicked—pulling off my clothes—dissolute—depraved! "Shit, darling— I've been fucked," I said, "in dirty lavatories—by men who would just as soon fuck sheep. I've been spread across tables in transport cafes . . . fucked in the dark by frightened little men . . . fucked in broad daylight—nearly torn in half . . ."

The sound blasts out of the twin speakers. The door of the flat opens and Harrison walks into the room, carrying a paper bag with a scotch bottle in it. He pushes the door shut behind him. He walks to counter, puts bag down, crosses to stereo, lifts arm off record, crosses to Weston. Silence.

HARRISON: What is it, Julie? For God's sake—what happened?

WESTON: Love me, Alan—please—make love.

Weston crosses to Harrison. They embrace. Curtain.

ACT II

An hour later, Harrison is sitting on the chair dressed in trousers and shirt open at the neck, and Weston is in his bathrobe, sitting on the bed. Weston is telling Harrison he'd like to make a real home for him somewhere, when the doorbell rings. They figure it is one of Weston's "callers," and Weston goes to the door to send him away. But when Weston comes back into the room he is accompanied by Harrison's wife Jacqueline (Jackie), 42, who has followed her husband to this flat and has insisted on being let in.

Jackie has read some letters to her husband signed "Julie," has followed her husband in order to confront her rival, She has trouble grasping the fact that this rival "Julie" is a man.

WESTON: My letters? You read my letters?

Harrison walks toward Jackie and she backs quickly away from him, stumbling against the foot stool. She falls heavily across it and rolls on to the floor. Harrison crouches beside Jackie, reaching to take hold of her.

JACKIE *(screaming):* Get away from me. Get away!

WESTON: Why did you let her read my letters? Why didn't you keep them safe? *Silence.*

JACKIE *(viciously, gathering herself together):* I thought at least you had a woman here. I didn't realise . . .

HARRISON *(reaches for her again):* Here—let me help you.

JACKIE *(rises, crosses away):* Don't touch me. Filth! You are—filthy!

WESTON *(at center chair):* I have a feeling, love—this could be sort of ugly.

(Brightly.) Tell you what—why don't we—right away now—all of us—pull ourselves together? Stop behaving like children. Remember where we are—and —God is always watching!—all those good things—and before we start this— stop! Why don't we do that?

JACKIE: You've been—to bed together?

WESTON: Could we do that?

JACKIE: You've been—what do you call it—surely not!—making love?

WESTON: No, we couldn't.

JACKIE: Is that what you've been doing?

WESTON *(crosses behind Harrison):* Darling—if you can't get it—don't knock it.

HARRISON *(crosses, gets coat, crosses to Jackie):* Jackie—why don't you let me take you home?

JACKIE *(harshly, backs away to dining table):* When I want to go home, I'll find my own way—thank you very much.

HARRISON: I don't see the point—staying here to fight.

JACKIE: Will it upset him? Is he sensitive—easily bruised?

WESTON: Alan—you can't just walk out of here.

HARRISON *(upstage of Jackie):* Be reasonable, Julie.

WESTON: You can't do that.

HARRISON: Try to understand.

WESTON: No.

HARRISON: I'll just take Jackie home.

WESTON: You won't come back.

Harrison is trying to get Jackie out because he wants to talk to her. Weston suggests (and Jackie agrees) that it would probably have been less painful if Jackie had found that "Julie" was a woman. Weston challenges Jackie: "What makes it normal—done to you—makes it so shameful—when it's done to me?"

Weston, whose anger is aroused by Jackie's scorn and Harrison's carelessness in having permitted her to read his letters, rubs in the awkwardness of the situation by comparing various physical sexual practises as between woman and man and man and man. He tells Jackie that Harrison hates her. Even Harrison is beginning to feel shame at some of Weston's all too explicit sarcasms. But Weston presses his attack on Jackie, accuses her of thinking about his relations with Harrison in stereotyped images. Turning to Harrison, Weston tells his friend he is only trying to save and protect him.

WESTON: . . . . . When she gets you out of here, she'll be so sympathetic. She'll say—"Darling, you're sick—a little bit insane"—no—some much kinder word. Unbalanced! Meaning the same thing—out of your bloody mind! She'll take you to a doctor and they'll try to cure you—'cause they don't want to think—they can't let themselves believe—you love me 'cause you love me . . . and the making love—something we do because it makes us happy. Look at her, love—she thinks we have some sort of orgy here—and do forbidden things! She thinks you want to fuck me 'cause it'd be different—sick—perverted—some new kind of thrill! She

thinks it can be cured—with help—and the love of a good woman! *(Sits in center chair.)* You won't make anything clear—taking her away—talking to her—telling her where you both went wrong and why it's better you should separate —she knows all that. *(Rises.)* Christ Almighty, Alan—aren't you here? You're separated. Maybe you haven't told each other—you've been separate for years.
      Embraces Harrison.
She has to know—you are in love with me—not 'cause I'm a fella—'cause you are in love.
      Silence.
   JACKIE *(calmly):* Alan—I think he's asking you a question.
      Silence.
   WESTON: Why do you want him back?
   JACKIE: Has he ever left?
   WESTON: Didn't you tell her?
   JACKIE: Isn't it obvious? He hasn't told me anything.
   WESTON: You came here and you didn't—what are you doing here?—you didn't tell her?
      Harrison puts head in hands.
   JACKIE: I simply thought you were a girl—another girl—and this time—for many personal and private reasons I won't discuss with you—I couldn't let him —get away with it.

Jackie found the address and telephone number in one of "Julie's" letters. Jackie counterattacks, informing Weston that her husband's physical relations with him cannot be classed as making love, Harrison is merely "using" Weston. Harrison tries to put an end to their confrontation, but to no avail.

Jackie derides her husband's claim that he needs time to think, accuses him of lack of consideration for his wife and children, of carrying on one extramarital affair after another. Harrison admits that maybe he should have left her 15 years before, when he was first unfaithful. He has stayed with her only because of their two children, Betty, now 16, and Michael, now 19.

Jackie suggests that he stayed with her because he can't bear to be alone. She boasts to Weston that she is a habit that Harrison will find difficult to break, and perhaps in the end Weston will lose Harrison because of her. She tells Weston: "He can't stay here with you. You're the excuse he needs to leave me—his 'grand amour!' He'll make you accept the guilt he cannot even recognize—and when he does—you think he'll stay? Surely—much easier—go to someone else. Leave all the guilt with you and run away again. At his age—forty-seven—forty-eight next month—can he change completely—make himself into another man—and start again? Living with some other woman—just the guilt would cripple him—with you—the same—contempt—disgust on people's faces—you think he won't despair?"

Weston invites Harrison to take Jackie away, but she goes on to boast of her husband's ardor until ten years before, when she noticed him beginning to disintegrate. She recalls that she herself was unfaithful, once, but it was all rather sad and unsatisfactory.

Finally Jackie asks Harrison to come home. Harrison tells her he wants to stay with Weston. Jackie and Weston find one point they can agree on: probably Harrison left the letters lying around because, somehow, he wanted Jackie to find out the truth.

Weston has had enough of this wrangling, and he decides that if they won't leave the flat he at least can make his escape. He leaves the flat, admonishing Jackie, "Take him home and keep him safe."

Alone with her husband, Jackie tells him she wishes he *had* made the break 15 years before, but Harrison insists he had no idea that he would ever want to leave her. Harrison mixes them drinks, and Jackie speculates on why they ever had the children. Harrison maintains that *she* had the children, he had no choice.

JACKIE: . . . . . Something you can be thankful for—you won't have to get a divorce. Save yourself a lot of money—and save me the . . . He won't insist you marry him?

Harrison crosses to fireplace, puts glass on mantel.

Sorry! (*She drinks some of her scotch.*) You see—if I once let myself—if I begin to take this—any of this—seriously—I might begin to scream—(*Crosses and sits on chest.*) You went to bed with him. You did—make love—to him. It could be rather funny. Can't you hear them—"Poor Jackie—did you know? Her husband left her for another man." Isn't that funny? I think it has a certain quality—you might say—surprise. Would you say—surprise?

Silence.

Alan!

Harrison walks to Jackie. She presses herself against Harrison, putting her arms around his back. Harrison accepts the embrace awkwardly.

Sit down, Please—will you?

HARRISON (*sits next to Jackie*): If you knew I was unfaithful . . .

JACKIE (*quickly*): I didn't know.

HARRISON: You had a pretty good idea.

JACKIE (*quietly*): Yes.

HARRISON: Why didn't you throw me out?

JACKIE: I thought it was probably my fault. I never was much good in bed. It didn't seem—well—altogether fair I should blame you entirely—and anyway—I never thought . . .

Silence. Smiling. Leans towards him.

You've got a kind face, sir. Give a poor girl a kiss.

Silence. Pulls back.

Actually, you've got rather a silly face. Sweet, of course. Look—you don't have to sit there—if you don't want to. God forbid—you should do anything . . .

She drinks some of her scotch, rises.

I thought this would help. Funny—you want to know something? It doesn't help a bit. What's on the telly?

Silence.

Jackie finally continues: when she first became aware of Harrison's unfaithful-ness she was angry, she considered leaving home with the children. Then she found herself standing outside the lighted windows of this flat, imagining what might be going on inside—but always with a girl.

Jackie believes that she could become the woman Harrison would like her to be, but he offers her no encouragement. Holding on to him tightly, Jackie asks that he state clearly just once whether he will stay with her or leave her, but Harrison is unwilling to make a final, sweeping commitment.

Jackie reviews the situation for Harrison. If he leaves her, she will divorce him, and he will see his children very infrequently—Betty perhaps not at all. Her briskness dissolves into a sort of tenderness as she begs Alan not to leave her alone, to help her to understand. Then when she kisses him fiercely and he pulls away, her tenderness turns to fury.

JACKIE: . . . You are queer, aren't you? I suppose you always were. Christ!— what sort of idiot . . . Did you ever make love to me—days when you made love to him?

Silence.

All the nights you couldn't make love—I blamed myself. I wasn't attractive— clever enough—I didn't know how to make you want me—how to seduce you! The times I went to sleep—knowing I was so inadequate a lover, I couldn't even make my husband hard. No wonder then you couldn't satisfy me. The years we've been married and you never left me really satisfied.

HARRISON *(quietly):* You came to bed smelling of children. You made love to me like a mother—comforting a child who made unreasonable demands—which had to be endured. One night I wanted to make love. I put my arms around you —kissed you—and you said—"Darling—before we start—will you just see—is Betty still asleep? She's been so odd today, I think she must be coming down with flu." I was halfway on top of you—and you said . . . The bed has never lost the smell of children. All your clothes—your body—the smell sticks to you. It has since they were born and you said—"I don't want any help. We can't afford it —anyway, I want to do it all myself."

JACKIE: Was that wrong?

HARRISON: We could afford it.

JACKIE: Doing it myself—was that wrong? Why didn't you tell me?

HARRISON: Why didn't you ask me? Eight years—talking to babies—when did you talk to me? Jackie—you dressed them—undressed them—walked with them in the park. You nursed them and your breasts still smell of milk. You changed them—held the messes in your hands. Smell your hands. Can you . . . on your hands—can you smell?

Silence.

The children are more secure now than I have ever been. They sleep in the dark. They hide in tiny cupboards. They run to strangers. I needed so much more than them. I needed you—and they had you—and couldn't let you go. Why should they? Children need their mother—and their mother . . . The trouble is—of course —I look like any other man—a reasonable and rational—adult, human being— able to cope with all his problems—buying a house—paying the bills—making the money for you all to spend—giving you presents—asking—*(Abruptly.)* love me. When was it ever quiet enough for you to hear? Where was the understanding

—help—I needed? Love and tenderness.
>*Silence.*

I knew it was foolish, weak—unmanly. I couldn't admit everything—each day of my life—frightened me to tears—and I couldn't even cry.
>*Silence.*

JACKIE *(hesitantly):* I love you.

HARRISON: I know—yes—of course.

JACKIE *(step toward Harrison):* If you could've told me . . . Alan—if you could have said you felt left out—you felt I was neglecting you . . .

HARRISON *(quietly):* I did say—Jackie—I told you—almost every day. You couldn't hear. *(Smiling.)* The children make more noise than Clapham Junction. How could you hear?

JACKIE (vehemently): I can't—Alan—please! Don't make me say—I could've kept you—we'd still be—together—if the children—if I hadn't . . . I love them. They are the best of me.

HARRISON *(crosses to Jackie):* I don't want you to say that. I don't think it's true. They're very probably—the best of me.

Jackie suggests that the children are now almost grown, the problem is almost solved, maybe they could try again to build a life together. Harrison has made up his mind to leave home, even though Jackie insists harshly: "You belong to me." Harrison does not love her, he says, he loves Weston; he is not even willing to stay on at home, in the loveless but unified pretense of the past 15 years of their marriage.

Jackie is beginning to accept the fact, if not the rationale, of the situation, and her mind turns to matters of ways and means: Harrison will tell the children, he will come to pick up his clothes, perhaps it will turn out that he and Jackie remain friends.

JACKIE *(abruptly):* Why did you wait so long?

HARRISON: I'm sorry.

JACKIE: Before you knew me—you must have known—eventually . . .

HARRISON *(smiling):* How could I know—before I knew you?

JACKIE: When you were a child—didn't you—play—with other boys? Didn't you know? Is it possible—you can be queer and not know? Live so long . . .

HARRISON *(quietly):* I don't know.

JACKIE: Well—you really had me fooled.
>*Silence.*

When will you see the children?

HARRISON: Tomorrow.

JACKIE *(opens door):* Saturday? Yes—all right. I'll see they both stay home. I won't be there. Will you manage?
>*Harrison nods his head.*

This is even smaller than the flat we used to live in. How will you survive?
>*Silence.*

You'll let me go? You won't even try to stop me? I keep expecting . . .

Jackie turns and walks out of the flat. She leaves the door open. Silence. There is the sound of the front door, as it opens and closes.

Harrison stands for a moment, then walks toward the door. He stares at the photomontage on the wall. He steps forward, kneels on the bed and reaches to tear the faces off the wall. He murmurs angrily to himself, grunting with the effort, exerting himself violently, tearing his fingernails across the photographs, rasping them down the wall. Curtain.

ACT III

Ten minutes later, Harrison is sitting in the center chair, smoking, when Powell comes in. Powell sizes up the situation, seeing the torn photomontage, guessing that Harrison plans to move in here with Weston (and approving this arrangement; Weston is the type who needs company), admitting that he is not Weston's brother. Powell thought he heard a woman's voice in this room this evening, and he says, "Do you like to make it with women as well? I make it with women. Not too often—just—when I have to."

Powell wonders whether Harrison's feelings about Weston are serious. He reminds Harrison that he and Weston have a date to spend the weekend together. Powell sits on the bed and pats it invitingly: "I'll show you things that make Julie look an amateur."

Infuriated, Harrison attacks Powell, half-strangles him before Powell breaks loose. This doesn't prevent Powell from continuing to comment in the same sarcastic vein about Harrison's feelings for Weston. "Starting life together—you shouldn't have any secrets," Powell says, and he goes to the armoire for Weston's notebooks. "I'll tell you a couple of Julie's secrets," Powell taunts Harrison, "Would you like that? No—I don't think you will. I'm going to tell you anyway."

Powell leafs through a notebook looking for the passages which reveal only too clearly that Weston has been a practising hustler, distributing his address and telephone number and promoting his body. The notebooks are a revelation of Weston's total promiscuity, his physical abandon.

POWELL *(reads quickly down the page):* "The man was awkward, hesitant. I opened the door. He almost turned away. It was ridiculous . . . I thought—at least —knowing he's come to fuck—all he has to do is pay . . . . ."
Turns the page, reading.
"Naturally—he assumed—I had all the experience. I would take control—seduce him. Offering all manner of mysterious delights. Five pounds down—and rapture guaranteed. I pulled the curtains—asked—what shall I do? What do you like? I thought—he's bound to notice—I don't even know the words. He wanted me to take off all my clothes . . . He wanted just to look at me, he said. At first—he wanted just to look. He began to get excited—and then—he took control. It was as I imagined it would be. No feeling—it wasn't my body—no guilt—I belonged to him—no self—I didn't exist."
Silence. Turns pages, looking.

I thought he'd give us some more detail.
> *Turns the page.*

(Reading.) "When the punishment is shame and there is no shame—how can the punishment begin? How can it ever end?"

Powell continues reading from Weston's notebooks about a succession of customers: what they wanted, how they behaved, how they felt, etc. He throws one of the notebooks at Harrison and picks up another one containing a reminiscence about someone called Gordon. Weston apparently was involved in an ongoing sado-masochistic relationship with this Gordon, and the diary fantasizes about killing him in bloody fashion.

Weston comes in and understands almost immediately the betrayal that is taking place. Powell boasts about having shown Harrison the notebooks, but he explains that it was Harrison, not he, who tore down the photomontage. Weston orders Powell out of the flat: "The fun starts when I get hold of you and cut your balls off—I mean—cut them off! I can imagine things to do with you that'd make anything you read sound like a fairy tale."

Harrison has come upon a paragraph dealing with Weston's diagnosis and treatment for venereal disease. Weston urges Harrison to read the whole passage, takes the notebook from Harrison and reads out loud himself.

WESTON *(reading):* " 'Yes—it sounds like gonorrhea. Let's have a look.' He was a very young man, detached, professional, not at all involved. I unzipped my trousers, showed myself to him. What did he see? 'I think we'll have a test. There's not a lot of doubt.' He turned away and wrote on bits of paper. 'Wash your hands.' He gestured with his head. He didn't look at me. The water in the tap ran very hot—scalding my hands. I held them in the water . . . . . He looked through a microscope—he looked at me—smeared across a narrow piece of glass. He looked inside me. What did he see? He made me bend across a high, hard couch and punched a hypodermic needle into my buttock—into my body—into my rotting soul—and shame—I was ashamed.

POWELL: Yes.

WESTON *(smiling to Powell):* Does that make you sick? Darling—that doesn't begin to tell you what it was like! I've done things that would really turn your stomach. I've been to bed with you. I've touched you. I've let you touch me. Think about that. If anything is going to make you sick! Have you any idea, darling—just how bad you smell? Has no one ever told you? Standing in the same room makes me want to take a bath in disinfectant. Your clothes stink. Don't you ever wash? Do you have any idea how ugly you are? Kissing you is like swimming under water in a sewer. Anyone goes to bed with you—he's got to be pretty desperate.

POWELL: You went to bed with me.

WESTON: Darling—last night—I would have fucked a pig. *(Starts to laugh.)*

Powell, angry, calls Weston "diseased," but Weston merely informs him calmly that he is now entirely cured and dismisses him loathingly. Powell has no alternative but to make his exit.

Alone with Weston, Harrison attacks the notebooks, tearing them as though he could destroy the past along with them. Harrison wishes that all the words in the books, all the pictures on the wall hadn't happened. Weston in his turn refuses to accept guilt or punishment for anything he did after Harrison deserted him.

Harrison left his wife and children tonight thinking that he would never return, but now, with all of these revelations, and with the pain left over from the scene with Jackie, he is beginning to waver. He is having doubts about his intentions.

Weston warns Harrison that he'd better think twice if he figures the two of them will just sit here indefinitely keeping each other company: "I won't be a comfort to you in your old age. There's nothing I hate more than old, painted queens—and you're a whole lot older, love, than I am. . . . . . What d'you think —I'm going to spend my life nursing an old man? Anyway, you'll soon get bored with me. I'm sort of stupid, when you get to know me."

Harrison might easily decide to go back to women some day or back to his wife, Weston continues. In any case, he isn't going to sit still for any accusing stare from Harrison. Weston accuses him: "Listen—you failed me tonight. You let her scream at me. You didn't stop her. You didn't try . . . . . I'm supposed to let her walk in here—say what she likes—scream at us? She called our making love— filthy! You wouldn't stand up for yourself—leave alone take care of me."

Harrison has a false romantic image of Weston as some sort of innocent, Weston believes. Harrison denies it, admits he realized Weston was no innocent from their first love-making.

HARRISON: . . . . . I'm not sure, if I'd known this whole night had to happen —I'm such a coward—I would most likely have stayed where I was. *(Bitterly.)* A strong man wouldn't have done all this. Only someone selfish—knowing what he wanted—disregarding other people's pain—his own responsibility—not looking any way but straight ahead—knowing if he looks around—he has to stop.
      Silence.
I used you, Julie. Leaving—I had to go somewhere—go—to someone. I wasn't ready—to go nowhere—on my own.
      WESTON: I'm glad you came here.
      HARRISON: I shan't go back. There's nothing there.
      WESTON: I'm sorry I said those things. I didn't mean them. I was so terrified —knowing you'd read that stuff.
      HARRISON: I could have stopped that happening to you. I can only think—
      WESTON *(hesitantly):* It didn't happen to me, love—not all of it. I went out and made it happen.
      HARRISON: I shall have trouble sometimes, when I think about it—
      Silence.
I may want to hurt you.
      WESTON: I know that. Christ! Whatever happens—one thing—right? You don't go away. It's worth it, love—I mean— *(Laughing.)* —speaking for myself, you understand— *(Doubtful.)* Isn't it worth it? That's what this is all about— yes? Staying together—being together—and no lies. *(Abruptly.)* Some lies—aren't

there always—and—some pain—but not so much—and maybe—less and less—
Love—I don't want to hurt you. I'm not angry any more. I just have to know
—right? Staying—you really are—and loving—whatever happens. We'll tidy all
this mess tomorrow—yes?

    HARRISON: Tomorrow—I have to see the children.

        Silence.

I can't think of Betty crying. I tell myself—she doesn't really care. She'll hardly
notice I'm not there. I can't think—tomorrow—when I tell her—she might cry.

    WESTON: Oh, love—my love.

        Silence. Curtain.

SHORT EYES

A Play in Two Acts

BY MIGUEL PIÑERO

Cast and credits appear on pages 351 & 386

MIGUEL PIÑERO was born in Puerto Rico Dec. 19, 1946 and came to New York City with his parents at age 4. A short while later, when his mother was pregnant with her fifth child, the father disappeared and mother and children were forced out into the street with nowhere to live until a friend made some room for them in a basement. The future playwright (whose full name is Miguel Antonio Gomez Piñero) sometimes attended Public School 97 and spent one year at Junior High School 22. At 11 he was picked up for truancy; at 13 he was into gang rumbles, shoplifting and finally burglary, for which he was at last caught and sentenced to three years on Riker's Island, where he was introduced to hard drugs. Paroled after a year, he kept on taking drugs and went from one job to another. At 24 he was caught and sentenced to five years in Sing Sing for an armed robbery of an apartment house which by coincidence is situated two blocks from the Public Theater, where his play was produced.

At Sing Sing, Piñero became interested in the prison's drama workshop run by Clay Stevenson. He started acting and went on to writing sketches about street and prison life for the prison shows. As the result of a New York Times *article about the Sing Sing workshop, the director of Theater of the Riverside Church, Arthur Bartow, got in touch with Piñero and learned that he was writing a full-length play,* Short Eyes, *in his cell. When he was paroled last summer after serving two and a half years of his sentence, he joined the Riverside group as a playwright in residence, director of the organization's Third World Projects, and member of The Family, an acting troupe of ex-convicts and ex-addicts under the direction of Marvin Felix Camillo.*

Soon The Family began rehearsing Short Eyes *under Camillo's direction. It was presented in January at Riverside in an off-off-Broadway production. It was so successful that Colleen Dewhurst brought it to the attention of Joseph Papp, whose New York Shakespeare Festival Public Theater mounted its off-Broadway premiere and then moved it uptown to the Broadway-sized Vivian Beaumont, with its* The Family *cast (all of whom are now members of Actors Equity) intact. The author, still on parole, is now writing another play.*

Time: The present

Place: The dayroom on one of the floors of the House of Detention

ACT I

SYNOPSIS: The dayroom is a large area, barren, furnished only with three tables, some chairs, a couple of trash cans and a TV set high up on a shelf. The barred door to the outside is at the right of the upstage wall, against which there is a ledge running the width of the room. Against the ledge is an open toilet. On a level above the dayroom, high up on the upstage wall, is a kind of balcony with exits at each end, representing access to the cells.

In early morning, after the morning meal, the dayroom is empty; the prisoners are all in their cells for a routine lock-in. An authoritative Voice can be heard calling the roll, with other voices answering by name and cell number. The Voice orders those that are due in court today to get ready. All others are then released for the morning lock-out.

The men come into the dayroom. Each group takes possession of its own private territory and table—the Puerto Ricans in one place, the blacks in another, the whites in a third. One of the younger Puerto Ricans, a lad named Julio Mercado, fresh-faced but not at all effeminate, resents the others calling him "Cupcakes" and simulating stripper music when he walks near.

El Raheem, a large and commanding black, seems to have his own personal territory along the upstage ledge, where he stands preaching damnation Muslim style down to the others—Omar, Juan Otero, "Ice" (John Wicker), Paco Pasqual and "Longshoe" (Charlie Murphy), as well as Mr. Nett, the guard on this floor, from whom Omar wants a favor.

OMAR: Mr. Nett, you know like I've been here over ten months—and I'd like to know why I can't get on the Help . . . like I've asked a dozen times . . . and guys that just come in are shot over me . . . and I get shot down . . . like why? Have I done something to you? Is there something about me that you don't like?

MR. NETT: Why? No, I don't have anything against you. But since you ask me I'll tell you. One is that when you first came in here you had the clap.

OMAR: But I don't have it any more. That was ten months ago.

MR. NETT: Two is that . . . well . . . how many fights have you had since the first day you came on the floor?

OMAR: But I haven't had a fight in a long time.

MR. NETT: How many?

OMAR: Seven.

MR. NETT: Seven? close to ten would be my estimation. No, if I put you on the Help, there would be trouble in no time. Now unless you give me your word that you would fight and stay cool, I'll give it some deep consideration.

OMAR: I can't give you my word on something like that . . . you know I don't stand for no lame coming out the side of his neck with me. Not my word . . . word is bond.

EL RAHEEM: Bond is life.

OMAR: That's why I can't give you my word. My word is my bond. Man in prison ain't got nothing but his word, and he's got to be careful who and how and for what he give it for . . . but I'll tell you this, I'll try to be cool.

MR. NETT: Well, you're honest about it anyway. I'll think it over.

Paco is sent out to a meeting, and Cupcakes complains that the TV set doesn't work. Cupcakes, Ice and Juan (who is something of a loner and often sits off in a corner by himself instead of at the Puerto Rican table) begin a game of cards. Paco comes back—it was a short meeting; he saw at once that his advisor was trying to trick him into making a deal with the D.A. El Raheem comments: "You still expect the white man to give you a fair trial in his court . . . don't you know what justice really means? Justice . . . just us . . . white folks."

Paco suggests that they play cards with hula dancing as a forfeit, the loser to put his shirt over his hips and do what Paco calls "ku-chi-kuchi." Cupcakes refuses; he has no complexes, he maintains, but he wants no part of this sort of game.

El Raheem and Longshoe, a white man, get to wrangling. Finally Longshoe infuriates the Muslim by making a slur at Allah. They begin to fight, and when Mr. Nett comes in to break it up he is advised by the others to leave the combatants alone and let them get their fury out of their systems in fair fight. They accompany their blows with racial slurs, and they are about even on both counts by the time they both become exhausted and break off.

The fighters go out to clean themselves up, and the Latins sit at their table and beat out a rhythmic song. When El Raheem comes back, Omar challenges him: if he is indeed God, why doesn't he melt down the walls and open the prison? El Raheem is a tangible God, he replies, he cannot perform "mysterious intangible deeds."

Cupcakes stands on the table and does an imitation of a night club M.C. The others urge him to give them one of his parodies. Cupcakes directs them to provide the background rhythm and chant "mambo tu le pop," then he recites: "It was a cold night before Christmas . . . and all thru the pad . . . cocaine . . . and heroin . . . was all the cats had. One cat in the corner . . . copping his nod . . . another scratching . . . thought he was God . . . I jumps on the phone

... and dials with care ... hoping my reefer ... would soon be there ... after awhile ... crowding my style ... there grew such a chatter ... in the parlor ... I ran to the door ... see what's the matter ... and to my surprise ... saw five police badges ... staring ... glaring in my eyes ... a couple of studs ... starts to get rough ... so I run to the bathroom ... get rid of the stuff ... narcs bang ... bang and bang ... but they banged in vain ... cause you see ... what didn't go in my veins ... went down the drain ... broke up the door ... knocked me to the floor ... and took me away ... that's how I spent ... my last Christmas Day ... like a dirty dog ... in a dark and dingy cell ... but I didn't care ... cause I was high as hell ... but I was cool ... you people are the fools ... cream off the top ... cause I got you saying something as stupid as 'mambo tu le pop.' "

Clark Davis, a white newcomer ("another devil" comments El Raheem), enters the dayroom and is taken under Longshoe's wing immediately. This is Clark's first time behind bars. Longshoe shows Clark which is the whites' table and explains to him the organization of prison life, as Mr. Nett lines the men up for chow.

LONGSHOE: Put your stuff on the table. Blacks go on the front of the line, we stay in the back ... it's O.K. to rap with the blacks but don't get too close with any of them. Ricans too. We're the minority here, so be cool. If you hate yams keep it to yourself. Don't show it. But also don't let them run over you. Ricans are funny people. Took me a long time to figure them out, and you know something, I found out that I still have a lot to learn about them. I rap spick talk. They get a big brother attitude about white folks in prison. But they'll also back the niggers, to the *T*. If a spick pulls a razor blade on you and you ain't got a mopringer in your hands ... run ... if you have static with a nigger and they ain't no white people around ... get a spick to watch your back, you may have a chance ... that ain't guarantee ... if you have static with a spick don't get no nigger to watch your back cause you be uptight. You a good-looking kid ... you ain't stuff ... don't wanna be stuff. Stay away from the bandits. Paco is one ... take no gifts from no one.

MR. NETT: Clark Davis ... Davis ...

CLARK: Yes, that me.

MR. NETT: Come here ... come here ... white trash ... filth ... let me tell you something and you better listen good cause I'm only gonna say it one time ... and one time only, this is a nice floor ... a quiet floor ... there has never been too much trouble on this floor ... with you I smell trouble ... I don't question the warden's or the captain's motive for putting you on this floor ... but for once I'm gonna ask as to why they put a sick fucking degenerate like you on my floor ... if you just look at me sideways one time ... if you talk out the side of your mouth one time ... if you mispronounce my name once, if you pick up more food than you can eat ... if you ever call me for something that I feel is unnecessary ... if you oversleep ... undersleep ... if ... if ... if ... you give me just one little reason ... I'm gonna break your face up so bad your own mother won't know you ...

LONGSHOE: Mr. Nett is being kinda hard . . .

MR. NETT: Shut up . . . I gotta eight-year-old daughter who was molested by one of you filthy . . . stinking sons of bitches and I just as well pretend that he was you, Davis . . . do you understand me . . .

PACO: Short eyes.

LONGSHOE: Short eyes? Short eyes . . . Clark, are you one of those short eyes freaks . . . are you a short eyes freak?

MR. NETT: Sit down, Murphy . . . I'm talking to this . . . this scumbag . . . yeah, he's a child rapist . . . a baby rapist, how old was she? How old? . . . Eight . . . seven.

The captain sends for Clark just outside the dayroom, and meanwhile Mr. Nett issues the orders for the after-lunch lock-in. Only Juan is left in the dayroom to sweep up, so that when Clark returns the two are alone. The Puerto Rican gives Clark something to eat and questions him about his crime. Clark says he doesn't know whether or not he did it: "What I mean is that I may have done it . . . or I may have not . . . I just don't remember . . . I remember seeing that little girl that morning . . . I sat in Bellevue 33 days and I don't remember doing anything like that to that little girl."

Juan senses that Clark has been involved in "something like that" previously, and Clark admits that he has. Juan is a good listener, and Clark needs someone to talk to. He has a wife and child whom he loves dearly, who might be hurt by any courtroom publicity, and he doesn't know what to do. Clark couldn't even tell his troubles to the prison psychiatrist, but now, with half an hour of privacy to go before lock-out, he is persuaded to pour his story into Juan's ear.

When Clark was about 15 or 16 (he tells Juan) he exposed himself to a little girl, a friend of his sister's who had come over to his house to watch TV. The incident happened when his sister left the room: "I came closer like a vampire . . . she started backing away . . . ran toward the door . . . stopped, looked at me again . . . never at my face . . . my body . . . I couldn't really tell whether or not the look on her face was one of fear . . . but I'll never forget that look."

Clark was afraid the little girl might tell her parents, but apparently she never did. Later on he had a full sexual experience with another little girl, the willing daughter of the Puerto Rican janitor next door, who enjoyed and wanted to repeat the experience. They did, three times a week, and Clark found himself becoming obsessed with children and their activities, "a professional degenerate . . . . . I couldn't help myself . . . something drove me to it . . . I thought of killing myself . . . but . . . I just couldn't go through with it . . . I don't really wanna die . . . I wanted to stop, really I did . . . I just didn't know how . . . I thought I may be crazy . . . but I read all types of psychology books . . . I heard or read somewhere that crazy people can't distinguish right from wrong . . . yet I can . . . I know what's right and I know what I'm doing is wrong, yet I can't stop myself . . ."

Clark couldn't go to the police, because he knew they would find some pretext to kill him for what he had done. Juan is making an effort to understand Clark, but he is in no way sympathic. He is just as much moved to anger and disgust by Clark's confession as the other men would have been—maybe even more so because Clark's first victim was Puerto Rican. Juan warns him: "If you remain on this floor you're asking to die . . . you'll be committing involuntary suicide."

Some of the others drift back into the dayroom. Whatever the racial or other differences among them, they are all in agreement that Clark is an untouchable, a pariah, a child-molester or "short eyes." Their hatred shows in every word addressed to Clark, who is "assigned" his proper place in the dayroom by a process of elimination.

OMAR *(to Clark):* Hey freak. You're standing on my Chinese handball court . . .

ICE: That there is where I hangs my wet clean clothes . . . and I don't wanna have them sprayed. Move . . .

EL RAHEEM: You're in God's walking space.

PACO: That Paco's walking space.

CUPCAKES: Hey, sicky . . . that spot's not taken . . . right over there . . . yeah, that's right . . . the whole toilet bowl and you go well together.

CLARK: I'm not going to stand for this treatment.

PACO: Did you say something out your mouth, greep . . .

OMAR: You talking to everyone or to someone in particular?

LONGSHOE: I know you ain't talking to me.

ICE: You got something you wanna say to some in this room, faggot?

CLARK: I was talking to myself.

EL RAHEEM: Well, don't talk to yourself out loud . . .

CUPCAKES: Talk to the shitbowl . . . you'll find you got a lot in common with each other.

JUAN: Drop it . . . cut it loose . . .

The others are somewhat surprised to find Juan talking Clark's part, Juan backs down under their scorn—he feels no real sympathy for Clark anyway—and the others continue tormenting their victim.

LONGSHOE *(goes over to toilet):* Hey, man . . . don't leave. I want you to hold it for me . . . while I pee.

CLARK: Wha . . . wha . . .

LONGSHOE: I want you to hold my motherfucking dick while I pee, sucker, so I don't get my hands wet . . .

Laughter.

Well??

CLARK: No . . . no . . . I can't do that . . .

LONGSHOE: Oh. You can't do that . . . but you can rape seven-year-old girls.

CLARK: I didn't rape anybody. I didn't do anything.

LONGSHOE: Shut up, punk. . . . .

Longshoe appropriates all Clark's cigarettes and a gold chain he's wearing that his mother gave him. One by one, Longshoe and the others pretend that Clark has affronted them in some way. Even El Raheem joins the pack closing in on Clark.

EL RAHEEM: Boy, I told you about being in God's walking space, didn't I?
ICE: You better answer God when he speaks, boy.
LONGSHOE: Don't you turn your back on me, motherfucker.
        Strikes Clark. Clark falls against El Raheem, who hits him too. Omar begins kicking him.
PACO: *Para . . . Para Eso . . . Lo van a matar . . .*
ICE: Cool it, brothers, cool it . . . you gonna end up killing this fool . . .
MR. NETT: You guys shouldn't whip up his face.
OMAR: Mr. Nett.
EL RAHEEM: Mr. Nett, the man started a fight with Omar and we just broke it up.
LONGSHOE: That's right, Mr. Nett.
MR. NETT: Sure, sure . . . I ain't never had any trouble from you boys. Omar, you and Juan are on the Help permanently. The Torres brothers beat their case this morning.
OMAR: Right on . . . bet them two are high as hell by now.
MR. NETT: Yeah, and they'll be back, mark my words . . . listen, get this man off the floor . . . you guys know the rules . . . no sleeping on the floor. *(Exit.)*

ICE: You guys ought to learn how to touch up a dude.
OMAR: I'll get a bucket of water.
LONGSHOE: Put the sucker's head in the toilet bowl. There's water there.
EL RAHEEM: You're still a devil . . . I won't do that to no man.
LONGSHOE: We could get it on again.
EL RAHEEM: That don't present me no problems . . .
ICE: Squash it, man . . . both of you . . .
LONGSHOE: Come on, Omar, grab his other side . . .
OMAR: Hey, there's piss in there still.
LONGSHOE: Put his head in and I'll flush it.
OMAR . . . let me put his head in there and you flush it.
LONGSHOE: Makes me no difference . . . flush the motherfucker, Omar.
        Curtain.

ACT II

Half an hour later, all are busy with various diversions: Juan playing chess with Ice, Omar and Cupcakes playing cards, El Raheem writing, Longshoe reading, Paco fiddling with the TV set. Clark has been taken away for a positive-identification (P.I.) session in the line-up.

The men are indulging in the customary banter to pass the time, consisting mostly of friendly insult, once in a while threatening to take a serious turn.

El Raheem accuses the other black men of wasting time they could be using to prepare themselves to take over the world from the white man, whose time is almost up. Ice answers him: "El, let me tell you something. I'm a hope-to-die dope fiend . . . not cause I'm black . . . or cause I have some personality disorder, but because I like being a dope fiend. And nothing is gonna change that in me . . . if Allah comes down from wherever he is . . . and he ain't doing good dope . . . I ain't gonna cop from him . . . and I'll put out a wire that his thing is cut with rat poison . . . why don't you go back into your lessons and git off my motherfucking back . . . cause I do as I please. When the day comes that I wanna become a black god, a panther or a Muslim then I will become one . . . right now all this shit you keep running about us being niggers—stupid and ignorant—ain't gonna get you nothing but a good kick in the ass."

Mr. Nett comes in to tell Juan and Longshoe they have visitors. Longshoe refuses to see anyone from the outside and begs Juan to do the same. Longshoe has some confused idea in his mind that somehow the presence among them of "the freak" makes it impossible for satisfactory contact with the outside world: "Don't you see, he has the mark on him . . . like I said before, it's the same thing as coming out of the joint . . . you're branded . . . a week . . . a month . . . sooner or later they're gonna take you off the count . . . you know that.. what makes you think his place is any different . . . it's all the same thing."

This confusion means nothing to Juan, who goes to see his visitors. In the shower area at left Cupcakes, dressed in underwear and socks, is drying his hair, when Paco sneaks up behind him and kisses him on the neck. Cupcakes reacts in instant fury, wanting no part of Paco, finally taking a swing at him. Paco, ducking, avoids the blow and connects with one of his own.

CUPCAKES: Leave me alone . . . *dejame.*

PACO: Listen little brother . . . I don't want nothing from you the hard way.

CUPCAKES: Well, that's all you gonna get out of me, a hard way to go . . . and don't you ever call me brother . . . if you considered me your brother, would you be trying this shit . . .

PACO: *Si mi hermano eras tan lindo como tu* . . . yeah . . .

CUPCAKES: You're sick . . .

PACO: I'm what? Sick . . . don't you say that to me . . . sick . . . Shit, I'm sick cause I'm in love with you . . .

CUPCAKES: Love me . . . you use words that you don't even know the meaning of. Brother . . . love . . . shit there's a gringo . . . who does it to a little girl . . . and you wanna mess with me . . . why don't you hit on him . . . why? Cause he's white . . . and you scare of the whitey . . . but you'll fuck over your own kind . . . he's the one you should be cracking on . . . he's the one. Not me . . . but you're scare of him . . .

PACO: I fear nobody . . . or anything, man . . . god or spirits . . . I don't want him, I want you . . .

CUPCAKES: But you can't have me.

PACO: Push comes to shove. I'll take you. But I don't wanna do that cause I know I'm gonna have to hurt you in the doing. Look man, I'll go both ways with you. Who you looking for? Juan is on the visit. And let me tell you this. Makes

me no difference if he does have your back or not. I'm gonna have you . . . if I want you . . . right now . . . I'm gonna show you I ain't scare of nobody . . . cause you need to know that you gotta man protecting you . . . I'm gonna take that honky and you're gonna help.
Enter Omar. Pause.
OMAR: What?
Exit Paco.
Why you let that creep talk to you that way? . . . all you gotta do is swing and keep swing. Fuck it if you lose. Fuck it if you win. Makes no change either way. Just let him know you's a man. I ain't the smartest guy in the world . . . but I do know that some people you can talk to . . . some people you gotta fight.

Omar advises Cupcakes to accept Juan's protection. In the dayroom, the men are whistling at "some fags" being brought on to another floor. Juan comes back —he had a most satisfactory visit with his woman. Soon they are all discussing the policies in other jails they have known.

JUAN: . . . . . it was terrible up there. Man, I still hear tell they got the old track system running.
CUPCAKES: What's the track system?
JUAN: Segregation between inmates . . . like black and white handball courts . . . water fountains, you know like . . .
ICE: If you're white you can't smoke after a black. Sit at the same table in the messhall, and if you do you can't eat your food. No taking anything from a black person. Like if you're a whitey and you're playing handball and your ball goes over on the black handball court and a black touches it, well you and the black have to fight. If you don't you go on the track and become a creep.
CUPCAKES: Break it down.
JUAN: For instance, the yard is broken down in three sections . . . four, really . . . one white . . . one black . . . one Spanish-speaking . . . and the track . . . If you're consider a good people you stay with your people and enjoy their protection. If you ain't good people and like go against the program that your people has set up—
ICE: Convicts law of survival. The codes of crime.
JUAN: Well anyway, you go to the track with the creeps . . . with no protection but your own two hands . . . dig.

Ice reminisces about the pornography circulated in prison, and about one wild time when, aroused, he imagined he was making love to a movie star so energetically and with such abandon that he attracted the attention of all the others on the floor to his orgiastic pleasures. Two guards tried to beat him up because the object of his imaginary fling was a white woman, but Ice managed to scare them out of it. Later on he was sent to the psychiatrist, not only because of his sexual activity but also for refusing to allow himself to be beaten.
Clark comes back into the dayroom. Mr. Nett announces sick call. The men line up, as Clark asks Juan to keep what he told him a secret.

CLARK: . . . . . Like, I don't know why I even said that, just . . . just that . . . man, like everything was just coming down on me . . . my wife . . . she was at the hospital . . . she . . . she didn't even look at me . . . once, not once . . . please . . . don't let it out . . . please . . . I'll really go for help this time . . . I promise.

JUAN: What happened at the P.I. stand?

CLARK: Nothing . . . nothing . . . happened . . .

JUAN: Did she identify you? Did she?

CLARK: I don't know. I didn't see anybody. They put me next to a bunch of the other men about my size-weight . . . You—the whole line-up routine. I didn't see anybody or anything but the people there and this voice that kept asking me to turn around to say "Hello, little girl." That's all.

JUAN: Nothing else?

CLARK: No.

JUAN: You mean they didn't make you sign some papers?

CLARK: No.

JUAN: Was there a lawyer for you there? Somebody from the courts?

CLARK: Juan, I really don't know . . . I didn't see anybody . . . and they didn't let me speak to anyone at all . . . they hustled me in and hustled me right out . . .

JUAN: That means you have a chance to beat this case . . . did they tell you what they are holding you for?

CLARK: No . . . no one told me anything.

Clark wants some kind of understanding from Juan, promising that if he goes free this time he will seek help and never molest anyone again. He senses Juan's rejection, and Juan tells him: "I don't hate you. I hate what you've done. What you are capable of doing. What you might do again."

Clark doesn't want Juan to judge him, he's had enough of judgment. He wants a companion to live and let live. He doesn't think he can bear the conditions and the relationships of prison life. Clark is on the verge of tears.

CLARK: . . . . . Why shouldn't I feel sorry for myself . . . I have a right to . . . I have some rights . . . and when these guys get back from the sick call . . . I'm gonna tell them what the captain said to me, that if anybody bothers me to tell him . . .

JUAN: Then you will die.

CLARK: I don't care one way or the other. Juan, when I came here I already had been abused by the police . . . threatened by a mob the newspaper created . . . then the judge, for my benefit and the benefit of society, had me committed to observation. Placed in an isolated section of some nut ward . . . viewed by interns and visitors like some abstract object, treated like a goddamn animal monster by a bunch of inhuman, incompetent, third-rate, unqualified, unfit psycopaths calling themselves doctors . . . electros—sedatives—hypnosis—therapy . . . humiliated by some crank nurses who strapped me to my bed and played with my penis to see if it would get hard for "big girls like us."

JUAN: Did it?

CLARK: Yeah . . . yes it did.

JUAN: My father used to say he would fuck 'em from eight to eighty, blind, cripple and/or crazy.

CLARK: Juan, you are the only human being I've met.

JUAN: Don't try to leap me up . . . cause I don't know how much of a human being I would be if I let you make the sidewalk. But there's no way I could stop you short of taking you off the count. I don't think I could do that.

The others return and draw Juan into a conference on what to do about Clark. Since the last riot, they have all agreed to settle any differences by means of a council.

JUAN: What's happening?

LONGSHOE: He white like I am . . . And you ain't got no right according to the rules to take his back . . . if he is stuff.

JUAN: Stuff? He ain't stuff.

LONGSHOE: Well we say he is.

JUAN: Who says he is.

PACO: I say he is. Anybody that has to rape little girls is a faggot. He's stuff . . . squeeze.

JUAN: I say he ain't.

ICE: You got no say in this.

PACO: Oh, he's got a say, not that it means anything, but he's got a say.

LONGSHOE: Paco, be cool.

JUAN: Yeah, Paco, be very cool.

LONGSHOE: That ain't necessary . . . and neither is your getting in the way of the council.

JUAN: The council was set up to help not to destroy.

Paco accuses Juan of being biased by a sexual interest in the newcomer as well as in Cupcakes—Paco imagines that all the others have designs on Cupcakes similar to his own. Paco assumes that Longshoe approves whatever they mean to do to Clark. Omar is on Paco's side, as is El Raheem: "He's a whitey. A devil. Anything goes." Cupcakes, too, chooses to side with Paco against Juan. Only Ice senses that Juan is right, they are behaving like animals, he wants no part of any action against Clark.

Juan tries to defend Clark from the others, but Paco grabs him and induces Ice to hold onto him. Clark calls for help.

CLARK: Mr. Nett. Mr. Nett. Juan.
        Runs toward the front. They grab him and beat him a little. He is still yelling. They drag him toward the back of the dayroom. Mr. Nett walks in, sees what's happening and turns to go.
O.K. O.K. Don't hurt me any more. Go 'head, do what you want. Go 'head, you filthy bastards. Go 'head, Mr. Nett, don't think you can walk away from this. Any

of you. Do what you want. Cause you'll pay. I'll tell the captain. I'll bring you all before the courts. You bastards. You too, you fat faggot.

JUAN: Shut up . . . shut up.

PACO: You gonna do what?

LONGSHOE: He gonna squeal. He's gonna rat us out.

JUAN: Ice, let him go.

EL RAHEEM: You're in this too, Ice. We'll all get more time.

CLARK: I'll make sure you get life, you son of a bitch.

MR. NETT: I'll lose my job.

CLARK: I'll make sure you go to jail. My father has money . . . plenty money.

JUAN: Shut up, Clark . . . shut up.

Paco pulls out a homemade knife.

PACO: I ain't doing no more time than I have to.

OMAR: Paco, that murder.

CUPCAKES: What are we going to do?

LONGSHOE: Kill the motherfucking rat.

MR. NETT: Kill him—it's self-defense.

Ice is still holding on to protesting Juan. All are agreed that Clark should die, and the knife is given to El Raheem, who brings the blade to Clark's throat but cannot bring himself to follow through and kill Clark while he is lying there helpless.

Clark begs for his life. The phone rings—it is probably the captain calling, and Mr. Nett goes to answer. Gripped by fury, Longshoe grabs the knife from El Raheem and cuts Clark's throat, killing him.

Everyone is silent.

OMAR: El Raheem . . . black god . . . leader of the black nation . . . faggot . . .

EL RAHEEM: I'm not a punk . . . I'm not a coward . . . Omar, believe me. It's just that I couldn't kill a man looking at me helpless.

LONGSHOE: You punk motherfucker you . . . you ain't nothing but a jiveass nigger. I'm gonna cut your black ass until you turn white, nigger.

ICE: Shoe . . . raise . . . or deal with me.

LONGSHOE: You want a part of this, too, Ice? . . . Nigger, you want a part of this.

ICE: Don't run it in the hole, Shoe.

LONGSHOE: You selling me a ticket, faggot?

ICE: That's right, honky. You feel you can cash it?

LONGSHOE: Come with it.

ICE: You bring it and bring your beat.

Longshoe rushes Ice, swings the knife. Ice jumps out of the way.

LONGSHOE: Come, nigger. What's the matter, jigg? You can't stand the sight of a knife. You bought this . . . now enjoy it. Come baby, don't run.

PACO: Ice.

Throws him a pipe.

LONGSHOE: Paco, you go up against me?

ICE: Come, punk, now we stand on equal grounds.

LONGSHOE: You'll only get one shot, faggot.

ICE: That's all I need.

PACO: Don't look at me, Longshoe. You wanna kill each other, then go ahead. *El que gane pierde.*

LONGSHOE: Whoever wins loses.

JUAN: Oh my god . . . is this really us?

        Curtain.

EPILOGUE: Captain Allard is seated in the dayroom reading Mr. Nett's report on the killing of the prisoner Clark Davis. The two men are alone in the room. Allard stares at Mr. Nett who protests too much that he is calm, not nervous, and has put all the facts in the report.

Allard calls in Cupcakes, who testifies that he knows nothing about the killing, he was watching "The Dating Game" on TV. Cupcakes is replaced by Longshoe, who also testifies he was watching "The Dating Game" when the killing occurred.

Allard dismisses Longshoe. Alone with Mr. Nett, Allard tells the guard that he knows the men are lying and why they are lying; and since Nett corroborates their story, he must be lying too, an accomplice of the inmates. It is perfectly clear to Allard that they couldn't have been watching TV, the set wasn't working.

Allard decides that for the good of the department he will suppress this damaging fact of the out-of-order TV set. The group will be broken up, assigned to other floors, and Juan, the only innocent, will be placed in protective detention for the remainder of his sentence. Mr. Nett is to write his reports and then apply for sick leave, get out of sight for awhile.

Allard calls the prisoners in to the dayroom and tells them what he has decided.

ALLARD: . . . . . I'm satisfied that it was a suicide. But I would also like to state that I hold all of you morally guilty. If you had taken some time out of your own problems to deal with this poor man who was placed in this position because of mistaken identity—

EL RAHEEM: What did he say? Mistaken identity? You mean he was not here because they caught him?

ICE: El.

ALLARD: Caught him doing what?

EL RAHEEM: With drugs, what else do people come to jail for?

ALLARD: No . . . Mr. Davis was not a drug addict . . . in fact he was a respectable member of society . . . working man with wife and kid. We took him down for a positive identification line-up . . . and the person who he had been supposed to have assaulted was not in their right mind . . . and had already pointed out two, maybe five other men as the men who assaulted her . . . Mr. Davis was just a victim of circumstances . . . innocent . . . good night, men . . . *(Exits.)*

ALL: Good night.

EL RAHEEM: Man, he was clean.

LONGSHOE: He was guilty. I could tell it in his eyes, man. I know.

CUPCAKES: What have we done?

ICE: Ain't no use crying over it now . . . Cupcakes, be cool . . . don't blow your cool.

PACO: Juan! Juan knows . . . Juan—

JUAN: I know nothing I was watching "The Dating Game."

All feel a share of guilt in the killing except Juan, of course, and possibly Paco, who remarks: "I saw him guilty. I feel nothing. Mistake? It happens. Some day I will be in the street walking. Shoot down by a policeman who will say mistake. I accept it as part of my *destino* . . . . ."

Cupcakes is getting out on bail today. He feels as much or more remorse for his part in the killing as any of the others, and he begs Juan for a word of absolution, of comfort to take with him.

CUPCAKES: . . . . . Juan? Give me something to go with, please.

ICE: What do you want, kid? What is it? If you . . . oh look, Juan, this kid thinks you're some kind of guru. If you don't tell him something, he's bound to go there and run this story to somebody that should hear it. Can you dig? Juan can you dig—where I'm coming from?

LONGSHOE: Cupcakes, I killed, and I'm not afraid to do it again. You understand me?

JUAN: Shoe. If you ever run some shit like that on him again I won't be afraid to kill, either.

EL RAHEEM: Neither would I.

JUAN: I'll give you something—a cheer . . . one final hurrah . . . that's you bylaw . . . cause you're leaving this place . . . and only because of that . . . I can't give you no cues . . . no lifestyle pearls . . . because you, like the rest of us, became a part of the walls . . . an extra bar on the gate . . . to remain a number for the rest of your life in the street world . . . Cupcakes, you went past the money and blew . . . yeah, this is a cop and blow . . . and you blew it . . . Cupcakes, you blew it because you placed yourself above understanding . . .

VOICE *(offstage):* On the bail . . . Mercado . . . get your ass out here now . . . Mercado . . . on the bail.

Juan turns on the TV set and the Watergate hearing comes on.

JUAN: Yoyo Cupcakes . . . just one thing . . . your fear for this place stole your spirit and this ain't no pawnshop.

Curtain.

CREEPS

A Play in One Act

BY DAVID E. FREEMAN

Cast and credits appear on page 389

DAVID E. FREEMAN was born Jan. 7, 1945 in Toronto, suffering from cerebral palsy which has affected his speech and the use of his limbs. He attended Sunny View School for the Handicapped until age 17. It was there that he began to become interested in writing, with the encouragement of his speech therapist. He founded the school newspaper, which is still being published. He left Sunny View in his tenth-grade year and drifted from job to job including garbage collection and sanding blocks for 75 cents a week in a "sheltered workshop."

In 1963 Freeman's stories began selling to magazines—including his "The World of Can't" in the July 1964 issue of Maclean's—and in 1966 he enrolled in McMaster University in Hamilton, Ont., graduating B.A. in political science and writing a satirical column for the campus publication. Freeman's first play, Creeps, was first produced in Canada, where it won the Chalmers Award for the best play of 1971–72 (its first draft was written in 1965 as a TV script). It was published by the University of Toronto Press in 1972 and had its American premiere at the Folger Theater in Washington. This season it was produced off Broadway for 15 performances, not a commercial success but clearly one of the Best Plays of its year.

Its author is equally clearly an accomplished playwright whose next work was Battering Ram, *produced at the Tarragon Theater, Toronto in 1972–73. Freeman's third play,* You're Gonna Be Alright, Jamie Boy, *is a hit this season in Canada.*

Time: The present

Place: The men's washroom of a sheltered workshop for cerebral palsy victims in a large industrial city in Canada

SYNOPSIS: The washroom contains urinals down right and stalls down left; a chair, a bench, basins, etc. It is ill cared-for, both dirty and messy, in this "sheltered workshop," a place where cerebral palsy victims and other disabled persons can work on projects at their own pace, more to pass the time than to earn a living.

One of the stalls is occupied. Michael, an 18-year-old mentally retarded victim of cerebral palsy, enters and sets about flushing the urinals and toilets one after the other. In the original production, the actor playing Michael *"staggered always, his head lolling, his body very loose, constantly on the edge of falling. He fell, or collapsed, rather than sat, and grinned most of the time. He had a speech problem, very slurred, not employing the facial muscles."*

The voice of Thelma, who will continue to be heard but never seen, cries out offstage, calling for a priest in tones that are spastic but clearly understandable.

Tom March enters—in the original production, the actor playing Tom *"walked with one hip thrust out to the side. Forward motion always began with the foot of the other leg, rising up on the toe, and then thrusting downward on the heel. His arms were held in front of him, his fingers splayed, upper arms and shoulders constantly being employed for balance."*

Michael leaves the washroom, and Tom watches Pete Cochran, the occupant of the stall, drop his cigarettes, his comic book and then his pants. In the original production, the actor playing Pete *"developed a way of speaking that is common to many spastics. The effort required to speak causes a distortion of the facial muscles. The actor was able to achieve this by thrusting his jaw forward and letting the lower jaw hang. The deformed hand was not held rigid in one position. The actor used the hand for many things, keeping the fist clenched and employing the fingers in a claw-like manner."*

Tom has been folding boxes and Pete has been weaving a rug (and offstage Thelma again calls "I want a priest!"). Both are bored with their occupations, which pay them 75 cents a week.

Sam rolls into the washroom in his wheel chair. *"Sam is a diaplegic, his body dead from the waist down (except for his genitals). Some spastics confined to wheel chairs wear belts around the waist to keep them in the chair, and without which they would fall out of it."* Sam is angry because his therapist has criticized the blocks he has been making—she wants the edges smoother. Finally Pete emerges from the stall.

PETE: I've been weaving that stupid rug beside that hot radiator every day for three months. And what has it got me? A big fat zero.

SAM: That's because you're a lazy bugger. You know what the stupid idiot who runs this dump says about you?

PETE: Yeah, I know. He says, "Peter, if you worked in my factory, you wouldn't last a day."

TOM: "But since you're a helpless cripple... I'll let you work in my workshop..."

SAM: "For free . . ."

PETE: "And the government will give me a pension just for breathing . . ."

TOM: "Because there's little else you can afford to do with it . . ."

PETE: "And the Rotary and the Shriners will provide hot dogs and ice cream."

SAM: And remember, boys . . . "If they won't do it . . ."

ALL TOGETHER: "Nobody else will."

Blackout.

Interlude #1: In ironic contrast to the central action of the play, there is a short interlude in which three symbols of physical romance—an astronaut, a football player and a beauty queen—join an M.C. (played by the actor who is playing Michael) in a telethon to raise money "to recycle these poor unfortunate cripples, or at least help us to get them off the streets. . . . . Come on folks, send us a check —one dollar, five dollars, ten dollars, anything. But please help us to help these poor blunders of God! . . . . ." Blackout.

The conversation in the washroom continues where it left off, as Tom tells the others he is coming to the end of his tolerance of box-folding, Thelma's cries, the Spastic Club. Tom longs to devote himself to his painting, and he is infuriated when Sam calls his abstract work "chickentracks."

SAM: Look, Tom, even if you do have talent, which I seriously doubt, what good is it to you? You know bloody well they aren't going to let you use it.

TOM: Who's they?

SAM: Who's they? The Rotary, the Shriners, the Kiwanis, the creeps who run this dump. In fact, the whole goddamn world. Hell, if we start making it, they won't have anyone to be embarrassed about.

PETE: Come on, Sam, there's always the blacks.

TOM: And the Indians.

SAM: Yeah, but we're more of a challenge. You can always throw real shit at a black man or an Indian. But at us you're only allowed to throw pityshit. And pityshit, boys, ain't visible.

Tom would have to "give someone's ass an extra big juicy kiss" in order to be permitted to use his talent, like Jim, who has an office job here at the workshop on a weekly salary and is president of the Spastic Club. Jim himself enters as though on cue; in the original production, the actor playing Jim "*walked with his knees almost touching, feet far apart, back bent much of the time, using his arms more than any other part of his body for balance.*"

Jim cautions the others that perhaps they are taking too much time away from work. Pete guesses that they are safe enough here. The therapist Miss Saunders won't come in here after them (though she once did invade these premises to break up the activity between a pair of homosexuals). Jim flares up at the insinuation that perhaps he may be her emissary—which in a way he is, though he hasn't come to spy on his friends. "Saunders saw me coming in," he tells them, "and she thought I might remind you that you'd been in here a long time."

Miss Saunders knocks on the washroom door, calling Jim's name. Jim calls out to her that he is using the toilet. The others shout defiance at her. She departs, warning "If you boys aren't back to work in five minutes I'm reporting you to Mr. Carson."

Jim understands the others' resentment of him; obviously they think he has gone over to the side of the authorities. Sam calls Jim a "white nigger."

SAM: You finished high school. You went to the university. You wrote all that crap for the paper about how shitty it was to be handicapped in this country. Then what do you do? You come running down here and kiss the first ass you can see. Now, that's what I mean by being a white nigger, and that's what fucking well pisses me off.

JIM: All right, Sam, now you listen to me. I still believe everything I wrote, and I intend to act on it, but you can't change things until you're in a position to call the shots. And you don't get there without being nice to people. By the way, what the heck are you doing about it? All I ever get from you is bitch, bitch, bitch.

SAM: I got every fuckin' right to bitch. You expect me to sand blocks and put up with the pityshit routine for ninety-nine years waiting for you to get your ass into a position of power? Fuck you, buddy! You give me a choice, and I'll stop bitching.

TOM: Now look who's taking himself seriously!

But Sam goes on: he has nothing but contempt for the look of martyrdom he sees time after time in the faces of his mother and father. Sam's parents are somewhat ashamed of him, and when they had the boss to dinner they wanted Sam to eat in the kitchen. Sam refused and deliberately vomited on the table in the middle of dinner. Jim warns that a stunt like that sets them all back 99 years and makes it very difficult for anyone trying to help them, like Carson, the head of this workshop.

Michael comes in to flush the toilets again but is stopped by Pete. They speculate on whether the workshop boss Carson is using them or helping them, and they are divided on this point. Jim has been invited to Carson's house for dinner once but never invited back (Sam considers this tokenism). The meetings of the Spastic Club with their free hot dogs are just another of the devices used to keep them all ripe for exploitation.

Miss Saunders calls again for them all to come out, but they merely curse her and pretend they are having a sex orgy behind the door through which she dares not enter.

Michael bums a cigarette and sits in the corner, eating it. Tom declares that he feels like the hero of an Edgar Allen Poe story—buried alive in this place and calling for help, but no one hears (and once again Thelma's cry "I need a priest!" is heard through the closed door). But the book Tom is actually carrying in his pocket is not Poe, but pornography. Tom gives the book to Sam, who reads some of it aloud and then tosses the book to Pete. Jim reminds Sam of the time he made love to a Rotarian's daughter at a picnic.

Again, Thelma calls out for a priest. This time, Sam calls back at her to be quiet, as though her cry were directed to him personally.

TOM: I'd like to know what the hell is going on.

PETE: This was before your time, Tom. Thelma was all right then. Cute kid, as a matter of fact. Until old horny here got his hands on her and drove her off her rocker.

SAM: That's a goddamn lie! The doctor said it wasn't my fault.

JIM: They only told you that to make it easy for you.

SAM: It wasn't my fault!

JIM: What you did sure didn't help any.

SAM: Why bring it up now?

PETE: Because we're sick and tired of hearing you put shit on everybody else. It's time somebody put shit on you for a change.

TOM: What did he do? Will someone please tell me?

PETE: From the first day Thelma got here, Sam was after her like a hot stud. He was being so nice to her, and then coming in here and bragging how she was letting him feel her up, and bragging how he was gonna fuck the ass off her soon.

THELMA (offstage): I want a priest!

PETE: Maybe you've heard, Tom, that Thelma's parents are religious. They're not just devout, they're real dingalings about it. Like they believe Thelma is the way she is because of some great sin they've committed. Anyway, one weekend Thelma was sick in bed with a cold, and Sam went over to visit her, and . . . her parents weren't out of the room two seconds before he was into her pants.

SAM: That's another goddamn lie, it didn't happen that way at all!

PETE: Well, maybe it took you a full minute. Why quibble over details?

SAM: Because I didn't want anything to happen that day, that's why. What do you think I am, stupid? In the first place, she had a cold, and in the second place, her parents were out on the porch. I just wanted to talk, but she starts fooling around, trying to grab my cannon and everything. Silly little bitch! Naturally I get a hard-on. What was I supposed to do? Anyway, we were just going real good when she changed her mind. One helluva time to exercise her woman's prerogative, eh? . . . She fell out of the bed. In a few seconds, in come Mommy and Daddy. They thought I'd fallen out of my chair or something. Well, there I am in bed with my joint waving merrily in the breeze, and poor Thelma on the floor minus her PJs, and all hell broke loose. You'd have thought they'd never seen a cock before. The old man bounced me out of bed and along the floor and into the hallway. The old lady, she dragged Thelma up behind. Then they held us in front of this little Jesus statue and asked it to forgive us 'cause we didn't know what we were doing. Even the doctors said it wasn't my fault.

JIM: They were only feeling sorry for a horny cripple in a wheel chair.

Simple-minded Michael picks up a refrain that sounds like mockery of Sam: "Thelma needs a priest, Thelma needs a priest." Furious, Sam tries to run Michael down with his wheel chair but is prevented by Pete.

Tom spies a cockroach in one of the urinals, and they all egg Michael on to "disintegrate" it with his "ray gun." Michael unzips and goes to the urinal.

Miss Saunders calls again for the men to come out. When they don't obey her this time, she comes into the room.

PETE: Have you no sense of decency?

SAUNDERS: All right, I don't know what you boys are doing in here, but I want you back to work immediately. Pete, you've still that rug. Tom, there's boxes to be folded. Sam, you'd better get busy and sand down the edges of those blocks if you expect to earn anything this week. As for you, Jim, well, I'm beginning to have second thoughts.

JIM: Yes, ma'am.

Pause. No one makes a move to go.

SAUNDERS: Well, get moving!

PETE: I have to take a crap.

He goes into one of the stalls.

TOM: Me too.

He goes into the other one.

SAM: I have to use the bottle.

SAUNDERS: And what do you have to do, Jim?

SAM: He has to hold the bottle for me.

SAUNDERS: He has to what?

PETE: Please, Miss Saunders, don't give him an opening.

SAUNDERS: Okay, I'll give you one more chance. When you're through here, I want you all back at work. Fast. Michael, you come with me.

Michael turns around from the urinal. His pants are open, his penis exposed.

Michael!

MICHAEL *(to Miss Saunders):* I'm gonna disintegrate you!

SAUNDERS: Oh you boys, you put him up to this, didn't you?

PETE: We did not.

SAUNDERS: Right! Mr. Carson will be here any minute. We'll see what he has to say!

She opens the door to leave.

SAM *(calling after her):* Hey, be careful. He's got one too!

Shocked again, she slams the washroom door, and her footsteps are heard running down the hall. Pete and Tom emerge from the stalls laughing. Jim zips up Michael's fly and sends him out the door.

Jim starts to pick up some of the trash that is lying on the washroom floor; he is not going to obey Miss Saunders's order to return to work.

Tom offers to have his father take a look at Jim's typewriter, which is out of order. Jim invites Tom to do this year's Christmas mural for the Spastic Club. Tom might do it if he were paid—but that's out of the question, Jim tells him.

All who work for the Spastic Club do so as volunteers—even Carson himself. In that case, Tom refuses to do the mural.

Disappointed, Jim puts the litter he has collected into the wastebasket, as Pete wants to know what the Spastic Club has planned for entertainment this year. Pete had suggested a lecture by a visiting university psychiatrist, but Carson has decided that some of the members might be bored by this. As for Sam's suggestion that they do something about having ramps installed in the subways, this is out of their jurisdiction.

TOM: Okay, Jim, what does the Spastic Club have up its sleeve for this year?

JIM: We've got a trip to the Science Center. One to the African Lion Safari. We're organizing a finger-painting contest, and a sorority is throwing a Valentine's Day party for us . . .

PETE: Oh boy, a party!

TOM: What's the entertainment, Jim?

JIM: Puffo the Clown, Merlin the Magician . . .

PETE: And Cinderella, and Snow White and the Seven fucking Dwarfs. Jesus Christ, Jim, Puffo the Clown! What do you and Carson think you're dealing with, a bunch of fucking babies?

Blackout.

Interlude #2: Puffo the Clown enters carring balloons. He is followed by a girl and two Shriners. The balloons are distributed, and on a signal from Sam all burst them. Blackout.

They are still discussing the Spastic Club program, mocking Jim's plans which include an educational trip through a glue factory. Jim knows that the program leaves something to be desired, but he is trying to improve it.

JIM: Okay, Tom, maybe the things we do aren't as exciting as you or I'd like them to be, but I'm doing the job as well as I can, and I can't do it all on my own. You guys bitch about the program, but you won't get off your asses and fight for something better. That idea of Pete's about the psychiatrist. I pushed it. I pushed it to the hilt . . .

PETE: But Carson didn't like it.

JIM: Carson didn't like it, and the more I pushed the firmer he got.

SAM: Why didn't you push it right up his ass?

JIM *(ignoring this):* So I told Pete to go down and talk to Carson. I even made him an appointment. But you never showed up, did you, Pete?

PETE: I was busy.

TOM: Why the hell should you or Pete or anyone else have to beg that prick for anything?

JIM: That's not fair, Tom. So he's a little stuffy and a bit inflexible at times, but at least he's interested. He does give us more than the passing time of day.

PETE: Yeah, he was in for a whole hour this morning.

JIM: Look, Pete, you may not like Carson, but just remember. If he, or the

Kiwanis, or any of the other service clubs decide to throw in the towel, we're in big trouble.

SAM: "If they won't do it . . . ."

JIM: If they won't do it, who will? You?

A long pause.

PETE: I've got nothing against the Rotary or the Kiwanis. If they want to give me a free meal just to look good, that's okay with me.

Jim suggests that if Pete wants something he should give something—but Pete still refuses to "jump through hoops" for Carson or anyone like him. Still, he knows how cold it is outside.

Pete remembers that 11 years ago, when he first came to this place, he wanted to be a carpenter despite his deformed hand. He found that the closest he could come to his ambition, in his doctor's and Miss Saunders's estimation, was to sand blocks. So he left the place after a few days; but on the outside he found every door closed against him. No one reached out to help him until one day he received an invitation to a meeting of the Spastic Club. Pete attended the meeting, found it as unstimulating as he'd expected—but "I got a free turkey dinner. When I got home I took a good look at myself. I ask myself what am I supposed to be fighting? What do these jokers expect me to do? The answer is, they want to make life easier for me. Is that so bad? I mean, they don't expect me to help keep you guys in your place or anything. They just want me to enjoy life. The government's paying me to do that. And if I take a job, I'll lose the pension, so what the fuck have I been bustin' my ass for looking for work? I got no answers for that one. So I joined."

Interlude #3: The actor playing Michael enters in the role of a barker, with a Girl. There is now no impediment in his speech as he goes into a pitchman's sell of life as a spastic: "The Shriners, the Rotary and the Kiwanis are just begging to wait on you hand and foot," to teach new skills like sanding blocks and folding boxes.

The Girl hands Michael a life-sized model of the human brain, so that Michael can illustrate how to qualify for a lifetime of being coddled: "All you do is simply adjust the motor area of the brain. Like this . . . . . Not too hard, now, we wouldn't want to lose you. *(He taps the brain gently.)* Having done that, you will have impaired your muscle coordination, and will suddenly find that you now 'talk with an accent.' *(The words in quotes are spoken with the speech defect of the character Michael.)* You will then be brought to our attention either by relatives who have no room for you in the attic, or by neighbors who are distressed to see you out in the street, clashing with the landscape."

There is still another solution for anyone who finds the subsequent lifetime of pampered leisure not to his taste, Michael adds. Just tap the brain a little harder. Blackout.

Sam is angry at Pete for feeling sorry for himself—Pete could make it as a carpenter if he tried a little harder, Sam believes. In addition to his physical handicap, Pete is embarrassed about the way he talks. Sam scoffs at him, Sam is above all that. He tells a story about flaunting a paper cup of urine in a movie theater men's room. Jim and Tom are not impressed; Sam sets their cause back with behavior like that.

Tom is determined to make it on the outside as an artist. Jim likes Tom's paintings, he finds them "colorful." But Jim reminds Tom that he cannot draw, that the lessons of the past teach that even good abstract painters are first of all good draftsmen. Jim cannot recall a single spastic painter—or writer either, for that matter.

Tom cites a letter he has received from an art critic. He produces the document. Pete tries to read it aloud to the others, but can't. Jim takes it and reads the art critic's comments aloud: "I was fascinated by the portfolio you submitted. I cannot recall an artist in whose work such a strong sense of struggle was manifest. You positively stab the canvas with bold color, and your sure grasp of the palette lends a native primitivism to your work. I am at once drawn to the crude simplicity of your figures and repulsed by the naive grotesqueries which grope for recognition in your tortured world. While I cannot hail you as a mature artist, I would be interested in seeing your work in progress this time next year."

They suggest that the writer must have been a friend of the family; but Tom tells them not so, the comment is completely objective. Pete suggests that maybe the critic is being deliberately easy on Tom because of his affliction, like the visitors who come through the workshop and "have an orgasm over my rug, no matter how shitty we both know it is." Tom denies this, claims the critic has a reputation for toughness and does not know Tom is spastic.

Once again Jim praises the workshop, seeing it as a sort of medium through which he is able to help unfortunates like Michael and Thelma, worthy of his efforts in its behalf even if he has to be very diplomatic in his relations with Carson in order to accomplish anything. But Tom has just about made up his mind to leave this place and strike out on his own, whatever the hazards. Jim pleads with Tom to wait until Christmas, do the mural, but Tom refuses. Jim warns him: "Look, I know this place isn't perfect. I agree. It's even pretty rotten at times. But, Tom, out there, you'll be lost. You're not wanted out there, you're not welcome. None of us are. If you stay here we can work together. We can build something."

Tom in his turn warns Jim that he is wasting his life and talent staying on here as Carson's private secretary.

TOM: . . . . . When was the last time you wrote something that you wanted to write?

JIM: Well, you know, my typewriter's busted . . .

TOM: Please, Jim, don't give me that crap about your typewriter. You don't want to get it fixed.

JIM: That's not true . . . *(He trails off.)*

TOM: Do you know what you're doing here? You're throwing away your talent for a lousy bit of security.

JIM: Tom, you don't understand . . .

TOM: You're wasting your time doing a patch-up job at something you don't even believe in.

Jim does not reply.

Jim, there are stacks of guys in the world who haven't the intelligence to know where they're at. But you have. You *know*. And if you don't *do* something with that knowledge, you'll end up hating yourself.

JIM: Do! What the hell could I do?

TOM: You could go into journalism, write a book. Listen, in this job, who can you tell it to? Spastics. Think of all the millions of jerks on the outside who have no idea of what it's really like in here. Hell, Jim, you could write a best-seller!

JIM: I've thought about it.

TOM: Well DO something about it!

JIM: Don't you think I want to?

TOM: Look, I know you're scared. I'm scared too. But if I don't take this chance, I don't have a hope in hell of making it. And if you keep on doing something you don't even really want to do, you're going to end up not even having a mind. Do you think if Michael had a mind like yours he'd be content to hang around this place flushing toilets all day?

PETE: He's right, Jim. You don't belong here. You and Tom should leave together.

TOM: Look, I'll help you. Now we'll go, and we'll get a place, and we'll do it together. Okay?

Before Jim can answer, Miss Saunders is heard in the hallway escorting Mr. Carson, who enters the washroom and orders them all out and back to work. Jim moves to obey, but when Tom informs Carson's he quitting, Jim says "I'm quitting too, sir. I'm going with Tom."

Carson refuses to believe them, telling them that if they carry on like this he ought to fire them. Sam calls for the urinating bottle, and when Carson refuses to hand it to him Pete does so, forcing an issue and telling Carson "Fuck you," setting Carson back on his heels a bit, so that he wonders, "What's wrong with you guys?" as he takes the bottle away from Sam.

Jim asks Carson listen to him. Carson tries to put him off, but Jim insists he wants to talk here and now. Sam, still needing the bottle, curses Carson.

CARSON *(to Jim):* What is it?

TOM: Jim, he's listening.

Long pause. Then, simultaneously:

CARSON: Well, Jim, you know   JIM: Shut up, damn you!
you've been a real disappointment to
me today.

Silence. Carson and Jim look at each other in disbelief.

JIM: I don't want to spend the rest of my life in this place.

CARSON: Fine, you probably won't. Now can we all get back to work?

SAM: NO, I NEED THAT FUCKING BOTTLE!

TOM: Didn't you hear what he said? He said he doesn't want to spend his whole goddamn life in this dump.

CARSON: Look, March, you've been in here all afternoon. You got Miss Saunders all upset because of Michael and . . .

SAM: HEY, I NEED THE BOTTLE.

CARSON: SHUT UP, SAM!

JIM: Did you ever think of why we're in here all afternoon? Ever think of that?

SAM: You are a prick! You want me to piss in my pants.

Carson practically throws the bottle at him.

TOM: Did it ever enter your mind that we may think of something besides the Spastic Club, the workshop and making you look good?

CARSON: Right now, I don't know what you think and I really don't care. All I'm concerned with is that you get out of the washroom and back to work.

JIM: No.

CARSON: What?

JIM: You heard me. We're going to settle this here and now.

Jim tells Carson he is determined to make his living as a writer, but Carson is deaf to understanding. He sneers at Tom's plan to join Jim in living on the outside somewhere on their government allowances. They couldn't afford to live on their own, he insists. In reply, Tom calls Carson a son of a bitch and Carson, angry, *"tries to usher Tom out, but Tom pushes him off, loses his balance and falls. Pete and Carson go to help him up, but Tom resists Carson's help."*

Tom challenges Jim to make up his mind here and now: come with him or remain in this trap. Jim wants more time to think it over while he carries out the Spastic Club Christmas program. Now Carson challenges Jim too: if Jim is going to leave, let him leave now.

PETE: Go, Jim! Go with Tom!

SAM: Don't let him do it to you, baby. Go, for Chrissake!

JIM: But Tom, it's Christmas!

TOM: Jim, please!

JIM: No, I can't let him down now. Maybe after Christmas . . .

SAM: Fuck Christmas! What about Tom?

JIM: But I've written all those letters and made all the arrangements . . .

SAM: Fuck the arrangements! Are you going to let him walk out that door alone?

PETE: If you don't go now, Tom will be alone, but you'll be more alone. Believe me, Jim, I know.

JIM: I CAN'T GO! I can't go, Tom, because, if you fall down, I'll be the only one there to pick you up. And I can hardly stand up myself.

Tom has gone.

SAM: How did you get around on campus, princess? Crawl on your belly? *(He wheels angrily to the door.)* Fuckin' door! Hey, Carson, how about one cripple helping another?

CARSON: Help him out, Pete.

> *Sam and Pete exit. They wait outside the door, listening. Jim staggers over to the bench and sits.*

Look, why don't we talk about this over dinner? At my place, if you like.

THELMA *(offstage):* I need a priest! Get me a priest! Someone get me a priest!

> *Slow fade to the sound of Thelma's sobbing. Pete wheels Sam down the hallway. Curtain.*

NOEL COWARD
IN TWO KEYS

A Program of Two Comedies

BY NOEL COWARD

Cast and credits appear on page 360

NOEL PEIRCE COWARD (1899–1973) was born in the Teddington section of London Dec. 16, 1899. Both his father, who worked for a music publisher, and his mother were interested in amateur theatricals and placed a toy theater among their infant son's playthings. The budding performer and dramatist made his first public appearance at the age of 6 in a school entertainment singing a song called "Coo" from a musical entitled The Country Girl *and accompanying himself on the piano. By 1910 young Coward was ready to answer an ad in the paper to audition for a children's show called* The Goldfish. *Coward got the part of Prince Mussel and played it at the Court Theater for a guinea and a half a week. He was soon cast in a fully professional adult play,* The Great Name, *at the Prince of Wales's Theater. One of the great careers of the modern stage had begun, as he continued to perform while finishing his education privately.*

A lung condition prevented Coward from active service in World War I until the beginning of 1918, when, apparently cured, he entered the British Army. He was discharged later that year, however, after a succession of serious illnesses and long stays in various hospitals. He immediately resumed his acting career, making the rounds of auditions, accompanying himself on the piano for songs he himself had written, including his first complete lyric, "Forbidden Fruit." In 1919 his stories were beginning to sell to magazines, and he was trying to write plays. Finally, on July 21, 1920, Noel Coward's professional playwriting debut took place with I'll Leave It to You *at the New Theater in London, following a Manchester tryout. It was not a success; his first hit was* The Vortex *at the Everyman theater in Hampstead in 1924.*

Coward's subsequent, illustrious career will surely continue to be a major focus of the theater historian's attention as it has been of the theatergoer's. In this space we will attempt to summarize only the New York authorship phase of it. Broadway premieres of shows written by Noel Coward, as listed in the Directory of the American Theater, were as follows: The Vortex, Hay Fever, Easy Virtue *(all 1925);* This Was a Man *(1926);* The Marquise, Fallen Angels *(both 1927);* This Year of Grace *(1928);* Murray Anderson's Almanac *(co-author of book),* Bitter Sweet *(both 1929);* Private Lives *(1931);* Design for Living *(1933, a Best Play);* Conversation Piece *(1934);* Point Valaine *(1935);* Tonight at Eight-Thirty *(1936);* Set to Music *(1939);* Blithe Spirit *(1942, a Best Play; Critics Award);* Present Laughter *(1946);* Quadrille *(1954);* Nude With Violin *(1957);* Look After Lulu *(1959);* Sail Away *(1961);* The Girl Who Came to Supper *(music and lyrics, 1963). In addition, his* The Young Idea *(1932),* Still Life *(1948) and* This Happy Breed *(1952) were produced off Broadway; his comedy* Blithe Spirit *was adapted into the musical* High Spirits *(1964); and his musical numbers have been assembled by Roderick Cook into two revues:* Noel Coward's Sweet Potato *(1968, on Broadway) and* Oh Coward! *(1972, off Broadway). His versatility was such that he wrote the songs as well as the books for his musicals and could perform the musical roles as well as the comic and dramatic ones in his own shows.*

Noel Coward's 23d new Broadway production and third Best Play, the program of comedies entitled Noel Coward in Two Keys, *was first produced in London in 1966 under the title* Suite in Three Keys. *The "suite" consisted of one full-length play* (A Song at Twilight) *and a program of two shorter works* (Come Into the Garden Maud *and* Shadows of the Evening), *presented in alternating performances. The plays shared the same Swiss luxury hotel suite setting, though they had different sets of characters, and Coward played all the leading roles. The "suite" was to have come to Broadway in the late 1960s, but its production was put off because of the illness of its author and star. The present New York version is a single program combining the short comedy* Come Into the Garden Maud *with the longer work* A Song at Twilight *and dropping* Shadows of the Evening, *a play about death.*

Coward has left a rich legacy of achievement in many areas of show business as well as on the theater library shelf. His best known screen plays were In Which We Serve *(for which Coward was director, star and co-producer as well as author and won a special Academy Award) and* Brief Encounter. *He performed with great distinction in every medium including cabaret. His autobiographies* Present Indicative *and* Future Indefinite *are to be followed by the as yet unpublished* Past Conditional. *Among his other works are the novel* Pomp and Circumstance, *four collections of short stories and a book of verse,* Not Yet the Dodo.

Noel Coward was knighted by Queen Elizabeth in 1970 for his services to the theater. In his last years he held a residence at Les Avants, sur Montreux, Switzerland, near his setting for Suite in Three Keys. *He died of a heart attack at his villa in Jamaica on March 26, 1973.*

COME INTO THE GARDEN MAUD

Time: The present

Place: The sitting-room of a private suite in a luxurious hotel in Switzerland

Scene 1: An evening in summer

SYNOPSIS: It is 7 o'clock on an early summer evening. The suite has a view of the mountains through windows leading onto a balcony at right. The door to the bedroom is down left and the door to the lobby and hall is up slightly left of center. The luxurious furnishings include a sofa upon which Anna-Mary Conklin is lying, polishing her nails, while the handsome floor waiter, Felix, stands ready for her orders. Anna-Mary is *"an exceedingly wealthy American matron in her late 40s or early 50s. At the moment she is wearing an elaborate blue peignoir, blue ostrich-feather mules and a hair-net through which can be discerned blue hair tortured in the grip of a number of metal curlers. Her expression is disagreeable because she happens to be talking to a member of the lower classes."*

Anna-Mary is complaining to Felix that he provided the wrong bottled water for her night table, and that the chambermaid served the wrong breakfast.

FELIX: Very well, madame.

ANNA-MARY: And you can tell her as well that I don't like being nattered at the first thing in the morning in a language that I can't understand. Neither Mr. Conklin nor I speak a word of Italian and the sooner the staff of this hotel realizes it, the better it will be for everybody concerned.

FELIX *(blandly):* Va bene, Signora.

ANNA-MARY: Are you being impertinent?

FELIX: Oh, no, madame. I most humbly beg your pardon. It's just a question of habitude.

ANNA-MARY: It may interest you to know that Mr. Conklin and I have stayed in most of the finest hotels in Europe, and when we pay the amount we do pay for the best service, we expect to get it.

FELIX: Very good, madame.

ANNA-MARY: That will be all for the moment.

Felix moves to depart, but Anna-Mary calls him back for a question about whether the water in the hotel is safe to drink. Finally Felix makes good his escape, polite and unruffled as always. Anna-Mary turns to the phone and complains in pidgin French to the beauty parlor about the quality of her hair-do and manicure.

Anna-Mary is eagerly but somewhat apprehensively looking forward to giving a dinner that evening—she has secured a prince as guest of honor. Her husband, Verner, is out playing golf. Anna-Mary phones her friend Mariette, who has rounded up the guests for her, for reassurance as to the etiquette of this princely occasion. She has no sooner replaced the receiver and gone into the bedroom than Verner Conklin enters. He is *"a tall, pleasant-looking man in his late 50s. There is little remarkable about him beyond the fact that he has spent the major portion of his life making a great deal of money. He is carrying a bag of golf clubs which he flings down on the sofa."*

Anna-Mary comes in and harries Verner about buying special cigars for the Prince. Verner couldn't get them, the shop was closed for lunch when he went to play golf, like all the others in this "lousy town." It was closed for the day when he came back.

ANNA-MARY: Clare Pethrington told me that the Prince likes a special sort of cigar which can only be got at one particular place here, and I, thinking it would be a nice gesture to have them served to him after dinner, am fool enough to ask you to take care of it for me—and what happens?

VERNER: Nothing happens. He does without 'em.

ANNA-MARY: Now look here, Verner . . .

VERNER: There's no sense in working yourself up into a snit. I guess the cigars you get in this hotel are liable to be good enough for anybody, and if His Royal Highness doesn't fancy 'em he can smoke his own, can't he?
He sits on the arm of the sofa.

ANNA-MARY *(bitterly):* You wouldn't care if the first dinner party we gave in this "lousy town" as you call it, were a dead failure, would you?

VERNER: Calm down, sweetheart—it won't be. Our parties ain't ever failures; they cost too damn much.

ANNA-MARY: You know, Verner, that's one of the *silliest* things I've ever heard you say. The sort of people we're entertaining tonight are interested in other things besides money.

VERNER: Like hell they are!

ANNA-MARY: I can't think what you came on this trip for.
She sits down and puts out her cigarette.
You can play golf in Minneapolis.

VERNER: And on a damn sight better course, too.

ANNA-MARY: You just about sicken me, Verner, you really do. Don't you get any kick at all out of travelling to new places and meeting distinguished people?

VERNER: What's so distinguished about 'em?

ANNA-MARY: Wouldn't you consider a royal prince distinguished?

VERNER: How do I know? I haven't met him yet.

ANNA-MARY: He just happens to be one of the most fascinating men in Europe, and one of the most sought after.

VERNER: Except in his own country, which he got thrown out of.

ANNA-MARY: You make me ashamed, saying things like that.

VERNER: Listen, sweetheart, Hows about you just stopping bawling me out and ringing for some ice? I want a drink.

ANNA-MARY: Ring for it yourself.
VERNER *(equably, rising):* Okay—Okay.

The phone rings to announce the imminent arrival of an acquaintance named Maud Caragnani who once had them to dinner in her small Rome apartment, and who has been asked to drop in for a drink. Verner remembers that he liked Maud a lot, she paid some attention to him, unlike most of the Europeans they meet.

ANNA-MARY: You've only got yourself to blame for that, Verner. It's just that you happen to be a "taker" and not a "giver." You won't make an *effort* with people. You just sit there looking grouchy and don't say a word.
VERNER: Maybe. But I do say the five most important words of the evening. "Garcon—bring me the check!"
ANNA-MARY: You know something, Verner? It's just that very attitude of mind that makes Europeans despise us Americans. Can't you think of anything but dollars and cents?
VERNER: *(mildly):* They're my dollars and cents, sweetheart, and I've spent the best part of my life pilin' 'em up, and if there didn't happen to be a hell of a lot of 'em you can bet your sweet ass we shouldn't be sitting here worrying about special cigars for royal princes and giving dinner parties to people who despise us.

Verner points out that at least Maud took the trouble to give them dinner. Anna-Mary speaks condescendingly of Maud, who has no money and is only a Sicilian princess but might turn out to be socially useful some time—that's why she's been invited up.

Anna-Mary goes into the bedroom to dress and Verner puts the golf bag behind the sofa, as Maud enters. *"She is an attractive-looking woman of about 47 or 48. Her appearance is a trifle baroque. She has style, but it is a style that is entirely her own. She wears no hat, and a number of heavy gold bracelets. She is English born and bred, and has acquired much of the jargon of what is known as 'The International Set.' Beneath this, however, she is a woman of considerable intelligence."*

Maud greets Verner warmly, obviously glad to see him. She has been invited to the dinner but can't come because she plans to drive all night to Rome, across the Simplon pass, in her Volkswagon. Besides, she doesn't much care for the Prince, "a great one for lavatory jokes and a bit of bottom-pinching on the side. The new wife's quite sweet and lovely to look at; she used to be a model, I believe. He insists on everyone bobbing to her and when they do she's liable to giggle."

Felix enters with the ice and exchanges greetings with Maud in Italian before leaving—they have met before at other hotels, and they are friends.

Anna-Mary makes an entrance with effusive cordiality, captures Maud and seats her on the sofa, while Verner fixes drinks. Maud, it seems, came here to Switzerland to visit her son (a beatnik left-wing painter) and his wife, whose company she enjoys very much. The wife, a ballet dancer, has just had a baby, making Maud a grandmother.

Anna-Mary boasts to Maud of the international celebrities who have accepted her dinner invitation, including the Prince. Maud knows most of these people and fills in some of the gaps for Anna-Mary left by her friend Mariette's vagueness —the Prince, for example is a Serene, not a Royal Highness.

Anna-Mary sends Verner out of the room so that she can talk to Maud (though Maud would prefer to chat with Verner). Verner leaves, carrying his golf clubs, assuring Maud that he'll "give a hundred dollars to each of the waiters and be right back."

Anna-Mary complains to Maud about Verner's indifference to the people and life she likes, flatters Maud about her popularity. In Anna-Mary's eyes, her husband Verner is "sharp enough in business, I'll grant you that, but he just won't open his eyes to *experience*. I mean he deliberately shuts his eyes to the *beauty* of things. You'd never credit it, but in the whole five months we've been in Europe this trip he's only been inside three churches!"

Maud sees Verner differently, as a sort of Buffalo Bill who has lost his horse and deserves a winged one, like Pegasus.

The phone rings. For Anna-Mary it is disaster: one of her fourteen guests has a temperature of 102 and can't come to dinner. Not only will he be unable to entertain them at the piano after dinner, as planned, but his absence will leave 13 at the table.

Anna-Mary is angry rather than sympathetic, as though in some way the guest's illness were a direct insult to her. She insists that Maud come to dinner after all, to become the 14th, but Maud makes it perfectly clear: she not only *can't* come because she's taking her son to dinner and won't be seeing him again for a long time; she also doesn't *want* to come because she dislikes the people Anna-Mary has invited. Maud cannot see why Anna-Mary should make so much fuss over the the Prince, who "would waive the most atavistic superstition for the sake of a free meal." As in the case of Verner, the two ladies are looking at the Prince from different points of view.

Frantically, Anna-Mary calls her friend Mariette, but Mariette has gone out to cocktails. Verner comes back and Anna-Mary pours out her woes to him. He cannot help smiling, although to Anna-Mary, in her state of nerves, winding up with 13 guests at her princely dinner seems like the end of the world. There is only one solution to her problem. Verner must skip the party and have his dinner alone in the suite, so that there will be only 12 at the table.

MAUD *(sitting on the arm of the sofa):* Won't that seem a little odd?

ANNA-MARY: It can't be helped. We'll pretend you're sick or something.

VERNER: You can say I've got a temperature of a hundred and three!

ANNA-MARY: You *could* be waiting for an important business call from New York.

MAUD: No, Anna-Mary, that would be *lèse-majesté*.

VERNER: You could always say I've got a galloping hernia.

ANNA-MARY *(losing her temper):* You think this is very funny, don't you? Both you and Maud? Well, all I can say is I'm very sorry I can't share the joke. Mariette's been just wonderful, making arrangements for this dinner for me tonight. We've been phoning each other back and forth for weeks. She's the only one who has taken the trouble to plan it all for *my* sake, and if only for *her* sake I'm going to see that it's a success if it's the last thing I do. And I'd like to say one thing more, because I just can't keep it in any longer. I'm bitterly disappointed in you, Maud, and it's no use pretending I'm not. I think it's real mean of you not to stand by me tonight and help me out of this jam. You could perfectly easily come to dinner if you wanted to.

MAUD *(calmly):* Certainly I could, but, as I have already explained to you, I don't want to, and, as you may remember, I also said why.

ANNA-MARY: I can remember that you were insulting about my guests and said the Prince was vulgar, and I just don't happen to think that's a nice way to talk.

VERNER: Listen, sweetheart, let's not have a brawl, shall we?

ANNA-MARY *(ignoring him, to Maud):* You've hurt me, Maud, more than I can say. You've let me down. And I thought you were a friend.

MAUD *(coldly):* Why?

VERNER: Holy mackerel!

MAUD *(inexorably, to Anna-Mary):* We have met casually three or four times and you have dined with me once. Is that, according to your curious behavior, sufficient basis for a lifelong affection?

ANNA-MARY *(with grandeur):* I do not give my friendship as easily as you seem to think, Maud, and when I do it is only to those who are truly sincere and willing to stand by me in time of trouble. After all, that is what friendship is for, isn't it? It's a question of give and take. However, I do not wish to discuss the matter any further . . . . .

Anna-Mary exits to the bedroom grandly, coldly, after directing Verner to order his dinner up here when and as he pleases. Verner persuades Maud—who is beginning to have qualms of contrition about her scene with Anna-Mary—to stay for another drink. Verner confides to Maud that he is just as happy to miss the dinner party, and that her dinner in Rome was the high spot of the whole trip for him, even if it's true, as Anna-Mary had implied, that Maud deliberately "laid herself out to be nice" to Verner for ulterior social motives.

Maud is curious about why Verner, if he is so rich, is continuously forced to do things he doesn't enjoy. Verner admits that for him this is the $64,000 question, to which he has found no answer. Maud calles Verner "Buffalo Bill" and suggests that he needs a horse.

VERNER: A horse? Are you out of your mind? What the hell should I do with a horse?

MAUD *(laughing):* Jump on its back and gallop away on it. Failing a horse, a dolphin would be better than nothing. There was a little boy in Greek mythology, I believe, who had an excellent seat on a dolphin. It took him skimming along over the blue waves of the Aegean, and he never had to go to any dinner parties or meet any important people, and whenever they came to rest on a rock or a little white beach, the dolphin would dive deep, deep down and bring him up a golden fish. It's high time somebody gave you a golden fish, Verner. It would mean nothing on the Stock Exchange, but it might light up your whole sad world.

VERNER *(astonished):* Well, I'll be God-damned!

MAUD *(rising purposefully):* I must go now. I promised my son I'd be at the hospital at seven-thirty.

VERNER *(with feeling):* Don't go yet, Princess. Please stay.

MAUD: I can't. I really can't. But we'll meet again.

> *She collects her bag from the desk, then returns to Verner.*

Goodbye for the moment, dear Buffalo Bill. Don't forget me too soon.

> *She kisses him unexpectedly on the cheek. She runs out as Verner sinks into a chair and the lights fade to black-out. Curtain.*

Scene 2: Later that night

In the same room, at about 11 o'clock that evening, Verner has finished his dinner and is reading when Felix enters to put Anna-Mary's bottled water in the bedroom. At Verner's request, Felix mixes him a bourbon on the rocks while Verner questions him about Princess Caragnani. Felix calls Maud "a lady much enchanted" and, serving the drink, tells Verner that everyone likes her. After questioning Felix about his private life (he has a girl back in Italy of whom he is fond, and maybe he'll marry her if he can save the money), Verner lets him go after tipping him a surprising $50.

The phone rings, and it is another surprise: Maud has come back and is in the lobby, Verner asks her up for one last brandy and goodbye before she takes off across the Alps in her car. Maud had a great evening with her son Faber, who shows signs of becoming a responsible, even doting, parent and has had his hair cut and his beard shaved off. Her son was born in Cornwall (Maud tells Verner) after his Italian father was killed in a car crash a year after they were married.

Maud found herself talking to her son about Verner this evening, much as Verner found himself talking to Felix about Maud. Maud stopped in to see Verner on "a sudden impulse. I was on my way to Pully to pick up my suitcase from Faber's flat and I was driving along, just out there by the lake, and I thought of you sitting up here all by yourself, so I turned the car round and came back. I thought you might be lonely."

Verner has a $64,000 question for Maud. Why did she kiss him earlier in the evening? It was an emotional impulse, Maud admits, not merely pity. It isn't long before Verner places her drink and his own on the table and kisses her long and purposefully on the mouth.

Maud is the first to push away from the embrace, but only to check on its effect on Verner. He seems sincerely affectionate, though somewhat afraid of making a fool of himself because he is much older than she is. Maud too is sincerely moved, not playing a role. This time it is she who puts her arms around Verner's neck, taking the initiative for another long kiss.

Impulsively, Verner declares himself in love with Maud, and she admits she could be in love with him too if only there weren't so many obstacles to their romance. Maud has no sympathy for Anna-Mary: "If any woman in the world asked for this situation to happen to her, she did." But she is afraid that Verner might get hurt.

They don't know much about each other, Verner admits, but they know enough for a beginning. Maud warns that she is a European, and "there is no innocence left in Europe"—she has a past. Verner has had a fling or two himself, he confesses. He insists that he is coming with her tonight, to Rome. Maud argues that he ought to take time to think things over.

MAUD: Everything's got out of hand.

VERNER: Now see here, Princess. It was you who went on about the horse and the dolphin and the golden fish. How can I get the golden fish if I'm scared of taking the ride?

MAUD: But you must have loved Anna-Mary once—in the very beginning, I mean?

VERNER: I guess I kidded myself that I did, but not for long. She got me on the rebound, anyway.

MAUD: The rebound?

VERNER: I was married before, to a girl I was crazy about.

He pauses.

Then, just after Pearl Harbor, when I'd been drafted into the Navy, she got stuck on another guy and went off with him to Mexico. The divorce was fixed up while I was in the Pacific. When I got home to Minneapolis in 1946 my old man died and I took over the business.

He sits on the arm of the sofa.

Anna-Mary was there, waiting to greet the conquering hero. I'd known her since she was a kid.

MAUD: Was she pretty?

VERNER: Yeah. That's just about what she was, pretty. Her mother and my mother had been in school together. Everybody put their shoulders to the wheel —it was a natural. We got married and lived happily ever after for all of seven months. There was a good deal of dough around even in those days. Then she got pregnant and had herself an abortion without telling me. I'd wanted a kid more than anything, so it was a kind of disappointment. She pretended at the time that it was a miscarriage, but I found out the truth later.

MAUD: What did she do that for?

VERNER: I don't know. She was scared, I guess. Also she didn't want to spoil her figure . . . . . Anna-Mary's eaten enough lettuce in her life to keep a million rabbits happy for a hundred years.

MAUD: Oh, Verner! What a dismal waste of time.

VERNER: You can say that again.

MAUD: And it never occurred to you to break away?

VERNER: Oh yes. It occurred to me once or twice, but it never seemed worth the trouble. We've led our own lives, Anna-Mary and me. She's had her social junketings and I've had my work, and a couple of little flutters on the side every now and again.

MAUD: Well, I'm glad to hear of that, anyhow.

VERNER: We might have jogged along all right indefinitely if we hadn't started taking these trips to Europe. *(He rises.)* Europe plays all hell with women like Anna-Mary; it gives 'em the wrong kind of ambitions.

MAUD *(moving to Verner):* I belong to Europe, Verner. I'm European from the top of my head to the soles of my feet. That's why I said just now that you ought to give yourself time to think—before you burn your boats.

VERNER: My boats wouldn't burn, honey; they're right down on the waterline anyways. What time do we leave?

Maud has to go get her suitcase at Faber's flat, while Verner packs a few things. Verner mentions divorce, but Maud cautions him not to make any promises or commitments, not to think beyond the present. Maud can imagine the headlines when it is discovered that an American millionaire has run off with a penniless shopkeeper (Maud has a little boutique in Rome). She can imagine the scene that Anna-Mary will make. But Verner doesn't plan to have a scene with Anna-Mary, or to tell her anything much except " 'Good night, sweetheart.' It's what I've been saying to her for nineteen years." Anna-Mary will be very angry when she finds out that Verner has left her, but Verner feels it's about time she had something really important to talk about.

Maud leaves to go get her suitcase. Verner phones the bar. Anna-Mary's dinner party is just breaking up. Verner takes off his jacket and tie and stretches out on the sofa, pretending sleep.

Anna-Mary enters, *"resplendent in a gown of sapphire-blue satin,"* with matching jewelry. She "wakes" Verner rudely, only to complain of his snoring and order him to fix her a drink. Anna-Mary is peeved with her friend Mariette for monopolizing the Prince all evening. She takes her anger out on Verner, criticizing his mussed hair, refusing to smile at a joke, at which point he tells her: "Yes, Anna-Mary, that was supposed to be funny. But—oh boy!—there's better to come!"

Anna-Mary won't permit Verner to get a word in edgewise about what's really on his mind. She criticizes his use of the word "booze."

ANNA-MARY: . . . It's vulgar and it grates on my nerves. You said it to Maud this evening, and I was mortified.

VERNER: She didn't seem to mind. Maybe her nerves ain't as sensitive as yours.

ANNA-MARY: I should think not, considering the sort of life she leads. You should have heard what Clare Pethrington was telling me about her tonight. I just couldn't believe my ears.

VERNER: That's the one with the buck teeth that we had lunch with today, isn't it?

ANNA-MARY: Verner!

VERNER: She looked as if she could eat an apple through a tennis racket.

ANNA-MARY: I'll have you know that Clare Pethrington is a highly cultured woman. She comes from one of the finest families in England. Her grandfather was the Earl of Babbercome and her great-grandfather was a close friend of Queen Victoria's. He used to stay at Balmor*al* every year, regular as clockwork.

VERNER: Bully for him.

ANNA-MARY: Just because she didn't throw herself at your head and butter you up and make you think how wonderful you were, like Maud did, you think it's funny to make snide remarks about her.

VERNER *(with deceptive gentleness):* I wouldn't like to make any snide remarks about any of your friends, Anna-Mary, but I would like to say, kind of off the record, that in my opinion this dame we happen to be talking about is a snooty, loud-mouthed, bad-mannered bitch.

ANNA-MARY: Verner Conklin, I just *don't want* to talk to you any more. And that's the truth. I just don't want to talk to you *any more!* I come back worn out after an exhausting evening and find you lying here drunk. Then you start making silly jokes and saying mean things about people I respect and admire. I'll tell you here and now I've had just about enough of it. You've changed lately, Verner, and it's no use pretending you haven't. You've changed beyond all recognition.

VERNER: You hit it right on the nose, baby. I sure have.

ANNA-MARY: You'd better go to your room, order some black coffee, and take an Alka-Seltzer.

VERNER *(rising, gaily):* Okay, sweetheart.
    He picks up his jacket and tie.
Did His Serene Highness enjoy his goddamned cigars?

ANNA-MARY *(sitting up straight, furiously):* Go away, Verner. Go away and leave me alone.

VERNER: Okay—okay. That's just exactly what I'm going to do.
    He opens the door.
Good night, sweetheart.
    Verner looks at her quizzically for a split second, then goes swiftly out of the room. Anna-Mary sits glaring after him balefully, as the curtain falls.

A SONG AT TWILIGHT

ACT I

SYNOPSIS: The scene is the same suite of the same Swiss luxury hotel as *Come Into the Garden Maud,* the opening play. Now, however, the occupants are Sir Hugo Latymer—an extremely eminent elderly writer—and his wife Hilde. The suite's furnishings have been augmented by some of Sir Hugo's prize possessions: impressionist paintings, a large writing-desk, a special armchair, books, medicines, a small gold clock and a vase full of ball-point pens.

It is evening, and seated at the writing-desk is Hilde Latymer, *"a faded woman in her early 50s. She has been married to Sir Hugo for nearly 20 years and was originally his secretary. Apart from being his official German translator, she is capable, dedicated and orders his life with considerable efficiency."*

Felix, the handsome floor waiter for this suite, is in attendance as he was in the opening play. He is holding notebook and pencil, taking orders from Hilde about this evening's dinner at which they expect a lady guest.

Felix exits, as Hilde turns to the telephone to arrange some matters of business. Sir Hugo will accept an honorary degree from an American university, but not a lecture tour; he is not up to it physically. Hilde is laying out some terms for a movie version of one of Sir Hugo's works, when the great man himself enters from the bedroom. *"He is a distinguished-looking man of 70. His figure is slim and erect. Sometimes, when he is in a good mood, he looks younger than he actually is by several years. At other times, when upset over some triviality or worried about his health, he becomes suddenly enfeebled and deliberately ancient. This, of course, is a pose, but it works like a charm on doctors and nurses or whoever happens to be looking after him at the moment. It even works on Hilde occasionally, notwithstanding the fact that she has had 20 years to grow accustomed to it. Sir Hugo is wearing a brocaded dressing gown, his white hair is slightly tousled and he looks irascible."*

The great man is in a mood to refuse permission to make the movie, even if they give him complete veto of script and adapter. He wonders what time it is and complains that he can't see the clock without his glasses.

HILDE: You said you were delighted with it when I gave it to you.

HUGO: Well, I'm not now.

HILDE: I'm sorry. I'll try and change it.

HUGO: And please don't look martyred. It draws your mouth down at the corners. Like a weary old camel.

HILDE: Thank you.

HUGO: With two unsymmetrical humps.

HILDE: That's a dromedary.

> *She rises, moves to the bureau and puts three books from it into the cupboard.*

Have you had your bath?

HUGO: No, I have not had my bath.

HILDE: Well, don't you think you should? She's due at eight.

HUGO: If I'm not ready, she can wait for me, can't she? An extra ten minutes tacked onto all those years can't matter all that much.

HILDE: You're in a very disagreeable mood.

HUGO: I'm nervous.

HILDE: It's your own fault if you are. You needn't have agreed to see her, and in fact, I still think it is a great mistake.

HUGO: Yes, I know you do. You've made that abundantly clear during the last three days. You've never been exactly adept at hiding your feelings.

HILDE: On the contrary, Hugo, that is one of the things I do best. Living with you for twenty years has been excellent training.

HUGO: Why are you so frightened of Carlotta?

HILDE *(calmly):* I am not in the least frightened of Carlotta.

HUGO: Oh, yes, you are. The very idea of her fills your soul with dread. Come on now, admit it.

HILDE: It is time for your blue pill.

Hilde gets the pill and gives it to Hugo, remarking that Carlotta wouldn't turn up like this unless she wanted something, and she will probably upset Hugo, causing a relapse of his high blood pressure and other ailments. Hilde sees clearly that Hugo has worked himself into a state about Carlotta's visit and is taking out his agitation on her. Hugo pretends to be keeping his cool: "My affair with Carlotta lasted exactly two years, and we parted in a blaze of mutual acrimony. That was centuries ago, and I haven't clapped eyes on her since, except once on the cinema screen when she appeared briefly as a Mother Superior in an excruciatingly bad film about a nun with a vast bust."

They haven't even corresponded over the years. If it is money Carlotta wants, Hugo will lend her some, but he fears she may be merely coming to gloat over him in his decrepitude. They were once very much in love (Hugo insists), but that isn't likely to be rekindled, although he suggests that Hilde is feeling jealous, perhaps, as she seems to be jealous of any of Hugo's friends.

HILDE *(with a show of spirit):* You have not so many friends for me to be jealous of.

HUGO: You hate Mariette. You are barely civil to Cedric Marcombe and David when they come here.

HILDE: They are barely civil to me.

HUGO: Cedric Marcombe is a man of brilliant intelligence and exquisite taste. He is also the greatest connoisseur of modern art alive today.

HILDE: And what is David?

HUGO *(defensively):* David is one of the most promising young painters that England has produced in the last twenty years. He also happens to be the son of Lord Tenterden.

HILDE: In that case he should have better manners. And his paintings I do not care for at all. They are ugly and cruel.

HUGO: *(viciously):* As a full-blooded German you are scarcely in a position to object to cruelty in art or anything else.

HILDE: It is wrong of you to speak to me like that, Hugo, and most unkind. When you are in a better mood you will see that this is so, and be sorry.

Hilde rises above this insult as she has so many others, and Hugo sees that he has gone too far. He tells Hilde he is sorry and begs her to stay and help him with Carlotta instead of going out to dinner with her friend Liesel and then to a movie, as planned. Hilde insists on going out, however, and does not even flinch when Hugo calls Liesel "a weatherbeaten old Lesbian." Hugo has gotten himself into this situation and is going to have to face Carlotta all by himself, though Hilde has arranged for the dinner and everything, including caviar and pink champagne.

Hilde rings for Felix and instructs him to make a vodka on the rocks for Hugo, then she goes to get ready to go out. Hugo chats with Felix, who had the day off yesterday and went swimming and to a movie with a friend. Hilde comes back, now wearing a hat, as Felix exits.

The phone rings—it is Carlotta, on her way up. Hilde sends Hugo to the bedroom to get dressed to receive his guest, then opens the door to admit Carlotta Gray, *"an attractive woman who at first glance would appear to be in her late 40s or early 50s. She is heavily made up and her hair is expertly tinted. She is wearing expensive costume jewelry, perhaps a little too much of it. Her dinner dress is simple and well cut. She carries a light coat over her arm."*

Hilde introduces herself and takes Carlotta's coat. Carlotta lights a cigarette, refuses a drink. Carlotta views Hilde as the great man's protector, which doesn't exactly please Hilde. She remains exceedingly cool to Carlotta.

Hugo comes in *"wearing an emerald green velvet smoking jacket over dark trousers. He has a cream shirt, a black tie, and his slippers are monogrammed in gold."* Hugo and Carlotta exchange compliments about each other's looks, as Hugo kisses her on both cheeks. Hilde pours a vodka for Carlotta, who tells them she too is staying at this hotel, taking a series of injections at a nearby clinic. Hilde manages to take this news in stride and goes off to have dinner with her friend.

Carlotta has plenty of money, it seems, in alimony from her last husband, her third. She likes Hilde, she confesses, better than she had though she would from reading Hugo's memoirs—but then Hugo poured out acid on everyone in his memoirs. Carlotta is no match for Hugo in the verbal sparring that takes place around this subject. Hugo once opened her eyes to many things: "You worked assiduously on my virgin mind and now I come to think of it, you didn't do so badly with my virgin body." But she acknowledges him her superior and she offers to leave at once if that is his wish. Hugo doesn't want her to leave, if only to avoid appearing discourteous, but he admits to being somewhat set in his ways; resigned to his life; valuing his dignity.

CARLOTTA: I think I know what you're up to.

HUGO *(still secure on Olympus):* I am open to any suggestions.

CARLOTTA: You are remodelling your public image. The witty, cynical author of so many best sellers is making way for the Grand Old Man of Letters.

HUGO: Supposing your surmise to be accurate, do you consider such a transition reprehensible?

CARLOTTA: Of course not, if the process is inevitable and necessary. But aren't you jumping the gun a little?

HUGO *(patiently):* No, Carlotta. I am not jumping the gun, or grasping Time by the forelock, or rushing my fences.

CARLOTTA: You must be prepared for a few cliches if you invite retired actresses to dinner.

HUGO *(ignoring her interruption):* I am merely accepting, without due dismay, the fact of my own mortality. I am an old man and I at least have the sense to realize it.

CARLOTTA: Don't be waspish, my dear. Just as we are getting along so nicely.

She crosses and stubs out her cigarette in the ashtray on the desk.

At least you can congratulate yourself on having had a fabulously successful career. How wonderful to have been able to entertain and amuse so many millions of people for such a long time. No wonder you got a knighthood.

HUGO: I begin to suspect that you are here as an enemy. I hoped for a friend.

CARLOTTA: Did you, Hugo? Did you really?

HUGO: Perhaps I was wrong.

CARLOTTA: Why did you write so unkindly about me in your memoirs?

HUGO: Aha! Now I'm beginning to understand.

CARLOTTA (cheerfully): Oh, no, you're not. You're merely jumping to conclusions. That was always one of your most glaring defects.

HUGO: Why can't we concentrate for a moment on some of my glaring assets? It might lighten the atmosphere.

CARLOTTA: We will, when you've answered my question.

HUGO: My autobiography was the assessment of the events and experiences of my life up to the date of writing it. I endeavored to be as objective and truthful as possible. If in the process I happened to hurt your feelings, I apologize. There was no unkindness intended. I merely wrote what I thought to be true.

CARLOTTA: Your book may have been an assessment of the *outward* experiences of your life, but I cannot feel that you were entirely honest about your inner ones.

HUGO: Why should I be? My inner feelings are my own affair.

CARLOTTA: In that case the book was sailing under false colors.

HUGO (nastily): And all this because I described you as a mediocre actress.

CARLOTTA (serenely): You don't happen to have any parchment lying about, do you?

HUGO: Parchment?

CARLOTTA: Yes. When zoological experts extract the venom from snakes they force them to bite on parchment.

Hugo suggests that they stop bickering, which ill becomes the old. Carlotta has decided not to *be* old, and she actually enjoys taking great pains with her physical appearance. She is curious as to how Hugo has spent the long years since their liaison, and Hugo is suspicious of her curiosity. He senses some hidden motive behind Carlotta's interest.

Felix enters with the dinner trolley. The meal, as it happens, is an exact duplicate of a dinner they once enjoyed at Ciro's when Carlotta tasted caviar for the first time. They sit down to it, and Hugo pours them vodka as Felix exits. Carlotta reminisces sadly about the demise of her first husband in a plane crash, and about the loss of her last remaining tooth (a subject which pains Hugo). Carlotta's second husband, a poor actor but a good lover, fathered her son and was killed in the war in the Pacific. Carlotta has lived most of her life in America, though she has made two London stage appearances since she saw Hugo last. Carlotta persuades Hugo to tell her a little about Hilde, whom she liked at first sight. Grudgingly, Hugo informs her that Hilde was a refugee from Nazi Germany. The love of her life was a young German poet who died in a concentration camp.

Felix comes in to remove dishes and pour more champagne. He serves the steak course and exits, as the diners reminisce about their past together. Hugo compliments Carlotta on her looks which, it turns out to his dismay, are the result of a face-lifting operation.

Hugo prods Carlotta as to her real reason for this visit, and she admits that she has come for an "irrelevant little favor." She advises Hugo: "Prepare yourself for a tiny shock," and informs him that she too has written an autobiography, written every word herself.

HUGO (*after a slight pause*): I suppose you want me to write an introductory preface.

CARLOTTA: No. I've already done that myself.

HUGO (*with a tinge of irritation*): What is it, then? What is it you want of me?

CARLOTTA: Permission to publish your letters.

HUGO (*startled*): Letters! What letters?

CARLOTTA: The letters you wrote to me when we were lovers. I've kept them all.

HUGO: Whatever letters I wrote to you at that time were private. They concerned no one but you and me.

CARLOTTA: I agree. But that was a long time ago. Before we'd either of us become celebrated enough to write our memoirs.

HUGO: I cannot feel that you, Carlotta, have even yet achieved that particular distinction.

CARLOTTA (*unruffled*): Doubleday and Heinemann do.

HUGO (*sitting back*): I believe that some years ago Mrs. Patrick Campbell made a similar request to Mr. George Bernard Shaw, and his reply was: "Certainly not. I have no intention of playing the horse to your Lady Godiva."

CARLOTTA (*stopping eating*): How unkind.

HUGO: It would ill become me to attempt to improve on Mr. George Bernard Shaw.

CARLOTTA (*helping herself to some more salad*): You mean you refuse?

HUGO: Certainly I most emphatically refuse.

CARLOTTA: I thought you would.

HUGO: In that case surely it was a waste of time to take the trouble to ask me?

CARLOTTA: I just took a chance. After all, life can be full of surprises sometimes, can't it?

HUGO: If your forthcoming autobiography is to be peppered with that sort of bromide, it cannot fail to achieve the best-seller list.

CARLOTTA: You can turn nasty quickly, can't you? You were quite cozy and relaxed a moment ago.

HUGO: I am completely horrified by your suggestion. It's in the worst possible taste.

Felix's entrance eases the situation for a moment, but Hugo resents the easy friendliness with which Carlotta chats with Felix about his background. Felix clears the table and leaves under orders to bring on the coffee at once. Hugo is becoming infuriated at what he considers Carlotta's rudeness, which is really only indifference to his pettish humors. Enraged at last when Carlotta points out a cliche in his own speech, Hugo suggests that perhaps she *had* better leave. He labels her request to publish his letters an impertinence and explains icily and condescendingly: "Not having read your book, I have naturally no way of judging whether it is good, bad or indifferent. I am perfectly aware, however, that, whatever its merits, the inclusion of private letters from a man in my position would enhance its value considerably. The impertinence, I think, lies in your assuming for a moment that I should grant you permission to publish them. We met and parted many years ago. Since then we have neither of us communicated with each other. You have pursued your career, I have pursued mine. Mine, if I may say so without undue arrogance, has been eminently successful. Yours, perhaps less so. Doesn't it strike *you* as impertinent that, after so long a silence, you should suddenly ask me to provide you with my name as a stepping-stone?"

Carlotta reacts to Hugo's overweening arrogance more in sorrow than in anger. The letters are so brilliantly written, she says, it will be a pity not to publish them. She goes to fetch her wrap, and Hugo manages to down two pills to calm his outrage before she returns to the sitting room.

CARLOTTA: Good night, Hugo. I am sorry the evening has ended so—so uncosily.

HUGO: So am I, Carlotta. So am I.

CARLOTTA *(turning on her way to the door):* To revert for a moment to the unfortunate subject of the letters. You may have them if you like. They are of no further use to me.

HUGO: That is most generous of you.

CARLOTTA: I'm afraid I can't let you have the others, though. That would be betraying a sacred promise.

HUGO: Others? What others?

CARLOTTA: Your letters to Perry.

HUGO *(visibly shaken):* My letters to Perry! What do you mean?

CARLOTTA: Perry Sheldon. I happened to be with him when he died.

HUGO: What do you know about Perry Sheldon?

CARLOTTA: Among other things, that he was the only true love of your life. Good night, Hugo. Sleep well.

Carlotta turns to exit as the curtain falls.

ACT II

A few minutes later, Hugo is sitting with his head in his hands, paralyzed by Carlotta's parting shot. After a moment he rises, pours himself a stiff brandy and calls Carlotta on the house telephone: "Quite a lot is the matter . . . Will you please come back? I must talk to you . . . Please, Carlotta . . . No, you know perfectly well that it can't wait until tomorrow. You've won your point—for God's sake have the grace not to exult too much. Please come . . . Yes, now—immediately."

Soon there is a knock on the door and Carlotta comes in and greets a now greatly chastened Hugo. Carlotta has ordered another bottle of champagne to suit her mood on this occasion, and Felix enters and serves it. After Felix goes out, Carlotta tells Hugo: "This is not a tragic situation, Hugo. All the tragedy was drained out of it when Perry died. There's only comedy left now. Rather bitter comedy, I admit, but not entirely unenjoyable."

Carlotta accuses Hugo of always taking himself too seriously; Hugo in his turn insinuates that Carlotta's purpose is blackmail, which she promptly denies.

HUGO: You said you were with Perry Sheldon when he died. Is that true?

CARLOTTA: Yes. *(She takes a sip of champagne.)*

HUGO: And you have in your possession letters written by me to him?

CARLOTTA: Yes. Love letters, most of them. They are less meticulously lyrical than the ones you wrote to me, but there is more genuine feeling in them. They were written in your earlier years, remember, before your mind had become corrupted by fame and your heart by caution. The last ones were written in the last years of his life. There are three of them. All refusals to help him when he was in desperate straits. They also are fascinating in their way, masterpieces of veiled invective. Pure gold for your future biographer.

HUGO *(controlling a quiver in his voice)*: Did you steal these letters?

CARLOTTA: No, Hugo, I didn't steal them. He gave them to me three days before he died.

HUGO: What do you propose to do with them?

CARLOTTA: I haven't quite decided yet. I made him a promise.

HUGO: What sort of promise?

CARLOTTA: I promised him that if he gave them to me I would keep them safe until the time came when they could be used to the best advantage.

HUGO: Used? To the best advantage! Used in what way?

CARLOTTA: By a suitable biographer.

HUGO: Are you intending to be that biographer?

CARLOTTA: Oh, no. I am not experienced enough. It would require someone more detached and objective than I am to write an accurate and unbiased account of you. My personal feelings would be involved.

HUGO: Your personal feelings would still be involved after more than half a lifetime?

CARLOTTA: Memory is curiously implacable. It can forget joy, but it seldom forgets humiliation.

HUGO *(putting out his cigarette in the ashtray on the cupboard)*: Your emotional tenacity is remarkable.

CARLOTTA: There is no longer any emotion in my feelings for you, Hugo.

Carlotta is not moved even by any desire for revenge. Her motive is rather that she wants to see justice done, a wrong righted. She has actually found a biographer, a former professor at Harvard, who can use these exceedingly valuable documents to the best literary and historical advantage. Hugo offers to buy the letters, and Carlotta merely laughs at him. He resigns himself to the fact that Carlotta is now in entire control of the situation, and the next move is to be dictated by her.

Carlotta reviews the legal situation: letters are the physical property of the recipient, though permission to publish them rests in the hands of the letter-writer. There is no plan to publish them as yet, but their very existence poses a continuing threat to Hugo's cherished reputation. Carlotta hasn't made a firm decision about what to do with the letters.

HUGO *(losing his temper):* This is intolerable.

CARLOTTA: Keep calm.

HUGO: I have been calm long enough. I am sick to death of this interminable witless skirmishing. Come to the point, if there is a point beyond your feline compulsion to torment me and insult me. The implications behind all the highfalutin rubbish you have been talking have not been lost on me. The veiled threat is perfectly clear.

CARLOTTA: What veiled threat?

HUGO: The threat to expose to the world the fact that I have had, in the past, homosexual tendencies.

CARLOTTA *(calmly):* Tendencies in the past! What nonsense! You've been a homosexual all your life and you know it.

HUGO *(shouting):* That is not true! *(He sits on the sofa.)*

CARLOTTA: Don't shout. It's waste of adrenalin. You've no idea what it does to the inside of your stomach when you work yourself into a state like that.

Carlotta offers him a brandy to help settle his nerves, but Hugo knocks the glass to the floor; in his anger he orders her to desist and depart, to publish and be damned. Calmly, Carlotta pours him another glass of brandy and assures him that she does not hate him, nor did she mean to insult him by calling him a homosexual. She does not consider it a crime or an insult. Hugo's crime, she tells him, "is something far worse than that. Complacent cruelty and moral cowardice . . . . . On the evidence of every book you've ever written and the dismal record of your personal relationships."

It is not hatred or revenge but irritation that has driven Carlotta to confront Hugo, and she means to get this irritation out of her system before it poisons her. They talk of Perry: he died about two years before in his late 50s or early 60s, of leukemia, without pain, with his only remaining vitality a look of hope in his eyes. Hugo has been living abroad and didn't know that Perry had died. He wants all the letters back, the three cruel ones as well as the love letters. He throws himself on Carlotta's mercy.

CARLOTTA: If you had the choice of having the earlier letters back or the later ones, which would you choose?

HUGO *(a little too quickly):* The earlier ones.

CARLOTTA: Yes. I was afraid you'd say that.

HUGO: You can also, I should imagine, understand my reasons.

CARLOTTA: Yes. I understand your reasons perfectly. You would prefer to be regarded as cynical, mean and unforgiving, rather than as a vulnerable human being, capable of tenderness.

HUGO: In these particular circumstances, yes.

CARLOTTA: Why?

HUGO: My private inclinations are not the concern of the reading public. I have no urge to martyr my reputation for the sake of self-indulgent exhibitionism.

CARLOTTA: Even that might be better than vitiating your considerable talent by dishonesty.

HUGO: Dishonesty? In what way have I been dishonest?

CARLOTTA: Subtly in all your novels and stories, but quite obviously in your autobiography.

HUGO: I have already explained to you that my autobiography was an objective survey of the events and experiences of my life in so far as they affected my career. It was never intended to be an uninhibited expose of my sexual adventures.

CARLOTTA: In that case why the constant implications of heterosexual ardor? Why those self-conscious, almost lascivious references to laughing-eyed damsels with scarlet lips and pointed breasts? And above all, why that contemptuous betrayal of Perry Sheldon?

HUGO *(with anger):* I forbid you to say any more. There was no betrayal.

CARLOTTA *(relentlessly):* He loved you, looked after you and waited on you hand and foot. For years he travelled the wide world with you. And yet in your book you dismiss him in a few lines as an "adequate secretary."

HUGO *(losing his temper again):* My relationship with Perry Sheldon is none of your God-damned business.

CARLOTTA: Considering that I have in my possession a bundle of your highly compromising letters to him, that remark was plain silly.

Carlotta demands unconditional surrender from Hugo, a moment of total, self-revealing truth, a sort of act of contrition. Carlotta decides to "roll up some heavier ammunition" and tells Hugo that in a way he is directly to blame for Sheldon's death, having first corrupted and then abandoned him. Hugo refuses to acknowledge any such guilt and declares that this meeting might as well adjourn because they are at an impasse. If Carlotta doesn't intend to sell or give him the Sheldon letters, he cannot see what can be gained by continuing the conversation, other than "a long-cherished, stale revenge for some imagined wrong I did you in the past."

Far from wronging Carlotta—Hugo insists—he launched her into an acting career which she has pursued ever since. Carlotta hints that Hugo got much more out of the affair than she did; for one thing, enhancement of his heterosexual reputation. Carlotta was truly in love with Hugo, and it was a year before she finally understood Hugo's "dishonesty and lack of moral courage." Hugo was using Carlotta to show the world that he was "a regular guy," using and finally betraying her as he has done to all who loved him. She tells him: "It wasn't your deception of the world that I found so unpardonable: it was your betrayal of me, and all the love and respect and admiration I felt for you. If you had had the courage to trust me, to let me share your uneasy secret, not in the first year perhaps, but later on, when things were becoming strained and difficult between us, if then you had told me the truth, I would very possibly have been your loyal and devoted friend until this very minute. As it was you let me gradually, bit by bit, discover what my instincts had already half guessed . . . . ."

Hugo remains unmoved by Carlotta's reminiscences, and she sees that he is

unregenerate. Hilde enters, her manner strangely altered as though she is probably *"what is described colloquially as a little 'high' "*. Hilde senses the tension in
the room but cannot quite put her finger on what the trouble is. She is on the edge
of the giggles anyway, taking off her hat (which Hugo doesn't like), talking about
her meeting with her friend Liesel (they decided to have a couple of stingers after
dinner instead of going to the movies).

Hilde decides that what she needs is another shot of brandy instead of black
coffee, and against Hugo's orders she downs a swig. She is emboldened to defend
Goethe and the whole German language against Hugo's deprecations. She even
recalls a mild little joke in German she and Liesel enjoyed that evening bearing
obliquely on Hugo's sexuality, as though perhaps both Hilde and Liesel were able
to guess Hugo's emotional secrets.

Hugo, now angry at Hilde too, reveals to her that Carlotta has come here to
blackmail him—but he does not name the grounds. Hilde cannot quite grasp what
Hugo is trying to tell her.

HILDE: I do not understand. I do not understand at all what is happening.

HUGO *(savagely):* If you had spent less time guzzling down stingers with that
leather-skinned old Sapphist your perceptions might be clearer.

HILDE *(with spirit):* You will *not* speak of Liesel like that. She is my close friend
and I am devoted to her.

HUGO: Then you should have more discrimination.

HILDE: Nor will I permit you to speak to me in that tone in front of a stranger.
It is in very bad taste and makes me ashamed of you.

CARLOTTA *(enjoying herself):* Hurray! A "sudden flood of mutiny!"

HILDE *(in full spate):* When you are ill and in discomfort I am willing to endure
your rudeness to me, but now you are no longer ill, you are perfectly well, and
I will stand no more of it. This very evening you accused me of being jealous of
your friends and of anyone who is close to you; you even said I was jealous of
Carlotta. But the truth of the matter is you have no friends; you have driven them
all away with your bitter tongue, and the only one who is close to you in the world
is me. And I will say one thing more. I will choose whatever friends I like and
I will drink as many stingers as I like, and so that there shall be no further
misunderstanding between us I am at this moment going to have some more
brandy.

Hilde suits her action to the words, then directs her attention to the "blackmail," taking charge, declaring that her mind is perfectly clear. Hugo recaps the
situation for her: how he refused Carlotta permission to print his love letters in
her memoirs, and how she plans to turn over other letters to a biographer. To
Hugo's astonishment, Hilde recognizes the name of the biographer and approves
of him, calling him "a very clever man and a brilliant writer." As Hugo's secretary, Hilde has had some correspondence with him and recognizes in him a true
admirer of Hugo. Hugo is furious at Hilde for communicating with a biographer
behind his back.

Hilde wants to know about the content of the letters, but neither Carlotta nor

Hugo will tell her. Hilde echoes Carlotta's previous complaint: "I think I can guess anyhow. But I would have liked you to tell me yourself. As a matter of fact, I would have liked you to have told me long ago; it would have shown me that even if you didn't love me, you were at least fond enough of me to trust me."

After 20 years of looking after Hugo, there isn't much that Hilde doesn't know about him, and she easily guesses that the letters in question were written to Perry Sheldon. The letters are not for sale—Carlotta informs Hilde—but she hasn't decided yet whether to turn them over to the biographer.

HILDE: As you know Hugo's feelings in the matter, Miss Gray, that would be a malicious and unforgivable thing to do.

CARLOTTA: I notice that you no longer call me Carlotta.

HILDE: I called you Carlotta when I thought we were to be friends. But I cannot possibly be friends with anyone who sets out deliberately to hurt my husband.

CARLOTTA: You are certainly magnanimous.

HILDE: It has nothing to do with magnanimity. It is a statement of fact.

CARLOTTA: I was thinking of Hugo's treatment of you.

HILDE: As you have only seen Hugo and me together this evening for the first time in your life, you cannot know anything about his treatment of me one way or the other.

CARLOTTA: You don't find it humiliating to have been used by him for twenty years not only as an unpaid secretary, manager and housekeeper, but as a social camouflage as well?

HUGO (violently): Once and for all, Carlotta, I forbid you to talk like that.

HILDE: You are a very forceful woman, Miss Gray, and Hugo is a complex and brilliant man, but it is beginning to dawn on me that I have a great deal more common sense than either of you. Your visit actually has little or nothing to do with permission to publish letters or threats or blackmail, has it?

CARLOTTA: No. No, it hasn't. I genuinely wanted to prove something to him. Something that, with all his brilliance and talent and eminence, he has never yet taken into account.

HILDE: What is it that he has failed to take into account?

CARLOTTA: You, being the closest to him, should know better than anybody. He has never taken into account the value of kindness and the importance of compassion. He has never had the courage or the humility to face the fact that it was not whom he loved in his life that really mattered but his own capacity for loving.

Hugo tries to laugh off Carlotta's statement, but Hilde silences him. Carlotta's mission has pretty much failed (both women admit) because Hugo is not a sentimentalist; he is a profound cynic whose inner defenses are impenetrable, who "is quite incapable of recognizing people as individuals. His mind classifies all human beings in groups and races and types." Hilde knew perfectly well Hugo's reasons for wanting to marry her and she in her turn, not loving Hugo but seeing in him a refuge from despair, viewed the marriage as "a sensible arrangement." If she has suffered from time to time over the years, so has he. Their lives might have been warmer had Hugo confided in her, but it would have been out of character for him to do so. Now Hugo is growing to rely on Hilde more and more, and this is all she asks, all she has been waiting for.

As to the letters—Hilde continues—Carlotta may do what she wishes. No biographer can publish them without Hugo's permission, and she doubts that any reputable one would even refer to them, because Perry Sheldon was unworthy of concern, "a creature of little merit; foolish, conceited, dishonest and self-indulgent." How does Hilde know? Because Liesel knew Sheldon years before in Hollywood and has told Hilde all about him.

Carlotta deliberates for a few moments, then goes to her handbag, takes out the bundle of Sheldon letters and holds them out to Hugo.

Hugo takes the letters. His face is expressionless.

HUGO: Thank you.

CARLOTTA: I cannot say that I entirely regret this evening. It has been most interesting, and almost embarrassingly revealing. If many of the things I have said have hurt you, I'm sorry. *(She gives a slight smile.)* I don't apologize, I'm just sorry. I'm also sorry for having kept you up so late.

HUGO: I will see that the permission you asked for earlier in the evening is delivered to you in the morning. Good night, Carlotta.

CARLOTTA *(looking at him, still with a quizzical smile):* Good night Hugo. *(She turns to Hilde.)* Good night, Lady Latymer. *(She moves toward the door.)*

HILDE *(rising):* Good night, Carlotta. I will see you out.

CARLOTTA *(stopping):* There is no necessity for that. My room is only just along the corridor.

HILDE: Nevertheless I should like to.

Hilde takes Carlotta by the arm and they exit, closing the doors. Hugo looks at the bundle of letters, then puts on his glasses, selects one at random and reads it. He puts the pile on the little table, takes another and starts to read it. After a moment he frowns slightly and looks up. It is apparent from his expression that he is deeply moved. He takes off his glasses, wipes away a tear, replaces the glasses and goes on reading. As he replaces his glasses, Hilde enters quietly. She stands looking at him for a moment, then moves down and sits silently on the edge of the sofa.

HUGO *(after a long pause):* I heard you come in.

HILDE *(almost in a whisper):* Yes. I thought you did.

Hugo continues reading the letter, as the curtain slowly falls.

JUMPERS

A Play in Two Acts and a Coda

BY TOM STOPPARD

Cast and credits appear on page 366

TOM STOPPARD was born in 1937 in Zlin, Czechoslovakia, where his family name was Straussler. When he was 18 months old his father, a physician, moved the family to Singapore, and from that time on Stoppard was brought up within the English-speaking culture. During World War II the doctor sent his wife and son to India for safety, and the boy attended an American school in Darjeeling. His father was killed in Singapore by the invading Japanese.

After the war Stoppard, age 9, and his mother (remarried to an English major) moved to England, where Stoppard attended school until age 17 and then entered upon a writing career, first as a journalist (at Bristol) and then as a free-lance whose credits include several TV and radio plays. His first stage play, A Walk on Water, *was produced on British TV in 1963 and on the stage in Hamburg and Vienna in 1964. Another early Stoppard work,* Enter a Free Man, *also a reworking of a TV play, was done in London in 1968. Stoppard is also the author of the television play* The Engagement *and the novel* Lord Malquist and Mr. Moon.

The first Stoppard play to appear on the New York stage was Rosencrantz and Guildenstern Are Dead. *It began as a one-act verse burlesque written in Berlin on a Ford Foundation grant in 1964, titled simply* Rosencrantz and Guildenstern. *The full-length version was produced by the Oxford Theater Group at the 1966 Edinburgh Festival before moving on to London and then to Broadway October 16, 1947 for a year's run, a Best Play citation and the Drama Critics Award for the best play of the season.*

Stoppard's The Real Inspector Hound *was produced in London in 1969, and his* After Magritte *appeared there the following year; combined on a single program, these two plays were produced off Broadway April 23, 1972 for 465 performances, followed by a national U.S. tour under the auspices of Kennedy Center. His* Albert's Bridge, *a version of a Prix Italia-winning drama, was produced in London in 1971. A year later* Jumpers *appeared at the National Theater and, in the words of Ossia Trilling's report in Best Plays, "introduced, unless I'm much mistaken, full frontal nudity for the first time on this august stage in the shape of the shapely Diana Rigg." It was produced in Washington in February, 1974 by Kennedy Center and brought to Broadway April 22, its author's second Best Play. It is such a volatile work that, in its author's own words in an introduction to its published script, "Each production will throw up its own problems and very often the solution will lie in some minor change to the text" according to the way in which it is directed and the kind of stage upon which it is played, so that we have used what the author calls his "basic version" of* Jumpers *for the synopsis which follows.*

Stoppard's playwriting career continued in 1973 with a new English version of Lorca's The House of Bernarda Alba, *staged in Greenwich, England. He lives near London with his wife and one child, a son.*

Time: *The present*

Place: *George and Dotty's flat in Mayfair, London*

ACT I

SYNOPSIS: The three major areas of the "flat" are the bedroom (right), the hall (center) and study (left), the hall capable of expansion to cover the whole setting as the other two rooms disappear on revolves. Above and behind this set is a large screen for the projection of photo images, and below and behind it is a wall-to-wall panoramic structure of mirrors. *"The apartment belongs to George, a professor of moral philosophy, married to a prematurely-retired musical comedy actress of some renown, Dorothy. The general standard of living suggested by the flat owes more, one would guess, to musical comedy than moral philosophy, and this is especially true of the bedroom . . . . ."* The study, however, is reasonably austere, though cluttered. It holds secretarial and professorial desks, books, papers, a tape recorder, etc.

In the opening scene, the large single open space of the hall occupies the whole area, with the audience reflected in the mirror panorama across the empty stage. Then there is the sound of a large gathering of people celebrating a political victory of the Radical Liberals. Their hostess, Dorothy Moore (a singer, *"very beautiful indeed"*) tries to sing for their entertainment—but suddenly she dries up on the lyrics of her song, "Shine on, Harvest Moon."

The young woman who will appear in later scenes as George's secretary (*"attractive but poker-faced, almost grim, even in her first appearance"*) comes into view on a swing attached to a chandelier, which moves back and forth through the spotlight as she strips off her articles of clothing one by one. Just as she is finally naked, the janitor of this flat serving as one of the waiters at the party, Crouch *("old and small and a bit stooped")*, blunders into the path of the trapeze. The scene blacks out.

An announcer's voice proclaims: "And now—ladies and gentlemen—the IN-CREDIBLE—RADICAL!—LIBERAL!!—JUMPERS!!" Eight gymnasts enter dressed in yellow tracksuit uniforms—*"and although they pass muster at first glance, they are not as universally youthful or athletic-looking as one might expect."* They tumble, somersault and finally form *"a tableau of modest pretension."*

Dorothy Moore wanders in front of the tableau. Her husband Professor George Moore—*"between 40 and 50 and still attractive enough to make it perfectly plausible that he should be married to Dotty, who is ten to 15 years younger"*—appears behind her carrying sheets of paper but obviously not part of the party and not dressed for it in shabby flannels, loose-hanging shawl and hair awry.

Dotty ignores her husband George, while calling for the Jumpers to do something not merely difficult, but unbelievable. Again, Dotty tries to sing but has great difficulty remembering the lyrics to songs about the moon. She keeps trying, as the Jumpers form a human pyramid.

> . . . . . *When the pyramid is completed it hides Dotty from view*
DOTTY *(sings):*

> You saw me standing in June
> January, Allegheny, Moon or July—

(Jeers.) Jumpers I've *had*—yellow, I've had them all! *Incredible, barely* credible, credible and all too bloody likely—When I say jump, *jump!*

> *From her tone now it should be apparent that Dotty, who may have appeared pleasantly drunk, is actually breaking up mentally. And from her position in the near-dark outside the Jumpers' light, it should be possible to believe that Dotty is responsible for what happens next— which is: a gun shot.*

> *One Jumper, bottom row, second from left, is blown out of the pyramid. He falls downstage, leaving the rest of the pyramid intact. The music has stopped. Dotty walks through the gap in the pyramid. The shot Jumper is at her feet. He starts to move, dying, pulling himself up against Dotty's legs. She looks at him in surprise as he crawls up her body. His blood is on her dress. She holds him under his arms and looks around in a bewildered way.*

(Whimpers.) Archie . . .

> *The pyramid has been defying gravity for these few seconds. Now it slowly collapses into the dark, imploding on the missing part, and rolling and separating, out of sight, leaving only the white spot.*

Dotty is still holding the murdered Jumper, but Archie *("a dandy, old as George or older")* fails to appear. Only his voice is heard announcing that the party's over. Archie's voice instructs Dotty to hide the corpse until morning and promises to return at 8 o'clock.

The flat's other two rooms appear on either side of the now-narrowed hall. Up on the large screen a TV newscast is telling the story of a disaster on the moon. The first two British astronauts have landed on the lunar surface, but their rocket was damaged on impact and now can carry only one of the two men back to earth. The two astronauts fought at the foot of the ladder for the single place. The mission commander, Scott, won the fight and took off in the rocket, leaving his comrade, Oates, "a tiny receding figure waving forlornly from the featureless wastes of the lunar landscape."

In the bedroom which has assembled around her, Dotty, still wearing her bloodstained dress, is wondering what to do with the corpse. George is in the study, working on a manuscript. Dotty hears someone come into the house and hopes it is Archie, but it is only the janitor Crouch.

Dotty changes channels on her bedroom TV set from the moon story to a report of the political victory procession, then a commercial. She takes off her dress while Crouch, in the hall, is cleaning away the debris of last night's party.

George's secretary runs in, stores her coat and hat downstage in the study closet and prepares to take George's dictation. It is almost 9 o'clock, Archie hasn't shown up yet and Dotty, desperate, is on point of crying for help when the bedroom blacks out.

In the study, George is in the midst of preparing a speech for an imminent meeting of the debating society. He scrawls notes on pieces of paper, assembles them in order and refers to them as he dictates to the Secretary. He makes a false start. Dotty, in the bedroom, does indeed call for help. George ignores her cries, however, and proceeds with his lecture. His method is to watch himself in a "mirror" on the downstage wall to check his delivery as he is speaking; but since there is no fourth wall, and hence no mirror, George is actually speaking directly to the audience as he dictates.

GEORGE: To begin at the beginning: is God? *(Pause.)* I prefer to put the question in this form because to ask "Does God exist?" appears to presuppose the existence of a God who may not, and I do not propose this late evening to follow my friend Russell, this evening to follow my late friend Russell, to follow my good friend the late Lord Russell, necrophiliac rubbish!, to begin at the beginning: is God? *(He ponders a moment.)* To ask "Is God?" appears to presuppose a Being who perhaps isn't . . . and thus is open to the same objection as the question "Does God exist?" . . . but until the difficulty is pointed out it does not have the same propensity to confuse language with meaning and to conjure up a God who may have any number of predicates including omniscience, perfection and four-wheel drive but not, as it happens, existence. This confusion, which indicates only that language is an approximation of meaning and and not a logical symbolism for it, began with Plato and was not ended by Bertrand Russell's theory that existence could only be asserted of descriptions and not of individuals, but I do not propose this evening to follow into the Theory of Descriptions my very old friend—now dead, of course—*ach!*—to follow into the Theory of Descriptions, the late Lord Russell—!

George continues his lecture as the Secretary diligently takes her notes. Suddenly Dotty is heard crying "Rape!" George tries to ignore her and keeps on going until she cries "Murder—rape—wolves!" This gives him pause, and he opens the study door and cries out to his wife to turn down her radio. He then continues his argument on the existence of God, taking out an archery target and a bow and arrow by way of illustration.

GEORGE: . . . . . Putting aside the God of Goodness, to whom we will return, and taking first the God of Creation—or to give him his chief philosophical *raison d'etre,* the First Cause—we see that a supernatural or divine origin is the logical consequence of the assumption that one thing leads to another, and that this series must have had a first term; that, if you like, though chickens and eggs may alternate back through the millenia, ultimately, we arrive at something which, while perhaps no longer resembling either a chicken or an egg, is nevertheless the first term of that series and can itself only be attributed to a First Cause—or to give it its theological soubriquet, God. How well founded is such an assumption? Could it be, for instance, that chickens and eggs have been succeeding each other in one form or another literally forever? My old friend—Mathematicians are quick to point out that they are familiar with many series which have no first term —such as the series of proper fractions between nought and one. What, they ask, is the first, that is the smallest, of these fractions? A billionth? A trillionth? Obviously not: Cantor's proof that there is no greatest number ensures that there is no smallest fraction. There is no beginning.

With a certain relish he notches his arrow into the bowstring.
But it was precisely this notion of infinite series which in the sixth century B.C. led the Greek philosopher Zeno to conclude that since an arrow shot towards a target first had to cover half the distance, and then half the remainder, and then half the remainder after that, and so on *ad infinitum,* the result was, as I will now demonstrate, that though an arrow is always approaching its target, it never quite gets there, and Saint Sebastian died of fright.

He is about to fire the arrow, but changes his mind.
Furthermore, by a similar argument he showed that *before* reaching the halfway point, the arrow had to reach the quarter-mark, and before that the eighth, and before than the sixteenth, and so on, with the result, remembering Cantor's proof, that the arrow *could not move at all!*
DOTTY *(offstage): Fire!*
George fires, startled before he was ready, and the arrow disappears over the top of the wardrobe.

George shouts at Dotty to be quiet, then sits down and examines his socks for philosophical revelations. He cites St. Thomas Aquinas's five proofs of God's existence. He promises to point out the fallacy on supposing that a tortoise, given a head start, could never be overtaken by a hare. By way of demonstration he produces a live tortoise and prepares also to produce a live hare, but when he goes to its box, he finds the animal missing.
George's search for his hare, Thumper, leads him into his wife's bedroom.

George switches off the TV, and reflexively they play a quick game of what is apparently a running match of charades. The corpse is not visible because it is hung up on the back of the closet door. But the closet door swings open when the bedroom door is shut, so that the corpse keeps appearing and reappearing to the audience, though not seen or noticed by George.

GEORGE: Do I say "My friend the late Bertrand Russell" or "My late friend Bertrand Russell"? They both sound funny.
        Pause.
DOTTY: Probably because he wasn't your friend.
GEORGE: Well, I don't know about that.
DOTTY *(angrily):* He was *my* friend. If he hadn't asked me who was that bloke always hanging about, you'd never have met him.
GEORGE: Nevertheless, I did meet him, and we talked animatedly for some time.
DOTTY: As I recall, *you* talked animatedly for some time about language being the aniseed trail that draws the hounds of heaven when the metaphysical fox has gone to earth; he must have thought you were barmy.
GEORGE *(hurt):* I resent that. My metaphor of the fox and the hounds was an allusion, as Russell well understood, to his Theory of Descriptions.
DOTTY: The Theory of Descriptions was not what was on his mind that night. For one thing it was sixty years since he'd thought it up, and for another he was trying to telephone Mao Tse Tung.
GEORGE: I was simply trying to bring his mind back to matters of universal import, and away from the day-to-day parochialism of international politics.
DOTTY: *Universal import!* You're living in dreamland!
GEORGE: Oh really? Well, I wouldn't have thought that trying to get the local exchange to put you through to Chairman Mao with the wine-waiter from the Pagoda Garden hanging on to the bedroom extension to interpret, showed a grasp of the real world.
        He goes to leave.
Thumper! Where are you, Thumper?
DOTTY: Georgie—I'll let you.
        He halts.
GEORGE: I don't want to be "let." Can't you see that it's an insult?
        Dotty drops back on to the bed in real despair, and perhaps a real contrition.
DOTTY: Oh God . . . if only Archie would come.

George is suspicious of Dotty's relations with Archie, who has been received here in her bedroom every day this week. Archie also happens to be vice-chancellor of George's university and a qualified psychiatrist who, Dotty claims, is closeted with her daily in the performance of his medical duties as her physician.

George is truly sorry to hear that Dotty has once again fallen into an ailing emotional state. She reassures him that she is all right as long as she can stay here in the sanctuary of the bedroom. She offers to stop seeing Archie and to pay more attention to George, who *"examines the new tone and decides the moment is genuine."* He takes his wife in his arms and remembers how they fell in love when she was a student and he her teacher. Soon after their marriage, though, Dotty "fell among theatricals," and everything seemed to go wrong between them—except once in a while when Dotty has nothing else to do.

Dotty asks George to go into the bathroom and shave before making love to her, and George gets as far as lathering his face. They exchange views on God and George's career; then, idly, Dotty takes the goldfish bowl into the bathroom and returns with it empty and over her head as she imitates an astronaut's stiff-legged moonwalk. When she mimes leaning over to pick up a small coin, George instantly guesses that she has drifted into a charade of "The Moon and Sixpence."

Outdoors can be heard military-sounding noises of the Radical Liberals parading in celebration of their election victory. They discuss the party and its prospects; Dotty favors the Radical Liberals, but George, leafing through a copy of the *Times,* is skeptical of their policies and ideals.

DOTTY: At least it's a government which keeps its promises.

GEORGE *(flinging down the paper):* This isn't political theory! To think that these simplistic score-settlers should have appropriated the battle-scarred colors of those true radicals who fought for universal suffrage and the repeal of the Corn Laws—! *(Raving.)* And how is the Church to pay its clergy? Are they going to pull down the churches?

DOTTY: Yes.

He gapes.
The Church is going to be rationalized.

GEORGE: *Rationalized? (Furiously.)* You can't rationalize the Thirty-Nine Articles!

DOTTY: No, no . . . not the faith, the fabric. You remember how they rationalized the railways?—well, now they're going to rationalize the Church. *(Pause.)* There was an announcement on television.

GEORGE: Who by?

DOTTY: The Archbishop of Canterbury. Clegthorpe.

GEORGE: *Clegthorpe? Sam Clegthorpe?*

DOTTY: It's been made a political appointment, like judges.

GEORGE: Are you telling me that the Radical Liberal spokesman for Agriculture has been made Archbishop of Canterbury?!!

DOTTY: Don't shout at *me* . . . I suppose if you think of him as a sort of . . . shepherd, ministering to his flock . . .

GEORGE: But he's an *agnostic.*

DOTTY *(capitulating):* I absolutely agree with you—*nobody* is going to have any confidence in him . . . . .

Dotty reflects on the news about the astronauts: "Poor moon man, falling home like Lucifer . . . . . Of course, to somebody *on* it, the moon is always full, so the local idea of a sane action may well differ from ours. *(Pause; stonily.)* When they first landed, it was as though I'd seen a unicorn on the television news . . . It was very interesting, of course. But it certainly spoiled unicorns. *(Pause.)* I tried to explain it to the analyst when everybody in sight was asking me what was the matter . . . 'What's the matter, darling?' . . . 'What happened, baby?' What could I say? I came over funny at work so I went home early. It must happen often enough to a working girl. And why must the damned show go on anyway? So it stopped right then and there, and in a way my retirement was the greatest triumph of my career."

Dotty visualizes that her retirement stretches out forever, with the audience out there still waiting for her to finish her song. Anyhow (she confides in George), it was the sight of the astronauts on TV that triggered her emotional upset this time, not any of the usual things like alcohol or overwork. But George is less concerned with Dotty's emotional state than with speculation about the new Archbishop.

DOTTY: Do you think it is . . . *significant* that it's impossible to imagine anyone building a church on the moon?

GEORGE: If God exists, he certainly existed before religion. He is a philosopher's God, logically inferred from self-evident premises. That he should have been taken up by a glorified supporters' club is only a matter of psychological interest.

DOTTY: Archie says the Church is a monument to irrationality.

GEORGE: If Archie ever chose to relinquish his position as an eminent vice-chancellor he would make an excellent buffoon; but since he manages to combine both roles without strain, I don't suppose he ever will.

He turns and shouts at her with surprising anger.

The National Gallery is a monument to irrationality! Every concert hall is a monument to irrationality!—and so is a nicely kept garden, or a lover's favor, or a home for stray dogs! You stupid woman, if rationality were the criterion for things being allowed to exist, the world would be one gigantic field of soya beans!

He picks up his tortoise and balances it lovingly on the palm of his hand, at the level of his mouth.

(Apologetically.) Wouldn't it, Pat? The irrational, the emotional, the whimsical . . . these are the stamp of humanity which makes reason a civilizing force. In a wholly rational society the moralist will be a variety of crank, haranguing the bus queue with the demented certitude of one blessed with privileged information —"Good and evil are metaphysical absolutes!" What did I come in for? *(Looking round.)*

Dotty remembers that she is hungry, and the cook has the day off for the national holiday. George starts to leave but Dotty doesn't want to be left alone. She picks up George's thread of thought about the appearances of good and evil and then weeps on his chest over the rape of the moon's romance. They are almost into an embrace when George remembers that he is looking for Thumper, which breaks the mood of intimacy.

George goes back to his study and his dictation (with foam remaining on his still-unshaven face). Meanwhile, Dotty takes down the Jumper's body and places it in a chair; so that when George suddenly goes back to fetch the tortoise Pat which he had left behind in the bedroom, Dotty must hide the corpse by sitting on it and covering it with the edges of her robe.

The doorbell rings. George supposes it is Archie come to see Dotty and answers the door, but it is Inspector Bones of Scotland Yard, carrying a bunch of flowers. He admires "Miss Moore" as an artist, thus the flowers, but he has come to investigate a complaint about her: "I mean, Jack, if the telephone call which set in motion this inquiry was the whim of a lunatic, as I myself suspect, then I will simply take the opportunity of presenting this token tribute to a fine actress, a great singer and a true lady—after which, I will take my leave, perhaps with her autograph on the cover of this much-played, much-loved gramophone record— *(from a capacious inside-pocket of his raincoat)*—and, who knows? the lingering touch of a kiss brushed against an admirer's cheek . . . *(Reverie . . .)* BUT!—if it so happens that there is any truth in the allegations concerning events in this luxury penthouse yesterday night, then there are going to be some bruised petals underfoot as the full majesty of the law comes down on her like a ton of bricks, you take my meaning, Ferdinand? *(Entering the study.)* Is this the scene of your morals?"

George is still carrying his tortoise and his archery kit, but he sets them down when he sees in the mirror that his face is still lathered. He wipes off the foam while introducing Inspector Bones to the Secretary and informing him that his wife is in bed awaiting the arrival of her doctor. Bones is looking for a room large enough to contain a group of acrobats and finds the Moores' hall possible for such a purpose.

George confesses to the Inspector that he himself placed the call complaining about the noise, the acrobats and a naked woman swinging from a chandelier. He did it because the Radical Liberal victory party in his own house, attended mostly by members of the academic community, disturbed and annoyed him, at a time when he was worrying how to meet the formidable arguments of his opponent in the upcoming debate, a Professor Duncan McFee.

George tries to get Bones to leave, but Bones questions him about McFee's views on murder, then goes to inspect the scene of the crime and to get a vase for his flowers. In the meantime, George informs his wife, to her considerable alarm, that there is a policeman in the house and tells her he'll get rid of him.

Inspector Bones comes back with his flowers now in a metal vase.

BONES: Tell me something—who *are* these acrobats?

GEORGE: Logical positivists, mainly, with a linguistic analyst or two, a couple of Benthamite Utilitarians . . . lapsed Kantians and empiricists generally . . . and of course the usual Behaviorists . . . a mixture of the more philosophical members of the university gymnastics team and the more gymnastic members of the Philosophy School. The close association between gymnastics and philosophy is I believe unique to this university and owes itself to the vice-chancellor, who is of course a first-rate gymnast, though an indifferent philosopher.

> Bones stares at him and then walks into the study and sits down like a man who needs to sit down. George follows him.

A curious combination of interests, but of course in ancient classical Greece—

BONES: We are not in ancient bloody classical Greece.

GEORGE: I absolutely agree with you. In fact, I will have nothing to do with it. And in spite of the vice-chancellor's insistence that I can jump better than I think, I have always maintained the opposite to be the case . . . In the circumstances I was lucky to get the Chair of Moral Philosophy. *(His tone suggests, rightly, that this is not much of a prize.)* Only the Chair of Divinity lies further below the salt, and *that's* been vacant for six months since the last occupant accepted a position as curate in a West Midland diocese.

BONES: Then why didn't you . . . jump along with the rest?

GEORGE: I belong to a school which regards all sudden movements as ill-bred. On the other hand, McFee, who sees professorship as a license for eccentricity, and whose chief delusion is that Edinburgh is the Athens of the North, very soon learned to jump a great deal better than he ever thought, and was rewarded with the Chair of Logic.

BONES: Are you telling me that the Professor of Logic is a part-time acrobat?

GEORGE: Yes. More of a gymnast, really—the acrobatics are just the social side.

BONES: I find this very hard to believe—

GEORGE: Oh, really? Why's that?

BONES *(rising):* I don't like it, Clarence! The way I had it, some raving nutter phones up the station with a lot of bizarre allegations starting off with a female person swinging naked from the chandeliers at Dorothy Moore's Mayfair residence and ending up with a professor picked off while doing handsprings for the cabaret, and as far as I'm concerned it's got fruit-cake written all over it; so I tell my sergeant to have a cup of tea and off I go thinking to myself, at last a chance to pay my respects in person, and blow me if it doesn't start to look straight up as soon as I put one foot in the door . . . . .

Bones knocks on the bedroom door and enters. Dotty receives him in pink romantic lighting, but as she holds out her arms to him the corpse falls from behind the curtains into the room.

The bedroom blacks out as George continues his dictation to his secretary in the study. His subject is the rebuttal of the paper he imagines McFee has just delivered, making arguments comparing primitive and sophisticated esthetics and social customs, accusing McFee of leading them all up a "deeply-rutted garden path."

George's train of though is interrupted by the sound of Dotty singing "Sentimental Jounrey" (it is actually Bones's record being played loudly in the bedroom, with Dotty miming singing it). George goes into the study as Bones leaves the bedroom, and the two men meet in the hall.

> *We can't hear what they say because the music is loud. George takes Bones downstage to the kitchen exit and goes off with him. Dotty continues to sway and mime. The dead Jumper is where he fell. The Secretary moves to the typewriter.*

The front door opens and Archie enters and stops just inside the door, almost closing it behind him. He stands listening—an impressive figure, exquisitely dressed: orchid in buttonhole, cigarette in long black holder, and everything which these details suggest. He carefully opens the door of the study. The Secretary looks up. She nods at him, but it is impossible to draw any conclusions from that. Archie withdraws, closing the door. He comes downstage and looks along the corridor into the kitchen wing. He returns to the front door and opens it wide.

Seven Jumpers in yellow tracksuits enter smoothly. Four of them carry a machine of ambiguous purpose: it might be a television camera. They also carry a couple of lights on tall stands, suitable for filming. Six enter the bedroom, Archie opening the door for them. One Jumper goes downstage to watch the kitchen exit.

In the bedroom, Dotty is surprised but pleased by the entry of Archie and the Jumpers. They put down the "camera" and the lights. They have come to remove the body. The song dominates the whole scene. Nothing else can be heard, and its beat affects the business of removing the body, for Dotty continues to sway and snap her fingers as she moves about welcoming the troops, and the Jumpers lightly respond, so that the effect is a little simple improvised choreography between the Jumpers and Dotty.

Archie moves downstage, facing front, and, like a magician about to demonstrate a trick, takes from his pocket a small square of material like a handkerchief, which he unfolds and unfolds and unfolds until it is a large plastic bag, six feet tall, which he gives to two Jumpers. These two hold the mouth of the bag open at the door; as the climax of the "dance" the four Jumpers throw the body into the bag: bag closes, bedroom door closes, Jumpers moving smoothly, front door closes, and on the last beat of the song only Archie and Dotty are left onstage. Blackout.

ACT II

A few minutes later, the bedroom is still blacked out, but music can be heard from there, the next number on Bones's record album. George emerges from the kitchen with Bones, who is wheeling a well-laden dinner cart. They are commenting on George's career and Dotty's retirement; her fans miss her, but they are resigned to the fact that she has suffered a breakdown. Bones hints to George that a competent psychiatric expert should easily be able to exonerate her from any blame for a sudden, violent, aberrant action, should she ever be in need of such help.

Bones suggests that George is shielding his wife and informs the philosopher that there is a dead body in his wife's bedroom. George, astonished, goes to see for himself. *"He opens the bedroom door. In the bedroom, Dotty is sitting on the bed. Archie is kneeling at her feet, holding one of her hands to his lips. They take no notice of George who, after a pause, retires, closing the door again, and returning to Bones . . . . . "*

George explains to Bones that the man in his wife's bedroom is very much alive *now*, at any rate, and what Bones saw before was probably one of those charades of which Dotty is so fond. Bones wheels the trolley into the bedroom. Dotty, hungry, is delighted to see him and introduces him to Archie. Archie gives Bones his card: "Sir Archibald Jumper," with a long list of degrees after it in medicine, philosophy, law, literature—and gymnastics.

ARCHIE: . . . . . I can still jump over seven feet.

BONES: High jump?

ARCHIE: Long jump. My main interest, however, is the trampoline.

BONES: Mine is show business generally.

ARCHIE: Really? Well, nowadays, of course, I do more theory than practise, but if trampoline acts appeal to you at all, a vacancy has lately occurred in a little team I run, mainly for our own amusement with a few social engagements thrown in—

BONES: Just a minute, just a minute!—what happened to Professor McFee?

ARCHIE: Exactly. I regret to tell you he is dead.

BONES: I realize he is *dead*—

ARCHIE: Shocking tragedy. I am entirely to blame.

BONES: You, sir?

ARCHIE: Yes, inspector.

BONES: Very chivalrous, sir, but I'm afraid it won't wash.

He approaches Dotty solemnly and takes her hand.

Miss Moore, is there anything you wish to say at this stage?

DOTTY *(in the sense of "pardon"):* Sorry?

BONES: My dear, we are all *sorry*—

ARCHIE: Just a moment! I will not have a patient of mine browbeaten by the police.

Archie explains to Bones that he is here in the capacity of doctor to examine his patient, Dotty, with the help of the machinery he has brought with him. Bones takes Archie into the hall for a private chat, and Archie tells him: "The plain facts are that while performing some modest acrobatics for the entertainment of Miss Moore's party-guests, Professor McFee was killed by a bullet fired from the outer darkness. We all saw him shot, but none of us saw who shot him. With the possible exception of McFee's fellow gymnasts, anybody could have fired the shot . . . . ."

Bones warns Archie to get Dotty a lawyer (Archie *is* her lawyer) and expert psychiatric evidence. But that is only half of the advice he has to offer.

BONES: . . . . . The other half is, get something on Mad Jock McFee, and if you don't get a Scottish judge it'll be three years' probation and the sympathy of the court.

ARCHIE: This is most civil of you, Inspector, but a court appearance would be most embarrassing to my client and patient; and three years' probation is not an insignificant curtailment of a person's liberty.

BONES: For God's sake, man, we're talking about a murder charge.

ARCHIE: You are. What I had in mind is that McFee, suffering from nervous strain brought on by the appalling pressure of overwork—for which I blame myself entirely—left here last night in a mood of deep depression, and wandered into the park, where he crawled into a large plastic bag and shot himself . . .

Pause. Bones opens his mouth to speak.

. . . leaving this note . . .

Archie produces it from his pocket.

. . . which was found in the bag together with his body by some gymnasts on an early morning keep-fit run.

Pause. Bones opens his mouth to speak.

Here is the coroner's certificate.

Archie produces another note, which Bones takes from him.

BONES: Is this genuine?

ARCHIE: *(testily):* Of course it's genuine. I'm a coroner, not a forger.

Archie probes to find what might induce Bones to go along with this version of the crime; not money, but prestige. Archie offers Bones the vacant Chair of Divinity at the university, even the coveted Chair of Logic, but Bones is not to be bribed. He wants to know where the gun is, if McFee shot himself inside the bag. He informs Archie: "This is a British murder enquiry and some degree of justice must seem to be more or less done."

In the bedroom, Dotty lets off steam with cries of "Help!" and "Murder!" Bones rushes to her side, but Archie drifts off into the kitchen.

In the study, George continues his dissertation, dealing with meanings of the word "good." Seeing Archie in the hall, he joins him, and the two philosophers are soon wrangling over the existence of God, atheism, and the possibility that the two are the same thing.

Archie informs George that his debating opponent-to-be, McFee, is dead. They will retain McFee's already-circulated written paper as the basis for the symposium, however, so that all George's preparations will not have been in vain. The vice-chancellor will frame his own reply during the two minutes of silence in memory of McFee which will open the proceedings.

George asks Archie how, as her doctor, he thinks Dorothy is, and what they do in there. Archie replies that his therapy takes many forms.

ARCHIE: . . . . . a bit of law, a bit of philosophy, a bit of medicine, a bit of gym . . . A bit of one and then a bit of the other.

GEORGE: You examine her?

ARCHIE: Oh yes, I like to keep my hand in. You must understand, my dear Moore, that when I'm examining Dorothy I'm not a lawyer or a philosopher. Or a gymnast, of course. Oh, I know, my dear fellow—you think that when I'm examining Dorothy I see her eyes as cornflowers, her lips as rubies, her skin as soft and warm as velvet—you think that when I run my hands over her back I am carried away by the delicate, contours that flow like a seashore from shoulder to heel—oh yes, you think my mind turns to ripe pears as soon as I press—

GEORGE *(viciously):* No, I don't!

ARCHIE: But to us medical men, the human body is just an imperfect machine. As it is to most of us philosophers. And to us gymnasts, of course.

DOTTY *(offstage; urgently):* Rape! *(Pause.) Ra—!*

> *Archie smiles at George and quickly lets himself into the bedroom, closing the door behind him. The bedroom lights up. Dotty is sobbing across the bed. Bones is standing by as though paralyzed. A wild slow smile spreads over his face as he turns to Archie, the smile of a man pleading, "It's not what you think." Archie moves in slowly.*

ARCHIE: Tsk tsk . . . Inspector, I am shocked . . . deeply shocked. What a tragic end to an incorruptible career . . .

BONES: . . . I never touched her—

ARCHIE: Do not despair. I'm sure we can come to some arrangement . . .

> *George has returned to the study.*

GEORGE: How the hell does one know what to believe?

The bedroom blacks out, and George proceeds with his dissertation, taking off from his last question and concluding: *"Cogito ergo deus est.* The fact that I cut a ludicrous figure in the academic world is largely due to my aptitude for traducing a complex and logical thesis to a mysticism of staggering banality. McFee never made that mistake, never put himself at risk by finding mystery in the clockwork, never looked for trouble or over his shoulder . . . . ."

George hears Dotty laugh and proceeds to the bedroom (where the lights come up, and where Archie and Dotty are enjoying lunch from the trolley). George asks the vice-chancellor for the Chair of Logic made vacant by McFee's death, but Archie is evasive. George drifts into the bathroom and returns shaking with rage, holding a dead goldfish—when Dotty used the bowl as a prop she merely poured its contents into the tub without bothering to see that the fish continued to have water. George is both emotionally and philosophically furious at Dotty for this act of wanton, careless destruction.

DOTTY: You bloody humbug!—the last of the metaphysical egocentrics! You're probably still shaking from the four-hundred-years-old news that the sun doesn't go round *you!*

GEORGE: We are *all* still shaking. Copernicus cracked our confidence, and Einstein smashed it; for if one can no longer believe that a twelve-inch ruler is always a foot long, how can one be sure of relatively less certain propositions, such as that God made the Heaven and the Earth . . .

DOTTY *(dry, drained):* Well, it's all over now. Not only are we no longer the still center of God's universe, we're not even uniquely graced by his footprint in man's image . . . Man is on the Moon, his feet on solid ground, and he has seen us whole, all in one go, *little—local* . . . and all our absolutes, the thou-shalts and the thou-shalt-nots that seemed to be the very condition of our existence, how did *they* look to two moonmen with a single neck to save between them? Like the local customs of another place. When that thought drips through to the bottom, people won't just carry on. There is going to be such . . . breakage, such gnashing of unclean meats, such coveting of neighbors' oxen and knowing of neighbors' wives, such dishonorings of mothers and fathers, and bowings and scrapings to images graven and incarnate, such killing of goldfish and maybe more—*(Looks up, tear-stained.)* Because the truths that have been taken on trust, they've never had edges before, there was no vantage point to stand on and see where they stopped. *(And weeps.)*

Dotty turns to George for comfort, but George cannot help her. Deliberately, she points out to him that the lunch dish she and Archie are enjoying so much is not casseroled, but "jugged." George is appalled at what this implies; at that moment they hear the front door. It is their janitor, Crouch, who goes to the study with George to commiserate with him on the shooting of Professor McFee, which Crouch witnessed and thinks probably was done by "Miss Moore." But George can think of nothing but the jugged hare being consumed with relish by his wife.

George returns to the bedroom, where Dotty and Archie are now concealed behind screens with the mechanical "dermatograph" projecting pictures of Dotty's skin onto the TV screen. George, who is somewhat annoyed by all this physical contact—"examining"—between Archie and his wife, is now convinced that Crouch's conclusion is the correct one, Dotty must have killed McFee and Thumper too.

George and Archie return to the study, where Crouch is reading George's paper and has come to the sentence "St. Sebastian died of fright." Commenting to the Secretary and unaware that he is being overheard by the others, Crouch observes: "Of course, the flaw in the argument *is* that even if the first term of his infinitely regressing series is zero rather than infinitesimal, the original problem remains in identifying the *second* term of the series, which however small must be *greater* than zero—you take my point? I grant you he's answered Russell's first point, I grant you that—the smallest proper fraction is zero—*but—*"

George snatches the paper from Crouch's hand and starts to argue with him. Crouch immediately falls back into his humble janitorial demeanor, but Archie has noticed that Crouch has a flair for logic. Philosophy is Crouch's hobby, and his mentor was Professor McFee, who at the time of his death was trying to reconcile the fact of the two astronauts fighting on the moon with his idea of a rational world.

The Secretary rises and prepares to go out for lunch, making use of the imaginary "mirror" on the downstage side of the room, *"a grim, tense, unsmiling young woman."* Meanwhile, Crouch is telling the others that he got to know the professor because McFee would come here to pick up his mistress "and as often as not Professor Moore kept her working a bit late." McFee's wife knew about the mistress, Crouch informs them, but the mistress didn't know about the wife.

CROUCH: . . . . . He was terrified to tell her, poor Duncan. Well, he won't be coming round here any more. Not that he would have done anyway, of course.
ARCHIE: Why's that?

CROUCH: Well obviously, he had to make a clean breast and tell her it was all off—I mean with him going into the monastery.

ARCHIE: Quite.

CROUCH: And now he's dead.

The Secretary snaps her handbag shut with a sharp sound and takes her coat out of the cupboard.

ARCHIE: A severe blow to Logic, Mr. Crouch.

CROUCH *(nodding):* It makes no sense to me at all. What do you make of it, sir?

ARCHIE: The truth to us philosophers, Mr. Crouch, is always an interim judgment. We will never even know for certain who did shoot McFee. Unlike mystery novels, life does not guarantee a denouement; and if it came, how would one know whether to believe it?

Archie and Crouch move out through the front door. The Secretary is also leaving, now wearing her white coat—which has a bright splash of blood on its back. George sees the blood as she leaves the study and the flat. In the unseen bedroom, Dotty's record of "Forget Yesterday" starts to play.

George realizes that the blood must have come from the top of the cupboard, i.e. wardrobe. He needs to stand on his desk or chair. He puts Pat, whom he had been holding, down now and climbs up to look into the top of the cupboard; and withdraws from the unseen depths his misfired arrow, on which is impaled Thumper. The music still continues.

Holding Thumper up by the arrow, George puts his face against the fur. A single sob. He steps backwards, down . . . CRRRRRUNCH!!! He has stepped, fatally, on Pat. With one foot on the desk and one foot on Pat, George looks down, and then puts up his head.

GEORGE *(cries out):* Dotty! Help! Murder!

The screen lights up with a picture: Dotty's naked skin. But the dermatograph is still ambiguous: in the presumed interests of medical research, the picture moves with erotic obsession over Dotty's body in a very big close-up: it is never a "pinup."

George falls to the floor. The song continues. The process which originally brought the set into view now goes into reverse. Only the screen remains, lit with Dotty's image. George's last sobs are amplified and repeated right into the beginning of the Coda.

CODA

The scheduled debate is taking place in dream form, Crouch presiding. After two minutes of silence dedicated to the late McFee, Sir Archibald Jumper is called on to begin the discussion of "Man—Good, Bad or Indifferent?"

Archie swings in on a rope and makes a statement that is gibberish, dotted with names like Darwin and Descartes. The ushers hold up score cards reading "9.7,"

"9.9" and "9.8," as though they were judging an athletic contest.

Archie calls for Captain Scott, the surviving astronaut, who enters on a red carpet. Archie demands that Scott describe his feelings "as you stood out there in the universe, on your own world, so to speak, looking at countless other worlds known and unknown, each of them being possibly a home of one kind of life or another, with certain customs or perhaps none, and I should like you to tell my lord exactly what were your instinctive considerations upon discovering that your defective vehicle had only enough power to lift one man off your world's surface; with special reference to your seniority over Captain Oates, your rational assessment of your respective usefulness to society on earth, your responsibility to yourself without which there can be no responsibility to others, and your natural response to a pure situation that robbed you of history and left you naked, an Adam in a treeless, leafless and fruitless present without a past."

Scott's reply is simply, "That's it." Archie has no further questions. Crouch invites George to question the witness, but George declines.

The next witness is the new Archibshop of Canterbury, Clegthorpe, who enters in Coronation regalia. He has been trying to discourage the faithful (the Archbishop testifies), but they insist on his giving them "the blood of the lamb . . . . . the bread of the body of Christ."

George has no questions for the Archbishop, either, and Archie calls in his Jumpers to move the prelate out of the way, which they do by making him part of one of their human pyramids. There is a shot which knocks Clegthorpe out of the pyramid as it previously did McFee, and the pyramid disintegrates.

Dotty Moore is called, and she makes her entrance on a spangled crescent moon. She expresses her philosophy to the music of "Sentimental Journey."

DOTTY (sings):
. . . . . Here is my consistent proposition,
Two and two make roughly four—
Gentlemen, that is my proposition,
Yours sincerely, Dorothy Moore . . . . .

Heaven, how can I believe in heaven?
Just a lying rhyme for seven!
Scored for violins on multi-track
That takes me back

To happy days when I knew how to make it
I knew how to hold a tune
Till the night they had to go and break it—
GEORGE (shouts): Stop!!
        Everything freezes.
A remarkable number of apparently intelligent people are baffled by the fact that a different group of apparently intelligent people profess to a knowledge of God when common sense tells them—the first group of apparently intelligent people —that knowledge is only a possibility in matters that can be demonstrated to be

true or false, such as that the Bristol train leaves from Paddington. And yet these same apparently intelligent people, who in extreme cases will not even admit that the Bristol train left from Paddington yesterday—which might be a malicious report or a collective trick of memory—nor that it will leave from there tomorrow —for nothing is certain—and will only agree that it did so today if they were actually there when it left—and even then only on the understanding that all the observable phenomena associated with the train leaving Paddington could equally well be accounted for by Paddington leaving the train—these same people will, nevertheless, and without any sense of inconsistency, claim to *know* that life is better than death, that love is better than hate, and that the light shining through the east window of their bloody gymnasium is more beautiful than a rotting corpse!—In evidence of which I ask you, gentlemen of the jury, to consider the testimony of such witnesses as Zeno Evil, St. Thomas Augustine, Jesus Moore and my late friend the late Herr Thumper who was as innocent as a rainbow . . .

ARCHIE: Do not despair—many are happy much of the time; more eat than starve, more are healthy than sick, more curable than dying; not so many dying as dead; and one of the thieves was saved. Hell's bells and all's well—half the world is at peace with itself, and so is the other half; vast areas are unpolluted; millions of children grow up without suffering deprivation, and millions, while deprived, grow up without suffering cruelties, and millions, while deprived and cruelly treated, none the less grow up. No laughter is sad and many tears are joyful. At the graveside the undertaker doffs his top hat and impregnates the prettiest mourner. Wham, bam, thank you Sam.

The light has reduced to a spot on Dotty.

DOTTY *(sings without music):*

Goodbye spoony Juney Moon.

Blackout.

THE GOOD DOCTOR

A Comedy with Music in Two Acts

BY NEIL SIMON

Adapted and suggested from stories by Anton Chekhov

Cast and credits appear on page 354

NEIL SIMON was born in the Bronx, N.Y., on July 4, 1927. He graduated from DeWitt Clinton High School, served in the Army where he managed to find some time for writing, which soon became his profession without the formalities of college, except for a few courses at New York University and the University of Denver. His first theater work consisted of sketches for camp shows at Tamiment, Pa., in collaboration with his brother Danny. He became a TV writer, supplying a good deal of material to Sid Caesar and Phil Silvers.

On Broadway, Simon contributed sketches to Catch a Star *(1955) and* New Faces of 1956. *His first Broadway play was* Come Blow Your Horn *(1961), followed by the book of the musical* Little Me *(1962). His comedy* Barefoot in the Park *was selected a Best Play of its season, as was* The Odd Couple *(1965). Neither of these had closed when the musical* Sweet Charity, *for which Simon wrote the book, came along early in 1966; and none of the three had closed when Simon's* The Star-Spangled Girl *opened the following season in December, 1966—so that Simon had the phenomenal total of four hit shows running simultaneously on Broadway during the season of 1966–67. When the last of the four closed the following summer, Simon's hits had played a total of 3,367 performances over four theater seasons.*

Simon immediately began stacking another pile of blue-chip Broadway shows. His Plaza Suite *(1968) was named a Best Play of its year; his book of the musical* Promises, Promises *(1969) was another smash, and* Last of the Red Hot Lovers *(1969) became his fourth Best Play and the third in still another group of Simon shows in grand simultaneous display on Broadway.* Plaza Suite *closed before* The Gingerbread Lady *(1970, also a Best Play) opened, so that Simon's second stack was three plays and 3,084 performances high.*

The next year Simon came up with still another Best Play, The Prisoner of Second Avenue, *and again last season with* The Sunshine Boys. *His 1973–74 adaptation of Chekhov material,* The Good Doctor, *is—let's see, now—Simon's 11th straight success and eighth Best Play. His last three plays also gave him two hits running simultaneously during the past two seasons, a tremendous feat of playwriting which by any other author would be acclaimed in the most powerful superlatives, but which in the unique case of Neil Simon seems scarcely worth mentioning alongside his other accomplishments.*

Simon lives in New York City where he can be close to all this action (he owns the Eugene O'Neill Theater, too). He has two daughters by his first marriage. His second wife is the actress Marsha Mason.

Our method of representing The Good Doctor *in these pages differs from that of the other Best Plays. Simon's comedy appears here in a series of photographs of ten of its 11 episodes adapted from Chekhov, to record the overall "look" of a Broadway show in 1973–74, with captions stating the situation of each sketch (one episode,* The Arrangement, *was never photographed).*

In addition, the text of one of the 11 sketches, The Seduction, *is presented here in its entirety, in order to illustrate as fully as possible its author's style in bringing his subject from page to stage. We are able to add the extra dimension of the full text in this single example, thanks to the kind permission of Random House, the publisher of* The Good Doctor *in its 11-episode entirety, and thanks to Neil Simon who designated* The Seduction *as representative of his work in the play.*

The photographs of The Good Doctor *depict scenes as produced by Emanuel Azenberg and Eugene V. Wolsk and directed by A.J. Antoon, as of the opening November 27, 1973 at the Eugene O'Neill Theater, with scenery and costumes by Tony Walton and lighting by Tharon Musser. Our special thanks are tendered to the producers and their press representatives, Merle Debuskey and Leo Stern, and to Martha Swope for making available these selections from Miss Swope's excellent photographs of* The Good Doctor.

THE GOOD DOCTOR

Act I

Scene 1: THE WRITER—The Narrator, a writer, presumably Anton Chekhov (in the person of Christopher Plummer, *above*), explains to the audience that he built his studio with his own hands and sits here writing, hour after hour, day after day, as though driven to it by some uncontrollable compulsion. He admits he enjoys writing while he's doing it but is always disappointed by the results. Just as he is about to reveal what he'd rather have done with his life, his train of thought is interrupted by an idea for a story which he will call *The Sneeze* . . .

Scene 2: THE SNEEZE—*On page at left,* One evening at the theater the Narrator observes a mild-mannered civil servant, Cherdyakov (Rene Auberjonois, back row *right*) with his wife (Marsha Mason) who happen to be seated behind his boss, Gen. Brassilhof, and his wife (Barnard Hughes and Frances Sternhagen, front row). By accident, the clerk sneezes embarrassingly and moistly on the back of his chief's neck. The General tries to overlook the unfortunate incident, but Cherdyakov's unremitting, exasperating efforts to apologize make this impossible and finally bring about the clerk's demise

Scene 3: THE GOVERNESS—An employer (Frances Sternhagen, *above right*) tries to teach her children's humble governess a lesson in standing up for her rights, by pretending to cheat her out of most of her wages. The governess's capacity for absorbing humiliation proves inexhaustible, however—and it may even be an asset in dealing with her proud mistress

Scene 4: SURGERY—Commenting on the nature of humor, the Narrator remarks that even pain can sometimes be the object of laughter. As an example, he sets a situation (*below*) in which a sexton (Barnard Hughes) is suffering agonies of toothache and seeks relief at the dentist's, only to find that the good doctor is away and there is only the assistant (Christopher Plummer), an inexperienced medical student. The assistant's well-meaning, energetic but hapless efforts to pull the offending tooth leave both doctor and patient exhausted

Scene 5: TOO LATE FOR HAPPINESS
—A man in his 70s and a woman in her
60s (Barnard Hughes and Frances Sternhagen, *above*) meet by chance on a park
bench. They express their inner feelings
in song. Each admires the other and
wonders whether they could get to know
each other better, but they stop short of
making any commitment

Scene 6: THE SEDUCTION—*Right,*
Marsha Mason as the wife in a scene
whose text appears in its entirety beginning on the page immediately following
this section of photographs

Scene 1: **THE DROWNED MAN**—Suffering from writer's block, the Narrator wanders down to the waterfront at night hoping to come upon an idea for a story. He meets a man (Rene Auberjonois, *above left*) who offers to jump in the water for a fee and act out a drowning for the Narrator's entertainment. The Narrator is repelled by the proposal until he learns that "drowning" is this man's regular occupation. The Narrator pays over the money for the man to do his act—for what, it develops, may very well be the last time

Scene 2: THE AUDITION—The Narrator's voice is heard issuing instructions to an auditioning actress (Marsha Mason, *left*) who pleases him with her rendering of a scene from *Three Sisters*

Scene 3: A DEFENSELESS CREATURE — A poor woman (Frances Sternhagen, *below*) whose husband is sick and out of work appeals to a gouty bank president for help, though none of her problems are remotely his responsibility. She so overwhelms him with her strident complaints, however, that he pays her the money she asks in a desperate effort to get rid of her

Scene 4: THE ARRANGEMENT (This scene was never photographed during the run of the original production)—The Narrator remembers when his father escorted him on his 19th birthday to have a professional teach him about love. Young Anton (played by Rene Auberjonois) is shy and fearful, while his father (played by Christopher Plummer) is impatient and matter-of-fact. The father strikes a bargain with one of the girls (played by Marsha Mason) to show his son the ways of love. But at the last minute the father has second thoughts about wanting his son, his little Antosha, to grow up suddenly; and much to Anton's relief they abandon the whole enterprise

Scene 5: THE WRITER—The Narrator still can't quite remember what it was he always wanted to do with his life . . . but on the whole he feels rather contented and fulfilled, so he may possibly be doing it already

THE SEDUCTION

Lights up on the Narrator. He is in suit and hat, pince nez and carrying his walking stick. There is a small public garden; a tree and a bench. He looks to the wings, as if waiting for someone, then out to the audience.

NARRATOR: . . . Peter Semyonych was the greatest seducer of other men's wives that I've ever met . . . He was successful with *all* women for that matter, but there was a special challenge to beautiful women married to prominent, rich, successful men . . . I could never do him justice, let him tell you in his own words . . .

He removes his glasses, puts them in his pocket, clears his throat, assumes a more debonair posture and becomes Peter Semyonych.

PETER: . . . If I may say so myself, I am the greatest seducer of other men's wives that I've ever met . . . I say this not boastfully, but as a matter of record. The staggering figures speak for themselves . . . For those men interested in playing this highly satisfying but often dangerous game, I urge you to take out pen and paper and take notes . . . I am going to explain my methods . . . In defense, married women may do likewise but it will do them little good if they happen to be the chosen victim . . . My method has never failed . . . Now then, there are three vital characteristics needed . . . They are, patience, more patience and still more patience . . . Those who do not have the strength to wait and persist, I urge you to take up bicycling . . . Rowing, perhaps . . . Seducing isn't for you . . . Now then, in order to seduce a man's wife, you must, I repeat *must,* keep as far away from her as possible . . . Pay her practically no attention at all . . . Ignore her if you must . . . We will get to her—through the *husband. (He looks at his watch, then off into the wings.)* You are about to witness a practical demonstration, for as it happens I am madly and deeply in love this week . . . My heart pounds with excitement knowing that she will pass through this garden in a few moments with her husband. Every fiber of my being tells me to throw my arms around her and embrace her with all the passion in my heart . . . But observe how a master works . . . I shall be cool almost to the point of freezing . . . My heart of hearts and spouse, approaches.

He turns the other way as the husband and his lovely, younger bride approach taking an afternoon stroll in the park. She carries an umbrella to shade the afternoon sun.

HUSBAND: Ahh Peter Semyonych, fancy meeting you here.

PETER *(doesn't look at wife):* My dear Nicolaich, how good to see you . . . you're looking well. *(To audience.)* Notice how I'm not looking at her.

HUSBAND: Thank you. And you, you gay devil, you're always looking well . . . Excuse me, have you met my wife, Irena? . . . Of course, you have . . . You sat next to her at dinner at the Vesinovs . . . Irena, I don't know what this charmer said to you at dinner, but I must warn you that he is a scoundrel, a notorious bachelor and an exceptional swordsman. That's the best I can say for you, Peter.

PETER: You exaggerate, Nicky. *(Glances at the wife.)* Madame. Good to see you again.

He doffs his hat but barely looks at her. She nods back, then turns and looks at the flowers.

HUSBAND: We were just taking a stroll. If you're not busy, why don't you walk with us?

PETER: That's very kind of you, Nikolaich, but as a matter of fact, I am riveted to this spot. A new romance has just entered my life and my legs are like pillars of granite . . . Until she is out of my sight, I will be incapable of movement. *(To audience.)* Too much, do you think? As I said, be patient.

HUSBAND: Fantastic! You never cease to amaze me. Pretty, I suppose?

PETER: Suppose *magnificent.* Suppose *glorious* and you will suppose correctly.

HUSBAND: Any . . . "complications?"

PETER: As usual, a husband. I'm afraid my cause looks hopeless.

HUSBAND: Nonsense. I'm placing my money on you, Peter. And you know I never bet unless I'm sure of winning. Well, we're off. Good hunting, my boy. Good hunting.

They start off.

PETER *(doffs his hat):* Madame! *(Turns to audience.)* . . . Beautifully done, don't you think? . . . I'm sometimes awed by the work of a true professional . . . Did you notice our eyes barely met, we exchanged hardly a word and yet how much she knows of me already. A) I am a popular bachelor, B) a man in love (always titillating to romantic women), C) a gifted sportsman (a nice contrast to her sedentary husband) and D), and this is most important, a dangerous man with the ladies . . . Quite frankly, at this point she is disgusted by me . . . A) because I'm a braggart and a scoundrel, B) because I am shamelessly frank as to my intentions and C) because she thinks she's not the one I'm interested in . . . Forgive me if I'm slightly overcome by my own deviousness . . . By the way, are you getting all this down? It gets tricky from here on in . . . Now then, next step, hypnosis . . . Not hypnosis with your eyes, but with the poison of your tongue much like a venomous snake moving in for the kill . . . and what's more, the best channel is the husband himself . . . Witness, as I "accidentally" run into him one day at the club . . .

He crosses to the "club". . . . The husband is sitting reading a newspaper . . . Peter takes up a newspaper and sits next to him . . . The husband looks up and notices him.

HUSBAND: . . . Peter . . . You're looking glum . . . I take it your pursuit isn't going well . . . *(He laughs.)*

PETER: Is it that obvious? I'm doomed, Nicky . . . I haven't seen her since last I met you and your dear wife . . . I sleep little and eat less. I've had all my shirt collars taken in a half inch. Ah, Nicky, Nicky, why do I waste my valuable youth chasing women I can never truly call my own . . . How I envy you.

HUSBAND: Me? . . . What's there about me that you envy?

PETER: Why, your marriage, of course. A charming woman your wife, let me tell you.

HUSBAND: Really? What is there about her that fascinates you so?

PETER: Her grace, her quiet charm, everything. But mostly it's the way she looks at you, Nicky. Oh, if only someone would look at me like that . . . with such adoring, loving eyes. It must send quivers through your body.

HUSBAND: Quivers? No, not really.

PETER: A tingle, perhaps? . . . Don't tell me you don't tingle when she looks at you.

HUSBAND: Oh, of course. By all means. I tingle all the time.

PETER: She's an ideal woman, Nicky, believe that from a lonely bachelor and be glad fate gave you a wife like that.

HUSBAND: Perhaps fate will be as kind to *you.*

PETER: That's what I'm counting on . . . Good heavens, I'm late for my doctor's appointment. *(He rises.)*

HUSBAND: What's he treating you for?

PETER: Melancholia . . . Please say hello to your extraordinary wife but I urge you not to repeat our conversation . . . It might embarrass her fragile sensitivities.

> *Sighs, as he walks away.*

Ahh, where oh where is the woman for me?

> *Out of earshot of the husband, he stops and turns to the audience . . . wicked smile.*

. . . I *know* where! . . . The question is: "How soon will she be mine?" . . . There is still work to be done . . . but not by me . . . That task falls to my aide and accomplice. Oh, by the way, I saw Peter Semyonych today . . .

> *Lights off on Peter and come up on the husband and the wife preparing for bed.*

HUSBAND: . . . Oh, by the way, I saw Peter Semyonych today . . .

WIFE *(putting up her hair):* Who?

HUSBAND: Peter Semyonych. The bachelor . . . we met him in the gardens last week. That attractive fellow . . . you remember.

WIFE: I remember what a loathesome man he is.

HUSBAND: You may not think so when you hear what he had to say about you.

WIFE: Nothing that braggart had to say would interest me.

HUSBAND: He spoke most enthusiastically about you . . . He was enraptured by your grace, your quiet charm . . . and he seemed to feel that you were capable of loving a man in some extraordinary way . . . It was something about your eyes and the way you looked so adoringly . . . He certainly had a lot to say about you . . . He went on and on . . . Well—good night, my dear.

WIFE: Good night . . . . What else?

HUSBAND: Hmm?

WIFE: What else did he have to say about me?

HUSBAND: Peter?

WIFE: Whatever that loathesome man's name is . . . What else did Peter Semyonych say about me?

HUSBAND: Well, that's more or less it . . . What I told you.

WIFE: But you said he went on and on.

HUSBAND: He did.

WIFE: But you stopped. If he went on and on, don't stop. Either go on and on or let's go to bed.

HUSBAND: Well, he said how much he envied me. How much he wanted someone to look at him the way you look at me.

WIFE: How does he know how I look at you?

HUSBAND: Well, that day in the gardens. He must have been looking at you when you were looking at me. It sent a tingle through my whole body.

WIFE: The way I looked at you?

HUSBAND: Exactly, my precious.

WIFE: But you were looking at him. So you couldn't have seen how I was looking at you. As a matter of fact, I was looking at the flowers because he made me nervous the way he kept avoiding looking at me . . . You must have tingled for some other reason.

HUSBAND: It's getting rather confusing . . . The point is, he found you fascinating. I thought it would please you.

WIFE: Well, it doesn't . . . I would rather you didn't tell me such stories . . . Are you planning to see him again soon?

HUSBAND: Tomorrow for lunch.

WIFE: . . . Well, I would rather not be discussed over lunch . . . Tell him that . . . And at dinner you can tell me what he said . . . Good night, Nicky.

HUSBAND: Good night, my angel.

    Lights up on Peter.

PETER: Good night, my love! *(To audience.)* I'm spellbound by my own powers . . . I succeeded in not only piquing her interest, but causing her heart to flutter at the mention of my name, the same man she called loathesome not two minutes ago . . . All this was accomplished, mind you, while I was home taking a pine-scented bath . . . Luncheon the next day was not only nourishing, but productive.

    He crosses and sits with the husband.

. . . By the way, old man, I ran into Nekrasov yesterday. The artist? . . . It seems he's been commissioned by some wealthy prince to paint the head of a typical Russian beauty . . . He asked me to look out for a model for him . . . I said I knew just the woman but I didn't dare ask her myself . . . What do you think of asking your wife?

HUSBAND: Asking my wife what?

PETER: To be the model, of course. That lovely head of hers. It would be a damn shame if that exquisite face missed the chance to become immortalized for all the world . . .

HUSBAND: For all the world. Really? . . . Hmm . . . I see what you mean . . .

PETER: Why don't you discuss it with her.

HUSBAND: Good idea. I'll discuss it with her.

    He gets up and crosses to the bedroom area. They are preparing for bed.

(To wife.) Well, I said I would discuss it with you. What do you think?

WIFE *(brushing her hair):* I think it's nonsense . . . How did he put it to you? I mean, did he actually say "a typical Russian beauty?"

HUSBAND: Precisely . . . And that it would be a damn shame if that exquisite face missed the chance to become immortalized for all the world . . . That's exactly what he said.

WIFE: He gets carried away by his own voice . . . Those *exact* words? You didn't leave anything out?

HUSBAND: Oh, yes . . . "That lovely face" . . . I left out "that lovely face" . . . He said that a number of times, I think . . .

WIFE: He *does* go on, doesn't he? . . . How many times did he say it? Once? Twice? What?

HUSBAND: Let me think. It's hard to remember.

WIFE: It's not important . . . but in the future I wish you would write these things down.

Blackout on them, light up on Peter.

PETER *(to audience):* . . . Have you seen me near her? . . . Have you heard me speak to her? . . . Has any correspondence passed between us? . . . No, my dear pupils . . . And yet she *hangs* on my every word uttered by her husband . . . Awesome, isn't it? . . . We apply this treatment from two to three weeks . . . Her resistance is weakening, weakening, weakening.

Back in bedroom.

HUSBAND *(as usual, preparing for bed):* I think his mind is elsewhere, if you ask me . . . On some woman, from the looks of him.

WIFE: What woman? Has he mentioned any woman in particular?

HUSBAND: Oh, no. He's too discreet for that. He'll protect her good name at any cost. Instead, he talks of you all day. Poor fool, I'm beginning to feel sorry for him.

WIFE: It's really none of our concern, Nicky, did you ask him to dinner tomorrow? *(There was no break in that last speech.)*

HUSBAND: He's busy.

WIFE: The day after, then.

HUSBAND: Busy.

WIFE: Next week. Next month. When? Doesn't the man eat?

HUSBAND: He says he's involved on a very important project and it will be months before he can see us . . . He did say that with patience and persistence, good things will come to him. By the way, he thinks you should go on the stage.

WIFE: The stage? Me, on the stage? Why, in heaven's name?

HUSBAND: Well, he said—just a moment. I don't want to misquote him.

He crosses to his jacket and takes a small notebook out.

WIFE: No, no. Take your time. Try to get it as accurately as possible.

HUSBAND *(reading):* Ah, yes. He said, "with such an attractive appearance, such intelligence, sensitiveness, it's a sin for her to be just a housewife."

WIFE *(hand to her heart):* Oh, dear, he said that?

HUSBAND: And that "Ordinary demands don't exist for such women."

WIFE: Nicky, I don't think I want to hear any more.

HUSBAND: "Natures like that should not be bound by time and space."

WIFE: Nicky, I implore you, please stop.

HUSBAND: And then he says, "If I weren't so busy, I'd take her away from you."

WIFE: He said that?

HUSBAND: Yes, right there. *(He points to notation.)*

WIFE: What did you say, Nicky? It's important I know what you said to him then.

HUSBAND *(laughs):* Well, I said, "Take her, then. I'm not going to fight a duel over her." *(He laughs again.)*

WIFE: Nicky, you mustn't discuss me with him any more. I beg you not to mention my name to him ever again.

HUSBAND: But I don't, my love. *He's* the one who always brings up the subject . . . He actually accused me of not understanding you . . . He shouted at me, "She's an exceptional creature, strong, seeking a way out . . . If I were Turgenev, I would put her in a novel . . . 'The Passionate Angel' I would call it" . . . The man is weird. Definitely weird.

> *The wife hangs her head disconsolately as we black out on them and come up on Peter.*

PETER *(to audience):* . . . He's delivering my love letters, sealing them with kisses and calls *me* weird . . . I ask you!! . . . So—let's see what we've got so far . . . The poor woman is definitely consumed with a passion to meet me. She is sure I am the only man who truly understands her. Her yawning, disinterested husband transmits my remarks but it is my voice she hears, my words that sing in her heart . . . The sweet poison is doing its work . . . I am relentless . . . There is no room for mercy in the seducing business . . . Observe how deftly the final stroke is administered . . . For the faint-hearted, I urge you, look away!

> *Light up on bedroom area . . . They are eternally preparing for bed.*

WIFE: *No,* Nicky! I don't want to hear. Not another word from him. Nothing.

HUSBAND: But exactly. That's what he said. He begged me to tell you *nothing.* He said he knew because of your sweet, sympathetic nature, you would worry to hear of someone else's distress.

WIFE: He's in distress?

HUSBAND: Worse . . . He's gloomy, morose, morbid, in the depths of despair.

WIFE: Oh, no . . . But why? What's the matter with him?

HUSBAND: Loneliness . . . He says he has no relatives, no true friends, not a soul who understands him.

WIFE: But doesn't he know I . . . *we* understand him perfectly? . . . Doesn't he know how much I . . . *we* appreciate him and commune with him daily? . . . Doesn't he know how much I . . . we yearn to be with him? . . . You and I.

HUSBAND: I tried to make that clear . . . I again urged him to come home to dinner with me . . . But he said he can't face people . . . He is so depressed he can't stay home . . . He paces in the public garden where we met him, every night.

WIFE: What time?

HUSBAND: Between eight and nine . . . By the way, we're invited to the Voscovecs tomorrow. Is eight o'clock all right for you?

WIFE: No, I'm visiting Aunt Sophia tomorrow. She's ill. I'll be there at nine . . . or a little after.

Lights off bedroom and come up on gardens where Peter is strolling, waiting for his prey.

PETER *(to audience):* . . . Please, no applause . . . I couldn't have done it alone . . . I share that honor with my good friend and collaborator, her husband . . . He wooed her so successfully, that there is no carriage fast enough for her to be in my arms . . . She ran all the way . . . Observe!

The wife, wearing a cloak, rushes in to the garden and then stops, breathless.

. . . Now for the conclusion . . . You *will* understand if I ask you to busy yourselves with your programs or such. These next few moments are private and I *am,* after all, a gentleman. *(He turns to wife.)* My dear . . . My sweet, dear angel . . . At last I can speak the words that I've longed—

WIFE: No! . . . Not a word! . . . Not a sound! . . . Please . . . I couldn't bear it . . . Not until you've heard what's in my heart. *(She takes a moment to compose herself.)* . . . For weeks now I've been in torment . . . You've used my husband as a clever and devious device to arouse my passions . . . which I freely admit, have been lying dormant these past seven years . . . Whether you are sincere or not, you have awakened in me desires and longings I never dreamt were possible . . . You appeal to my vanity and I succumb. You bestir my thoughts of untold pleasures and I weaken. You attack my every vulnerability and I surrender. I am here, Peter Semyonych, if you want me.

He starts to reach for her but she holds up her hand for him to stop. But let me add this. I love my husband dearly. He is not a passionate man, nor even remotely romantic. Our life together reaches neither the heights of ecstasy nor the depths of anguish. We have an *even* marriage. Moderate and comfortable . . . and in accepting this condition and the full measure of his devoted love, I have been happy . . . I come to you now knowing that once you take me in your arms, my marriage and my life with Nicky will be destroyed for all time . . . I am too weak and too selfish to make the choice . . . I rely on your strength of character . . . The option is yours, my dear Peter . . . Whichever one you choose will make me both miserable and eternally grateful . . . I beg of you not to use me as an amusement . . . although even with that knowledge, I would not refuse you. I am yours to do as you will. Peter Semyonych . . . If you want me, open your arms now and I will come to you . . . If you love me, turn your back and I will leave, and never see or speak to you again . . . The choice, my dearest, sweetest love of my life is yours . . . I await your decision.

Peter looks at her, then turns his head and looks full face at the audience . . . He wants some advice but none is coming . . . He turns back to the wife . . . He starts to raise his arms for her but they will not budge. It is as though they weighed ten tons each . . . He struggles again with no results. He makes one final effort and then quickly changes his mind and turns his back on her.

. . . God bless you, Peter Semyonych . . . I wish life brings you the happiness you have just brought to me.

She turns and runs off. Peter then turns out to the audience . . . then reaches into his pocket, puts on his glasses and becomes the Narrator again . . . a little older and with none of the dash and charm of Peter.

NARRATOR: . . . Peter Semyonych, the *former* seducer of other men's wives, from that day on turned his attentions to single, unmarried women only . . . Until one day, the perfect girl came along, and the confirmed bachelor married at last.

He starts to walk off.

He is today a completely happy man . . . except possibly on those occasions when some dashing young officer tells him how attractive he finds his lovely young wife . . .

Dimout. Curtain.

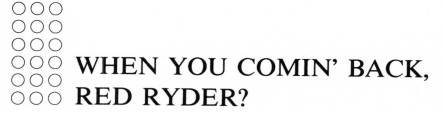

WHEN YOU COMIN' BACK, RED RYDER?

A Play in Two Acts

BY MARK MEDOFF

Cast and credits appear on page 390

MARK MEDOFF was born in 1940 in Mt. Carmel, Ill., the son of a physician (his father) and a psychologist (his mother). He grew up in Florida and spent his undergraduate years at the University of Miami, moving on to Stanford in California for his M.A. in English. His first play, The Kramer, *was produced in 1973 under an Office for Advanced Drama Research grant at American Conservatory Theater in San Francisco and subsequently in the New Theater for Now series at the Mark Taper Forum in Los Angeles. His next,* The Wager, *was done at Stanford Repertory Theater and the Berghof Playwright's Workshop. His third,* When You Comin' Back, Red Ryder?, *appeared off off Broadway at the Circle Repertory Theater before moving into commercial production for its author's New York professional theater debut, in which it has been named a Best Play.* The Wager *was also produced off off Broadway this season, at the Manhattan Theater Club.*

Medoff lives in Las Cruces, New Mexico, where he is an associate professor of English at New Mexico State University. He and his wife Stephanie have a daughter, Debra.

Time: The end of the 1960s

Place: A diner in Southern New Mexico

ACT I

SYNOPSIS: A counter with six stools occupies the center of the stage and the focus of attention inside a desert spa, a diner which is clean but has lived a hard life and has seen better days. There are two tables at left and a table and a juke box at right. The door to the highway is at left beside a window with the lettering "Foster's Diners."

Stephen, 19, sits at the counter reading a newspaper, his back against the wall and his feet resting on one of the stools. *"He is plain looking in an obtrusive way —small, his hair slicked straight back off his forehead. He wears a short-sleeved sports shirt open one too many buttons at the top, the sleeves rolled several times toward his shoulders—in the last of the 1960s, an unconscious parody in his dress of the mid-1950s. He smokes Raleigh cigarettes and has a tattoo 'Born Dead' on his forearm."* He has a habit of making a sucking sound through his teeth.

It is just after 6 A.M., on a Sunday morning, the juke box is playing. Stephen turns it off as Angel enters. She is *"obese, her white uniform stretched across the rolls of her body,"* the diner's daytime cook and waitress who is now six minutes late in coming to take over from Stephen, the night man. He lets her know that she is late, and she reproaches him for drinking his morning coffee in a paper cup, which is used only when customers want coffee to go, and costs a nickel extra.

Angel begins her morning routine of sprucing up the place for the daytime customers. Stephen reaches under the counter for a fresh pack of Raleighs.

ANGEL: What're ya gonna get with your cigarette coupons, Stephen?
Stephen reads his paper, smokes, sips his coffee.
Stephen?
STEPHEN *(lowers the newspaper with an edge of irritation):* How many times I gotta yell ya to don't call me Stephen.
ANGLL: I don't like callin ya Red. It's stupid—callin somebody with brown hair Red.
STEPHEN: It's my name, ain't it? I don't like Stephen. I like Red. When I was a kid I had red hair.
ANGEL: But ya don't now. Now ya got brown hair.
STEPHEN *(exasperated):* But *then* I did, and then's when counts.
ANGEL: Who says *then's* when counts?
STEPHEN: The person that's doin the *countin!* Namely yours truly! I don't call you . . . Caroline or . . . *Madge,* do I?
ANGEL: Because those aren't my name. My name's Angel, so—
STEPHEN: Yeah, well ya don't look like no angel to me.

ANGEL: I can't help that, Stephen. At least I was named my name at birth. Nobody asked me if I'd mind bein named Angel, but at least—

STEPHEN: You could change it, couldn't ya?

ANGEL: What for? To what?

STEPHEN *(thinking a moment, setting her up):* To Mabel.

ANGEL: How come Mabel?

STEPHEN: Yeah . . . Mabel.

ANGEL: How come? You like Mabel?

STEPHEN: I *hate* Mabel. *(Stares at her, sucks his teeth.)*

Angel takes the insult in stride, prods him again about what he intends to get with his coupons. Grudgingly, he tells her: a back pack for his travels. Stephen plans to leave this place in any direction he can thumb a ride, "and when I get to some place that don't still smella Turdville here I'm gonna get me a decent job and I'm gonna make me some bread."

Angel pours him a fresh cup of coffee and advises him that he had better adopt a more with-it look if he expects to be given a ride—grow his hair longer and get some more stylish clothes. They argue about the fate of this diner since the new by-pass opened. If it weren't for the gas station and motel across the way, they might not have any night-time customers.

Lyle Striker, the owner of the motel and gas station, comes into the diner— *"He is a man in his early 60s. He wears a brace on one leg and uses an aluminum crutch—the type with wrist and forearm supports. In his relationship to Angel there is a distant sexual undertone."* All eight of Lyle's units were full the past evening, but most of the customers have now gone. His new high-rise sign is pulling them in off the by-pass, and he kids his diner friends about their signs dotting the highway, advertising steak and eggs, which is every other place's specialty too.

Stephen notices through the window that Lyle's remaining customers have drawn up to the pump in their big Cadillac and are waiting for gas. Lyle leaves to take care of them (from the diner window they look too affluent to feel at home in a place like Lyle's). Red envies Lyle his occupation and wishes he were working for him—except that he plans to go away soon and work only for Number One. Angel wonders what kind of work Stephen plans to do.

STEPHEN: Don't you worry about me. Okay?

ANGEL: Yeah, but what're ya gonna *do*, Stephen?

STEPHEN: What am I gonna do? I'm gonna come drivin up to your door one day in a Chevrolet Corvette Sting Ray convertible the color of money is what I'm gonna do. Then I'm gonna rev up that four-ten engine through my glass-pack mufflers and I'm gonna lay about four hundred feet a rubber down your street.

Pause. He looks from a distance to her.

Anybody pull a stunt like that on your street one day, you be sure and tell 'em who it was. You tell 'em it was Red Ryder, everybody, drivin a Chevrolet Corvette Sting Ray convertible the color of money and livin in his own apartment. You be sure and tell 'em.

ANGEL: I'll tell them, Stephen.

STEPHEN: You tell 'em it was Red Ryder and from now on he's working for Number One.

ANGEL: What kinda work's Number One gonna be *doin* though, Stephen?—

STEPHEN: And I'll tell ya one thing. When I'm ready to go, I'm gonna write a letter to the goddamn *com*pany tellin 'em what the hell kinda deal I think Clark's givin us out here.

ANGEL: Hey, do me a favor. Never mind the company. Just get Mr. Clark in here when I'm around and tell him off. I'd pay money to see that.

STEPHEN: I ain't gonna waste my time talkin to Clark. He's just runnin a lousy franchise. When I quit, I'm writin a *registered* letter to the *com*pany. I'm writin a registered letter to ole man Foster hisself.

ANGEL: I'd pay twenty bucks to see ya read off Mr. Clark.

STEPHEN You ain't got twenty bucks.

ANGEL *(sticking out her hand):* You wouldn't care to bet on that, would ya?

STEPHEN: How much money you got?

> Angel sticks her tongue into her cheek and takes a crack at a haughty look.

You probably got three, four thousand stored up. Ya never do a damn thing but come to work, watch television with that ole cripple out there, and go home to get ready to do the same goddamn thing all over again.

> He snaps the newspaper up. His remark is true enough to hurt her just visibly.

Angel has been working here 14 months and has asked for but never received a raise. Angel speculates that Stephen might find it possible to get a raise out of Mr. Clark because he couldn't find anyone else to work the graveyard shift and would have to do it himself. At this point, Clark himself comes in carrying two bags of red chile pods for the Sunday lunch special. Clark checks the cash register, then rebukes Stephen for using a nickel paper cup for his coffee and for putting his feet on the stool. Stephen removes his feet, says nothing. Clark leaves, promising to return soon.

Angel puts up the Sunday Special sign advertising the enchilada lunch, as she wonders why Stephen's stepfather Ray isn't picking him up today. Ray, it seems, has gone away following a legal separation, leaving the family carless and virtually penniless.

The owners of the Cadillac, Clarisse and Richard Ethredge, enter for breakfast. *"They are an attractive, informally well-dressed couple in their late 30s, early 40s . . . . . There is about both of them the bearing of youthful success simply adjusted to. There does not seem to be anything intentionally pretentious about them."* Clarisse moves toward one of the tables, but her husband steers her to the counter. She is a violinist, and she carries her instrument with her in its case, setting it down carefully on the counter. They decline steak and eggs and instead order a more fastidious breakfast. When they ask for a newspaper, Angel gives them Stephen's.

Lyle comes in and gives Richard his change from the gasoline money—Lyle has left the keys in the car. Stephen draws himself another cup of coffee, while

Angel tells Lyle that Stephen wants a change and maybe Lyle could hire him next door. Lyle—who calls Stephen "Redbird"—allows as how he could; in fact, he has offered him the job three times. But Stephen is determined to leave town, explaining: "A girl that I went to high school with's old lady that moved to Baton Rouge said when they were in for a visit at Christmas that if I was ever leavin here and wanted to go to work for her that I could come on over to Baton Rouge and they'd put me to work in a *decent* job."

Angel points out that the girl's mother, a Mrs. Williams, owns a restaurant, so that Stephen will be jumping from the frying pan into the fire, however more elaborate the new place may be. Stephen vows he is leaving after he attends to one last detail. When Lyle suggests this detail is buying a car for his mother, and offers to help, Stephen storms out of the diner.

Angel apologizes to the Ethredges for Stephen's behavior. Stephen comes back almost immediately carrying a fresh newspaper and reporting the arrival of a VW van at the gas station. Lyle starts to get up, but the van's occupants enter the diner. They are Teddy (*"30–35, wears an army fatigue jacket and has long hair"*) and Cheryl (*"no more than 20, wears a long dress and a light shawl. She is pretty in a straight-haired, unwashed, no-makeup way. She is bra-less, a fact which generates helpless interest in Stephen, an interest which he tries all too obviously to hide"*). Angel greets the new customers, and Teddy is silent a long moment before replying.

TEDDY: *(affecting a stereotyped Southwestern accent):* Mornin, neighbors.
   Teddy holds another moment, then starts down the counter, past Lyle and the Ethredges toward the far table. As he passes Clarisse he suddenly stops and turns to her.
Pardon me, m'am, but . . .
   Clarisse looks up at him. She obviously does not know him. Teddy holds fleetingly on her and then averts his gaze . . .
'Scuse me.
   . . . as if he's trying to suggest that he doesn't recognize her when in fact he really wants to suggest that he does. Clarisse and Richard exchange bewildered glances, and a strange dormant seed is planted in Richard's mind.
Well now . . . who runs that yere fillin station next door?
LYLE: Right here. Lyle Striker, owner, proprietor and janitor.
TEDDY: Well, sir, need a rebuilt generator for a VW van.
LYLE: Nothin open today. Sunday.
TEDDY: Sunday, is it?
LYLE: Ever'body sleepin it off or out prayin forgiveness for it.
TEDDY: Tell ya what I had in mind. Thought maybe in a town such as yours a man with a service station, and a good natured crippled man to boot, would be in a position to call up a parts store on a Sunday mornin and get a part anyhow.
LYLE *(pause):* S'pose I could.
TEDDY: We surely would appreciate it.
LYLE: Let's have a look at your van first and make sure—

TEDDY *(accentless):* Don't have to look at the van.

LYLE: Wouldn't want ya to spend—

TEDDY *(accentless):* Generator's gone, sir. If you'll be kind enough to get us a rebuilt, I'll install it myself.

LYLE: Well, that sounds like a tough offer to beat.

He meets Teddy's eyes and then has to avert his gaze.

Lyle departs on his errand, and Teddy and Cheryl sit at one of the tables. Teddy tries to make small talk with the others in the diner, calls Stephen "kid," and Stephen replies by calling Teddy "dad." Teddy is by way of putting them all on, and Cheryl tells him to stop it, orders coffee. Questioned about where they're from, Teddy replies "Istanbul." Stephen has noticed they have California plates, and Teddy tells them all he is headed for Mexico.

After ordering steak and eggs, Teddy addresses the Ethredges. He has noticed the Cadillac and the San Diego faculty sticker. Teddy makes a pretense that Clarisse reminds him of his cousin. Richard tells him they are headed for New Orleans.

TEDDY *(nodding at the violin case):* Packin a submachine gun?

RICHARD: Only a violin, I'm afraid.

TEDDY: Prefer a submachine gun, would ya?

RICHARD *(laughing):* I didn't mean I was literally afraid—

TEDDY: Yes, m'am, I don't mind saying that you tend to remind me a whole helluva lot of my cousin Fern.

Teddy's and Clarisse's eyes hold a moment.

That must be a mighty fine fiddle to get took to breakfast with ya.

RICHARD: It's a Guarnerius. *(Smiling.)* Sometimes I think my wife has an added appendage.

TEDDY: Lady playin the hoe-down circuit, is she?

CLARISSE: No, I'm—

Richard stops her from answering by touching her shoulder.

RICHARD: She's going to be with the New Orleans Philharmonic this summer.

TEDDY: Uncle Clyde Bob and Aunt Cissy must be mighty proud of you, Cousin Freda. *(To Richard.)* And you just goin along to answer the tough questions for her? Just livin off the little woman's residuals, as it were.

RICHARD: Not quite.

TEDDY: Not quite. Doctor, lawyer or Indian chief?

Richard smiles indulgently.

Don't mean to be nosey.

RICHARD: No?

TEDDY: Just curious. Just makin a little roadside diner conversation. Pass the time. Hope ya don't mind.

RICHARD: As of yet I don't.

TEDDY: But at some future date you might . . . Gonna jot that down here.

RICHARD: That accent you're affecting seems a form of condescension aimed at all of us.

TEDDY: Surely not. No law against havin fun, is there. Leastways, not yet.

Teddy smiles broadly at Richard, who smiles coolly back and goes on with his breakfast.
RICHARD: No. Not yet.

Teddy is sure Richard must be an osteopath, but Richard discloses that he's in the textile importing business. Teddy turns the focus of his condescension onto Stephen, ridiculing his slicked-down hair and his rolled-up sleeves. When Stephen doesn't respond, Angel draws Teddy's attention.

Lyle returns with the good news that the parts man is coming with a generator, marked down two dollars and a half from list price. Lyle has an inflated feeling of accomplishment, which Teddy promptly punctures.

Lyle turns to Stephen and offers to lend him the $30 he still needs to buy his mother a car, but Stephen refuses the loan. As Lyle is leaving the diner, Teddy bores in on the subject of his crippled leg. Lyle good-naturedly tells him the handicap came about as a result of a stroke.

As Lyle exits, Teddy remarks that Lyle seems anxious to get Stephen out of town. He has heard Lyle call Stephen "Red" and wonders why. Angel lets the cat out of the bag: Stephen's last name is Ryder. When Teddy grasps the name "Red Ryder," he explodes in laughter.

TEDDY *(to Richard):* You remember Red Ryder, Doc?
RICHARD: Yes. Very well.
TEDDY: Boy, I do too. There was one straight shooter. Didn't dress like a fag and sing like Roy and Hoppy. And that Little Beaver—I tell you, there was a little redskin could handle a bow and arrow. What in the hell happened to those people, Doc?
RICHARD *(off-hand):* Gone.
TEDDY: Gone, sir, or displaced?
        Pause.
I'll tell ya one thing for sure, Red—those boys had guts. You got guts, Red? How would you rate your own self on a *gut* scale?
        Stephen sucks his teeth. Suddenly Teddy crashes his hand down on the counter. Everyone starts. Teddy moves toward Stephen gunslinger fashion.
There ain't room enough in this yere town for you and me, Red Ryder.
        Pause.
So I'm leavin.
        Teddy laughs robustly at himself.
Just as soon as I get my hoss a new generator.
        Pause.
You're a real chickenshit, ain't ya, boy?
STEPHEN: Takes one to know one.
        Teddy laughs happily.

Teddy ribs Stephen about his tattoo, calls him "a walking metaphor." Richard tries to quiet Teddy down, to no avail. Finally Stephen admits "You scare me," and Teddy replies in deadly earnest, "You bet your ass I scare you." He pries the facts of the tattoo out of Stephen: it was done when Stephen went to a carnival with a friend name Davidson and Davidson's girl. His friend had the girl's name tattooed on his arm, and Stephen selected "Born Dead." Of course Teddy belittles Stephen for not facing up to Davidson and having the girl's name tattooed on his own arm too.

Richard and Clarisse move to depart, but Teddy delays them, asking to see the violin. As an act of appeasement, Clarisse opens the case and shows it to Teddy. Richard admits that it is $11,000 worth of instrument.

Teddy suggests that Clarisse favor them with a tune (she refuses of course); then, menacingly, he demands that they make him a present of the violin: "I want that violin, cousin, and I swear to God you'd be wiser than you can imagine to give it to me." Richard of course refuses; but Teddy makes no move to stop the Ethredges from paying their check and leaving, though he watches them through the window as Angel brings him and Cheryl their breakfast order.

Teddy suggests to Angel that she and Stephen probably do more than just talk when they're alone in the diner, and he pulls one of Angel's breasts to make his point. *"Angel gets stuck between anger and amusement."*

Lyle comes into the diner with Richard—the ignition keys which Lyle left in the Cadillac seem to be missing. Richard goes right out again to search for them, but Lyle stays to inform Teddy that in dismounting the air cooling shroud to install the new generator in the VW he has found something taped there which might interest the Mexican border guards. Lyle advises Teddy not to make matters worse by stealing the Ethredges' car keys. Lyle offers to pretend that he had the keys in his pocket all the time, if Teddy will give them back to him at once. Teddy warns Lyle that if he keeps on interfering he'll "cut your tongue right out of your throat."

The Ethredges return, not having found their keys. When Lyle informs them "The boy's got 'em," Teddy grabs Stephen off his stool and upends him, pretending he's trying to shake the keys loose. Finally Richard understands that Teddy is "the boy" who has taken his keys and is not ready to give them back even if Richard were willing to ransom them—which he isn't. Lyle decides the situation is such that it's time to phone the sheriff to come straighten it out.

TEDDY: I pray to the very funny lord that you don't attempt that, sir.

LYLE: Then give the man his keys back!

TEDDY: Darn it all, I can't do that.

> *Lyle starts for the phone on the wall. Teddy drops all traces of the affected accent.*

Do *not* touch that phone!

> *Lyle stops.*

Now, when I say don't do something the way I just said it . . . don't do it. *(To Richard.)* All right, let's cut the crap, friend. We're forty-five minutes from the Mexican border and permanently out of your lives. But we've got no money to pay for our breakfast, let alone a generator. We need money.

LYLE: Have the breakfast on me, son. Put their breakfast on my tab, Angel. Have the generator on me too. Let's just don't do anything you'll be sorry for. My offer still stands. You go calmly outta here and—

TEDDY: We accept breakfast and the generator with thanks but we've still got to have money. In the hand. Now I'm damn sure that there's not enough money in this register or yours, ole man, to make cleanin them out worth my while, so if Gentleman Jim here doesn't come up with, say, three hundred dollars in cash, I'm going to be very upset. What do you say, Jim?

Teddy has slipped the keys from his jacket and approaches Richard, holding the keys out in his palm. Suddenly Richard leaps for the keys but Teddy, anticipating, secures them in a closed fist.

See that move, Red Ryder. Fastest fist in the West. Can I sign on as Little Beaver with moves like that?

Richard breaks for the door. Teddy leaps between Richard and the door. Like a basketball player, Richard tries to fake one way and go the other around Teddy, but Teddy stays between him and the wall. Richard loses his balance as Teddy moves at him and falls against the table with Teddy's and Cheryl's dishes on it.

Suddenly Angel breaks for the door, but Cheryl leaps up and blocks the way with what is, in fact, a nearly totally ineffectual stance against Angel's bulk should she decide to bust through.

CHERYL: Please don't do anything.

ANGEL *(screaming in Cheryl's face, close to tears):* They're nice people!

TEDDY *(to Angel):* You just shift your tank in reverse and back over behind that counter—

During Teddy's exchange with Angel, Richard has stepped close enough to Teddy to hit him. Rather than coldcocking him, however, Richard slaps him across the face. Teddy drops the keys and Richard grabs them.

Christ, Jim, what if I'd been wearing contact lenses?

RICHARD: We're walking out of here. We're going over to Mr. Striker's station and we're getting in our car. You have as long as it takes us to locate the sheriff and get him out here to get your car fixed and be gone.

Richard puts an arm around Clarisse's shoulders and starts them for the door. Teddy pulls a small caliber revolver from his jacket.

TEDDY: Hold it!

The Ethredges hold it.

CHERYL: Teddy . . .

RICHARD: Don't you *dare* point that thing at me.

TEDDY: Empty your pockets on that table.

RICHARD: I will not.

TEDDY: Friend, I don't need to shoot you, but if that's what it's going to take to make clear who's controlling this, then that's the way it's going to have to be.

RICHARD: That's the way it's going to have to be then.

Teddy fires the gun at Richard and, simultaneously, the stage goes black.

ACT II

Some minutes later, Lyle is binding up a flesh wound in Richard's torso with material from a first-aid kit. Teddy is at the table, his revolver beside him, Richard will be all right, but Teddy now dominates the situation totally. He amuses himself wondering where all the old-time Western heroes have gone.

Cheryl accuses Stephen and Lyle of staring at her breasts. Teddy glares at Stephen, then tells him: "But then she's got 'em right out there for you *to* look at, don't she? She don't want you to look at her bosom, she oughta cover the thing up. Ain't that right?" Stephen nods. Teddy sends Lyle out to finish installing the generator and Cheryl to cover him with the revolver, which he gives to her. He orders Cheryl to bring back some friction tape. Lyle exits, covered by Cheryl. Teddy continues baiting Stephen.

TEDDY (*to Stephen*): Shame on you, boy.
> *Pause; he stares deeply into Stephen.*

What's goin on in your mind, boy?—way back there in the corners where you never been before? Don't let it touch ya, boy, ya hear me? Ya do and it's just liable to eat you whole.
> *Silence. Stephen is unsure how to respond to what seems an almost intimate tone. He meets Teddy's eyes a moment, then drops his eyes into Teddy's fatigue jacket. Teddy continues to stare at him, to stay tight to him. Stephen glances back up at Teddy's eyes.*

Go ahead, boy. Ask me somethin.
> *Pause.*

STEPHEN: Were you in the war?
TEDDY: Yeah. You?
STEPHEN: Uh-uh.
TEDDY: Unfit . . . or pull a lucky number?
STEPHEN: Three-twenty-four.
TEDDY: That's too bad, ain't it? Ya mighta got yourself shot to shit and mailed home in a plastic garbage bag and buried down the road there. Ever'body woulda come to the funeral. You'da *been* somebody then, Red.
STEPHEN: Boy I went to high school with got killed in the war.
TEDDY: Uh-huh.
> *Pause. Stephen can't remember the boy's name. He finally turns to Angel.*

ANGEL: Billy Simon.
STEPHEN: Billy Simon.
TEDDY: Yeah—you'da been somebody, Red. I knew a *lotta* good ole boys who *became* somebody by gettin their good ole asses shot off . . . I can't remember their names either.
> *Teddy stares at Stephen, then turns abruptly away.*

I wanted to go away once too, boy. Figured one place was as bad as another. Went to college. Ya know what I remember? How to do the tired swimmer's carry —which ain't much use, say, here in the desert—and the succession of Tudor-

Stuart kings and queens—which ain't *no* use even if ya happen to be close to water.

> *He turns back to Stephen.*

Yeah . . . you might as well stay here, boy. Maybe someday they'll make ya head of the parkin lot.

Angel brings over a pot of coffee at Teddy's command, asks Teddy about Cheryl. Teddy doesn't know exactly how old Cheryl is but remembers they met at a dance. Teddy turns the questioning in the other direction and asks Angel about her weight.

ANGEL *(pause):* When did I start to get fat?
TEDDY: That's right, darlin.
ANGEL: When I was little.
TEDDY: Glands, was it?
ANGEL: Uh-huh.
TEDDY: How come ya wear that weddin right on your right hand? You married to Mrs. Christ's boy?
ANGEL: My daddy gave it to me.
TEDDY: How is your daddy these days?
ANGEL *(pause):* I don't know. He went away a long time ago.
TEDDY: Cause a you?
ANGEL *(pause):* Cause of my momma and my gran'ma,I think.
> *Pause.*
TEDDY: You think anybody's ever gonna marry you, Angel?
ANGEL *(pause):* I don't know.
TEDDY *(pause; without malice):* No. Nobody ever is.
RICHARD: What the hell's the *matter* with you, man?
TEDDY: Generally, Jim, or in particular?
RICHARD: What's the matter with *all* of you?
TEDDY: Ah! All of us. You mean us here disaffected youth of the United States of America?
RICHARD: *Yes!*
TEDDY: We disaffected, Jim.
RICHARD: What happened to all of that Love and Peace garbage?
TEDDY: Ah! That was another group, sir. That was these other fellas. No—us, we're not in favor of Love and Peace.
> *Pause.*
How about you, Jim? You filled with Love and Peace, are ya?
RICHARD: Not right now.

Teddy addresses the same question to Angel, who allows she loves only her mother and grandmother; Stephen she only *likes.* Teddy tries to bait Stephen on this subject, and when Stephen won't cooperate, Teddy, furious, knocks him off the stool and goes after him: "My God, the unspeakable audacity of a punk like you wearing a tattoo like that. The real Red Ryder would've hung 'em up if anyone were to tell him he was associated with pigshit like that. And I'll tell you somethin else: you *never* would've found the real Ryder sitting around a dump like this staring at some tourist lady's tits. I swear to goddamn Christ I'm tempted to take those eyes out of your head and cut that tattoo out of your arm."

Instead, he orders Stephen to make himself ridiculous by pretending to ride the range in the diner's open space. Stephen "gallops" around and around, making noises as though addressing his horse. Teddy orders Stephen to "dismount" and Angel to "welcome him home" with a kiss. Angel presents her face, and Stephen kisses her on the cheek.

Teddy likes this scene so much he decides to play it himself with Clarisse. She refuses until Teddy takes her precious violin from its case and threatens to harm it. Over Richard's futile objection, Teddy goes through the motion of galloping up and dismounting. *"Teddy leans across the counter but Clarisse turns her head away. Teddy grabs her through her pullover by the brassiere, twists the brassiere, and yanks her toward him. With the hand holding the violin, Teddy snaps her head back around and kisses her full on the mouth. Richard comes for Teddy. Teddy raises the violin over his head as if he would smash it on the counter. Richard stops. Teddy stares at him a moment, then still holding the violin over his head he kisses Clarisse again, taking his time."*

Clarisse demands her violin back, but Teddy orders her to play some "range-ridin music" with a fork on a tray while Stephen goes through the scene as demonstrated with Angel. Stephen refuses, but Teddy forces him. Stephen goes through the motions reluctantly, kissing Angel lightly on the mouth. They are all somewhat ashamed of their easy humiliation, but now Teddy is warming to his cruel task and has decided that Stephen and Angel will continue acting out their roles as though in a movie, and are to make love to each other on the counter, with Clarisse continuing her accompaniment.

TEDDY: . . . Now here's the way we're gonna play it. Red, you'll say to nubs here that you're goin away and she'll ask ya, Why ya goin away, Red Ryder?— and you'll say, I don't know, cause you're Red Ryder and you don't know a goddamn thing unless someone tells ya—and that's a great way to be, wouldn't you say, Jim? Memmer how it used to be? Oh yeah, none a this horseshit you're into, boy, about re-sponsibility and ex-is-tential choice. All's the ole Ryder knew is he got sealed orders to go away, so he was goin; and so you'll say, I don't know why I'm goin away; and she'll say, Is it because of me?; and you'll say, I don't know if it's because of you—because no one told ya whether that's it or not; and she'll say, I have to know why; and all's you'll be able to say is, I don't know. Say it!

STEPHEN: I don't know.

TEDDY *(showing him how):* I don't know.

STEPHEN: I don't know.

TEDDY: And then, sweet cheeks, you'll say, When you comin back, Red Ryder?; and whudduyou say, Red?

STEPHEN: I don't know.

TEDDY: Uh-uh, no, that's wrong. Because at this juncture, some unknown but officious individual steps to your ear and whispers: Never. You ain't never comin back, Red Ryder. And you say to your little dumplin here: I ain't never comin' back. And nubs here's eyes fill up and she says, Make love to me, Ryder, before ya go; and you, bless ya, Red, you say, We ain't married, Missy Nubs, it wouldn't be right. I couldn't! I mustn't! *Goddamn it! (Turning on Richard.)* You a Dodger fan Jim?

RICHARD *(startled):* No.

TEDDY *(to Stephen): Base*ball! Game men used to play when Jim and me was boys and you weren't the only Red Ryder around. Who'd you root for, Jamie?

RICHARD *(unsettled):* Yankees.

TEDDY *(laughing distantly):* You shitbrick. Yeah—we ain't gonna forget Roger Maris's flattop overnight, are we? Ya stick with 'em when you moved West, Jimmy? I'll tell ya what happened to me: When they moved the Duker outta Brooklyn and into that frigging L.A. Coliseum, they ruined the career of the only man I ever loved. I'm talkin to you, you Jimble. You speak to that!

RICHARD: I . . . lost interest when they traded Maris, and Mantle retired.

TEDDY: The Micker, Jesus. Yeah—yeah, maybe that was the end of it. And that goddamn Yogi Berra. Jesus, I hated that little bastard. What's they used to call him?

RICHARD: Mr. Clutch.

TEDDY: Mr. Clutch, my ass.

RICHARD: The Dodgers were losers. You belong together.

TEDDY: Don't you ever imply in my presence that the Duke was a loser. *(Laughing distantly.)* Ah, the Duker. Edward Donald Snider, friends, the Duke of Flatbush, pokin 'em into Bedford Avenue. *(Pause; turning on Stephen.)* Oh there was another time, boy, I know it . . .

Caught somewhere deep inside himself, Teddy stops, retreats.
Yeah. But that was yesteryear and this is today . . . . .

Teddy returns to the subject of Stephen and Angel making love on the counter, and he orders them to procede. Richard corrects Teddy: it was *Edwin,* not Edward Snider—and he tells Teddy to stop degrading the two young people. Teddy offers Stephen Clarisse as a substitute for Angel, but Stephen's reply to Teddy is "You're a queer!" Clarisse's is "You are an obscenity." She is not impressed, she will not be demeaned by this "mass of filth" named Teddy. She thinks that Richard should *do* something, that he too is being belittled by the continuing situation, because he is unable to stop Teddy. A quarrel flashes between them, subsiding only when they suddenly realize that they have now openly demeaned each other in front of everybody else.

Teddy, enjoying the others' disintegration under pressure, starts up the juke box as Lyle and Cheryl enter. Repairs to the van have been completed. Teddy orders Stephen and Angel (who has been crying since the Ethredge's quarrel) to dance, and they obey. With Richard's compliance, Teddy chooses Clarisse as a dancing partner and hands Richard the violin. Teddy forces Clarisse into close physical contact: *"He digs his fingers into her buttocks, pressing her to his groin with such force that his arms quiver slightly."* Clarisse continues to defy him in every way.

Teddy orders a change of partners. Angel choses Lyle. Teddy commands

Stephen and Cheryl to pair off, and when Cheryl refuses Teddy warns her that being his companion affords her no privileges: "You functional too, darlin. Nothin else really. Now you dance."

Slowly she obeys, after handing Teddy the revolver. Clarisse and Richard obey Teddy's orders to dance together.

> *Teddy stamps his foot and sings with the music, his stamping and singing becoming maniacal. Suddenly he leaps at Richard and Clarisse and spins them round and round.*
>
> TEDDY *(screaming at them):* DANCE! DANCE! GODDAMN IT, DANCE!
> *He derives no satisfaction from this and now throws Richard to the floor and against Clarisse's cries of resistance, he clamps her arms above her head and peels her pullover up over her head and yanks her brassiere up, exposing her breasts. He bears her blindly to Stephen.*
>
> THERE, BOY, TITS! TITS!
> *And now across to Lyle who backs away as if bitten.*
>
> THERE, OLE MAN, TITS!
> *Richard has risen by now and reached Teddy, As he grips Teddy's shoulder from the rear, Teddy rifles his elbow into Richard's stomach, turns and kicks Richard in the groin. Richard drops like a sack of cement. Teddy is panting. He looks about him a moment, then with an animal cry he tears the juke box plug from its socket. The music winds to a stop, the lights go out on the machine.*

Teddy's frenzy has subsided too, as Clarisse goes to comfort Richard. Teddy orders Stephen to help him tape the others' hands and feet. Stephen obeys. When he needs a knife to cut the tape, Teddy passes him one. Stephen has a brief notion about using the knife on Teddy, but Teddy faces him down.

Taping the others' mouths with a wider strip of adhesive, Teddy condemns Lyle for his "ass-kissing" hypocrisy and Clarisse and Richard for having nothing beyond the violin and the Cadillac. In equal contempt, he orders Stephen to take the knife and cut the tattoo out of his arm. *"Stephen yanks the knife out of the counter, screams his insides long and open, and rushes with deadly earnestness at Teddy's belly. Teddy catches Stephen's wrists, heaves him backward onto the floor and draws and cocks the revolver, He presses the revolver's muzzle into Stephen's face."*

But Teddy has no intention of shooting Stephen. He sentences Stephen "to live, looking back on that inept charge across this room as the high spot of your life's prime," made in ignorance that it is now much too late for anything like old-fashioned, Red Ryder-type heroism to save any situation.

Teddy rifles Richard's pockets, as Cheryl expresses her fears about how much trouble they have piled on themselves. Teddy challenges Cheryl to stay there and teach these loveless people something about love. Cheryl gets some food together including a box of Wheaties, and Teddy comments: "Breakfast of Champions. That where it all started to go bad, ya think, Jim? The Reverend Bob Richards polevaulting into our churches and hearts for . . . *Wheaties!*"

Cheryl has decided that she isn't going with Teddy. Teddy gathers up his belongings, tears the receiver out of the phone, orders Stephen to tell him one more time that Red Ryder is *never* coming back. Then Teddy tapes Stephen's mouth and exits without a backward glance.

Cheryl isn't quite ready to make the commitment of untaping the others, but the problem is settled by Clark's entrance. After getting over his shock and ascertaining that the money in the cash register hasn't been touched, Clark starts the untaping. He orders Lyle to go across the street and call the police and the sheriff. Richard makes the point that Teddy must be heading *away* from Mexico with his load of drugs, not *toward* it, and Cheryl admits that they were going to San Diego.

Lyle hurries away on his errand, as Richard seats Cheryl on one of the stools.

CLARK: Don't you worry yourself none—we'll get this fella.

RICHARD: I'm not worried.

CLARK *(to Stephen):* Three men here and one fella did this?

ANGEL: He had a gun.

CLARK *(ignoring her):* And what'd you do, Redbird? Just sit here on your butt drinkin up my coffee and greasin up the customer newspaper?

STEPHEN *(powerfully):* Up your hole, Clark, with a ten foot pole.

ANGEL: Stephen tried to do something. He—

CLARK: All right, boy, that's all for you. You're as of here and now fired. *(Turning to Angel.)* You sure that's all he took?

RICHARD: He took some money from me. About a hundred and seventy dollars.

CLARK *(turning back to Stephen, ignoring Richard):* To tell ya the honest to God truth, boy, after that by-pass open, I wanted to shut down at night, but cause a your momma, I kept you on and I stayed open, to the detriment of my nearly major source of income.

STEPHEN: You're a goddamn charity organization, Clark, no question about it.

CLARK: Boy, somebody oughta wash your mouth out with lye soap.

STEPHEN *(stepping up to Clark, face to face):* Yeah, and I suppose you're the one's gonna try it.

Clark doesn't dare push Stephen any farther. Richard tells them all to shut up, Clarisse included, and seizes the violin as though to smash it. Stephen confronts him, takes the instrument from him and returns it to its case.

Lyle comes in to report that the highway police are after Teddy, and Richard is needed at the police station to sign papers—they will have a doctor there to look at his wound. To Richard's irritation, they aren't going to report Cheryl's part in the affair.

Richard and Clarisse turn to go. Stephen stops them and asks for a ride as far as Baton Rouge. Richard refuses, but it is clear that Clarisse is going to overrule him. Stephen turns to Lyle, hands him $40 and accepts his offer of a loan of enough more to buy his mother a car—Lyle will see to it. Stephen has now cut the last tie holding him to this place, and Clarisse makes up her mind: she will take Stephen as far as Baton Rouge on their way to New Orleans, and if Richard wants to come along, so much the better. Richard has no choice but to acquiesce.

Stephen hurls a final insult at Clark. Clark, infuriated but helpless, grabs Cheryl and pushes her ahead of him out the door.

> *Stephen comes out from behind the counter with his carton of Raleighs and a current Playboy magazine. He goes around to his stool, smiling at Lyle and Angel as if he has just conquered the world. He stuffs his pockets with his pack of cigarettes and his matches, snaps up a light-weight flannel shirt, and heads for the door.*

ANGEL: Stephen!—

> *Stephen stops between Lyle and Angel. Pause.*

You take care of yourself now. Okay?

> *Stephen doesn't know what to do, though he knows he must do something.*

STEPHEN: Don't you worry about ole Number One here.

> *Pause. Then he walks self-consciously over to her and in lieu of kissing her or hugging her, he kind of mushes her with both hands on the shoulder.*

You just worry about your own self.

> *Pause. Then he crosses to Lyle, stops, gives Lyle a little elbow in the chest.*

So long, suckers. *(Exits.)*

ANGEL: G'bye.

> *Lyle looks at her but she can't look at him. He starts toward her; as he gets close, Angel moves away from him. Silence.*

LYLE: It's good. He'll be better off.

ANGEL *(nodding vigorously):* Oh—I agree.

LYLE: Yep, got himself a real good future in stock if he can get goin with Mizzes Williams.

ANGEL: I'll be it's a real nice place she's got.

LYLE: Oh yeah—no doubt about that. Ya don't have a restaurant in Baton Rouge where the help wears tuxedos less'n you're runnin a high class establishment.

ANGEL: I'll say.

> *Silence.*

LYLE: Welp, guess I'd better get to cleanin some rooms. *(Pause.)* Comin over for TV tonight? Sunday. Got "Bonanza".

ANGEL: Oh—gee, I don't think so, Lyle. I think . . . My mom and me, we had a extra special good one this morning. Maybe I oughta just go on home and spend the evenin with her and gran'ma.

LYLE: Sure. Sure. No need to explain. *(Pause.)* Maybe tomorrow night. *(Angel smiles thinly.)* You know you're welcome anytime, kid. Any-time.

ANGEL: Car just pulled into the station.

LYLE: Hmm?

ANGEL: A car.

LYLE: Ah.

ANGEL: For gas, it looks like.

LYLE: Welp . . . see ya at lunch, kid.

Angel cannot meet his eyes. He stares at her head.

(*Quietly, almost inaudibly.*) Okay, okay . . . I'm comin . . . (*Exits.*)

Angel looks into space, then around the diner. Pause. She moves to Stephen's area, looks at it, takes his stool. She picks up the remnant of his stale donut. She looks at it, then tears off a small piece of it and puts it in her mouth. She lifts her head, staring toward the window, chewing. The lights fade.

THE SEA HORSE

A Play in Two Acts

BY EDWARD J. MOORE

Cast and credits appear on page 399

EDWARD J. MOORE was born in Chicago June 2, 1935. His father was a truck driver. He attended Nobel Grammar School and studied to become an auto mechanic at Washburne Trade School but went off to join the U.S. Navy at age 19. After a four-year hitch Moore decided that he wanted to become an actor and made his way into the theater via the school run by the Goodman Theater in Chicago.

After six years acting with such regional theater groups as the Hartford Stage Company, Cincinnati's Playhouse in the Park and the Cleveland Play House, Moore came to New York City in 1963 but at first couldn't seem to get a career going there. While studying with Uta Hagen, Moore and an actress friend Susan Riskin (a large woman like Gertrude in The Sea Horse) *decided they needed a kind of showcase for auditioning their talents. Moore worked up a ten-minute scene called* The Sea Horse *which the two auditioned for the class on March 11, 1969 (it was the scene in which Harry speaks of the son he longs for—c.f. the synopsis following in this section of this volume). A 40-minute version of this showcase was put on at the 13th Street Theater that summer; Alan Arkin saw it and cast Moore in* The White House Murder Case *on the strength of it, so that it served its purpose as an acting vehicle.*

Moore acted in several TV serials while working The Sea Horse *into a full-length play, rewriting it six times. When it was at last produced off off Broadway at the Circle Theater this season Miss Riskin was occupied elsewhere, and Conchata Ferrell played the part of Gertrude. Moore played Harry, of course, but opened the script under the* nom de plume *"James Irwin." Soon after the off-Broadway*

302

opening, however, the true authorship became known of this, Moore's first play, not only a Best Play but also the best American play of 1973–74.

Time: The present

Place: The Sea Horse, a bar on the West Coast waterfront

ACT I

SYNOPSIS: It is about 2:30 A.M., after closing time at The Sea Horse, *"a dimly-lit, musty, drafty, dreary, unpleasant place"* furnished with three tables at right, a bar and shelves with bottles on display in the center and a stove and refrigerator at left. The stairway to the bedroom loft is up left, the door to the back room up right and the street door down right.

The bar is empty, but a clatter of bottles is heard coming from the back room. Gertrude Blum enters, cursing. *"She is in her late 30s, a big woman, about 200 pounds, fat, but firm, not flabby, and stands five foot seven or eight. Gertrude has a strong, sensitive face that hasn't been distorted by her bulk. Her hair is pulled back in a ponytail, she is wearing dark green men's work pants, a long-sleeved grey work shirt and black shoes. Her clothes are grubby and she looks tired, work-weary after a long day."*

As Gertrude begins mopping the floor, Harry Bales runs up to the front door. He carries a seabag over his shoulder and is dripping wet from the rain. He pounds on the door and calls for Gertrude, who pretends not to hear him. Finally she lets him in but goes back to her mopping, trying to ignore Harry, who complains about being left out in the wet. Harry is *"almost athletic in appearance. He is a powerful, compassionate man in his late 30s. He is wearing a light weight blue jacket, dark green sweat shirt, tan gabardine pants, logger's low top lace boots and an Army jeep cap."*

Harry hangs up his sopping cap and jacket, wrings his sweat shirt and grabs a bar towel to dry his hair, while in mock anger he accuses Gertrude of failing to hear his knocking because she was in the back room with another man (and trembles for a moment as he considers this might be true, then rejects the thought). Gertrude is accusatory in her turn: Harry's ship, the Sister Katingo, docked at 6 o'clock in the morning, and Harry didn't turn up until now.

> *Harry puts his arms around her waist. Furious, she shakes him off.*
GERTRUDE: You bastard!!!
HARRY: Hey . . . wait a minute . . . I stayed aboard the ship!
GERTRUDE *(putting stools back in place):* Of all the crap!!
HARRY: I did, I had to secure!

GERTRUDE: And that took all day!!

HARRY: No . . . I was thinking!

GERTRUDE *(stools in place):* Thinking!
Crosses, picks up pail and mop.
You were thinking!! You're gone almost two months and you sit in dock thinking!!
(Turning to him.) Since when do you think?! . . . You want to stay here, you show
me *respect!*
Mop and pail in hand, she exits through curtain to back room.

HARRY *(crosses after her):* The crew tell ya I was in on the Sister? *(Stops at
doorway.)* Okay, fine! . . . They tell ya they seen me on the pier? . . . In town?
. . . No, they didn't! . . . 'Cause I stayed aboard! *(A moment.)* Gertrude??

GERTRUDE *(offstage):* Warm up the coffee!!

HARRY: Yeah . . . *(Calls to her as he goes behind the bar.)* Turn on the heat,
will ya, it's freezing in here!

Harry lights the gas under the coffee and pours a shot of Gertrude's best
whiskey from a bottle behind the bar. At Gertrude's insistence, Harry takes off
his wet sweat shirt and wraps himself in a blanket she finds for him (he had left
his slicker behind by mistake this trip; it is hanging in the upstairs room with some
more of his things).

Gertrude decides to believe his story about staying aboard, as she totals up the
day's receipts. Harry waited until after closing time to come to The Sea Horse
because he didn't want to share his homecoming with others; he has brought
Gertrude a special present. Now he has aroused her curiosity, but he withholds
the present, telling Gertrude he left it aboard ship, insisting that he has something
important to tell her first. Gertrude permits Harry to kiss her, then pushes him
away.

Gertrude stores the money in a canvas bag (it was a good day—this bar does
a good business because the customers like Gertrude, Harry assures her) and puts
it away. Harry has heard that a certain shrimp fisherman named Hank wants to
sell his boat—there has been a "For Sale" notice posted here on The Sea Horse
bulletin board for months—and Harry thinks he might like to buy it and go into
business for himself taking out fishing parties. He has saved up enough for a down
payment, but Gertrude, pouring coffee, thinks Harry will be wasting his money
on a worthless enterprise. Harry insists that he doesn't want to go to sea in rust
buckets any more and spend all his life down in the hot engine room in the grease
and grime. He wants to own his own boat, be his own man.

Seeing that Harry is determined, Gertrude offers to make the deal for him with
Hank (obviously Harry is accustomed to rely on Gertrude's support, both moral
and financial). But this time Harry means to arrange the whole matter on his own.
He has it all figured out, right down to the color he's going to paint his boat when
he refurbishes it. He plans to work out of Vallejo up the coast, but Gertrude insists
that he would be better off right here, where his room and board at The Sea Horse
wouldn't cost him anything.

Harry hands Gertrude a drink, and they toast the new boat—*their* boat, since
Harry intends to give Gertrude half even though he doesn't want her to chip in
on the purchase price. Gertrude suggests that Harry is "crazier than ever," and

he admits that an important change has come over him. It happened one night aboard ship when he came up out of the hot engine room onto the cool deck and stared out at the glassily calm sea, feeling the ship vibrate under him.

HARRY: . . . . . And I started thinking of a kid . . . ya see, I imagined myself sitting there with a little boy next to me . . . and he was my son . . . and it was so real I could see him. He had a tiny pair of non-skids on, and khakis, and a little striped sweater, I remember it was blue. And he had on one of my old watch caps, it was cut down and pulled over his ears to keep out the night cold. And he was sitting on a cushion next to me and I had my arm around him and I was tellin' him all about the sea and everything . . . you know I must have sat there for over an hour just talkin' to him . . . and that's when I started making my plans . . . ya see, I want that kid! And I want my own boat, that's why it's so important I talk to Hank, so I don't have to be away from him so long. And I'd like to get an old beat-up house somewhere, that way it would be cheap, and I could fix it up. And when he gets old enough, I want him to go out with me . . . on the boat, and his old man will teach him how to be the best damn little salt! *(He leans toward her. Smiles.)* And he'll have a great mom! *(A moment.)* Well . . . what do ya think?!

GERTRUDE *(a moment, then):* I think you're full of shit!
> *Laughs, gets up, takes her coffee cup, cookies, goes behind bar.*

HARRY *(taken aback):* I'm full of shit? . . . I tried to tell ya how I feel about a little kid and ya tell me I'm full of shit? . . . That's not funny!
> *He gets up, crosses to bar.*

Look, you don't understand . . . let me finish telling ya . . .

GERTRUDE: No! I don't want to hear any more crap about kids and that sentimental crud!!
> *Puts cookies back in tin.*

HARRY: It's not crud!

GERTRUDE: Well, I don't want to hear it!!

HARRY: If I can't tell ya how I feel, then what's the use to anything?!

GERTRUDE *(angry):* Well, feel something else!!
> *Harry turns away in disgust, crosses back to table, takes pour spout out of bottle, pours himself a shot. Gertrude watches him.*

Bring that bottle over here! You drank enough!!

HARRY: I'll pay ya for it!
> *Downs the shot. With bottle and glass he starts crossing to window.*

GERTRUDE: You couldn't begin to pay me for all the booze you sopped down around here!!

HARRY *(stops, looks at her):* Oh . . . and I don't do nothing for it?!
> *Crosses to bar.*

I'm always working around here, helping out, fixing stuff . . . *(Gesturing upstairs.)* . . . not counting the work I do upstairs in that bed!!

GERTRUDE *(glares at him, then with quiet intensity):* Oh . . . that's work, is it?! *(He doesn't answer.)* . . . Is it!!?

HARRY: No! . . . . . you just boiled me, that's all.

Harry pours himself another shot, still grumbling about being laughed at. Finally Gertrude half-apologizes, albeit rather brusquely, for hurting his feelings. Harry keeps on drinking and insisting that this time he has a workable plan. Gertrude is too tired to discuss it any further now.

Harry also wants to tell Gertrude about a time the reciprocating pump broke on board ship, but she doesn't want to hear about that right now, either.

> *Disgusted, Harry puts the bottle on the bar, then, glass in hand, he starts up the stairs. He stops, leans on the stairwell.*

HARRY: When we go upstairs tonight . . . and I get in that sack, ya know what's going to happen?!

She doesn't answer. Her back to him, she busily washes glasses.

. . . I'm going to take all my clothes off!

GERTRUDE *(matter of factly):* Well I certainly hope so.

HARRY: I'm gonna lean over to ya . . . and I'm gonna put my *big* . . .

He stops, watches her intently. She continues washing. He finally sees her smile.

. . . *arms!* . . . around ya . . .

Gertrude is grinning now, busily washing.

(*Sexily.*) . . . and I'm gonna run my tongue all the way down your back . . . I'm gonna blow hot air in your ear . . . and then I'm gonna say . . . you know when that reciprocating pump broke aboard ship!

Harry wins his point—Gertrude will listen to the story now. He tells her how the pump broke and had to be pulled up and down by hand, until he devised an ingenious way of adding the weight of a bucket of water so that the pump worked better than ever before. Gratified by his own ability to solve problems, he decided then and there to solve the problem of where he and Gertrude should live, and he decided on Vallejo. But Gertrude refuses to listen to him further, accuses him of drunken pipe dreaming. Harry threatens to go to Vallejo without her. He knows she dislikes having him leave her, because once, recently, she deliberately withheld information about a job that would have taken Harry to sea for a six-month stretch.

Gertrude is reluctant to admit that she likes to have Harry around, tries to change the subject to the leakiness of The Sea Horse's roof (she has moved her mattress from the loft into the back room in order to keep dry). Harry boasts of his attractiveness to other women. Gertrude invites Harry to join her on the mattress in the back room, but Harry doesn't like the idea of sleeping on the floor with all the rats. He is feeling good from the drink, and he is coaxed by Gertrude into singing a song that is now current along the waterfront, a blunt but affectionate ditty about The Sea Horse and its proprietress. In the song, she is "Two Ton Dirty Gerty" whose place is crumbling and rat-infested, but . . . . .

"She makes me laugh, she makes me sad,
Takes my money, but I'm always glad,
Makes me forget all my trouble and strife,
Makes me forget of ever taking a wife."

. . . . . and, the song concludes, she kicks you out at dawn but "if she likes ya special" might let you go upstairs with her after closing.

Gertrude loves the song which, Harry said, was made up by his friends. They kiss, and Gertrude goes upstairs to get her phonograph so they can dance. In her absence, Harry confesses aloud to himself: "I hate that song!"

Gertrude comes back with the phonograph and plays her favorite record, "Little Music Box." Harry is slumped across a table watching her as she revolves to the music slowly like a figurine on a music box, at the same time declaring that she wishes she could have been a dancer: "They kind of float, ya know . . . like their feet don't touch."

Gertrude's moment of warmth warms Harry too, and he tries to persuade her to tell him something of her past. He has heard that Gertrude was once married —but she warns him away from this subject. He remembers the first time he came to The Sea Horse; he had a girl with him and Gertrude sent him away, no women except herself are permitted in her barroom. Harry returned that very evening, alone, and Gertrude too remembers "That was the first time I brought anyone upstairs, the same night I met 'em."

Harry can't quite remember why he went upstairs with Gertrude, she wasn't his type, but he clearly remembers saying to himself, "Harry . . . you don't do it right, you could get killed." Gertrude allows as how Harry did it right.

Gertrude sees that Harry has had more than enough and takes his drink away from him. Meanwhile Harry insists on telling her about his ship's shaft alley.

HARRY: I go down this ladder, see . . . (Although a little drunk, he is still articulate, not slurring his words.) Way down below the water line . . .
      Gertrude goes to refrigerator, pours a glass of soda.
. . . and there's the shaft . . . it turns the screw . . . the propellor. And I go down there to check the bearings . . . and it's quiet down there . . . and I like to sit for a bit, alone, and think. I like to listen to the shaft . . . it talks.

GERTRUDE (she has taken off the record and unplugged the phonograph, winds up the cord): It does what?

HARRY (smiles): It talks! . . . I mean it rumbles . . . It's rusty in places and it squeaks . . . and it kinda says stuff . . . like . . . (Gesturing with his hand, indicating the turning shaft.) "I'm old . . . I'm old" and I'd answer 'n' say "Oh, yeah . . . oh, yeah."
      Gertrude, leaning on end of bar, drinks some soda, begins to get caught up in what he's saying.
. . . then she'd speed up 'n' say other things, like . . . (Again gestures.) "I'm so long at sea, I'm so long at sea" and I'd answer, 'n' say "Your bearings'll be fine, your bearings'll be fine" . . . and then, that strange night, you know, the one I told ya about, the glass ocean . . . well, later that same night, I went down to the shaft alley, to think about it. And that old shaft is rumbling away again, and this time she's saying "Gertrude Blum . . Gertrude Blum" . . . and I started saying it "Gertrude Blum . . . Gertrude Blum" . . . but then she starts speeding up, and my saying "Gertrude Blum" . . . doesn't fit the rumble . . . and it started saying . . . (Indicates the speed of the shaft, spinning his arm rapidly and talking with

compulsive intensity.) "I love Gertrude Blum, I love Gertrude Blum" and I
started sayin' it—

Harry repeats "I love Gertrude Blum" again and again, while Gertrude is
telling him to shut up. Finally she throws the soda in his face, but this doesn't
stop him. He wants to run off with Gertrude to Vallejo, he declares, where there
will be no one to inhibit or interfere with them starting a new life.

GERTRUDE: You wanna hide me!
    Both roar with laughter.
HARRY: Yeah!! *(Realizing what he said.)* I mean no . . . I mean . . .
GERTRUDE: You mean I'm a blubberball and you wanna hide me!
    Both laugh.
HARRY: . . . It's just that . . .
GERTRUDE: I been sleeping around so you wanna hide me . . .
HARRY: No, that's . . .
GERTRUDE: And all your buddies know!
HARRY *(still laughing):* They won't find out! . . . I mean . . . you're mixing me
up . . .
GERTRUDE: You wanna hide me!!
HARRY *(suddenly explodes, jumps up, his fist clenched):* Quit making fun of
me!!!
GERTRUDE *(glares at him):* You don't have any balls, Harry, you belong in a
dress! Who'd wanna run away with you!

Harry, now furious, orders her to be silent, insults her, calls her "a lard ass"
and "a fat pig" and accuses her even of hating little kids. Gertrude attacks him
with her fists. Harry tries to cover up but then, swinging back wildly and reflexively, connects with a hard blow to the stomach which sends Gertrude to the
floor, her breath knocked out.
Harry is immediately contrite. After she gets her breath back, Gertrude begins
swinging wildly at Harry once again, screaming accusations at him. Harry is now
in a panic, trying to calm her down, shouting back: "I WON'T HIDE YA!! I'M
NOT GONNA HIDE YA!!! I LOVE YA!!! YOU'RE NOT A LARD ASS!!! I'M
NOT GONNA HIDE YA!!! I WON'T HIDE YA!!! I'M NOT GONNA HIDE
YA!!!" Curtain.

ACT II

At 11 o'clock the following morning it is still raining outside. Harry has slept
on the floor with his seabag for a pillow, and now he is cooking oatmeal for
breakfast, having changed into a red plaid shirt and white sweat socks, but
wearing the same pants he had on the night before.
Gertrude comes in from the back room. Her hair is down, and this morning
she has put on a dress—not out of choice but because Harry has taken her

working clothes to soak in a pail of water and has pressed and set out the dress for her. Gertrude takes over the cooking chore from Harry (the cereal is stale oatmeal Gertrude keeps to feed the birds, but they figure they will eat it anyway). Last night Harry rigged a hammock for Gertrude in the back room so she wouldn't have to sleep on the floor. He is relieved to learn that Gertrude's stomach feels O.K. this morning.

Gertrude serves oatmeal to Harry but wants no breakfast herself. She sits at the table to keep him company.

> *Harry sticks the spoon straight up in his oatmeal, lets it go. It doesn't move.*

HARRY: I think this stuff has set.

GERTRUDE *(gets up):* I'll get ya some flakes.

HARRY: No, no, sit down . . . sit down! Don't bother, I'll eat later when you get hungry.

> *Gertrude sits, looking at him quizzically, irritated at all this attention. He smiles.*

I can't get over it . . . you look beautiful!

> *Gertrude pulls her hair back, starts to put a rubber band that she had on her wrist around it.*

What ya doing?

> *Stopping her.*

Don't do that, it looks so pretty down!

GERTRUDE *(angry):* Cut it out!

> *Gets up, goes behind the bar, continues fixing her hair.*

What is all this crap?!? . . . You got me hanging up in the air back there! . . . you cook my bird seed! . . . you've been fussing, nosing around, so you belted me one, that mean you gotta please me or something?!!?

HARRY: No, that's . . .

GERTRUDE: Look, don't flatter yourself, I've been hit a lot harder!!! . . . I just got a little sick, that's all, so knock it off!!!!

HARRY: Hell, I wasn't . . .

GERTRUDE: Don't scratch! . . . Don't ever scratch!! Not for anyone or anything, without your guts ya go under, I'm telling ya, you do something, it's over, forget it!!! *(Then, almost to herself.)* You start scratching a little, giving a little, then they . . . *(She catches herself.)*

HARRY *(unable to tell her that she has misunderstood all his intentions, he tries to connect what she is saying now with what happened last night; a moment, then, with quiet intensity):* I'll beat the hell out of him!

GERTRUDE: What?

HARRY: The guy that beat you bloody! That's what you meant last night, wasn't it? It wasn't me you was afraid of!

GERTRUDE *(a beat; then):* You gonna help me today?

> *Gertrude reaches for a coffee cup under the bar. Harry crosses to her.*

HARRY: That guy you was married to, was he the one who hurt you?!

GERTRUDE *(viciously, she slams the cup on the bar):* I SAID!!!! *(With frightening intensity.)* . . . Are you going to help me today?
HARRY: . . . Yeah . . . sure . . . I'm gonna help ya . . .

Harry admires Gertrude's dress, which makes her even more embarrassed to be wearing it. Harry makes love to her and tries to coax her into bed, but she has her bar-opening chores to perform. Harry teases her by making love to his seabag, coaxing her near enough so he can grab her and pull her down onto the blanket with him. She is feeling playful, until Harry tells her again that he loves her, which makes her uncomfortable. She breaks away—but she takes her rival the seabag with her.

Harry opens the front door and shouts out as loud as he can, "I LOVE GERTRUDE BLUM!!!!!" This infuriates Gertrude, but Harry persists, and at least this time she can't accuse him of wanting to hide their relationship. Harry suggests they both take off all their clothes and go swimming at the end of the pier, so that everyone'll know how it is with them. They will stay here instead of moving to Vallejo and fix up the place with red streamers (because red is Gertrude's favorite color) and lanterns. They'll invite everybody in for music and dancing. And, Harry informs Gertrude, "You'll be all dressed up in lace! . . . And I'll be behind the bar, ya see . . . and I'll be settin' up all the drinks . . . and everyone will be toastin'! . . . And if anyone sings that song about you, I'll throw 'em through a wall, 'cause you'll be my wife! *(Gertrude stares at him. A beat.)* That's right, we're getting married! . . . We're just gonna do it! . . . Ya see, I know what I want, and I don't give a Humping Houdini about nothing else! . . . We're going to be so happy, we'll have little Gerties runnin' all over the place . . . I got so many plans!"

Gertrude denies that she loves Harry, even though she often lets jealousy show when Harry pays attention to other women. She pushes Harry away, declares vehemently that she wants things between them to stay exactly as they are, even threatens Harry with the sawed-off baseball bat she keeps behind the bar for use on bums. She orders him to take out a pile of newspapers and bring in a case of liquor for the bar. *"He exits. She looks after him. Alone now, we see that Gertrude is wearing down, the confrontations with Harry are beginning to take their toll."*

To calm her nerves, Gertrude takes a swig of vodka, then prepares Corn Flakes and coffee, which she serves to Harry when he comes back. Harry remembers how his father, the driver of a coal truck, loved his Corn Flakes. He feels like talking, and he asks Gertrude about her husband. Grudgingly, she informs him that her husband was a sailor too, a bosun. Harry tries to pry her open on this subject. All she will tell him is that the man is still living, then she forces him to change the subject. They discuss needed repairs to The Sea Horse, and when Harry refers to his plan to buy a boat, she offers to pay him more to help her here at the bar than he could earn on his own, even with a boat.

Gertrude begins to believe she is making some headway talking Harry out of his foolishness about the boat and his dreams, and she decides to make a concession. She will bring no one upstairs from now on except Harry: ". . . Not that

I have since you been staying here. *(A little embarrassed that she revealed this fact, covers it.)* I mean, when ya like playing the tuba . . . you don't trade it in for a flute!" She even offers to open the place late today and spend the day upstairs with Harry; but at this point Harry has more than sex on his mind. He puts his arms around Gertrude, closes her eyes and persuades her to imagine that a ship is getting ready to put to sea, hauling up its anchor chain. Gertrude, in turn, believes that *"things are getting back to normal, and so grateful for it that she indulges him."* Harry imagines that the ship is now putting to sea, the propellor has begun to turn.

Harry gets up now, stands behind her chair, his arms around her.

HARRY: . . . . . We're out of the breakwater now . . . and you can feel the first roll . . . and you can smell the salt . . . *(Inhales deeply.)* . . . smell it, Gert? . . . Smell that salt?? . . . Bridge rings down all ahead half. *(Sounds three bells.)* . . . I'm down in the engine room, see . . . my hands on the throttles . . . I'm watching that PSI gauge holding steady at 450 . . . I get a bell, "Clang—clang." All ahead full!! *(He moves away, spinning an imaginary valve.)* I spin the throttle valve open!! I'm losin' pressure, I spin 'er back, I yell down to the boiler room . . . *(Stomps his foot on the floor, calls down to boiler room.)* Hey!! Come on, you guys!!! Main steam pressure is dropping!! Shove in another burner!! For Christ's sake, tell 'em Gert, we're losin' pressure!!

GERTRUDE *(having a great time):* Come on! come on! ya horse's ass! shove in another burner!!

HARRY: She's coming up now. *(To Gertrude.)* Watch the gauge, watch the gauge! . . . 430 . . . 440 . . . there she is!! There she is!!!

Both laugh.

GERTRUDE *(very excited, gets up):* What do I do?!? What do I do?!!?

HARRY *(moves to her, takes her hand):* Hell, Gert . . . you're the Captain!! . . . Captain blows the ship's whistle!

He takes her hand, makes the sound of the ship's whistle, pulling an imaginary rope.

Come on, you do it!

She joins in, both blowing the whistle. Then he blows the whistle in her face, getting her wet.

GERTRUDE *(breaks away, laughing):* I don't want to be the Captain!

HARRY *(laughing):* Sure ya do!

GERTRUDE: No, I want to be a seaman!

HARRY: No, you want to be a Captain!!

GERTRUDE: I want to be a *seaman!* I always have, ever since I was a little girl!

Gertrude's father used to bring her to sit on the end of this pier and watch the ships, longing to be a seaman some day. Harry raises the subject of Gertrude's husband again and assures her that now they are partners and he will protect her if the guy ever shows up again. Harry is still curious about The Sea Horse. Grudgingly Gertrude tells him the place was her father's, not her husband's. After her father died the place was boarded up, and at 18 Gertrude married a seaman who was good to her until he was barred from the union for drinking on duty and turned mean. Gertrude's husband pulled the boards off The Sea Horse and they moved into the loft upstairs. Gertrude hated it, especially when he would get drunk and beat her. She was pretty then, she admits, and finally her husband set her to waiting on tables: "I was good for business! . . . Yeah, real good . . . he left me alone one night . . . I had to close up . . . couple of guys kept hanging around, wouldn't leave . . . they slapped me to the floor and took turns on top of me . . . I think that's funny, don't you? . . . I mean, can you imagine anyone trying that now!"

When she told her husband, he just laughed. But she stayed on here and learned to make the business work. Gertrude senses that Harry is having his way with her in forcing her to tell him about her past; in a way, Harry is no different from her husband. Harry protests: "I'm a man!!! . . . I never hurt no one like that!!!" He insists that Gertrude loves him and should tell him so. This thought frightens Gertrude, and once again she takes up the sawed-off baseball bat to defend herself. Harry struggles with her, takes the bat away from her and orders her to calm down.

Gertrude cools off, but in doing so she calls out for her father and is led to admit that she still misses him terribly. He would tell her stories about the sea and about her dead mother, and give her a bell to ring in case she needed him, while he went inside to run The Sea Horse. He told her that The Sea Horse was no place for her, which made it very hard for Gertrude to move into the building at her husband's insistence.

Harry remembers something like that happened to him, too. As a devoutly religious little boy, he took it literally when a nun told him that every evil thought or deed formed a cobweb inside. Harry began to imagine himself sick with a mass of cobwebs until his father reassured him that the Sister didn't mean her words literally.

But Gertrude has memories even harder to bear: "I was sitting on the pier one day, doing my homework with some friends . . . waiting for my Dad to take me home. I heard all this shouting coming from the Horse. I saw my Dad throw this man out, a couple of other men came out too. This man was trying to hit my Dad . . . I got up and started running towards him . . . crying 'Daddy, Daddy!' My Dad turned to me, and the man stabbed him . . . he died . . . I held him, and he died."

For a long time afterward, Gertrude, who went to live with an aunt, could remember all the details of the incident but couldn't remember her own name. When she was grown, Gertrude would come down here to watch the ships, but she never went back inside The Sea Horse until her husband forced her to. After he walked out on their marriage, leaving the place debt-ridden, the customers would take advantage of Gertrude until she got angry and hit one of them with a bottle. After that, she demanded and received respect: ". . . And I didn't *need* . . . *anyone* . . . any more."

Harry goes to his seabag where he has concealed a box containing Gertrude's present, takes the box out and hands it to her. She refuses to open it, so Harry does so, as he tells her: "You could never be happy here, Gert . . . so we'll be leaving . . . No! Not to hide from anyone! . . . But to start fresh! . . . this is no place to bring up kids!" Harry takes the cover off the box and pulls out the present: an old-fashioned, lacy, frilly wedding dress. Gertrude just stares at Harry, hardly responding.

HARRY *(strongly, without anger):* . . . . . It's a wedding dress! I had it made special, with a lot of lace! I told the guy to put plenty 'a that on, 'cause you'd like it! *(Crossing to her.)* Ya see . . . I've been planning this for a long time now . . .

Lays the dress across one of the stools.

. . . and I know I made a lot of mistakes, I know that . . . but I got the hang of it now . . . ya see, I want you to marry me, have our kids and live with me! *(Quiet determination.)* And you can't tell me you don't love me . . . no matter what you do, something tells me you love me . . . it's all over you . . . you know I can see it in your face right now . . . even your back says you love me . . . don't ya?

GERTRUDE *(moved by his warmth, his sincerity):* All the years I've been down here, I never seen it once . . . where someone wasn't all bullshit . . . but maybe you changed . . .

HARRY: Oh, I did!

GERTRUDE *(gets up):* I don't know! . . . *Maybe* you have!

HARRY: Of course I have!!

GERTRUDE *(stops, terribly frustrated, trying not to hurt him. but believing it would never work):* I'd be too much for you!

HARRY: No, you wouldn't!!

GERTRUDE: Too many things happened!! . . .

HARRY: That stuff doesn't matter to me!!

GERTRUDE: I can't even have kids! *(A moment.)* I was hurt once.

A long pause. She sits at downstage center table.

. . . You don't want someone like me . . . I'm not right for what you want . . . I mean I can get ya laughing, and I know I'm a good bounce . . . but I'm not right for that other . . . family stuff. I like the good times too, and I wouldn't want to change that . . . but you'd never make it with me . . . I'm fat 'n' ugly . . . and it would get to ya . . . in time, it would get to ya . . . you'll make it, but not with me . . . you go.

A pause.

HARRY: When I was in Kobe, I saw this little joker hanging around the shipyard . . . just a wee tyke of a guy . . . you know he took to me right off . . . and I know he doesn't have anyone, and you'd like him . . . and if that didn't work out, I'm sure . . .

Turns, looks at her.

I know it's not gonna be easy, I know that . . . but we can do it!

Crosses to her.

And you're not fat! You're well built! And I don't ever want to hear you talking about yourself like that again!

Gertrude tries to pretend that she doesn't care, that she wants Harry to leave so that she can start her day's work, or that he can stay here on condition that he doesn't mention the subject of marriage again. Yet when Harry agrees disgustedly to abandon his dream of marriage with Gertrude, she cries "Talker!" at him again and again, more and more loudly. He can hardly bear this implied accusation that he has been pipe dreaming about his plans; in crying "Talker!" she is attacking Harry's very sincerity, which he wears on his sleeve and is all too painfully genuine.

Now furious, Harry stuffs his gear into his seabag and prepares to leave; he has finally had enough. Gertrude solicitously collects his cap and jacket and promises him that when he finally does come back some day with a wife and child she will break her lifelong rule and allow Harry's wife to enter The Sea Horse.

Gertrude goes upstairs to collect Harry's slicker, reminding him to take away the wedding dress. He cannot bear to put it back into the bag and throws it on a chair as Gertrude returns with his slicker. Harry stows the slicker in his seabag, puts on his cap, zips up his jacket, as Gertrude puts a rock 'n' roll number on the juke box. She tells him to leave the door open for her expected morning customers, as she goes behind the bar.

> *Harry puts his seabag over his shoulder, crosses to front door, stops a few moments, then he turns.*

HARRY: I ain't going! . . . *(He crosses to bar.)* You hear me?! . . . I said I ain't going!!

> *Gertrude crosses to juke box.*

. . . 'cause you need me!!

> *She turns the volume up full, the music is deafening. Harry throws down his seabag.*

No I ain't going!! You hear me!!

> *Takes off his cap and jacket, throws them down violently.*

YOU'RE GONNA MARRY ME!!! *(Crosses right up to her.)* YOU'RE GONNA MARRY ME!!!!

> *He goes to juke box, yanks out the plug. There is a dead silence.*

GERTRUDE *(quietly):* . . . I don't trust you . . .

HARRY *(crosses slowly toward her):* You will . . .

GERTRUDE: I don't trust you . . . I don't trust you . . .

> *Harry is moving close to her, Gertrude is backing away.*

I don't trust you, I don't trust you . . .

> *He gently takes her arms, drawing her close to him.*

I don't trust you . . .

> *She's in his arms now.*

HARRY: You will . . . I know you will!

> *Curtain.*

A GRAPHIC GLANCE

NOEL COWARD

RALPH CARTER AND VIRGINIA CAPERS (CENTER) SURROUNDED
BY ERNESTINE JACKSON, JOE MORTON, DEBORAH ALLEN AND
ROBERT JACKSON IN THE MUSICAL "RAISIN"

KARIN WOLFE (GIGI), AGNES MOOREHEAD, MARIA KARNILOVA,

ALFRED DRAKE AND DANIEL MASSEY IN THE LERNER AND LOEWE MUSICAL "GIGI"

"MUSIC! MUSIC!" WAS A CAVALCADE OF AMERICAN MUSIC
PRODUCED BY THE CITY CENTER OF MUSIC AND DRAMA

CAROL CHANNING AS LORELEI LEE IN THE MUSICAL "LORELEI"

GLORIA ROSSI, DAVID CRYER, CHRIS CALLAN, BRITT SWANSON, JERRY
REVIVAL OF SIGMUND ROMBERG'S OPERETTA "THE DESERT SONG"

DODGE, MICHAEL KERMOYAN AND SHEPPERD STRUDWICK IN THE

DAVID DOWNING, HATTIE WINSTON AND AL FREEMAN JR. IN THE NEGRO
ENSEMBLE COMPANY'S PRODUCTION OF "THE GREAT MACDADDY"

GEORGE GRIZZARD AND EILEEN HERLIE IN "CROWN MATRIMONIAL"

NICOL WILLIAMSON, CATHLEEN NESBITT, ELIZABETH WILSON,
THE REVIVAL OF CHEKHOV'S "UNCLE VANYA"

JULIE CHRISTIE, GEORGE C. SCOTT AND LILLIAN GISH IN

ZERO MOSTEL AS LEOPOLD BLOOM IN "ULYSSES IN NIGHTTOWN"

HENRY FONDA IN "CLARENCE DARROW"

HAL LINDEN, BARBARA MCNAIR, CAB CALLOWAY AND SHARRON

MILLER IN THE REVIVAL OF "THE PAJAMA GAME"

SAMMY DAVIS JR. IN THE REVUE "SAMMY"

JAMES WHITMORE IN "WILL ROGERS' U.S.A."

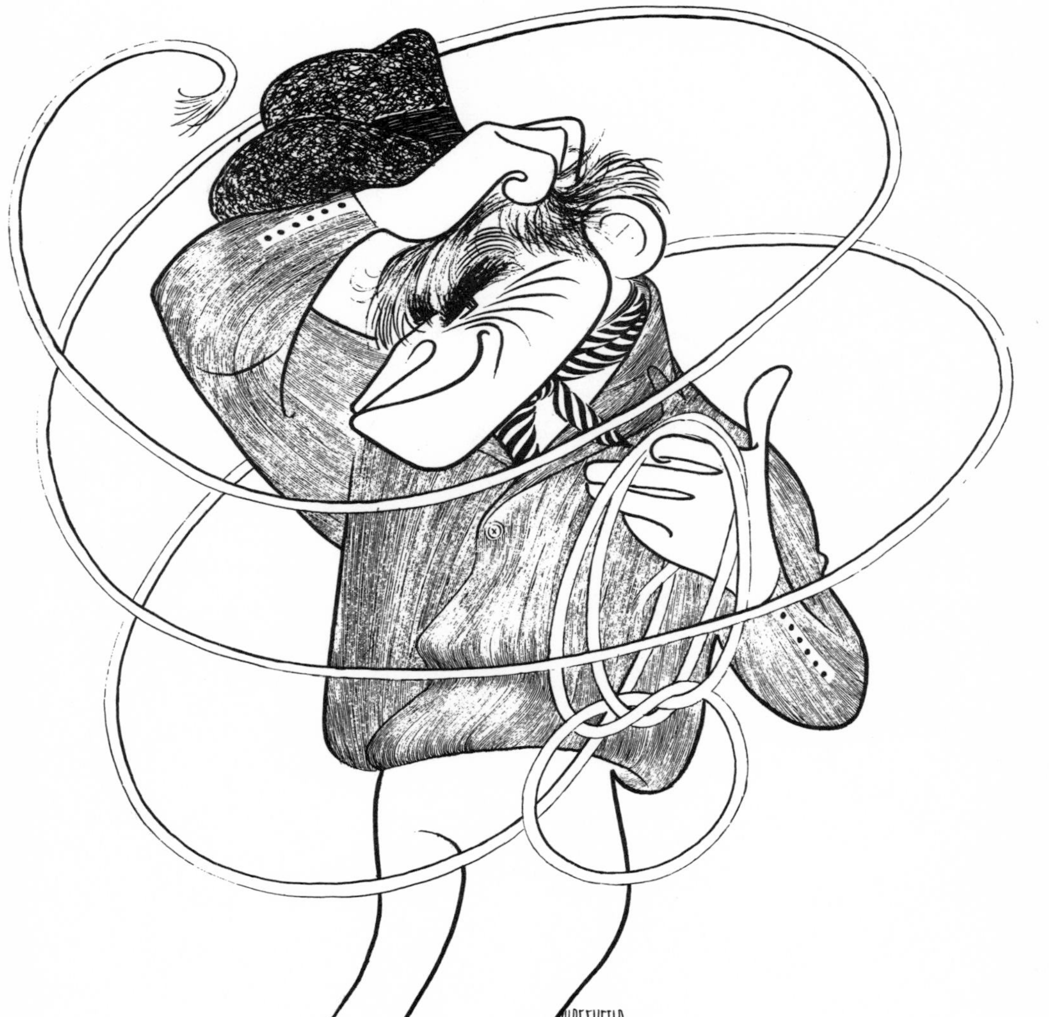

JULIE HARRIS AND CHARLES DURNING IN "THE AU PAIR MAN"

KAY BALLARD IN THE TITLE ROLE OF THE MUSICAL "MOLLY"

MICHAEL REDGRAVE IN THE ROYAL SHAKESPEARE COMPANY'S REVIVAL OF "THE HOLLOW CROWN" AT THE BROOKLYN ACADEMY OF MUSIC OPERA HOUSE

LYNN REDGRAVE AND GEORGE ROSE IN "MY FAT FRIEND"

MADELINE KAHN (CENTER) SURROUNDED BY FREDERICK COFFIN,
MARY WORONOV, CHARLES DURNING, CHARLOTTE RAE AND ROBERT
LOGGIA IN "BOOM BOOM ROOM"

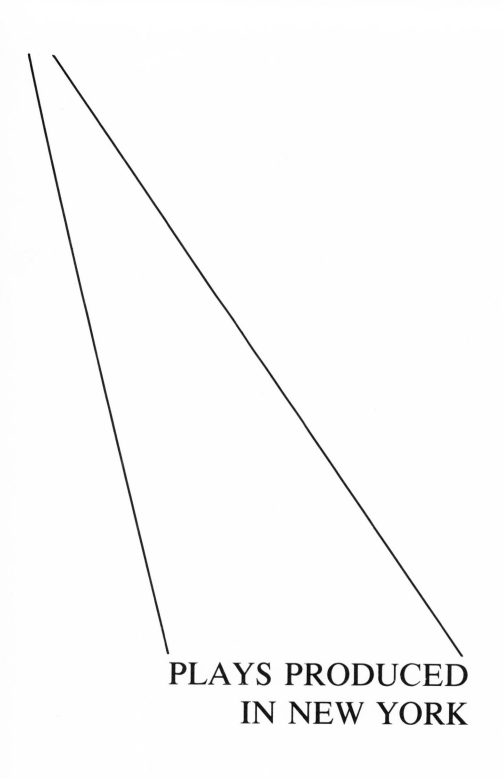

PLAYS PRODUCED
IN NEW YORK

PLAYS PRODUCED ON BROADWAY

Figures in parentheses following a play's title indicate number of performances. The figures are acquired directly from the production office in each case and do not include previews or extra non-profit performances.

Plays marked with an asterisk (*) were still running on June 3, 1974. Their number of performances is figured from opening night through May 31, 1974.

In a listing of a show's numbers—dances, sketches, musical scenes, etc.—the titles of songs are identified by their appearance in quotation marks (").

HOLDOVERS FROM PREVIOUS SEASONS

Plays which were running on June 1, 1973 are listed below. More detailed information about them appears in previous *Best Plays* volumes of appropriate years. Important cast changes since opening night are recorded in a section of this volume.

Sleuth (1,222). By Anthony Shaffer. Opened November 12, 1970. (Closed October 13, 1973)

Jesus Christ Superstar (720). Musical based on the last seven days in the life of Jesus of Nazareth; conceived for the stage by Tom O'Horgan; music by Andrew Lloyd Webber; lyrics by Tim Rice. Opened October 12, 1971. (Closed June 30, 1973)

The Prisoner of Second Avenue (780). By Neil Simon. Opened November 11, 1971. (Closed September 29, 1973)

* Grease (957). Musical with book, music and lyrics by Jim Jacobs and Warren Casey. Opened February 14, 1972.

Sugar (505). Musical based on the screen play *Some Like It Hot* by Billy Wilder and I.A.L. Diamond (based on a story by Robert Thoeren); book by Peter Stone; music by Jule Styne; lyrics by Bob Merrill. Opened April 9, 1972. (Closed June 23, 1973)

* Don't Bother Me, I Can't Cope (914). Musical revue by Micki Grant. Opened April 19, 1972.

That Championship Season (844). By Jason Miller. Opened May 2, 1972 off Broadway, where it played 144 performances through September 3, 1972; transferred to Broadway September 14, 1972 for 700 additional performances. (Closed April 21, 1974)

* Pippin (669). Musical with book by Roger O. Hirson; music and lyrics by Stephen Schwartz. Opened October 23, 1972.

The River Niger (400). By Joseph A. Walker. Opened December 5, 1972 off Broadway, where it played 120 performances through March 3, 1973; transferred to Broadway March 27, 1973 for 280 additional performances. (Closed November 25, 1973)

The Sunshine Boys (538). By Neil Simon. Opened December 20, 1972. (Closed April 21, 1974)

Finishing Touches (164). By Jean Kerr. Opened February 8, 1973. (Closed July 1, 1973)

* **A Little Night Music** (527). Musical suggested by Ingmar Bergman's film *Smiles of a Summer Night;* book by Hugh Wheeler; music and lyrics by Stephen Sondheim. Opened February 25, 1973.

The Changing Room (192). By David Storey. Opened March 6, 1973. (Closed August 18, 1973)

* **Irene** (590). Revival of the musical with book by Hugh Wheeler and Joseph Stein; from an adaptation by Harry Rigby; based on the original play by James Montgomery; music by Harry Tierney; lyrics by Joseph McCarthy; additional lyrics and music by Charles Gaynor and Otis Clements. Opened March 13, 1973.

Seesaw (296). Musical based on the play *Two for the Seesaw* by William Gibson; written by Michael Bennett; music by Cy Coleman; lyrics by Dorothy Fields. Opened March 18, 1973. (Closed December 8, 1973)

The Women (63). Revival of the play by Clare Boothe Luce. Opened April 25, 1973. (Closed June 17, 1973)

The Repertory Theater of Lincoln Center. 1972–73 schedule of four programs concluded with **A Streetcar Named Desire** (110). Revival of the play by Tennessee Williams. Opened April 26, 1973. (Closed July 29, 1973). Reopened at the St. James Theater on October 4, 1973 (see its entry in the "Plays Produced on Broadway" section of this volume).

Cyrano (49). Musical with book based on Anthony Burgess's adaptation of *Cyrano de Bergerac* by Edmond Rostand; music by Michael J. Lewis; lyrics by Anthony Burgess. Opened May 13, 1973. (Closed June 23, 1973)

Nash at Nine (21). Musical revue with verses and lyrics by Ogden Nash; conceived by Martin Charnin; music by Milton Rosenstock. Opened May 17, 1973. (Closed June 2, 1973)

Smith (17). Musical with book by Dean Fuller, Tony Hendra and Matt Dubey; music and lyrics by Matt Dubey and Dean Fuller; Opened May 19, 1973. (Closed June 3, 1973)

PLAYS PRODUCED, JUNE 1, 1973–MAY 31, 1974

Circle in the Square. 1972–73 schedule of four revivals concluded with **Uncle Vanya** (64). By Anton Chekhov; translated by Albert Todd and Mike Nichols. Produced by Circle in the Square, Inc., Theodore Mann artistic director, Paul Libin managing director, at the Circle in the Square Joseph E. Levine Theater. Opened June 4, 1973. (Closed July 28, 1973; see note)

Marina	Lillian Gish	Sonya	Elizabeth Wilson
Michael Astrov	George C. Scott	Elena	Julie Christie
Ivan Voinitsky	Nicol Williamson·	Mrs. Voinitsky	Cathleen Nesbitt
Alexander Serebryakov	Barnard Hughes	Yefim	Rod Loomis
Ilya Telyegin	Conrad Bain	Workmen	Tom Tarpey, R. Mack Miller

Standbys: Misses Gish, Nesbitt—Anne Ives; Miss Wilson—Joanna Merlin; Miss Christie—Taina Elg; Mr. Scott—Michael Higgins. Understudies: Mr. Hughes—R. Mack Miller; Mr. Bain—Tom Tarpey.

Directed by Mike Nichols; scenery and costumes, Tony Walton; lighting, Jules Fisher; production stage manager, Randall Brooks; press, Merle Debuskey, Leo Stern.

Place: Serebryakov's estate. The play was presented in two parts.

The most recent professional New York revivals of *Uncle Vanya* were the Roundabout's off Broadway 1/24/71 for 50 performances and David Ross's off Broadway during the season of 1955–56. Its most recent Broadway revival was in Old Vic repertory 5/13/46 for 5 performances.

Note: *Uncle Vanya* played one extra performance 7/29/73 for the benefit of the Actors Fund.

The Desert Song (15). Musical revival with book and lyrics by Otto Harbach, Oscar Hammerstein II and Frank Mandel; music by Sigmund Romberg. Produced by Moe Septee in association with Jack L. Wolgin and Victor H. Potamkin in the Lehman Engel production at the Uris Theater. Opened September 5, 1973. (Closed September 16, 1973)

Mindar . . . . .Nicholas Scarpinati	Sgt. Boussac . . . . William Leyerle
Sid El Kar . . . . .John Ribecchi	Azuri . . . . Gloria Rossi
Hadji . . . . Dick Ensslen	Edith . . . . .Osceola Davis
Palace Guard . . .Frederick G. Sampson III	Susan . . . . .Britt Swanson
Hassi . . . . .Mandigo Shaka	Gen. Birabeau . . . . . . Shepperd Strudwick
Neri . . . . Ruby Greene Aspinall	(Margot Bonvalet) . . . . Chris Callan,
Red Shadow; Pierre Birabeau . . David Cryer	Carol Jeanne Tenney
Benjamin Kidd . . . . .Jerry Dodge	Clementina . . . . Gloria Zaglool
Capt. Paul Fontaine . . . . . Stanley Grover	Ali Ben Ali . . . . .Michael Kermoyan
Lt. Davergne . . . . Kent Cottam	

(Parentheses indicate role in which the actresses alternated, Miss Tenney playing Wednesday and Saturday matinee performances)

Azuri Dancing Girls: Kita Bouroff, Lana Caradimas, Urylee Leonardos, Jane Lucas, Sandra Mannis, Dundi Wright.

Ensemble: Ruby Greene Aspinall, Marsha Bagwell, Rita Oney Best, Kita Bouroff, Lana Caradimas, Jacqueline Clark, Osceola Davis, Karen Ford, Bonnie Hinson, Urylee Leonardos, Rona Leslie, Jane Lucas, Sandra Mannis, Berdeen E. Pigorsh, Brenda Schaffer, Dundi Wright, Donald Coleman, Bill Collins, Austin Colyer, Kent Cottam, Ronald De Felice, Dennis Dohman, Dick Ensslen, William Leyerle, Frederick G. Sampson III, Nicholas Scarpinati, Peter Schroeder, Arthur Shaffer, Anthony Tamburello, David Vogel, David Weatherspoon.

Principal Understudies: Mr. Cryer—Stanley Grover; Misses Callan, Tenney—Gloria Zaglool; Mr. Strudwick—David Vogel; Messrs. Kermoyan, Ensslen—Anthony Tamburello; Mr. Grover—Peter Schroeder.

Directed by Henry Butler; choreography, David Nillo; musical direction, Al Cavaliere; scenery and lighting, Clarke Dunham; costumes, Sara Brook; dance arrangements, Dorothea Freitag; production stage manager, Lee Murray; stage manager, Patricia Drylie; press, Ellen Levene, Betty Lee Hunt Associates.

Time: The 1930s. Place: Northern Africa.

This operetta was first produced on Broadway 11/30/26 for 228 performances and was previously revived at the City Center 1/8/46 for 45 performances.

ACT I

Scene 1: Retreat of the Red Shadow in the Riff Mountains, evening
"Prelude," "Feasting Song" . . . . Sid, Riffs
"The Riff Song" . . . . Red Shadow, Sid, Riffs
"Feasting Song" (Reprise) . . . . Sid, Riffs
"The Riff Song" (Reprise) . . . . Red Shadow, Sid
"Margot" . . . . Paul, Soldiers
Scene 2: Outside Gen. Birabeau's house, the same evening
"Has Anybody Seen My Bennie?" . . . . Susan
(new lyrics by Edward Smith)
Scene 3: A room in Gen. Birabeau's house, a few minutes later
"Why Did We Marry Soldiers?" . . . . French Girls

"French Military Marching Song" . . . . Margot, French Girls, Soldiers
"Romance" . . . . Margot, French Girls
"Then You Will Know" . . . . Margot, Pierre, Ensemble
"I Want a Kiss" . . . . Margot, Pierre, Paul, Ensemble
"It" . . . . Bennie, Susan
  (new lyrics by Edward Smith)
"The Desert Song" . . . . Red Shadow, Margot
Azuri Dance . . . . Azuri, Azuri Girls
  "Soft as a Pigeon" . . . . Sid, Paul Ensemble
  "The Desert Song" (Reprise) . . . . Red Shadow, Margot, Ensemble
Entr'acte

ACT II

Scene 1: The harem of Ali Ben Ali, afternoon of the following day
  "My Little Castagnette" . . . . Clementina, Spanish Girls
  "Song of the Brass Key" . . . . Clementina, Spanish Girls
  "One Good Boy Gone Wrong" . . . . Bennie, Clementina
    (new lyrics by Edward Smith)
Eastern and Western Love
  "Let Love Go" . . . . Ali, Male Ensemble
  "One Flower in Your Garden" . . . . Sid, Male Ensemble
  "One Alone" . . . . Red Shadow, Sid, Ali, Male Ensemble
Scene 2: A corridor, a few minutes later
Scene 3: The room of the Silken Couch, a few minutes later
  "The Sabre Song" . . . . Margot, Red Shadow
  "The Desert Song" (Reprise) . . . . Margot, Red Shadow
Scene 4: Edge of the desert, the following morning half an hour before dawn
  "One Alone" (Reprise) . . . . Red Shadow, Male Ensemble
Scene 5: A room in Gen. Birabeau's house, two days later
  "The Desert Song" (Reprise) . . . . Margot
  "It" (Reprise) . . . . Bennie, Susan
    (new lyrics by Edward Smith)
Dance of Triumph . . . . Azuri
"One Alone" (Reprise) . . . . Pierre, Margot

* **Circle in the Square.** 1973–74 schedule of four programs. **The Waltz of the Toreadors**
(85). Revival of the play by Jean Anouilh; translated by Lucienne Hill. Opened September
13, 1973. (Closed November 25, 1973) **The Iceman Cometh** (85). Revival of the play by
Eugene O'Neill. Opened December 13, 1973. (Closed February 24, 1974) **An American
Millionaire** (17). By Murray Schisgal. Opened April 20, 1974. (Closed May 5, 1974)
* **Scapino** (15). Adapted from Molière's *Les Fourberies de Scapin* in The National Theater
of Great Britain Young Vic production. Opened May 18, 1974. Produced by Circle in the
Square, Inc., Theodore Mann artistic director, Paul Libin managing director, at the Circle
in the Square Joseph E. Levine Theater.

THE WALTZ OF THE TOREADORS

Mme. St. Pe	. . . . Anne Jackson	Leontine	. . . . Mary Hara
Gen. St. Pe	. . . . Eli Wallach	Mlle. de Ste. Euverte	. . Diana Van Der Vlis
Gaston	. . . . Benjamin Masters	Mme. Dupont-Fredaine	. . . . Miriam Burton
Sidonia	. . . . Laura Esterman	Father Ambrose	. . . . . . Earl Montgomery
Estelle	. . . . Maia Danziger	Pamela	. . . . Charon Lee Cohen
Dr. Bonfant	. . . . William Roerick		

Understudies: Miss Jackson—Mary Hara; Miss Van Der Vlis—Laura Esterman; Misses Esterman,
Danziger—Charon Lee Cohen; Misses Cohen, Hara, Burton—Nancy Sellin; Messrs. Masters, Mont-
gomery—Thomas Vivian.
  Directed by Brian Murray; scenery, Clarke Dunham; costumes, Joseph F. Bella; lighting, Thomas
Skelton; production stage manager, Gerald Nobles; press, Merle Debuskey, Leo Stern.

Place: The study of Gen. St. Pe and his wife's adjoining bedroom in a small garrison town somewhere in southern France. Act I, Scene 1: The study, a spring morning. Scene 2: The study, a few minutes later. Act II, Scene 1: The study, later that afternoon. Scene 2: The bedroom, immediately following. Act III: The study, that evening.

The Waltz of the Toreadors was first produced on Broadway 1/17/57 for 132 performances, in this same translation, and was named a Best Play of its season and won the Critics Award for best foreign play. It was revived on Broadway the following season 3/4/58 for 31 performances and was done off Broadway during the 1958–59 and 1959–60 seasons.

THE ICEMAN COMETH

Rocky Pioggi . . . . .Joseph Ragno	Pat McGloin . . . . Rex Everhart
Larry Slade . . . . Michael Higgins	Ed Mosher . . . . Patrick Hines
Hugo Kalmar . . . . David Margulies	Margie . . . . Marcia Savella
Willie Oban . . . . .Walter McGinn	Pearl . . . . Jenny O'Hara
Harry Hope . . . . .Stefan Gierasch	Cora . . . . Lois Smith
Joe Mott . . . . Arthur French	Chuck Morello . . . . . .Pierrino Mascarino
Don Parritt . . . . Stephen McHattie	Theodore Hickman . . . . James Earl Jones
Cecil Lewis . . . . Jack Gwillim	Moran . . . . .Gene Fanning
Piet Wetjoen . . . . George Ebeling	Lieb . . . . Ronald Siebert
James Cameron . . . . Tom Aldredge	

General understudies: Gene Fanning, Ronald Siebert, Robin Kronstadt.

Directed by Theodore Mann; scenery, Clarke Dunham; costumes, Carrie F. Robbins; lighting, Jules Fisher; production stage manager, Randall Brooks.

Time: Summer, 1912. Place: The back room of the bar at Harry Hope's on the downtown West Side of New York. Act I: Early morning. Act II: Around midnight of the same day. Act III: Morning of the following day. Act IV: Around 1:30 the next day. The play was presented in three parts, with intermissions following Acts I and II.

O'Neill's play was first presented on Broadway 10/9/46 for 136 performances and was named a Best Play of its season. It was revived off Broadway by Circle in the Square during the 1955–56 season with Jason Robards as Hickey (Theodore Hickman).

AN AMERICAN MILLIONAIRE

Jake Jackson . . . . .Joseph Bova	Professor Bobby Rudetsky . Austin Pendleton
Nathaniel Schwab . . . . Paul Sorvino	Arnold Brody . . . . .Bob Dishy
Messenger . . . . Joshua Mostel	Jennifer Schwab . . . . .Lee Lawson
Debbie Schwab . . . . Linda Eskenas	

Directed by Theodore Mann; scenery, Douglas W. Schmidt; costumes, Theoni V. Aldredge; lighting, Martin Aronstein; production stage manager, Randall Brooks; stage manager, Maxine Taylor; press, Merle Debuskey, Susan L. Schulman.

Time: The present, an early October evening. Place: The suburban home of Nathaniel Schwab. The play was presented in two parts.

A circus of zany, absurdist comedy characters cavorting around a millionaire whose life is being threatened in a number of ways.

SCAPINO

Scapino . . . . Jim Dale	Giacinta . . . . Tammy Ustinov
Headwaiter . . . . Hugh Hastings	Argante . . . . Ian Trigger
Waiter . . . . .Alan Coates	Geronte . . . . .Paul Brooke
Waitress . . . . Jenny Austen	Leandro . . . . .Jeremy James-Taylor
Carlo . . . . Raymond Platt	Zerbinetta . . . . .Cleo Sylvestre
Ottavio . . . . .Christopher Hastings	Nurse . . . . .Lotti Taylor
Sylvestro . . . . Gavin Reed	

Directed by Frank Dunlop; designed by Carl Toms; lighting, David Watson; music, Jim Dale; production stage manager, Lawrence Spiegel; stage manager, Gordon Monsen.

Place: Naples. The play was presented in two parts.

This Young Vic production of *Scapino* appeared in New York earlier this season in an off-Broadway presentation in repertory at the Brooklyn Academy of Music, 3/12/74 for 10 performances; see its entry in the "Plays Produced off Broadway" section of this volume.

Melanie Chartoff replaced Tammy Ustinov.

Crown Matrimonial (79). By Royce Ryton. Produced by Lester Osterman Productions (Lester Osterman and Richard Horner) in association with Michael Codron at the Helen Hayes Theater. Opened October 2, 1973. (Closed December 9, 1973)

Queen Mary	Eileen Herlie	Mary, Princess Royal	Paddy Croft
Page	Richard Sterne	Duchess of Gloucester	Elizabeth Swain
Lady-in-Waiting	Eleanor Phelps	Duke of York	Patrick Horgan
Lady-in-Waiting	Enid Rodgers	Duchess of York	Ruth Hunt
King Edward VIII	George Grizzard		

Standbys: Miss Herlie—Carol Teitel; Mr. Grizzard—Anthony Call; Misses Croft, Hunt, Swain—Diana Kirkwood.

Directed by Peter Dews; scenery and costumes, Finlay James; lighting, Neil Peter Jampolis; production stage manager, Ben Janney; stage manager, Richard Sterne; press, Seymour Krawitz, Patricia McLean Krawitz.

Place: Queen Mary's private sitting room on the second floor of Marlborough House, overlooking the Mall, in London. Act I, Scene 1: Late morning, September 1936. Scene 2: Before dinner, November 1936. Scene 3: After dinner, the same night. Act II, Scene 1: Late evening, two weeks later. Scene 2: Early evening, two days later. Scene 3: An afternoon in November 1945.

Crown Matrimonial views the persons and events surrounding the abdication of King Edward VIII (later the Duke of Windsor) from the point of view of the ex-King's mother. A foreign play previously produced in London.

A Streetcar Named Desire (53). Return engagement of a revival of the play by Tennessee Williams. Produced by Jules Irving in association with Lucille Lortel and Alan Mandell, by arrangement with Lincoln Center for the Performing Arts, at the St. James Theater, Opened October 4, 1973. (Closed November 18, 1973)

A Woman	Rosetta LeNoire	Steve Hubbell	Robert Symonds
Stanley Kowalski	Alan Feinstein	Pablo Gonzales	Santos Morales
Harold Mitchell	John Newton	Young Collector	Alan Cauldwell
Stella Kowalski	Barbara Eda-Young	Mexican Woman	Antonia Rey
Eunice Hubbell	Priscilla Pointer	Doctor	Ray Fry
Blanche Du Bois	Lois Nettleton	Nurse	Sandra Seacat

Habitues of the Quarter: Robert Phalen, Alyce E. Webb, Frank Dwyer.

Directed by Jules Irving; scenery, Douglas W. Schmidt; lighting, John Gleason; costumes, Nancy Potts; music, Cathy MacDonald; sound, Gary Harris; production stage manager, Frank Bayer; stage manager, Barbara-Mae Phillips; press, Sol Jacobson, Lewis Harmon.

Time: Spring, summer and early fall. Place: New Orleans. The play was presented in two parts.

This is a repeat production, under Jules Irving's direction with a different cast, of last season's Lincoln Center revival of this play under Ellis Rabb's direction 4/26/73 for 110 performances.

* Raisin (265). Musical based on Lorraine Hansberry's *A Raisin in the Sun;* book by Robert Nemiroff and Charlotte Zaltzberg; music by Judd Woldin; lyrics by Robert Brittan. Produced by Robert Nemiroff at the Forty-sixth Street Theater. Opened October 18, 1973.

Pusher	Al Perryman	Beneatha Younger	Deborah Allen
Victim	Loretta Abbott	Lena Younger	Virginia Capers
Ruth Younger	Ernestine Jackson	Bar Girl	Elaine Beener
Travis Younger	Ralph Carter	Bobo Jones	Ted Ross
Mrs. Johnson	Helen Martin	Willie Harris	Walter P. Brown
Walter Lee Younger	Joe Morton	Joseph Asagai	Robert Jackson

African Drummer . . . . Chief Bey   Pastor's Wife . . . . Marenda Perry
Pastor . . . . Herb Downer   Karl Lindner . . . . Richard Sanders

People of the Southside: Chuck Thorpes, Eugene Little, Karen Burke, Zelda Pulliam, Elaine
Beener, Renee Rose, Paul Carrington, Marenda Perry, Gloria Turner, Don Jay, Glenn Brooks,
Marilyn Hamilton.

Understudies: Miss Jackson—Gloria Turner; Master Carter—Paul Carrington; Messrs. Morton,
Jackson—Herb Downer; Miss Allen—Renee Rose; Misses Capers, Martin—Marenda Perry; Mr.
Sanders—Will Mott; Messrs. Brown, Ross, Downer—Don Jay.

Directed and choreographed by Donald McKayle; musical director and conductor, Howard A.
Roberts; scenery, Robert U. Taylor; costumes, Bernard Johnson; lighting, William Mintzer; orches-
trations, Al Cohn, Robert Freedman; vocal arrangements, Joyce Brown, Howard A. Roberts; dance
arrangements, Judd Woldin; incidental arrangements, Dorothea Freitag; associate producers, Sydney
Lewis, Jack Friel; production stage manager, Helaine Head; production associates, Irving Weltzer,
Will Mott; stage manager, Nate Barnett; press, Max Eisen, Maurice Turet.

Time: The 1950s. Place: Chicago.

Raisin is a musicalization of Miss Hansberry's play about a black family making its way in
pre-civil-rights-movement Chicago, first produced 3/11/59 for 530 performances on Broadway,
where it was named a Best Play of its season and received the Drama Critics Award as best American
play. The musical version was previously produced at the Arena Stage in Washington, D.C.

ACT I

Prologue . . . . Company
"Man Say" . . . . Walter Lee
"Whose Little Angry Man" . . . . Ruth
"Runnin' to Meet the Man" . . . . Walter Lee, Company
"A Whole Lotta Sunlight" . . . . Mama
"Booze" . . . . Bar Girl, Bobo, Walter Lee, Willie, Company
"Alaiyo" . . . . Asagai, Beneatha
"African Dance" . . . . Beneatha, Walter, Company
"Sweet Time" . . . . Ruth, Walter Lee
"You Done Right" . . . . Walter Lee
   (Recording of "Same Old Color Scheme" sung by Elaine Beener)

ACT II

"He Come Down This Morning" . . . . Pastor, Pastor's Wife, Mama, Mrs. Johnson,
                                                               Ruth, Travis, Company
"It's a Deal" . . . . Walter Lee
"Sweet Time" (Reprise) . . . . Ruth, Walter Lee
"Sidewalk Tree" . . . . Travis
"Not Anymore" . . . . Walter Lee, Ruth, Beneatha
"Alaiyo" (Reprise) . . . . Asagai
"It's a Deal" (Reprise) . . . . Walter Lee
"Measure the Valleys" . . . . Mama
"He Come Down This Morning" (Reprise)

Children of the Wind (6). By Jerry Devine. Produced by Shepard Traube and Buff Cobb
at the Belasco Theater. Opened October 24, 1973. (Closed October 27, 1973)

Daniel A. Brophy . . . . . . James Callahan   John Brophy . . . . Barry Goss
May Walker . . . . Ann Thomas   Marvo the Wonder Dog . . . . Himself
Kitty Brophy . . . . Sarah Hardy

Understudies: Mr. Callahan—Ray Parker; Misses Thomas, Hardy—Nancy Devlin; Mr. Goss—
John Page.

Directed by Shepard Traube; scenery and lighting, Leo Kerz; costumes, Sara Brook; production
stage manager, Larry Forde; stage manager, Ray Parker; press, Sol Jacobson, Lewis Harmon.

Time: The early 1930s. Place: The front parlor of a theatrical boarding house in New York City.
Act I, Scene 1: A late summer day. Scene 2: A few hours later. Act II, Scene 1: Several weeks later.

Scene 2: Two days later. Act III, Scene 1: The following evening. Scene 2: Later that evening. Scene 3: The next night.

An actor struggles with career, alcohol and family problems.

Veronica's Room (75). By Ira Levin. Produced by Morton Gottlieb at The Music Box. Opened October 25, 1973. (Closed December 29, 1973)

The Woman	Eileen Heckart	The Girl	Regina Baff
The Man	Arthur Kennedy	The Young Man	Kipp Osborne

Standbys: Miss Heckart—Nancy Marchand; Mr. Kennedy—Sydney Walker; Miss Baff—Amy Levitt; Mr. Osborne—Everett McGill

Directed by Ellis Rabb; scenery, Douglas W. Schmidt; costumes, Nancy Potts; lighting, John Gleason; stage manager, Everett McGill; press, Ruth Cage, Joshua Ellis.

Time: The present, an evening in spring. Place: A room in a house about half an hour's drive from Boston.

Thriller about a strange masquerade brought to a fatal conclusion by warped and menacing evildoers.

Molly (68). Musical based on characters from "The Goldbergs" by Gertrude Berg; book by Louis Garfinkle and Leonard Adelson; music by Jerry Livingston; lyrics by Leonard Adelson and Mack David. Produced by Don Saxon, Don Kaufman and George Daley in association with Complex IV at the Alvin Theater. Opened November 1, 1973. (Closed December 29, 1973)

Angelina Frazini	Suzanne Walker	Michael Stone	Swen Swenson
Mrs. Sullivan	Camilla Ashland	Cousin Simon	Mitchell Jason
Mr. Sullivan	Eddie Phillips	Max	Martin Garner
Mrs. Frazini	Justine Johnston	Ensemble:	
Molly	Kay Ballard	Skeeter	Don Bonnell
Mrs. Kramer	Molly Stark	Ralph	Rodney Griffin
Belle Seidenschneer	Ruth Manning	Reggie	Bob Heath
Mrs. Bloom	Hazel Weber Steck	Harold	Don Percassi
Mrs. Dutton	Toni Darnay	Vinnie	Sal Pernice
Rosalie	Lisa Rochelle	Sheala	Linda Rose
Jake	Lee Wallace	George	Leland Schwantes
Uncle David	Eli Mintz	Walter	Gerald Teijelo
Sammy	Daniel Fortus	Ellen	Mimi Wallace
Stella Hazelcorn	Connie Day	Sarah	Miriam Welch

Understudies: Miss Ballard—Molly Stark; Mr. Wallace—Mitchell Jason; Messrs. Mintz, Jason—Martin Garner; Mr. Fortus—Bob Heath; Miss Rochelle—Ellie Smith; Messrs. Swenson, Garner—Gerald Teijelo; Miss Day—Miriam Welch; Mr. Phillips—Don Percassi; Misses Manning, Steck, Johnston, Stark, Ashland—Toni Darnay.

Directed by Alan Arkin; choreography, Grover Dale; musical direction and vocal arrangements, Jerry Goldberg; scenery Marsha L. Eck; costumes, Carrie F. Robbins; lighting, Jules Fisher; sound, Gary Harris; orchestrations, Eddie Sauter; dance arrangements, Arnold Gross; associate producers, Larry Fallon, Richard Vonella; musical consultant, Ronald Snyder; production stage manager, Martin Gold; stage manager, Jean Weigel; press, Saul Richman, Sara Altshul.

Time: Spring 1933. Place: The Bronx.

The lovable Molly Goldberg of radio fame guides her children Samuel and Rosalie through adolescence, her husband Jake through unemployment and her entire Bronx neighborhood through the Depression and its attendant but—for Molly—always solvable problems.

ACT I

(Lyrics by Leonard Adelson unless otherwise specified)
Scene 1
"There's a New Deal on the Way" .... Angelina, Company
"If Everyone Got What They Wanted" .... Molly, Company

Scene 2: The Goldberg apartment
"A Piece of the Rainbow" . . . . Molly
Scene 3: The front sidewalk
"Cahoots" . . . . Michael, Molly
Scene 4: The rooftop
"Sullivan's Got a Job" . . . . Company
    (lyrics by Mack David)
"In Your Eyes" . . . . Sammy
Scene 5: The front sidewalk
"Cahoots" (Reprise) . . . . .Belle, Molly
Scene 6: Belle's apartment
Scene 7: A street
Scene 8: The Goldberg apartment
"High Class Ladies and Elegant Gentlemen" . . . . .Michael, Stella, Goldbergs
"So I'll Tell Him" . . . . Molly
Scene 9: The Goldberg apartment, the following day
"Appointments" . . . . Uncle David
    (lyrics by Mack David)
"There's Gold on the Trees" . . . . .Jake, Molly, Company

ACT II

Scene 1: The Mandarin Palace
"The Mandarin Palace on the Grand Concourse" . . . . Company
"I Want to Share It With You" . . . . Michael, Stella, Company
Scene 2: Outside the Mandarin Palace
"In Your Eyes" (Reprise) . . . . Sammy
Scene 3: The Goldberg apartment
"I Was There" . . . . Molly, Jake
"Oak Leaf Memorial Park" . . . . Molly
    (lyrics by Mack David)
"If Everyone Got What They Wanted" (Reprise) . . . . Uncle David, Rosalie
"I See a Man" . . . . Molly
    (lyrics uncredited)
Scene 4: The Goldberg kitchen
Scene 5: The Goldberg apartment
"The Tremont Avenue Cruisewear Fashion Show" . . . . Company
    (lyrics by Mack David)
"I've Got a Molly" . . . . Jake
    (lyrics by Mack David)
"Go in the Best of Health" . . . . Molly
    (lyrics by Mack David)

Full Circle (21). By Erich Maria Remarque; adapted by Peter Stone. Produced by Otto Preminger and The John F. Kennedy Center at the ANTA Theater. Opened November 7, 1973. (Closed November 24, 1973)

Anna . . . . Bibi Andersson   Mack; Russian Sergeant . . . . . Peter Weller
Grete . . . . Linda Carlson   Schmidt . . . . .Josef Sommer
Koerner . . . . .Max Brandt   Katz . . . . .James Tolkan
Rohde . . . . .Leonard Nimoy   Russian Captain . . . . .David Ackroyd
Maurer; Russian Soldier . . . . . Stan Wiklin

Understudies: Misses Andersson, Carlson—Paula Wagner; Mr. Nimoy—David Ackroyd; Mr. Sommer—Stan Wiklin; Mr. Ackroyd—Peter Weller; Messrs. Brandt, Tolkan, Wiklin, Weller—Marnel Sumner.
Directed by Otto Preminger; scenery, Robin Wagner; costumes, Hope Bryce; lighting, Jules Fisher; sound, Gary Harris; produced for Kennedy Center Productions, Inc. by Roger L. Stevens; associate producer, Bud Rosenthal; stage manager, William Dodds; press, Frank Goodman, Arlene Wolf.
Time: April 30 and May 1, 1945. Place: A third-floor room in Berlin. The play was presented without intermission.

Drama of the fall of Berlin drawing ironic parallels between the defeated Nazis and the victorious Communists. A foreign play previously produced in Germany and Washington, D.C.

* New York Shakespeare Festival Lincoln Center. Schedule of five programs. **Boom Boom Room** (37). By David Rabe. Opened November 8, 1973. (Closed December 9, 1973). **The Au Pair Man** (37). By Hugh Leonard. Opened December 27, 1973. (Closed January 27, 1974) **What the Wine-Sellers Buy** (37). By Ron Milner. Opened February 14, 1974. (Closed March 17, 1974) **The Dance of Death** (37). Revival of the play by August Strindberg: adapted by A. J. Antoon from the Elizabeth Sprigge translation. Opened April 4, 1974. (Closed May 5, 1974) *** Short Eyes** (80; see note). By Miguel Piñero. Opened May 23, 1974. Produced by New York Shakespeare Festival Lincoln Center, Joseph Papp producer, at the Vivian Beaumont Theater.

ALL PLAYS—Associate producer, Bernard Gersten; press, Merle Debuskey, Faith Geer.

BOOM BOOM ROOM

Chrissy	Madeline Kahn	Harold	Charles Durning
Susan	Mary Woronov	Guy	Peter Bartlett
Vikki	Margaret Davies	Eric	Michael Kell
Melissa	Barbara Monte-Britton	Al	Robert Loggia
Sally	Cissy Colpitts	Ralphie	Frederick Coffin
Carol	Madeleine Swift	LeRoy; Man	Warren Finnerty
Eileen	Lani Sundsten	Helen	Charlotte Rae

Standby: Mr. Durning—Will Hare. Understudies: Miss Kahn—Lynne Lipton; Miss Rae—Sloane Shelton; Miss Woronov—Barbara Monte-Britton; Messrs. Loggia, Coffin—Jack Ryland; Mr. Durning—Warren Finnerty; Misses Monte-Britton, Colpitts—Margaret Davies; Miss Davies—Madeleine Swift; Messrs. Bartlett, Kell—John Spencer.

Directed by Joseph Papp; scenery, Santo Loquasto; costumes, Theoni V. Aldredge; lighting, Martin Aronstein; sound, Roger Jay; go go dances staged by Raymond Bussey; production stage manager, D.W. Koehler; stage manager, Jeff Hamlin.

Time: 1967. Place: Philadelphia. The play was presented in three parts.

The life of a go-go girl viewed as one of the dead ends of the human experience. Joseph Papp took over the direction from Julie Bovasso in the final week of rehearsal.

THE AU PAIR MAN

Mrs. Rogers	Julie Harris	Eugene Hartigan .... Charles Durning

Standbys: Miss Harris—Betty Miller; Mr. Durning—Curt Dawson.

Directed by Gerald Freedman; scenery, John Conklin; costumes, Theoni V. Aldredge; lighting, Martin Aronstein; special sound, James Reichert; production stage manager, Dean Compton; stage manager, John Beven.

Place: The home of Mrs. Elizabeth Rogers, London, England. Act I: Sometime in the not-too-distant present. Act II, Scene 1: A few months later. Scene 2: Several months later. Act III: Sometime later.

An allegory of the relationship between crumbling England and exploited Ireland, as a queenly woman living in seedy grandeur takes in a rough-edged "au pair" man, shaping and forcing him to various household chores. A foreign (Irish) play previously produced in London.

WHAT THE WINE-SELLERS BUY

Slim; Cab Driver	Steve Laws	Hustler; Old Bob	Frank Adu
Tate; Pete	Ron Rayford	Voice (offstage); Mrs. Harris	Jean DuShon
Steve Carlton	Glynn Turman	Jim Aaron	Sonny Jim Gaines
Joe	Ray Vitte	Melvin	Lonny Stevens
Rico	Dick A. Williams	Francis	Berlinda Tolbert
Mrs. Laura Carlton	Marilyn B. Coleman	Helen	Debbie Morgan
Mae Harris	Loretta Greene	Marilyn	Sheilah Goldsmith

Phyllis; Make-up	Starletta Depaur	Candy; Mrs. Copeland	.Gloria Edwards
Red	Kyle Duncan	George	. . Kirk Kirksey
Hunt	Harris David	White Cop; Coach	. Bill Wintersole
Bill	Herbert Rice	Black Cop	Garrett Morris

Understudies: Mr. Williams—Frank Adu; Mr. Turman—Herbert Rice; Miss Greene—Berlinda Tolbert; Miss Coleman—Jean DuShon; Miss Edwards—Sheilah Goldsmith; Mr. Adu—Steve Laws; Mr. Gaines—Garrett Morris; Mr. Stevens—Ron Rayford; Messrs. Vitte, Kirksey—Harris David; Miss DuShon—Starletta Depaur; Miss Depaur—Debbie Morgan; Mr. Laws—Kirk Kirksey; Mr. Rayford—Lonny Stevens.

Directed by Michael Schultz; scenery, Santo Loquasto; lighting, Martin Aronstein; costumes, Judy Dearing, supervised by Edward Burbridge; production stage manager, D.W. Koehler; stage manager, Fred Seagraves.

Time: Now. Place: Detroit, Michigan. The play was presented in three parts.

Young man growing up in the black ghetto is tempted by the apparently large material rewards of a life as a pimp and drug-pusher.

THE DANCE OF DEATH

Edgar	Robert Shaw	Kurt	. Hector Elizondo
Alice	Zoe Caldwell		

Standbys: Mr. Shaw—Robert Pastene; Miss Caldwell—Betty Miller; Mr. Elizondo—Marco St. John.

Directed by A.J. Antoon; scenery, Santo Loquasto; costumes, Theoni V. Aldredge; lighting, Ian Calderon; production stage manager, Frank Bayer; stage manager, John Beven.

Time: Late autumn. Place: Inside a fortress on an island off the coast of Sweden. The play was presented in two parts.

The last New York production of the Strindberg material was the Friedrich Duerrenmatt adaptation *Play Strindberg* 6/3/71 for 65 performances at the Lincoln Center Forum. The play itself was last produced on Broadway 4/28/71 for 9 performances.

SHORT EYES

Mr. Brown	Hollis Barnes	Blanca	.Chu Chu Malave
Juan Otero	Bimbo	Mr. Frederick Nett	. Robert Maroff
Charlie "Longshoe" Murphy	Joseph Carberry	Gypsy	.Rick Reid
Clark Davis	.William Carden	Omar Blinker	. Kenny Steward
Julio "Cupcakes" Mercado	Tito Goya	Paco Pasqual	. Felipe Torres
John "Ice" Wicker	Ben Jefferson	Sgt. Morrison	.Chuck Bergansky
William "El Raheem" Johnson .	J. J. Johnson	Capt. Allard	. H. Richard Young

Understudies: Messrs. Carberry, Young, Maroff—Chuck Bergansky; Messrs. Jefferson, Steward—Hollis Barnes; Messrs. Johnson, Barnes—Alan Chilly; Messrs. Bimbo, Torres—Eduardo Figueroa; Messrs. Carden, Bergansky—David Hausman; Mr. Goya—Chu Chu Malave.

Directed by Marvin Felix Camillo; scenery, David Mitchell; costumes, Paul Martino; costumes supervised by David Mitchell; lighting, Spencer Mosse; production stage manager, Robert Kellogg.

Time: The present. Place: The dayroom of one of the floors of the House of Detention. The play was presented in two parts, Act I and Act II plus Epilogue.

Short Eyes is a slice-of-life prison drama, mostly about sexual relations among inmates and their anathematizing hatred of an inmate charged with child molestation. The play's author is an ex-convict and it is performed by a cast of former members of a theater workshop at Bedford Hills, N.Y., Correctional Facility, who call themselves "The Family."

NOTE: *Short Eyes* was previously produced off off Broadway at the Theater of the Riverside Church. This New York Shakespeare production was presented off Broadway at the Public Theater 2/28/74 for 54 performances before being transferred to Lincoln Center; see its entry in the "Plays Produced off Broadway" section of this volume.

A best play; see page 208

Gigi (103). Musical based on the novel by Colette; book and lyrics by Alan Jay Lerner; music by Frederick Loewe. Produced by Saint-Subber in The Los Angeles and San

Francisco Light Opera Production, Edwin Lester producer, at the Uris Theater. Opened November 13, 1973. (Closed February 10, 1974)

Honore Lachailles . . . . Alfred Drake	Waiter; Law Clerk . . . . . . Thomas Stanton
Gaston Lachailles . . . . Daniel Massey	Liane's Dance Partner . . . . Thomas Anthony
Liane d'Exelmans . . . . . Sandahl Bergman	Artist . . . . Andy Bew
Inez Alvarez (Mamita) . . . Maria Karnilova	Count . . . . Joel Pressman
Gigi . . . . Karin Wolfe	Sandomir . . . . Randy Di Grazio
Aunt Alicia . . . . Agnes Moorehead	Dancing Teacher . . . . Gregory Drotar
Charles . . . . Gordon De Vol	Manuel . . . . Truman Gaige
Head Waiter; Receptionist; Telephone	Maitre Du Fresne . . . . Richard Woods
Installer; Maitre d'Hotel . . . . . Joe Ross	Maitre Duclos . . . . John Dorrin
Waiter; Law Clerk . . . Leonard John Crofoot	

The Ensemble: Thomas Anthony, Alvin Beam, Russ Beasley, Robyn Blair, Leonard John Crofoot, Judy Cummings, Gordon De Vol, Randy Di Grazio, Gergory Drotar, Margit Haut, Andy Keyser, Clyde Laurents, Diane Lauridsen, Merilee Magnuson, Jean McLaughlin, Kelley Maxwell, Vickie Patik, Susan Plantt, Joel Pressman, Thomas Stanton, Marie Tillmans, Sallie True.

Standbys: Miss Wolfe—Patricia Arnell; Mr. Drake—Larry Keith; Misses Karnilova, Moorehead —Louise Kirtland. Understudies: Mr. Massey—Gordon De Vol; Messrs. Woods, Gaige—John Dorrin; Miss Bergman—Marie Tillmans; Mr. Ross—Joel Pressman; Swing Dancer—Bjarne Buchtrup.

Directed by Joseph Hardy; dances and musical numbers staged by Onna White; musical direction, Ross Riemueller; scenery, Oliver Smith; costumes, Oliver Messel; lighting, Thomas Skelton; orchestrations, Irving Kostal; dance arrangements, Trude Rittmann; musical associate, Harper MacKay; associate dance director, Martin Allen; production manager, Bill Holland; production stage manager, M. William Lettich; press, Martin Shwartz, Ben Washer.

Time: The turn of the century. Place: Paris (mostly).

This musical is a stage version of the Lerner-Loewe movie musical Gigi, starring Leslie Caron, Maurice Chevalier, Hermione Gingold and Louis Jourdan, also based on the Colette story about a young girl being trained for a career as a demi-mondaine.

Arlene Francis replaced Agnes Moorehead 1/24/74.

ACT I

"Thank Heaven for Little Girls" . . . . Honore	
"It's a Bore" . . . . Honore, Gaston	
"The Earth and Other Minor Things" . . . . Gigi	
"Paris Is Paris Again" . . . . Honore, Ensemble	
"She's Not Thinking of Me" . . . . Gaston	
"It's a Bore" (Reprise) . . . . Honore, Gaston, Manuel, Aunt Alicia	
"The Night They Invented Champagne" . . . . Gigi, Gaston, Mamita	
"I Remember It Well" . . . . Honore, Mamita	
"I Never Want to Go Home Again" . . . . Gigi, Ensemble	

ACT II

"Gigi" . . . . Gaston	
"The Contract" . . . . Alicia, Mamita, Duclos, Du Fresne	
"I'm Glad I'm Not Young Anymore" . . . . Honore	
"In This Wide, Wide World" . . . . Gigi	
"Thank Heaven for Little Girls" (Reprise) . . . . Honore	

* Good Evening (228). Two-man revue with music; written and performed by Peter Cook and Dudley Moore. Produced by Alexander H. Cohen and Bernard Delfont at the Plymouth Theater. Opened November 14, 1973.

Directed by Jerry Adler; design, Robert Randolph; produced in association with Donald Langdon for Hemdale, Ltd.; production stage manager, Alan Coleridge; press, David Powers.

Comic commentary on our life and times in the manner of Beyond the Fringe, entitled Behind the Fridge in its London run. A foreign play previously produced in London.

ACT I—Hello, On Location, "Madrigal," Six of the Best, "Die Flabbergast," Down the Mine, One Leg Too Few, "Chanson," Soap Opera.

ACT II—Gospel Truth, Mini-Drama, "The Kwai Sonata," The Frog and the Peach, An Appeal, Tea for Two.

The New Phoenix Repertory Company. Repertory of three revivals. **The Visit** (32). By Friedrich Duerrenmatt; adapted by Maurice Valency. Opened November 25, 1973. **Chemin de Fer** (42). By Georges Feydeau; adapted by Suzanne Grossmann and Paxton Whitehead. Opened November 26, 1973. **Holiday** (28). By Philip Barry. Opened December 26, 1973. Produced by The New Phoenix Repertory Company, a project of Theater Incorporated, T. Edward Hambleton and Michael Montel managing directors, Harold Prince and Stephen Porter artistic directors, at the Ethel Barrymore Theater. (Repertory closed February 16, 1974)

PERFORMER	"THE VISIT"	"CHEMIN DE FER"	"HOLIDAY"
Ralph Drischell	Painter; Doctor	Police Secretary	
David Dukes	Husbands #7, #8, #9; Athlete	Coustouillu	Nick Potter
George Ede	Mayor	Hubertin	Edward Seton
Peter Friedman	Carpenter	Auguste	
Bonnie Gallup	Mayor's Wife; 2d Woman	Cecille	Susan Potter
John Glover	Teacher	Planteloup	Johnny Case
Merwin Goldsmith	Pastor	Lapige	
Nicholas Hormann	Loby	Mover; Deliveryman	Charles
Curt Karibalis	Policeman	Belgence	Seton Cram
Chip Lucia	Max		
Valentine Mayer	Mike; Truck Driver	Mover; Deliveryman	
John McMartin	Schill	Fedot	
Bill Moor	Station Master	Germal	Henry
Charlotte Moore	Frau Schill	Sophie	Linda Seton
George Pentecost	Koby	Etienne	
Rachel Roberts	Clara Zachanassian	Francine	
Robin Pearson Rose	Ottilie		Julia Seton
Thomas A. Stewart	Conductor; Karl	Mover; Deliveryman	Ned Seton
Ellen Tovatt	1st Woman; Reporter	Madeleine	Laura Cram
Richard Venture	Boby	Chanal	

ALL PLAYS—Scenery, Edward Burbridge; lighting, Ken Billington; production stage manager, Murray Gitlin; stage manager, Louis Pulvino; press, Mary Bryant, Shirley Herz, Bill Evans.

THE VISIT—Understudies: Miss Roberts—Bonnie Gallup; Mr. McMartin—George Ede; Messrs. Moor, Goldsmith—Nicholas Hormann; Messrs. Friedman, Stewart, Pentecost—Valentine Mayer; Mr. Venture—Bill Moor.

Directed by Harold Prince; costumes, Carolyn Parker; assistant director, Ruth Mitchell; music consultant, Paul Gemignani; incidental music based on work by Edgar Varese and guitar transcriptions by Julian Bream.

Time: Some time ago. Place: In and around the little town of Güllen. The play was presented in three parts.

The Visit was first produced on Broadway 5/5/58 for 189 performances and was named a Best Play of its season. It was revived at the City Center 3/8/60 for 16 performances.

CHEMIN DE FER—Understudies: Miss Roberts—Ellen Tovatt; Mr. McMartin—Kurt Karibalis; Mr. Venture—Bill Moor; Mr. Ede—Merwin Goldsmith; Mr. Dukes—Peter Friedman; Misses. Moore, Gallup, Tovatt—Robin Pearson Rose; Mr. Pentecost—Ralph Drischell; Messrs. Goldsmith, Glover—Nicholas Hormann; Messrs. Friedman, Karibalis—Thomas A. Stewart; Mr. Moor—Valentine Mayer.

Directed by Stephen Porter; costumes, Nancy Potts; music, Bernardo Segall.

Act I, Scene 1: Francine's drawing room, afternoon. Scene 2: Bedroom at 21 Rue du Colisee, late that night. Act II, Scene 1: Fedot's apartment, early next morning. Scene 2: Francine's drawing room, a year later.

As in most Feydeau farces, lovers both married and unmarried are shuffled and dealt through assignations like cards in the game of the play's title. *Chemin de Fer* was previously produced at the Mark Taper Forum in Los Angeles. It has never been produced in New York under this title.

HOLIDAY—Understudies: Mr. Glover—David Dukes; Mr. Stewart—Nicholas Hormann; Mr. Ede—Bill Moor; Mr. Karibalis—Peter Friedman; Mr. Dukes—Valentine Mayer.

Directed by Michael Montel; costumes, Donald Brooks; musical consultant, Paul Gemignani.

Time: December, 1928. Place: New York City. Act I: A room on the third floor of Edward Seton's house. Act II: A room on the top floor, New Year's Eve. Act III: A room on the third floor, twelve days later.

Holiday was first produced on Broadway 11/26/28 for 229 performances and was named a Best Play of its season. This is its first professional New York revival.

NOTE: In addition to its regular programs, The New Phoenix Repertory Company presented a series of special "Side Shows" at Playhouse II for 5 performances each, as follows: *Miracle Play* by Joyce Carol Oates, directed by Dan Freudenberger, with Robert Guillaume, Marcella Lowery, 12/30/73; *The Removalists* by David Williamson, directed by Michael Montel, with Patrick Horgan, Munson Hicks, Susan Browning, Sharon Spelman, Ken Baker, Michael Irving, 1/20/74; *In the Voodoo Parlor of Marie Leveau* program of one-act plays by Frank Gagliano—*Gris-Gris* directed by Michael Montel, with Stephanie Cotsirlos, Delores Gaskins, Bill Cobbs, John Cullum, and *The Commedia World of Lafcadio Beau* directed by David Dukes, with Rhoda Gemignani, Stephed D. Newman, Tony Palmer—4/19/74; and *Pretzels*, music and lyrics by John Forster, directed by Philip Adelman, with Judy Kahan, Fred Grandy, Jane Curtin, 5/17/74.

The Good Doctor (208). By Neil Simon; adapted from and suggested by stories by Anton Chekhov. Produced by Emanuel Azenberg and Eugene V. Wolsk at the Eugene O'Neill Theater. Opened November 27, 1973. (Closed May 26, 1974)

Rene Auberjonois	Christopher Plummer
Barnard Hughes	Frances Sternhagen
Marsha Mason	

Directed by A.J. Antoon; scenery and costumes, Tony Walton; lighting, Tharon Musser; music and orchestrations, Peter Link; lyrics, Neil Simon; sound, Sandy Hacker; production stage manager, Tom Porter; stage manager, George Rondo; press, Merle Debuskey, Leo Stern.

Human foibles as depicted by a Chekhov-like "writer" in a series of episodes taking place in Russia and preceded by a mood- and style-setting musical concert.

THE CONCERT—Oop Tymbali, Good Doctor Opus #1, Trans Siberian Railroad, Father and Son, Good Doctor Opus #2, Morning Dance (Dance for the Gathering I, Dance for the Gathering II). Musicians: Stan Free conductor, marimba, trumpet concertina, accordian; Herbert Sorkin violin, viola, associate conductor; Richard Meldonian flute, piccolo; Armen Halburian percussion; Bernard Moore balalaika, guitar; Jack Messing bass, tuba.

ACT I—*The Writer*—Christopher Plummer; *The Sneeze*—Plummer, Rene Auberjonois, Marsha Mason, Barnard Hughes, Frances Sternhagen; *The Governess*—Misses Sternhagen, Mason; *Surgery* —Plummer, Hughes; *Too Late for Happiness*—Hughes, Miss Sternhagen; *The Seduction*—Plummer, Auberjonois, Miss Mason.

ACT II—*The Drowned Man*—Plummer, Auberjonois, Hughes; *The Audition*—Plummer, Miss Mason; *A Defenseless Creature*—Plummer, Hughes, Miss Sternhagen; *The Arrangement*—Plummer, Auberjonois, Miss Mason; *The Writer*—Plummer.

Kathryn Walker replaced Marsha Mason 2/74.

A Best Play; see page 275

The Pajama Game (65). Musical revival with book by George Abbott and Richard Bissell; music and lyrics by Richard Adler and Jerry Ross; based on the novel *7½ Cents* by Richard Bissell. Produced by Richard Adler and Bert Wood in association with Nelson Peltz at the Lunt-Fontanne Theater. Opened December 9, 1973. (Closed February 3, 1974)

Hines	Cab Calloway	Mabel	Mary Jo Catlett
Prez	Marc Jordan	1st Helper	David Brummel
Joe	Gerrit de Beer	2d Helper	John Engstrom
Hasler	Willard Waterman	Charlie	Tiger Haynes
Gladys	Sharron Miller	Babe Williams	Barbara McNair
Sid Sorokin	Hal Linden	Mae	Margret Coleman

Brenda . . . . Chris Calloway		Salesman . . . . Hal Norman	
Poopsie . . . . Wyetta Turner		Pop . . . . Baron Wilson	

Dancers: Dru Alexandrine, Eileen Casey, Vicki Frederick, Mickey Gunnersen, Jo Ann Ogawa, P.J. Benjamin, Hank Brunjes, Jon Engstrom, Ben Harney, Randal Harris, David Kresser Jr., Cameron Mason, Chester Walker.

Singers: Chalyce Brown, Susan Dyas, Rebecca Hoodwin, Patricia Moline, Marie Santell, Cynthia White, Gerrit de Beer, David Brummel, Doug Carfrae, Stan Page, Ward Smith, Teddy Williams.

Standby: Mr. Calloway—Tiger Haynes. Principal Understudies: Miss McNair—Chris Calloway; Mr. Linden—David Brummel; Miss Miller—Wyetta Turner; Mr. Waterman—Hal Norman; Miss Catlett—Chalyce Brown; Mr. Jordan—Gerrit de Beer.

Directed by George Abbott; choreography and musical numbers reproduced by Zoya Laporska; musical numbers originally staged by Jerome Robbins and Bob Fosse; original choreography, Bob Fosse; musical direction, Joyce Brown; production design, David Guthrie; lighting, John Gleason; orchestrations, Don Walker; assistant to Mr. Abbott, John Allen; stage managers, Bert Wood, Stan Page, James Sarnoff; press, Jay Bernstein Public Relations, Ted Goldsmith, Jeffrey Richards.

Place: A small town in the Middle West.

The Pajama Game was first produced on Broadway 5/13/54 for 1,063 performances. It was revived by the New York City Center Light Opera Company 5/15/57 for 23 performances.

The list of musical numbers in *The Pajama Game* appears on page 354 of *The Best Plays of 1953–54*.

City Center Acting Company. Repertory of five revivals. **Three Sisters** (7). By Anton Chekhov; translated by Tyrone Guthrie and Leonid Kipnis. Opened December 19, 1973 (see note). **The Beggar's Opera** (6). By John Gay. Opened December 22, 1973 (see note). **Measure for Measure** (7). By William Shakespeare. Opened December 26, 1973 (see note). **Scapin** (1). By Molière. Opened December 28, 1973 in one matinee performance for children. **Next Time I'll Sing to You** (2). By James Saunders. Opened January 2, 1974 (see note). (Repertory closed January 11, 1974) Produced by City Center Acting Company, John Houseman artistic director, at the Billy Rose Theater.

PERFORMER	"THREE SISTERS"	"THE BEGGAR'S OPERA"	"MEASURE FOR MEASURE"	"NEXT TIME I'LL SING TO YOU"
Nita Angeletti		Mrs. Trapes	Julietta	
Gisela Caldwell	Anfisa	Suky Tawdry	Mother Superior; (Mariana)	
Leah Chandler	Dounyasha	Dolly Trull	(Isabella)	
Joel Colodner		Harry Paddington	1st Gentleman; Barnardine	
Peter Dvorsky	Ferapont	Jemmy Twitcher	Claudio	
Benjamin Hendrickson	Prozorov	Beggar	Elbow	Meff
Cynthia Herman	Natasha	Polly Peachum		
Patti LuPone	Irina	Lucy Lockit	A Boy	Lizzie
Kevin Kline	Vershinin	Macheath	Friar Peter	
John Michalski			2d Gentleman; Abhorson	
Mary-Joan Negro	Masha	Jenny Diver	(Isabella); (Mariana)	
Richard Ooms		Matt	Exscalus	
Mary Lou Rosato	Olga	Mrs. Peachum; Betty Coaxer	Mistress Overdone	
Jared Sakren	Rode	Jack	Pompey	Hermit
David Schramm	Chebutykin	Wat Dreary	Angelo	Rudge
Gerald Shaw	Fedotik	Ned	Froth	
Norman Snow	Tusenbach	Filch	Provost	Dust
David Ogden Stiers	Kulygin	Peachum	Duke	
Sam Tsoutsouvas	Solyony	Lockit	Lucio	

(Parentheses indicate roles in which the performers alternated)

Three Sisters—Members of the Prozorov Household: Nita Angeletti, Joel Colodner, John Michalski, Richard Ooms.

The Beggar's Opera—Instrumentalists: Gerald Shaw organ, Benjamin Hendrickson and Jared Sakren guitar, Peter Dvorsky reed and percussion.

Measure for Measure—Servitors: Joel Colodner, John Michalski, Gerald Shaw; Ladies of the Town: Gisela Caldwell, Cynthia Herman, Patti LuPone, Mary-Joan Negro, Rebecca Reynolds; Nuns: Rebecca Reynolds, Judy Smith.

SCAPIN

Octave	Gerald Shaw	Hyacinthe	Patti LuPone
Sylvestre	Sam Tsoutsouvas	Zerbinette	Cynthia Herman
Scapin	Jared Sakren	Carle; Nerine	Leah Chandler
Argante	David Schramm	Geronte	David Ogden Stiers
Leandre	Kevin Kline		

ALL PLAYS—Producing director, Margot Harley; executive director, Porter Van Zandt; lighting, Martin Aronstein; stage manager, Peter B. Mumford; press, Sol Jacobson, Lewis Harmon.

THREE SISTERS—Understudies: Misses. Rosato, Negro, Chandler—Nita Angeletti; Misses LuPone, Herman, Caldwell—Leah Chandler; Mr. Hendrickson—Sam Tsoutsouvas; Messrs. Schramm, Stiers, Kline—Richard Ooms; Mr. Snow—Peter Dvorsky; Mr. Tsoutsouvas—Joel Colodner; Messrs. Shaw, Sakren—John Michalski; Mr. Dvorsky—Jared Sakren.

Directed by Boris Tumarin; scenery, Douglas W. Schmidt; costumes, John David Ridge; musical direction, Gerald Shaw; dances arranged by Elizabeth Keen.

Time: The turn of the century. Place: A provincial town in Russia. Act I: The drawing room of the Prozorov home, noonday in spring. Act II: The same, two years later, a winter evening. Act III: Olga and Irina's room, two years later, 3 a.m. in early spring. Act IV: The garden of the house, noonday in autumn of the same year. The play was presented in two parts with the intermission following Act II.

Three Sisters was last presented on Broadway by American Conservatory Theater 10/9/69 for 11 performances.

THE BEGGAR'S OPERA—Understudies: Mr. Hendrickson—Peter Dvorsky; Mr. Stiers—Richard Ooms; Mr. Tsoutsouvas—David Schramm; Mr. Kline—Joel Colodner; Mr. Snow—Jared Sakren; Miss Herman—Mary-Joan Negro; Misses LuPone, Negro—Nita Angeletti; Misses Rosato, Angeletti—Gisela Caldwell.

Directed by Gene Lesser; musical direction and arrangements, Roland Gagnon; scenery, Robert Yodice; costumes, Carrie F. Robbins; dances arranged by Elizabeth Keen.

Time: The 18th century. Place: London, in and around Newgate Prison.

This John Gay musical, first performed at the Theater Royal, Drury Lane, London in 1728 and recently the basis for a new version called *The Threepenny Opera,* was last produced professionally in New York 3/21/72 for 253 performances by the Chelsea Theater Center.

MEASURE FOR MEASURE—Understudies: Mr. Dvorsky—Richard Ooms; Messrs. Ooms, Sakren—Peter Dvorsky; Messrs. Schramm, Snow—Benjamin Hendrickson; Messrs. Dvorsky, Shaw—Joel Colodner; Messrs. Tsoutsouvas, Colodner—Kevin Kline; Messrs. Hendrickson, Kline—John Michalski; Mr. Michalski—Gerald Shaw; Miss Rosato—Cynthia Herman; Miss Caldwell—Nita Angeletti; Miss Negro—Patti LuPone.

Directed by John Houseman; music, Virgil Thomson; scenery, Douglas W. Schmidt; costumes, John David Ridge; assistant to Mr. Houseman, Gerald Shaw.

Place: The city of Vienna. Act I, Scene 1: The palace. Scene 2: Before the palace. Scene 3: A street in the red light district. Scene 4: A nunnery. Scene 5: A courtroom in the palace. Act II, Scene 1: An apartment in the palace. Scene 2: The prison. Scene 3: The moated grange. Act III, Scene 1: The prison. Scene 2: Before the gates of the city.

Measure for Measure last appeared in New York in the season of 1966–67 in two productions: the New York Shakespeare Festival's in Central Park 7/12/66 for 17 performances and the Bristol Old Vic's on Broadway 2/14/67 for 7 performances.

SCAPIN—Directed by Pierre Lefevre; lyrics, Sam Tsoutsouvas; costumes, John David Ridge.

Molière's comedy of a trickster was last seen in New York in a musical adaptation 1/8/73 for 8 performances. The straight version was last done in French off Broadway 5/7/67 for 4 performances and in English off Broadway 3/9/64 for 10 performances.

NEXT TIME I'LL SING TO YOU—Understudies: Messrs. Snow, Schramm—Peter Dvorsky; Miss LuPone—Leah Chandler; Mr. Sakren—David Ogden Stiers; Mr. Hendrickson—Sam Tsoutsouvas.

Directed by Marian Seldes; costumes, John David Ridge.

This play was first performed in England at the Questors Theater, Ealing, in 1962 and the following year at the Arts Theater in London. Its American premiere took place off Broadway in the Phoenix Theater production 11/27/63 for 23 performances, when it was named a Best Play of its season. It was revived last season by City Center Acting Company 10/25/72 for 2 performances.

NOTE: In addition to its official 23 performances, City Center Repertory presented 6 preview performances as follows: *Three Sisters* 2, *The Beggar's Opera* 2, *Measure for Measure* 1 and *Next Time I'll Sing to You* 1.

* A Moon for the Misbegotten (175). Revival of the play by Eugene O'Neill. Produced by Elliot Martin and Lester Osterman Productions at the Morosco Theater. Opened December 29, 1973.

Josie Hogan	Colleen Dewhurst	James Tyrone Jr.	Jason Robards
Mike Hogan	Edwin J. McDonough	T. Stedman Harder	John O'Leary
Phil Hogan	Ed Flanders		

Standbys: Mr. Robards—James Karen; Miss Dewhurst—Jacqueline Brooks. Understudies: Mr. Flanders—John O'Leary; Messrs. McDonough, O'Leary—James Struthers.

Directed by Jose Quintero; scenery and lighting, Ben Edwards; costumes, Jane Greenwood; associate producer, Richard Horner; production stage manager, Jane E. Neufeld; press, Seymour Krawitz, Patricia McLean Krawitz.

Time: Early September, 1923. Place: A farmhouse. Act I: Around noon. Act II: 11 o'clock that night. Act III: Immediately after. Act IV: Dawn of the following morning. The play was presented in two parts with the intermission following Act II.

A Moon for the Misbegotten was first produced on Broadway 5/2/57 for 68 performances and was named a Best Play of its season. It was revived off Broadway by Circle in the Square 6/12/68 for 199 performances.

Tom Clancy replaced Ed Flanders 5/20/74.

An Evening With Josephine Baker (7). Revue devised as a showcase for the solo performance of Josephine Baker. Produced by the Palace Theater, the Messrs. Nederlander directors, at the Palace Theater. Opened December 31, 1973. (Closed January 6, 1974)

Josephine Baker	Norman Hawkins
Roberto Lorco and Company	Ricardo Portlette
Paco Juanas guitarist	Charlene Ricks
Domingo Alverado singer	Barbara Rolle
Michael Powell Ensemble	Calvin Van Meter
Michael Powell	Esther Westbrook
Joey Coleman	Peggy Williams
Leeroy Cooks	Shirley Williams
Vinson Cunningham	Baby Laurence
Bernadette Doctor	G. Keith Alexander (M.C.)
Dorthea Doctor	

Choreography of "Mira Bra", Maria Rosa Merced; stage director, Patrick Horrigan; press, Gifford/Wallace, Inc.

Engagement limited to one week by the noted cabaret entertainer Josephine Baker, in a revue context. Miss Baker last appeared in a revue on Broadway 2/4/64 for 16 performances.

ACT I—"People," "Sourire," "Impossible," "Avec," "Love Story," "Hello Young Lovers," Medley. ACT II—"Lend Your Ear," "Si Me Faltas Tu," "My Fair Lady," "Demain," "La Vie en Rose," "Yesterday," "J'ai Deux Amours," "My Sweet Lord."

Find Your Way Home (135). By John Hopkins. Produced by Rick Hobard at the Brooks Atkinson Theater. Opened January 2, 1974. (Closed April 28, 1974)

Julian Weston	Michael Moriarty	Alan Harrison	Lee Richardson
David Powell	John Ramsey	Jacqueline Harrison	Jane Alexander

Understudy: Mr. Moriarty—Joseph Lambie.
Directed by Edwin Sherin; scenery, William Ritman; costumes, Theoni V. Aldredge; lighting, Marc B. Weiss; associate producer, Peter Wright; production stage manager, Elizabeth Caldwell; press, Max Eisen, Maurice Turet, Barbara Eisen.
Time: The present. Place: A small flat in a large town in the south of England. Act I: Evening. Act II: One hour later. Act III: Ten minutes later.
Explicitly exposed emotions of a homosexual hustler, a married man who wants to live with him, and the abandoned wife. A foreign play making its world premiere in this production.
A Best Play; see page 192

Liza (23). One-woman show performed by Liza Minnelli; written by Fred Ebb; original musical material by Fred Ebb and John Kander. Produced by The Shubert Organization in association with Ron Delsener at the Winter Garden. Opened January 6, 1974. (Closed January 26, 1974)

Dancers: Pam Barlow, Spencer Henderson, Jimmy Roddy, Sharon Wylie.
Directed by Bob Fosse; choreography, Bob Fosse, Ron Lewis; musical coordinator, Marvin Hamlisch; conductor, Jack French; lighting, Jules Fisher; audio design, Phil Ramone; sound, Stan Miller; production coordinator, Bill Liberman; press, Betty Lee Hunt Associates, Harriett Trachtenberg, Maria Pucci.
The show, a collection of more than 20 songs sung by Miss Minnelli plus a few production numbers with four dancers, was presented in two parts.

* Lorelei (143). Musical based on the musical *Gentlemen Prefer Blondes* (book by Anita Loos and Joseph Fields, music by Jule Styne, lyrics by Leo Robin, based on Miss Loos's collection of stories); new book by Kenny Solms and Gail Parent; new music by Jule Styne; new lyrics by Betty Comden and Adolph Green. Produced by Lee Guber and Shelly Gross at the Palace Theater. Opened January 27, 1974.

Lorelei Lee	Carol Channing	Charles; Master of Ceremonies	Robert Riker
Henry Spofford	Lee Roy Reams	Robert Lemanteur	Bob Fitch
Mrs. Ella Spofford	Dody Goodman	Louis Lemanteur	Ian Tucker
Lord Francis Beekman	Jack Fletcher	Lobster	Brenda Holmes
Lady Phyllis Beekman	Jean Bruno	Caviar	Linda McClure
Josephus Gage	Brandon Maggart	Pheasant	Aniko Farrell
Dorothy Shaw	Tamara Long	Salade	Marie Halton
Gus Esmond	Peter Palmer	Dessert	Carol Channing
Bartender; Pierre; Announcer	Ray Cox	Maitre D	Willard Beckham
Frank	Steve Short	Simone Duval	Sherrill Harper
George; Engineer	Bob Daley	Mr. Esmond	David Neuman

Bridesmaids: Aniko Farrell, Marie Halton, Sherrill Harper, Linda McClure. Ship's Personnel, Passengers, Tourists, Olympic Team Members, Waiters, Wedding Guests: Aniko Farrell, Joela Flood, Marie Halton, Marian Haraldson, Sherrill Harper, Brenda Holmes, Linda Lee MacArthur, Linda McClure, Susan Ohman, Gina Ramsel, Roxanna White, Willard Beckham, Ray Cox, Bob Daley, Bob Fitch, Gregg Harlan, Wayne Mattson; Jonathan Miele, Jeff Richards, Robert Riker, Rick Schneider, Steve Short, Don Swanson, Ian Tucker.
Understudies: Miss Channing—Sherrill Harper; Miss Long—Gina Ramsel; Misses Goodman, Bruno—Marian Haraldson; Messrs. Palmer, Maggart—Ray Cox; Mr. Reams—Wayne Mattson; Mr. Fletcher—David Neuman; Messrs. Short, Daley, Tucker—Jonathan Miele; Mr. Fitch—Robert Riker; Mr. Neuman—Bob Daley.
Directed by Robert Moore; choreography, Ernest O. Flatt; musical direction, Milton Rosenstock; scenery, John Conklin; costumes, Alvin Colt; Miss Channing's costumes, Ray Aghayan, Bob Mackie; lighting, John Gleason; orchestrations, Philip J. Lang, Don Walker; vocal arrangements, Hugh Martin, Buster Davis; dance music arrangements, Jay Thompson; production stage manager, Ben D. Kranz; stage manager, George Boyd; press, Solters/Sabinson/Roskin, Inc., Milly Schoenbaum, Myrna Post.
Act I, Scene 1: The pier of the Ile de France. Scene 2: The deck of the Ile de France. Scene 3: Lorelei's suite on the Ile de France. Scene 4: The Eiffel Tower. Scene 5: Lorelei's suite, the Ritz Hotel in Paris. Act II, Scene 1: Pre-Catalin Nightclub. Scene 2: A Paris street. Scene 3: Lorelei's suite, the

Ritz Hotel in Paris. Scene 4: On the way home. Scene 5: The Central Park Casino, New York. These scenes were preceded by a Prologue and followed by an Epilogue.

Subtitled *Gentlemen Still Prefer Blondes,* this musical presents Lorelei Lee looking back on her 1920s escapades from the viewpoint of the present, in which she has become the wealthy widowed Mrs. Esmond. The 1920s scenes are largely excerpted from the musical *Gentlemen Prefer Blondes* which was presented on Broadway 12/8/49 for 740 performances, with Carol Channing creating the role of Lorelei.

ACT I

(Songs marked with an asterisk (*) are new numbers by Jule Styne, Betty Comden and Adolph Green; others are from the original show, *Gentlemen Prefer Blondes.*)

"Looking Back"* . . . . .Lorelei
"Bye, Bye, Baby" . . . . Gus, Lorelei, Passengers, Tourists
"High Time" . . . . Dorothy, Mrs. Spofford, Passengers
"Little Rock" . . . . .Lorelei
"I Love What I'm Doing" . . . . .Dorothy
"It's Delightful Down in Chile" . . . . .Lorelei, Lord Francis, Stewards
"I Won't Let You Get Away"* . . . . Henry, Dorothy
"Keeping Cool With Coolidge" . . . . Henry, Dorothy, Mrs. Spofford, Guests
"Men"* . . . . .Lorelei
Dance supervised by Robert Tucker

ACT II

"Coquette" . . . . Dorothy, Lorelei, Showgirls
"Mamie Is Mimi" . . . . Lorelei, Robert, Louis
"Diamonds Are a Girl's Best Friend" . . . . .Lorelei
"Homesick" . . . . .Lorelei, Gus
"Miss Lorelei Lee"* . . .Henry, Dorothy, Mrs. Spofford, Gage, Robert, Louis, Wedding Guests
"Button Up With Esmond" . . . . Lorelei, Bridesmaids
"Diamonds Are a Girl's Best Friend" (Reprise) . . . . .Lorelei

Rainbow Jones (1). Musical with book, music and lyrics by Jill Williams. Produced by Rubykate, Inc. in association with Phil Gillin and Gene Bambic at The Music Box. Opened and closed at the evening performance, February 13, 1974.

Rainbow Jones . . . . .Ruby Persson   Cardigan . . . . .Stephanie Silver
Leona . . . . .Peggy Hagen Lamprey   Joey Miller . . . . .Peter Kastner
Bones . . . . Andy Rohrer   Aunt Felicity . . . . Kay St. Germain
C.A. Fox . . . . .Gil Robbins   Uncle Ithaca . . . . .Daniel Keyes

Directed by Gene Persson; musical staging, Sammy Bayes; musical direction and vocal arrangements, Danny Holgate; scenery, Richard Ferrer; costumes, James Berton-Harris; lighting, Spencer Mosse; production stage manager, Kate Pollock; press, Michael Alpert, Marilynn LeVine, Ellen Levene, Anne Weinberg.

Time: The present. Act I, Scene 1: Noon, Central Park. Scene 2: Later, Aunt Felicity's apartment. Scene 3: A few hours later, Joey Miller's office. Scene 4: Minutes later, Central Park. Scene 5: That evening, Aunt Felicity's apartment. Scene 6: The next day at noon, Central Park. Act II, Scene 1: A few minutes later, Central Park. Scene 2: A week later, Uncle Ithaca's farm. Scene 3: A moment later, Central Park. Scene 4: A week later, the parlor car of the Ohio Express/Felicity's apartment. Scene 5: A few hours later, Central Park.

A lonesome young lady consoles herself with imaginary animal friends until Mr. Right comes along.

ACT I

Prologue: "A Little Bit of Me in You" . . . . Leona, Bones, C.A. Fox, Cardigan
"Free and Easy" . . . . .Rainbow
"Do Unto Others" . . . . Rainbow, Leona, Bones, C.A. Fox, Cardigan
"I'd Like to Know You Better" . . . . Joey

"Bad Breath" . . . . Leona, Cardigan, Bones, C.A. Fox
"I'd Like to Know You Better" (Reprise) . . Joey, Rainbow, Leona, C.A. Fox, Cardigan, Bones
"Alone, at Last, Alone" . . . . Aunt Felicity
"Free and Easy" (Reprise) . . . . .Rainbow
"Her Name Is Leona" . . . . Rainbow, Bones, Cardigan, C.A. Fox, Leona
"We All Need Love" . . . . Cardigan, Bones, C.A. Fox, Leona

ACT II

"We All Need Love" (Reprise) . . . . Cardigan, C.A. Fox, Bones, Leona
"The Only Man for the Job" . . . . Bones
"It's So Nice" . . . . Aunt Felicity, Uncle Ithaca
"Wait a Little While" . . . . Leona
"It's So Nice" (Reprise) . . . . Rainbow, Aunt Felicity, Uncle Ithaca, Joey
"One Big Happy Family" . . . . .Joey, C.A. Fox, Bones, Cardigan, Leona
"Who Needs the Love of a Woman" . . . . Joey, Rainbow
"We All Need Love"/"A Little Bit of Me in You" (Reprise) . . . . .Joey, Rainbow,
Cardigan, Bones, C.A. Fox, Leona

The Freedom of the City (9). By Brian Friel. Produced by Konrad Matthaei and Hale Matthews, by arrangement with the Goodman Theater Center, Chicago, at the Alvin Theater. Opened February 17, 1974. (Closed February 23, 1974)

Police Constable;	Soldier;
Prof. Cuppley . . . . . . Edward Holmes	Pressman . . . . Reno Roop
Judge . . . . Maurice D. Copeland	Liam O'Kelly . . . . Gordon Gould
Dr. Dodds . . . . Joe Ponazecki	Barkeep; Dr. Winbourne . . . Howard Honig
Skinner . . . . Lenny Baker	Balladeer . . . . Robert Swan
Lily . . . . Kate Reid	Priest . . . . Henderson Forsythe
Michael . . . . Allan Carlsen	Pressman;
Soldier;	Brig. Johnson-Handsbury . . William Bogert
Army Press Officer .J. Kenneth Campbell	

Understudies: Miss Reid—Kip McArdle; Mr. Baker—J. Kenneth Campbell; Messrs. Carlsen, Campbell—Reno Roop; Messrs. Copeland, Bogert, Honig—Edward Holmes; Messrs. Forsythe, Honig, Holmes—Harry Young; Messrs. Ponazecki, Swan—Howard Honig; Mr. Gould—William Bogert.

Directed by William Woodman; scenery, David Jenkins; lighting, F. Mitchell Dana; costumes, Alicia Finkel; produced in association with Roger L. Stevens and Richard Crinkley for Kennedy Center Productions, Inc.; dance consultant, Elizabeth Kean; production stage manager, Warren Crane; stage manager, Harry Young; press, Max Eisen, Maurice Turet, Barbara Eisen.

Time: February 1970. Place Londonderry, Northern Ireland. The play was presented in two parts.

Three non-violent protesters who have taken refuge in the Lord Mayor's office are killed unmercifully and needlessly by a large force of British troops brought in to keep order, in an incident reportedly based on real events in the recent disturbances. A foreign play previously produced in Dublin, London and the Goodman Theater Center in Chicago.

* Noel Coward in Two Keys (106). Program of two plays by Noel Coward: *Come Into the Garden Maud* and *A Song at Twilight*. Produced by Richard Barr and Charles Woodward in association with Michael Frazier at the Ethel Barrymore Theater. Opened February 28, 1974.

PERFORMER	"COME INTO THE GARDEN MAUD"	"A SONG AT TWILIGHT"
Anne Baxter	Maud Caragnani	Carlotta Gray
Thom Christopher	Felix	Felix
Hume Cronyn	Verner Conklin	Hugo Latymer
Jessica Tandy	Anna-Mary Conklin	Hilde Latymer

Standbys: Mr. Cronyn—Shepperd Strudwick; Misses Baxter, Tandy—Jan Farrand; Mr. Christopher—Joel Parks.

Directed by Vivian Matalon; scenery and lighting, William Ritman; costumes, Ray Diffen; associate producer, Michael Kasdan; production stage manager, Mark Wright; press, Betty Lee Hunt Associates, Harriett Trachtenberg.

Time: The present. Place: A private suite in a luxurious hotel in Switzerland. *Come Into the Garden Maud*—Scene 1: An evening in summer. Scene 2: Later that night. *A Song at Twilight*—Act I—Evening. Act II— A few minutes later.

In *Come Into the Garden Maud*, a middle-aged American millionaire leaves his intensely selfish, social-climbing wife and runs off with a congenial countess. In *A Song at Twilight*, a world-famous, aging writer finds it difficult to admit even to himself that he is a latent homosexual. Both plays are comedies (the former a one-acter, the latter near full length), both are played in the same setting with different sets of characters, and both are foreign plays previously produced in London.

A Best Play; see page 234

Sextet (9). Musical with book by Harvey Perr and Lee Goldsmith; music by Lawrence Hurwit; lyrics by Lee Goldsmith. Produced by Balemar Productions and Lawrence E. Sokol at the Bijou Theater. Opened March 3, 1974. (Closed March 10, 1974)

David	Robert Spencer	Kenneth	Harvey Evans
Ann	Dixie Carter	Paul	John Newton
Fay	Mary Small	Leonard	Jerry Lanning

Directed and choreographed by Jered Barclay; musical direction and orchestrations, David Frank; scenery, Peter Harvey; costumes, Zoe Brown; lighting, Marc B. Weiss; assistant choreographer, Mary Jane Houdina; production stage manager, May Muth; stage manager, Bob Burland; press, Milly Schoenbaum, Solters/Sabinson/Roskin, Inc.

Time: The present. Place: An apartment in New York City. The play was performed without intermission.

Shifting hetero and homosexual sands among a group of six friends.

MUSICAL NUMBERS

"Nervous"	Company
"What the Hell Am I Doing Here?"	Paul
"Keep on Dancing"	David, Kenneth, Fay, Paul
"Spunk"	Fay, David, Kenneth
"Visiting Rights"	Ann
"Going-Staying"	Company
"I Wonder"	Ann, Fay
"Women and Men"	Leonard, David, Kenneth
"I Love You All the Time"	Leonard
"Keep on Dancing" (Reprise)	Company
"Hi"	Kenneth
"It'd Be Nice"	Fay
"Roseland"	Company
"How Does It Start?"	David
"Someone to Love"	Company

* Over Here! (100). Musical with book by Will Holt; music and lyrics by Richard M. Sherman and Robert B. Sherman. Produced by Kenneth Waissman and Maxine Fox at the Sam S. Shubert Theater. Opened March 6, 1974.

Norwin Spokesman	Douglass Watson	Maggie	Ann Reinking
Make-out	Jim Weston	Mitzi	Janie Sell
Father	MacIntyre Dixon	Misfit	John Travolta
Mother	Bette Henritze	Utah	Treat Williams
Rankin	William Griffis	Lucky	John Mineo
Donna	Marilu Henner	Sarge	William Newman
Wilma	Phyllis Somerville	Sam	Samuel E. Wright

June . . . . April Shawhan   Pauline de Paul . . . . Maxene Andrews
Bill . . . . .John Driver   Paulette de Paul . . . . Patty Andrews

The Big Band Soloists: Joseph Klein leader; Jimmy Sedlar lead trumpet; Bernie Berger lead saxophone; Mike Cavin lead clarinet; Harry DiVito lead trombone; Teddy Sommer drums; Clay Fullum piano/accordion; Doc Solomon bass; Harvey Estrin, Michael Schuster, Sol Schlinger saxophones; Merv Gold, Jack Gale, Vincent Forchetti trombones; Bob Millikan, Jay Brower, Charles Sullivan trumpets; Ruben Rivera cello; Hal Schaefer piano; Warren Hard percussion; Carmen Mastren guitar/banjo.

Understudies: Misses Maxene and Patty Andrews, Sell, Henritze—Chevi Colton; Messrs. Dixon, Watson, Griffis, Newman—Jack Naughton; Misses Shawhan, Reinking, Henner, Somerville—Chris Callan; Messrs. Driver, Weston, Mineo, Travolta—John Fennessy; Mr. Wright—Edmond Wesley.

Directed by Tom Moore; musical numbers and dances staged by Patricia Birch; musical director, Joseph Klein; scenery, Douglas W. Schmidt; costumes, Carrie F. Robbins; lighting, John Gleason; musical coordination, vocal arrangements, special dance music, Louis St. Louis; orchestrations, Michael Gibson, Jim Tyler; media design, Stan J. Goldberg, Jeanne H. Livingston; sound, Jack Shearing; associate producer, Lou Kramer; production stage manager, T. Schuyler Smith; stage manager, Martha Knight; press, Betty Lee Hunt Associates, Maria Pucci, Harriett Trachtenberg.

Nostalgic musical reminiscences of the home front in World War II—training and entertaining the troops—starring two of the three singing Andrews Sisters (the third, LaVerne Andrews, died six years ago).

ACT I

The Beat Begins (Overture) . . . . The Big Band, Company
"Since You're Not Around" . . . . Make-out, Company
"Over Here"* . . . . Paulette, Pauline
"Buy a Victory Bond" . . . . Company
"My Dream for Tomorrow" . . . . June, Soldiers
"Charlie's Place" . . . . Pauline, Maggie, Lucky, The Big Band, Company
"Hey Yvette/The Grass Grows Green" . . . . Spokesman, Rankin, Father
"The Good-Time Girl" . . . . Paulette, Company
"Wait for Me Marlena" . . . . Mitzi, Company
"We Got It"* . . . . Paulette, Pauline, Mitzi, Company

ACT II

The Beat Continues (Entre'act) . . . . The Big Band, Company
"Wartime Wedding" . . . . Paulette, Pauline, Company
"Don't Shoot the Hooey to Me, Louie" . . . . Sam
"Where Did the Good Times Go?" . . . . Paulette
"Dream Drummin/Soft Music" . . . . Misfit, The Big Band, Company
"The Big Beat"* . . . . Paulette, Pauline, Mitzi
"No Goodbyes" . . . . Paulette, Pauline, Company
*Messrs. Sherman and St. Louis wish to acknowledge the creative contribution of Walter Wechsler on these numbers.

* Candide (149; see note). Musical revival with new book by Hugh Wheeler adapted from Voltaire; music by Leonard Bernstein; lyrics by Richard Wilbur; additional lyrics by Stephen Sondheim and John Latouche. Produced by The Chelsea Theater Center of Brooklyn in conjunction with Harold Prince and Ruth Mitchell at the Broadway Theater. Opened March 10, 1974 matinee; see note.

Dr. Voltaire; Dr. Pangloss; Governor; Host; Sage . . . . Lewis J. Stadlen
Chinese Coolie; Westphalian Soldier; Priest; Spanish Don;
  Rosary Vendor; Sailor; Lion; Guest . . . . Jim Corti
Candide . . . . Mark Baker
Huntsman; 1st Recruiting Officer; Agent; Spanish Don;
  Cartagenian; Priest; Sailor; Eunuch . . . . David Horwitz
Paquette . . . . .Deborah St. Darr
Baroness; Harpsichordist; Penitente; Steel Drummer; Houri . . . . Mary-Pat Green

Baron; Grand Inquisitor; Slave Driver; Captain; Guest . . . . Joe Palmieri
Cunegonde . . . . Maureen Brennan
Maximillian . . . . Sam Freed
Servant; Agent of Inquisition; Spanish Don; Cartagenian Sailor . . . . Robert Hendersen
2d Recruiting Officer; Aristocrat; Cartagenian . . . . Peter Vogt
Penitente; Whore; Houri . . . . Gail Boggs
Penitente; Cartagenian; Houri . . . . Lynne Gannaway
Aristocrat; Cartagenian; 2d Sheep . . . . Carolann Page
Bulgarian Soldier; Aristocrat; Fruit Vendor; Sailor; Pygmy; Cow . . . . Carlos Gorbea
Bulgarian Soldier; Penitente; Cartagenian; Sailor; Cow . . . . Kelly Walters
Westphalian Soldier; Agent; Governor's Aide; Pirate; Guest . . . . Chip Garnett
Rich Jew; Judge; Man in Black; Cartagenian; Pirate; German; Botanist; Guest . . . . Jeff Keller
Aristocrat; Cartagenian; Houri . . . . Becky McSpadden
Aristocrat; Whore; Houri; Cunegonde Alternate . . . . Kathryn Ritter
Lady With Knitting; Cartagenian; 1st Sheep . . . . Renee Semes
Old Lady . . . . June Gable
Swing Girl . . . . Rhoda Butler

Understudies: Mr. Stadlen—Sam Freed; Mr. Baker—Kelly Walters; Miss Brennan—Kathryn Ritter; Mr. Freed—Robert Hendersen; Miss Gable—Renee Semes; Miss St. Darr—Lynne Gannaway; Mr. Palmieri—Peter Vogt.

Directed by Harold Prince; choreography, Patricia Birch; design, Eugene and Franne Lee; lighting, Tharon Musser; musical direction, John Mauceri; orchestrations, Hershy Kay; production stage manager, James Doolan; press, Betty Lee Hunt Associates, Maria Pucci, Harriett Trachtenberg.

The play was presented without intermission.

A musical version of Voltaire's *Candide* with music by Leonard Bernstein, lyrics by Richard Wilbur, John Latouche and Dorothy Parker and book by Lillian Hellman was produced on Broadway 12/1/56 for 73 performances and was named a Best Play of its season. A version of this work with book adapted by Sheldon Patinkin was produced 10/26/71 for 32 performances at the John F. Kennedy Center's Opera House in Washington, D.C. but never reached New York.

NOTE: This production of *Candide* was presented by The Chelsea Theater Center of Brooklyn at the Brooklyn Academy of Music 12/11/73 for 48 performances before being transferred to Broadway; see its entry in the "Plays Produced off Broadway" section of this volume.

MUSICAL NUMBERS—"Life Is Happiness Indeed"—Mark Baker, Maureen Brennan, Sam Freed, Deborah St. Darr; "The Best of All Possible Worlds"—Lewis J. Stadlen, Baker, Freed, Misses Brennan, St. Darr; "Oh Happy We"—Baker, Miss Brennan; "It Must Be So"—Baker; "O Miserere" —Carolann Page, Lynne Gannaway, Gail Boggs, Robert Hendersen; "Oh Happy We" (Reprise)— Baker, Miss Brennan; "Glitter and Be Gay"—Miss Brennan; "Auto Da fe (What a Day)"—Company; "This World"—Baker; "You Were Dead, You Know"—Baker, Miss Brennan; "I Am Easily Assimilated"—June Gable, Jim Corti, David Horwitz, Hendersen; "I Am Easily Assimilated" (Reprise)—Baker, Misses Gable, Brennan; "My Love"—Stadlen; "Alleluia"—Company; "Sheep's Song" —Renee Semes, Corti, Baker, Misses St. Darr, Page; "Bon Voyage"—Stadlen, Company; "The Best of All Possible Worlds" (Reprise)—Baker, Misses Gable, St. Darr, Semes, Page; "You Were Dead, You Know" (Reprise)—Baker, Miss Brennan; "Make Our Garden Grow"—Company.

Ulysses in Nighttown (69). Revival of the play by Marjorie Barkentin; dramatized from James Joyce's *Ulysses*. Produced by Alexander H. Cohen and Bernard Delfont at the Winter Garden. Opened March 10, 1974. (Closed May 11, 1974)

Narrator . . . . W.B. Brydon
Buck Mulligan; 2d Watch; Dr. Mulligan; Bishop of Erin . . . . David Ogden Stiers
Stephen Dedalus . . . . Tom Lee Jones
Coachman; Lynch; Spy; Tom Kernan; Hollybush . . . . Douglas Anderson
Martin Cunningham; Pvt. Carr; Harry Rumbold; Man in Macintosh;
  Dr. Madden; Brother Buzz . . . . Norman Barrs
Leopold Bloom . . . . Zero Mostel
Simon Dedalus; 1st Watch; J.J. O'Molloy; Bishop of Down & Connor;
  Dr. Dixon; Rev. Love . . . . Michael Clarke-Laurence
Molly Bloom; Crone; Mary Driscoll; Mrs. Bellingham; Applewoman . . . . Fionnuala Flanagan
Blazes Boylan; Drunken Navvy; Pvt. Compton; Dark Mercury;
  Pavior & Flagger; Orator; Elijah . . . . Danny Meehan

Sprawled Figure; Mrs. Breen; Mrs. Yelverton Barry; Old Resident;
Mrs. Riordan; Mrs. Thornton; Bella Cohen . . . . Beulah Garrick
Child; Gnome; Whore; Female Infant . . . . Barbara Blair
Child; Wellington; Davy Stephens; Acolyte; Attendant; Rudy . . . . Scott Gordon
Idiot; Gladstone; Balladeer; Attendant . . . . Danny Ruvolo
Pygmy Woman; Blushing Bride; Nymph . . . . Joanna de Varona
Zoe . . . . Carolyn Kirsch
Whore; Virago; Florry . . . . Margery Beddow
Cissy Caffrey; Kitty . . . . Gale Garnett
Blind Man; Prof. Maginni . . . . .Bert Michaels
Mrs. Mervin Talboys; Stephen's Mother . . . . Robin Howard
Sir Frederick Falkiner; Mayor Harrington; Father Farley; Hornblower . . . . . . Kevin O'Leary
Bella-Bello . . . . Swen Swenson

The Yews: Margery Beddow, Barbara Blair, Gale Garnett, Carolyn Kirsch.
Musicians: Peter Phillips musical director and keyboards; Howard Collins guitar and banjo; Irwin Cooper percussionist; Leo Kahn violinist; Wallace Kane woodwinds; Austin Wallace bass and tuba.
Standbys: Messrs. Jones, Stiers, Meehan, Anderson—Richard Morse. Principal Understudies: Messrs. Clarke-Laurence, Barrs—Kevin O'Leary; Messrs. Michaels, Gordon—Danny Ruvolo; Miss Flanagan—Gale Garnett; Miss Kirsch—Joanna de Varona; Misses Garnett, Blair, Beddow, Mr. Swenson—Robin Howard.
Directed by Burgess Meredith; score and arrangements, Peter Link; scenery, Ed Wittstein; costumes, Pearl Somner; lighting, Jules Fisher; dance movement, Swen Swenson; assistant director, Tom Clancy; sound, Sandy Hacker; production associate, Hildy Parks; production supervisor, Jerry Adler; associate producer, Roy A. Somlyo; production stage manager, Donald W. Christy; stage manager, Alisa Jill Adler; press, David Powers.
Time: June 16, 1904. Place: Dublin. The play was presented in two parts.
Sexual and other fantasies of Leopold Bloom, Molly Bloom, Stephen Dedalus, etc., are acted out explicitly, largely in the red-light-district scene of Joyce's novel. The play was originally produced off Broadway during the 1958–59 season with Zero Mostel as Leopold Bloom, and it was revived in the 1963–64 season by Equity Library Theater. This is its first Broadway production.

Clarence Darrow (22). One-man performance by Henry Fonda in a play by David W. Rintels; based on *Clarence Darrow for the Defense* by Irving Stone. Produced by Mike Merrick and Don Gregory at the Helen Hayes Theater. Opened March 26, 1974. (Closed April 23, 1974)

Directed by John Houseman; scenery and lighting, H.R. Poindexter; production stage manager, George Eckert; stage manager, Berny Baker; press, Seymour Krawitz, Patricia McLean Krawitz.
A one-character play in which Fonda, as the noted defense lawyer Clarence Darrow, is sometimes telling the audience about his life and career and sometimes addressing juries, witnesses, etc. as though they were actually present onstage. The play was presented in two parts.

* My Fat Friend (70). By Charles Laurence. Produced by James Nederlander, Inc. (James Nederlander, Elizabeth I. McCann) by arrangement with Michael Codron at the Brooks Atkinson Theater. Opened March 31, 1974.

James . . . . John Lithgow   Vicky . . . . Lynn Redgrave
Henry . . . . George Rose   Tom . . . . James Ray Weeks

Standbys: Miss Redgrave—Jill Tanner; Mr. Rose—Geoff Garland; Messrs. Lithgow, Weeks—Allen Williams.
Directed by Robert Moore; scenery, William Ritman; costumes, Sara Brook, Lighting, Martin Aronstein; production associate, Richard Lehmann; production stage manager, Ben Janney; stage manager, George Rondo; press, Michael Alpert, Marilynn LeVine, Ellen Levene.
Time: The present. Place: Vicky's house and bookshop in a North section of London. Act I, Scene 1: An August morning. Scene 2: That evening. Scene 3: The next day. Act II, Scene 1: Sunday, four months later. Scene 2: Christmas Eve. Scene 3: Later that evening.
A fat girl's two friends and boarders persuade her to slim down in order to fascinate a certain man —who, it turns out, doesn't like slim women. A foreign play previously produced in London, South America and elsewhere.

* **Thieves** (62). By Herb Gardner. Produced by Richard Scanga and Charles Grodin at the Broadhurst Theater. Opened April 7, 1974.

Charlie . . . . Dick Van Patten	Johnny MacDonald . . . . . William Hickey
Harry; Perez . . . . .Pierre Epstein	Carlton Danfield II . . . . . Haywood Nelson
Flo . . . . .Alice Drummond	Joe Kaminsky . . . . .Irwin Corey
Martin Cramer . . . . .Richard Mulligan	Gordon . . . . .David Spielberg
Sally Cramer . . . . Marlo Thomas	Street Lady . . . . Sudie Bond
Nancy . . . . .Ann Wedgeworth	Devlin . . . . .Sammy Smith
Stanley; Policeman . . . . George Loros	

Standby: Misses Thomas, Wedgeworth—Susan Browning. Understudies: Mr. Corey—Sammy Smith; Mr. Nelson—Julio Herrera; Messrs. Loros, Van Patten, Hickey—Pierre Epstein; Miss Bond—Alice Drummond; Messrs. Spielberg, Epstein—George Loros.

Directed by Charles Grodin; scenery, Peter Larkin; costumes, Joseph G. Aulisi; lighting, Jules Fisher; sound, Sandy Hacker; production stage manager, Bud Coffey; stage manager, Robert Corpora; press, Merle Debuskey, Leo Stern.

Time: The present, between 1 A.M. and 7 A.M. on a warm June night. Place: The Upper East Side of Manhattan (we see pieces of a piece of the city; the upper reaches of the buildings rise directly out of the streets around them). The play was presented in two parts.

Comic slices of life in New York: panhandling in the gutters and assignations and troubled marriages in the high-rises.

Pierre Epstein replaced Dick Van Patten 5/27/74.

Music! Music! (37). Cavalcade of American music with footnotes by Alan Jay Lerner. Produced by The City Center of Music and Drama, Inc., Norman Singer executive director, and Alvin Bojar at the City Center 55th Street Theater. Opened April 11, 1974. (Closed May 12, 1974)

Robert Guillaume	Gail Nelson
Larry Kert	Gene Nelson
Will Mackenzie	Ted Pritchard
Donna McKechnie	Arnold Soboloff
Karen Morrow	Russ Thacker

Singing and Dancing Ensemble: Renée Baughman, Trish Garland, Denise Mauthé, Michon Peacock, Tom Offt, Michael Radigan, Yolanda R. Raven, Freda Soiffer, Thomas J. Walsh. Standbys: Women—Barbara Broughton; Men—Ken Cory. Dance Alternate—Penelope Richards. Dance Understudy for Miss McKechnie—Renée Baughman.

Directed and staged by Martin Charnin; choreography, Tony Stevens; musical direction and vocal arrangements, John Lesko; scenery, David Chapman; costumes, Theoni V. Aldredge; lighting, Martin Aronstein; orchestrations, Elliot Lawrence, Men—Ken Cohn, William Elton; dance arrangements, Wally Harper; producers for City Center, Robert P. Brannigan, Chuck Eisler; associate producer, Howard Effron; production stage manager, Janet Beroza; stage manager, Donald King; press, Dan Langan.

Act I: Storyville, The Great White Way, World War I, The Princess Theater, Those #%*!$20s, Tin Pan Alley, Prohibition, The Boom, The Bust, Catfish Row, NY to LA. Act II: World War II, The Great White Way Revisited, Rock and Roll, New Haven and Broadway, The New Frontier, The Great Society? Yesterday's Children, To Be Continued . . .

A survey of American music from 1895 to the present, in a series of musical numbers.

* **Words and Music** (53). Revue by Sammy Cahn; lyrics by Sammy Cahn; music by various composers. Produced by Alexander H. Cohen and Harvey Granat at the John Golden Theater. Opened April 16, 1974.

Sammy Cahn	Shirley Lemmon
Kelly Garrett	Jon Peck

Directed by Jerry Adler; musical direction, Sammy Cahn, Richard Leonard; design, Robert Randolph; lighting, Marc B. Weiss; production stage manager, Murray Gitlin; press, David Powers, William Schelble.

Standbys: Misses Garrett, Lemmon—Christine Andreas; Mr. Peck—Williams James.

The noted lyricist Sammy Cahn plays and sings his own songs and discusses his career in an embellished one-man show presented in two parts.

Jumpers (48). By Tom Stoppard. Produced by the John F. Kennedy Center for the Performing Arts, Frederick Brisson and Roger L. Stevens producers, with the cooperation of the Billy Rose Foundation at the Billy Rose Theater. Opened April 22, 1974. (Closed June 1, 1974)

Archie . . . . .Remak Ramsay	Duncan McFee . . . . Robert Rhys
Dotty . . . . .Jill Clayburgh	George . . . . .Brian Bedford
Secretary . . . . Joan Byron	Bones . . . . .Ronald Drake
Crouch . . . . Walter Flanagan	Clegthorpe . . . . .William Rhys

Jumpers, Chaplains, Ushers, etc: Larry Bailey, Larry Breeding, Mark Hanks, Bobby Lee, James Litten, Eddie Mekka, Ross Miles, Dale Muchmore, Stan Picus, George Ramos, Robert Rhys, William Rhys, Jason Roberts, Russell Robertson, Gordon Weiss.
Standbys: Messrs. Bedford, Ramsay—Colin Hamilton; Messrs. Flanagan, Drake—Alex Reed; Misses Clayburgh, Byron—Lisa Richards.
Directed by Peter Wood; choreography and tumbling, Dennis Nahat; scenery, Josef Svoboda; costumes, Willa Kim; Miss Clayburgh's special bedroom costumes, Fernando Sanchez; lighting, Gilbert V. Hemsley Jr.; musical arrangements, Claus Ogerman; original lyrics, Tom Stoppard; "Beyond My Reach" music by Claus Ogerman, lyrics by Mort Goode; production stage manager, Mitchell Erickson; stage managers, John Hardy, Frank Marino; press, Gifford/Wallace, Inc.
Time: The present. Place: George and Dotty's flat in Mayfair, London.
Absurdist farce with a dash—but only a dash—of murder, bearing down on the contrast between the mental gymnastics of a professor preparing to debate whether God is dead and the literal physical acrobatics of a group of gymnasts; they are "jumpers" all, in their private and professional lives. A foreign play previously produced in London by the Old Vic and in Washington, D.C.
A Best Play; see page 257

Sammy (14). Revue devised as a showcase for the solo performance of Sammy Davis Jr. Produced by Nederlander at the Uris Theater. Opened April 23, 1974. (Closed May 4, 1974)

Sammy Davis Jr.   Freda Payne
The Nicholas Brothers

Musical conductor, George Rhodes; produced in association with Sy Marsh; stage director, Darrell Giddens; press, Michael Alpert, Ellen Levene, Anne Weinberg.
A night club show transposed to Broadway for a limited engagement, with Sammy Davis Jr. as the main attraction.

* My Sister, My Sister (36). By Ray Aranha. Produced by Jay J. Cohen, Myra L. Burns and Chesmark Productions at the Little Theater. Opened April 30, 1974.

Sue Belle . . . . Seret Scott	Jesus . . . . Lowell Copeland
Mama . . . . Barbara Montgomery	Eddie . . . . .David Downing
Evalina . . . . Jessie Saunders	

Spectres: Frank Adu, Trazana Beverley, Diane Bivens, Rosanna Carter, Larry Pertilla.
Understudies: Mr. Downing—Frank Adu; Miss Montgomery—Trazana Beverley; Misses Saunders, Scott—Diane Bivens.
Directed by Paul Weidner; scenery, Lawrence King; lighting, Larry Crimmins; costumes, Kathleen Ankers; lighting design supervised by John Gleason; production stage manager, Bette Howard; press, Les Schecter.
A black Southern childhood in the 1950s. Previously produced by the Hartford, Conn. Stage Company and off off Broadway.

* Bad Habits (126; see note). By Terrence McNally. Produced by Adela Holzer at the Booth Theater. Opened May 5, 1974; see note.

PERFORMER	"RAVENSWOOD"	"DUNELAWN"
F. Murray Abraham	Roy Pitt	Mr. Blum
Emory Bass	Hiram Spane	Mr. Ponce
Paul Benedict	Jason Pepper, M.D.	Hugh Gumbs
Cynthia Harris	April Pitt	Ruth Benson, R.N.
Michael Lombard	Harry Scupp	Mr. Yamadoro
J. Frank Lucas	Francis Tear	Dr. Toynbee
Doris Roberts	Dolly Scupp	Becky Hedges, R.N.
Henry Sutton	Otto	Bruno

Standby: Misses Harris, Roberts—Doris Belack. Understudies: Messrs. Bass, Lucas—Skedge Miller; Messrs. Sutton (Otto), Abraham (Blum), Lombard (Yamadoro)—James Carruthers; Messrs; Lombard (Harry), Benedict, Sutton (Bruno)—Paul B. Price.

Directed by Robert Drivas; scenery and costumes designed by Michael H. Yeargan and Lawrence King; lighting, Ken Billington; production stage manager, Robert Vandergriff; press, Michael Alpert, Ellen Levene, Marilynn LeVine, Anne Weinberg.

Both plays on this program of two one-acters are set in nursing homes, in the present, and both are black or gray-comedy comments on common personal neuroses of our times. In *Ravenswood,* several couples are suffering wrenchingly obvious emotional and ego problems, which the doctor seeks to cure by total permissiveness. In *Dunelawn,* drugs and gibberish are offered as the solution to several deep-seated ills.

NOTE: This production of *Bad Habits* was presented off Broadway at the Astor Place Theater 2/4/74 for 96 performances before being transferred to Broadway; see its entry in the "Plays Produced off Broadway" section of this volume.

Paul B. Price replaced Paul Benedict 5/12/74.

A Best Play; see page 173

Will Rogers' U.S.A. (8). One-man show adapted by Paul Shyre; with James Whitmore. Produced by George Spota at the Helen Hayes Theater. Opened May 6, 1974. (Closed May 11, 1974)

Directed by Paul Shyre; production designed by Eldon Elder; associate producer, Bryan Sterling; presented in association with Lester Osterman Productions (Lester Osterman, Richard Horner); production stage manager, Bernard Pollack; press, Seymour Krawitz, Patricia McLean Krawitz, Fred Hoot.

The noted performer, philosopher and humorist Will Rogers, impersonated by James Whitmore and speaking in selections from his own material. The play was presented in two parts. Previously produced in a cross-country tour.

Ride the Winds (3). Musical with book, music and lyrics by John Driver. Produced by Berta Walker and Bill Tchakirides at the Bijou Theater. Opened May 16, 1974. (Closed May 18, 1974 matinee)

Musashi	Irving Lee	Banzo	Tom Matsusaka
Yamada	Sab Shimono	Ya Ta	Fanny Cerito Assoluta
Sensei Takuan	Ernesto Gonzalez	Lan	Elaine Petricoff
Joshu	Nate Barnett	Toki	Marion Jim
Inari	Chip Zien	Oda	Alexander Orfaly

Tellers: Laura May Lewis, John Gorrin. Priests, Kendo Students, Soldiers: Kenneth Frett, John Gorrin, Richard Loreto, Ken Mitchell.

Musicians: Robert Brandzel conductor, woodwinds, percussion; Lawrence J. Blank keyboard, Joseph Deluca percussion, David Moore bass.

Directed by Lee D. Sankowich; choreography, Jay Norman; musical direction, orchestration, vocal arrangements, Robert Brandzel; scenery and costumes, Samuel C. Ball; lighting, Jeff Davis; technical advisor, Sensei Yoshiteru Otani, production stage manager, Victor Straus; stage manager, S.L. Smith; press, Shirley Herz.

Place: A feudal country in the Far East. Act I: Around a monastery along a mountain road. Act II: Four years later.

The story of an 11th century Japanese warrior and swordsman, or Samurai.

ACT I

"Run Musashi, Run" . . . . Company
"The Emperor Me" . . . . Musashi
"The Gentle Buffoon" . . . . Joshu, Inari,
"Those Who Speak" . . . . Musashi, Joshu, Inari
"Flower Song" . . . . Takuan, Lan, Joshu, Ensemble
"You're Loving Me" . . . . Musashi
"Breathing the Air" . . . . Toki
"Remember That Day" . . . . Takuan, Yamada
"Tengu" . . . . Ensemble

ACT II

"Ride the Winds" . . . . Company
"Are You a Man" . . . . Lan
"Ride the Winds" (Reprise) . . . . Company
"Every Days" . . . . Lan, Toki, Inari Priests
"Loving You" . . . . Lan, Musashi
"Pleasures" . . . . Oda
"Someday I'll Walk" . . . . Musashi
"That Touch" . . . . Lan
Finale . . . . Company

* **The Magic Show** (5). Musical with book by Bob Randall; music and lyrics by Stephen Schwartz; magic by Doug Henning. Produced by Edgar Lansbury, Joseph Beruh and Ivan Reitman at the Cort Theater. Opened May 28, 1974.

Manny	Robert Lupone	Doug	Doug Henning
Feldman	David Ogden Stiers	Mike	Ronald Stafford
Donna	Annie McGreevey	Steve	Loyd Sannes
Dina	Cheryl Barnes	Charmin	Anita Morris
Cal	Dale Soules	Goldfarb	Sam Schacht

Musicians: Stephen Reinhardt conductor, keyboards; Paul Shaffer keyboards; Brian McCormick guitars; Jerry Wiener guitars; Steve Manes bass; Joseph Saulter drums; Charles Birch Jr. percussion.

Understudy: Messrs. Stafford, Sannes: Justin Ross.

Directed and choreographed by Grover Dale; musical direction, Stephen Reinhardt; scenery, David Chapman; costumes, Randy Barcelo; lighting, Richard Nelson; dance arrangements, David Spangler; associate producer, Nan Pearlman; production stage manager, Herb Vogler; stage manager, John Actman; press, Gifford/Wallace, Inc.

Place: The Passaic Top Hat, a night club in New Jersey. The play was presented without intermission.

A suburban night club hires a new magician to replace its worn-out old act; the new man turns out to be an amazing performer whose illusions are part of the show's spectacle.

MUSICAL NUMBERS

"Up to His Old Tricks" . . . . Entire Company
"Solid Silver Platform Shoes" . . . . Dina, Donna
"Lion Tamer" . . . . Cal
"Style" . . . . Feldman, Company
"Charmin's Lament" . . . . Charmin
"Two's Company" . . . . Dina, Donna
"The Goldfarb Variations" . . . . Dina, Feldman, Donna, Manny, Charmin
Doug's Act . . . . Doug
"A Bit of Villainy" . . . . Feldman, Dina, Donna
"West End Avenue" . . . . Cal
"Sweet, Sweet, Sweet" . . . . Charmin, Manny, Mike, Steve
"Before Your Very Eyes" . . . . Dina, Donna, Feldman

PLAYS WHICH CLOSED
PRIOR TO BROADWAY OPENING

Plays which were organized in New York for Broadway presentation, but which closed during their tryout performances, are listed below.

The Student Prince. Musical revival with book and lyrics by Dorothy Donnelly; music by Sigmund Romberg. Produced by Moe Septee in association with Jack L. Wolgin and Victor H. Potamkin, in the Lehman Engel production, in a pre-Broadway tour at the Academy of Music, Philadelphia; Mechanic Theater, Baltimore; Opera House, Washington, D.C.; Shubert Theater, Chicago; Royal Alexandra Theater, Toronto; Clowes Theater, Indianapolis and the State Fair in Dallas. Opened June 5, 1973. (Closed in Dallas October 21, 1973)

Prime Minister	Robert Symonds	Count Hugo	Ed Dixon
Dr. Engel	Richard Torigi	Kathie	Bonnie Hamilton
Ruder	John Mintun	Grand Duchess	Fran Stevens
Gretchen	Patti Allison	Princess Margaret	Sandra Thornton
Toni	Warren Galjour	Capt. Tarnitz	William Covington
Lutz	George Rose	Baron Arnheim	Peter Atherton
Hubert	Theodore Tenley	Countess	Mary Roche
Von Asterberg	Brad Tyrell	Prince Karl Franz (evenings)	Harry Danner
Lucas	Don Estes	Prince Karl Franz (matinees)	Jon Garrison

Lackeys: Eric Ellenberg, Homer Foil, Wayne Scherzer, Michael Merrill.

Singers, Dancers: Neal Antin, Peter Atherton, Marta Brennan, Michael Carrier, Peter Damon, Doreen DeFeis, Eric Ellenberg, Tricia Ellis, Patti Farmer, John Franz, Homer Foil, James Fredericks, George Holland, Mark Jacoby, Howard Johnson, Robert Kunar, Valerie Lemon, George Maguire, Jason McAuliff, Michael Merrill, Sal Mistretta, Mary Roche, Anthony Santelmo, Wayne Scherzer, Dana Talley, David Varnum, Richard Walker, John West, Peter Whitehead, Parker Willson.

Directed by George Schaefer; choreography, David Nillo; musical direction, John Lesko (premiere conducted by Lehman Engel); scenery and lighting, Clarke Dunham; costume supervision, Winn Morton, Sara Brook; stage managers, Pat Tolson, Robert Vandergriff, Parker Willson; press, Gene Palatsky.

The play was presented in a prologue and two acts.

This Romberg operetta was first produced in New York 12/2/24 and has been revived twice on Broadway (1/29/31 for 42 performances and 6/8/43 for 153 performances) and off Broadway in the season of 1960–61.

Ray Walston replaced George Rose. Robert Rounseville replaced William Covington.

MUSICAL NUMBERS: "By Our Bearing So Sedate," "Golden Days," "To the Inn We're Marching," "Drinking Song," "I'm Coming at Your Call," "Come Boys," "Entrance of the Prince and Engel," "Gaudeamus Igitur," "Golden Days" (Reprise), "Deep in My Heart, Dear," "Serenade," "Student Life," "Just We Two," "The Flag That Flies," "To the Inn We're Marching" (Reprise), "Serenade" (Reprise), "Come Boys" (Reprise).

The One-Night Stand. By Bruce Jay Friedman and Jacques Levy. Produced by David Merrick in a pre-Broadway tryout at the Fisher Theater, Detroit and the Forrest Theater, Philadelphia. Opened August 6, 1973. (Closed in Philadelphia September 22, 1973)

Phil Corning	Tony Curtis	Rose	Judith Tillman
Vendor: Lou Corning	Sammy Smith	Girl; Henrietta	Carolyn Mignini
1st Jogger; Dugan; Dr. Atkins;		Timothy Keefe	William Devane
Charlie	Marty Davis	Valerie Cushing	Leslie Charleson
2d Jogger; Froehlich; Mr. Hoxie	Ken Olfson	Sgt. O'Mara; Doorman	Barney Martin
Girl Jogger; Sister Allison;		Dave Corning	Harold Gary

Directed by Jacques Levy and Bruce Jay Friedman; scenery, Peter Larkin; costumes, Sara Brook; lighting, Roger Morgan; incidental music, Stanley Walden; production assistant, Lucia Victor; production stage manager, May Muth; stage manager, Bob Burland; press, Michael Alpert, Anne Weinberg.

Time: The present. Place: New York City. Act I, Scene 1: Central Park. Scene 2, Police Station. Scene 3: Central Park. Scene 4: St. Luke's Hospital. Scene 5: Phil Corning's apartment. Scene 6: An office at Christian Dior. Scene 7: Corning's apartment, Scene 8: Corning's apartment. Act II: Scene 1: A restaurant. Scene 2: The showroom at Dave-Lou Knitwear, Inc. Scene 3: Corning's apartment. Scene 4: Corning's apartment.

Once entitled *Turtlenecks,* a comedy about a severely dedicated writer whose friends try to distract him with sex horseplay.

The Day After the Fair. By Frank Harvey; based on a story by Thomas Hardy. Produced by Arthur Cantor by arrangement with Frith Banbury and Jimmy Wax in a touring production. Opened at the Auditorium Theater, Denver, September 4, 1973. (Closed at the John F. Kennedy Center for the Performing Arts, Washington, D.C., January 20, 1974)

Arthur Harnham	W.B. Brydon	Sarah	Marie Tommon
Letty	Brenda Forbes	Anna	Vickery Turner
Edith	Deborah Kerr	Charles Bradford	Michael Shannon

Directed by Frith Banbury; scenery, Reece Pemberton; costumes, Robin Fraser Paye; lighting, H.R. Poindexter; production stage manager, Mitchell Erickson; stage manager, Robert Crawley; press, Gertrude Bromberg.

Time: Three months during the summer of 1900. Place: The front room of "The Brewer's House" in a West Country cathedral city in England. Act I, Scene 1: May, evening. Scene 2: Ten days later, morning. Scene 3: Six weeks later, Sunday evening. Act II, Scene 1: Two weeks later, Saturday afternoon. Scene 2: Three days later, Tuesday morning. Scene 3: The first Saturday in August, morning.

Stage adaptation of Thomas Hardy's story *On the Western Circuit* about the Victorian embarrassment of a well-to-do family's suddenly pregnant young ward. A foreign play previously produced in London. Nineteen-week American road tour included Los Angeles, San Francisco, Chicago, Boston and Toronto.

Rachael Lily Rosenbloom and Don't You Ever Forget It. Musical with book by Paul Jabara and Tom Eyen; music and lyrics by Paul Jabara. Produced by Robert Stigwood and Ahmet Ertegun in previews at the Broadhurst Theater. Opened November 26, 1973. (Closed in previews December 1, 1973)

Richard Cooper Bayne	Anita Morris
Carole Bishop	Michon Peacock
Kenneth Carr	Marion Ramsey
André De Shields	Jozella Reed
Judy Gibson	Jane Robertson
Ellen Greene	Thomas Walsh
Paul Jabara	Anthony White

Swing Girl—Rhoda Farber. Swing Boy—Wayne Cilento.

Directed by Tom Eyen; choreography and music numbers staging, Tony Stevens; choreographic supervision, Grover Dale; scenery, Robin Wagner; costumes, Joseph G. Aulisi; lighting, Jules Fisher; sound, Abe Jacob; dance music arrangements, Bill Cunningham; production supervisor, Galen McKinley; production coordinator, Jeffrey Mont; music supervision, Gordon Lowry Harrell; associate producers, Gatchell & Neufeld; stage manager, William Schill; press, Betty Lee Hunt Associates, Harriett Trachtenberg, Maria Pucci.

Time: The present. Act I, Scene 1: The 46th annual Academy Awards presentation. Scene 2: Brooklyn garbage cans. Scene 3: Fulton Fish Market. Scene 4: Rachael's bedroom in Brooklyn. Scene 5: The Rachael Rosenbloom Radio Show. Scene 6: Travelling cross country. Scene 7: Hollywood's own Lolo Lounge. Scene 8: A park near Beverly Hills. Scene 9: Stella's bathroom. Scene 10: Stella's Southern California party. Act II, Scene 1: The 46th annual Academy Awards presentation. Scene

2: Rachael's Hollywood bedroom. Scene 3: Barbra's reception room. Scene 4: Rachael's Hollywood bedroom. Scene 5: Ocho Rios. Scene 6: Sam Dago's Bar. Scene 7: On location in the depths of North Africa. Scene 8: Sam Dago's Bar. Scene 9: In the gutter outside Sam Dago's. Scene 10: Fulton Fish Market. Scene 11: In the streets. Scene 12: The Rachael Rosenbloom Concert.

A would-be star (who spells her name Rachael in order to pick up the "a" dropped by Barbra Streisand) winds up as a gossip columnist.

ACT I—"Academy Awards Theme"—Company; "Dear Miss Streisand"—Ellen Greene; "Delivery Boys' Lament"—Richard Cooper Bayne, Kenneth Carr, André De Shields, Thomas Walsh, Anthony White; "Me and My Perch" (lyrics by Paul Jabara and David Debin)—Miss Greene, Bayne, Carr, De Shields, Walsh, White; "Gorgeous Lily"—Miss Greene, Michon Peacock, Carole Bishop, Paul Jabara; "Get Your Show Rolling"—Marion Ramsey, Miss Greene, De Shields, White, Company; "Hollywood! Hollywood!"—Misses Ramsey, Greene, Messrs. Jabara, De Shields, White; "East Brooklyn Blues"—Carr, Bayne, De Shields, Misses Greene, Peacock, Bishop, Jozella Reed, Company; "Broadway Rhythm"—Anita Morris, Girls; "Hollywood Is Dying"—Boys; "Broadway I Love You"—Miss Morris; "Raymond's Song"—Jabara, Miss Greene; "Seduction Samba"—Miss Peacock, De Shields, White, Company; "Rona, Mona and Me"—Jabara, Miss Bishop, Jane Robertson; "Working for Stella"—Misses Morris, Greene; "Silver Diamond Rhinestone Glasses"—Miss Greene; "Party Sickness"—Company; "Take Me Savage"—Misses Morris, Gibson, Reed; "Overdose"—Company; "Get Your Show Rolling" (Reprise)—Misses Ramsey, Greene, Company.

ACT II—"Academy Awards Theme" (Reprise)—Company; "Change in Raquel"—Miss Greene, Jabara, Bayne, Carr, White, De Shields; "Raquel Gives the Dish"—Misses Greene, Peacock, Messrs. White, Carr, Walsh, De Shields, Bayne; "Gorgeous Lily" (Reprise)—Misses Greene, Peacock, Bishop, Mr. Jabara; "Ochos Rios" (Lyrics by Paul Jabara and Paul Issa)—Misses Greene, Morris, Messrs. De Shields, Jabara, Walsh, Company; "Cobra Woman"—Miss Greene, Company; "Things" —Miss Greene, Carr, Walsh, Bayne, White; "One Man"—Misses Greene, Morris, Ramsey, Girls; "We'll Be There" (lyrics by Paul Jabara and Paul Issa)—Misses Ramsey, Reed, Gibson, Messrs. De Shields, White—"One Man" (Reprise)—Misses Morris, Ramsey; "Broadway Rhythm" (Reprise)— Company; "We'll Be There" (Reprise)—Company.

Brainchild. Musical with book by Maxine Klein; music by Michel Legrand; lyrics by Hal David. Produced by Adela Holzer in a pre-Broadway tryout at the Forrest Theater in Philadelphia. Opened March 25, 1974. (Closed April 6, 1974)

Adrian:	Irving . . . . Mark Siegel
Adrian's Self Image . . . . Tovah Feldshuh	Her Teacher;
Adrian's Emotional Self . . Marilyn Pasekoff	Telephone Operator . . . . . Louise Hoven
Adrian's Mental Self . . . . . Barbara Niles	Sally Ensalada . . . . Signa Joy
Adrian's Memories:	Adrian's Fantasies:
Her Father, Raymond . . Dorian Harewood	Hag; New York Lady . . . . . Louise Hoven
Her Mother . . . . Barbara Niles	Rock Singer . . . . Dorian Harewood
Jim . . . . Gene Lindsey	Weatherball Mermaid . Nancy Ann Denning
Bonnie; Nun . . . . Nancy Ann Denning	Low Bottom Woman . . . . Signa Joy

Adrian's Nerve Cells: Francesca Bartoccini, Nancy Dalton, Ben Harney, Scott Johnson, Tony Padron, Justin Ross, Harriet Scalici.

Directed by Maxine Klein; musical direction and supervision, Thomas Pierson; scenery, Kert Lundell; costumes, Joseph G. Aulisi; lighting, Thomas Skelton; musical concepts and arrangements, Michel Legrand; choreographic assistant to the director, Leigh Abdallah; sound, Lou Gonzalez; production stage manager, Frank Hartenstein; stage manager, Robert Vandergrift; press, Michael Alpert, Ellen Levene, Marilynn LeVine.

Time: Now. Adrian is waiting for her lover. He is late as usual. Place: In Adrian's mind. She is a composer. Like most composers, she is always somewhere in between procrastinating and writing a song. The play was presented without intermission.

Self-described as "a musical in the mind," the fantasies and other thoughts occupying the mind of a woman songwriter.

MUSICAL NUMBERS—"Everything That Happens to You" (unfinished)—Tovah Feldshuh; "I'm Tired of Me"—Marilyn Pasekoff, Barbara Niles, Miss Feldshuh; "No Faceless People"—Nancy Dalton, Nancy Ann Denning, Signa Joy, Harriet Scalici; "The First Time I Heard a Bluebird"—Miss Pasekoff; "I Know You Are There"—Dorian Harewood, Ben Harney, Scott Johnson, Tony Padron, Justin Ross; "Don't Talk, Don't Think"—Miss Denning, Gene Lindsey; "Low Bottom Woman"— Miss Joy; "I've Been Starting Tomorrow"—Messrs. Harewood, Harney, Miss Joy; "I've Been Starting Tomorrow" (Reprise)—Misses Feldshuh, Joy, Messrs. Harewood, Harney; "Everything That Hap-

pens to You" (unfinished)—Misses Feldshuh, Pasekoff, Niles; "Let Me Think for You"—Misses
Pasekoff, Niles; "I Never Met a Russian I Didn't Like"—Messrs. Harney, Johnson, Padron, Ross;
"Sally Ensalada"—Miss Joy, Messrs. Harney, Padron, Harewood, Johnson, Ross; "Let Me Be Your
Mirror"—Harewood; "Just a Little Space Can Be a Growing Place"—Miss Niles; "What Is It?"—
Misses Feldshuh, Pasekoff, Niles; "Don't Pull Up the Flowers"—Miss Feldshuh, Company; "Every-
thing That Happens to You"—Miss Feldshuh, Company.

PLAYS PRODUCED
OFF BROADWAY

Some distinctions between off-Broadway and Broadway productions at one end of the scale and off-off-Broadway productions at the other end were beginning to blur in the New York theater of the 1970s. For the purposes of this *Best Plays* listing, the term "off Broadway" signifies a show which opened for general audiences in a mid-Manhattan theater seating 299 or fewer during the time period covered by this volume and 1) employed an Equity cast, 2) planned a regular schedule of 7 or 8 performances a week and 3) offered itself to public comment by critics at opening performances.

Occasional exceptions of inclusion (never of exclusion) are made to take in visiting troupes, borderline cases and a few non-qualifying productions which readers might expect to find in this list because they appear under an off-Broadway heading in other major sources of record.

Figures in parentheses following a play's title indicate number of performances. These figures are acquired directly from the production office in each case and do not include previews or extra non-profit performances.

Plays marked with an asterisk (*) were still running on June 1, 1974. Their number of performances is figured from opening night through May 31, 1974.

In a listing of a show's numbers—dances, sketches, musical scenes, etc.—the titles of songs are identified by their appearance in quotation marks (").

Most entries of off-Broadway productions which ran fewer than 20 performances are somewhat abbreviated.

HOLDOVERS FROM PREVIOUS SEASONS

Plays which were running on June 1, 1973 are listed below. More detailed information about them appears in previous *Best Plays* volumes of appropriate years. Important cast changes since opening night are recorded in a section of this volume.

* **The Fantasticks** (5,863; longest continuous run of record in the American theater). Musical suggested by the play *Les Romantiques* by Edmond Rostand; book and lyrics by Tom Jones; music by Harvey Schmidt. Opened May 3, 1960.

One Flew Over the Cuckoo's Nest (1,025). Revival of the play by Dale Wasserman. Opened March 23, 1971. (Closed September 16, 1973)

The Proposition (1,109). Improvisational revue conceived by Allan Albert. Opened March 4, 1971; order and method of presentation somewhat rearranged for "new" editions beginning September 16, 1971 and September 13, 1972. (Closed April 14, 1974)

* **Godspell** (1,270). Musical based on the Gospel according to St. Matthew; conceived by John-Michael Tebelak; music and lyrics by Stephen Schwartz. Opened May 17, 1971.

The Real Inspector Hound and After Magritte (465). Program of two one-act plays by Tom Stoppard. Opened April 23, 1972. (Closed June 3, 1973)

Oh Coward! (294). Musical revue with words and music by Noel Coward; devised by Roderick Cook. Opened October 4, 1972. (Closed June 17, 1973)

National Lampoon's Lemmings (350). Musical revue with words and lyrics by David Axlerod, Anne Beatts, Henry Beard, John Boni, Tony Hendra, Sean Kelly, Doug Kenny, P.J. O'Rourke and the cast; music by Paul Jacobs and Christopher Guest. Opened January 25, 1973. (Closed November 25, 1973)

* **El Grande de Coca-Cola** (668). Musical revue in the Spanish language written by the cast; based on an idea by Ron House and Diz White. Opened February 13, 1973.

The Tooth of Crime (123). By Sam Shepard; music by The Performance Group; lyrics by Sam Shepard. Opened March 7, 1973. (Closed July 29, 1973)

* **The Hot l Baltimore** (499). By Lanford Wilson. Opened March 22, 1973.

What's a Nice Country Like You Doing in a State Like This? (543). Cabaret revue based on an original concept by Ira Gasman, Cary Hoffman and Bernie Travis; music by Cary Hoffman; lyrics by Ira Gasman. Opened April 19, 1973. New edition opened March 25, 1974. (Closed May 12, 1974)

The American Place Theater. 1972–73 schedule of four programs concluded with Baba Goya (25). By Steve Tesich. Opened May 9, 1973. (Closed June 2, 1973; reopened 10/3/73 under the title *Nourish the Beast;* see its entry in the "Plays Produced Off Broadway" section of this volume)

Hot and Cold Heros (16). Musical revue conceived by Joe Jakubowitz. Opened May 9, 1973. (Closed June 2, 1973)

PLAYS PRODUCED JUNE 1, 1973—MAY 31,1974

The Boy Who Came to Leave (1). By Lee Kalcheim. Produced by Lymehouse Productions at the Astor Place Theater. Opened and closed at the evening performance, June 6, 1973.

Directed by William E. Hunt; scenery and lighting, William Strom; press, Max Eisen, Warren Pincus. With Fred Grandy, Jordan Charney, Arthur Sellers, Mary Hamill.

Two young men, a poet and a composer of widely differing characters, share an apartment and an abrasive relationship.

The Faggot (182). Musical revue with words and music by Al Carmines. Produced by Bruce Mailman and Richard Lipton at the Truck and Warehouse Theater. Opened June 18, 1973. (Closed November 25, 1973)

Peggy Atkinson	Bruce Hopkins
Essie Borden	Julie Kurnitz
Lou Bullock	Philip Owens
Al Carmines	David Pursley
Marilyn Child	Bill Reynolds
Tony Clark	Ira Siff
Frank Coppola	David Summers
Lee Guilliatt	

Directed by Al Carmines; choreography, David Vaughan; piano, John R. Williams; scenery and costumes, T.E. Mason; lighting, Gary Weathersbee; production stage manager, Gary Weathersbee; press, Saul Richman, Sara Altshul.

Vignettes of homosexual lives and attitudes in songs and sketches. Previously produced off off Broadway at Judson Poets Theater.

ACT I: Movie House—Frank Coppola, Lou Bullock, Company; Overture—Company; "Women With Women—Men With Men"—Company; "The Hustler: A Five-Minute Opera"—David Pursley (The Score), Bill Reynolds (The Hustler); "I'll Take My Fantasy"—Tony Clark (Secretary of State), David Summers (Aide), Company; Mothers-in-Law—Julie Kurnitz (Jenny), Marilyn Child (Sadie); "Hari Krishna"—Ira Siff, Philip Owens, Reynolds, Bruce Hopkins; "Desperation"—Hopkins, Essie Borden, Company; "A Gay Bar Cantata"—Miss Child (Adele), Messrs. Bullock, Clark, Coppola, Owens Pursley (Businessmen), Summers (The New Boy in Town).

ACT II: "Nookie Time"—Lee Guilliatt (Narrator), Company; "Your Way of Loving"—Pursley (Oscar Wilde), Siff (Bosie); Fag Hag—Miss Borden; Puddin 'N' Tame—Bullock (Host), Coppola (Guest); "Ordinary Things"—Miss Guilliatt (Gertrude Stein), Peggy Atkinson (Alice B. Toklas); "Art Song"—Misses Kurnitz (Catherine the Great), Borden, Child (Ladies-in-Waiting); "What is a Queen"—Owens, Company; "Women With Women—Men With Men" (Reprise)—Company; Finale —Misses Guilliatt (Gertrude Stein, Atkinson (Alice B. Toklas), Kurnitz (Catherine the Great), Messrs. Pursley (Oscar Wilde), Siff (Bosie), Company.

Antiques (8). Musical with special material by Dore Schary; music and lyrics by Alan Greene and Laura Manning. Produced by Video Techniques, Inc. in association with Dore Schary Productions, Inc. at the Mercer-O'Casey Theater. Opened June 19, 1973. (Closed June 24, 1973)

Directed by Marco Martone; choreography, Jeffrey K. Neill; scenery, Bruno C. Scordino; costumes, William Christians; lighting, R.H. Rizzio; press, Cheryl Sue Dolby. With Charles Hudson, Laura Manning, Richard Marr, Betty Oakes, Eugene Smith, Ward Smith, Molly Stark.

Variations on the theme of the generation gap. Previously produced on cable TV.

New York Shakespeare Festival. Summer schedule of outdoor programs of two revivals of plays by William Shakespeare and one revival of a musical adaptation of a play by William Shakespeare. **As You Like It** (28). Opened June 21, 1973; see note. (Closed July 21, 1973) **King Lear** (28). Opened July 26, 1973; see note. (Closed August 26, 1973). Produced by New York Shakespeare Festival, Joseph Papp producer, at the Delacorte Theater in Central Park. **Two Gentlemen of Verona** (24). Adapted by John Guare and Mel Shapiro; music by Galt MacDermot; lyrics by John Guare. Opened July 31, 1973. (Closed August 26, 1973). Produced by New York Shakespeare Festival, Joseph Papp producer, in a Mobile Theater production in a citywide tour of parks and playgrounds.

ALL PLAYS: Associate producer, Bernard Gersten; produced in cooperation with the City of New York, Hon. John V. Lindsay mayor, Hon. Richard M. Clurman administrator parks, recreation and cultural affairs, Phyllis Robinson deputy commissioner of cultural affairs; costumes, Theoni V. Aldredge; press, Merle Debuskey, Norman L. Berman.

AS YOU LIKE IT

Orlando	Raul Julia	1st Senior Lord	Albert Hall
Adam	Lou Gilbert	2d Senior Lord	Frankie Faison
Oliver	David Clennon	1st Frederick Lord	Albert Quinton
Dennis; 2d Page	Douglas Hughes	2d Frederick Lord	Philip Polito
Charles	Henry Baker	Corin	Joe Fields
Celia	Marybeth Hurt	Silvius	Will Mackenzie
Rosalind	Kathleen Widdoes	Jaques	Frederick Coffin
Touchstone	John Harkins	Audrey	Kelly Wood
Le Beau; Sir Oliver Mar-Text	Neil Flanagan	Phebe	Susan Browning
Duke Frederick	Edward Zang	William	Bill McIntyre
Duke Senior	Douglass Watson	1st Page	Colin Garrey
Amiens	Meat Loaf	Jaques de Boys	Luis Avalos

Lords, Ladies, Attendants: Saax Bradbury, Cherie Carter, Steve Mendillo, James West III, Anne Marie Zinn.

Directed by Joseph Papp; scenery, Santo Loquasto; lighting, Martin Aronstein; music, David Shire; production stage manager, Dyanne Hochman; stage manager, John Beven.

The play was presented in two parts. New York's last professional production of *As You Like It* was by New York Shakespeare Festival in Central Park 7/11/63 for 21 performances.

KING LEAR

Kent	Douglass Watson	Oswald	Frederick Coffin
Gloucester	Paul Sorvino	Lear's Fool	Tom Aldredge
Edmund	Raul Julia	Knight; 1st Servant	J.W. Harper
Lear	James Earl Jones	Gentleman	George Dzundza
Goneril	Rosalind Cash	Curan	John Tobinski
Cordelia	Lee Chamberlin	2d Servant	Anthony Chisholm
Regan	Ellen Holly	3d Servant	Frank Seales
Albany	Robert Stattel	Old Man	Charles Pegues
Cornwall	Robert Lanchester	Messenger	Redvers Jeanmarie
Burgundy	Louis Quinones	Doctor	William Hart
King of France;		French Messenger	Gregory Mosher
French Gentleman	Jean-Pierre Stewart	Captain	Frankie Faison
Edgar	Rene Auberjonois	Herald	George Addison

Knights, Soldiers, Attendants: Jose Machado, Simpson Markson, Kevin Maung, John W. Salat, James West III.

Directed by Edwin Sherin; scenery, Santo Loquasto; lighting, Martin Aronstein; music, Charles Gross; production stage manager, Jason Steven Cohen; stage manager, Elizabeth Holloway.

The play was presented in two parts. *King Lear's* most recent professional New York revival was by The Repertory Theater of Lincoln Center 11/7/68 for 72 performances.

TWO GENTLEMEN OF VERONA

Thurio	Chesley Uxbridge	Launce	Greg Antonacci
Speed	Jose Fernandez	Antonio; Tavern Host	William McClary
Valentine	Larry Marshall	Crab	Hildagarde
Proteus	Carlos Cestero	Duke of Milan	Judd Jones
Julia	Louise Shaffer	Silvia	Rozaa Wortham
Lucetta	Carol Jean Lewis	Eglamour	Alvin Lum

Citizens of Verona and Milan: Joanna Albrecht, Melvin Barnett, Susie Chin, Josie Haskin, Paul Hoskins, Harold Johnson, Ursuline Kairson, Barbara Korey, William Lindner, Clifford Lipson, William McClary, Lonnie McNeil, Howard Porter, Bonnie Schneider, Graciela Simpson, John-Ann Washington.

Musicians: Margaret Harris conductor, Ray Copeland Trumpet, Don McIntosh trumpet, Billy Nichols guitar, Norman Pride drums, Louis Risbrook bass.

Directed by Kim Friedman; scenery, Ming Cho Lee; lighting, Lawrence Metzler; choreography, Dennis Nahat, restaged by Wendy Mansfield; musical direction, Margaret Harris; orchestrations, Harold Wheeler; associate set designer, Leo Yoshimura; original production directed by Mel Shapiro, choreographed by Jean Erdman; production stage manager, John Beven; stage manager, Anthony Neely.

The play was presented without intermission. This musical version of the Shakespeare play was first produced 7/22/71 by New York Shakespeare Festival at the Delacorte Theater in Central Park for 14 performances and was transferred to Broadway 12/1/71 for 613 additional performances.

The list of musical numbers in *Two Gentlemen of Verona* appears on pages 325–6 of *The Best Plays of 1971–72*.

In addition to the regular programs, New York Shakespeare Festival presented *Please Don't Let It Rain!*, a midnight concert with music by Peter Link and lyrics by A.J. Antoon, Michael Cacoyannis, C. C. Courtney, Ragan Courtney, Euripides, Peter Link, Susan McGonagle and William Shakespeare, for 1 performance 7/13/73 at the Delacorte Theater. Joseph Papp co-produced with 4 Astor Place Writers Workshop *Olú Clemente—The Philosopher of Baseball*, a bilingual play by Miguel Algarín and Jesús Abraham Laviera, for 1 performance 8/30/73 at the Delacorte Theater.

NOTE: In this volume, certain programs of off-Broadway companies like the New York Shakespeare Festival are exceptions to our rule of counting the number of performances from the date of the press coverage. When the official opening night takes place late in the run of a play's public performances (after previews), we count the first performance of record, not the press date, as opening night. Press date for *As You Like It* was 6/27/73, for *King Lear* 7/31/73.

* Roundabout Theater Company. Schedule of five programs. **The Caretaker** (36). Revival of the play by Harold Pinter. Opened June 23, 1973; see note. (Closed July 22, 1973). **Miss Julie,** revival of the play by August Strindberg, adapted by Henry Pillsbury, and **The Death of Lord Chatterly** by Christopher Frank, translated by Henry Pillsbury (16). Opened July 31, 1973; see note. (Closed August 12, 1973) **The Father** (97). Revival of the play by August Strindberg; adapted by Gene Feist. Opened September 11, 1973; see note. (Closed December 2, 1973). **The Seagull** (105). Revival of the play by Anton Chekhov; adapted by Gene Feist. Opened December 18, 1973; see note. (Closed March 17, 1974) * **The Circle** (71). Revival of the play by W. Somerset Maugham. Opened March 26, 1974; see note. Produced by Roundabout Theater Company, Gene Feist producing director, Michael Fried executive director, at the Roundabout Theater.

ALL PLAYS: Scenery, Holmes Easley; press, Michael Fried.

THE CARETAKER

Mick	Philip Campanella	Davies	William Prince
Aston	W.T. Martin		

Directed by Gene Feist; costumes, Theodora Skipitares; lighting, Barry Arnold; original score, Philip Rosenberg; stage manager, David Alexander.

Place: A house in West London. Act I, Scene 1: A night in winter. Scene 2: The next morning. Act II, Scene 1: Later that night. Scene 2: The next morning. Scene 3: Afternoon, two weeks later. Scene 4: That night. Scene 5: The next evening.

The Caretaker was first produced on Broadway 10/4/61 for 165 performances and subsequently revived off Broadway 1/30/64 for 94 performances.

MISS JULIE

Christine	Mary Alice	Miss Julie	Linda Carlson
Jean	Albert Hall		

THE DEATH OF LORD CHATTERLY

Madam	Linda Carlson	Butler	Philip Campanella

Directed by Henry Pillsbury; costumes, Carole M. Gersten; lighting, Barry Arnold; original score, Philip Rosenberg; producer Directions 73, Roger Cunningham; stage manager, David Alexander.

Miss Julie—Time: At the end of the 19th century. Place: The kitchen of a large estate in the southern part of the United States. *The Death of Lord Chatterly*—Time: Between 1920 and 1940, Place: A summer castle.

Miss Julie was last revived off Broadway 11/10/65 for 11 performances. Its Scandinavian setting was changed to the U.S. South in this production. *The Death of Lord Chatterly* is a foreign play, a French farce about a butler and a chatelaine whose husband is on his death bed.

THE FATHER

The Captain	Robert Lansing	Old Margret	Dorothy Blackburn
Laura	Elizabeth Owens	Nojd	Philip Campanella
Bertha	Francesca James	Dr. Ostermark	James Mitchell
The Pastor	Fred Stuthman		

Directed by Gene Feist; costumes, Mimi Maxmen; lighting, Robert L. Rayne; production stage manager, Robert L. Rayne; stage manager, Ron Antone.

Time: The 1880s. Place: The Captain's quarters at a regimental post in a Swedish country town. Act I, Scene 1: Early evening. Scene 2: Later that night. Act II: The next evening.

The Father was last revived in a Broadway production by the Royal Dramatic Theater of Sweden 5/14/62 for 3 performances.

THE SEAGULL

Irina Arkadina ....Dolores Sutton	Masha ....Laura Esterman
Konstantin Treplev ....Christopher Lloyd	Boris Alexeyevitch Trigorin ....Tom Klunis
Pyotr Sorin ....Erik Rhodes	Yevgeny Dorn ....Stephen Scott
Nina Zaretchny ....Linda De Coff	Semyon Medvedenko ......Robert Stattel
Ilya Shamraev ....William Myers	Yakov ....David Guc
Polina Andreyevna ......Paula Laurence	Dunyasha ....Jacqueline Bennett

Directed by Gene Feist; costumes, Mimi Maxmen; lighting, John McLain; sound, Gary Harris; original score, Philip Campanella; production stage manager, Robert L. Rayne; stage manager, Ron Antone.

Place: Sorin's country estate. The play was presented in four acts with intermissions following Acts II and III (an interval of two years elapses between Acts III and IV).

The Seagull was last produced on Broadway by the National Repertory Theater 4/5/64 for 16 performances. Its Roundabout Theater opening date, Dec. 17, coincided with the 75th anniversary of the play's first performance by the Moscow Art Theater Company 12/17/98. .

THE CIRCLE

Arnold Champion-Cheney, M.P. ....Brian Davies	Edward Luton ....Brian McKeon
	Clive Champion-Cheney ...David Atkinson
Butler ....Rand Mitchell	Lady Catherine
Mrs. Shenstone ....Mary Cooper	Champion-Cheney ......Natalie Schafer
Elizabeth ....Erika Slezak	Lord Porteous ......Christopher Hewett

Directed by Gene Feist; lighting, Richard Winkler; costumes, Charles Gelatt; original score, Philip Campanella; sound, Gary Harris; presented by special arrangement with Sheldon Abend; stage manager, Ron Antone.

Time: Early summer, the late 1920s. Place: The drawing room at Ashton Edey, Arnold Champion-Cheney's house in Dorset. Act I: Morning. Act II: The afternoon, two days later. Act III: Evening, the same day.

Maugham's play about the pros and cons of living in sin was first produced in 1921 at the Haymarket in London and in New York at the Selwyn Theater 9/12/21. It was revived on Broadway 4/18/38 for 72 performances and was staged by the Equity Library Theater in its 1946–47 season.

Nicol Williamson's Late Show (30). One-man program performed by Nicol Williamson. Produced by Norman Twain at the Eastside Playhouse. Opened June 26, 1973. (Closed July 28, 1973)

Musicians: Ray Kane leader, bass; Bill Bremner lead guitar; Rod Derefinko piano, vibes; Al Rogers drums; Stan Free organ; Bill Schwartz, guitar.

Lighting, Jene Youtt; production stage manager, Charles Roden; press, Gifford/Wallace, Inc.

A program of poetry excerpts and popular music presented in two parts and performed by Nicol Williamson late in the evening, following his nightly performances on Broadway in *Uncle Vanya*. The program was selected from works by e.e. cummings, Samuel Beckett, Dylan Thomas, T.S. Eliot, Dorothy Parker, T.A. Daly, John Betjeman, E.B. White, Spike Mulligan, William Shakespeare, Carl Lee Perkins, Hoagy Carmichael, Kris Kristofferson, Tim Hardin, Johnny Dankworth, Kurt Weill and Marc Blitzstein, John Killigrew, Jimmy Webb, Jimmy McHugh and Dorothy Fields, Barry Robbins and Maurice Gibbs, J.P. Richardson, Fred Neil.

I Love Thee Freely (23). By Benjamin Bernard Zavin; based entirely on the works of Robert and Elizabeth Browning. Produced by The Candlelight Co. at the Astor Place Theater. Opened September 17, 1973. (Closed October 7, 1973)

Robert Browning .... Gregory Abels   Elizabeth Barrett .... Janet Kapral

Directed by Moni Yakim; scenery and costumes, Don Jensen; lighting, Ian Calderon; production stage manager, Norman Marshall; press, Saul Richman, Dick Falk.
Time: Jan. 10, 1845 to Sept. 19, 1846. Place: England. The play was presented in two parts.
Dramatization of the love letters of Robert Browning and Elizabeth Barrett.

Nellie Toole & Co. (32). By Peter Keveson. Produced by Sally Sears and Primavera Productions, Ltd. In association with Richard Dulaney at Theater Four. Opened September 24, 1973. (Closed October 21, 1973)

Benny .... Vincent Baggetta   Moke .... Stefan Gierasch
Paul .... Lou Tiano   Nellie .... Sylvia Miles

Directed by Jeremiah Morris; scenery, Hal Tiné; costumes, Walter Florell; lighting, Spencer Mosse; production stage manager, Victor Straus; press, Howard Newman.
Time: The present. Place: A cafe off Second Ave. Act I: The cafe, 2 A.M. Act II: Same as Act I, a few minutes later.
A psychological thriller set in a New York East Side bar. Previously produced in Cologne, West Germany.

Sisters of Mercy (15). Musical revue with words and music by Leonard Cohen; additional music by Zizi Mueller. Produced by Martin J. Machat, by special arrangement with Lucille Lortel productions, at the Theater de Lys. Opened September 25, 1973. (Closed October 7, 1973)

Conceived and directed by Gene Lesser; musical director, Zizi Mueller; scenery, Robert U. Taylor; costumes, Carrie F. Robbins; lighting, Spencer Mosse; production stage manager, Ginny Freedman; press, Betty Lee Hunt. With Gale Garnett, Emily Bindiger, Michael Calkins, Nicholas Surovy, Pamela Paluzzi, Rosemary Radcliffe. Musicians: Zizi Mueller, Dean Kelso.
Self-described as "a musical journey into the words of Leonard Cohen" presenting the author as a poet and a lover.

Nourish the Beast (54). Return engagement of the play (formerly entitled *Baba Goya*) by Steve Tesich. Produced by Edgar Lansbury and Joseph Beruh in the American Place Theater Production at the Cherry Lane Theater. Opened October 3, 1973. (Closed November 18, 1973)

Goya .... Olympia Dukakis   Adolf .... Ken Tigar
Mario .... John Randolph   Criminal .... Randy Kim
Old Man .... Lou Gilbert   Studly .... Stephen Mendillo
Bruno .... R.A. Dow   Client .... James Greene
Sylvia .... Peggy Whitton

Directed by Edwin Sherin; scenery, Karl Eigsti; lighting, Roger Morgan; costumes, Whitney Blausen; production stage manager, Gigi Cascio; press, Max Eisen & Co., Maurice Turet.
Time: The present. Place: A house in Queens. The play was presented in two parts.
Comedy originally produced under the title *Baba Goya* by and at the American Place Theater 5/9/73 for 25 performances (see its entry in the "Plays Produced off Broadway" section of *The Best Plays of 1972-73*).

A Breeze From the Gulf (48). By Mart Crowley. Produced by Charles Hollerith Jr. and Barnard S. Straus at the Eastside Playhouse. Opened October 15, 1973. (Closed November 25, 1973)

Michael .... Robert Drivas   Teddy .... Scott McKay
Lorraine .... Ruth Ford

Directed by John Going; scenery, Douglas W. Schmidt; costumes, Stanley Simmons; lighting, Ken Billington; associate producer, Arthur Gorton; production stage manager, Philip Cusack; press, Michael Alpert, Marilynn LeVine, Anne Weinberg.

The play was presented in two acts representing the passage of 15 years, 1950–1965. A young man grows up in the midst of family strife with a neurotic mother and alcoholic father.

The American Place Theater. Schedule of four programs. **House Party** (42). By Ed Bullins. Opened October 16, 1973; see note. (Closed November 24, 1973) **Bread** (32). By David Scott Milton. Opened January 12, 1974; see note. (Closed February 9, 1974) **A Festival of Short Plays** (29). Program of four one-act plays: *Shearwater* by William Hauptman, *Cream Cheese* by Lonnie Carter, *Dr. Kheal* by Maria Irene Fornes, *Love Scene* by Robert Coover. Opened March 6, 1974; see note. (Closed March 30, 1974) * **The Year of the Dragon** (10). By Frank Chin. Opened May 22, 1974; see note. Produced by The American Place Theater, Wynn Handman director, at The American Place Theater.

ALL PLAYS—Associate director, Julia Miles; press, David Roggensack.

HOUSE PARTY

Cast: Girlfriend, Woman Poet, Loved One—Mary Alice; Seduced and Abandoned, Fun Lovin', Wile Chile, Fried Brains—Verona Barnes; Dopeseller, Working Man—Gary Bolling; Soul Sister, Rememberer, Confused and Lazy, Harlem Mother—Rosanna Carter; Go-Go, Quitter, Virgin—Starletta De Paur; Harlem Politician, Scrap Book Keeper, Black Critic, Reconciler—Earle Hyman; Corner Brother, Explainer, Black Writer—Andre Mtumi; MC, Groover, Rapper—Jimmy Pelham; Lover Man, West Indian Revolutionary—Basil Wallace.

Musicians: Steve Berrios drums, Bill Hardman trumpet, Pat Patrick saxophone; Cedar Walton piano, Roland Wilson bass.

Directed by Roscoe Orman; production concept, Robert MacBeth; music composed and arranged by Pat Patrick; scenery, Kert Lundell; lighting, Roger Morgan; cinematography, Karma Stanley; choreographer, Clay Stevenson; visual environment, Romare Bearden; production stage manager, Grania M. Hoskins; stage manager, Fred Seagraves.

Time: In the nostalgic past and now. Place: Black America. The play was presented without intermission.

Subtitled *A Soulful Happening,* the show is a revue of vignettes of the black experience, some with music and singing.

BREAD

Lou . . . . Rudy Bond	Stanley . . . . Dolph Sweet
George . . . . Mike Kellin	Mark . . . . John Peter Barrett
Dagmar . . . . .Marilyn Chris	Jake . . . . Constantine Katsanos

Directed by Martin Fried; scenery, Kert Lundell; lighting, Roger Morgan; costumes, Ruth Morley; production stage manager, Gigi Cascio; stage manager, Grania M. Hoskins.

Place: A bakery on the south side of Pittsburgh. Act I, Scene 1: Late night. Scene 2: Midnight, a day later. Scene 3: The next night. Act II, Scene 1: The next evening. Scene 2: Several weeks later. Act III, Scene 1: A month later. Epilogue: Sometime later.

Difficulties and hostilities in the operation of a bakery symbolize the wider problems of life itself.

A FESTIVAL OF SHORT PLAYS

PERFORMER	"SHEARWATER"	"CREAM CHEESE"	"DR. KHEAL"	"LOVE SCENE"
Hy Anzell		Blintzkrieg		
Susan Bjurman	Reporter	Pepsi		
James Greene	Shearwater	Lecherpawn;		
		Immigration official		
Richard Hamilton		Boss Tweedy Pie		

PERFORMER	"SHEARWATER"	"CREAM CHEESE"	"DR. KHEAL"	"LOVE SCENE"
Andrew Jarkowsky	Sailor		Dr. Kheal	
Arthur Morey		Millard Raker		
Ann Sachs	Rita			Woman
Lin Shaye		Ann Crist		
Robert B. Silver		D.A.; Androidi		
Kenneth Tigar		Foreman		Man
Matthew Tobin	Rodney	Justice		

ALL PLAYS—Scenery, Charles Cosler; lighting, Edward M. Greenberg; costumes, Liz Covey; production stage manager, Gigi Cascio; stage manager, Grania M. Hoskins.

SHEARWATER—Based on the death of Donal Crowhurst while attempting to sail around the world in an open boat.

CREAM CHEESE—Directed by Isaiah Sheffer; music by Bobby Paul and Lanny Meyers; musical direction, Lanny Meyers.

Time: 1899. Place: Pittsburgh. About labor troubles in a cream cheese factory at the turn of the century.

DR. KHEAL—Directed by Maria Irene Fornes. An eccentric professor's philosophical monologue.

LOVE SCENE—Directed by Caymichael Patten. Two actors rehearse a love scene, under orders from an offstage voice.

THE YEAR OF THE DRAGON

Fred	Randall (Duk) Kim	Ross	Doug Higgins
China Mama	Lilah Kan	Pa Eng	Conrad Yama
Ma Eng	Pat Suzuki	Johnny Eng	Keenan Shimizu
Sissy	Tina Chen		

Directed by Russell Treyz; scenery, Leo Yoshimura; lighting; Victor En Yu Tan; costumes, Susan Hum Buck; production stage manager, Grania M. Hoskins.

Family portrait of two generations of a Chinese-American family living in San Francisco's Chinatown.

NOTE: In this volume, certain programs of off-Broadway companies like The American Place Theater are exceptions to our rule of counting the number of performances from the date of the press coverage. When the official opening night takes place late in the run of a play's public performances (after previews) we count the first performance of record, not the press date, as opening night. Press date for *House Party* was 10/29/73, for *Bread* 1/28/74, for *A Festival of Short Plays* 3/20/74, for *The Year of the Dragon* 6/3/74.

Bil Baird's Marionettes. Schedule of two marionette programs. **The Whistling Wizard and the Sultan of Tuffet** (36). Revival with book by Alan Stern; songs by Bil Baird and Alan Stern. And **Bil Baird's Variety.** Opened October 17, 1973. (Closed December 2, 1973). **Pinocchio** (134). Book by Jerome Coopersmith; music by Mary Rodgers; lyrics by Sheldon Harnick. And **Bil Baird's Variety.** Opened December 15, 1973. (Closed April 21, 1974). Produced by The American Puppet Arts Council, Arthur Cantor executive producer, in the Bill Baird's Marionettes production at the Bil Baird Theater.

PERFORMER	"THE WHISTLING WIZARD"	"PINOCCHIO"
Peter Baird	Akimbo; Sasha; Flying Carpet	Alex; Harlequin; Policeman
Olga Felgemacher	Princess Peekaboo; J.P.	Pinocchio
Jonathan E. Freeman	Sultan; Turtle	Mr. Fireball; Pierrot; Policeman; Mrs. Bluestone
John O'Malley	Dooley; Wizard; Dooley Bird; Camel Driver	
Sean O'Malley		Cat; Numerous Fish
Bill Tost	Casbah; Pasha; Dragon	Geppetto; Magistrate
Byron Whiting	Heathcliff; Camel; Magic Lamp	Fox; Carlos; Columbine

BOTH PROGRAMS—Designed and produced by Bil Baird; lighting, Peggy Clark; production manager, Carl Harms; artistic associate, Frank Sullivan; theater manager, Frank Rowley; press, Arthur Cantor, C. George Willard.

THE WHISTLING wizard and the sultan of tuffet—Directed by Frank Sullivan and Lee Theodore; musical director, Alvy West.

Place: The country of Tuffet and the Land of Beyond. The play was presented in two parts.

This fairy tale in which the Whistling Wizard saves the Sultan's throne from an evil servant, Casbah, was first presented by Bil Baird's Marionettes 12/20/69 for 167 performances and was repeated 10/17/70 for 33 performances.

PINOCCHIO—Singing voice of Pinocchio—Margery Gray; Voice of Mrs. Bluestone—Marcia Rodd; Singing voice of Carlos—Robert Gorman.

Directed by Lee Theodore; musical conductor and arranger, Alvy West; scenery, Howard Mandel.

Scene 1: Geppetto's workshop. Scene 2: The street. Scene 3: Fireball's theater. Scene 4: The woods. Scene 5: A courtroom. Scene 6: The street. Scene 7; Land of Toys. Scene 8: A mountain top. Scene 9: The deep, deep sea. Scene 10: Geppetto's workshop. The play was presented in two parts.

Fairy tale of a wooden puppet who turns into a real boy, based on the story by C. Collodi.

BILL BAIRD'S VARIETY—Perennial exhibition of "puppet virtuosity embodying many styles and types."

The Chelsea Theater Center of Brooklyn. Schedule of four programs. **The Contractor** (72). By David Storey. Opened October 17, 1973 at the Chelsea Theater Center of Brooklyn in Manhattan. (Closed December 9, 1973) **Candide** (48). Musical revival with new book by Hugh Wheeler adapted from Voltaire; music by Leonard Bernstein; lyrics by Richard Wilbur; additional lyrics by Stephen Sondheim and John Latouche. Opened December 11, 1973; see note. (Closed January 20, 1974 and transferred to Broadway; see its entry in the "Plays Produced on Broadway" section of this volume) **Total Eclipse** (32). By Christopher Hampton. Opened February 23, 1974. (Closed March 10, 1974) **The Wild Stunt Show** (21). Revue by The Madhouse Company. Opened April 9, 1974. (Closed April 28, 1974). Produced by The Chelsea Theater Center of Brooklyn, Robert Kalfin artistic director, Michael David executive director, Burl Hash productions director, at the Brooklyn Academy of Music (unless otherwise noted above).

THE CONTRACTOR

Kay	Reid Shelton	Claire	Lynn Ann Leveridge
Marshall	Michael Finn	Glendenning	Kevin O'Connor
Mr. Ewbank	John Wardwell	Old Mr. Ewbank	Neil Fitzgerald
Fitzpatrick	Joseph Maher	Maurice	Rudolph Willrich
Bennett	George Taylor	Old Mrs. Ewbank	Anne Ives
Paul	John Roddick	Mrs. Ewbank	Kate Wilkinson

Directed by Barry Davis; scenery, Lawrence King; costumes, Susan Hum Buck; lighting, Richard Devin; production stage manager, Shan Covey; press, Leslie Gifford, Gordon Forbes.

Time: The present. Place: The lawn of Ewbank's house in Yorkshire. Act I: Morning, late summer. Act II: Afternoon of the same day. Act III: Morning, two days later.

The raising and razing of a tent for the wedding party of a contractor's daughter symbolizes the human life-cycle. A foreign play previously produced in London and at the Long Wharf Theater in New Haven, Conn.

A Best Play; see page 153

CANDIDE

Dr. Voltaire, Dr. Pangloss, Governor, Host, Sage—Lewis J. Stadlen; Chinese Coolie, Westphalian Soldier, Priest, Spanish Don, Rosary Vendor, Sailor, Lion, Guest—Jim Corti; Candide—Mark Baker; Huntsman, 1st Recruiter, Agent, Executioner, Spanish Don, Cartagenian, Priest, 3d Sailor, Eunuch —David Horwitz; Paquette—Deborah St. Darr; Baron, Grand Inquisitor, Slave Driver, 1st Sailor— Joe Palmieri; Baroness, Harpsichordist, Penitente, Steel Drummer, Houri, Cow—Mary-Pat Green; Cunegonde—Maureen Brennan; Maxmillian—Sam Freed; Servant, Bulgarian Sergeant, Agent of the

Inquisition, Executioner, Spanish Don, Cartagenian, Sailor—Robert Hendersen; 2d Recruiter, Rich Jew, Judge, Man in Black, Cartagenian, Pirate, German Botanist, Penitente, Cartagenian, Houri—Lynne Gannaway; Aristocrat, Guest—Jeff Keller; Pentitente, Whore, Houri—Gail Boggs; Cartagenian, 2d Sheep—Marti Morris; Westphalian Soldier, Agent, Guard, Governor's Aide, Pirate, Guest—Chip Garnett; Bulgarian Soldier, Aristocrat, Fruit Vendor, 2d Sailor, Pygmy, Cow—Carlos Gorbea; Lady With Knitting, Cartagenian, 1st Sheep—Renee Semes; Aristocrat, Whore, Houri, Cunegonde (alternate)—Kathryn Ritter; Old Lady—June Gable.

Musicians: Tom Pierson, Joseph D. Lewis, Albin Konopka piano; O.T. Myers trombone; David Sella cello; Rick Cohen percussion; Dennis Masuzzo double bass; Ruth Millhouse, Yuval Waldman violin, viola; Grant Keast, Scott Wharton trumpet; Charles O'Kane clarinet, flute, piccolo, alto recorder; Phil Bashor clarinet, saxophone, bass clarinet; Virginia Hourigan clarinet, oboe, bassoon.

Directed by Harold Prince; choreographer, Patricia Birch; musical director, John Mauceri; production designed by Eugene and Franne Lee; orchestrations, Hershy Kay; assistant director, Ruth Mitchell; production stage manager, James Doolan; stage manager, Errol Selsby.

A musical version of Voltaire's *Candide* with music by Leonard Bernstein, lyrics by Richard Wilbur, John Latouche and Dorothy Parker and book by Lillian Hellman was produced on Broadway 12/1/56 for 73 performances and was named a Best Play of its season. A version of this work with book adapted by Sheldon Patinkin was produced 10/26/71 for 32 performances at the John F. Kennedy Center's Opera House in Washington, D.C. but never reached New York. The new version at the Chelsea Theater Center was presented without intermission.

MUSICAL NUMBERS—"Life Is Happiness Indeed"—Mark Baker, Maureen Brennan, Sam Freed, Deborah St. Darr; "The Best of All Possible Worlds"—Lewis J. Stadlen, Baker, Freed, Misses Brennan, St. Darr; "O Happy We"—Baker, Miss Brennan; "It Must Be So"—Baker; "O Miserere" —Lynne Gannaway, Gail Boggs, Marti Morris; "O Happy We" (Reprise)—Baker, Miss Brennan; "Glitter and Be Gay"—Miss Brennan; "Auto Da fe (What a Day)"—Company; "This World"—Baker; "You Were Dead, You Know"—Baker, Miss Brennan; "I Am Easily Assimilated"—June Gable, Jim Corti, Robert Hendersen, David Horwitz; "I Am Easily Assimilated" (Reprise)—Baker, Misses Gable, Brennan; "My Love"—Stadlen; "Fons Pietatis"—Company; "Sheep's Song"—Misses Morris, Renee Semes, St. Darr, Messrs Corti, Baker; "Bon Voyage"—Stadlen, Company; "The Best of All Possible Worlds" (Reprise)—Baker, Misses Gable, St. Darr, Semes, Morris; "You Were Dead, You Know" (Reprise)—Baker, Miss Brennan; "Make Our Garden Grow"—Company.

TOTAL ECLIPSE

Paul Verlaine	Christopher Lloyd	M. Maute de Fleurville;	
Mme. Maute de Fleurville;		Jean Aicard	Ronald Bishop
Eugenie Krantz	Dorothy Chace	Maid	Linda Bowden
Mathilde Verlaine	Maia Danziger	Etienne Carjat; Clerk	George Morfogen
Arthur Rimbaud	Michael Finn	Ernest Cabaner; Judge Theodore	
Charles Cros; Barman	Lou Trapani	T'Serstevens	James Cahill
		Isabelle Rimbaud	Tanny McDonald

Directed by Robert Kalfin; scenery, Doug Higgins; costumes, Nancy Potts; lighting, William Mintzer; poetry by Verlaine and Rimbaud read in French by Alex Szogyi; production stage manager, Ginny Friedman; stage manager, Philip Himberg.

Act I—Scene 1: The Paris home of M. Maute de Fleurville, Sept. 1871. Scene 2: The same, Sept. 1871. Scene 3: Charles Cros's apartment, Nov. 1871. Scene 2: The same, Sept. 1871. Scene 3: Charles Cros's apartment, Nov. 1871. Scene 4: Café du Théâtre du Bobino, Dec. 1871. Scene 5: Café du Rat Mort, June 1872. Act II—Scene 6: A hotel room in Brussels, July 1872. Scene 7: 34–5 Howland St., London, Nov. 1872. Scene 8: 8 Gt. College St., London, July 1873. Scene 9: A hotel room in Brussels, July 1873. Act III—Scene 10: Hospital and courtroom, Brussels, July 1873. Scene 11: The Black Forest, near Stuttgart, Feb. 1875. Scene 12: A cafe in Paris, Feb. 1892.

Historical drama of the strong homosexual attachment between the French poets Verlaine and Rimbaud. A foreign play previously produced at the Royal Court Theater in London.

THE WILD STUNT SHOW

The Madhouse Company:	Boris Quill
Hamlet MacWallbanger	Tommy Shand
Nina Petrova	Marcel Steiner

A revue evolved in April 1971 by former performers in The Ken Campbell Show (an entertainment which toured London's pubs and streets), of which only one charter member, Marcel Steiner, appears in this company. A foreign play previously produced in London at the Royal Court and elsewhere.

NOTE: In this volume, certain programs of off-Broadway companies like The Chelsea Theater Center of Brooklyn are exceptions to our rule of counting the number of performances from the date of the press coverage. When the official opening night takes place late in the run of a play's public performances (after previews) we count the first performance of record, not the press date, as opening night. Press date for *Candide* was 12/21/73.

New York Shakespeare Festival Public Theater. Schedule of six programs. **Lotta** (54). By Robert Montgomery; songs by Robert Montgomery. Opened October 18, 1973; see note. (Closed December 2, 1973) **More Than You Deserve** (63). Musical with book by Michael Weller; lyrics by Michael Weller and Jim Steinman; music by Jim Steinman. Opened November 21, 1973; see note. (Closed January 13, 1974) **Barbary Shore** (48). By Jack Gelber; adapted from the novel by Norman Mailer. Opened December 18, 1973; see note. (Closed January 27, 1974) **Les Femmes Noires** (57). By Edgar White. Opened February 21, 1974; see note. (Closed April 14, 1974). **Short Eyes** (54). By Miguel Piñero. Opened February 28, 1974; see note. (Closed April 14, 1974; see note) **The Killdeer** (48). By Jay Broad. Opened March 12, 1974; see note. (Closed April 21, 1974) Produced by New York Shakespeare Festival Public Theater, Joseph Papp producer, at the Public Theater.

ALL PLAYS—Associate producer, Bernard Gersten; press, Merle Debuskey, Bob Ullman, Norman L. Berman.

LOTTA

Priestess	Irene Cara	Repairman One	Ronald Silver
Priest	David Gunnip	Repairman Two	R.H. Thomson
Bub	MacIntyre Dixon	Repairman Three	John Long
Doctor	Paula Larke	Tracy Shamus	Richard Ramos
Trixie	Bette Henritze	Glenn; Overvoice	Jerrold Ziman
Limester	Jeffrey Duncan Jones	Mrs. Diddly; Dr. Olving	Jill Eikenberry
Lotta	Dale Soules	Dr. Gray Medulla	Sean Barker

Performing Choir: Sean Barker, Irene Cara, Jill Eikenberry, David Gunnip, Paula Larke, Jerrold Ziman.

Musicians: Conductor, piano Clay Fullum; bass guitar Jaime Austria; cello Avron Coleman; drums Al Rogers; guitar Scott Kuney; french horn Priscilla McAfee.

Directed by David Chambers; musical staging, Dennis Nahat; musical direction and orchestrations, Ken Guilmartin; scenery, Tom H. John; costumes, Nancy Adzima, Richard Graziano; lighting, Roger Morgan; additional music and vocal supervison, Mel Marvin; sound, Roger Jay; production stage manager, Ken Glickfeld.

Time: Lotta was born tomorrow. Place: Eastern U.S.A. The play was presented without intermission.

A play with music, subtitled *The Best Thing Evolution's Ever Come Up With,* a metaphysical fantasy about a magically gifted woman.

MORE THAN YOU DESERVE

Nurse; Nin Hua	Leata Galloway	Costucci; Lt. Maddox	Edward Zang
Nurse; Uncle Remus	Marybeth Hurt	Spooky 1; Vietnamese	Justin Ross
Nathan; Herbie; Pilot	Steve Collins	Spooky 2; Vietnamese;	
Dr. Smith; Sgt. Price	Graham Jarvis	Radioman	Eivie McGehee
Luke; Lance Moriarity	Seth Allen	Melvin	Terry Kiser
Mike; Brown; Gerald Moore	Larry Marshall	Maj. Michael Dillon	Fred Gwynne
Perrine; Rabbit	Meat Loaf	Fiona Markhan	Kimberly Farr
Wiley; Trout	Kim Milford	Gen. Chet Eastacre	Ronald Silver
Owlsy; Joe	Tom Leo	Vietnamese	Dale Soules

Musicians: Steve Margoshes piano, conductor; Bill Blount soprano, alto and tenor sax, clarinet; David Bradnum acoustic guitar; David Dutemple bass; Mike Redding drums; Billy Schwartz lead guitar.

Directed by Kim Friedman; choreography, Scott Salmon; scenery, Miguel Romero; costumes, Lowell Detweiler; lighting, Martin Aronstein; musical arrangements and direction, Steve Margoshes; sound, Abe Jacob; production stage manager, Dyanne Hochman.

Musical comment on the Vietnam War by means of comic emphasis on such proclivities as drug-taking, torture, racism, etc., inflated for satirical effect.

ACT I

Scene 1: B-Ward, Zama Army Hospital, Japan
"Give Me the Simple Life"—Larry Marshall, Meat Loaf, Kim Milford, Company
Scene 2: Camp Sally, parade grounds, Mekong Delta
"Could She Be the One"—Fred Gwynne, Kimberly Farr
Scene 3: The Hootch
Scene 4: A clearing
"Where Did It Go?"—Seth Allen; "Come With Me . . . We Know Love"—Leata Galloway, Allen; "Mama You Better Watch Out for Your Daughter"—Milford, Marshall, Miss Farr
Scene 5: Dillon's Office
"O, What a War"—Gwynne, Ronald Silver, Graham Jarvis, Edward Zang
Scene 6: Supply grounds
"More Than You Deserve"—Meat Loaf, Company
Scene 7: Dillon's office
"Song of the City of Hope"—Miss Galloway, Milford, Gwynne, Miss Farr

ACT II

Scene 1: Dillon's office
"To Feel So Needed"—Misses Galloway, Farr
Scene 2: A clearing
Scene 3: Lo Dinh Temple
"Go, Go, Go Guerillas"—Marshall, Allen, Silver
Scene 4: Helicopter pad
"What Became of the People We Were?"—Miss Farr, Terry Kiser
Scene 5: Supply grounds
"If Only" Gwynne, Miss Farr
Scene 6: Parade Ground B
"Midnight Lullabye"—Miss Galloway
Scene 7: A clearing
"Song of the Golden Egg"—Milford, Company
Scene 8: The radio shack
Scene 9: Hospital
Finale—Company

BARBARY SHORE

William McLeod	Rip Torn	Leroy Hollingsworth	Lane Smith
Mike Lovett	Lenny Baker	Guinevere	Estelle Parsons

Directed by Jack Gelber; design, David Mitchell; lighting, Roger Morgan; sound, Roger Jay; production stage manager, Paul Richard Beck.

Time: Late August, some years ago. Place: A Brooklyn rooming house. The play was presented in three parts.

A Marxian argument transferred from printed page to stage with a thin seasoning of mystery drama.

LES FEMMES NOIRES

King Alfa	Neil Harris	Voice II; Didi	Judyie Brandt
Hounsi	Gylan Kain	Mary Alice	Juanita Clark
Miss Telephone Lady;		Rita; Jackie	Anna Horsford
Laverne	Norma Jean Darden	Roberta	Barbara Montgomery
Carolyn	Rosemary Stewart	Erlene; Carolyn's Mother	. . Trazana Beverley
High School Girl; Carla	Laurie Carlos	Cipo	Marshall Hutchinson
Cop; Pee Wee	Bob Diamond	Prophet	Dewayne Oliver
Mrs. Fowler	Rosanna Carter	Naphtali	Willard Reece
Mrs. Thompson	Ethel Ayler	Hamm	Bill Cobbs
Voice I; Psychiatrist; Verna . . .	Florene Wiley		

Expressions of the Spirit in the City: Leopoldo—conga, talking drum, Lukembe, Kalimba, other sounds of night and day; Gregory St. Strickland—piano, strings and all, flute; Ed White—bamboo cross flute, Chinese flute, flute; Obara-Wali Rahman—music director, Obara's horn, bamboo flutes, sansa, Kalimba, Haitian drum, Indian drum.

Directed by Novella Nelson; scenery, George Smith; costumes, Judy Dearing; lighting, Sati Jamal; choreography, Otis Sallid; production stage manager, Osborn Scott.

Scene Structure: The Entrance to Ife (Hounsi and King Alfa); (The city of Life); Study for Cop; Study for High School Girl; Study for Business Administrator; Study for Numbers Woman; The Workers return home (Mary Alice and Carla); Study for two Ladies in Love; Study for Father and Son (King Alfa and Hounsi); Carolyn's space (Study for Black Bourgeoisie); Golgotha; Laverne in the Subway; Mary Alice and Carla; Hamm (Study for Butcher); The Leaving of Ife—Nightworld; (The Voyage to the Grotto). The play was presented without intermission.

Series of vignettes of the black experience at various levels of American life.

SHORT EYES

Mr. Brown	Hollis Barnes	William "El Raheem"	
Juan Otero	Bimbo	Johnson	Johnny Johnson
Charlie "Longshoe" Murphy	Joseph Carberry	Mr. Frederick Nett	Robert Maroff
Clark Davis	William Carden	Omar Blinker	Kenny Steward
Julio "Cupcakes" Mercado	Tito Goya	Paco Pasqual	Felipe Torres
John "Ice" Wicker	Ben Jefferson	Sgt. Morrison	J.C. Quinn
		Capt. Allard	H. Richard Young

Directed by Marvin Felix Camillo; scenery, David Mitchell; costumes supervised by Paul Martino; lighting, Spencer Mosse; production stage manager, Robert Kellogg.

Time: The present. Place: The dayroom of one of the floors in the House of Detention. The play was presented in two parts, Act I and Act II plus Epilogue.

Short Eyes is a slice-of-prison-life drama, mostly about sexual relations among inmates and their anathematizing hatred of an inmate charged with child molestation. The play's author is an ex-convict and it is performed by a cast of former members of a theater workshop at Bedford Hills, N.Y., Correctional Facility, who call themselves "The Family." Previously produced off off Broadway at the Theater of the Riverside Church.

NOTE: This production of *Short Eyes* was transferred to the Vivian Beaumont Theater for an additional run 5/23/74; see its entry in the "Plays Produced on Broadway" section of this volume.

A Best Play; see page 208

THE KILLDEER

Ted	Ralph Waite	Marty	Franklin Cover
Sparky	Barbara Barrie	Charlie Revere	William Bogert
Huck	Timothy Nissen	Otto Beethoven	George Voskovec
Spike	Michael-Raymond O'Keefe	Tony Kraver	Jack Ramage
Georgia	Dolores Kenan		

Directed by Melvin Bernhardt; scenery, Marjorie Kellogg; costumes, Theoni V. Aldredge; lighting, Jennifer Tipton; production stage manager, Dyanne Hochman.

Stresses and strains on a modern suburbanite husband and father include a drinking problem and the ever-present threat of failure. A program note states: "The killdeer is a monogamous family bird (genus: plover) found in the pastures of North America. When under attack it attempts to lead danger away from its nest by feigning a broken wing and uttering a plaintive cry." The play was presented in two parts.

In Joseph Papp's Public Theater there are many separate auditoriums. *Lotta, Barbary Shore* and *Short Eyes* played the Florence S. Anspacher Theater, *More Than You Deserve* and *The Killdeer* played the Estelle R. Newman Theater, *Les Femmes Noires* played The Other Stage.

Workshop or work-in-progress productions by the Public Theater at Martinson Hall this season included Douglas Dyer's *The Company Stow* 12/4/73, David Rabe's *Burning* 4/13/74 and John Ford Noonan's *Where Do We Go From Here?* 4/28/74.

NOTE: In this volume, certain programs of off-Broadway companies like the New York Shakespeare Festival Public Theater are exceptions to our rule of counting the number of performances from the date of the press coverage. When the official opening night takes place late in the run of a play's public performances (after previews) we count the first performance of record, not the press date, as opening night. Press date for *Lotta* was 11/21/73, for *More Than You Deserve* 1/3/74, for *Barbary Shore* 1/10/74, for *Short Eyes* 3/13/74, for *Les Femmes Noires* 3/17/74, for *The Killdeer* 3/28/74

The Indian Experience (1). Revue by Wayne Johnson and John Kauffman. Produced by the Zean Production Company at Playhouse 2. Opened and closed at the evening performance October 23, 1973.

Directed by Gregory A. Falls; scenery, Bill Forrester; lighting, Jody Briggs; press, Michael Alpert, Marilynn LeVine. With John Kauffman, John Aylward.

Vignettes of 300 years of Indian culture, virtually a one-man show by John Kauffman.

The Man From the East (8). Musical in the Japanese language with words and music by Stomu Yamash'ta. Produced by Gordon Crowe, by arrangement with Looner Enterprises, in Stomu Yamash'ta's Red Buddha Rock Theater production, at the Brooklyn Academy of Music. Opened October 23, 1973. (Closed October 28, 1973)

Directed by Stomu Yamash'ta; scenery, Takeo Adachi; scenery coordinator, Chuck Murawski; lighting, Mitzuru Ishii; press, Rod Jacobson, Jane Friedman. With Akiko Komaki, Kimihiro Reizei, Kuniyuki Ohgari, Asako Akashi, Nadia Nguyen, Fufuo Fujiwara, Machiko Fukuda, Yukiko Hashimoto, Kazuko Hattori, Eiichi Ho, Akira Kobayshi, Eiji Kusuhara, Masao Kuwabara, Michelle Liao, Michi Matsuzaki, Kuniko Okamura, Bambi Okubo, Tsutomu Sakai, Sheila Tankiovitch, Toshiaki Tanaka.

Rock operetta reflections on the Japanese past, climaxed with the bombing of Hiroshima. A foreign play previously produced in Japan and elsewhere.

Medea (40). Revival of the play by Euripides; translated by Rex Warner; adapted by George Arkas. Produced by the Greek Art Theater of New York at The Players Theater. Opened October 30, 1973. (Closed December 2, 1973)

Nurse	Parker McCormick	Jason	Joseph Corral
Tutor	Conrad McLaren	Messenger	Grant Stewart
Medea	Yula Gavala	Chorypheus	Maria Russo
Creon; Aegeus	Oliver Malcolmson		

Children of Jason and Medea: Wayne Harding, Anthony or Steven Grandinetti. Soldiers: Grant Stewart, George Patterson. Leaders: Judith Jablonka, Ann Mathews. Members: Carolyn Lenz, Hillary Wyler.

Directed by George Arkas; scenery and lighting, George Patterson; music, Dimitris Dragatakis; costumes, Dimitri Smolens; production stage manager, Jerry Zafer; press, Les Schecter.

The Euripides play was last revived on Broadway 1/17/73 for 70 performances.

* Moonchildren (244). Revival of the play by Michael Weller. Produced by Steve Steinlauf in association with Jay Kingwill, by special arrangement with Lucille Lortel Productions, Inc., at the Theater De Lys. Opened November 4, 1973.

Mike	James Seymour	Ralph	Jack Honor
Ruth	Elizabeth Lathram	Mr. Willis	Kenneth McMillan
Cootie (Mel)	Jim Jansen	Lucky	Peter Iacangelo
Norman	Michael Sacks	Effing	Emmett Walz
Dick	Robert Phelps	Bream	Shev Rodgers
Kathy	Carol Williard	Uncle Murry	Wil Albert
Bob Rettie	Richard Cox	Cootie's Father	George Spelvin
Shelly	Renee Tadlock		

Directed by John Pasquin; scenery, William F. Matthews; costumes, Mary Warren; lighting, Joseph Dziedzic; production stage manager, Robert Keegan; press, Merlin Group, Sandra Manley.

The first professional New York production of *Moonchildren* took place on Broadway 2/21/72 for 16 performances. It was named a Best Play of its season. This revival production was presented in three acts.

New York Shakespeare Festival Lincoln Center. Schedule of two programs of revivals by William Shakespeare. **Troilus and Cressida** (57). Opened November 10, 1973; see note. (Closed December 30, 1973 matinee) **The Tempest** (81). Opened January 26, 1974; see note. (Closed April 7, 1974) And **Macbeth**, a revival of the play by William Shakespeare, which opened in previews 4/13/74 but cancelled its scheduled opening 5/5/74 and closed in previews 6/23/74. Produced by New York Shakespeare Festival Lincoln Center, Joseph Papp producer, at the Mitzi E. Newhouse Theater.

BOTH PLAYS—Associate producer, Bernard Gersten; press, Merle Debuskey, Faith Geer.

TROILUS AND CRESSIDA

Troilus	John Christopher Jones	Menelaus; Ajax	Richard Masur
Pandarus; Calchas	William Hickey	Aeneas; Servant	Dan Deitch
Cressida; Cassandra;		Thersites; Diomedes	Charles Kimbrough
Helen	Madeleine Le Roux	Achilles	Christopher Walken
Agamemnon	Jack Hollander	Patroclus; Paris	Richard Kline
Nestor; Priam	Ron Faber	Hector	Beeson Carroll
Ulysses	Leonard Frey		

Directed by David Schweizer; scenery and costumes, Paul Zalon; lighting, Ian Calderon; music, Richard Peaslee; production stage manager, Jason Steven Cohen.

The last professional New York revival of *Troilus and Cressida* was by New York Shakespeare festival in Central Park, 8/4/65 for 23 performances. It was last presented on Broadway by the Old Vic 12/26/56.

THE TEMPEST

Alonso	Tom Atkins	Francisco	Jeffrey Duncan Jones
Sebastian	K.C. Wilson	Caliban	Jaime Sanchez
Prospero	Sam Waterston	Trinculo	Randy Kim
Antonio	Christopher Walken	Stephano	Richard Ramos
Ferdinand	Mark Metcalf	Miranda	Carol Kane
Gonzalo	James Tolkan	Ariel	Christopher Allport
Adrian	Ray Xifo		

Musicians: David Tofani conductor, woodwinds; Robert Steen woodwinds; Eric Wilson cello; Rick Cutler percussion.

Directed by Edward Berkeley; scenery, Santo Loquasto, costumes supervised by Hilary M. Rosenfeld; lighting, Jennifer Tipton; music, James Milton; production stage manager, Jason Steven Cohen.

Place: An uninhabited island. The play was presented in two parts.

The Tempest was last revived in New York by the New York Shakespeare Festival in Central Park 7/16/62 for 18 performances.

NOTE: In this volume, certain programs of off-Broadway companies like the New York Shakespeare Festival Lincoln Center at the Mitzi E. Newhouse Theater are exceptions to our rule of counting the number of performances from the date of the press coverage. When the official opening night takes place late in the run of a play's public performances (after previews) we count the first performance of record, not the press date, as opening night. Press date for *Troilus and Cressida* was 12/2/73, for *The Tempest* 2/10/74. *Macbeth* opened in previews 4/13/74 and was never offered to the press for review, in a production directed by Edward Berkeley, scenery and costumes by Santo Loquasto, lighting by Jennifer Tipton, music by William Penn, with Victor Arnold, Peter Burnell, Stephen Collins, Cara Duff-MacCormick, Laura Esterman, Clarence Felder, Cecelia Hart, John Heard, David Jay, Carol Kane, Christopher Lloyd, M.B. Miller, John Roddick, Neva Small, Scott Thomson, James Tolkan, Christopher Walken, Peter Weller, K.C. Wilson.

The Foursome (24). By E.A. Whitehead. Produced by Huttleston Productions in association with Jon Pierre at the Astor Place Theater. Opened November 12, 1973. (Closed December 2, 1973)

Harry	Matthew Coles	Marie	Lindsay Crouse
Tim	Timothy Meyers	Sheila	Carole Monferdini

Directed by Jacques Levy; scenery, Edward Charles Terrel II; lighting, Ian Calderon; costumes, Bernard Roth; assistant to the producer, Salem Ludwig; stage manager, Philip Price; press, Saul Richman, Dick Falk.

Time: A day in summer. Place: A deserted beach outside of Galveston, Tex. Scene 1: Morning. Scene 2: Noon. Scene 3: Late afternoon.

An Americanized version of Whitehead's play about the sexual battle between men and women. A foreign play previously produced in London by the Royal Court.

The Enclave (22). By Arthur Laurents. Produced by Edgar Lansbury, Joseph Beruh and Clinton Wilder at Theater Four. Opened November 15, 1973. (Closed December 2, 1973)

Eleanor	Rochelle Oliver	Wyman	Tom Happer
Bruno	Don Gantry	Oliver	Laurence Hugo
Cassie	Peg Murray	Roy Lee	Fred Morsell
Donnie	Steve Elmore	Janet	Ann Sweeny
Ben	Barton Heyman		

Directed by Arthur Laurents; scenery and lighting, Robert Randolph; costumes, Robert Mackintosh; incidental music, Stephen Sondheim; musical direction, Paul Gemignani; production stage manager, Robert W. Pitman; press, Gifford/Wallace, Inc.

Time: The present. The play was presented in two parts.

Plans of a group of friends to create an enclave for themselves in a city mews are unsettled by the decision of one of them to live openly as a homosexual. Previously produced by the Washington, D.C. Theater Club.

Creeps (15). By David E. Freeman. Produced by Orin Lehman in association with the Folger Theater Group, Louis W. Scheeder producer, Richmond Crinkley founder, at Playhouse 2. Opened December 4, 1973. (Closed December 16, 1973)

Pete	Steven Gilborn	Astronaut; Shriner	Stefan Peters
Michael; M.C.; Puffo the Clown;		Girl	Ronni Richards
Barker	Philip Charles MacKenzie	Jim	Richard DeFabees
Tom	Mark Metcalf	Saunders; Voice of Thelma	Robin Nolan
Sam	Bruce Weitz	Carson	Peter Vogt
Football Player; Shriner	Richard Fancy		

Directed by Louis W. Scheeder; production design, David Chapman; movement consultant, Virginia Freeman; production stage manager, Bud Coffee; press, Michael Alpert, Marilynn LeVine.

Time: The present. Place: The men's washroom of a sheltered workshop for cerebral palsy victims in a large industrial city in Canada. The play was presented without intermission.

Spastics as victims not only of their disease but also of prejudice because they are "different." A foreign (Canadian) play previously produced in Toronto and Washington, D.C.

A Best Play; see page 223

* When You Comin' Back, Red Ryder? (201). By Mark Medoff. Produced by Elliot Martin in The Circle Repertory Theater Production at Eastside Playhouse. Opened December 6, 1973.

Stephen	Bradford Dourif	Clarisse	Robyn Goodman
Angel	Elizabeth Sturges	Richard	James Kiernan
Lyle	Addison Powell	Teddy	Kevin Conway
Clark	Joe Jamrog	Cheryl	Kristin Van Buren

Directed by Kenneth Frankel; scenery, Bill Stabile; costume coordination, Penny Davis; lighting, Cheryl Thacker; associate producer, E.J. Oshins; production associate, Marjorie Martin; production stage manager, William Weaver; press, Michael Alpert, Marilynn LeVine.

Time: The end of the 1960s. Place: A diner in southern New Mexico. The play was presented in two parts.

A drug-smuggling criminal and bully shatters the egos and the illusions of a group of people in a small-town diner. Previously produced off off Broadway by The Circle Repertory Theater Company.

John Lisbon Wood replaced Bradford Dourif 3/74.

A Best Play; see page 285

* Let My People Come (194). Musical revue with music and lyrics by Earl Wilson Jr. Produced by Phil Oesterman at the Village Gate. Opened January 8, 1974.

Christine Andersen	Joe Jones
Tobie Columbus	James Moore
Daina Darzin	Ian Naylor
Lorraine Davidson	Larry Paulette
Marty Duffy	Peachena
Alan Evans	Jim Rise
Lola Howse	Denise Connolley

Band: Jim Cox organ, Austin Wallace bass, Hank Jaramillo drums, Billy Cunningham piano.

Directed by Phil Oesterman; music arranged and conducted by Billy Cunningham; choreography, Ian Naylor; lighting, Centaur Productions; production stage manager, Anguss Moss; press, Saul Richman.

Self-described as "A sexual musical," began performances 1/8/74 but never invited critics to a formal opening (though it has been reviewed occasionally during the course of its run).

ACT I—"Opening Number"—Company; "Mirror"—Lola Howse, Daina Darzin, Alan Evans; "Whatever Turns You On"—Company; "Give It to Me"—Lorraine Davidson; "Giving Life"— Misses Howse, Darzin, Tobie Columbus, Denise Connolley, Messrs. Evans, Larry Paulette, Joe Jones, Ian Naylor; "The Ad"—James Moore; "Felatio 101"—Miss Connolley, Students; "I'm Gay"— Messrs. Jones, Marty Duffy; "Linda Georgina Marilyn & Me"—Christine Andersen; "Dirty Words" —Company; "I Believe My Body"—Company.

ACT II—"The Show Business Nobody Knows"—Company; "Take Me Home With You"— Paulette; "Choir Practise"—Naylor, Company; "And She Loved Me"—Misses Howse, Peachena, Darzin, Columbus; "Poontang"—Company; "Come in My Mouth"—Miss Columbus; "The Cunnilingus Champion of Co. C"—Jones, Paulette, Miss Andersen; "Doesn't Anybody Love Anymore" —Peachena, Company; "Let My People Come"—Company.

Royal Shakespeare Company. Repertory of two programs. **Richard II** (22). Revival of the play by William Shakespeare. Opened January 9, 1974. **Sylvia Plath** (14). Dramatization of writing by Sylvia Plath. Opened January 15, 1974. (Repertory closed January 27, 1974) Produced by the Brooklyn Academy of Music in association with Brooklyn College and presented by the Governors of the Royal Shakespeare Theater, Stratford-Upon-Avon, England, in the productions of the Royal Shakespeare Company, Peggy Ashcroft, Peter Brook and Trevor Nunn directors (Trevor Nunn artistic director), Peter Daubeny and Peter Hall consultant directors, at the Brooklyn Academy of Music.

RICHARD II

(Richard II) . Ian Richardson, Richard Pasco	Abbot of Westminster . . . .Robert Ashby
(Bolingbroke) . Richard Pasco, Ian Richardson	Sir Henry Greene . . . . . .Ray Armstrong
Queen Isabel . . . . Janet Chappell	(Bishop of
John of Gaunt . . . . Tony Church	Carlisle . . . .Brian Glover, Tony Church
Duke of York . . . . Sebastian Shaw	Of Bolingbroke's Party:
Duchess of York;	Earl of
Duchess of Gloucester . . .Janet Whiteside	Northumberland . . . . Clement McCallin
Mowbray; 1st Gardener . . . . .Denis Holmes	Harry Percy . . . . John Abbott
Earl of Salisbury . . . . Richard Mayes	Lord Ross . . . . Charles Keating
Messenger . . . . Peter Machin	Lord Willoughby . . . . Gavin Campbell
Of the King's Party:	Sir Piers of Exton . . . . . Anthony Pedley
Duke of Aumerle . . . . . Nickolas Grace	2d Gardener . . . . Leon Tanner
Sir John Bushy;	3d Gardener . . . . Wilfred Grove

(Parentheses indicate roles in which the actors alternated)

Councillors, Grooms, Soldiers, Welsh Captains, Monks, Ladies: John Abbott, Ray Armstrong, Janet Chappell, Michael Ensign, Brian Glover, Nickolas Grace, Wilfred Grove, Denis Holmes, Catherine Kessler, Peter Machin, Colin Mayes, Lloyd McGuire, Leon Tanner, Gwynne Whitby, Janet Whiteside.

Musicians: Gordon Bennett, Bernard Galton, Nigel Garvey, William Grant, Roger Hellyer, Peter Morris, Robert Pritchard, John Riley, David Statham, Michael Tubbs.

Directed by John Barton; designed by Timothy O'Brien and Tazeena Firth; lighting, David Hersey; music adapted from traditional sources by James Walker; assistant to the director, Patrick Tucker; stage manager, Roger Gregory; press, Charles Ziff, Nigel Redden.

The play was presented in two acts. Segments of *Richard II* have been presented here in recent years in such pot pourri programs as *Homage to Shakespeare* (3/15/64 for 1 performance), *Ages of Man* (12/28 58 for 40 performances and 4/14/63 for 8 performances) and Royal Shakespeare Company's *The Hollow Crown* (1/29/63 for 46 performances). Its last full New York staging was by New York Shakespeare Festival in Central Park 8/28/61 for 12 performances.

SYLVIA PLATH

Voice 1 . . . . .Brenda Bruce	Voice 3 . . . . .Louise Jameson
Voice 2 . . . . Estelle Kohler	

Directed by Barry Kyle; designed by Gordon Sumpter; music composed and played by Jeremy Barlow; lighting, Brian Harris; stage manager, Peter Sofroniou.

Act I: Works by Sylvia Plath used are *Contusion, Daddy, The Applicant, Johnny Panic and the Bible of Dreams, Lady Lazarus, Ariel, Morning Song, Tulips, The Bee Box, Mothers, Nick and the Candlestick, Lesbos, Balloons, Death and Company, Edge.* Act II: *Three Women,* a play by Sylvia Plath, set in and around a maternity ward.

Poems and other writings, including a radio play about birth, by the late Sylvia Plath, presented as stage setpieces and describing some elements of her personality and beliefs.

Of the various auditoria under the Brooklyn Academy of Music roof, the Opera House housed *Richard II* and the Leperq Space *Sylvia Plath.*

Felix (6). By Claude McNeal. Produced by Ted Ravinett at the Cherry Lane Theater. Opened January 17, 1974. (Closed January 20, 1974)

Directed by Robert Mandel; music by Robert Dennis; scenery, Robert Mitchell; costumes, Juliellen Weiss; lighting, Arden Fingerhut; production stage manager, Elizabeth Stearns; press, Merlin Group, Stanley F. Kaminsky. With Dick O'Neill, James Staley, Greg Antonacci, Robert Weil, John Perkins, Sloane Shelton, Ed Setrakian, Penelope Milford, Sydnee Devitt, Ramiro Ray Ramirez, Gerry Black, Eugene Kallman.

Study of a loser pitilessly destroyed by the modern materialistic environment.

Actors Company. Repertory of four programs. **The Wood Demon** (10). Revival of the play by Anton Chekhov; translated by Ronald Hingley. Opened January 29, 1974. **Knots** (5). Adapted by Edward Petherbridge from the book by R.D. Laing. Opened January 30, 1974.

King Lear (10). Revival of the play by William Shakespeare. Opened February 2, 1974.
The Way of the World (5). Revival of the play by William Congreve. Opened February
13, 1974. (Repertory Closed February 24, 1974) Produced by the Brooklyn Academy of
Music in association with Brooklyn College, in the Actors Company production, at
Brooklyn Academy of Music Opera House.

PERFORMER	"THE WOOD DEMON"	"KING LEAR"	"THE WAY OF THE WORLD"
John Bennett		Chief Knight; King of France	
Caroline Blakiston		Goneril	Millamant
Milton Cadman	Vassili		Messenger
Marian Diamond	Helen		Mrs. Fainall
Paola Dionisotti			Marwood
Sharon Duce	Julia	Cordelia	Foible
Robert Eddison	Serebryakov	King Lear	Billy
Robin Ellis	Theodore	Albany; Gloucester Servant	Fainall
Tenniel Evans	Voynitsky	Oswald; Captain	Waitwell
Peter Holt		Cornwall Servant	
Matthew Long		Edmund	Petulant
Margery Mason	Mme. Voynitsky	Old Woman	Lady Wishfort
Ian McKellen	Khruschov	Edgar	Footman
John Moreno	Zheltukin	Cornwall; Doctor; Herald	Chauffeur
Edward Petherbridge	Simon	Fool	Mirabell
Ronald Radd		Gloucester	
Sheila Reid	Sonya	Regan	Mincing
Elaine Strickland	Servant		Peg
John Tordoff	Dyadin	Burgundy; Gloucester Servant	Witwoud
John Woodvine	Orlovsky	Kent	Sir Willful

Servants, Knights, attendants in *King Lear:* Marian Diamond, Paola Dionisotti, Margery Mason,
Peter Holt, Milton Cadman, Patrick Cadell, Elaine Strickland.

KNOTS

Organist, vocalist—Caroline Blakiston; Speaker, cello, pipe, Juggler's Assistant "Pierretti"—Paola
Dionisotti; Speaker, pipe, Tap Dancer—Sharon Duce; Compere, "Professor"—Robert Eddison;
drums, male voice quartet—Robin Ellis; male voice quartet—Tenniel Evans; Speaker, percussionist,
Comedian, Singer—Matthew Long; Speaker, percussionist, male voice quartet, "Puppet Manipula-
tor"—Ian McKellen; Speaker, Juggler, Tap Dancer, drummer, male voice quartet, "Harlequin"—
John Moreno; pipe, Comedian's Stooge, "Pierrot"—Edward Petherbridge; Singer (including final
song)—Sheila Reid.

THE WOOD DEMON—Directed by David Giles; scenery, Kenneth Mellor; costumes, Stephen
and Wendy Doncaster; lighting, Howard Eldridge; stage manager, Clare Fox; press, Charles Ziff,
Nigel Redden.
Act I: At Zheltukin's. Act II: At Serebryakov's. Act III: At Serebryakov's. Act IV: at Dyadin's.
The play was presented in two parts with the intermission following Act II.
The Wood Demon was last presented in the Alex Szogyi translation by Equity Theater in the
1966–67 season. The Actors Company, a British ensemble group, made its first appearance at the
Edinburgh Festival in 1972 and toured Britain prior to a six-week season in Cambridge. The majority
of the company reassembled for the 1973 season.
KNOTS—Directed by Edward Petherbridge; music composed by Martin Duncan; lighting, Clare
Fox.
Logical and psychological paradoxes and propositions advanced in the words of the psychia-
trist and author R.D. Laing (except for a Compere's speech to the audience, written by the adap-
tor). A foreign play previously produced in England. The play was presented without intermis-
sion.
KING LEAR—Directed by David William; designed by Alan Barlow in association with Brenda
Hartill Moores; lighting, Howard Eldridge; swordplay, Derek Ware.
Time: Long ago. Place: Albion. The play was presented in three parts.

King Lear was last produced 7/26/73 at the Delacorte Theater in Central Park for 28 performances; see its entry in this section of this volume.

THE WAY OF THE WORLD—Directed by David William; scenery, Karen Mills; lighting, Howard Eldridge; choreography, Geraldine Stephenson.

Time: During the course of one day. Place: London. Act I, Scene I: A London club. Scene 2: St. James's Park. Scene 3: Lady Wishfort's drawing room. Act II: Lady Wishfort's drawing room.

The Way of the World was last produced in New York off Broadway during the 1960–61 season and on Broadway in a Players Club revival 6/1/31 for 8 performances.

Bad Habits (96). Program of two one-act plays by Terrence McNally: *Ravenswood* and *Dunelawn*. Produced by Adela Holzer at the Astor Place Theater. Opened February 4, 1974. (Closed April 28, 1974; see note)

PERFORMER	"RAVENSWOOD"	"DUNELAWN"
F. Murray Abraham	Roy Pitt	Mr. Blum
Emory Bass	Hiram Spane	Mr. Ponce
Paul Benedict	Jason Pepper, M.D.	Hugh Gumbs
Cynthia Harris	April Pitt	Ruth Benson, R.N.
Michael Lombard	Harry Scupp	Mr. Yamadoro
J. Frank Lucas	Francis Tear	Dr. Toynbee
Doris Roberts	Dolly Scupp	Becky Hedges, R.N.
Henry Sutton	Otto	Bruno

Directed by Robert Drivas; scenery, costumes and lighting by Michael H. Yeargan and Lawrence King; production stage manager, Robert Vandergriff; press, Michael Alpert, Marilynn LeVine, Anne Weinberg.

Both plays on this program of one-actors are set in expensive nursing homes, in the present, and both are gray-comedy comments on common personal neuroses of our times. In *Ravenswood,* several couples are suffering wrenchingly obvious emotional and ego problems, which the doctor seeks to cure by total permissiveness. In *Dunelawn,* drugs and gibberish are offered as the solution to similarly deep-seated ills.

NOTE: This production of *Bad Habits* was transferred to Broadway 5/5/74; see its entry in the "Plays Produced on Broadway" section of this volume.

A Best Play; see page 173

* The Ridiculous Theatrical Company. Schedule of two programs. **Hot Ice** (94). By Charles Ludlam. Opened February 7, 1974. (Closed April 28, 1974). *** Camille** (15). Revival of the play by Alexandre Dumas; adapted by Charles Ludlam. Opened May 13, 1974. Produced by The Ridiculous Theatrical Company at the Evergreen Theater.

HOT ICE

Narrator	Bill Vehr	Irmtraut "Moms"		
Tank Irish	Richard Currie	Mortimer	Lola Pashalinski
Ramona Malone	Black-Eyed Susan	Max Mortimer	John D. Brockmeyer
Lt. Sczutcaretski	Jack Mallory	Piggie	Robert Beers
Buck Armstrong	Charles Ludlam	Lady With the Poodle	Susan Kapilow
Miss Enright	Stephen Sterne	Fifi	Endust
Bunny Beswick	Georg Osterman	The Kid	Randy Hunt

With: Cathy Badomi, Robert Reddy, Sydney Chandler Faulkner.

Directed by Charles Ludlam; scenery and costumes, Edward Avedisian; lighting, Richard Currie; production stage manager, Richard Gibbs; press, Alan Eichler.

Time: Now. Place New York. The play was presented in two parts.

Lampoon of science fiction-gangster-sex dramas, in a melee of jokes and tomfoolery about frozen corpses and stolen jewels.

CAMILLE

Baron de Varville	. . . . John D. Brockmeyer	Saint Gaudens	. . . . .Robert Reddy
Nanine	. . . . Jack Mallory	Prudence Duvernoy	. . . . . Lola Pashalinski
Marguerite Gautier	. . . . . Charles Ludlam	Gston Roue	. . . . Robert Beers
Nichette	. . . . .George Osterman	Armand Duval	. . . . Bill Vehr
Butler	. . . . Stephen Sterne	Duval Sr.	. . . . Richard Currie
Olympe de Taverney	. . . Black-Eyed Susan		

Directed by Charles Ludlam; scenery, Boblack Calejo; lighting, Richard Currie; costumes, Mary Brecht; production stage manager, Richard Gibbs.

A take-off of *Camille,* with a male actor (but not a female impersonater) playing the heroine.

The Negro Ensemble Company. Schedule of three programs. **The Great Macdaddy** (72). By Paul Carter Harrison; music by Coleridge-Taylor Perkinson. Opened February 12, 1974. (Closed April 14, 1974) **A Season-Within-a-Season** (32). Schedule of four limited engagements of new plays: **Black Sunlight** (8) by A.I. Davis, opened March 19, 1974 (closed March 24, 1974); **Nowhere to Run, Nowhere to Hide** (8) by Herman Johnson, opened March 26, 1974 (closed March 31, 1974); **Terraces** (8) by Steve Carter, opened April 2, 1974 (closed April 7, 1974); **Heaven and Hell's Agreement** (8) by J.E. Gaines, opened April 9, 1974 (closed April 14, 1974). And *In the Deepest Part of Sleep* by Charles Fuller, to open 6/4/74. Produced by The Negro Ensemble Company, Inc., Douglas Turner Ward artistic director, Robert Hooks executive director, Frederick Garrett administrative director, at St. Marks Playhouse.

THE GREAT MACDADDY

Phylicia Ayers-Allen	Alton Lathrop
Marjorie Barnes	Howard Porter
Graham Brown	Alvin Ronn Pratt
Adolph Caesar	Martha Short-Goldsen
David Downing	Freda T. Vanterpool
Al Freeman Jr.	Charles Weldon
Dyane Harvey	Victor Willis
BeBe Drake Hooks	Hattie Winston
Sati Jamal	

Musicians: Herb Bushler conductor, bass; Omar Clay percussion; Sue Evans drums; Neal Tate keyboards.

Directed by Douglas Turner Ward; choreography, Dianne McIntyre; scenery, Gary James Wheeler; costumes, Mary Mease Warren; lighting, Ken Billington; production stage manager, Clinton Turner Davis; production assistant, Sandra Ross; press, Howard Atlee, Clarence Allsopp, Meg Gordean.

Time: The 1930s during Prohibition (however, succeeding episodes do not conform to strict time). The play was presented in two parts with an intermission following Beat Two.

An odyssey with music, with Macdaddy progressing from one symbolic episode to another searching for a lost character named "Wine" and fighting off one named "Scag," in a form described by its author in a program note as "a ritualized African/American event inspired by the African story-telling technique advanced by Amos Tutuola in his world-famous novel, *The Palm Wine Drinkard.*"

Robert Hooks replaced Al Freeman Jr. 3/4/74. Cleavon Little replaced David Downing 3/12/74.

ACT I—Primal Rhythm (Los Angeles): Macdaddy—David Downing; Scag/Photographer—Al Freeman Jr.; Old Woman—BeBe Drake Hooks; Deacon Jones—Adolph Ceasar; Young Woman—Marjorie Barnes; Wine—Graham Brown; Other Community Members—Phylicia Ayers-Allen, Sati Jamal, Alton Lathrop, Howard Porter, Alvin Ronn Pratt, Martha Short-Goldsen, Freda T. Vanterpool, Charles Weldon, Victor Willis. Beat One (Nevada Desert): Old Grandad, Soldier (Wine)—Brown; Momma—Miss Short-Goldsen; Shine—Jamal; Scag—Freeman. Beat Two (Las Vegas): Fast Life Dudes—Caesar, Jamal, Porter, Weldon; Leionah—Hattie Winston; Skull (Scag)—Freeman; Skuletons—Caesar, Weldon; Signifyin' Baby—Willis; Song—Miss Barnes; Dance—Dyane Harvey; Drum—Omar Clay; Other Community Members—Company.

ACT II—Beat Three (Arizona, Dog Races): Four Jackles—Jamal, Lathrop, Weldon, Pratt; White

Track Man—Caesar. Beat Four (Texas): Sheriff (Scag)—Freeman; Bartender—Caesar; Cowboy—Porter; Niggertoe—Jamal; Beast of Prey—Pratt, Lathrop, Miss Harvey. Beat Five (Arkansas): Scarecrow (Scag)—Freeman; Mr. Middlesex—Caesar; Mrs. Middlesex—Miss Short-Goldsen; Eagle—Lathrop; Spirit of Woe—Brown, Jamal, Porter, Pratt, Weldon. Beat Six (St. Louis): Mother Faith—Miss Hooks; Stagolee/Scagolee—Weldon; Poppa (Wine)—Brown; Community at Rest—Company. Beat Seven (Louisiana): Red Woman/Tree/Dance—Miss Vanterpool; Blood Leader/Tree (Wine)—Brown; Benny—Porter; Red—Jamal; Humdrum (Scag)—Freeman; Blood Son—Pratt; Drum—Clay; Blood Folk—Company. Terminal Rhythm (South Carolina): Macdaddy—David Downing; Leionah—Miss Winston; Wine—Brown. Terminal Coda (Los Angeles)—Company.

A SEASON-WITHIN-A-SEASON

ALL PLAYS—Coordinator, Steve Carter; lighting, Sandra Ross; sound, Dik Krider; costume supervision, LaDonna Brown; set supervision, Steve Carter; stage manager, Harrison Avery.

BLACK SUNLIGHT

MHandi . . . . Richard Jackson
MHandi's Wife . . . . Mary Alice
Wajji . . . . Robert Stocking

Police Commissioner Kuunsa . . Gary Bolling
Cabinet Member NKundi . . Robert Christian

Directed by Kris Keiser.
Influences of dictatorship on the year-old government of an emerging African nation.

NOWHERE TO RUN, NOWHERE TO HIDE

Sam Wilde . . . . Frankie Faison
Frank Wilson . . . . Leon Morenzie
Jesse Graves . . . . Roland Sanchez
Willie Stewart . . . . Todd Davis
Lucia Ferguson . . . . Joyce Hanley

Ida Mae Stewart . . . . Lea Scott
Chester Pearce . . . . Samm Williams
Clarissa Ferguson . . . . Michele Shay
Paul Ferguson . . . . Robert Stocking
Newscaster's Voice . . . . . Adolph Caesar

Directed by Dean Irby.
Time: Right now. Place: Harlem. Act I, Scene 1: Street, police car. Scene 2: Willie's apartment. Scene 3: An alley. Scene 4: Street. Act II, Scene 1: Street: Wilson's car. Scene 2: A bench in the park. Scene 3: Lucia's apartment. Scene 4: Street: police car. Scene 5: Lucia's apartment. Scene 6: By the Hudson River, Wilson's car. Scene 7: An alley. Scene 8: An alley.
A rebellious young man is framed for murder by dishonest cops.

TERRACES

First:
Manager . . . . Leon Morenzie
Wife-To-Be . . . . Joyce Hanley
Husband-To-Be . . . . . . Roland Sanchez
Second:
Wife . . . . Michele Shay
Husband . . . . Robert Christian
Third:
Older Wife . . . . Mary Alice

Older Husband . . . . Leon Morenzie
Fourth:
Fleur . . . . Joyce Hanley
Zan . . . . Roland Sanchez
Octavia . . . . Mary Alice
Marigold . . . . Michele Shay
Nicky . . . . Robert Christian
Man . . . . Leon Morenzie

Directed by Frances Foster.
Time: The present. Place: A pseudo-posh, multi-terraced housing complex smack in the middle of the sorrow of Harlem, U.S. of A.
Three satiric and one melodramatic sketches of well-to-do black domesticity.

HEAVEN AND HELL'S AGREEMENT

Mr. Jackson . . . . Nick Latour
Miss Vi . . . . Lea Scott

Norma Jean . . . . Michele Shay
Bert . . . . Leon Morenzie

Buddy . . . . Gary Bolling   Mrs. Moore . . . . Mary Alice
Poor Boy . . . . Roland Sanchez   Western Union Boy . . . . Todd Davis

Directed by Anderson Johnson.
A soldier presumed dead in Vietnam returns and tries to find his place again with his wife and mother in the family environment.

Fashion (94). Musical based on the play by Anna Cora Mowatt; adapted by Anthony Stimac; music by Don Pippin; lyrics by Steve Brown. Produced by R. Scott Lucas at the McAlpin Rooftop Theater. Opened February 18. 1974. (Closed May 12, 1974)

Evelyn/Mrs. Tiffany . . . . .Mary Jo Catlett   Nan/Adam Trueman . . . . .Henrietta Valor
Jean/Millinette . . . . Sydney Blake   Pat/Mr. Anthony Tiffany . . . . Jan Buttram
Edwina/Frankson . . . . . . Susan Romann   Suzanne/Joseph Snobson . . . . Rhoda Butler
Rita/Seraphina Tiffany . . . Sandra Thornton   Marion/Gertrude . . . . . . Joanne Gibson
Richard/Count Jolimaitre . . . Ty McConnell   Kim/Colonel Howard . . . . . Holland Taylor

Directed by Anthony Stimac; musical director, Susan Romann; scenery, Robert U. Taylor; costumes, Bieff-Herrera; lighting, Spencer Mosse; musical arrangements, Don Pippin; additional musical staging, Gene Kelton; production associate, Richard Lehmann; production stage manager, Clarke W. Thornton; press, the Merlin Group, Cheryl Sue Dolby, Stanley F. Kaminsky.
Time: Nippy fall 1973. Place: A high fashion living room on Long Island, the home of Evelyn and Allen Rich. The play was presented in two parts.
The "Long Island Masque and Wig Society" of ladies is putting on an early American comedy (Miss Mowatt's *Fashion,* about a social climber hoodwinked by impostors) in a musical version. The ladies play "themselves" and their roles in the play, including all the male roles except one, that of an impostor posing as a French count, played by the "director" helping them put on the play.
Patti Perkins replaced Rhoda Butler 3/5/74.

ACT I

Prologue: Pearl's Hat Shoppe
"Rococo Rag" . . . . Pearl, Girls
Scene 1: Mrs. Tiffany's drawing room
"You See Before You What Fashion Can Do" . . . . Jolimaitre, Mrs. Tiffany, Seraphina
Scene 2: Mr. Tiffany's counting house
"It Was for Fashion's Sake . . . . Mr. Tiffany
"The Good Old American Way" . . . . .Mr. Trueman, Mr. Tiffany
Scene 3: The conservatory
"What Kind of Man Is He?" . . . . Gertrude
Scene 4: Mrs. Tiffany's drawing room
"My Daughter the Countess' . . . . Mrs. Tiffany
"Take Me" . . . . .Jolimaitre, Seraphina
Scene 5: Chambermaid's pantry
"Why Should They Know About Paris?" . . . . .Jolimaitre, Millinette
"I Must Devise a Plan" . . . . Company

ACT II

Scene 1: Mrs. Tiffany's ballroom
"Meet Me Tonight" . . . . Company
"My Title Song" . . . . Mrs. Tiffany, Company
Scene 2: Chambermaid's pantry
"A Life Without Her" . . . . .Mr. Trueman
Scene 3: Mrs. Tiffany's drawing room
"My Daughter the Countess' (Reprise) . . . . Mrs. Tiffany
"My Title Song" (Reprise) . . . . Company

Dear Nobody (71). One-woman play with Jane Marla Robbins; by Terry Belanger and Jane Marla Robbins; based on the diaries of Fanny Burney. Produced by Albert Poland at the Cherry Lane Theater. Opened February 19, 1974. (Closed April 28, 1974)

Directed by Leon Russom; costumes, Patricia Zipprodt; lighting, Martin Aronstein; production stage manager, Duane F. Mazey; press, Saul Richman.

Time: 1768–1795. Place: In and around London.

The life and times of Fanny Burney, noted 18th century wit, novelist and woman-about-London, from her 15th birthday to the birth of her first son in her early 40s, based on her own record, with Miss Robbins portraying Miss Burney and a score of her contemporaries both male and female.

Once I Saw a Boy Laughing (5). By Scott Mansfield. Produced by Lawrence E. Davis at the Westside Theater. Opened February 21, 1974. (Closed February 24, 1974)

Directed by Gail Mansfield; scenery, David Chapman; lighting, Martin Aronstein; costumes, Ann Kelleher; sound, Peter J. Fitzgerald; musical direction, John Randall Booth; orchestrations, Ron Frangipane, Wally Harper, Peter Howard, Ron Kristy, Stephen Metcalf, Lee Norris, Horace Ott; production stage manager, Robert J. Fahey; press, Gifford/Wallace, Inc. With Jerry Plummer Chesnut, Michael Glenn-Smith, Scott Mansfield, Dennis Simpson, Russ Thacker, Rick Warner.

Six American soldiers on "a piece of land in nowhere" are killed off one by one. The script and staging included the following songs: "Gee, I Got the Blues," "So Long, Suzanne/A Song for Boni," "Lonely as the Wind," "Morning Child," "Once I Saw a Boy Laughing," "Again, My Friend," "Why."

The Young Vic. Repertory of three revivals. **The Taming of the Shrew** (12). By William Shakespeare. Opened March 6, 1974; see note. **Scapino** (10). Adapted from Molière's *Les Fourberies de Scapin*. Opened March 12, 1974; see note. **French Without Tears** (8). By Terence Rattigan. Opened March 15, 1974; see note. (Repertory closed March 31, 1974). Produced by The National Theater of Great Britain and presented by The Brooklyn Academy of Music in association with Brooklyn College, in The Young Vic productions, Frank Dunlop director, Bernard Goss associate director, at the Brooklyn Academy of Music.

PERFORMER	"THE TAMING OF THE SHREW"	"SCAPINO"	"FRENCH WITHOUT TEARS"
Jenny Austen	Widow	Waitress	Marianne
Paul Brooke	Biondello	Geronte	
Ian Charleson	Lucentio	Ottavio	Brian Curtis
Alan Coates	Policeman	Waiter	
Denise Coffey	Bianca	Zerbinetta	Jacqueline Maingot
Jim Dale	Petruchio	Scapino	
Douglas Elliott			Lord Heybrook
Richard Gere	Pedant		
Hugh Hastings	Baptista	Waiter	M. Maingot
Joan Heal	Curtis		
Jeremy James-Taylor	Tailor	Leandro	Kenneth Lake
Jane Lapotaire	Katharina		
Alan Lewis	Grumio		Kit Neilan
Mel Martin		Giacinta	Diana Lake
Gavin Reed	Hortensio	Sylvestro	Lt. Cmdr. Rogers
Andrew Robertson	Tranio	Carlo	Hon. Alan Howard
Ian Taylor	Vincentio		
Lotti Taylor		Nurse	
Ian Trigger	Gremio	Argante	

ALL PLAYS—Production, Frank Dunlop; design, Carl Toms; lighting, David Watson; production stage manager, Rosemary Hoare; press, Charles Ziff, Nigel Redden.

THE TAMING OF THE SHREW—Servants, Musicians, Horses, etc.—James Hunter-Lisle and the Company; music, Michael Lankester.

The play was presented in two parts. It was last produced in New York by The Roundabout Repertory Company 1/30/72 for 29 performances.

SCAPINO—Music, Jim Dale.
Place: Naples. The play was presented in two parts. Written in 1671, it was last produced in New York last season in a musical version entitled *Tricks*, 1/8/73 for 8 performances.
NOTE: This production of *Scapino* was presented on Broadway by Circle in the Square, opening 5/18/74; see its entry in the "Plays Produced on Broadway" section of this volume.
FRENCH WITHOUT TEARS—Assistant to director, Bernard Goss.
Place: "Miramar," a villa in a small seaside town in the South of France. Act I: A morning in July. Act II, Scene 1: Two weeks later (July 14), early afternoon. Scene 2: Six hours later. Act III, Scene 1. A few hours later. Scene 2: Next morning.
Rattigan's play about young Englishmen studying French in romantic surroundings was first produced on Broadway 9/28/37 for 11 performances. This is its first professional revival.
NOTE: In this volume, certain programs of off-Broadway companies like The Young Vic are exceptions to our rule of counting the number of performances from the date of the press coverage. When the official opening night takes place following the first public performances (after previews) we count the first performance of record, not the press date, as opening night. Press date for *The Taming of the Shrew* was 3/7/74, for *Scapino* 3/13/74, for *French Without Tears* 3/16/74.
Of the various auditoria under the Brooklyn Academy of Music's roof, the Opera House housed *The Taming* of the Shrew and the Leperq Space the other two plays.

I Am a Woman (32). One-woman show by Viveca Lindfors; conceived and arranged by Viveca Lindfors and Paul Austin. Produced by Theater in Space, Gene Frankel artistic director, at Theater in Space. Opened April 2, 1974. (Closed April 28, 1974)

Directed by Paul Austin; lighting, Beverly Emmons; costumes, Joe Eula; music, David Horowitz; metal sculpture, Suzanne Benton; sound, Gary Harris; choreographic consultant, Gui Andrisano; associate producer, Bob MacDonald; song "I Am Woman" by Reddy & Burton, sung by Helen Reddy; production stage manager, Douglas Laidlaw; press, Gifford/Wallace, Inc.
Miss Lindfors in a series of character portraits from life and literature.
PART I—Lillian (*Pentimento* by Lillian Hellman); Anne (*The Diary of Anne Frank* by Frances Goodrich and Albert Hackett); Brenda (*Lovers and Other Strangers* by Renee Taylor and Joseph Bologna); Eve (*A Conversation Against Death* by Eve Merriam); Polly (*The Threepenny Opera* by Bertolt Brecht and Kurt Weill, translated by Marc Blitzstein); Barbara (*The Liberated Orgasm* by Barbara Seaman); Constance (*Lady Chatterley's Lover* by D.H. Lawrence); Lina (*Misalliance* by George Bernard Shaw); Unknown Woman (*As You Desire Me* by Luigi Pirandello, translated by Marta Abba); Marie (*In the Jungle of the Cities* by Bertolt Brecht, translated by Anselm Hollo); Pati (poem by Pati Trolander); Anne (*Little Girl, My Stringbean, My Lovely Woman* by Anne Sexton); Portia (*The Merchant of Venice* by William Shakespeare); Shen-Te (*The Good Woman of Setzuan* by Bertolt Brecht, translated by Eric Bentley); Judy (*I Want a Wife* by Judy Syfers); Sally (*Cutting Loose* by Sally Kempton); Sido (*In My Mother's House* by Colette, adapted by Bert Green); Aurelia (*The Madwoman of Chaillot* by Jean Giraudoux, translated by Maurice Valency).
PART II—Revolutionary; Dr. Freud; Queenie (*Queenie* by Hortense Calisher; Nora (interview with G.I. by Nora Sayre); Sally; Nora (*A Doll's House* by Henrik Ibsen); Louise (interview with Louise Nevelson); Marilyn (*Marilyn Monroe* by Gloria Steinem); Alexandra (*Sweet Bird of Youth* by Tennessee Williams); Betty (*The Feminine Mystique* by Betty Friedan); A Hungarian Mother (*A Boy Changed Into a Stag Clamors at the Gate of Secrets* by Juhasz); A German Mother (*Song of a German Mother* by Bertolt Brecht, translated by George Tabori); Charlie's Mother (interview with Mrs. Manson); A Member of Charlie's Family (testimony of Patricia Krenwinkel); Sylvia (*Spinster* by Sylvia Plath); Anna (*Mother Courage and Her Children* by Bertolt Brecht and Paul Dessau, translated by George Tabori); A German Mother; Ngo Thi (Paris Peace Conference, 1968); Anne; Helen ("I Am Woman" by Reddy & Burton); Fran (*Dear Black Man* by Fran Sanders); Anais (diary of Anais Nin).

Pop (1). Musical with book and lyrics by Larry Schiff and Chuck Knull; music by Donna Cribari. Produced by Brad Gromelski in association with William Murphy III at the Players Theater. Opened and closed at the evening performance, April 3, 1974.

Directed by Allen R. Belknap; choreography, Ron Spencer; additional music, Larry Schiff; musical direction and arrangements, Donna Cribari; scenery and costumes, Pat Gorman; lighting, Hallam B. Derx; production stage manager, Kenneth Williams. With Frank W. Kopyc, Anna Gianiotis, Lois Greco, Karen Magid, Frank Juliano, Stephan Dunne, T. Galen Girvin, Dennis Ferden, Bill Nightingale, Richard Forbes, Larry Lowe, Dolores Elena Garcia, Lyman Jones.
Free musical adaptation of *King Lear*.

Le Roi Se Meurt (Exit the King) (9). Revival of the play by Eugene Ionesco in the French language. Produced by The French Institute/Alliance Française under the auspices of L'Association d'Action Artistique of the Government of the French Republic, with the patronage of the Cultural Counselor to the French Embassy, in Le Tréteau de Paris production, Jean de Rigault executive director, Yves Berthiau general administrator, at The American Place Theater. Opened April 15, 1974. (Closed April 20, 1974)

Béranger the First	Oliver Hussenot	Doctor	Jean Dalmain
Queen Marguerite	Hélène Duc	Juliette	Monique Saintey
Queen Marie	Christiane Desbois	Guard	Jacques Tessier

Directed by Jacques Mauclair; scenery and costumes, Jacques Noel; incidental music, George Delerue; technical director, Francisco de Castro; tour administrator, Francis Aubert; press, David Roggensack.

The action takes place in a kingdom and a time both imaginary. The play was presented in two parts.

Exit the King was last revived in English, on Broadway, in APA repertory 1/9/68 for 45 performances.

* The Sea Horse (52). By Edward J. Moore; see note. Produced by Kermit Bloomgarden, Max Allentuck and Orin Lehman in The Circle Repertory Theater Company production at the Westside Theater. Opened April 15, 1974.

Harry Bales	Edward J. Moore	Gertrude Blum	Conchata Ferrell

Directed by Marshall W. Mason; scenery, David Potts; costumes, Jennifer von Mayrhouser; lighting, Cheryl Thacker; stage manager, Peter Schneider; press, Herb Striesfield, Gary Feinstein.

Time: The present. Place: The Sea Horse, a bar on the West Coast waterfront. Act I: After closing. Act II: Following morning.

The love song of an embittered barmaid, game for a fling but not for any solid commitment of any kind, and a sailor determined to marry her. Previously produced off off Broadway.

NOTE: The author of *The Sea Horse* used the *nom de plume* James Irwin in the off-off-Broadway production and in the off-Broadway production until shortly after the opening, when it became known that he, the play's co-star, was also its author.

A Best Play; see page 303

Royal Shakespeare Company. Repertory of two programs. **The Hollow Crown** (7). Revival of the anthology devised by John Barton. Opened April 18, 1974. **Pleasure and Repentance** (5). Anthology devised by Terry Hands. Opened April 21, 1974. (Repertory closed April 28, 1974) Produced by the Brooklyn Academy of Music in association with Brooklyn College, and by Paul Elliott and Duncan C. Weldon by arrangement with the governors of the Royal Shakespeare Company, Stratford-Upon-Avon, England, in The Royal Shakespeare Theater production at the Brooklyn Academy of Music Opera House.

With Michael Redgrave, Sara Kestelman, James Grout, Paul Hardwick and Martin Best (songs, guitar and lute).

Directed by Patrick Tucker; designed by Anna Steiner; stage manager, Ian Drake; press, John A. Carter, Charles Ziff, Nigel Redden.

THE HOLLOW CROWN

Self-described as "an entertainment by and about the kings and queens of England—music, poetry, speeches, letters and other writings from the chronicles, from plays and in the monarchs' own words; also music concerning them and by them." It was last presented on Broadway 1/29/63 for 46 performances.

PART I—Kings According to Legend and the Chroniclers: Prologue, *The Hollow Crown* (William

Shakespeare); *The Death of Kings*—William I and II, Henry I, Stephen (Stow and Anglo-Saxon Chronicle); Anonymous ballad—Henry II, Elinor; 16th and 17th century chronicles—Henry II and III, Richard I, John, Edward I and II (Holinshed, Hall, Baker, Churchill); Ballade (by Richard I); Richard II surrenders at Flint Castle to Henry IV, from Froissart's Chronicles (Lord Berners); *A Partial, Prejudiced and Ignorant Historian*—Henry IV, V, VI, VII and VIII, Edward IV, V and VI, Richard III, Mary, Elizabeth, James I, Charles I (Jane Austen aged 15); "The Agincourt Song." The Monarchs Speak for Themselves: Edward III writes a love-letter to the Countess of Salisbury (William Shakespeare); Henry VII sends a secret memorandum to his ambassadors concerning a proposed marriage between himself and the Queen of Naples, and they reply to it; Mary Tudor (speech) denounces the rebellion of Sir Thomas Wyatt raised in protest against her proposed marriage with Philip of Spain; "The King's Hunt" (song)—Henry VIII; Henry VIII (letter) proposes to Anne Boleyn; Anne Boleyn—a lady in waiting at court (letter) writes to Henry from the Tower before her execution; "Ballad of Jane Seymour"; poems—Henry VI and VIII, Elizabeth, Charles I; "Here's Health Unto His Majesty."

PART II— The Stuarts: James I blows a "Counterblast to Tobacco"; Charles I confronts John Bradshaw, president of the court, at his trial for high treason and is condemned to death; *Ayre* (Charles I); Charles II addresses Parliament, writes a letter to his Lord Chancellor and is anatomised by the Marquis of Halifax; the Vicar of Bray upholds the Protestant Succession—Charles II, James II, William and Mary, George I. The Illustrious House of Hanover: the death of Queen Caroline (Lord Hervey); George II is buried in Westminster Abbey (Horace Walpole); George III discusses the arts (Fanny Burney); George IV is unswathed and interpreted (William Makepeace Thackeray); a Scottish medley; the madness of George III (Marianne Thornton to E.M. Forster); William IV makes a good start (the Greville Memoirs). The Victorian Age: "A Ballad to an Absent Friend" (music by Albert, Prince Consort, words by his brother Ernest); Victoria describes her coronation at age 19 (private journal); Epilogue (from *Morte d'Arthur* by Thomas Malory).

PLEASURE AND REPENTANCE

Self-described as "a lighthearted look at love," in the words of various authors.

PART I—A description of love (Sir Walter Raleigh); "Cotton Eye Joe" (American traditional); *Song to Be Sung by the Father of Infant Children*—Ogden Nash; *The New-Born Baby's Song* from the private journal of Marjory Fleming, aged 8 (Frances Cornford); "When I Was a Little Wolf Cub" (Paddy Robberts); *Come Down Oh Maid* (Alfred Tennyson); *Fain Would I Wed* (Thomas Campion); *Love Letter* (John Keats); excerpt from *The Pickwick Papers* (Charles Dickens); *Satisfaction* (The Rolling Stones); *Perils of the Dance* (William Prynne); *Prayer to St. Catherine* (anonymous); "If My Complaints" (John Dowland); *The Flea* (John Donne); "Westron Wind" (traditional); excerpt from *I the Jury* (Mickey Spillane); "Norwegian Wood" (John Lennon, Paul McCartney); excerpt from *The Importance of Being Earnest* (Oscar Wilde); *Letter to Her Lover* (Sarah Johnson); "Gloire de Dijon" (Lawrence & Oldfield); *To His Mistress Going to Bed* (John Donne); *Night: Vendice* (Tourneur); *may i feel said he* (e.e. cummings); Forbidden Fruit (from the Book of Genesis).

PART II— *There Was a Little Man Came From the West* (traditional ballad); *Ballad Upon a Wedding* (John Suckling); *A Young Wife* (D.H. Lawrence); *The Pooters at Home* (George and Weedon Grossmith); excerpt from *The Merchant of Venice* (William Shakespeare); *A Bachelor's Complaint About Married People* (Charles Lamb); *Der Noble Ritter Hugo* (Hans Breitmann); "The Grey Cock" (traditional Birmingham); *Victor* (W. H. Auden); "Died for Love" (traditional Somerset); *The Mess of Love* (D.H. Lawrence); *To Women as Far as I'm Concerned* (D.H. Lawrence); *I Am as I Am* (Jacques Prevert); *The Arrow in the Heart* (William Hazlitt); *A Wife and Another* (Thomas Hardy); "So We'll Go No More A'Roving" (Byron, music by Martin Best); *At Castle Boteral* (Thomas Hardy); *Cocoa* (S.J. Sharpless); letter (George Bernard Shaw); *Now Sleeps the Crimson Petal, Now the White* (Alfred Tennyson); "She Moved Through the Fair" (traditional Irish); a description of love (Sir Walter Raleigh).

Ionescopade (14). Vaudeville musical taken from the works of Eugene Ionesco; music and lyrics by Mildred Kayden. Produced by Kermit Bloomgarden and Roger Ailes at Theater Four. Opened April 25, 1974. (Closed May 5, 1974).

Conceived and directed by Robert Allan Ackerman; choreography, Merry Lynn Katis; scenery and lighting, David Sackeroff; costumes, Patricia Adshead; arrangements, Michael Gibson, Mildred Kayden; musical direction, Ed Linderman; production stage manager, Andie Wilson Kingwill. With Joseph Abaldo, Gary Beach, Jerry Beal, Veronica Castang, Richard Crook, Connie Danese, Maron McCorry, Bob Morrissey, Stephanie Satie, Howard L. Sponseller Jr.

Plays and other Ionesco material, presented in two parts. Previously produced off off Broadway by the New Repertory Company.

Kaboom! (1). Musical with book and lyrics by Ira Wallach; music by Doris Schwerin. Produced by Joseph Rhodes, Alice Shuman associate producer, at the Bottom Line Theater. Opened and closed at the evening performance, May 1, 1974.

Directed and choreographed by Don Price; scenery, Peter Harvey; costumes, Lohr Wilson; lighting, Timmy Harris; musical direction, Arnold Gross; orchestrations, Eddie Sauter; stage manager, Charles A. Roden; press, Shirley Herz. With James Donahue, Marjorie Barnes, Tom Matthew Tobin, Bernice Massi, Charles Hudson, Jack Blackton, Corinne Kason.

Lampoon of American institutions, from supermarket to rocket ship.

* Jacques Brel Is Alive and Well and Living in Paris (22). Revival of the revue based on Jacques Brel's lyrics and commentary; production conception, English lyrics and additional material by Eric Blau and Mort Shuman; music by Jacques Brel. Produced by 3 W Productions, Inc. and Lily Turner at the Astor Place Theater. Opened May 17, 1974.

Jack Blackton	Stan Porter
Barbara Gutterman	Henrietta Valor

Musicians: Bertha Melnik conductor, piano; Wayne Wright guitar, classical guitar; Andy Sieff drums, marimba, chimes; Joe Davis bass, fender bass.

Directed by Moni Yakim; musical direction, Mort Shuman; scenery and costumes, Don Jensen; lighting, Ian Calderon; arrangements, Wolfgang Knittel; production stage manager, Philip E. Price; press, Saul Richman.

This material was first presented off Broadway as a cabaret revue 1/22/68 for 1,847 performances.

ACT I: "Marathon"—Company; "Alone"—Jack Blackton; "Madeleine"—Company; "I Loved" --Henrietta Valor; "Mathilde"—Stan Porter; "Bachelor's Dance"—Backton; "Timid Frieda"—Barbara Gutterman; "My Death"—Miss Valor; "Girls & Dogs"—Porter, Blackton; "Jackie"—Porter; "The Statue"—Blackton; "Desperate Ones"—Company; "Sons Of"—Miss Valor; "Amsterdam"—Porter.

ACT II: "The Bulls"—Blackton; "Old Folks"—Miss Valor; "Marieka"—Miss Valor; "Brussels" —Miss Gutterman; "Fannette"—Blackton; "Funeral Tango"—Porter; "Middle Class"—Porter, Blackton; "You're Not Alone"—Miss Valor; "Next"—Porter; "Carousel"—Miss Valor; "If We Only Have Love"—Company.

A Look Back at Each Other (2). By Paul Pagano. Produced by Jen-Laura Productions at the Masque Theater. Opened May 21, 1974. (Closed May 22, 1974)

Directed and produced by Lester Goldman; scenery, Gene Becker; costumes, Nancy Carney; lighting, Charles Diaz. With Paul Phillips. Steve Weiser, Irving Piper, Shirley Lamb, Mitch Lee, John Vallone, John Burns, Hattie Crystal, Steve Feinstein.

Two homosexuals attempt to raise a child.

Off Off Broadway
and Additional Productions

Here is a comprehensive sampling of off-off-Broadway and other experimental or peripheral 1973–74 productions in New York. There is no definitive "off-off-Broadway" area or qualification. To try to define or regiment it would be untrue to its fluid, exploratory purpose in an estimated 1,500 or more programs annually.

The listing below is as inclusive as possible, however, and includes almost all Manhattan-based, new-play-producing, English-language organizations listed by the Theater Development Fund and the Off-Off-Broadway Alliance—plus many others about which reliable information is available.

Producing groups are identified in **bold face type,** in alphabetical order, with artistic policies and the name of the managing director given when these are a matter of record. Examples of outstanding 1973–74 programs of each group are listed with the play titles in capital letters. In many cases these are works in progress with changing scripts, casts and directors, usually without an engagement of record (but an opening date or early performance date of record is included in the entries when available).

Actors' Experimental Unit. Material chosen for quality, relevance and performance by a group of actors. John Davis, director.

THE TRACKS HOME by Ed Baierlein. January 6, 1964. Directed by Robert Breuler.
STOP, YOU'RE KILLING ME by James Leo Herlihy. April 11, 1974.
THE TOWER by Peter Weiss. April 24, 1974. Directed by John Davis; with Robert Capece, Judith Carroll, Philip Merker, Paul Ricci, Leta Ridolfo, Neil Sawyer, Chris Stavropolis, Suzanne Volkman.

Actor's Place at St. Luke's. Emphasis on audience involvement, Frank Mosier, director.

THE TWO SISTERS by Frank Mosier.
UNTITLED liturgical drama. April 1, 1974. Directed by Frank Mosier.
THREE SERMONS FOR TODAY written and directed by Frank Mosier. May 11, 1974.

The Actors Studio. Development of talent in productions of new and old works. Arthur Penn and Lee Strasberg, artistic directors.

THE ASSIGNMENT by Gertrude Samuels.
LONG DAY'S JOURNEY INTO NIGHT by Eugene O'Neill, adapted by Will Hare, Vivian Nathan, J.J. Quinn, Jean-Pierre Stewart, Mary Anisi. December 10, 1973.
AMERICAN NIGHT CRY by Phillip Hayes Dean. March 7, 1974. Directed by Richard Ward; with Sylvia Miles, Josephine Premice, Lenka Peterson, Don Blakely.
PEOPLE OF THE SHADOWS program of two one-act plays: MRS. MINTER by Donald Kvares, with Lenka Peterson, and AN EVENING IN SONG AND STORY by Norman Rosten in association with Harry Davis, with Harry Davis. April 18, 1974.
OH GLORIOUS TINTINNABULATION book and lyrics by June Havoc, music by Cathy MacDonald. May 23, 1974. Directed by June Havoc; with Estelle Parsons, Madeleine Sherwood, Frank Bennett, Wayne Flower, Louise Stubbs.

Afro-American Studio. Express the black experience in terms of theater. Ernie McClintock, artistic director.

THE CHIP WOMAN'S FORTUNE by Willis Richardson.
JOHANNAS by Bill Gunn.

Afro-American Total Theater. Developing and producing the work of black artists. Hazel Bryant, artistic director.

SHEBA book by Hazel Bryant, music by Jimmy Justice. April 19, 1974. Directed by Helaine Head; choreography, Milo Timmons.

Amas Repertory Theater. Interracial theater group, with the accent on original material. Rosetta LeNoire, founder and artistic director.

HEROES AND FAILURES translated by Simon Hanson and others, adapted and directed by Warren Kliewer. November 2, 1973.
THE JITNEY VEHICLE by Eloise Baker and LITTLE B.S. adapted by Charles Briggs. November 30, 1973. Directed by Charles Briggs.
THE GLASS MENAGERIE by Tennessee Williams. February 23, 1974. Directed by Conrad McLaren.
HAIKU (multimedia) conceived and directed by Robert Walker. May 17, 1974.

American Center for Stanislavski Theater Art (ACSTA). Development of the Stanislavski method in the American theater. Sonia Moore, director.

A DEED FROM THE KING OF SPAIN by James Baldwin. January 24, 1974. Directed by Sonia Moore; with Donna Stark, Philip G. Bennett, Phyllis Gibbs, Barbara Frick, Len Silver, Ray Matthews.
THE MAN WITH THE FLOWER IN HIS MOUTH by Luigi Piandello, THE STRONGER by August Strindberg and THE SLAVE by Imamu Amiri Baraka. February 7, 1974.
DESIRE UNDER THE ELMS by Eugene O'Neill. March 9, 1974.
THE BOOR, THE ANNIVERSARY and THE MARRIAGE PROPOSAL by Anton Chekhov. March 21, 1974.
THE CRUCIBLE by Arthur Miller. May 16, 1974. Directed by Sonia Moore.

American Theater Company. New works done, but accent on the American theater's heritage. Richard Kuss, artistic director.

HUGHIE by Eugene O'Neill and HERE WE ARE by Dorothy Parker. November 9, 1973. Directed by Stephen B. Finnan.
THE MALE ANIMAL by James Thurber and Elliott Nugent. April 20, 1974. Directed by Ellis Santone.
PONTEACH, OR THE SAVAGES OF AMERICA by Maj. Robert Rogers. May 30, 1974. Directed by Richard Kuss.

Brooklyn Academy of Music. In addition to its commercial-theater schedule, this organization occasionally finds room for experimental productions of the avant garde. Harvey Lichtenstein, executive director.

THE LIFE AND TIMES OF JOSEPH STALIN by Robert Wilson. December 15–16, 1973 (7 P.M. to 7 A.M., 12 hours' duration). Directed by Robert Wilson; choreography, Andrew de Groat; with a cast of 144.
THE CHIP WOMAN'S FORTUNE by Willis Richardson and JOHANNAS by Bill Gunn (Black Theater Alliance Festival).

Byrd Hoffman School of Byrds. Usually concentrates on one sizeable production annually. Robert Wilson, director (c.f. Brooklyn Academy of Music entry).

THE SAME OLD STORY (THE SAME OLD HISTORY) RIGHT by Elizabeth Pasquale. Directed by Elizabeth Pasquale.

Central Arts Cabaret Theater. Accent on religion as expressed in the arts. Albert Louis DuBose, executive producer.

INNER CITY by Eve Merriam and Helen Miller, conceived by Randall Hoey.
HALLELUJAH! by James Elward. November 29, 1973. Directed by Harry Eggart; with Jim Jensen.
FRIENDS OF MINE by Robert Preston. February 14, 1974. Directed by Jack Chandler.
MOTHER & SON & CO. by Bruce Peyton. March 21, 1974.
CANTICLE book and lyrics by Michael Champagne, music by William Penn.
THE LATTER DAYS OF A CELEBRATED SOUBRETTE (new version of *The Gnadiges Fraulein*) by Tennessee Williams. May 16, 1974. Directed by Luis Lopez-Cepero; with Robert Frink, Anne Meacham, Roddy O'Connor, William Pritz, Roger Sewall, Bill Waters.

Circle Repertory Theater Company. Has gained renown for its productions of new plays transferred to the commercial theater. Marshall W. Mason artistic director.

WHEN YOU COMIN' BACK, RED RYDER? by Mark Medoff. November 5, 1973. Directed by Kenneth Frankel; with Kevin Conway, Brad Dourif, Elizabeth Sturges, Jim Kiernan, Joe Jamrog, Kristin Van Buren, Robyn Goodman, Addison Powell.
PRODIGAL by Richard Lortz. December 16, 1973. Directed by Marshall W. Mason; with Cathryn Damon, Salem Ludwig, Zane Lasky, Judd Hirsch, Ted Leplat.
THE AMAZING ACTIVITY OF CHARLEY CONTRARE AND THE NINETY-EIGHTH STREET GANG by Roy London. January 20, 1974. Directed by Richard A. Steel; with Zane Lasky, Jonathan Hogan, Rob Thirkfield, Tanya Berezin, Sharon Madden, David Hooks, Alice Drummond, Andy Leavitt, Bonnie Herron.
THE SEA HORSE by James Irwin (Edward J. Moore). March 3, 1974. Directed by Marshall W. Mason; with Conchata Ferrell, Edward J. Moore.
him by e.e. cummings, music by Norman L. Berman. April 14, 1974. Directed by Marshall Oglesby: with Tanya Berezin, Trish Hawkins, Sharon Madden, Marilyn Amaral, Neil Flanigan, Baxter Harris.
THE PERSIANS by Aeschylus. May 19, 1974.

Clark Center for the Performing Arts (Playwrights' Horizons). New works developed and redeveloped to bring out all their possibilities. Robert Morse, director.

STORKWOOD by Mark Dunster.
SANTA ANITA '42 by Allan Knee.
MARRY ME! MARRY ME! by Dennis Andersen. October 17, 1973. Directed by Robert Moss.
HARD NEWS by D.B. Gilles. November 6, 1973. Directed by David Trainer.
THE HARLOT AND THE HUNTED by Arnold Meyer. November 9, 1973. Directed by Michael Clarke-Laurence.
SALTED ARROWS by Tony Brazina. November 13, 1973. Directed by Robert O'Rourke.
SISSIES' SCRAPBOOK by Larry Kramer. November 14, 1973. Directed by Alfred Gingold.
ATHEIST IN A FOX HOLE by Eric Thomson. February 1, 1974. Directed by Craig Barish.
JEALOUSY by Steven Shea. February 6, 1974. Directed by Paul Cooper.
PASSING BY by Martin Sherman. March 5, 1974. Directed by Joseph Cali.
THE CONDITIONING OF CHARLIE ONE by Robert Karmon.
THE MINISTER'S BLACK VEIL by Allan Knee. March 21, 1974. Directed by Steven Robman.
URLICHT by Albert Innavrato. March 26, 1974. Directed by Edward M. Cohen.
BIOGRAPHY FOR A WOMAN (multimedia) written and directed by Jo Ellen Sheffield. April 27, 1974.
SIGMUND by Richard Preston. May 4, 1974. Directed by Mel Freeland.
A LATE SNOW by Jane Chambers. May 5, 1974. Directed by Nyla Lyon.
THE GRAND AMERICAN EXHIBITION by Len Jenkins. May 5, 1974. Directed by Garland Wright.
GREATEST SHOW ON EARTH by David Rimmer. May 14, 1974. Directed by Frank Askin.
MAMAS CRAZYHORSE ROCKIN' AGAIN by Bess Codling. May 15, 1974. Directed by I. Allen Lee.
BLUE ISLAND by Hal Craven. May 16, 1974. Directed by Bill Bond.

Common Ground. Developing theater programs by a collaborative process known as "progression". Norman Taffel, artistic director.

CREATING A CRECHE. December 8, 1973. Directed by Norman Taffel.
THE GRID by Sorge. January 19, 1974. Directed by Sal Rasa.
HOPPER a biography. February 27, 1974. Directed by Norman Taffel.

The Courtyard Players. Eclectic policy of searching for "a good play," new ones preferred but not exclusively. Ken Eulo, artistic director.

ITS CALLED THE SUGAR PLUM by Israel Horovitz. January, 1974. Directed by Ken Eulo.

CSC Repertory Theater. Permanent repertory of classics, with emphasis on production quality. Christopher Martin, artistic director.

MOBY DICK verse adaptation by Christopher Martin. September 12, 1973.
TWELFTH NIGHT by William Shakespeare. September 26, 1973. Directed by Christopher Martin.
THE MISANTHROPE by Molière, adapted by Robert Hall and Lorraine Ross. November 6, 1973. Directed by Robert Hall; with Christopher Martin, Karen Sunde, Harris Laskawy, Dennis Lipscomb.
MISS JULIE by August Strindberg, adapted by Julianne Boyd. November 20, 1973. Directed by Christopher Martin; with Esther Koslow, Harris Laskaway, Linda Varvel.
THE HOMECOMING by Harold Pinter. December 11, 1973. Directed by Robert Hall.
ROSENCRANTZ AND GUILDENSTERN ARE DEAD by Tom Stoppard. January 22, 1974. Directed by Christopher Martin; with Paul E. Doniger, Howard Lucas, Paul Meacham, Francois de Giroday, Harris Laskawy.
THE REVENGER'S TRAGEDY by Cyril Tourneur. February 27, 1974.
HEDDA GABLER by Henrik Ibsen. April 24, 1974. Directed by Christopher Martin; with Karen Sunde, John C. Vennema, Harris Laskaway, Susan Sadler, Christopher Martin.
THE DWARFS directed by Marlene Swartz and THE DUMBWAITER directed by Christopher Martin, by Harold Pinter. May 3, 1974.

The Cubiculo and **Cubiculo III**. Experiments in the use of theater, dance, music, etc., housed in four studios and two stages. Philip Meister, artistic director.

ALCESTIS by Euripides. November 2, 1973. Directed by Maurice Edwards.
WIGLAF: A MYTH FOR ACTORS by the Rutgers Theater Arts Workshop, based on *Beowulf.* November 8, 1973. Directed by Joseph Hart.
FORTY written and directed by Keith Aldrich. January 9, 1974.
. . . AND SHOULD A BLIMP FALL THE TOURISTS WILL BE SILHOUETTED, CAUSING THEM TO BECOME MOBILE STONES . . . by David A. Nunemaker and Members of a Cloud February 1, 1974. Directed by David A. Nunemaker.
HEDDA GABLER by Henrik Ibsen. February 20, 1924. Directed by Philip Meister; with Elaine Sulka, Neil Flanagan, William Shust, Darrie Lawrence, Toby Tompkins, Patricia Mertens.
NIGHT SONG lyrics by Gene Rempel, music by Dave Bobrowits. April 3, 1974. Directed by Andy Thomas and Luba Ash.
KLYTEMNESTRA by Eniale Aklus. April 18, 1974. Directed by Philip Meister.
THE DOGS OF PAVLOV by Danny Abse. May 2, 1974. Directed by Maurice Edwards; with Thayer David, Brenda Currin, Saylor Creswell, Bruce Gray, Munson Hicks.
EROS IN EXILE by Luigia Morgoglione Miller. May 16, 1974.
THE COLOR OF A WORLD by Roma Greth. Directed by Martin Oltarsh.

The Demi Gods. A company with special training in dance and music as well as theater. Joseph A. Walker, director.

YIN YANG written and directed by Joseph A. Walker, music by Dorothy A. Dinroe. October 4, 1973.

Direct Theater. A professional company of actors and other stage artists exploring new techniques. Allen R. Belknap, artistic director.

During 1973–74 presented no formal programs but conducted experiments in movement; programs to resume in September 1974.

Drama Tree Players. Productions focussing the efforts of a whole production unit. Anthony Mannino, artistic director.

COME INTO MY WORLD by Paul Pierog. Directed by Frank A. Ammirati.
COME BLOW YOUR HORN by Neil Simon. January 4, 1974. Directed by Robert Day.
EVERYBODY ELSE by Marvin Starkman. Directed by Frank Ammirati.

Dramatis Personae. A showcase for new, specifically oriented material.

BOYS, BOYS, BOYS by Wayne Corliss. October 5, 1973. Directed by Steven Baker.
ROUND AND ROUND THE NAKED ROUND written and directed by A.R. Bell. October 6, 1973.

A MIDSUMMER NIGHT'S DREAM by William Shakespeare, in a gay adaptation written and directed by George Stevenson. April 6, 1974.

Drifting Traffic. The production of new plays, often by new playwrights. Sande Shurin, artistic director.

THE DOLPHIN DREAMER by Betty Jean Lifton. November 5, 1973. Directed by Sande Shurin.
AH! WINE! by Leonard Melfi. January 14, 1974. Directed by Sande Shurin.
BEAUTIFUL! by Leonard Melfi. May 16, 1974. Directed by Sande Shurin

Ensemble Studio Theater. Workshop for the development of professional theater talent and new scripts. Curt Dempster, artistic director.

STUDS EDSEL by Percy Granger. March 7, 1974. Directed by Kent Paul; with Richard Backus, Valerie French, Brian Farrell.
ACTORS by Conrad Bromberg. May 19, 1974. Directed by Harold Stone; with Martin Shakar, Roberts Blossom.

Equity Library Theater. Actors Equity produces a series of revivals each season as showcases for the work of its actor-members. George Wojtasik, managing director.

BROADWAY by Philip Dunning and George Abbott. October 18, 1973. Directed by Ken Eulo; with Bernard Erhard, Lonnie Burr, Susan Harney, Carey Connell, David Toll, Martin Donegan.
CALL ME MADAM by Howard Lindsay and Russel Crouse, music and lyrics by Irving Berlin. November 8, 1973. Directed by Janet McCall; with Grace Keagy, David Vogel, John Holly, Linda Byrne.
RASHOMON by Fay and Michael Kanin, based on stories by by Ryunosuke Akutagawa. December 6, 1973. Directed by Tito Shaw; with Kitty Chen, Faizul Khan, Count Stovall, Ken Tigar, Joi Staton, Rose Lischner.
LOOK: WE'VE COME THROUGH by Hugh Wheeler. January 10, 1974. Directed by Richard Mogavero; with Pamela Hall, Kelly Walters, Margaret Impert, Michael Martins, Joseph Brockett, Richard Council.
CAROUSEL by Richard Rodgers and Oscar Hammerstein II. February 7, 1974. Directed by Russell Treyz; with Suellen Estey, Robert Manzari, Carole Doscher, George Hall, Dick Bonelle, Iris Acker.
OH, LADY! LADY! by Jerome Kern, Guy Bolton, and P.G. Wodehouse. March 13, 1974. Directed by Clinton Atkinson; with Kelly O'Brien, Gary Brubach, Robert Lunny, Donna Theodore, Robert Lydiard, Ann Hodapp.
BLOOMERS by Carl Sternheim, translated by M.A. McHaffie. April 18, 1974. Directed by Roger Hendricks Simon; with Chet Hoherty, Marjorie Erdreich, Dana Gladstone, Joan Pape, Stephen Pearlman, Albert Sanders.
MAN WITH A LOAD OF MISCHIEF by John Clifton and Ben Tarver, based on a play by Ashley Dukes. May 9, 1974. Directed by Joseph F. Leonard; with Avril Gentles, Edward Penn, Casper Roos, Freyda Ann Thomas, Brad Tyrrell, Gloria Zaglool.

Folk City. A night club which presents plays in the early evening, prior to folk and rock concerts.

LONELY FRIENDS program of four one-act plays by Edna Schappert. Directed by Sammy Eneff.

Gene Frankel Theater Workshop (Theater in Space). Development of new works for the theater. Gene Frankel, artistic director.

THE INTERVIEW by Peter Swet. July 10, 1973. Directed by Ted Story; with Joey Fitter, Richard Creamer.
I AM A WOMAN conceived by Paul Austin and Viveca Lindfors. January 9, 1974. Directed by Paul Austin; with Viveca Lindfors.
SPLIT LIP by John Cromwell, music by Lee Pockriss. May 14, 1974. Directed by Gene Frankel; choreography, Doug Rogers; with Gilda Mulette, Seth Allen, Ruth Manning, William Pierson.

Greenwich Mews Theater. Encourage and promote understanding among all people, through the arts. William Glenesk, artistic director.

THE DISPOSAL by William Inge, music by Anthony Caldarella, lyrics by Judith Gero. September 22, 1973. Directed by Barry Feinstein.
FASHION adapted by Anthony Stimac from the play by Anna Cora Mowatt, music by Don Pippin, lyrics by Steve Brown. December 6, 1973. Directed by Anthony Stimac.
FOUR'S COMPANY by Davi Napoleon.
STREET JESUS and THE BLIND JUNKIE by Peter Copani.

Hamm and Clov Stage Company. International repertory of plays, tours abroad. David Villaire, director.

THE VILLAGE WOOING by George Bernard Shaw. January 10, 1974.
DARTS by Ladewijk de Boer. January 16, 1974. Directed by David Villaire.

Interart Theater. Provide opportunities for women to participate in theatrical activity. Margot Lewitin, coordinater.

BECAUSE I WANT TO by Myrna Lamb. January 11, 1974. Directed by Marjorie de Fazio.
MINE by Jane Chambers, directed by Nancy Rhodes, and THE WIFE by Jane Chambers, directed by Margot Lewitin. March 29, 1974.
GIFTS written and directed by Marge Helenchild. May 4, 1974.

Jean Cocteau Theater. A small house in the Bowery experimenting with seldom-performed classics. Eve Adamson, artistic director.

MEDEA by Jean Anouilh. October 5, 1973. Directed by Eve Adamson.
THE LESSON by Eugene Ionesco. October 6, 1973. Directed by Eve Adamson.
WAITING FOR GODOT by Samuel Beckett. October 7, 1973. Directed by Eve Adamson.
THE MAN WHO MARRIED A DUMB WIFE by Anatole France. October 21, 1973. Directed by Eve Adamson.
AN EVENING WITH EDNA ST. VINCENT MILLAY adapted and directed by Jere Jacob. February 9, 1974.
NO EXIT by Jean-Paul Sartre. February 15, 1974. Directed by Eve Adamson.
ASTONISHMENTS experiments and magic by Samuel Beckett, T.S. Eliot, Jeff Sheridan. March 15, 1974. Directed by Eve Adamson.
GHOSTS by Henrik Ibsen. April 26, 1974. Directed by Eve Adamson.

Jones Beach Marine Theater. Each summer, a musical classic is presented in this huge outdoor theater on Long Island. Guy Lombardo, producer.

CAROUSEL by Richard Rodgers and Oscar Hammerstein II. June 22, 1973. Directed by John Fearnley; with John Cullum, Barbara Meister, Bonnie Franklin.

Joseph Jefferson Theater Company. An eclectic policy of production, housed in the annex of The Little Church Around the Corner. Cathy Roskam, founder.

WHAT! AND LEAVE BLOOMINGDALE'S? program of four one-act plays by Marion Fredi Towbin and David Finkle. July 21, 1973. Directed by Robert Reiser; with Leigh Woods, Linda Swenson.
THE FIREBUGS by Max Frisch, adapted by Lou Trapani. February 18, 1974. Directed by Lou Trapani; with Cathy Roskam.

The Judson Poets' Theater. The theater arm of Judson Memorial Church and its pastor, Al Carmines, who creates a series of new, unconventional musicals which are sometimes transferred to the commercial theater. Al Carmines, director.

RELIGION oratorio by Al Carmines. October 28, 1973. Directed by Al Carmines. With Joan Montgomery, Reuben Schafer, Semina DeLaurentis, Trisha Long, Al Carmines.

THE FUTURE by Al Carmines. March 25, 1974. Directed by Al Carmines; choreography, Dan Wagoner; with David Pursley, Essie Borden, Ira Siff, Lee Guilliatt, Reathel Bean.

La Mama Experimental Theater Club (ETC). A busy workshop and showcase for experimental theater of all kinds. Ellen Stewart, director.

GETOUT book and lyrics by Joseph Renard, music by Joseph Blunt. February 24, 1974. Directed by Joseph Renard; choreography, Joaquin La Habana; with Joseph Renard, Margaret Benczak, Gary Swartz, Gretel Cummings, Ellwoodson Williams, James Hilbrandt.
CALL ME CHARLIE by Michael Moran, music and lyrics by Sam Burtis and Jane Blackstone. April 1974. With Danny Devito.

Lincoln Center for the Performing Arts. Third annual Community/Street Theater Festival of performances in Lincoln Center Plaza by troupes from the various boroughs of New York City and from other U.S. cities, opening August 21, 1973, some of whose programs are listed below. Leonard de Paur, producer.

BLACK LOVE presented by Theater West, Dayton, Ohio.
TO BE YOUNG, GIFTED AND BLACK and OLD JUDGE MOSE IS DEAD presented by Stamford, Conn., Street Theater.
THE FLAT HEAD CYCLE AND DRAGON PARADE presented by the Puppet Theater of War, Dragons and Children, Brooklyn.
THE AGE OF KALI and ADVENT OF LORD KRISHNA presented by the Vaikuntha Players, Brooklyn.
URSULA UNDERDOG MEETS THE MONEYGRABBER presented by the Mass Transit Street Theater, New York City.
THE WAY IT HAPPENED presented by the Weusi Kuumba Troupe, Brooklyn.
TOTAL TOGETHERNESS presented by the Brownsville Lab Theater Arts, Inc., Brooklyn.
PRI-GHETTO-SON presented by the Ossining, N.Y., Street Theater.
A COMMUNITY HAPPENING/BLACK CREATIVITY presented by the Brownsville Theater Project, Brooklyn.
A STORY presented by the Washington, D.C., Workshop for Careers in the Arts.
STREET JESUS presented by The People's Union Betterment Performing Company, Brooklyn.
WILLIE HEAVY SHOES and OPEN AND SHUT MAGIC COMPANY presented by Theater for the New City, New York City.
Program of four short plays presented by the Hispanic Theater Company, Boston, Mass.
LAZARUS: SOMETHING ABOUT LOVE presented by Reality, New York.
DUVALIER presented by the Harlem Everyman Company.

Lolly's Theater Club. Low-admission professional productions on a schedule of new scripts, specialties, revivals, visiting troupes, etc. Laura Bivens, director.

TONIGHT WE IMPROVISE AT LOLLY'S directed by Mort Siegel. August 1, 1973.
NUDE WITH VIOLIN by Noel Coward. August 2, 1973. Directed by June Plager; with Lynne E. Moss, Cynthia Kaplan, Elizabeth Reavey.
FEIFFER'S PEOPLE. August 2, 1973.
HUGHIE by Eugene O'Neill. August 9, 1973.
TONIGHT AT 8:30 by Noel Coward. August 15, 1973.
THE PORTABLE CIRCUS. September 25, 1973.
THE MATES by Bernard Mendillo, with Norman Lind and Louis Venturini, and HOW HE LIED TO HER HUSBAND by George Bernard Shaw, with Micheline Muselli. October 18, 1973.
TISTOU by Rafael V. Blanco, based on a story by Maurice Duron. December 4, 1973. Directed by Rafael V. Blanco.
THREE BY TENNESSEE program of one-act plays by Tennessee Williams: THE LADY OF LARKSPUR LOTION, TALK TO ME LIKE THE RAIN and SOMETHING UNSPOKEN. December 6, 1973. Directed by Dick Gaffield and Cindy Kaplan; with Josy Fox, Gerald M. Kline, Lacy J. Thomas, Cindy Kaplan.
THE SPIDER'S WEB by Agatha Christie. January 15, 1974. Directed by Anthony De Vito, with Ellen Gross, Robb McIntire, Fran Harris, Norman Lind.

The Manhattan Project. Development of theater by means of group improvising. Andre Gregory, director.

OUR LATE NIGHT by Wallace Shawn (open rehearsals). March 6, 1974.
ALICE IN WONDERLAND adapted from the book by Lewis Carroll. March 7, 1974.
ENDGAME by Samuel Beckett. April 11, 1974.

Manhattan Theater Club. A producing organization with three stages for productions, readings, workshop activities and cabaret. Lynne Meadow, artistic director.

YUCCA FLATS by Adam Le Fevre. October 2, 1973. Directed by J. Ranelli.
MIRACLE PLAY by Joyce Carol Oates. January 6, 1974. Directed by Dan Freudenberger.
THE WAGER by Mark Medoff. January 17, 1974. Directed by Lynne Meadow.
THE REMOVALISTS by David Williamson. January 20, 1974. Directed by Michael Montel.
THE CRETAN BULL by Kenneth H. Brown and ALLERGY by Cecil Taylor. February 1, 1974. Directed by Ronald Roston.
HOCUS, POCUS, DOMINOCUS by Jim Doyle.
BY MUTUAL CONSENT by Jeff Kindley.
MASHA by Tim Kelly.
BIRDBATH by Leonard Melfi.
THE QUESTIONING OF NICK by Arthur Kopit.
HOPSCOTCH, SPARED and OUR FATHER'S FAILING by Israel Horovitz.
SUDDENLY LAST SUMMER by Tennessee Williams.
BORN YESTERDAY by Garson Kanin.
THE SIRENS by Richard Wesley. May 2, 1974. Directed by Bill Lathan; with Roscoe Orman, Loretta Greene, Deborah Morgan, Roger Hill, Veronica Redd.
MORNING AFTER OPTIMISM by Thomas Murphy. May 10, 1974. Directed by Bob Mandel.

Matinee Theater Series. Revivals of American theater classics for two performances each at the Theater de Lys. Lucille Lortel, artistic director.

THREE ON BROADWAY anthology of American musical theater, with special tribute to George Gershwin. November 12, 1973. With Ronald Rogers, Jan McArt, Tichard Otto.
THE INTERVIEW by Peter Swet, directed by Ted Story, and THE EPIC OF BUSTER FRIEND by Richard Lenz, directed by Michael Kahn. December 3, 1973. With Caroline McWilliams, David Rounds.
SCOTT AND ZELDA by Paul Hunter. January 7, 1974. Directed by Herbert Machiz; with Nicholas Pryor, Kathryn Loder.

The New Dramatists. An organization devoted to playwrights; member writers may use the facilities for anything from private cold readings of their material to workshop stagings. Letha Nims, executive director.

GHOST DANCE by Stuart Vaughan.
THE OFF SEASON by Harding Lemay.
THE RAPISTS by Dennis Turner.
THE RABINOWITZ GAMBIT by Rose Leiman Goldemberg.
VEIL OF INFAMY by Stuart Vaughan.
HELLO I LOVE YOU by Barry Berg.

New Federal Theater. The Henry Street Settlement's training and showcase unit for new playwrights, mostly black and Puerto Rican. Woodie King Jr., director.

LADIES IN WAITING by Peter DeAnda. October 14, 1973. Directed by Shauneille Perry; with Yolanda Karr, Saundra Kelley.
BRISBURIAL by Edward Pomerantz. February 15, 1974. Directed by Richard Vos.
CANDIDATE by Charles Fuller. March 14, 1974. Directed by Hal DeWindt: with J.A. Preston, Zaida Coles, Maxwell Glanville, Arthur French, Chet Doherty, Hall Holden.

New Phoenix Repertory Company. Schedule of experimental "Side Shows" in addition to its regular Broadway repertory. T. Edward Hambleton and Michael Montel, directors. (For its 1973–74 "Side Shows," see the New Phoenix Repertory Company entry in the "Plays Produced on Broadway" section of this volume.)

New Repertory Company. Popular classics in repertory. Robert Allan Ackerman, artistic director.

THIEVES' CARNIVAL by Jean Anouilh. December 13, 1973. Directed by Robert Brink: with Tarina Lewis, Lisa Inserra, Keith McDermott.
IONESCOPADE revue of excerpts from the work of Eugene Ionesco, music and lyrics by Mildred Kayden, with Harrison Sommerville, Myra Malkin, Marion McCorry, Joanna Ferraro, Jerry Beal, and PICNIC ON THE BATTLEFIELD by Fernando Arrabal, with Joseph Abaldo, Ruth Wallman, Richard Catesby, Ian Stulberg. July 26, 1973.
THE LADY FROM THE SEA by Henrik Ibsen. September 18, 1973. Directed by Robert Kalfin; with Jerrold Ziman, Myra Malkin, Philip Himberg, Marion McCorry, Paul Sparer, Richard Crook, Marilyn Chris, Harvey Solin.

New York Shakespeare Festival. Schedule of experimental workshop or work-in-progress productions in addition to its regular schedules at the Public, Vivian Beaumont and Forum Theaters. Joseph Papp, producer. (For its 1973–74 workshop programs, see the New York Shakespeare Festival Public Theater entry in the "Plays Produced off Broadway" section of this volume.)

New York Theater Ensemble. Organization encouraging the playwright to develop his work in progress. Oswald Daljord, director.

CASHMERE LOVE by F.V. Hunt.
AS YOU WAIT by Arthur Williams and Lois Dengrove, music by Jay Woody.
FREAKY PUSSY by Harvey Fierstein. February 15, 1974. Directed by Harvey Tavel.
GLAMOR, GLORY AND GOLD—THE LIFE AND LEGEND OF NOLA NOONAN—GODDESS AND STAR by Jackie Curtis. March 1, 1974. Directed by Ron Link.

New York Theater Strategy. Organization of playwrights for the production of their own works. Maria Irene Fornes, president.

PLAY-BY-PLAY by Robert Patrick and THE STRING GAME by Rochelle Owens. June 6, 1973.
2,008½ (A SPACED ODDITY) book and lyrics by Tom Eyen, music by Gary William Friedman. February 10, 1974. Directed by Tom Eyen; with Madeleine le Roux, Mary-Jennifer Mitchell, Clark Gardner, Marion Ramsey, William Duff-Griffin, Debbie Wright.

The Nighthouse. Eclectic policy of outreaching theater. David Gaard, producer.

COMING OUT! compiled by Jonathan Katz, directed by David Roggensack, with Deanna Alida, Elizabeth Rosen, Michael O'Connor, Charlie Brown; and THE WOMEN'S REPRESENTA-TIVE by Sun Yu, adapted by David Gaard, directed by Pamela DeSio, with Linda Kampley, Dolores Kenan, Lisa Shreve, Roberta Pikser. May-June 1973.
UBU ROI AND UBU BOUND by Alfred Jarry, adapted by Gerald Mast and B.Y. Sitterly. November 18, 1973. Directed by B.Y. Sitterly; with Peter Burnell, Linda Kampley, Deanna Alida, Chris Erickson.
PIGJAZZ (vaudeville). January 22, 1974. Directed by Michael James Nee, with Bella Darvonne, Danny Corcoran, Frodo Godeaux, Ivory Snow.

Omni Theater Club. Develop a repertory of classics and present new plays in the interest of assisting playwrights to develop their work. Viktor Allen, director.

NUCLEAR HECUBA by Robert Reinhold.
THE TAMING OF THE SHREW by William Shakespeare.
GOT A MATCH? by Viktor Allen and Valerie Owen. Directed by Viktor Allen.
AMBROSE THE GREAT by Valerie Owen. May 5, 1974. Directed by Viktor Allen.

Ontological-Hysteric Theater. Avant garde theater productions written, directed and designed by the group's founder, Richard Foreman.

PAIN(T) and VERTICAL MOBILITY: SOPHIA—(WIDSOM) PART IV by Richard Foreman. April 1, 1974. Directed by Richard Foreman; with Kate Manheim, Nora Manheim.

The People's Performing Company. New, socially significant musicals. Peter Copani, Vince Gugliotti, Tony Bastiano, directors.

THE OPPOSITE SIDE OF SONNY book and lyrics by Peter Copani, music by John Roman and Peter Copani.
POWER book and lyrics by Peter Copani, music by David McHugh.

The Performance Group. Experiments with new collaborative and non-verbal creative techniques. Richard Schechner, director.

THE BEARD by Michael McClure. October 25, 1973. Directed by Stephen Borst; environmental-ist and technical director, James Clayburgh.
THE TOOTH OF CRIME by Sam Shepard. February 2, 1974. Directed by Richard Schechner.

The Performing Garage. The theater used by Richard Schechner's Performance Group sometimes houses visiting companies or productions.

THE TAMING OF THE SHREW by William Shakespeare. September 11, 1973. With Shakes-peare and Company, Tina Packer artistic director.
CALL ME CHARLIE by Michael Moran, music and lyrics by Sam Burtis and Jane Blackstone. May 11, 1974.

Players' Workshop. Mixture of new and classical productions drawing on Lower East Side audiences. Clay Stevenson, director.

NATIVE SON by Paul Green. October 19, 1973. Directed by Clay Stevenson.
TRAPS by James Whitten. January 4, 1974. Directed by Clay Stevenson.
THE MARRIAGE by Donald Greaves. April 12, 1974. Directed by James Whitten.

Ron Dener Ensemble. Dinner theater featuring improvisations and new plays. Ron Dener, artistic director.

BARROOM THEATER an improvisation developed in workshop. January 15, 1974. Conceived and directed by Ron Dener.

Root Theater of Trinity Church. Lunchtime programs in the Wall Street area. Jean Forrest, director.

SHAKESPEAREAN SONGS AND DIALOGUE. January 9, 1974. Directed by Cecile Bruns-wick.
DR QUAKENBUSH'S TRAVELLING MEDICINE SHOW AND MAGIC CIRCUS by the company. April 5, 1974. Directed by John Grimaldi.

Section Ten. New material developed through improvisation. Omar Shapli, artistic direc-tor.

A GREAT HOSS PISTOL by the company. November 1, 1973. Directed by Omar Shapli and Andrea Balis.
LULU by Frank Wedekind, adapted by Ron Cowan. May 1, 1974. Directed by Andrea Balis.

The Shade Company. Accent on the classics and modern plays of established merit. Edward Berkeley, director.

A MIDSUMMER NIGHT'S DREAM by William Shakespeare. October 4, 1973. Directed by Edward Berkeley.
THE GAMBLER by Ugo Betti. October 18, 1973. Directed by Edward Berkeley.
TARTUFFE by Molière. November 8, 1973. Directed by Edward Berkeley.
THE MARRIAGE OF MR. MISSISSIPPI by Friedrich Duerrenmatt. February 1, 1974. Di-

rected by James Milton; with Richard Yarnell, Jerrold Ziman, Rozana Stuart, Paul Jordan, Peter Victor, Alan Nebelthau.
TILL EULENSPIEGEL AND HIS MERRY PRANKS by Don Ferguson. May 4, 1974. Directed by Dale Fuller.

Stage Directors & Choreographers Workshop. Experimental showcase operated by the directors' and choreographers' organization. Madolin Cervantes, director.

HOMEFRONT BLUES by Jack Gilhooley.

T. Schreiber Studio. Establishing a close bond with the audience with all productions. Terry Schreiber, director.

OF MICE AND MEN by John Steinbeck. October 11, 1973. Directed by Terry Schreiber.
TARTUFFE by Molière. November 29, 1973. Directed by M.M. Streicher.
48 WEST 87TH by John Bishop. January 31, 1974. Directed by Terry Schreiber.
UNCLE VANYA by Anton Chekhov. March 14, 1974. Directed by Lee Wallace.
PINOCCHIO (children's rock musical). April 27, 1974. Directed by Isaac Dostis.

Theater Arts Repertory Company. An acting company concentrating on American classics but open to selected new works. Philip Nolan, artistic director.

EVERYTHING IN THE GARDEN by Edward Albee. Directed by Gene Gavin.
IDIOT'S DELIGHT by Robert E. Sherwood. Directed by Philip Nolan.

Theater at Noon. A lunchtime theater with an eclectic policy. Miriam Fond, artistic director.

A DAY IN THE PORT AUTHORITY by Gloria Gonzalez.
MARJORIE DAW book, music and lyrics by Sally Dixon Weiner. Directed by Miriam Fond.

Theater at St. Clements. New plays, guest bookings and revivals on a highly professional level, utilizing American Place's old space. Kevin O'Connor, artistic director.

NIGHT THOUGHTS by Corinne Jacker.
TWO GIRLS AND A SAILOR by Edward M. Cohen.
OPEN THEATER repertory of three programs: NIGHTWALK a collective work by the Open Theater and Jean-Claude van Itallie, Sam Shepard and Megan Terry, directed by Joseph Chaikin, September 8, 1973; TERMINAL, September 15, 1973; and THE MUTATION SHOW, September 19, 1973. With Raymond Barry, Shami Chaikin, Ralph Lee, Tom Lillard, Ellen Maddow, Jo Ann Schmidman, Tina Shepard, Paul Zimet.
SECRETS OF THE CITIZENS CORRECTION COMMITTEE by Ronald Tavel. October 17, 1973. Directed by John Chapman; with Grayson Hall.
THE RICHARD MORSE MIME THEATER. November 1, 1973. With Richard Morse, Pilar Garcia.
THEATER ASYLUM COMPANY program: BABEL-BABBLE by Joel Stone. November 8, 1973. Directed by Joel Stone; with Pete Emmons, Jeffrey Knox, Deborah Nadel, Trudy Rudin, Eleanor Schlusselberg, Wende D. Sherman, David Sternberg, Phil Therrien.
THE GREATEST FAIRY STORY EVER TOLD by Donald Howarth, from a play by Kathleen Hounsell-Roberts. November 26, 1973. With Robert Dale Martin, Gale Garnett, Sal Viscuso, Carleton Carpenter, Helen Bourne, Alix Elias, Garnett Smith.
MOON MYSTERIES program of three one-act plays by William Butler Yeats, original music by Teijo Ito. December 19, 1973. Directed and choreographed by Jean Erdman.
THE PETRIFIED FOREST by Robert E. Sherwood. January 22, 1974. Directed by Len Cariou; with George Loros, Daniel Davis, Brooke Adams.
DISQUIETING MUSES theatrical collage developed by N.Y.U. School of the Arts. February 11, 1974.
ALIVE AND WELL IN ARGENTINA by Barry Pritchard. March 4, 1974. Directed by Kevin O'Connor; with Bill Moor, Stephen McHattie, Diane Kagan, J.T. Walsh, Kevin O'Connor.
STUDIO II (Theater Laboratory of Denmark) program of two works: POSSESSION and HUH. March 20, 1974. With Yves Lebreton, Gilles Maheu.

DUET and TRIO program of two one-act plays by Nathan Teitel. March 28, 1974. Directed by Nick Havinga; with Kevin O'Connor, Carol Teitel.
BREAD AND PUPPET THEATER program of two works: GREY LADY CANTATA #4 and MEADOWS GREEN. April 26, 1974. Directed by Peter Schumann.
IN OUR TIME by Jory Johnson, adapted from short stories by Ernest Hemingway. May 6, 1974. Directed by Stephen Roylance; with Arlene Banas, Susan Bredoff, Gene Gebauer, David Himes, Jorge Johnson.
U.S.A. by John Dos Passos. May 6,1974. Directed by Jack McClure.
ELECTRA collaborative work by Joseph Chaikin, Robert Montgomery, Michele Collison, Paul Zimet, Shami Chaikin. May 27, 1974.

Theater for the New City. Specializing in experimental productions. Crystal Field, artistic director.

WOMEN ONLY WOMEN by Helen Duberstein.
TEN BEST MARTYRS OF THE YEAR by Seymour Simckes. November 1, 1973. Directed by Crystal Field.
AUNT HARRIET book by Galt MacDermot, Julie Orimus, Barbara Loden, music by Galt MacDermot. November 21, 1973. Directed by Barbara Loden.
BUCK BANION'S BIG STORY by Stanley Seidman. January 10, 1974. Directed by Norman Marshall.
ELECKTRA by Hugo von Hoffmannsthal, translated by Cari Richard Mueller. February 3, 1974. Directed by Barry Keating.
THE CHILDREN'S ARMY IS LATE by Arthur Sainer. March 8, 1974. Directed by Crystal Field.
UNDER THE BRIDGE THERE IS A LONELY SPOT by Helen Duberstein. April 25, 1974. Directed by Neil Flanagan.
PRESENTING: AUSCHWITZ by David Libman.
DOOMED LOVE by Bruce Serlen.

Theater Genesis. Production of new American plays. Walter Hadler, artistic director.

HOW JACQUELINE KENNEDY BECAME QUEEN OF GREECE by Ronald Tavel. November 2, 1973. Directed by Caymichael Patten.
PRUSSIAN SUITE by Michael Smith, music by John Smead. February 14, 1974. Directed by Michael Smith; with Ondine, Georgia Lee, Jimmy Centola, Charles Stanley.

Theater in Space (see Gene Frankel Theater Workshop).

Theater of the Riverside Church. A community theater which maintains high professional standards. Arthur Bartow, administrative director.

ARE YOU NOW OR HAVE YOU EVER BEEN by Eric Bentley. November 27, 1973. Directed by Jay Broad; with Clarence Felder, Anne Francine, Albert Hall, James Hilbrandt, Joseph Leon, Allan Miller, Michael Nader, William Newman, Arnold Soboloff, Peter Thompson.
SHORT EYES by Miguel Piñero. January 3, 1974. Directed by Marvin Felix Camillo; with The Family (Ben Jefferson, J.J. Johnson, Andrew Butler, Kenny Steward, Felipe Torres, Robert Maroff).
WHITE NIGHTS book and lyrics by Paul Zakrzewski, music by Wally Harper, a program of two musicals: WHITE NIGHTS based on the short story by Feodor Dostoyevsky and THE LOVES OF ALONZO FITZ CLARENCE AND ROSANNAH ETHELTON based on the short story by Mark Twain. February 6, 1974. Directed by Paul Zakrzewski; with Curt Dawson, Livia Genise, Kay Cole, Jonathan Hadary, Marlene Hammerling, Michael Misita.
MOURNING HERCULES by Howard Brown. May 3, 1974. Directed by Allan Beck.

Theater 77. New plays preferred. Rod Clavery and Dolores McCullough, artistic directors.

ROCK THE WORLD by Louise Naughton.
POE: FROM HIS LIFE AND MIND by Stanley Nelson. Directed by Marjorie Melnick.
MUSHROOMS by Donald Kvares. Directed by Ted Mornel.

Thirteenth Street Repertory Company. The city's only musical repertory company focusing on new work; also children's programs. Edith O'Hara, artistic director and producer.

THE COWGIRL AND THE TIGER by Wallace Gray, music and lyrics by Hank Beebe. Directed by Howard Lipson.
HABITUEES by T.J. Camp, November 19, 1973. In repertory with 100 MILES FROM NOWHERE by Bill Solly, choreography by Brian MacDonald, December 4, 1973. With Mama Hare's Tree (Edith O'Hara, founder).

Time and Space Ltd. Experiments in writing and production. Linda Mussman, artistic director.

HEDDA GABLER, modernized version of the play by Henrik Ibsen. October, 1973. Directed by Linda Mussman.
THE LOST ONES adapted from the Samuel Beckett short story by Linda Mussman. February, 1974. Directed by Linda Mussman.

Urban Arts Corps. Dedicated to the development of theater arts and crafts skills in the black community. Vinnette Carroll, artistic director.

THE FLIES by Jean-Paul Sartre. Directed by Vinnette Carroll.
ALL THE KING'S MEN by Robert Penn Warren, adapted by Vinnette Carroll, music and lyrics by Malcolm Dodds. May 14, 1974. Directed by Vinnette Carroll; with Palmer Dean, Maryce Carter, Barbara Clarke, John Danelle, Everett Ensley, Russ Gustafson.

U.R.G.E.N.T. Staging of new works and works in progress. Ronald Muchnick and Nathan George, directors.

THE ANNIVERSARY by Bill MacIlwraith. August 1, 1973. Directed by Allan Miller; with Terry Alexander, Laura Zucker, Marshall Harris, Nathan George, Marge Eliot, Louise Stubbs.
THE BALDING AFFAIR (formerly *Conflict of Interest*) by Jay Broad. October 3, 1973. Directed by Tunc Yalman; with William Mooney, Earl Hammond, Lawrence Keith.
THE WINNER by Clement Fowler. December 12, 1973. Directed by Frederick Rolf; with Sam Gray, Ruth Livingstone, Hugh Hurd.
BREAK A LEG by Ira Levin. May 13, 1974. Directed by Sheldon Patinkin; with Paul Dooley, Barbara Dana, Timothy D. Lewis, Martin Harvey Friedberg, Frank Bongiorno.
MY SISTER, MY SISTER by Ray Aranha.

Voices, Inc. Productions organized for touring colleges and universities. Josephine Jackson, artistic director.

HARLEM HEYDAY by Josephine Jackson, directed by Roger Furman, and JOURNEY INTO BLACKNESS by Josephine Jackson, directed by Rod Rogers. September 1973.

West Side Community Repertory Theater. Contemporary approaches to classical plays. Andres Castro, director.

THE MISTRESS OF THE INN by Carlo Goldoni. October 5, 1973. Directed by Andres Castro.
HEDDA GABLER by Henrik Ibsen. November 23, 1973. Directed by Andres Castro.
ANOTHER EVENING WITH CHEKHOV: THE ANNIVERSAY, A SUMMER IN THE COUNTRY, SWAN SONG by Anton Chekhov. March 1, 1974. Directed by Andres Castro.
THE PLAYBOY OF THE WESTERN WORLD by John Millington Synge. May 3, 1974. Directed by Andres Castro.

Westbeth Playwrights' Feminist Cooperative. Develop artists and audiences for feminist theater. Dolores Walker, artistic administrative director.

WE CAN FEED EVERYBODY HERE by Patricia Horan, Sally Ordway, Dolores Walker, others.
ALL THEM WOMEN by Patricia Horan, Sally Ordway, Megan Terry, Dolores Walker, others. January 11, 1974. Directed by Marjorie Melnick.
WHAT TIME OF NIGHT IT IS by Marjorie DeFazio and Patricia Horan. May 3, 1974.

Workshop of the Players Art (WPA Theater). A 200-member company presenting works of quality, both traditional and experimental. Harry Orzello, artistic director.

NEW PLAYS FESTIVAL schedule included: GOALIE by Louis Phillips, directed by Michael Lessac, with Charlie Stavola; SIDE SHOW by Joseph Renard, directed by Hugh Gittens, with Gary Swartz, J. LaHabana; ALL OVER AGAIN by William Kushner, with Valerie Beaman, Neil Flanagan; THE FLAME PLAY by Christopher Mathewson, directed by Hugh Gittens, with Karen Hendel, Cindy Ames, Amanda Davies; FEAR by Jacov Lind, directed by Leonard Peters, with Mitch Kreindel; ROBERT BENCHLEY'S LOCOMOTIVE written and directed by William Van Gieson, with Cathy Boyd, Nicki Kaplan; FAR FROM THE SUMMER, FAR FROM THE SEA by Israel Eliraz, directed by Rina Elisha, with Barbara Ball, John Schak. July 7, 1973.
THE DEATH OF THE SIAMESE TWINS by Louis Phillips.
THE TRIAL by Franz Kafka. Directed by David Q. Gale.
CHOKING UP written and directed by Joseph Renard. November 18, 1973.
KEYHOLES by Frank Marcus. November 20, 1973. Directed by Hugh Gittens, Tom Hatcher, Dennis Morre.
THE AMERICAN WAR WOMEN by Roma Greth. February 1, 1974. Directed by Pat Mullin.
ROCKS: HIGHTIME by Aura Petrides, directed by Richard Townsend, and ON THE ROCKS written and directed by Diane Kagan. February 2, 1974.
GERONIMO by John Stuehr. March 1, 1974. Directed by Leonard Peters.
A SHRIEK TO MELT THE TEXAS MOON by Christopher Mathewson. April 14, 1974. Directed by Hugh Gittens.
OLI'S ICE CREAM FANTASY by Richard Ploetz. April 30, 1974. Directed by Craig Barish.
THE RODEO STAYS IN TOWN FOR AT LEAST A WEEK by Jerry Stubblefield. May 21, 1974. Directed by David Gantreaux.

CAST REPLACEMENTS AND TOURING COMPANIES

Compiled by Stanley Green

The following is a list of the more important cast replacements in productions which opened in previous years, but were still playing in New York during a substantial part of the 1973–74 season; or were still on a first class tour in 1973–74 (casts of first class touring companies of previous seasons which were no longer playing in 1973–74 appear in previous *Best Plays* volumes of appropriate years).

The name of each major role is listed in *italics* beneath the title of the play in the first column. In the second column directly opposite appears the name of the actor who created the role in the original New York production (whose opening date appears in *italics* at the top of the column). Indented immediately beneath the original actor's name are the names of subsequent New York replacements, together with the date of replacement when available.

The third column gives information about first-class touring companies, including London companies (produced under the auspices of their original Broadway managements). When there is more than one roadshow company, #1, #2, #3, etc., appear before the name of the performer who created the role in each company (and the city and date of each company's first performance appears in *italics* at the top of the column). Their subsequent replacements are also listed beneath their names, with dates when available.

A note on bus-truck touring companies appears at the end of this section.

BUTLEY

	New York 10/31/72	Washington 10/15/73
Ben Butley	Alan Bates	Brian Bedford

THE FANTASTICKS

New York 5/3/60

El Gallo	Jerry Orbach
	Gene Rupert
	Bert Convy
	John Cunningham
	Don Stewart 1/63
	David Cryer
	Keith Charles 10/63
	John Boni 1/13/65
	Jack Mette 9/14/65
	George Ogee
	Keith Charles
	Tom Urich 8/30/66
	John Boni 10/5/66
	Jack Crowder 6/13/67
	Nils Hedrick 9/19/67
	Keith Charles 10/9/67
	Robert Goss 11/7/67
	Joe Bellomo 3/11/68
	Michael Tartel 7/8/69
	Joe Bellomo 2/15/72
	David Cryer 5/2/72
	Michael Vidnovic 6/12/72
	Joe Bellomo 11/12/72
	David Rexroad 6/73
	David Snell 12/73
	Hal Robinson 4/2/74
Luisa	Rita Gardner
	Carla Huston
	Liza Stuart 12/61
	Eileen Fulton
	Alice Cannon 9/62
	Royce Lenelle
	B.J. Ward 12/1/64
	Leta Anderson 7/13/65
	Carole Demas 11/22/66
	Leta Anderson 8/7/67
	Carole Demas 9/4/67
	Anne Kaye 1/23/68
	Carole Demas 2/13/68
	Anne Kaye 5/28/68
	Carolyn Magnini 7/29/69
	Virginia Gregory 7/27/70
	Leta Anderson
	Marty Morris 3/7/72
	Sharon Werner 8/1/72
Matt	Kenneth Nelson
	Gino Conforti
	Jack Blackton 10/63
	Paul Giovanni
	Ty McConnell
	Richard Rothbard

Gary Krawford
Bob Spencer 9/5/64
Erik Howell 6/28/66
Gary Krawford 12/12/67
Steve Skiles 2/6/68
Craig Carnelia 1/69
Erik Howell 7/18/69
Samuel D. Ratcliffe 8/5/69
Michael Glenn-Smith 5/26/70
Jimmy Dodge 9/20/70
Geoffrey Taylor 8/31/71
Erik Howell 3/14/72
Michael Glenn-Smith 6/13/72
Phil Killian 7/4/72
Richard Lincoln 9/72
Bruce Cryer 7/24/73
Phil Killian 9/11/73

FINISHING TOUCHES

	New York 2/8/73	*Los Angeles 12/4/73*
Katy Cooper	Barbara Bel Geddes	Barbara Bel Geddes
Jeff Cooper	Robert Lansing	Robert Lansing

GODSPELL

	New York 5/17/71	*Pittsburgh 10/27/72*
Jesus	Stephen Nathan Andy Rohrer 6/6/72 Don Hamilton Ryan Hilliard Don Scardino 1/73 Jeremy Sage 2/74	Mark Shera Robert Brandon Tom Rolfing
Judas	David Haskell Bart Braverman 5/72 Lloyd Bremseth	Mark Ganzel Tom Rolfing Michael Hoit

GREASE

	New York 2/14/72	#1 *New Haven 1/22/73* #2 *London 6/26/73* #3 *Philadelphia 4/7/74*
Danny Zuko	Barry Bostwick Jeff Conaway 6/73	#1 Jeff Conaway Barry Bostwick 6/73 #2 Richard Gere #3 John Lansing
Sandy Dumbrowski	Carole Demas Eileen Graff 3/73	#1 Pamela Adams Candice Earley #2 Stacey Gregg #3 Marcia McClain
Betty Rizzo	Adrienne Barbeau Elaine Petrokoff 3/73 Randee Heller 5/74	#1 Judy Kaye #2 Jacqui-Ann Carr #3 Karren Dille

THE HOT L BALTIMORE

New York 3/22/73

| *Jackie* | Mari Gorman |
| | Jennifer Harmon 10/24/73 |

IRENE

New York 3/13/73

Irene O'Dare	Debbie Reynolds
	Jane Powell 2/6/74
Mrs. O'Dare	Patsy Kelly
	Mary McCarty 8/2/73
	Patsy Kelly 8/20/73
Donald Marshall	Monte Markham
	Ron Husmann 6/4/73

A LITTLE NIGHT MUSIC

	New York 2/25/73	*Philadelphia 2/26/74*
Desiree Armfeldt	Glynis Johns	Jean Simmons
Fredrik Egerman	Len Cariou	George Lee Andrews
	William Daniels 2/25/74	
Madame Armfeldt	Hermione Gingold	Margaret Hamilton

PIPPIN

	New York 10/23/72	*London 10/30/73*
Pippin	John Rubinstein	Paul Jones
Charles	Eric Berry	John Turner
Catherine	Jill Clayburgh	Patricia Hodge
	Betty Buckley 6/11/73	
Fastrada	Leland Palmer	Diane Langdon
	Priscilla Lopez 1/6/74	
Berthe	Irene Ryan	Elisabeth Welch
	Lucie Lancaster 4/73	
	Dorothy Stickney 6/11/73	
Leading Player	Ben Vereen	Northern J. Calloway
	Northern J. Calloway 2/18/74	
	Ben Vereen 5/7/74	

THE PRISONER OF SECOND AVENUE

	New York 11/11/71	*#1 Los Angeles 10/17/72* *#2 Baltimore 9/15/73*
Mel Edison	Peter Falk	#1 Art Carney
	Art Carney 6/5/72	Jack Somack
	Hector Elizondo 10/2/72	Art Carney
	Gabriel Dell 6/25/73	#2 Shelley Berman

Edna Edison	Lee Grant Barbara Barrie 6/5/72 Phyllis Newman 10/2/72 Barbara Barrie 1/29/73 Rosemary Prinz 6/25/73	#1 Barbara Barrie Rosemary Prinz 1/29/73 #2 Mimi Hines
Harry Edison	Vincent Gardenia Jack Somack 5/22/72 Harry Goz 10/2/72	#1 Jack Somack Harry Goz Bill Morev #2 Jack Hanrahan

THE REAL INSPECTOR HOUND and AFTER MAGRITTE

	New York 4/23/72	*Philadelphia 2/18/74*
Moon (Hound)	David Rounds Lenny Baker	Robert Vaughn
Harris (Magritte)	Konrad Matthaei Christopher Bernau Donegan Smith 1/73 Ted Danson Christopher Bernau	Robert Vaughn

THE RIVER NIGER

	N.Y. Off-Bway. 12/5/72 *N.Y. Bway. 3/27/73*	*Philadelphia 10/16/73*
Johnny Williams	Douglas Turner Ward Arthur French 5/29/73	Douglas Turner Ward

SEESAW

	New York 3/18/73	*Boston 4/15/74*
Gittel Mosca	Michele Lee Patti Karr 10/1/73 Michele Lee 10/15/73 Patti Karr 10/29/73	Lucie Arnaz
Jerry Ryan	Ken Howard Nicholas Coster 6/11/73 John Gavin 6/18/73	John Gavin
David	Tommy Tune	Tommy Tune

SLEUTH

	New York 11/12/70	*Toronto 10/6/71*
Andrew Wyke	Anthony Quayle Paul Rogers 9/27/71 Patrick Macnee 7/3/72 George Rose 4/9/73 Patrick Macnee 5/21/73	Michael Allinson
Milo Tindle	Keith Baxter Donal Donnelly 8/16/71 Keith Baxter 9/20/71 Brian Murray 3/27/72 Jordan Christopher 11/7/72 Curt Dawson 8/6/73	Donal Donnelly

THE SUNSHINE BOYS

	New York 12/20/72	Detroit 12/3/73
Al Lewis	Sam Levene Lou Jacobi 11/19/73	Sam Levene
Willie Clark	Jack Albertson Jack Gilford 10/16/73	Jack Albertson Ned Glass
Ben Silverman	Lewis J. Stadlen John Batiste 7/23/73	Stephan Mark Weyte

THAT CHAMPIONSHIP SEASON

	New York 5/2/72	#1 Los Angeles 12/3/73 #2 London 5/6/74
Tom Daley	Walter McGinn Peter Masterson	#1 Philip R. Allen #2 Walter McGinn
George Sikowski	Charles Durning Emmet Walsh 10/73 Charles Durning	#1 George Dzundza #2 Ron McLarty
James Daley	Michael McGuire Nicholas Pryor	#1 Bernie McInerney #2 Bernie McInerney
Phil Romano	Paul Sorvino Joseph Mascolo Paul Sorvino 6/27/72 Carmine Caridi	#1 Joseph Mascolo #2 Joseph Mascolo
Coach	Richard A. Dysart Pat Hingle 6/18/73 Harry Bellaver 2/25/74 Pat Hingle 3/20/74	#1 Forrest Tucker #2 Broderick Crawford

THE WALTZ OF THE TOREADORS (Revival)

	New York 9/13/73	Chicago 2/25/74
Mme. St. Pe	Anne Jackson	Anne Jackson
Gen. St. Pe	Eli Wallach	Eli Wallach

BUS-TRUCK TOURS

These are touring productions designed for maximum mobility and ease of handling in one-night and split-week stands (with occasional engagements of a week or more). Among Broadway shows on tour in the season of 1973–74 were the following bus-truck troupes:

Godspell, 81 cities, 9/6/73–2/21/74
No, No, Nanette with Evelyn Keyes, Benny Baker, Betty Keane, 93 cities, 9/14/73–3/12/74
Two Gentlemen of Verona, 102 cities, 9/20/73–4/27/74.
No Sex Please, We're British with Noel Harrison, 46 cities, 10/7/73–12/9/73
Grease, 95 cities, 10/8/73–4/5/74 (converted to regular touring company 4/7/74)
The Prisoner of Second Avenue with Imogene Coca and King Donovan, 100 cities, 10/12/73–4/10/74
Twigs with Vivian Blaine, 18 cities, 1/4/74–4/1/74
Camelot with John Raitt, 51 cities, 2/1/74–4/9/74

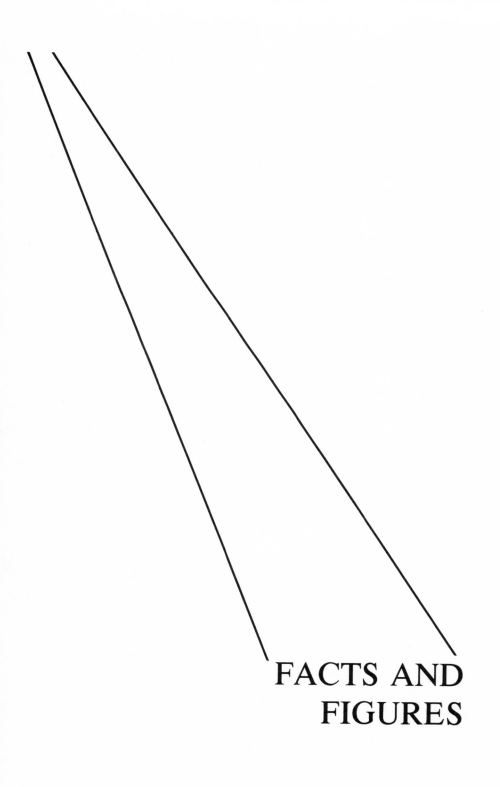

FACTS AND
FIGURES

LONG RUNS ON BROADWAY

The following shows have run 500 or more continuous performances in a single production, usually the first, not including previews or extra non-profit performances, allowing for vacation layoffs and special one-booking engagements, but not including return engagements after a show has gone on tour. Where there are title similarities, the production is identified as follows: (p) straight play version, (m) musical version, (r) revival.

THROUGH MAY 31, 1974

(PLAYS MARKED WITH ASTERISK WERE STILL PLAYING JUNE 1, 1974)

Plays	Number Performances	Plays	Number Performances
Fiddler on the Roof	3,242	Mister Roberts	1,157
Life With Father	3,224	Annie Get Your Gun	1,147
Tobacco Road	3,182	The Seven Year Itch	1,141
Hello, Dolly!	2,844	Butterflies Are Free	1,128
My Fair Lady	2,717	Pins and Needles	1,108
Man of La Mancha	2,328	Plaza Suite	1,097
Abie's Irish Rose	2,327	Kiss Me, Kate	1,070
Oklahoma!	2,212	The Pajama Game	1,063
South Pacific	1,925	The Teahouse of the August	
Harvey	1,775	Moon	1,027
Hair	1,750	Damn Yankees	1,019
Born Yesterday	1,642	Never Too Late	1,007
Mary, Mary	1,572	Any Wednesday	982
The Voice of the Turtle	1,557	A Funny Thing Happened on	
Barefoot in the Park	1,530	the Way to the Forum	964
Mame (m)	1,508	The Odd Couple	964
Arsenic and Old Lace	1,444	Anna Lucasta	957
The Sound of Music	1,443	*Grease	957
How To Succeed in Business		Kiss and Tell	956
Without Really Trying	1,417	The Moon Is Blue	924
Hellzapoppin	1,404	Bells Are Ringing	924
The Music Man	1,375	*Don't Bother Me, I	
Funny Girl	1,348	Can't Cope	914
Oh! Calcutta!	1,314	Luv	901
Angel Street	1,295	Applause	896
Lightnin'	1,291	Can-Can	892
Promises, Promises	1,281	Carousel	890
The King and I	1,246	Hats Off to Ice	889
Cactus Flower	1,234	Fanny	888
Sleuth	1,222	Follow the Girls	882
1776	1,217	Camelot	873
Guys and Dolls	1,200	The Bat	867
Cabaret	1,165	My Sister Eileen	864

Plays	Number Performances	Plays	Number Performances
No, No, Nanette (r)	861	Peg o' My Heart	692
Song of Norway	860	The Children's Hour	691
A Streetcar Named Desire	855	Purlie	688
Comedy in Music	849	Dead End	687
That Championship Season	844	The Lion and the Mouse	686
You Can't Take It With You	837	White Cargo	686
La Plume de Ma Tante	835	Dear Ruth	683
Three Men on a Horse	835	East Is West	680
The Subject Was Roses	832	Come Blow Your Horn	677
Inherit the Wind	806	The Most Happy Fella	676
No Time for Sergeants	796	The Doughgirls	671
Fiorello!	795	The Impossible Years	670
Where's Charley?	792	Irene	670
The Ladder	789	Boy Meets Girl	669
Forty Carats	780	*Pippin	669
The Prisoner of Second		Beyond the Fringe	667
Avenue	780	Who's Afraid of Virginia	
Oliver	774	Woolf?	664
State of the Union	765	Blithe Spirit	657
The First Year	760	A Trip to Chinatown	657
You Know I Can't Hear You		The Women	657
When the Water's Running	755	Bloomer Girl	654
Two for the Seesaw	750	The Fifth Season	654
Death of a Salesman	742	Rain	648
Sons o' Fun	742	Witness for the Prosecution	645
Gentlemen Prefer Blondes	740	Call Me Madam	644
The Man Who		Janie	642
Came to Dinner	739	The Green Pastures	640
Call Me Mister	734	Auntie Mame (p)	639
West Side Story	732	A Man for All Seasons	637
High Button Shoes	727	The Fourposter	632
Finian's Rainbow	725	Two Gentlemen	
Claudia	722	of Verona (m)	627
The Gold Diggers	720	The Tenth Man	623
Jesus Christ Superstar	720	Is Zat So?	618
Carnival	719	Anniversary Waltz	615
The Diary of Anne Frank	717	The Happy Time (p)	614
I Remember Mama	714	Separate Rooms	613
Tea and Sympathy	712	Affairs of State	610
Junior Miss	710	Star and Garter	609
Last of the Red Hot Lovers	706	The Student Prince	608
Company	705	Sweet Charity	608
Seventh Heaven	704	Bye Bye Birdie	607
Gypsy (m)	702	Broadway	603
The Miracle Worker	700	Adonis	603
Cat on a Hot Tin Roof	694	Street Scene (p)	601
Li'l Abner	693	Kiki	600

Plays	Number Performances	Plays	Number Performances
Flower Drum Song	600	Milk and Honey	543
Don't Drink the Water	598	Within the Law	541
Wish You Were Here	598	The Music Master	540
A Society Circus	596	Pal Joey (r)	540
Blossom Time	592	What Makes Sammy Run?	540
*Irene (r)	590	The Sunshine Boys	538
The Me Nobody Knows	586	What a Life	538
The Two Mrs. Carrolls	585	The Unsinkable Molly Brown	532
Kismet	583	The Red Mill (r)	531
Detective Story	581	A Raisin in the Sun	530
Brigadoon	581	*A Little Night Music	527
No Strings	580	The Solid Gold Cadillac	526
Brother Rat	577	Irma La Douce	524
Show Boat	572	The Boomerang	522
The Show-Off	571	Follies	521
Sally	570	Rosalinda	521
Golden Boy (m)	568	The Best Man	520
One Touch of Venus	567	Chauve-Souris	520
Happy Birthday	564	Blackbirds of 1928	518
Look Homeward, Angel	564	Sunny	517
The Glass Menagerie	561	Victoria Regina	517
I Do! I Do!	560	Half a Sixpence	511
Wonderful Town	559	The Vagabond King	511
Rose Marie	557	The New Moon	509
Strictly Dishonorable	557	The World of Suzie Wong	508
A Majority of One	556	The Rothschilds	507
The Great White Hope	556	Sugar	505
Toys in the Attic	556	Shuffle Along	504
Sunrise at Campobello	556	Up in Central Park	504
Jamaica	555	Carmen Jones	503
Stop the World—I Want to Get Off	555	The Member of the Wedding	501
Florodora	553	Panama Hattie	501
Ziegfeld Follies (1943)	553	Personal Appearance	501
Dial "M" for Murder	552	Bird in Hand	500
Good News	551	Room Service	500
Let's Face It	547	Sailor, Beware!	500
		Tomorrow the World	500

LONG RUNS OFF BROADWAY

Plays	Number Performances	Plays	Number Performances
*The Fantasticks	5,863	Jacques Brel Is Alive and Well and Living in Paris	1,847
The Threepenny Opera	2,611		

Plays	Number Performances	Plays	Number Performances
You're a Good Man		The Knack	685
Charlie Brown	1,597	The Balcony	672
The Blacks	1,408	*El Grande de Coca-Cola	668
*Godspell	1,270	America Hurrah	634
Little Mary Sunshine	1,143	Hogan's Goat	607
One Flew Over the		The Trojan Women (r)	600
Cuckoo's Nest (r)	1,025	Krapp's Last Tape and	
The Boys in the Band	1,000	The Zoo Story	582
Your Own Thing	933	The Dumbwaiter and	
Curley McDimple	931	The Collection	578
Leave It to Jane (r)	928	Dames at Sea	575
The Mad Show	871	The Crucible (r)	571
The Effect of Gamma Rays on		The Iceman Cometh (r)	565
Man-in-the-Moon Marigolds .	819	The Hostage (r)	545
A View From the Bridge (r) . . .	780	Six Characters in Search of an	
The Boy Friend (r)	763	Author (r)	529
The Pocket Watch	725	The Dirtiest Show in Town . . .	509
The Connection	722	Happy Ending and Day of	
Adaptation and Next	707	Absence	504
Oh! Calcutta!	704	The Boys From Syracuse (r) . . .	500
Scuba Duba	692		

DRAMA CRITICS CIRCLE VOTING, 1973–74

The New York Drama Critics Circle voted the British play *The Contractor* the best play of the season by a majority of 13 first choices of the 22 voting members on the first ballot. The votes on this ballot were distributed as follows: *The Contractor* (13)—Clive Barnes, John Beaufort, Brendan Gill, William H. Glover, Henry Hewes, Ted Kalem, Emory Lewis, Edith Oliver, George Oppenheimer, William Raidy, John Simon, Marilyn Stasio, Allan Wallach; *Freedom of the City* (4)—Jack Gaver, Walter Kerr, Douglas Watt, Richard Watts Jr.; *Boom Boom Room* (2)—Harold Clurman, Martin Gottfried; *Jumpers* (2)—Jack Kroll, Norman Nadel; Abstain (1)—Hobe Morrison.

Having named a foreign play best of bests, the Critics Circle proceeded to vote on a best American play, the first ballot of first choices producing no majority in a division as follows: *Boom Boom Room* 5, *Short Eyes* 4, *Bad Habits* 2, *The Good Doctor* 2, *Clarence Darrow* 1, *Creeps* 1, *Thieves* 1, *When You Comin' Back, Red Ryder* 1, Abstain 5. A vote was then taken to decide by simple majority whether or not to present an award to a best American play. The ayes had it in a close vote, 12 to 10. The Circle then proceeded to choose *Short Eyes* the best American play by a 1-point margin over *Boom Boom Room,* on a second ballot weighted to produce a consensus measured by points, with 3 points given to each critic's first choice, 2 for his second and 1 for his third. The point scores on this second ballot were *Short Eyes* 22, *Boom Boom Room* 21, *Bad Habits* 19, *The*

Good Doctor 9, *What the Wine-Sellers Buy* 8, *Creeps* 7, *Red Ryder* 5, *The Great Macdaddy* 3, *A Breeze From the Gulf* 2, *Going Through Changes* 2, *My Sister, My Sister* 2, *The Sea Horse* 2.

The critics voted *Candide* the best musical of the season by a majority of 14 first choices on the first ballot. The votes on this ballot were distributed as follows: *Candide* (14)—Barnes, Clurman, Gill, Hewes, Kalem, Kerr, Lewis, Miss Oliver, Oppenheimer, Raidy, Simon, Miss Stasio, Wallach, Watts; *Raisin* (2)—Beaufort, Morrison; *The Life and Times of Josef Stalin* (1)—Gottfried; *Over Here* (1)—Kroll; Abstain (4)—Gaver, Glover, Nadel, Watt.

At the beginning of the meeting the critics had considered the eligibility of various works. It was decided that *Ulysses in Nighttown* hadn't been sufficiently altered from its previous production to be considered a new work, but that *Candide,* with its new book, had.

Here's the way the Critics Circle members' votes were distributed on the weighted second ballot for best American play:

SECOND BALLOT FOR BEST PLAY

Critic	1st Choice (3 pts.)	2d Choice (2 pts.)	3d Choice (1 pt.)
Clive Barnes *Times*	Short Eyes	Bad Habits	When You Comin' Back, Red Ryder?
John Beaufort *Monitor*	The Good Doctor	What the Wine-Sellers Buy	Short Eyes
Harold Clurman *The Nation*	Boom Boom Room	Creeps	My Sister, My Sister
Jack Gaver *UPI*	Abstain		
Brendan Gill *New Yorker*	Bad Habits	Wine-Sellers	Boom Boom Room
William H. Glover *AP*	Short Eyes	Bad Habits	Creeps
Martin Gottfried *Women's Wear*	Boom Boom Room	Going Through Changes	Short Eyes
Henry Hewes *Sat. Review/World*	Abstain		
Ted Kalem *Time*	Abstain		
Walter Kerr *Times*	Short Eyes	A Breeze From the Gulf	The Great Macdaddy
Jack Kroll *Newsweek*	Boom Boom Room	Short Eyes	Red Ryder
Emory Lewis *Bergen Record*	Boom Boom Room	Bad Habits	Short Eyes
Hobe Morrison *Variety*	Abstain		
Norman Nadel *Scripps-Howard*	Abstain		
Edith Oliver *New Yorker*	Bad Habits	Boom Boom Room	Wine-Sellers
George Oppenheimer *Newsday*	The Good Doctor	Bad Habits	Creeps
William Raidy *Newhouse*	Red Ryder	Boom Boom Room	Short Eyes
John Simon *New York*	Creeps	Bad Habits	Short Eyes

Marilyn Stasio *Cue*	Boom Boom Room	Bad Habits	My Sister, My Sister
Allan Wallach *Newsday*	Short Eyes	Wine-Sellers	Boom Boom Room
Douglas Watt *Daily News*	Short Eyes	The Sea Horse	Bad Habits
Richard Watts Jr. *Post*	The Good Doctor	The Great Macdaddy	Wine-Sellers

CHOICES OF SOME OTHER CRITICS

Critic	*Best Play*	*Best Musical*
Judith Crist	Jumpers	Candide
Leonard Harris WCBS-TV	Boom Boom Room	Candide
Leonard Probst	Scapino	Candide
Virgil Scudder WINS Radio	Boom Boom Room	Candide
Stewart Klein	Ulysses in Nighttown	Abstain

NEW YORK DRAMA CRITICS CIRCLE AWARDS

Listed below are the New York Drama Critics Circle Awards from 1935–36 through 1972–73, classified as follows: (1) Best American Play, (2) Best Foreign Play, (3) Best Musical, (4) Best, regardless of category (this category was established by new voting rules in 1962–63 and did not exist prior to that year).

1935–36—(1) Winterset
1936–37—(1) High Tor
1937–38—(1) Of Mice and Men, (2) Shadow and Substance
1938–39—(1) No award, (2) The White Steed
1939–40—(1) The Time of Your Life
1940–41—(1) Watch on the Rhine, (2) The Corn Is Green
1941–42—(1) No award, (2) Blithe Spirit
1942–43—(1) The Patriots
1943–44—(2) Jacobowsky and the Colonel
1944–45—(1) The Glass Menagerie
1945–46—(1) Carousel
1946–47—(1) All My Sons, (2) No Exit, (3) Brigadoon
1947–48—(1) A Streetcar Named Desire, (2) The Winslow Boy
1948–49—(1) Death of a Salesman, (2) The Madwoman of Chaillot, (3) South Pacific
1949–50—(1) The Member of the Wedding (2) The Cocktail Party, (3) The Consul
1950–51—(1) Darkness at Noon, (2) The Lady's Not for Burning, (3) Guys and Dolls
1951–52—(1) I Am a Camera, (2) Venus Observed, (3) Pal Joey (Special citation to Don Juan in Hell)
1952–53—(1) Picnic, (2) The Love of Four Colonels, (3) Wonderful Town
1953–54—(1) Teahouse of the August Moon, (2)

Ondine, (3) The Golden Apple
1954–55—(1) Cat on a Hot Tin Roof, (2) Witness for the Prosecution, (3) The Saint of Bleecker Street
1955–56—(1) The Diary of Ann Frank, (2) Tiger at the Gates, (3) My Fair Lady
1956–57—(1) Long Day's Journey Into Night, (2) The Waltz of the Toreadors, (3) The Most Happy Fella
1957–58—(1) Look Homeward, Angel, (2) Look Back in Anger, (3) The Music Man
1958–59—(1) A Raisin in the Sun, (2) The Visit, (3) La Plume de Ma Tante
1959–60—(1) Toys in the Attic, (2) Five Finger Exercise, (3) Fiorello!
1960–61—(1) All the Way Home, (2) A Taste of Honey, (3) Carnival
1961–62—(1) The Night of the Iguana, (2) A Man for All Seasons, (3) How to Succeed in Business Without Really Trying
1962–63—(4) Who's Afraid of Virginia Woolf? (Special citation to Beyond the Fringe)
1963–64—(4) Luther, (3) Hello, Dolly! (Special citation to The Trojan Women)
1964–65—(4) The Subject Was Roses, (3) Fiddler on the Roof
1965–66—(4) The Persecution and Assassina-

tion of Marat as Performed by the Inmates of the Asylum of Charenton Under the Direction of the Marquis de Sade, (3) Man of La Mancha
1966–67—(4) The Homecoming, (3) Cabaret
1967–68—(4) Rosencrantz and Guildenstern Are Dead, (3) Your Own Thing
1968–69—(4) The Great White Hope, (3) 1776
1969–70—(4) Borstal Boy, (1) The Effect of Gamma Rays on Man-in-the-Moon Marigolds, (3) Company

1970–71—(4) Home, (1) The House of Blue Leaves, (3) Follies
1971–72—(4) That Championship Season, (2) The Screens, (3) Two Gentlemen of Verona (Special citations to Sticks and Bones and Old Times)
1972–73—(4) The Changing Room, (1) The Hot 1 Baltimore, (3) A Little Night Music
1973–74—(4) The Contractor, (1) Short Eyes, (3) Candide

PULITZER PRIZE WINNERS, 1916–17 TO 1973–74

1916–17—No award
1917–18—Why Marry?, by Jesse Lynch Williams
1918–19—No award
1919–20—Beyond the Horizon, by Eugene O'Neill
1920–21—Miss Lulu Bett, by Zona Gale
1921–22—Anna Christie, by Eugene O'Neill
1922–23—Icebound, by Owen Davis
1923–24—Hell-Bent fer Heaven, by Hatcher Hughes
1924–25—They Knew What They Wanted, by Sidney Howard
1925–26—Craig's Wife, by George Kelly
1926–27—In Abraham's Bosom, by Paul Green
1927–28—Strange Interlude, by Eugene O'Neill
1928–29—Street Scene, by Elmer Rice
1929–30—The Green Pastures, by Marc Connelly
1930–31—Alison's House, by Susan Glaspell
1931–32—Of Thee I Sing, by George S. Kaufman, Morrie Ryskind, Ira and George Gershwin
1932–33—Both Your Houses, by Maxwell Anderson
1933–34—Men in White, by Sidney Kingsley
1934–35—The Old Maid, by Zoë Akins
1935–36—Idiot's Delight, by Robert E. Sherwood
1936–37—You Can't Take It With You, by Moss Hart and George S. Kaufman
1937–38—Our Town, by Thornton Wilder
1938–39—Abe Lincoln in Illinois, by Robert E. Sherwood
1939–40—The Time of Your Life, by William Saroyan
1940–41—There Shall Be No Night, by Robert E. Sherwood
1941–42—No award
1942–43—The Skin of Our Teeth, by Thornton Wilder
1943–44—No award
1944–45—Harvey, by Mary Chase
1945–46—State of the Union, by Howard Lindsay and Russel Crouse
1946–47—No award.
1947–48—A Streetcar Named Desire, by Tennessee Williams
1948–49—Death of a Salesman, by Arthur Miller
1949–50—South Pacific, by Richard Rodgers, Oscar Hammerstein II and Joshua Logan
1950–51—No award
1951–52—The Shrike, by Joseph Kramm
1952–53—Picnic, by William Inge
1953–54—The Teahouse of the August Moon, by John Patrick
1954–55—Cat on a Hot Tin Roof, by Tennessee Williams
1955–56—The Diary of Anne Frank, by Frances Goodrich and Albert Hackett
1956–57—Long Day's Journey Into Night, by Eugene O'Neill
1957–58—Look Homeward, Angel, by Ketti Frings
1958–59—J. B., by Archibald MacLeish
1959–60—Fiorello!, by Jerome Weidman, George Abbott, Sheldon Harnick and Jerry Bock
1960–61—All the Way Home, by Tad Mosel
1961–62—How to Succeed in Business Without Really Trying, by Abe Burrows, Willie Gilbert, Jack Weinstock and Frank Loesser
1962–63—No award
1963–64—No award
1964–65—The Subject Was Roses, by Frank D. Gilroy
1965–66—No award
1966–67—A Delicate Balance, by Edward Albee
1967–68—No award
1968–69—The Great White Hope, by Howard Sackler
1969–70—No Place to Be Somebody, by Charles Gordone
1970–71—The Effect of Gamma Rays on Man-in-the-Moon Marigolds, by Paul Zindel
1971–72—No award
1972–73—That Championship Season, by Jason Miller
1973–74—No award

ADDITIONAL PRIZES AND AWARDS, 1973–74

The following is a list of major prizes and awards for theatrical achievement. In all cases the names of winners—persons, productions or organizations—appear in **bold face type.**

VILLAGE VOICE OFF-BROADWAY (OBIE) AWARDS for off-Broadway excellence, selected by a committee of judges whose members were Clive Barnes, Emory Lewis, Dick Brukenfeld and Arthur Sainer. Best American play, *Short Eyes* by Miguel Piñero. Best foreign play, *The Contractor* by David Storey. Distinguished plays, *Bad Habits* by Terrence McNally, *When You Comin' Back, Red Ryder?* by Mark Medoff, *The Great Macdaddy* by Paul Carter Harrison. Distinguished direction, **Marvin Felix Camillo** for *Short Eyes*, **Robert Drivas** for *Bad Habits*, **David Licht** for *Hard To Be a Jew*, **John Pasquin** for *Moonchildren*, **Harold Prince** for *Candide*. Distinguished performances, **Barbara Barrie** in *The Killdeer*, **Joseph Buloff** in *Hard To Be a Jew*, **Kevin Conway** and **Elizabeth Sturges** in *When You Comin' Back, Red Ryder?*, **Conchata Ferrell** in *The Sea Horse*, **Loretta Greene** in *The Sirens*, **Barbara Montgomery** in *My Sister, My Sister*, **Zipora Spaizman** in *Stepenyu*. Best music, **Bill Elliott** for *C.O.R.F.A.X.* Best costumes, **Theoni V. Aldredge** for Public Theater productions. Best set design, **Holmes Easley** for Roundabout Theater productions, **Christopher Thomas** for *The Lady From the Sea.* Special citations to **The Bread & Puppet Theater, The Brooklyn Academy of Music** for its British theater season, the **CSC Repertory Company, Robert Wilson** for *The Life and Times of Josef Stalin.*

ELIZABETH HULL-KATE WARRINER 1973 AWARD (to the playwright whose work produced within each year dealt with controversial subjects involving the fields of political, religious or social mores of the time, selected by the Dramatists Guild Council). **Joseph A. Walker** for *The River Niger.*

MARGO JONES AWARD (for the most significant contribution to the theater through a continuing policy of producing new plays). **Douglas Turner Ward** and the **Negro Ensemble Company.**

VERNON RICE AWARD (for outstanding contribution to the off-Broadway season, voted by Drama Desk). **The Circle Repertory Theater Company.**

JOSEPH MAHARAM FOUNDATION AWARDS (for distinguished New York theatri-

cal design). Best 1973–74 scene design, **Eugene** and **Franne Lee** for Candide; **Ed Wittstein** for *Ulysses in Nighttown.* Best 1973–74 costume design, **Franne Lee** for *Candide.*

GEORGE JEAN NATHAN AWARD (for criticism). **Stanley Kauffmann.**

SAM S. SHUBERT FOUNDATION AWARD (for outstanding contribution to the American Theater). **Robert Whitehead.**

THEATER WORLD AWARDS (30th annual awards to the most promising new performers in Broadway and off-Broadway productions). **Mark Baker** and **Maureen Brennan** in *Candide,* **Ralph Carter, Ernestine Jackson** and **Joe Morton** in *Raisin,* **Thom Christopher** in *Noel Coward in Two Keys,* **John Driver, Ann Reinking** and **Janie Sell** in *Over Here,* **Conchata Ferrell** in *The Sea Horse,* **Michael Moriarty** in *Find Your Way Home,* **Mary Woronov** in *Boom Boom Room.* Special award to **Sammy Cahn.**

LOS ANGELES DRAMA CRITICS CIRCLE AWARDS for distinguished 1973–74 productions in Los Angeles. *Cyrano de Bergerac* produced by Center Theater Group, *Dominus Marlowe/A Play on Dr. Faustus* produced by ProVisional Theater, *Bus Stop* produced by MET Theater.

BRANDEIS UNIVERSITY CREATIVE ARTS AWARD. **Helen Hayes.**

OUTER CIRCLE AWARDS (voted by critics of out-of-town and foreign periodicals for distinctive achievement in New York Theater). Best play, *Noel Coward in Two Keys.* Best musical, *Candide.*

NATIONAL THEATER CONFERENCE AWARD for distinguished service to the American Theater. **Ruth Mayleas.**

THEATER AWARDS '74 (voted by the National Academy of the Living Theater Foundation and presented at the Tony ceremonies). **Actors Equity Association** for "60 years of forceful and tireless effort on behalf of American actors and actresses;" the **Theater Development Fund** for "imaginative and energetic array of programs designed to nurture and enlarge the audience for the living theater;" **John F. Wharton** for "over 50 years of sagacious legal counsel to the entire theatrical industry;" **Harold Friedlander** for "more than 40 years of expert counsel in the design and preparation of display material for the theater."

THE TONY AWARDS

The Antoinette Perry (Tony) Awards are voted by members of the League of New York Theaters, the governing bodies of the Dramatists Guild, Actors, Equity, the American Theater Wing, the Society of Stage Directors and Choreographers, the United Scenic Artists Union, and members of the first and second night press, from a list of up to five nominees in each category. Nominations are made by a committee serving at the invitation of the League of New York Theaters, which is in charge of the Tony Awards procedure, with the committee's personnel changing every year. The 1973–74 nominating committee was composed of Mel Gussow, Ted Kalem, Elliot Norton, William Raidy, Lee Silver, Marilyn Stasio and Isabelle Stevenson. Their list of nominees follows, with winners listed in **bold face type.**

BEST PLAY. *The Au Pair Man* by Hugh Leonard, produced by Joseph Papp; *Boom Boom Room* by David Rabe, produced by Joseph Papp; *The River Niger* by Joseph A. Walker, produced by Negro Ensemble Company; *Ulysses in Nighttown* by Marjorie Barkentin, produced by Alexander H. Cohen and Bernard Delfont.

BEST MUSICAL: *Over Here* produced by Kenneth Waissman and Maxine Fox; *Raisin* produced by Robert Nemiroff; *Seesaw* produced by Joseph Kipness, Lawrence Kasha, James Nederlander, George M. Steinbrenner III, Lorin Price.

BEST BOOK OF A MUSICAL. *Candide* by **Hugh Wheeler;** *Raisin* by Robert Nemiroff and Charlotte Zaltzberg; *Seesaw* by Michael Bennett. BEST SCORE: *Gigi,* music by **Frederick Loewe,** lyrics by **Alan Jay Lerner;** *The Good Doctor,* music by Peter Link, lyrics by Neil Simon; *Raisin,* music by Judd Woldin, lyrics by Robert Brittan; *Seesaw,* music by Cy Coleman, lyrics by Dorothy Fields.

BEST ACTOR—PLAY. **Michael Moriarty** in *Find Your Way Home,* Zero Mostel in *Ulysses in Nighttown,* Jason Robards in *A Moon for the Misbegotten,* George C. Scott and Nicol Williamson in *Uncle Vanya.*

BEST ACTRESS—PLAY. Jane Alexander in *Find Your Way Home,* **Colleen Dewhurst** in *A Moon for the Misbegotten,* Julie Harris in *The Au Pair Man,* Madeline Kahn in *Boom Boom Room,* Rachel Roberts in New Phoenix repertory.

BEST ACTOR—MUSICAL. Alfred Drake in *Gigi,* Joe Morton in *Raisin,* **Christopher Plummer** in *Cyrano,* Lewis J. Stadlen in *Candide.*

BEST ACTRESS—MUSICAL. **Virginia Capers** in *Raisin,* Carol Channing in *Lorelei,* Michele Lee in *Seesaw.*

BEST SUPPORTING ACTOR—PLAY: Rene Auberjonois in *The Good Doctor,* **Ed Flanders** in *A Moon for the Misbegotten,* Douglas Turner Ward in *The River Niger,* Dick A. Williams in *What the Wine-Sellers Buy.*

BEST SUPPORTING ACTRESS—PLAY. Regina Baff in *Veronica's Room,* Fionnuala Flanagan in *Ulysses in Nighttown,* Charlotte Moore in *Chemin de Fer,* Roxie Roker in *The River Niger,* **Frances Sternhagen** in *The Good Doctor.*

BEST SUPPORTING ACTOR—MUSICAL. Mark Baker in *Candide,* Ralph Carter in *Raisin,* **Tommy Tune** in *Seesaw.*

BEST SUPPORTING ACTRESS—MUSICAL. Leigh Beery in *Cyrano,* Maureen Brennan and June Gable in *Candide*, Ernestine Jackson in *Raisin*, **Janie Sell** in *Over Here*.

BEST DIRECTOR—PLAY. Burgess Meredith for *Ulysses in Nighttown*, Mike Nichols for *Uncle Vanya*, Stephen Porter for *Chemin de Fer*, **Jose Quintero** for *A Moon for the Misbegotten*, Edwin Sherin for *Find Your Way Home*.

BEST DIRECTOR—MUSICAL. Michael Bennett for *Seesaw*, Donald McKayle for *Raisin*, Tom Moore for *Over Here*, **Harold Prince** for *Candide*.

BEST SCENIC DESIGNER. John Conklin for *The Au Pair Man*, **Franne** and **Eugene Lee** for *Candide*, Santo Loquasto for *What the Wine-Sellers Buy*, Oliver Smith for *Gigi*, Ed Wittstein for *Ulysses in Nighttown*.

BEST COSTUME DESIGNER. Theoni V. Aldredge for *The Au Pair Man*, Finlay James for *Crown Matrimonial*, **Franne Lee** for *Candide*,

Oliver Messel for *Gigi*, Carrie F. Robbins for *Over Here*.

BEST LIGHTING DESIGNER. Martin Aronstein for *Boom Boom Room*, Ken Billington for *The Visit*, Ben Edwards for *A Moon for the Misbegotten*, **Jules Fisher** for *Ulysses in Nighttown*, Tharon Musser for *The Good Doctor*.

BEST CHOREOGRAPHER. **Michael Bennett** for *Seesaw*, Patricia Birch for *Over Here*, Donald McKayle for *Raisin*.

SPECIAL AWARDS (voted by the Tony Administration Committee). *A Moon for the Misbegotten* as "an outstanding dramatic revival of a major American play"; *Candide* as "an outstanding contribution to the artistic development of the musical theater"; **Peter Cook** and **Dudley Moore** for "a unique contribution to the theater of comedy"; **Bette Midler** and **Liza Minnelli** for "superior concert entertainment on the Broadway stage."

THE DRAMA DESK AWARDS

The Drama Desk Awards for outstanding contribution to the theater season are voted by the critics, editors and reporters who are members of Drama Desk, a New York organization of theater journalists in all media. Selections are made from a long list of nominees covering Broadway, repertory theater, off Broadway and off off Broadway. In order that work in productions seen only by a portion of the voters can compete fairly with that seen by almost all, the ballots ask each voter to check only those candidates whose work they actually saw. This makes it possible to compute the proportion of those who voted for the show to those who saw the show, determining winners by percentages rather than total votes received.

Winners of 1973–74 Drama Desk Awards are listed below in the order of percentages received. The actual percentage figure is given for those who scored highest in each category.

OUTSTANDING PERFORMANCES. **Colleen Dewhurst** (85.3 per cent) in *A Moon for the Misbegotten*, **Jim Dale** in *Scapino*, **Michael Moriarty** in *Find Your Way Home*, **Barbara Barrie** in *The Killdeer*, **Henry Fonda** in *Clarence Darrow*, **Jason Robards** in *Moon*, **Brian Bedford** in *Jumpers*, **Madeline Kahn** in *Boom Boom Room*, **Kevin Conway** in *When You Comin' Back, Red Ryder?* **Ruby Lynn Reyner** in *La Bohemia*, **Ed Flanders** in *Moon*, **Elizabeth Sturges** in *Red Ryder*, **Seret Scott** in *My Sister, My Sister*, **Ian McKellen** in *The Wood Demon* and *King Lear*, **Kevin O'Connor** in *The Contractor*, **Conchata Ferrell** in *The Sea Horse*, **George**

Rose in *My Fat Friend*, **Joseph Buloff** in *Hard To Be a Jew*, **Dick A. Williams** in *What the Wine-Sellers Buy*, **Zero Mostel** in *Ulysses in Nighttown*, **Veronica Redd** in *The Sirens*, **Nicol Williamson** in *Uncle Vanya*.

OUTSTANDING DIRECTORS. **Frank Dunlop** for *Scapino* (88.9 per cent), **Jose Quintero** for *A Moon for the Misbegotten*, **Harold Prince** for *Candide* and *The Visit*, **Marvin Felix Camillo** for *Short Eyes*.

OUTSTANDING SCENE DESIGNERS. **Franne** and **Eugene Lee** for *Candide* (66.7 per cent), **David Mitchell** for *Short Eyes,* **Douglas W. Schmidt** for *Over Here* and *Veronica's Room.*

OUTSTANDING COSTUME DESIGNERS. **Franne Lee** for *Candide* (56.6 per cent), **Carrie F. Robbins** for *Over Here* and *The Iceman Cometh.*

OUTSTANDING CHOREOGRAPHER. **Patricia Birch** for *Candide* (73.3 per cent).

OUTSTANDING COMPOSER. **Al Carmines** for *The Faggot* (47.6 per cent).

OUTSTANDING LYRICIST. **Al Carmines** for *The Faggot* (78.5 per cent).

OUTSTANDING BOOK WRITER. **Hugh Wheeler** for *Candide* (70 per cent).

OUTSTANDING NEW PLAYWRIGHTS. **Edward J. Moore** (James Irwin) for *The Sea Horse* (76.2 per cent), **Miguel Piñero** for *Short Eyes,* **Mark Medoff** for *When You Comin' Back, Red Ryder?,* **David E. Freeman** for *Creeps,* **David W. Rintels** for *Clarence Darrow,* **Ray Aranha** for *My Sister, My Sister.*

1973–1974 PUBLICATION OF RECENTLY-PRODUCED PLAYS

AC/DC and *The Local Stigmatic.* Heathcote Williams. Viking (also paperback).
Alfred the Great. Israel Horovitz. Harper & Row.
Alpha Beta. E. A. Whitehead. Faber & Faber (paperback).
And They Put Handcuffs on the Flowers. Fernando Arrabal. Grove (paperback).
Approaching Simone. Megan Terry. Feminist Press (paperback).
Cato Street. Robert Shaw. Chatto & Windus (paperback).
Changing Room, The. David Storey. Random House.
Equus. Peter Shaffer. Andre Deutsch.
Finishing Touches. Jean Kerr. Doubleday.
Full Circle. Erich Maria Remarque, adapted by Peter Stone. Harcourt Brace Jovanovich.
Green Julia. Paul Abelman. Grove Press.
Hot l Baltimore, The. Lanford Wilson. Hill & Wang (also paperback).
Idiot, The. Simon Gray. Methuen (paperback).
In Celebration and *The Contractor.* David Storey. Penguin (paperback).
Increased Difficulty of Concentration, The. Vaclav Havel. J. Cape (paperback).
Jumpers. Tom Stoppard. Faber & Faber (paperback). Grove (paperback).
Karl Marx Play, The and Others. Rochelle Owens. Dutton (paperback).
Kean. Jean-Paul Sartre. Davis-Poynter (paperback).
Little Night Music, A. Hugh Wheeler and Stephen Sondheim. Dodd, Mead.
Macbett. Eugene Ionesco. Grove.
Making of Americans, The. Leon Katz. Something Else Press.
Mother Adam. Charles Dyer. Davis-Poynter (paperback).
No Sex, Please—We're British. Anthony and Alistair Foot (paperback).
Not I. Samuel Beckett. Faber & Faber (paperback).
Oh Coward! Roderick Cook. Doubleday.
Old Boys, The. William Trevor (paperback).
Out Cry. Tennessee Williams. New Directions (also paperback).
Painters, The. Davis-Poynter. Heinrich Henkel (paperback).
Pilgrimage. Louis Phillips. Colonnades Theatre Lab (paperback).
River Niger, The. Joseph A. Walker. Hill & Wang (also paperback).
Striker Schneiderman. Jack Gray. University of Toronto (paperback).
Sunshine Boys, The. Neil Simon. Random House.
This Jockey Drives Late Nights. Henry Livings. Methuen (paperback).
Three Arrows, The and *The Servants and the Snow.* Iris Murdoch. Viking.
Trotsky in Exile. Peter Weiss. Methuen (paperback). Pocket Books (paperback).
Tyger. Adrian Mitchell. J. Cape.
Veronica's Room. Ira Levin. Random House.

A SELECTED LIST OF OTHER PLAYS PUBLISHED IN 1973–74

Beggar's Opera, The. John Gay. Dover (paperback).
Best Short Plays 1973, The. Stanley Richards, editor. Chilton.
Best Short Plays of the World Theater, The: 1968–1973. Volume 2. Stanley Richards, editor. Chilton.
Black Theater USA. James V. Hatch and Ted Shine, editors. Free Press (Macmillan).
Candle in the Wind. Aleksandr Solzhenitsyn. University of Minnesota.
Collected Plays of Wole Soyinka, Volume 1. Oxford.
Dream Play, A. Ingmar Bergman. Dial Press.
Exiles. James Joyce. J. Cape.
Fantasticks, The and *Celebration.* Tom Jones and Harvey Schmidt. Drama Book Specialists.
Four Plays. Gunter Grass. Penguin (paperback).
Great American Life Show, The. Collection of nine plays from the avant-garde theater. John Lahr and Jonathan Price, editors. Bantam (paperback).
Last Days of Mankind, The. Karl Kraus. Frederick Ungar.
Marquee: Ten Plays by American and British Playwrights. James E. Miller Jr. and Robert Hayden, editors. Scott, Foresman.
New Lafayette Theater Presents, The. Anthology of six plays by black playwrights. Ed Bullins, editor. Anchor.
Off-Broadway Plays 2. Introduction by Charles Marowitz. Penguin (paperback).
Ten Great Musicals of the American Theater. Stanley Richards, editor. Chilton.

MUSICAL AND DRAMATIC RECORDINGS OF NEW YORK SHOWS

Title and publishing company are listed below. Each record is an original New York cast album unless otherwise indicated. An asterisk (*) indicates recording is also available on cassettes. Two asterisks (**) indicate it is available on eight-track cartridges.

Little Night Music, A. Columbia. (*) (**).
Black Nativity. Trip. (**).
Candide. Columbia (**).
Dear World. Columbia Special Record.
Do I Hear a Waltz? Columbia Special Record.
El Grande de Coca-Cola. The Bottle.
First Impressions. Columbia Special Record.
Gigi. RCA. (**)
Gone With the Wind. RCA.
Gypsy. (Original London Cast). RCA. (*) (**).
Karl Marx Play, The. Kilmarnock.
Let My People Come. Libra.
Lorelei. MGM-Verve. (*) (**).
Oliver. London Decca.
Over Here. Columbia.
Raisin. Columbia. (*) (**).
Streetcar Named Desire, A. (Repertory Theater of Lincoln Center). Caedmon.

THE BEST PLAYS, 1894–1973

Listed in alphabetical order below are all those works selected as Best Plays in previous volumes in the *Best Plays* series. Opposite each title is given the volume in which the play appears, its opening date and its total number of performances. Those plays marked with an asterisk (*) were still playing on June

1, 1974 and their number of performances was figured through May 31, 1974. Adaptors and translators are indicated by (ad) and (tr), and the symbols (b), (m) and (l) stand for the author of the book, music and lyrics in the case of musicals.

NOTE: A season-by-season listing, rather than an alphabetical one, of the 500 Best Plays in the first 50 volumes, starting with the yearbook for the season of 1919–1920, appears in *The Best Plays of 1968–69.*

PLAY	VOLUME	OPENED	PERFS.
ABE LINCOLN IN ILLINOIS—Robert E. Sherwood	38–39	Oct. 15, 1938	472
ABRAHAM LINCOLN—John Drinkwater	19–20	Dec. 15, 1919	193
ACCENT ON YOUTH—Samson Raphaelson	34–35	Dec. 25, 1934	229
ADAM AND EVA—Guy Bolton, George Middleton	19–20	Sept. 13, 1919	312
ADAPTATION—Elaine May; and NEXT—Terrence McNally	68–69	Feb. 10, 1969	707
AFFAIRS OF STATE—Louis Verneuil	50–51	Sept. 25, 1950	610
AFTER THE FALL—Arthur Miller	63–64	Jan. 23, 1964	208
AFTER THE RAIN—John Bowen	67–68	Oct. 9, 1967	64
AH, WILDERNESS!—Eugene O'Neill	33–34	Oct. 2, 1933	289
AIN'T SUPPOSED TO DIE A NATURAL DEATH—(b,m,l) Melvin Van Peebles	71–72	Oct. 7, 1971	325
ALIEN CORN—Sidney Howard	32–33	Feb. 20, 1933	98
ALISON'S HOUSE—Susan Glaspell	30–31	Dec. 1, 1930	41
ALL MY SONS—Arthur Miller	46–47	Jan. 29, 1947	328
ALL THE WAY HOME—Tad Mosel, based on James Agee's novel *A Death in the Family*	60–61	Nov. 30, 1960	333
ALLEGRO—(b,l) Oscar Hammerstein II, (m) Richard Rodgers	47–48	Oct. 10, 1947	315
AMBUSH—Arthur Richman	21–22	Oct. 10, 1921	98
AMERICA HURRAH—Jean-Claude van Itallie	66–67	Nov. 6, 1966	634
AMERICAN WAY, THE—George S. Kaufman, Moss Hart	38–39	Jan. 21, 1939	164
AMPHITRYON 38—Jean Giraudoux, (ad) S. N. Behrman	37–38	Nov. 1, 1937	153
ANDERSONVILLE TRIAL, THE—Saul Levitt	59–60	Dec. 29, 1959	179
ANDORRA—Max Frisch, (ad) George Tabori	62–63	Feb. 9, 1963	9
ANGEL STREET—Patrick Hamilton	41–42	Dec. 5, 1941	1,295
ANIMAL KINGDOM, THE—Philip Barry	31–32	Jan. 12, 1932	183
ANNA CHRISTIE—Eugene O'Neill	21–22	Nov. 2, 1921	177
ANNA LUCASTA—Philip Yordan	44–45	Aug. 30, 1944	957
ANNE OF THE THOUSAND DAYS—Maxwell Anderson	48–49	Dec. 8, 1948	286
ANOTHER LANGUAGE—Rose Franken	31–32	Apr. 25, 1932	344
ANOTHER PART OF THE FOREST—Lillian Hellman	46–47	Nov. 20, 1946	182
ANTIGONE—Jean Anouilh, (ad) Lewis Galantière	45–46	Feb. 18, 1946	64
APPLAUSE—(b) Betty Comden and Adolph Green, (m) Charles Strouse, (l) Lee Adams, based on the film *All About Eve* and the original story by Mary Orr	69–70	Mar. 30, 1970	896
APPLE TREE, THE—(b), (l) Sheldon Harnick, (b), (m) Jerry Bock, add'l (b) Jerome Coopersmith, based on stories by Mark Twain, Frank R. Stockton and Jules Feiffer	66–67	Oct. 18, 1966	463
ARSENIC AND OLD LACE—Joseph Kesselring	40–41	Jan. 10, 1941	1,444
AS HUSBANDS GO—Rachel Crothers	30–31	Mar. 5, 1931	148
AUTUMN GARDEN, THE—Lillian Hellman	50–51	Mar. 7, 1951	101
AWAKE AND SING—Clifford Odets	34–35	Feb. 19, 1935	209
BAD MAN, THE—Porter Emerson Browne	20–21	Aug. 30, 1920	350
BAD SEED—Maxwell Anderson, based on William March's novel	54–55	Dec. 8, 1954	332
BARBARA FRIETCHIE—Clyde Fitch	99–09	Oct. 23, 1899	83
BAREFOOT IN ATHENS—Maxwell Anderson	51–52	Oct. 31, 1951	30
BAREFOOT IN THE PARK—Neil Simon	63–64	Oct. 23, 1963	1,530

PLAY
                                                        VOLUME   OPENED   PERFS.
FIDDLER ON THE ROOF—(b) Joseph Stein, (l) Sheldon Harnick, (m)
  Jerry Bock, based on Sholom Aleichem's stories . . . . 64–65 . . Sept. 22, 1964 . . 3,242
FINISHING TOUCHES—Jean Kerr . . . . 72–73 . . Feb. 8, 1973 . . 164
FIORELLO!—(b) Jerome Weidman, George Abbott, (l) Sheldon Har-
  nick, (m) Jerry Bock . . . . 59–60 . . Nov. 23, 1959 . . 795
FIREBRAND, THE—Edwin Justus Mayer . . . . 24–25 . . Oct. 15, 1924 . . 269
FIRST LADY—Katharine Dayton, George S. Kaufman . . . . . . 35–36 . . Nov. 26, 1935 . . 246
FIRST MRS. FRASER, THE—St. John Ervine . . . . 29–30 . . Dec. 28, 1929 . . 352
FIRST YEAR, THE—Frank Craven . . . . 20–21 . . Oct. 20, 1920 . . 760
FIVE FINGER EXERCISE—Peter Shaffer . . . . 59–60 . . Dec. 2, 1959 . . 337
FIVE-STAR FINAL—Louis Weitzenkorn . . . . 30–31 . . Dec. 30, 1930 . . 175
FLIGHT TO THE WEST—Elmer Rice . . . . 40–41 . . Dec. 30, 1940 . . 136
FLOWERING PEACH, THE—Clifford Odets . . . . 54–55 . . Dec. 28, 1954 . . 135
FOLLIES—(b) James Goldman, (m, l) Stephen Sondheim . . . . . . 70–71 . . Apr. 4, 1971 . . 521
FOOL, THE—Channing Pollock . . . . 22–23 . . Oct. 23, 1922 . . 373
FOOLISH NOTION—Philip Barry . . . . 44–45 . . Mar. 3, 1945 . . 104
FORTY CARATS—Pierre Barillet and Jean-Pierre Gredy, (ad) Jay
  Allen . . . . 68–69 . . Dec. 26, 1968 . . 780
FOURPOSTER, THE—Jan de Hartog . . . . 51–52 . . Oct. 24, 1951 . . 632
FRONT PAGE, THE—Ben Hecht, Charles MacArthur . . . . . . 28–29 . . Aug. 14, 1928 . . 276

GENERATION—William Goodhart . . . . 65–66 . . Oct. 6, 1965 . . 299
GEORGE WASHINGTON SLEPT HERE—George S. Kaufman, Moss
  Hart . . . . 40–41 . . Oct. 18, 1940 . . 173
GIDEON—Paddy Chayefsky . . . . 61–62 . . Nov. 9, 1961 . . 236
GIGI—Anita Loos, based on Colette's novel . . . . 51–52 . . Nov. 24, 1951 . . 219
GINGERBREAD LADY, THE—Neil Simon . . . . 70–71 . . Dec. 13, 1970 . . 193
GIRL ON THE VIA FLAMINIA, THE—Alfred Hayes,
  based on his novel . . . . 53–54 . . Feb. 9, 1954 . . 111
GLASS MENAGERIE, THE—Tennessee Williams . . . . 44–45 . . Mar. 31, 1945 . . 561
GOLDEN APPLE, THE—(b, l), John Latouche, (m) Jerome Mor-
  oss . . . . 53–54 . . Apr. 20, 1954 . . 125
GOLDEN BOY—Clifford Odets . . . . 37–38 . . Nov. 4, 1937 . . 250
GOOD GRACIOUS ANNABELLE—Clare Kummer . . . . 09–19 . . Oct. 31, 1916 . . 111
GOODBYE, MY FANCY—Fay Kanin . . . . 48–49 . . Nov. 17, 1948 . . 446
GOOSE HANGS HIGH, THE—Lewis Beach . . . . 23–24 . . Jan. 29, 1924 . . 183
GRAND HOTEL—Vicki Baum, (ad) W. A. Drake . . . . 30–31 . . Nov. 13, 1930 . . 459
GREAT DIVIDE, THE—William Vaughn Moody . . . . 99–09 . . Oct. 3, 1906 . . 238
GREAT GOD BROWN, THE—Eugene O'Neill . . . . 25–26 . . Jan. 23, 1926 . . 271
GREAT WHITE HOPE, THE—Howard Sackler . . . . 68–69 . . Oct. 3, 1968 . . 556
GREEN BAY TREE, THE—Mordaunt Shairp . . . . 33–34 . . Oct. 20, 1933 . . 166
GREEN GODDESS, THE—William Archer . . . . 20–21 . . Jan. 18, 1921 . . 440
GREEN GROW THE LILACS—Lynn Riggs . . . . 30–31 . . Jan. 26, 1931 . .   64
GREEN HAT, THE—Michael Arlen . . . . 25–26 . . Sept. 15, 1925 . . 231
GREEN JULIA—Paul Ableman . . . . 72–73 . . Nov. 16, 1972 . . 147
GREEN PASTURES, THE—Marc Connelly, based on Roark Bradford's
  Ol Man Adam and His Chillun . . . . 29–30 . . Feb. 26, 1930 . . 640
GUYS AND DOLLS—(b) Jo Swerling, Abe Burrows, based on a story
  and characters by Damon Runyon, (l, m) Frank Loesser . . . . 50–51 . . Nov. 24, 1950 . . 1,200
GYPSY—Maxwell Anderson . . . . 28–29 . . Jan. 14, 1929 . .   64

HADRIAN VII—Peter Luke, based on works by Fr. Rolfe . . . . . 68–69 . . Jan. 8, 1969 . . 359
HAMP—John Wilson; based on an episode from a novel by J.L. Hod-
  son . . . . 66–67 . . Mar. 9, 1967 . . 101
HAPPY TIME, THE—Samuel Taylor, based on Robert Fontaine's
  book . . . . 49–50 . . Jan. 24, 1950 . . 614

PLAY	VOLUME	OPENED	PERFS.
ST. HELENA—R. C. Sherriff, Jeanne de Casalis	36–37	Oct. 6, 1936	63
SATURDAY'S CHILDREN—Maxwell Anderson	26–27	Jan. 26, 1927	310
SCREENS, THE—Jean Genet, (tr) Minos Volanakis	71–72	Nov. 30, 1971	28
SCUBA DUBA—Bruce Jay Friedman	67–68	Oct. 10, 1967	692
SEARCHING WIND, THE—Lillian Hellman	43–44	Apr. 12, 1944	318
SEASON IN THE SUN—Wolcott Gibbs	50–51	Sept. 28, 1950	367
SECOND THRESHOLD—Philip Barry	50–51	Jan. 2, 1951	126
SECRET SERVICE—William Gillette	94–99	Oct. 5, 1896	176
SEPARATE TABLES—Terence Rattigan	56–57	Oct. 25, 1956	332
SERPENT, THE—Jean-Claude van Itallie	69–70	May 29, 1970	3
SEVEN KEYS TO BALDPATE—George M. Cohan	09–19	Sept. 22, 1913	320
1776—(b) Peter Stone, (m,l) Sherman Edwards, based on a conception of Sherman Edwards	68–69	Mar. 16, 1969	1,217
SHADOW AND SUBSTANCE—Paul Vincent Carroll	37–38	Jan. 26, 1938	274
SHADOW OF HEROES—(see *Stone and Star*)			
SHE LOVES ME—(b) Joe Masteroff, based on Miklos Laszlo's play *Parfumerie*, (l) Sheldon Harnick, (m) Jerry Bock	62–63	Apr. 23, 1963	301
SHINING HOUR, THE—Keith Winter	33–34	Feb. 13, 1934	121
SHOW-OFF, THE—George Kelly	23–24	Feb. 5, 1924	571
SHRIKE, THE—Joseph Kramm	51–52	Jan. 15, 1952	161
SILVER CORD, THE—Sidney Howard	26–27	Dec. 20, 1926	112
SILVER WHISTLE, THE—Robert E. McEnroe	48–49	Nov. 24, 1948	219
SIX CYLINDER LOVE—William Anthony McGuire	21–22	Aug. 25, 1921	430
6 RMS RIV VU—Bob Randall	72–73	Oct. 17, 1972	247
SKIN GAME, THE—John Galsworthy	20–21	Oct. 20, 1920	176
SKIN OF OUR TEETH, THE—Thornton Wilder	42–43	Nov. 18, 1942	359
SKIPPER NEXT TO GOD—Jan de Hartog	47–48	Jan. 4, 1948	93
SKYLARK—Samson Raphaelson	39–40	Oct. 11, 1939	256
SLEUTH—Anthony Shaffer	70–71	Nov. 12, 1970	1,222
SLOW DANCE ON THE KILLING GROUND—William Hanley	64–65	Nov. 30, 1964	88
SMALL CRAFT WARNINGS—Tennessee Williams	71–72	Apr. 2, 1972	192
SOLDIER'S WIFE—Rose Franken	44–45	Oct. 4, 1944	253
SQUAW MAN, THE—Edwin Milton Royle	99–09	Oct. 23, 1905	222
STAGE DOOR—George S. Kaufman, Edna Ferber	36–37	Oct. 22, 1936	169
STAIRCASE—Charles Dyer	67–68	Jan. 10, 1968	61
STAR-WAGON, THE—Maxwell Anderson	37–38	Sept. 29, 1937	223
STATE OF THE UNION—Howard Lindsay, Russel Crouse	45–46	Nov. 14, 1945	765
STICKS AND BONES—David Rabe	71–72	Nov. 7, 1971	367
STONE AND STAR—Robert Ardrey, also called *Shadow of Heroes*	61–62	Dec. 5, 1961	20
STOP THE WORLD—I WANT TO GET OFF—(b,l,m) Leslie Bricusse, Anthony Newley	62–63	Oct. 3, 1962	555
STORM OPERATION—Maxwell Anderson	43–44	Jan. 11, 1944	23
STORY OF MARY SURRATT, THE—John Patrick	46–47	Feb. 8, 1947	11
STEAMBATH—Bruce Jay Friedman	70–71	June 30, 1970	128
STRANGE INTERLUDE—Eugene O'Neill	27–28	Jan. 30, 1928	426
STREET SCENE—Elmer Rice	28–29	Jan. 10, 1929	601
STREETCAR NAMED DESIRE, A—Tennessee Williams	47–48	Dec. 3, 1947	855
STRICTLY DISHONORABLE—Preston Sturges	29–30	Sept. 18, 1929	557
SUBJECT WAS ROSES, THE—Frank D. Gilroy	64–65	May 25, 1964	832
SUMMER OF THE 17TH DOLL—Ray Lawler	57–58	Jan. 22, 1958	29
SUNRISE AT CAMPOBELLO—Dore Schary	57–58	Jan. 30, 1958	556
SUNSHINE BOYS THE—Neil Simon	72–73	Dec. 20, 1972	538
SUN-UP—Lula Vollmer	22–23	May 25, 1923	356
SUSAN AND GOD—Rachel Crothers	37–38	Oct. 7, 1937	288

NECROLOGY

MAY 1973—JUNE 1974

PERFORMERS

Abbott, Bud (78)—April 25, 1974
Adler, Harriet (55)—April 23, 1974
Akeman, David "Stringbean" (57)—November 11, 1973
Allan, Andrew (66)—January 15, 1974
Almonte, Marie A.—June 25, 1973
Amore, James (27)—May 17, 1974
Andra, Fern (80)—February 8, 1974
Antonova, Helene A. (75)—December 31, 1973
Applewhite, Eric Leon (76)—May 20, 1973
Arlington, Eleanor—December 28, 1973
Ashton, Florence (69)—September 16, 1973
Ballerino, Virginia—February 19, 1974
Barbette, Yander (68)—August 5, 1973
Bass, Helen Kennedy—October 21, 1973
Baum, Harry (58)—January 31, 1974
Bausman, Nellie Dutton (85)—April 15, 1974
Beal, Scott (83)—July 10, 1973
Beatty, Raymond (70)—December 5, 1973
Beck, James (41)—August 6, 1973
Benoit, Denise (53)—June, 1973
Berk, Juanita Saun (73)—August 29, 1973
Berman, Harry (76)—March 25, 1974
Blackmer, Sidney (78)—October 5, 1973
Blue, Rita (68)—October 13, 1973
Boles, Athena Lorde (57)—May 23, 1973
Borg, Veda Ann (58)—August 16, 1973
Boskovic, Natasha (62)—June 30, 1973
Bouvier, Corinne (31)—June 5, 1973
Bradford, Lane (50)—June 7, 1973
Bradshaw, Fanny (76)—June 26, 1973
Brady, Kenneth Darryl "Ish" (27)—April 28, 1974
Brandies, Bob (71)—August 1, 1973
Braswell, Charles (49)—May 17, 1974
Britt, Jacqueline (29)—March 6, 1974
Brown, Joe E. (82)—July 6, 1973
Brunot, Andre (93)—August 6, 1973
Burgess, Hazel (63)—December 11, 1973
Bush, Anita—February 16, 1974
Butler, Royal "Roy" (80)—July 28, 1973
Campeau, June Harrison (48)—March 10, 1974
Cansino, Eduardo Jr. (54)—March 11, 1974
Carr, Mary (99)—June 24, 1973
Carsey, Mary (35)—August 27, 1973
Casals, Pablo (96)—October 22, 1973
Castle, Peggy (47)—August 11, 1973
Cervi, Gino (72)—January 3, 1974

Chaney, Lon Jr. (67)—July 12, 1973
Checchi, Andrea (57)—March 31, 1974
Claire, Helen (68)—January 12, 1974
Clitheroe, Jimmy (50s)—June 6, 1973
Colleano, Con (73)—November 13, 1973
Collinge, Patricia (81)—April 10, 1974
Compson, Betty (77)—April 18, 1974
Conway, Curt (59)—April 10, 1974
Corbett, Mary (48)—April 28, 1974
Coyle, Joe (56)—September 3, 1973
Crafts, Charley (78)—September 5, 1974
Crafts, Griffin (73)—August 7, 1973
Crane, Norma (42)—September 28, 1973
Cranko, John (45)—June 26, 1973
Crisp, Donald (93)—May 25, 1974
Crowe, Ellen Beatrice (78)—March 20, 1974
D'Angelo, Carlo (54)—June 1973
Darin, Bobby (37)—December 20, 1973
Dash, Pauly (55)—February 2, 1974
David, Pete (80)—May 1974
David, Virginia (47)—July 21, 1973
Davis, Lee—August 14, 1973
Davis, Phil (78)—January 16, 1974
Deane, Doris (73)—March 24, 1974
De Cordova, Arturo (66)—November 3, 1973
Delgado, Roger (53)—June 19, 1973
Delmonte, Jack (84)—June 8, 1973
der Abrahmian, Arousiak (82)—July 2, 1973
De Wolfe, Billy (67)—March 5, 1974
Dodd, Claire (50s)—November 23, 1973
Donn, Marie (74)—July 16, 1973
Dooley, Jed (89)—September 4, 1973
Dorree, Bobbie (Babette) (68)—January 10, 1974
Dumbrille, Douglass (84)—April 2, 1974
Dunn, Michael (39)—August 29, 1973
Edstrom, Katherine (72)—June 2, 1973
Emerick, Robert (57)—June 1, 1973
Errolle, Ralph (82)—August 31, 1973
Evans, Helen Hartz (77)—March 30, 1974
Evans, Joe (57)—September 12, 1973
Falgi, Nick (40's)—August 15, 1973
Feldman, Gladys (82)—February 12, 1974
Ferguson, Howard (78)—January 18, 1974
Field, Betty (55)—September 13, 1973
Fitzharris, Coralie (74)—August 15, 1973
Fokine, Leon (68)—November 19, 1973
Frampton, Eleanor (77)—October 8, 1973
Frasca, Mary—July 24, 1973
Fritsch, Willy (72)—July 13, 1973
Gallagher, Dan—November 16, 1973

Gardner, Renee (43)—November 26, 1973
Georges, Katherine—May 28, 1973
Gilbert, Bobby (75)—September 19, 1973
Giordmaine, John (75)—January 19, 1974
Gold, Sid (67)—January 18, 1974
Goldman, Isaac (80)—August 19, 1973
Gordon, Frank Odell (95)—September 30, 1973
Gordon, Kitty (96)—May 26, 1974
Gordon, Rose M.—December 11, 1973
Goth, Trudy—May 12, 1974
Grable, Betty (56)—July 3, 1973
Granada De Carlos, Perla (70)—June 8, 1973
Greaza, Walter N. (76)—June 1, 1973
Greene, Billy M. (76)—August 24, 1973
Hackman, William H. (62)—July 23, 1973
Haines, William (73)—December 26, 1973
Haltiner, Fred (37)—December 7, 1973
Hanley, Jack (50)—December 30, 1973
Hannoch, Dan (69)—March 14, 1974
Hardie, Russell (69)—July 21, 1973
Harlan, Russell B. (70)—February 28, 1974
Hartman, Paul (69)—October 2, 1973
Harvey, Laurence (45)—November 26, 1973
Haskins, Douglas N. (45)—June 8, 1973
Hawkins, Jack (62)—July 18, 1973
Hayakawa, Sessue (83)—November 23, 1973
Herskovits, Bela (54)—May 8, 1974
Hewitt, Alice (102)—September 18, 1973
Holden, Fay (79)—June 23, 1973
Hubbard, Didrikke—February 1, 1974
Huff, Louise (77)—August 22, 1973
Illingworth, Elsie (87)—July 19, 1973
Imboden, David C. (87)—March 19, 1974
Jackson, Henry Conrad (46)—July 30, 1973
Jaffe, Carl (72)—April 12, 1974
Johnston, Daisy B. (94)—March 10, 1974
Jones, Joan Granville—January 3, 1974
Joyce, James (53)—May 17, 1974
Judge, Arline (61)—February 7, 1974
Kannon, Jackie (54)—February 1, 1974
Katz, Herman (73)—May 28, 1973
Keene, Elsie—December 29, 1973
Kegley, Kermit (54)—February 19, 1974
Kennedy, Anne G. (38)—January 12, 1974
Kerr, Anne (48)—July 29, 1973
King, Omega J. (81)—December 11, 1973
Kirby, Helen DuVall (81)—July 30, 1973
Kirby, John (41)—July 3, 1973
Klein, Miriam Lillian (78)—July 16, 1973
Knight, Frank (79)—October 18, 1973
Kornman, Mary (56)—June 1, 1973
Lake, Veronica (53)—July 7, 1973
Lamond, Stella (62)—July 5, 1973
Lane, Allan (Rocky) (64)—October 27, 1973
Lashanska, Hulda (80)—January 17, 1974
Lauher, Bob (42)—August 22, 1973
Laurence, Baby (53)—April 2, 1974
Lee, Bruce (32)—July 20, 1973
Lee, Lila (68)—November 13, 1973
Lee, Madaline—January 10, 1974
Lerner, Carl (61)—August 26, 1973
Lesley, Carole (38)—February 28, 1974
Leslie, Noel (85)—March 10, 1974

Lewis, Larry (106)—February 1, 1974
Linn, Margaret (39)—September 12, 1973
Lloyd, Morris (83)—January 5, 1974
Lupo, George G. (49)—August 8, 1973
Lynn, Charlotte—May 1974
Machado, Lena (70)—January 22, 1974
Macready, George (73)—July 2, 1973
Magnani, Anna (65)—September 26, 1973
Makletzova, Xenia (81)—May 18, 1974
Malkin, Beata (82)—September 25, 1973
Mall, Dr. Richard (54)—August 28, 1973
Mann, Billy—April 14, 1974
Mantia, Charles (85)—May 17, 1974
Marks, Joe E. (82)—June 14, 1973
Martin, Pete (74)—May, 1974
Marx, Marie Simard—January 17, 1974
Mason, Edith (80)—November 26, 1973
Mass, Joseph E. (62)—March 19, 1974
Masters, Harry (79)—May 12, 1974
Matsui, Suisei (73)—August 1, 1973
May, Harold R. (70)—September 16, 1973
McGill, Wallace Read (67)—August 12, 1973
McIntyre, Duncan (66)—December 1973
McVey, Patrick (63)—July 6, 1973
Mercer, Tony (51)—July 14, 1973
Merrige-Abrams, Salway (43)—July 19, 1973
Meyer, Frederic (63)—September 16, 1973
Michael, Mickie (30)—November 18, 1973
Middleton, Guy (65)—July 30, 1973
Mills, Grant—August 4, 1973
Mishima, Masao (67)—July 18, 1973
Monroe, Ann Swinburne (87)—November 17, 1973
Moodie, Douglas (64)—November 1973
Moore, Cleo (44)—October 25, 1973
Moore, Henrietta (50)—October 22, 1973
Moorehead, Agnes (67)—April 20, 1974
Moreland, Mantan (72)—September 28, 1973
Morton, John (84)—May 2, 1974
Murphy, Juliette (71)—September 28, 1973
Mutch, James E. (84)—January 17, 1974
Myers, Michaele (49)—January 10, 1974
Nagiah, V. (70)—December 30, 1973
Nelson, Skip (53)—March 31, 1974
Nicholson, Nora (86)—September 18, 1973
Nilsson, Anna Q. (85)—February 11, 1974
Noemi, Lea (90)—November 6, 1973
Nye, Carroll (72)—March 17, 1974
Oborin, Lev (66)—December, 1973
O'Leary, Willie (69)—July 1973
O'Malley, Grania (75)—June 14, 1973
O'Shea, Michael (67)—December 4, 1973
Page, Paul (70)—April 28, 1974
Pampanini, Rosetta (72)—August 2, 1973
Pandelakis, Beatrice (52)—June 11, 1973
Parish, James (69)—January 1974
Parsons, Gram (27)—September 19, 1973
Patzak, Julius (75)—January 26, 1974
Peers, Donald (64)—August 9, 1973
Percy, Eileen (72)—July 29, 1973
Peters, Gunnar—March 11, 1974
Pierson, Rennie (75)—August 10, 1973
Plant, Jack (77)—October 22, 1973

Platt, Edward (58)—March 20, 1974
Poe, Aileen (79)—September 22, 1973
Powers, Marie (60s)—December 29, 1973
Prescott, Norman (81)—November 11, 1973
Price, Dennis (58)—October 7, 1973
Price, Jesse (64)—April 19, 1974
Pritchard, Richard Valentine (Cardini) (79)—
     November 11, 1973
Pryor, Roger (72)—January 31, 1974
Qualters, Tot (79)—March 27, 1974
Quinn, Joe (75)—May 20, 1974
Rabagliati, Alberto (67)—March 8, 1974
Raeburn, Henzie (72)—October 27, 1973
Raft, Tommy Moe (59)—January 7, 1974
Raynaud, Fernand—September 28, 1973
Reddy, Max (59)—September 1973
Reed, Billy (60)—February 4, 1974
Reichow, Werner (51)—August 17, 1973
Renard, David (52)—August 19, 1973
Rice, Florence (67)—February 23, 1974
Ritchie, Carl (64)—March 16, 1974
Ritter, Blake (58)—September 21, 1973
Ritter, Tex (67)—January 2, 1974
Robinson, Edward G. Jr. (40)—February 26,
     1974
Roels, Marcel (80)—December 27, 1973
Roquevert, Noel (81)—December 1973
Rosay, Francoise (82)—March 28, 1974
Ross, Babs (62)—July 1973
Ruick, Barbara (42)—March 3, 1974
Runnel, Albert F. (82)—January 4, 1974
Ryan, Robert (63)—July 11, 1973
St. Cyr, Lillian Red Wing (90)—March 12, 1974
St. John, Howard—March 13, 1974
Sakharoff, Clothilde (80)—January 11, 1974
Sand, Inge (45)—February 3, 1974
Sands, Diana (39)—September 21, 1973
Satz, Lillie (78)—April 11, 1974
Schmeling, Walter B. (73)—September 2, 1973
Scordley, Jack (59)—September 23, 1973
Seeley, Blossom (82)—April 17, 1974
Senn, Ken (51)—December 9, 1973
Serreau, Jean-Marie (59)—May 1973
Shanahan, Elva (48)—August 1, 1973
Shane, Jerry (42)—January 19, 1974
Shannon, Msgr. William J. (62)—May 31, 1973
Sheehan, Jack (53)—July 30, 1973
Sherman, Allan (49)—November 21, 1973
Shtraukh, Maxim (73)—January 1974
Shuman, Roy (48)—July 30, 1973
Simon, Joan Baim (41)—July 11, 1973
Singerman, Bernard (61)—September 1973
Slattery, James (Candy Darling) (26)—March
     21, 1974
Smith, J. Stanley (69)—April 13, 1974
Sokolova, Lydia (77)—February 2, 1974
Somigli, Franca—May 16, 1974
Sonnemann, Emmy (80)—June 8, 1973
Sonneveld, Wim (56)—March 8, 1974
Speicher, Ann Drew (83)—February 6, 1974
Spitz, Mrs. Leo (72)—February 13, 1974
Starr, Frances (92)—June 11, 1973
Stehli, Edgar (89)—July 25, 1973

Stephen, John (62)—April 3, 1974
Stone, Harvey (61)—March 4, 1974
Strange, Glenn (74)—September 20, 1973
Strassberg, Morris (76)—February 8, 1974
Strength, William T. (45)—October 1, 1973
Striker, Joseph (74)—February 24, 1974
Stroud, Clarence G. Sr. (66)—August 15, 1973
Summers, Ann (54)—January 14, 1974
Sunderland, Nan—November 23, 1973
Sutherland, A. Edward (77)—January 1, 1974
Swanson, Marcella (80s)—August 24, 1973
Talmadge, Constance (73)—November 23, 1973
Tannen, Don (60s)—April 5, 1974
Tarjan, George (63)—December 25, 1973
Taylor, Alma (79)—February 1974
Taylor, Louise (89)—March 24, 1974
Terhune, Max (82)—June 5, 1973
Thalin, Vivien Parker (77)—February 2, 1974
Tharpe, Rosetta (57)—October 9, 1973
Tornatore, Michael (53)—July 5, 1973
Tourel, Jennie (63)—November 23, 1973
Trow, William (82)—September 2, 1973
Truex, Ernest (82)—June 27, 1973
Van, Billy (61)—August 22, 1973
Van Rooten, Luis d'Antin (66)—June 17, 1973
Velazquez, Conchita—February 17, 1974
Ventura, Dick (80s)—November 8, 1973
Vogel, Eleanore (70)—June 26, 1973
Vyvyan, Jennifer (49)—April 5, 1974
Waldis, Otto (68)—March 25, 1974
Weissman, Dora—May 21, 1974
Welch, Harry Foster (74)—August 16, 1973
Wendling, Pete (85)—April 7, 1974
Wengraf, John E. (77)—May 4, 1974
Whalen, Michael (72)—April 14, 1974
Wheeler, Jimmy (63)—October 7, 1973
Wilbur, Crane (83)—October 18, 1973
Wilcox, Frank (66)—March 3, 1974
Williams, Paul (34)—August 17, 1973
Williams, Vanilla (35)—December 3, 1973
Winstone, Eric (61)—May 1, 1974
Wiziarde, Lou (83)—September 28, 1973
Wolfe, R. Driskill (72)—August 11, 1973
Wolfson, Martin (69)—September 11, 1973
Worlock, Frederick (87)—August 1, 1973
Yarnell, Bruce (35)—November 30, 1973
Zeitz, Daisy (67)—April 29, 1974
Ziga, Casey (56)—May 15, 1974

PLAYWRIGHTS

Arundel, Honor—June 1973
Auerbach, George (68)—November 1973
Backer, George (70s)—May 1, 1974
Barkentin, Marjorie (80s)—February 27, 1974
Behn, Harry—September 5, 1973
Behrman, S.N. (80)—September 9, 1973
Block, Ralph (84)—January 2, 1974
Bontemps, Arna (70)—June 4, 1973
Buffington, Adele (73)—November 23, 1973
Clarke, Austin (77)—March 20, 1974
Driver, Harry (46)—November 25, 1973
Crean, Robert (50)—May 6, 1974

Duff, Warren (69)—August 5, 1973
Fimberg, Harold A. (67)—April 6, 1974
Gipson, Fred (65)—August 14, 1973
Hatch, Eric (71)—July 4, 1973
Heininger, Francis (62)—June 13, 1973
Hurley, Dunlea (64)—July 17, 1973
Inge, William (60)—June 10, 1973
Kafka, John H. (71)—February 6, 1974
Kedobra, Maurice (88)—June 1973
Levinson, Leonard Louis (69)—January 30, 1974
Levy, Benn W. (73)—December 7, 1973
Lively, William E. (66)—September 29, 1973
MacDougall, Ranald (58)—December 12, 1973
MacMullen, Charles (C.K. Munro) (84)—July 20, 1973
Marcel, Gabriel (83)—October 8, 1973
McKay, Ted (55)—November 8, 1973
McLaughlin, Robert (65)—October 28, 1973
Miller, Seton I. (71)—March 29, 1974
Moberg, Vilhelm (74)—August 9, 1973
Moore, Jenny (50)—October 3, 1973
Orlovitz, Gil (55)—July 10, 1973
Pagnol, Marcel (79)—April 18, 1974
Phillips, Irna (72)—December 23, 1973
Pulitzer, Margaret Leech (80)—February 22, 1974
Rittenberg, Barbara (42)—June 16, 1973
Ruby, Harry (79)—February 23, 1974
Sachs, Mary P.K. (91)—December 24, 1973
Seligman, Marjorie (73)—March 15, 1974
Sirkin, Stephen (30)—January 19, 1974
Yelvington, Ramsey (60)—July 25, 1973
Zaltzberg, Charlotte (49)—February 24, 1974

COMPOSERS AND LYRICISTS

Allen, Neal (22)—February 18, 1974
Auden, W.H. (66)—September 28, 1973
Bargy, Roy (79)—January 15, 1974
Barlow, Nevett (39)—November 20, 1973
Beecher, William G. Jr. (69)—December 7, 1973
Belasco, Jacques (56)—June 12, 1973
Berg, Harold C. (73)—July 24, 1973
Busser, Henri (101)—December 30, 1973
Carroll, Adam (76)—February 28, 1974
Citkowitz, Israel (65)—May 4, 1974
Duclos, Pierre (44)—November 25, 1973
Eckstein, Maxwell (69)—May 16, 1974
Edwards, Clara (95)—January 17, 1974
Ellington, Duke (75)—May 24, 1974
Etler, Alvin D. (60)—June 13, 1973
Fields, Dorothy (68)—March 28, 1974
Gannon, James (73)—April 29, 1974
Hattori, Raymond (65)—August 5, 1973
Hutchinson, Jody (57)—October 23, 1973
Kaufman, Alvin S.—December 21, 1973
Klemperer, Otto (88)—July 7, 1973
Labroca, Mario (76)—July 1, 1973
Lillie, Muriel (81)—August 19, 1973
Maderna, Bruno (53)—November 13, 1973
Maganini, Quinto (77)—March 11, 1974
Malipiero, Gian Francesco (91)—August 1, 1973

Manno, Anthony P. (34)—November 12, 1973
Phillips, Sid (65)—May 25, 1973
Piket, Frederick (71)—February 28, 1974
Ritchey, Buck (58)—December 23, 1973
Rockwell, Donald S. (75)—March 29, 1974
Ruby, Harry (79)—February 23, 1974
Savino, Domenico (91)—August 8, 1973
Sherman, Allan (76)—September 16, 1973
Snyder, Agnes Tilton (90s)—March 4, 1974
Vann, Al (73)—June 17, 1973
White, Paul T. (77)—May 31, 1973
Wrubel, Allie (68)—December 13, 1973

PRODUCERS, DIRECTORS, CHOREOGRAPHERS

Allegret, Marc (73)—November 3, 1973
Bacon, Walter Scott (82)—November 7, 1973
Ball, Donald I. (69)—January 7, 1974
Benson, Alex (46)—March 12, 1974
Carlin, Roger (62)—April 5, 1974
Carruth, Richard (53)—August 22, 1973
Cole, Jack (60)—February 17, 1974
Colligan, James (70)—January 21, 1974
Conn, Maurice H. (67)—October 16, 1973
Coon, Gene L. (49)—July 8, 1973
Cott, Ted (55)—June 12, 1973
De Orduna, Juan (67)—February 3, 1974
Di Blasio, Joe (62)—October 12, 1973
Dowling, Robert W. (77)—August 28, 1973
Dudley, Carl (63)—September 2, 1973
Elorrieta, Jose Maria (52)—February 22, 1974
Ford, John (78)—August 31, 1973
Fowler, Bruce (80)—September 21, 1973
Freed, Fred (53)—March 31, 1974
Freeman, Leonard (53)—January 20, 1974
Friedman, Phil (83)—March 30, 1974
Gelber, Eugene (46)—March 21, 1974
Goldstein, Robert (70)—April 6, 1974
Goldwyn, Samuel (91)—January 31, 1974
Golenpaul, Dan (73)—February 13, 1974
Gosch, Martin A. (62)—October 20, 1973
Haberstroth, Alex (67)—December 8, 1973
Hammerstein, Theodore M. (72)—October 6, 1973
Hart, Walter (67)—July 31, 1973
Hurok, Sol (85)—March 5, 1974
Hyman, Walter A. (51)—October 11, 1973
Jacobs, Arthur P. (51)—June 27, 1973
Kamahara, Takeshi (63)—October 3, 1973
Kaps, Arthur (66)—January 23, 1974
Katzell, William R. (68)—January 16, 1974
Katsman, Sam (72)—August 4, 1973
King, Robert M. (54)—April 22, 1974
Kirk, William T. (65)—January 7, 1974
Kuhl, H. Calvin (66)—August 7, 1973
Lehmann, Maurice (79)—May 17, 1974
Lesan, David E. (64)—May 1974
Lilley, Edward (86)—April 3, 1974
Lods, Jean (71)—April 1974
Martin, Philip Jr. (57)—March 14, 1974
Melville, Jean-Pierre (55)—August 2, 1973
Mendes, Lothar (79)—February 25, 1974

Morton, Alfred H. (76)—April 9, 1974
Moss, Marty—December 7, 1973
Myerberg, Michael (67)—January 6, 1974
Phillips, Sidney (82)—August 18, 1973
Pignieres, Rene (68)—November 1973
Pittman, Frank (50s)—August 18, 1973
Previn, Charles (86)—September 22, 1973
Proser, Monte (69)—October 5, 1973
Reed, Joseph Verner (71)—November 25, 1973
Rogell, Sid (73)—November 15, 1973
Rothman, Benjamin (76)—July 27, 1973
Ruskin, Leonard (51)—December 22, 1973
Salkind, Michel (83)—January 1974
Somlo, Josef (89)—November 29, 1973
Specter, Edward (73)—March 13, 1974
Stephenson, Paul (75)—April 22, 1974
Talmon-Gros, Walter (62)—September 22, 1973
Viehoever, Joseph (47)—August 12, 1973
Weber, Leonard S. (45)—October 27, 1973
White, Edward J. (76)—September 24, 1973
Whyte, Jerome (65)—March 14, 1974
Wigman, Mary (86)—September 18, 1973
Wolf, Gerd (50)—November 28, 1973
Youngson, Robert (56)—April 8, 1974

CONDUCTORS

Ancerl, Karel (65)—July 3, 1973
Davies, Gareth (41)—May 27, 1973
Mahler, Fritz (72)—June 1973
Paul, Tibor (64)—November 11, 1973
Schmidt-Isserstadt, Hans (73)—May 28, 1973
Steinberg, Benjamin (58)—January 29, 1974
Winterhalter, Hugo (64)—September 17, 1973

DESIGNERS

French, Park M. (93)—March 18, 1974
Gentile, Gerard L. (62)—June 11, 1973
Gerard, Manny (47)—October 23, 1973
Greer, Howard (78)—April 17, 1974
Gulbrandsen, Charles (83)—March 22, 1974
Holzager, Toni Ward (66)—December 5, 1973
Ingram, Mrs. Clyde Rapp (75)—May 19, 1974
Joseph, Will C. (88)—September 24, 1973
Kenny, Sean (40)—June 11, 1973
Oliver, Harry (85)—July 5, 1973
Schiaparelli, Elsa (83)—November 13, 1973
Unruh, Walter (75)—August 28, 1973

CRITICS

Aldridge, John Stratten (59)—November 28, 1973
Brown, Ivor (82)—April 22, 1974
Carmody, Jay (72)—June 18, 1973
Dragosei, Italo (58)—July 1973
Elwell, Herbert (75)—April 17, 1974
Eversman, Alice M. (88)—February 1, 1974
Finkelstein, Sidney (64)—January 13, 1974
Griffin, John David (45)—June 2, 1973
Hall, Mordaunt (94)—July 3, 1973
Hartung, Philip T. (70)—July 24, 1973

Hass, Willy (82)—September 4, 1973
Holt, Nora (89)—January 25, 1974
Kempf, Paul Jr. (64)—September 5, 1973
Lewis, Mel (53)—April 19, 1973
MacArthur, Harry (62)—September 12, 1973
Rahv, Philip—December 22, 1973
Reisner, Robert (53)—February 19, 1974
Schonberg, Rosalyn (60)—June 18, 1973
Shira, Jerry (28)—August 11, 1973
Smith, Delos (68)—May 31, 1973
Trautman, William E. (75)—August 28, 1973

MUSICIANS

Adams, E. Crawford (83)—August 25, 1973
Allen, Ed (75)—January 28, 1974
Almeida, Pua (57)—February 9, 1974
Asunto, Frank (42)—February 25, 1974
Bedetti, Jean (89)—July 20, 1973
Bender, Dave (55)—October 29, 1973
Benjamin, Joseph (54)—January 26, 1974
Bickel, Bill (58)—March 9, 1974
Botkin, Perry Sr. (66)—October 14, 1973
Boxon, Lillian (40)—August 9, 1973
Braun, Karl E.—October 30, 1973
Burr, Minerva (81)—January 30, 1974
Campion, William E. (61)—June 5, 1973
Candrix, Fud (65)—April 11, 1974
Carlton, William (50)—August 15, 1973
Carr, Mickey—July 17, 1973
Carroll, Adam (77)—February 28, 1974
Casals, Pablo (96)—October 22, 1973
Cherb, George W. (50)—January 14, 1974
Christian, Frank J. (86)—November 28, 1973
Collins, Peter—July 25, 1973
Concepcion, Cesar (64)—March 11, 1974
Condon, Eddie (67)—August 4, 1973
Cowan, Lynn F.—August 29, 1973
Cullum, Jim Sr. (59)—June 7, 1973
D'Alexander, Silvio (87)—May 20, 1974
Donahue, Sam—March 22, 1974
Elgar, Anthony C. (94)—July 30, 1973
Eliot, June Cowley (71)—September 21, 1973
Englund, Arthur W. (86)—March 1974
Fagerquist, Don (47)—January 1974
Gary, David Stuart (22)—June 24, 1973
Geoffrion, Victor (89)—May 14, 1974
Geraldo (Bright, Gerald) (69)—May 4, 1974
Glenn, Tyree (61)—May 18, 1974
Gonsalves, Paul (53)—May 15, 1974
Harding, Walter N.H. (90)—December 13, 1973
Hayes, Tubby (38)—June 8, 1973
Heifetz, Benar (74)—April 5, 1974
Horgan, James J. (46)—June 2, 1973
Houdini, Wilmoth—August 6, 1973
Houser, John Garnett Jr. (54)—March 8, 1974
Hutsell, Robert M. (Bobby) (67)—August 23, 1973
Impellitter, Louis (92)—June 18, 1973
Jackson, Jiggs (65)—June 1973
Jacquet, Linton (63)—May 9, 1974
Jeffrey, Samuel D. (76)—June 21, 1973
Jimenez, José A. (47)—November 23, 1973

Kabos, Ilona (75)—May 27, 1973
Krupa, Gene (64)—October 16, 1973
Labunski, Wiktor (78)—January 26, 1974
Layfield, Arthur (83)—March 1, 1974
Lewis, Jerry Lee Jr. (19)—November 13, 1973
Lindemann, William L. (61)—February 14, 1974
Lunsford, Bascom Lamar (91)—September 4, 1973
Madriguera, Enric (71)—September 7, 1973
Moore, Brew (49)—August 19, 1973
Newman, Ruby (70)—September 20, 1973
Nicholas, Albert (73)—September 3, 1973
Niven, Roger (41)—November 8, 1973
Noge, John F. (69)—November 24, 1973
Nugent, Buddy (57)—July 24, 1973
Phillips, Reuben L. (53)—February 13, 1974
Pierce, De De (69)—November 22, 1973
Plunkett, Malcome Scott (19)—July 29, 1973
Price, Jesse (64)—April 20, 1974
Quittner, George F. (53)—February 7, 1974
Radcliffe, Jimmy (36)—July 27, 1973
Regules, Marisa (48)—July 13, 1973
Rimac, Ciro Campos (79)—September 8, 1973
Seagraves, C. Roy (72)—June 6, 1973
Shaw, Elliott (86)—August 13, 1973
Smith, John J. (75)—February 21, 1974
Solis, Max (62)—March 19, 1974
Spencer, Eleanor (84)—October 12, 1973
Spencer, Tim (65)—April 26, 1974
Stapleton, Cyril (60)—February 25, 1974
Strongin, Lillian (72)—January 5, 1974
Sweeney, Patrick (27)—August 20, 1973
Taylor, Vinnie (25)—April 19, 1974
Timmons, Bobby (38)—March 1, 1974
Titmarsh, Gurney (70)—April 14, 1974
Topper, Henry (74)—April 9, 1974
Varola, Richie (30)—April 29, 1974
Vaughn, Elma K. (77)—September 23, 1973
Walton, Jerry Lowell (18)—July 29, 1973
Ward, Jack (75)—July 26, 1973
Wayne, Artie (60)—February 14, 1974
Webster, Ben (64)—September 20, 1973
Wellington, John (70)—November 15, 1973
Wendt, George (Fats) (64)—August 31, 1973
Wiles, Charles C. (75)—March 16, 1974
Williams, Casco (79)—January 19, 1973

OTHERS

Abbe, James (91)—November 11, 1973
Photo journalist, reporter
Adler, Benjamin (84)—February 25, 1974
Investor
Adler, Seymour Lewis (58)—June 4, 1973
TV executive
Allan, Christopher (46)—November 4, 1973
Agent
Alvarez, Joseph (58)—August 3, 1973
WNBC-TV editorial manager
Bacon, Stuart Leslie (67)—August 9, 1973
Deputy gen. mgr., Festival Hall, London
Balaban, Carrie (85)—January 10, 1974

Widow of A.J. Balaban
Banner, Jack (67)—March 18, 1974
Journalist, publicist
Barcella, Ernest L. (63)—January 19, 1974
Publicist
Bartle, Colin (58)—July 2, 1973
Founder, Wakefield Theater Club
Bates, H.E. (68)—January 29, 1974
Author
Beck, Mary Ridgely Carter (72)—April 16, 1974
Founder, Newport Music Carnival
Befus, Roy (44)—August 10, 1973
Stage manager
Beinhorn, Nat (55)—February 28, 1974
Investor
Berceller, Oscar (74)—January 30, 1974
Toronto restaurateur
Bienstock, David (29)—July 24, 1973
Curator of films
Blanchard, Edwin H. (78)—November 30, 1973
Journalist, publicist
Bloom, Ben (79)—September 3, 1973
Music publisher
Bluem, A. William (48)—April 16, 1974
Author and educator
Bock, Harold J. (Hal) (68)—August 10, 1973
Publicist, KNBC-TV manager
Bodkin, Thomas V. (87)—April 16, 1974
Company manager
Boughner, Daniel E. (65)—May 8, 1974
Historian
Breed, Mrs. William (81)—March 20, 1974
Member of musical organizations
Broude, Irving (63)—June 22, 1973
Music publisher
Brylawski, Fulton (88)—November 23, 1973
Copyright attorney
Bush, Anita—February 16, 1974
Founder of Harlem stock company
Butler, Albert W. (84)—November 4, 1973
Publicist for circuses
Cannon, Jimmy (63)—December 6, 1973
Journalist
Carson, Jean-Philippe (49)—October 21, 1973
Cinematographer
Carver, Davis (70)—May 10, 1974
British sec'y gen. of P.E.N.
Cassagne, Margot S.—March 1974
Co-head of Janco Films
Cazin, Leon Sr.—September 17, 1973
Tampa entrepreneur
Charriere, Henri (66)—July 29, 1973
Author
Chasen, Dave (74)—June 16, 1973
Hollywood restaurateur
Coar, Robert J. (68)—January 23, 1974
Radio, TV engineer
Cochrane, Robert H. (94)—May 31, 1973
Founding partner, Universal Pictures
Cock, Gerald (86)—November 10, 1973
BBC executive
Cohen, Abe (76)—May 7, 1974
Company manager

Cohen, Sidney I. (64)—September 12, 1973
Consultant
Connor, Allen (75)—June 3, 1973
Talent agent
Contner, J. Burgi (67)—May 20, 1973
Cameraman, engineer, inventor
Conway, J. Rudolph (80)—November 2, 1973
Dix Bros., Reo Bros. circuses
Costello, Charles (Roxy) (83)—October 1973
Stage manager
Creasy, John (64)—June 9, 1973
Author
Cristiani, Ernesto (91)—October 23, 1973
Patriarch of Cristiani circus family
Crosby, Edward John (Ted) (73)—December 10, 1973
Newspaperman, publicist
Deane, Martha (65)—December 9, 1973
News-talk show hostess
Denenholz, Reginald (59)—July 10, 1973
Publicist
de Renzie, Leonard (73)—February 1974
Theater manager
Deutsch, Milt (56)—May 25, 1974
Manager and agent
Domela, Jan (62)—August 1, 1973
Matte artist at Paramount
Eichelbaum, M. Martin (65)—August 7, 1973
Owner of Bagel Delicatessen, Detroit
Fitzpatrick, Thomas (73)—September 19, 1973
Restaurateur
Fortier, Frank—February 26, 1974
Showman
Frank, Marvin (48)—January 11, 1974
Publicist
Friedman, Samuel J. (62)—April 26, 1974
Publicist
Gabriel, Gus (63)—July 20, 1973
Showman
Geddes, George E. (68)—July 1973
Founder of Dundee Repertory
Gee, Jack (84)—June 4, 1973
Manager
Gelman, Betty—March 28, 1974
Admin., Motion Picture Country Home
Gilligan, Edmund (75)—December 29, 1973
Novelist
Gillmor, Noelle (58)—August 20, 1973
Author of subtitles for foreign films
Godfrey, George (80s)—April 15, 1974
Talent scout
Gordon, David (64)—June 21, 1973
Journalist
Gore, Larry (50)—August 1, 1973
Publicist
Greenberg, Herman (77)—July 15, 1973
Assistant gen. mgr., ASCAP
Groshev, Alexander (69)—February, 1974
Director, Moscow Film School
Gustave, Henry (63)—August 24, 1973
London hotelier
Hall, Edwin S. (54)—November 18, 1973
Sound technician

Halperin, Michael (71)—March 28, 1974
Theatrical lawyer
Hapgood, Elizabeth (80)—February 27, 1974
Editor, translator
Handwerker, Nathan (83)—March 24, 1974
Co-founder, Nathan's
Helscher, Fern (73)—March 3, 1974
Publicist
Hirsch, Georges (79)—May 14, 1974
Administrator of Paris Opera
Hitchens, Dolores (65)—August 1, 1973
Novelist
Hoover, Richard A. (59)—September 4, 1973
Performing Arts Center, Milwaukee
Horrigan, John P. (47)—June 2, 1973
Publicist
Hulett, Ralph (58)—January 15, 1974
Disney background artist
Huntley, Chet (62)—March 20, 1974
TV journalist
Ingals, Miles (71)—February 14, 1974
Agent
Jahns, Robert—February 23, 1974
Film editor
Kalmenson, Benjamin (75)—January 18, 1974
President, Warner Bros. Pictures
Keeler, Jane (93)—February 9, 1974
Educator
Kelly, Walt (60)—October 19, 1974
Cartoonist
Kline, Ben (79)—January 7, 1974
Cameraman
Kocsis, Charles Jr. (31)—November 7, 1973
Film editor
Kriendler, Mac (65)—August 7, 1973
President of 21 Club
Lance, Leon O. (76)—September 7, 1973
Talent agent
Lawrence, Viola (78)—November 20, 1973
Film editor
Levi, Pilade (61)—November 15, 1973
Italian film executive
Lindgren, Ernest (62)—July 22, 1973
Britain's National Film Archive
Littler, Prince (72)—September 13, 1973
British impresario
Lyon, William A. (71)—March 18, 1974
Film editor
Mann, Joseph (79)—June 6, 1973
Mgr., Peoples Symphony Concerts
McAlpin, Hal A. (73)—June 28, 1973
Cameraman
McGee, Frank (52)—April 17, 1974
TV journalist
McHugh, Edward A. (81)—October 24, 1973
Stage manager
McKay, Evelyn C. (75)—May 29, 1973
Founder, Louis Braille Foundation
McMahon, Charles W. Sr. (93)—August 4, 1973
Booking agent
McSpadden, Kate (91)—November 14, 1973
Inspired "K-K-K-Katie"
Minsky, Jack (85)—July 15, 1973
Theater manager

Mitford, Nancy (68)—June 30, 1973
  Author
Mohr, Hal (79)—May 11, 1974
  Cinematographer *(The Jazz Singer)*
Montgomery, John R. (80)—September 8, 1973
  Pres., Peabody Conservatory, Baltimore
Morris, Russell E.—June 30, 1973
  International trustee, IATSE
Morrison, Leo (75)—April 19, 1974
  Publicist
Mundy, Frank (65)—February 6, 1974
  Manager, Royal Albert Hall
Nafash, William (69)—August 22, 1973
  Chief projectionist, Music Hall
Offin, Phil (70)—April 26, 1974
  Agent
Parado, Eleanore—February 19, 1974
  Wardrobe mistress
Paris, Robert Graham (68)—February 19, 1974
  Drama coach
Penotti, Franco (81)—April 1974
  Italian film executive
Peters, Cyril (60s)—July 15, 1973
  Radio journalist
Podell, Jules (74)—September 27, 1973
  Copacabana operator
Post, Marjorie (86)—September 12, 1973
  Patron, Washington National Symphony
Pratt, Thomas P. (74)—August 4, 1973
  Film editor
Prouty, Charles (64)—May 10, 1974
  Shakespearean scholar
Prouty, Olive Higgins (92)—March 24, 1974
  Author
Ramsey, William M. (73)—October 3, 1973
  Advertising director
Raym, Maxmilian E. (71)—January 9, 1974
  Publicist
Reisner, Bob (53)—February 19, 1974
  Writer, humorist
Rescher, Jay (80)—August 11, 1973
  Cinematographer
Rissetto, Bartolomeo (84)—February 22, 1974
  Restaurateur
Rittenberg, Arnold (78)—March 28, 1974
  Showman
Rosen, Joel (29)—March 13, 1974
  TV production manager
Rosher, Charles A. (89)—January 15, 1974
  Cinematographer
Russell, Diarmuid (71)—December 16, 1973
  Agent
Sacconi, Fernando (78)—June 26, 1973
  Violinmaker
Sanford, Jay (65)—March 22, 1974
  Story editor
Saphier, James L. (67)—April 9, 1974
  Business agent
Scanlan, James F. (51)—July 13, 1973
  Publicist
Schaffer, Max (83)—February 13, 1974
  Operator, Hubert's Museum
Schiffman, Frank (80)—January 15, 1974
  Operator, Apollo Theater

Schoengarth, Russell F.—March 30, 1974
  Film editor
Schrott, Eugene (62)—June 2, 1973
  Publicist
Schwalberg, Alfred W. (75)—December 7, 1973
  President, Paramount Distributors
Sedgwick, Mrs. Ruth (82)—May 27, 1974
  Journalist
Senz, Edward (74)—November 4, 1973
  Makeup man
Shnayerson, Lydia Todd (46)—August 26, 1973
  Music teacher
Small, Seldon (72)—March 6, 1974
  Costume supplier
Smith, Edward A. (85)—April 27, 1974
  Theater manager
Snethan, Robert E. Jr. (44)—December 11, 1973
  Film editor
Staniland, Albert (71)—July 28, 1973
  Theater operator
Stauffer, Ivan Rex (72)—May 4, 1974
  Publicist
Stein, Harold (79)—August 13, 1973
  Photographer
Stinnett, Ray J. (92)—August 1974
  Theater owner
Stogel, Syd (60)—May 12, 1974
  Publicist
Strausberg, Morris O. (62)—April 17, 1974
  President, Interboro Circuit
Sutherland, Everett (63)—February 23, 1974
  Film editor
Teitel, Abraham (85)—April 24, 1974
  Film distributor
Thall, Al (63)—November 14, 1973
  Publicist
Tregaskis, Richard (56)—August 15, 1973
  Author, war correspondent
Van Pelt, Homer—September 3, 1973
  Photographer
Vaughan, Olwen (68)—August 18, 1973
  British Film Society
Weber, Fred (67)—August 30, 1973
  Founder, Mutual Broadcasting System
Weir, Milton R. (75)—November 9, 1973
  Theatrical lawyer
Westmore, George (Bud) (55)—June 24, 1973
  Makeup man
Westmore, Walter J. (Wally) (57)—July 3,
1973
  Makeup man
White, William L. (73)—July 26, 1973
  Author, journalist
Wilbur, Norman (Lucky) (82)—July 6, 1973
  Vocal coach, song plugger
Wolfson, Abraham (65)—June 18, 1973
  Agent
Wren, Harry (57)—August 30, 1973
  Showman
Zakowski, Rita (43)—March 1, 1974
  Agent
Zimanich, Josef (Zimmy)—June 11, 1973
  Russian musical supervisor

INDEX

Play titles are in **bold face** and **bold face italic** page numbers refer to pages where cast and credit listings may be found.

466   INDEX

De Cordova, Arturo, 448
de Fazio, Marjorie, 407
De Felice, Ronald, 343
De Filippo, Eduardo, 104, 125, 137
De Funès, Louis, 141, 143
de Ghelderode, Michel, 148
de Giroday, Francois, 405
de Groat, Andrew, 403
de Hartog, Jan, 66, 75
de Jongh, Holly, 117
de la Croix, Yves, 149
de Laiglesia, Alvaro, 143
de Lavallade, Carmen, 71, 72
De Lullo, Giorgio, 137
de Mandiargues, André-Pieyre, 145
de Motherlant, Henry, 145
de Musset, Alfred, 145
de Obaldia, René, 126
De Orduna, Juan, 451
De Paur, Leonard, 408
De Paur, Starletta, 351, 380
de Ré, Michel, 144, 147
de Ré, Pierre, 142
de Renzie, Leonard, 454
de Rigault, Jean, 399
de Roja, Fernando, 42
de Sade, Marquis, 124
De Salvio, Joseph V., 52
De Santis, John, 63, 64
de Schryver, Jean, 146
de Seynes, Catherine, 148
De Shields, André, 370, 371
de Varona, Joanna, 364
De Vito, Anthony, 408
De Vol, Gordon, 352
De Wolfe, Billy, 448
Deacon, Brian, 119
Dead Easy, 115
Dean, Isobel, 110, 117
Dean, Libby, 70
Dean, Martha, 454
Dean, Palmer, 414
Dean, Phillip Hayes, 402
DeAnda, Peter, 409
Deane, Doris, 448
DeAngelis, Rosemary, 56, 90, 91
Dear Black Man, 398
Dear Liar, 39
Dear Luger, 59
Dear Nobody, 9, 28, 396–397
Dearborn, Dalton, 51
Dearing, Judy, 351, 386
Dearth, Lynn, 108
Death, 124
Death and the Devil, 126
Death of Lord Chatterly, The, 24, 28, 377
Death of the Siamese Twins, The, 415
DeBaer, Jean, 56
Debayo, Jemoko, 127
Debin, David, 371

Debrakel, Louise, 145
Debuskey, Merle, 343, 344, 350, 354, 365, 375, 384, 388
Decameron, 111
Deck, Terry, 55
Decline and Fall of the Entire World as Seen Through the Eyes of Cole Porter, 61
Deed From the King of Spain, A, 403
Deegan, Denise, 120
Deen, Nedra, 64
DeFabees, Richard, 89, 389
DeFazio, Marjorie, 414
DeFeis, Doreen, 369
Deforges, Corinne, 146
Defossez, Roger, 148
DeFrank, Bob, 75, 76
Deighton, Gordon, 116
Deishsel, Wolfgang, 129
Deitch, Dan, 388
DeKay, Victoria, 66
del Valle-Inclan, Ramon, 130
Delamare, Lise, 145
Delaney, Pauline, 110
Delaney, Thom, 125
DeLaurentis, Semina, 407
Delbo, Charlotte, 145
Delerue, George, 399
Delfont, Bernard, 123, 125, 352, 363, 431
Delgado, Roger, 448
Delicate Balance, A, 77
Délirante Sarah, La, 136, 144
Dell, Gabriel, 418
Delmet, Paul, 146
Delmonte, Jack, 448
Delsener, Ron, 358
Deluca, Joseph, 367
Delve, David, 114
DeMaio, Peter, 92
Demas, Carole, 416, 417
Demi Gods, The, 405
Demler, Steve, 54
Dempsey, Jerome, 71, 72
Dempster, Curt, 406
DeMunn, James, 53
Dench, Judi, 125
Dendy, Michael, 58
Denenholz, Reginald, 454
Dener, Ron, 411
Dengrove, Lois, 410
Denison, Michael, 112
Denker, Carl, 116
Denker, Henry, 88
Denning, Nancy Ann, 371
Denning, Richard, 112
Dennis, Gil, 65, 66
Dennis, John, 63, 64
Dennis, Robert, 71, 391
Dennison, George, 69
Denson, Cheryl, 58, 60
Depardieu, Gérard, 147
der Abrahmian, Arousiak, 448
Derefinko, Rod, 378

Dermer, Bob, 94, 95
DeRusso, Richard, 89
Dervieus, Jean-Pierre, 144
Derx, Hallam B., 398
Desailly, Jean, 147
Desalles, Gérard, 144
Desbois, Christiane, 399
Desert Song, The, 4, 8, 23, 25, 88, 343–344
Design for Living, 105, 113
DeSio, Pamela, 42, 410
Desire Under the Elms, 403
Desmarets, Sophie, 143
Desmeliers, Georges, 145
Desmond, Dan, 52, 72
Desmond, Nancy A., 89
Dessau, Paul, 398
Destoop, Jacques, 143
Destrez, Thierry, 145
Detective Story, 75
Detweiler, Lowell, 73, 79, 385
Deutsch, Milt, 454
Deutsches Requiem, 144
Deux Clowns, 145
Deux-Chaises Company, 147
Devane, William, 369
Devant la Porte, 147
Deveraux, Ed, 123
Devereaux, Diana, 58, 60
Devereaux, Greg, 58, 59
Devils, The, 139
Devil's General, The, 77
Devin, Richard, 73, 74, 382
Devine, George, 101, 118, 121
Devine, Jerry, 18, 63, 347
Devito, Danny, 408
DeVito, Harry, 362
Devitt, Sydnee, 391
Devlin, Nancy, 347
Dewhurst, Colleen, 8, 20, 21, 41, 357, 431, 432
DeWindt, Hal, 409
Dews, Peter, 346
Dexter, John, 106, 107, 112, 117
Di Blasio, Joe, 451
Di Grazio, Randy, 352
Diamond, Bob, 386
Diamond, I. A. L., 341
Diamond, Marian, 127, 392
Diamond, Michael, 54
Diaries of Adam and Eve, The, 69
Diary of Anne Frank, The, 398
Diary of a Superfluous Man, 67
Diaz, Charles, 401
Dick, 114
Dick Deterred, 115
Dick Whittington and His Cat, 114
Dickens, Charles, 95, 114, 400
Dickson, Robert, 58, 59
Diderot, Denis, 140
Diercks, Shirley, 75
Dietz, Kyra, 119